CRIMES AGAINST HUMANITY
IN INTERNATIONAL CRIMINAL LAW

CRIMES AGAINST HUMANITY IN INTERNATIONAL CRIMINAL LAW

by

M. Cherif Bassiouni

Professor of Law, President, International
Human Rights Law Institute, DePaul University;
President, International Association of Penal Law;
President, International Institute of Higher
Studies in Criminal Sciences

MARTINUS NIJHOFF PUBLISHERS
DORDRECHT / BOSTON / LONDON

Library of Congress Cataloging-in-Publication Data

Bassiouni, M. Cherif, 1937-
    Crimes against humanity in international criminal law / M. Cherif
Bassiouni.
      p.   cm.
    Includes index.
    ISBN 0-7923-1737-8 (HB : alk. paper)
    1. Crimes against humanity. 2. War crimes. I. Title.
JX5418.B38   1992
341.7'7--dc20   92-13220

ISBN 0-7923-1737-8
0191083

Published by Martinus Nijhoff Publishers,
P.O. Box 163, 3300 AD Dordrecht, The Netherlands.

Sold and distributed in the U.S.A. and Canada
by Kluwer Academic Publishers,
101 Philip Drive, Norwell, MA 02061, U.S.A.

In all other countries, sold and distributed
by Kluwer Academic Publishers Group,
P.O. Box 322, 3300 AH Dordrecht, The Netherlands.

Printed on acid-free paper

Printed in the Netherlands

TABLE OF CONTENTS

CHAPTER 1

EMERGENCE AS AN INTERNATIONAL CRIME

CHAPTER 2

THRESHOLD ISSUES OF LEGAL PHILOSOPHY

TABLE OF CONTENTS

CHAPTER 3

PRINCIPLES OF LEGALITY

CHAPTER 4

HISTORICAL LEGAL FOUNDATIONS: INTERNATIONAL HUMANITARIAN LAW AND THE REGULATION OF ARMED CONFLICTS

CHAPTER 5

INDIVIDUAL CRIMINAL RESPONSIBILITY AND INTERNATIONAL PROSECUTIONS

CHAPTER 6

PREREQUISITE LEGAL ELEMENTS: PUBLIC LAW CONNECTION AND INTERNATIONAL COGNIZABLE HARM

TABLE OF CONTENTS

CHAPTER 7

IDENTIFYING THE SPECIFIC CRIMES IN "GENERAL PRINCIPLES OF LAW" AT THE TIME OF THE CHARTER

CHAPTER 8

THE CONTENTS OF THE SPECIFIC CRIMES FROM THE CHARTER UNTIL NOW

CHAPTER 9

ELEMENTS OF CRIMINAL RESPONSIBILITY

TABLE OF CONTENTS

CHAPTER 10

DEFENSES AND EXONERATIONS

CHAPTER 11

POST-CHARTER LEGAL DEVELOPMENTS

CHAPTER 12

CONCLUDING ASSESSMENT

DOCUMENTS

INDEX

PREFACE

In 1989, the Canadian Department of Justice asked me to serve as its legal expert in *R. vs. Finta*, Canada's first prosecution of "Crimes Against Humanity" under a 1987 statute incorporating this international crime into Canadian criminal law. This statute, which is retrospective but not retroactive, requires that "Crimes Against Humanity" be established under international law at the time the alleged crime was committed and that the specific crimes charged also constitute a violation of Canadian criminal law when the alleged criminal conduct occurred. There are also other jurisdictional requirements needed to satisfy the Canadian law.

The former Hungarian Gendarmerie Captain Imre Finta was charged, *inter alia*, with the deportation of 8,617 Jews from Szeged, Hungary to Auschwitz, Poland, and Strasshof, Austria, in June 1944 as part of Nazi Germany's plan to exterminate Jews. No one knows how many of these deportees died in transit, in that death camp, or in slave-labor camps. Reviewing such horrors even forty five years later was deeply moving.

Since the facts in this case occurred in 1944, I could not rely on the Law of the Charter for precedent. Thus, working on the *Finta* case was my own small "Nuremberg" -- a daunting task.

As I tried to establish that "crimes against humanity" existed as an international crime in 1944, the insight of many scholars' published works greatly benefited me. But the reams of pages I read about Nuremberg, Tokyo and their sequels left me with more questions than I had to begin with. It also left me with the realization that my previous work on "crimes against humanity"; as well as that of so many others, including the work of the International Law Commission, needed to be revisited. My conclusion is that the case for the legal validity and viability of "crimes against humanity" still needs to be made; Nuremberg and Tokyo notwithstanding, or perhaps despite these precedents. This conclusion leads me to believe that nothing short of a new comprehensive convention can resolve the problems devolved to us by the Nuremberg and Tokyo legacy.

The research I did in preparation for the *Finta* case, in addition to my many years of international criminal law work, led to this book. Hopefully, it will contribute to a better understanding of the many complex legal issues relating to this category of international crimes.

As I point out throughout the text, the Law of the Charter was driven by the facts. Indeed the facts were so horrendous that no law, no matter how prescient, could have anticipated them. But this was not a case where no law existed, but rather that no specific positive law on point had been elaborated. And how could it? No law can divine the absurd, the grotesque or the inhumane. Thus, the law

vise, trapped between its legality technique and the moral content which characterizes its social purpose.

How can one intellectually criticize on technical legal terms that which conscience so eloquently supports? The answer is that the Rule of Law, which is the only difference between justice and tyranny, and thus between civilization and barbarism, always needs to be defended.

The memory of yesterday's victims are haunting, and yet the images of our contemporary world's victims pass before us with relative indifference. My *Concluding Assessments* Chapter best expresses my feelings and beliefs on this question.

This Preface would not be complete, if I did not also express my belief that the world community must develop a commitment to the prosecution of those who committed "crimes against humanity," irrespective of time, place and the identity of the perpetrators' status or that of the hapless victims. The motivation for that urging is not vindictiveness, but a belief in the compelling need to express opprobrium against such human depredations. Prosecutions for "crimes against humanity," when and where they may occur, should evidence, if nothing else, our human solidarity with the victims of such crimes -- that is the least we can do for them--as well as for upholding our own humanity. Along with this urging, I must also add a word of caution, not to say admonishment, to all those engaged in such proceedings -- the greater the magnitude of human depredation, the less it can countenance trivialization.

The words of John Donne seem appropriate to end this Preface:

No man is an island, entire of itself; every man is a piece of the continent, a part of the main. ...Any man's death diminishes me because I am involved in mankind, and therefore never send to know for whom the bell tolls; it tolls for thee.

M. Cherif Bassiouni
Chicago, April 7, 1992

x

ACKNOWLEDGMENTS

I wish to express my appreciation to the Canadian Department of Justice and to those in the Section on War Crimes and Crimes Against Humanity, for having given me the opportunity to assist in the prosecution of this case. The experience was the impetus for this book.

My thanks to John Roberts, Dean, DePaul University College of Law, for giving me the support I needed to accomplish this task, and to DePaul University for giving me the time to complete this book.

To George Gullo, my research assistant, who did so much legwork chasing after so many unwieldy footnotes, and his successor, Mark Bennett, to Helena Kapjon and Lorraine Hewett who typed the numerous drafts of each Chapter, my thanks for their dedication and patience, and to Paula Clark who set the type for this book.

I also want to thank Howard Levie, Emeritus Professor of International Law, Saint Louis University, for having read the Chapter on the international regulation of armed conflicts and giving me the benefit of his thoughts on it. Lastly, I wish to express my appreciation to the publisher, Martinus Nijhoff, and to Alan Stephens, this is my fourth book they have published.

INTRODUCTION

The legal literature on post-WWII prosecutions is abundant, but it is mostly on the Nuremberg trials. And it is in this context that "crimes against humanity" are dealt with, but more particularly in connection with war crimes. In contrast, the Tokyo trials are the subject of significantly fewer books and articles, and the treatment within them of "crimes against humanity" is very limited.

While there are very few books that deal exclusively with "crimes against humanity" in connection with European prosecutions, there are none in a European language to this writer's knowledge, in connection with far-east prosecutions. Most of these books are redundant since they overwhelmingly focus on the Nuremberg trials. Few among them include Allied prosecutions subsequent to Nuremberg and among those the emphasis is on U.S. Subsequent Proceedings. There are no books known to this writer on Allied proceedings subsequent to the Tokyo trials dealing exclusively or even significantly with "crimes against humanity." The *Yamashita* trial in the Philippines is probably the case most widely written about, but it does not deal with "crimes against humanity."

In this abundant legal literature one hardly finds books that comprehensively cover all the issues raised by the London Charter's Article 6(c), the Tokyo Charter's Article 5(c) and Control Council Law No. 10 Article II(c), as well as these and other prosecutions. Those authors who are critical of this legislation and its application focus more on the "principles of legality," the Achille's heel of these legal formulations, their interpretation and application. Their criticism is muted, however, because of the enormity of the harm committed. Authors who support these formulations and their application avoid the more technical legal arguments which could likely undermine their legality. But, while "principles of legality" and some specific legal issues, like "command responsibility" and "obedience to superior orders" received the lion's share of commentators' attention, other important issues have been largely ignored. Just as the Law of Charter was driven by the facts, both in its formulation and application, so was the tenor of the legal literature.

As stated in the Preface, it is difficult to contemporaneously critically appraise, support, advocate continued viability, and urge significant reform and yet remain consistent, particularly because the intellectual analysis, methodology, and writing style for each of these goals are different.

One of the particular difficulties I encountered was with the starting point and the sequence of issues. I elected the classical continental legal approach of starting with the law and then going from the general to the specific. Thus, Chapter 1 covers the legislative history of Articles 6(c), 5(c) and II(c) respectively of the London and Tokyo Charters and Control Council Law No. 10. Consistent with this approach, Chapter 2 deals with questions of legal philosophy. Logically, this leads to the "principles of legality" covered in Chapter 3, whose issues permeate the entire subject of this book.

INTRODUCTION

Chapters 4 and 5 deal with the history of international humanitarian law, the international regulation of armed conflicts and the history of international and national prosecutions of war crimes and "crimes against humanity." Had I chosen a chronological approach for the emergence of "crimes against humanity" in international criminal law, these two Chapters would have been the first ones in the book. But, while Chapter 4 serves as the historical basis for the emergence of this international category of crimes as a jurisdictional extension of war crimes, Chapter 5, which deals with enforcement, is unrelated to Chapter 4 as a source of law. But it is nevertheless logically dependent on Chapter 4 since enforcement is a consequence of the normative legal development. It would have, therefore, been incongruous to have started with these two Chapters and then follow them with the chapters on the legislative history of the Charter, issues of legal philosophy and "principles of legality." Thus, I opted to start with the more general and pervasive issues, after positing the initial normative legislative basis, and then to go to the more specific ones.

Chapters 4 and 5 do not only serve as a historical-legal foundation for the initial normative legislation discussed in Chapter 1, but they are also the basis for what penalists call the special part, namely, the specific crimes. These specific crimes, however, emerge from more than one source of international law, and thus, they do not exclusively arise out of the international regulation of armed conflicts. It is in this context that the multi-disciplinary nature of international criminal law has proven particularly intractable. Indeed, to reconcile several sources of international law, which includes "general principles of law recognized by civilized nations," as well as other "general principles" of criminal law recognized in the world's major criminal justice systems, particularly the "principles of legality," is a significant intellectual and methodological challenge.

The fact that a particular crime is recognized in the world's major criminal justice systems does not make it an international crime. A link is needed to connect what would otherwise be common crimes under the exclusive national jurisdiction of states to an international crime. That link is what I call "state action or policy." Few writers on the subject have dealt with this dimension which so particularly characterizes "crimes against humanity." As I see that link, it is an indispensable constitutive element of this category of international crimes. Some penalists may view it as belonging more with the general part discussed in Chapter 9 than with the special part discussed in Chapters 7 and 8. I concluded, however, that such a pre-requisite legal element is a foundation for the special part, though it partakes of some characteristics of the general part. Consequently, it was sequentially placed before the discussion of the special parts.

The specific contents of this category of international crimes follows the pre-requisite legal element discussed in Chapter 6, but they are divided into two chapters because of the analysis' sequence. Chapter 7 examines "general principles" as a source of international law through which one can identify certain national proscriptions which support international criminalization. But, as I point out in that chapter such a source of international law, while useful and, at times, necessary, to justify international criminalization, cannot be deemed legally sufficient in accordance with "principles of legality" to transform national crimes into international crimes. Chapter 7 also serves to argue in support of the post-WWII international legislation and in mitigation of the positivist position which holds that such legislation violates the "principles of legality." The arguments presented in Chapter 7 are retrospectively and prospectively valid. They also form the basis for Chapter 8. The latter, however, is more prospective in its approach, and its analysis extends to post-WWII international legislation. Thus, while Chapter 7 serves essentially to support the post-WWII legislation, Chapter 8 reinforces the legacy of that period and supports continued legal viability.

Chapters 9 and 10 deal with general part issues of responsibility and defenses. They also analyse the post-WWII *lacunae* and reveal that most of them have remained as such since then.

Chapter 11 is, from a legal perspective, the saddest analysis I had to make. To find legal weaknesses in the legislative formulation developed in the wake of the discoveries of WWII's horrors is probably inevitable. But to find only woefully deficient international legislation since then is shocking.

The Concluding Assessment Chapter further discloses the reasons why the continued viability of "crimes against humanity" is necessary.

The Documents section is both historical and contemporary. Most of its contents are readily available to researchers with access to well supplied law libraries. But that is not the case for most countries of the world. Thus, it serves as an easy reference source to those who can find these documents but only in scattered sources, and above all it serves as an almost exclusive source for so many who cannot have access to these documents.

The term, "crimes against humanity" is almost as much a part of worldwide popular usage as murder. Yet, unlike murder, "crimes against humanity" is far from having the benefit of international and national legislation which provides it with the necessary legal specificity and particularity which has come to be expected of major national common crimes. Popular perceptions and expectations have thus outdistanced positive law.

INTRODUCTION

The Preface and Conclusion clearly state my goals, purposes, and values, this Introduction serves only to explain why and how I developed the sequence of this book.

In doing this book, I tried to be my worst critic and argued with myself on so many questions of method, substance, and form, which led to my rewriting every chapter many times, and to repeatedly changing the order of presentation. In my final review of the manuscript, I felt that every chapter could have been a book in itself and, for better or worse, the publisher wanted the manuscript and wanted it in a size that would not be too cumbersome and too onerous to the reader.

TABLE OF ABBREVIATIONS

1899 Hague Convention

Convention With Respect to the Laws and Customs of War on Land, The Hague, 26 July 1899, 26 Martens (2d) 949, 32 Stat. 1803, T.S. No. 403. *Reprinted in* 1 AJIL 129 (1907) (Supp.); 1 Friedman 221; Schindler/Toman 57. *See* (excerpts) Document Section D.3.

1907 Hague Convention

Convention Respecting the Laws and Customs of War on Land, The Hague, 18 October 1907, 3 Martens (3d) 461, 36 Stat. 2277, T.S. No. 539. *Reprinted in* 2 AJIL 90 (1908) (Supp.); 1 Bevans 631; 1 Friedman 308. *See* (excerpts) Document Section D.5.

1919 Commission Report

Report Presented to the Preliminary Peace Conference by the Commission on the Responsibilities of the Authors of the War and on Enforcement of Penalties (Conference of Paris 1919 Carnegie Endowment for International Peace, Division of International Law), Pamphlet No. 32 (1919). *Reprinted in* 14 AJIL 95 (1920) (Supp.); 1 Friedman 842. *See* (excerpts) Document Section A.2.

1949 Geneva Conventions
(also Geneva Conventions)

Conventions signed at Geneva, 12 August 1949:
(a) Convention for the Amelioration of the Condition of the Wounded and Sick in Armed Forces in the Field (Geneva I), 75 U.N.T.S. 31, 6 U.S.T. 3114, T.I.A.S. 3362. *Reprinted in* 1 Friedman 525; Schindler/Toman 305. *See* (excerpts) Document Section D.9.
(b) Convention for the Amelioration of the Condition of Wounded, Sick, and Shipwrecked Members of the Armed Forces at Sea (Geneva II), 75 U.N.T.S. 85, 6 U.S.T. 3217, T.I.A.S. No. 3363.

Reprinted in 1 Friedman 570; Schindler/Toman 333. *See* (excerpts) Document Section D.10.
(c) Convention Relative to the Treatment of Prisoners of War (Geneva III), 75 U.N.T.S. 135, 6 U.S.T. 3316, T.I.A.S. No. 3364. *Reprinted in* 1 Friedman 589; Schindler/Toman 355. *See* (excerpts) Document Section D.11.
(d) Convention Relative to the Protection of Civilian Persons in Time of War (Geneva IV), 75 U.N.T.S. 287, 6 U.S.T. 3516, T.I.A.S. 3365. *Reprinted in* 1 Friedman 641; Schindler/Toman 427. *See* (excerpts) Document Section D.12.

1977 Additional Protocols (also Protocols)	(a) Protocol I Additional to Geneva Conventions of 12 August 1949, (Relating to the Protection of Victims of International Armed Conflicts), 12 December 1977, U.N. Doc. A/32/144 Annex I. *Reprinted in* 16 ILM 1391 (1977); Schindler/Toman 551. *See* (excerpts) Document Section D.13. (b) Protocol II Additional to Geneva Convention of 12 August 1949, (Relating to the Protection of Victims of Non-International Armed Conflicts), 12 December 1977, U.N. Doc. A/32/144 Annex II. *Reprinted in* 13 ILM 1391 at 1442 (1977); Schindler/Toman 619. *See* (excerpts) Document Section D.14.
1954 Draft Code of Offences	Draft Code of Offences Against the Peace and Security of Mankind, 28 July 1954, 9 U.N. GAOR Supp. (No. 9) at 11, U.N. Doc. A/2693 (1954). *Reprinted in* 45 AJIL 123 (1954) (Supp.); 2 Ferencz 460. *See* Document Section F.4.
1991 Draft Code of Crimes	Draft Code of Crimes against the Peace and Security of Mankind, 19 July 1991, in [1991] *Report of the ILC*, Supp.No. 10 (A/46/10) 238. *See* Document Section F.5.

ABAJ — AMERICAN BAR ASSOCIATION JOURNAL

Affirmation of Nuremberg Principles — Affirmation of the Principles of International Law Recognized by the Charter of the Nuremberg Tribunal, 11 December 1946, U.N. G.A. Res. 95(I), 1 U.N. GAOR (Part II) at 188, U.N. Doc. A/64/Add. 1(1946). *Reprinted in* 2 Friedman 1027; Schindler/Toman 833. *See* (excerpts) Document Section C.11.

AJIL — AMERICAN JOURNAL OF INTERNATIONAL LAW

AM. J. CRIM. L. — AMERICAN JOURNAL OF CRIMINAL LAW

AM. J. COMP. L. — AMERICAN JOURNAL OF COMPARATIVE LAW

AM. J. JURIS. — AMERICAN JOURNAL OF JURISPRUDENCE

AM. POL. SCI. REV. — AMERICAN POLITICAL SCIENCE REVIEW

AM. SOC. INT'L L. PROC. — AMERICAN SOCIETY OF INTERNATIONAL LAW PROCEEDINGS

AM. U.J. INT'L L. & POL'Y — AMERICAN UNIVERSITY JOURNAL OF INTERNATIONAL LAW AND POLICY

AM. U.L. REV. — AMERICAN UNIVERSITY LAW REVIEW

Apartheid Convention — International Convention on the Suppression and Punishment of the Crime of *Apartheid*, 30 November 1973, U.N. G.A. Res. 3068 (XXVIII), 28 U.N. GAOR Supp. (No. 30) at 75, U.N. Doc. A/9030 (1973). *Reprinted in* 13 ILM 50 (1974). *See* (excerpts) Document Section F.2.

ARIZ. L. REV. — ARIZONA LAW REVIEW

TABLE OF ABBREVIATIONS

Article 6(c)
The "crimes against humanity" provision in the Charter of the International Military Tribunal Annexed to the London Agreement, 8 August 1945.

AUST. Y.B. INT'L L.
AUSTRALIAN YEARBOOK OF INTERNATIONAL LAW

BASSIOUNI DIGEST
M.C. BASSIOUNI, INTERNATIONAL CRIMES: DIGEST/INDEX OF CONVENTIONS AND RELEVANT PENAL PROVISIONS (2 vols. 1986).

BASSIOUNI DRAFT CODE
M.C. BASSIOUNI, A DRAFT INTERNATIONAL CRIMINAL CODE & DRAFT STATUTE FOR AN INTERNATIONAL CRIMINAL TRIBUNAL (1987).

BASSIOUNI ICL
M.C. BASSIOUNI, INTERNATIONAL CRIMINAL LAW (Vol. I--Crimes; Vol. II--Procedure; Vol. III--Enforcement, 1986).

BASSIOUNI AND NANDA TREATISE
A TREATISE ON INTERNATIONAL CRIMINAL LAW (M.C. Bassiouni and V.P. Nanda eds., 1973, 2 vols.).

Bevans
TREATIES AND OTHER INTERNATIONAL AGREEMENTS OF THE UNITED STATES OF AMERICA, 1776-1949 (C.F. Bevans ed., 1970, 13 vols.).

BRIT. J. OF CRIMINOLOGY
BRITISH JOURNAL OF CRIMINOLOGY

BRIT. Y. B. INT'L L.
BRITISH YEARBOOK OF INTERNATIONAL LAW

B. V. INT'L L. J.
BOSTON UNIVERSITY INTERNATIONAL LAW JOURNAL

CALIF. L. REV.
CALIFORNIA LAW REVIEW

CALIF. W. INT'L L. J.	CALIFORNIA WESTERN INTERNATIONAL LAW JOURNAL
CAMBRIDGE L.J.	CAMBRIDGE LAW JOURNAL
CAN. B. REV.	CANADIAN BAR REVIEW
CAN. Y. B. INT'L L.	CANADIAN YEARBOOK OF INTERNATIONAL LAW
CASE W. RES. J. INT'L L.	CASE WESTERN RESERVE JOURNAL OF INTERNATIONAL LAW
CCL 10 (*See also* Subsequent Proceedings)	Allied Control Council Law No. 10, Punishment of Persons Guilty of War Crimes, Crimes Against Peace and Against Humanity, 20 December 1945, OFFICIAL GAZETTE OF THE CONTROL COUNCIL FOR GERMANY, No. 3, Berlin, 31 January 1946. *Reprinted in* 1 Ferencz 488; 1 Friedman 908. *See* Document Section C.5.
CCL Trials	Trials of War Criminals Before the Nuremberg Military Tribunals Under Control Council Law No. 10, (U.S. Govt. Prtg. Office, 1952).
Charter (see also London Agreement)	Annex to Agreement for the Prosecution and Punishment of Major War Criminals of the European Axis (London Agreement), London, 8 August 1945, 82 U.N.T.S. 279, 59 Stat. 1544, E.A.S. No. 472. *Reprinted in* 39 AJIL 257 (1945) (Supp.); 1 Ferencz 454; 1 Friedman 883; Schindler/Toman 823. *See* Document Section C.2.
CINC. L. REV.	CINCINNATI LAW REVIEW
COLO. L. REV.	COLORADO LAW REVIEW
COLUM. J. TRANSNAT'L L.	COLUMBIA JOURNAL OF TRANSNATIONAL LAW

TABLE OF ABBREVIATIONS

Protocols to the European Human Rights Convention	Protocol to the European Convention for the Protection of Human Rights and Fundamental Freedoms, 20 March 1952, 213 U.N.T.S. 262; Protocols 2, 1963, E.T.S. No. 44; 3, 1963, E.T.S. No. 45; 4, 1963, E.T.S. No. 46; 5, 1966, E.T.S. No. 55.
European Convention on Non-Applicability of Statutory Limitations	European Convention on the Non-Applicability of Statutory Limitations to Crimes Against Humanity and War Crimes, 25 January 1974, E.T.S. No. 82. *Reprinted in* 13 ILM 540 (1974). *See* Document Section E.4.
I.G. Farben Case	United States v. Krauch et al., 7 CCL Trials and 8 CCL Trials.
Far East Military Proceedings	Trials held in connection with the post-World War II Far East Military Activities conducted by: (a) the United States, as special military trials; and (b) other countries including Great Britain, Soviet Union, China, Netherlands, Australia and other Commonwealth nations.
Ferencz	B. FERENCZ, AN INTERNATIONAL CRIMINAL COURT - A STEP TOWARDS WORLD PEACE (2 vols. 1980).
The Flick Case	United States v. Flick et al., 6 CCL: Trials (1947). *Reprinted in* 2 Friedman 1281.
FOR. REL.	(U.S.) FOREIGN RELATIONS (United States Dep't of State publication).
FORDHAM INT'L L. J.	FORDHAM INTERNATIONAL LAW JOURNAL
FORDHAM L. REV.	FORDHAM LAW REVIEW

TABLE OF ABBREVIATIONS

The Hostage Case	*United States v. List et al.*, 11 CCL Trials (1948). *Reprinted in* 2 Friedman 1303.
HOUS. J. INT'L L.	HOUSTON JOURNAL OF INTERNATIONAL LAW
HUDSON	M.O. HUDSON, INTERNATIONAL LEGISLATION (9 vols. 1931-1950).
HUMAN RIGHTS COMPILATION	HUMAN RIGHTS: A COMPILATION OF INTERNATIONAL INSTRUMENTS, U.N. DOC. ST/HR-/1/REV. 2, U.N. SALES NO. E. 83. X IV./(1983).
HUMAN RIGHTS J. INT'L & COMP. L.	HUMAN RIGHTS JOURNAL OF INTERNATIONAL & COMPARATIVE LAW
ICJ	International Court of Justice
ILC	International Law Commission
ILM	International Legal Materials
IMT (also Nuremberg Trials)	International Military Tribunal sitting at Nuremberg. Reported in TRIAL OF THE MAJOR WAR CRIMINALS BEFORE THE INTERNATIONAL MILITARY TRIBUNAL (1949); commonly known as the "Blue Series."
IMTFE (also Tokyo Trials)	International Military Tribunals for the Far East. Trial of the Major War Criminals, Proceedings of the International Military Tribunal for the Far East at Tokyo. *Reprinted in* 4 Bevans 20; 2 B. FERENCZ, DEFINING INTERNATIONAL AGGRESSION 522 (1975). *See* (excerpts) Document Section C.9.
IND. INT'L & COMP. L. REV.	INDIANA INTERNATIONAL AND COMPARATIVE LAW REVIEW

TABLE OF ABBREVIATIONS

The Justice Case	United States v. Altstoelter et al., 3 CCL Trials (1947). *Reprinted in* 2 Friedman 1196.
KY. L. J.	KENTUCKY LAW JOURNAL
The Krupp Case	United States v. Krupp et al., 9 CCL Trials (1948). *Reprinted in* 2 Friedman 1344.

Law of the Charter — Refers to:
(a) London Agreement and the Charter;
(b) Indictments, Proceedings and Judgment of the International Military Tribunal at Nuremberg;
(c) Tokyo Charter;
(d) Indictments, Proceedings and Judgment of the International Military Tribunal at Tokyo;
(e) Subsequent Proceedings CCL 10;
(f) Allied Tribunals;
(g) Post-Charter Legal Developments.

LAW & CONTEMP. PROB.	LAW AND CONTEMPORARY PROBLEMS
LAW GUILD REV.	LAW GUILD REVIEW
Leipzig Trials	The trials of German war criminals after World War I held before the German Supreme Court (*Reichsgericht*) Sitting at Leipzig. *See generally* C. MULLINS, THE LEIPZIG TRIALS (1921); *see also* 16 AJIL 696 *et seq.* (1922).
LIA	London International Assembly, *See* The Punishment of War Criminals: Recommendations of the London International Assembly (1944) (Report of Commission I). *See* (excerpts) Document Section B.1.

TABLE OF ABBREVIATIONS

Lieber Code

U.S. Dept. of War, Instructions for the Government of the Armies of the United States in the Field, General Orders No. 100 (1863); *reprinted in* 1 Friedman 158; 3 Schindler/Toman. *See* (excerpts) Document Section C.1.

London Agreement
(see also, Charter)

Agreement for the Prosecution and Punishment Of Major War Criminals of the European Axis (London Agreement), London, 8 August 1945, 82 U.N.T.S. 279, 59 Stat. 1544, E.A.S. No. 472. *Reprinted in* 39 AJIL 257 (1945) (Supp.); 1 Ferencz 454; 1 Friedman 883; Schindler/Toman 823. *See* Document Section C.1.

LOY. L. REV.

LOYOLA LAW REVIEW

L.N.T.S.

League of Nations Treaty Series

L.Q.

LAW QUARTERLY

L.Q. REV.

LAW QUARTERLY REVIEW

L. REV.

LAW REVIEW

Martens

Nouveau Recueil Général des Traités

MD. L. REV.

MARYLAND LAW REVIEW

The Medical Case

United States v. Brando et al., 1 CCL Trials and 2 CCL Trials.

ME. L. REV.

MAINE LAW REVIEW

MICH. J. INT'L L.

MICHIGAN JOURNAL OF INTERNATIONAL LAW

MICH. L. REV.

MICHIGAN LAW REVIEW

xxvii

The Milch Case	United States v. Milch, 2 CCL Trials.
MIL. L. REV.	MILITARY LAW REVIEW
The Ministries Case	United States v. Van Weizsaecker et al., 12 CCL Trials, 13 CCL Trials, and 14 CCL Trials (1948). *Reprinted in* 2 Friedman 1373.
MINN. L. REV.	MINNESOTA LAW REVIEW
MOD. L. REV.	MODERN LAW REVIEW
Moscow Declaration	The Moscow Conference, October 19-30, 1943 (Declaration of German Atrocities, 1 November 1943), 1943 FOR. REL. (I) 749 at 768. *Reprinted in* 38 AJIL 3, at 7 (1944) (Supp.); 3 Bevans 816, at 834. *See* Document Section B.3.
National Prosecutions	Post World War II prosecutions held in different states predicated on the Law of the Charter, but, based on national legislation and conducted before military tribunals, special tribunals and ordinary courts.
NAT. L. F.	NATURAL LAW FORUM
NAVAL WAR COL. REV.	NAVAL WAR COLLEGE REVIEW
NETH. INT'L L. REV.	NETHERLANDS INTERNATIONAL LAW REVIEW
NETH. Y.B. INT'L L.	NETHERLANDS YEARBOOK OF INTERNATIONAL LAW
NEW ENGLAND J. MED.	NEW ENGLAND JOURNAL OF MEDICINE
NOVA L.J.	NOVA LAW JOURNAL

TABLE OF ABBREVIATIONS

The Pohl Case	United States v. Pohl et al., 5 CCL Trials (1947). *Reprinted in* 2 Friedman 1254.
POLISH Y.B. INT'L L.	POLISH YEARBOOK OF INTERNATIONAL LAW
Post-Charter Legal Developments	Refers to: (a) Affirmation of Nuremberg Principles; (b) Genocide Convention; (c) ILC Nuremberg Principles; (d) U.N. Non-Applicability of Statutory Limitations to War Crimes; (e) Resolutions on War Criminals, 15 December 1970, U.N.G.A. Res. 2583 (XXIV). *Reprinted in* 1 Friedman 754; (f) *Apartheid* Convention; (g) International Co-operation in Extradition; (h) European Non-Applicability of Statutory Limitations to War Crimes.
Potsdam Conference	The Berlin (Potsdam) Conference (Protocol of Proceedings), 2 August 1945, 1945 FOR. REL. Conference of Berlin (Potsdam II) 1499. *Reprinted in* 3 Bevans 1207; 39 AJIL 245 (1945) (Supp.). *See* (excerpts) Document Section B.5.
RECUEIL DES COURS	RECUEIL DES COURS DE L'ACADEMIE DE DROIT INTERNATIONAL DE LA HAYE
RIDP	REVUE INTERNATIONALE DE DROIT PÉNAL
The Rusha Case	United States v. Greifelt et al., 4 CCL Trials and 5 CCL Trials.
RUT. L. J.	RUTGERS LAW JOURNAL
RUT.-CAM. L.J.	RUTGERS-CAMDEN LAW JOURNAL

TABLE OF ABBREVIATIONS

SANTA CLARA L. REV.   SANTA CLARA LAW REVIEW

S. CALIF. L. REV.   SOUTHERN CALIFORNIA LAW REVIEW

Schindler/Toman   THE LAW OF ARMED CONFLICTS (D. Schindler &
                             J. Toman eds. 1981).

STAN. L. REV.   STANFORD LAW REVIEW

Stat.   United States Statutes at Large

Subsequent Proceedings   Proceedings by the Allied Powers held pursuant to
(*See also* CCL Trials)   Control Council Law No. 10, (Punishment of
                             Persons Guilty of War Crimes, Crimes Against
                             Peace and Against Humanity), 20 December 1945,
                             OFFICIAL GAZETTE OF THE CONTROL COUNCIL FOR
                             GERMANY, No. 3, Berlin, 31 January 1946. *Re-
                             printed in* 1 Ferencz 488; 1 Friedman 908. The
                             Proceedings involved 12 Trials:
                             (a) *The "Einsatzgruppen" Case*
                             (b) *The I.G. Farben Case*
                             (c) *The Fleck Case*
                             (d) *The High Command Case*
                             (e) *The Hostage Case*
                             (f) *The Justice Case*
                             (g) *The Krupp Case*
                             (h) *The Medical Case*
                             (i) *The Milch Case*
                             (j) *The Ministries Case*
                             (k) *The Pohl Case*
                             (l) *The Rusha Case*

Tehran Conference   The Tehran Conference, (Declaration of the Three
                             Powers), 1 December 1943, Dep't. of State Bull.
                             409-410 (Dec. 11, 1943). *Reprinted in* 1943 FOR.
                             REL. 640; 3 BEVANS 859; A DECADE OF AMERI-

	CAN FOREIGN POLICY: BASIC DOCUMENTS 1941-1949 21-22 (1985). *See* Document Section B.4.
TEMP. L.Q.	TEMPLE LAW QUARTERLY
TEMPLE L. REV.	TEMPLE LAW REVIEW
TEX. INT'L L. J.	TEXAS INTERNATIONAL LAW JOURNAL
TEX. L. REV.	TEXAS LAW REVIEW
T.I.A.S.	(U.S.) Treaties and Other International Acts Series
Tokyo Charter	International Military Tribunal for the Far East: (a) Proclamation by the Supreme Commander for the Allied Powers, 19 January 1946, T.I.A.S. 1589: *Reprinted in* 4 Bevans 20; 1 B. FERENCZ, DEFINING INTERNATIONAL AGGRESSION 522 (1975); Friedman 894. *See* Document Section C.7. (b) Charter of the International Military Tribunal for the Far East, 19 January 1946, T.I.A.S. 1589; *Reprinted in* 1 B. FERENCZ, DEFINING INTERNATIONAL AGGRESSION 523; 1 Friedman 895. *See* Document Section C.8.
Tokyo Judgment	1 B. FERENCZ, DEFINING INTERNATIONAL AGGRESSION 539 (2 vols. 1975). *See* Document Section C.9. (excerpts).
Torture Convention	Convention Against Torture and Other Cruel, Inhuman or Degrading Treatment or Punishment, 10 December 1984, U.N. G.A. Res. 39/46. *Reprinted in* 24 ILM 535 (1985); 23 ILM 1027 (1984). *See* Document Section C.3.
Treaty of Versailles	Treaty of Peace Between the Allied and Associated Powers and Germany (Treaty of Versailles), 28

TABLE OF ABBREVIATIONS

UNWCC	United Nations War Crimes Commission. *See* A. WRIGHT, HISTORY OF THE UNITED NATIONS WAR CRIMES COMMISSION (1948). *See* (excerpts) Document Section B.2.
Universal Declaration	Universal Declaration of Human Rights, 10 December 1948, G.A. Res. 217A (III).
U. PA. L. REV.	UNIVERSITY OF PENNSYLVANIA LAW REVIEW
U. RICH. L. REV.	UNIVERSITY OF RICHMOND LAW REVIEW
U.S.T.	United States Treaty Series
VA. J. INT'L L.	VIRGINIA JOURNAL OF INTERNATIONAL LAW
VA. L. REV.	VIRGINIA LAW REVIEW
VAL. U.L. REV.	VALPARAISO UNIVERSITY LAW REVIEW
VAND. J. TRANSNAT'L L.	VANDERBILT JOURNAL OF TRANSNATIONAL LAW
VAND. L. REV.	VANDERBILT LAW REVIEW
WAYNE L. REV.	WAYNE LAW REVIEW
Y.B. INT'L L. COMM'N	YEARBOOK OF THE INTERNATIONAL LAW COMMISSION
YALE J. INT'L L.	YALE JOURNAL OF INTERNATIONAL LAW
YALE J. WORLD PUB. ORD.	YALE JOURNAL OF WORLD PUBLIC ORDER
YALE L. J.	YALE LAW JOURNAL

TABLE OF ABBREVIATIONS

ZSTW   ZEITSCHRIFT FÜR DIE GESAMTE STRAFRECHTS
                              WISSENSCHAFT

The term "he" and other pronouns refer to masculine and feminine for lack of any appropriate gender neutral terms in the English language.

CHAPTER 1

EMERGENCE AS AN INTERNATIONAL CRIME

Mens aequa in ardius

Introduction

The Charter of the International Military Tribunal for the Trial of the Major War Criminals[1] was appended to the London Agreement of August 8, 1945.[2] Article 6 defined the crimes -- committed in the European theater by certain "major war criminals" -- which the Allies would prosecute. They were: "Crimes Against Peace," "War Crimes," and "Crimes Against Humanity." The Charter defined this last criminal category in Article 6(c) as:

> murder, extermination, enslavement, deportation, and other inhumane acts committed against any civilian population, before or during the war, or persecutions on political, racial or religious grounds in execution of or in connection with any crime within the jurisdiction of the Tribunal, whether or not in violation of the domestic law of the country where perpetrated.

Subsequently, two other formulations defining "crimes against humanity" were developed, they are: Article 5(c) of the Tokyo Charter[3] and Article II(c) of the Allied Control Council Law No. 10.[4] Notwithstanding the fact that these two subsequent formulations differed slightly from that of the Charter's Article 6(c), as discussed below, the same legal issues pertaining to Article 6(c) apply to them. More importantly, the Charter was first in time and served as the model and legal basis for these subsequent developments. Consequently, the analysis which follows throughout this book is predicated essentially on the Charter.

The Charter's Article 6(c) formulation was the first instance in positive international criminal law in which the specific terms "crimes against humanity" were used. It was

---

[1] *See* Document Section C.2.

[2] *See* Document Section C.1.

[3] *See* Document Section C.8.

[4] *See* Document Section C.5.

also the first time that this international criminal category was defined. It should be noted, however, that the notion of protecting civilians in time of war is historically well established in the international regulation of armed conflicts and precedes the Charter, as discussed in Chapter 4.

The major Allies first broadcasted a proclamation on December 17, 1942, followed by a second one on January 5, 1943, indicating their intention to hold Germans and Germany accountable for war crimes and atrocities committed during the war. Then on February 11, 1943 at the Yalta Conference, Roosevelt, Churchill and Stalin adopted a similar resolution. Lastly on November 1, 1943, the Moscow Declaration[5] made explicit the policy and intentions of the Allies to hold post-war trials. After Germany's unconditional surrender on May 8, 1945, the Potsdam Agreement[6] asserted that war criminals were to be punished. But neither the policy nor the precise legal basis was laid out in any of these proclamations, declarations or the Potsdam Agreement.

The existence of two theaters of operation, one in Europe and the other in the Far-East, imposed the need to have two different approaches, which resulted in the London Charter and its Tokyo counterpart. The former was in the nature of an Agreement signed by the Four Major Allies -- France, the United Kingdom, the United States of America and the Union of Soviet Socialist Republics -- and acceded to by 19 others.[7] The latter was proclaimed by General Douglas MacArthur in his capacity as Supreme Allied Commander in that theater of operation.[8] No one ever adequately explained why in one case an international agreement was needed and in the other a military proclamation by a theater military commander was deemed sufficient. But as is frequently the case in international affairs, a variety of political considerations, some international and some domestic, bring about an outcome which upon reflection may neither be good law nor sound policy. But the political decision of the Allies to provide a legal process for the prosecution and punishment of those who committed crimes in connection with World War II was essentially a principled one.

---

[5]   *See* Document Section B.3.

[6]   *See* Document Section B.5.

[7]   London Agreement accompanied by the Charter; *see also* JACKSON'S REPORT at 410. The nineteen were: Australia; Belgium; Czechoslovakia; Denmark; Ethiopia; Greece; Haiti; Honduras; India; Luxembourg; the Netherlands; New Zealand; Norway; Panama; Paraguay; Poland; Uruguay; Venezuela; and Yugoslavia. *See* JACKSON'S REPORT at viii.

[8]   *See* Document Section C.5.

Both the London and Tokyo Charters provided only for the prosecution of what the Allies considered to be major war criminals in the two separate theaters of military operations. The London Charter established the International Military Tribunal at Nuremberg, and the Tokyo Charter established the International Military Tribunal for the Far East at Tokyo.

In the European theater, the Allies established a joint body to administer Germany, the Control Council, and pursuant to that body's supreme control over Germany it passed CCL 10. That law was a hybrid between international law and national law and was made applicable to Germany by the Allied occupying powers. Under that law, the Allies in the European theater were to try, in their respective zones of occupation, Germans and others accused of the crimes contained in CCL 10. There was no such counterpart in Japan where sovereign authority over Japan was *de facto* exercised by the United States through General Douglas MacArthur.

The Allies in Germany and in Asia were also permitted to set up their own military courts to try war criminals, and formerly occupied countries could also exercise their jurisdiction whether through their military, or through ordinary criminal courts applying their respective laws. There are no published records of the reasons for these and other legal and policy decisions that were taken by the Allies; one can assume that they were made for pragmatic reasons and, given the times, surely in haste.

The only published record that exists of the negotiations leading to the London Agreement of August 8, 1945 and its annexed Charter is contained in the *Report of Robert H. Jackson, United States Representative to the International Conference on Military Trials to the President of the United States of America* (1945). It consists of the transcription of stenographic notes made by Justice Robert Jackson's secretary. These notes were not, however, verbatim transcriptions but edited summaries which contained selective quotations of some of the drafters' statements.[9] A book by Professor A.N. Trainin, who was the alternate Russian delegate at the London Conference, published in Moscow in 1944, also provides insight as to the question of aggression.[10] These sources are insufficient to assess the reasons for the policies and

---

[9]   *See* JACKSON'S REPORT. *See also* R.H. JACKSON, THE NÜRNBERG CASE (1947, 2d printing 1971). Another insightful report of a senior participant is that of Brg. Gen. Telford Taylor who was Jackson's deputy and then his successor, and who also headed the U.S. prosecution team under CCL 10. T. TAYLOR, FINAL REPORT TO THE SECRETARY OF THE ARMY ON THE NUREMBERG WAR CRIMES TRIALS UNDER CONTROL COUNCIL LAW No. 10, 1-32 (1949). *See also* B. SMITH, THE AMERICAN ROAD TO NUREMBERG: THE DOCUMENTARY RECORD (1982); and B. SMITH, REACHING JUDGMENT AT NUREMBERG 20-73 (1977).

[10]   *See* A.N. TRAININ, HITLERITE RESPONSIBILITY UNDER CRIMINAL LAW (A. Rothstein trans. 1945

critical decisions that led to the newly established law-making process, the reasons for the legal decisions made by the drafters, and the multiplicity of applicable legal sources and adjudicative bodies which emerged from that process. A more revealing document about the Allies' policies, however, is contained in the American Memorandum presented at San Francisco, April 30, 1945, excerpts of which appear below. It shows quite clearly that the United States' views and policies ultimately prevailed in the formulation of the London and Tokyo Charters and in the conduct of the IMT and IMTFE prosecutions, as well as in the formulation of CCL 10 and the Subsequent Proceedings. Beyond that, the United States apparently had no interest in what the other Allies did in their respective zones of occupation in Germany and even less about what they did or did not do to Germans and to their collaborators in their respective national territories. Subsequently, however, the United States became interested in the continuation of prosecutions by Germany (at the time, the Federal Republic of Germany) of those accused of "crimes against humanity" against Jews and it pursued a belated national policy of denaturalization and extradition of such persons. But the United States has not demonstrated any particular interest in pursuing national prosecutions for "crimes against humanity," unlike such countries as Canada, France and Israel.

The horrendous crimes committed against millions of innocent civilians and lawful combatants and the devastation inflicted on so many countries was not the context in which to raise legal arguments, no matter how valid. Everything paled in comparison to what had happened. Indeed this was a case in which the facts drove the law, more specifically they drove the making of the law. Whatever law existed, it did not, and could not have foreseen the horrors that had taken place. This was truly a situation so extreme that no law, however prescient, could have fantasized the horrors that occurred. It was truly a case so maximal that it was beyond foreseeability. And law is not an exercise in fantasy. Consequently by reversing the Roman Law maxim *de minimus non curat praetor*, it can be said that *de maxima non curat lex*.[11]

---

from a Moscow 1944 ed.). In 1946, Trainin wrote an article that gave some insight into the IMT and the Charter. *See, Le Tribunal Militaire International et le Procés de Nuremberg*, 17 RIDP 263 (1946).

[11] *See* Cohn, *The Problems of War Crimes Today*, 26 TRANS. GR. SOC'Y 125, 141 (1940); and JACKSON'S REPORT 198-99.

The Making of the Charter: Law and Policy Considerations

The four major Allies delegated to the legal ingenuity of their able representatives the task of establishing a legal process and the codification of the specific crimes for which the vanquished would be tried.[12] The political decision of the Allies to provide a legal process for the prosecution and punishment of those who committed crimes in connection with World War II was essentially a principled one. What they also had to accomplish was to serve as a model for other prosecutions and a precedent for the future. But not all the participants in this process were so motivated. Some were only concerned with the immediate task at hand of prosecuting and punishing the Germans and the Japanese.

The first major substantive legal issue was whether "crimes against humanity" existed under any one of the sources of international law specified in Article 38 of the Statute of the PCIJ, namely: conventions, customs, and "general principles of law recognized by civilized nations."[13] The second issue, which was predicated on the first one, was to ascertain the legal contents of such crimes in accordance with the sources

---

[12] Each country had a team of jurists, whose principals were:

The United States: Justice Robert H. Jackson;
The United Kingdom: Sir David Maxwell Fyfe, who was succeeded by Lord Jowitt;
France: Judge Robert Falco and Professor André Gros;
The Union of Soviet Socialist Republics: General I.T. Nikitchenko and Professor A.N. Trainin.

As stated by Bradley Smith:

"The U.S. and British documents show clearly that there never was a fixed or well-defined Nuremberg plan or policy. The Allies stumbled and compromised their way into the business of a major trial of war criminals, and neither the government leaders nor the prosecutors clearly grasped the uncertainties inherent in the enterprise. There was much talk of the need for a trial, together with an admonition about possible hazards, but few expected that it would open a Pandora's box so wide that the proceedings would threaten to pass beyond the control of the governments. So the Allied leaders and prosecutors plunged ahead, piling uncertainty upon complexity until the case became so confused that clarity and order could be imposed only from on high -- which is to say that the Nuremberg judges, not the government leaders or prosecutors, ultimately had to produce the necessary order in the case so that they could write a general opinion and render a series of verdicts."
B. SMITH, REACHING JUDGMENT AT NUREMBERG xvii (1977).

See JACKSON'S REPORT at xii.

[13] *See* Chapter 7.

of international law under which they would be deemed to exist. This issue involved not only public international law but also comparative military law and comparative criminal law.[14] The third was a cluster of legal issues pertaining to the basis and elements of criminal responsibility[15] and the grounds for exoneration from criminal responsibility.[16] These questions essentially involved comparative criminal law, and they also had international law dimensions.

Conventional and customary international law dealt with some of these legal issues, but no conventional text or precedent existed that was by itself sufficient or specific enough to be relied upon. The drafters of the Charter thus had to stitch together different elements of pre-existing law and to extrapolate therefrom new legal elements while satisfying the requirements of the "principles of legality."[17] More particularly, in this context, the drafters had to resolve the problems of the impermissible retrospective application of the new codification and justify the removal, *ex post facto*, of legal defenses arising under pre-existing national positive law, including the defense of "obedience to superior orders," which was also a defense under customary international law.[18] Indeed, the laws of Nazi Germany either commanded or justified the acts deemed to constitute "crimes against humanity," and in any event the acts in question were committed pursuant to the *Führerprinzip* or by command of superior orders. The latter was, at that time, deemed to constitute a valid legal defense under customary international law and was considered by some jurists as an absolute defense, while others viewed it as a qualified one.[19]

These and other technical problems, not to speak of the political ones, confronted the drafters under the pressing exigencies of circumstances surrounding the end of the war. Furthermore, the drafters did not have the comfort and guidance of a similar precedent to rely upon. Above all, they had to resolve these problems in short order. Thus, the outcome reflected the need to rapidly produce a workable system for a specific purpose.

---

[14] *See* Chapters 7, 8, 9 and 10.

[15] *See* Chapter 9.

[16] *See* Chapter 10.

[17] *See* Chapter 3.

[18] *See* Chapter 10.

[19] *Id.*

6

The drafters may have been concerned with the legal nature of "crimes against humanity," but if that was the case, there is no evidence of it. Instead they, and later the IMT, found that "crimes against humanity" are simply an extension of war crimes because the category of protected persons is the same in the two crimes, the difference being whether the violators were of the same or another nationality. Thus, the historical-legal foundation of "crimes against humanity" is found in international humanitarian law and in the normative aspects of the international regulation of armed conflicts, as discussed in Chapter 4.

The Charter's drafters were also confronted with certain basic questions of law and policy that commonly arise under national criminal law, such as: what to criminalize; why criminalize; how to criminalize; whom to punish; why punish; and how to punish. The drafters, however, were not hampered by the characteristic weakness of international criminal law, namely: enforcement.[20] Thus, whereas international criminal law has always had to temper its goals with the realization of its own enforcement limitations, the drafters of the Charter had all the enforcement powers and capabilities needed to carry out their plans for international prosecutions. But they posited the legitimacy of their powers on the grounds that the Allies were the sovereign power over a Germany which had surrendered unconditionally. On that point, the IMT in its judgment stated:

> The making of the Charter was the exercise of the sovereign legislative power by the countries to which the German Reich unconditionally surrendered; and the undoubted right of these countries to legislate for the occupied territories has been recognized by the civilized world. The Charter is not an arbitrary exercise of power on the part of the victorious nations. ... The Signatory Powers created this Tribunal, defined the law it was to administer, and made regulations for the proper conduct of the trial. In doing so, they have done together what any one of them might have done singly.[21]

One of the implications of this postulate could have been for the Charter to become the new German law of the land, and have national legal validity and territorial jurisdictional application, but that was not the case. The Allies deemed the Charter part of international law. Conversely, however, the Allies developed a legislative system for

---

[20] *See generally* 3 BASSIOUNI ICL.

[21] 22 IMT 461.

occupied Germany, the Control Council, which provided in its CCL 10 the basis for the Allies to prosecute for "crimes against humanity."[22] Thus, the Charter was neither intended to be national German law, nor was it applied as such. Instead, it was to be part of international law and applied by a specially established international military tribunal that would try only a selected number of accused, while others would be tried by the Allies under CCL 10. In addition, the military tribunals, or court martials of the Allies prosecuted German military personnel in their custody and under their respective laws, which was a departure of the agreement to have all such prosecutions conducted under CCL 10. It should, however, be noted that the 1929 Geneva Convention recognized the right of belligerents to prosecute, but only for certain violations of this Convention.[23]

Formerly occupied Allied countries also prosecuted German occupation personnel in accordance with their national military or criminal laws, or other laws specifically enacted for that purpose.

In the Far East, the Allies set up another international military tribunal at Tokyo in 1946 and patterned its Charter after the London Charter. Thus, as stated above, the legal issues pertaining to the formulation of Article 6(c) crimes arise also with respect to the Tokyo Charter's Article 5(c).

All these prosecutions are discussed in Chapter 5.

The drafters of the Charter had to devise a new legal process, as well as to formulate the general and special parts of the new codification, with a view that it would apply to an *ad hoc* tribunal. But they also had to link this new development to the evolutionary chain of international criminal law in order that the formulation they were elaborating be linked to the past and become a basis for the future. The drafters, however, faced many difficulties, such as the assimilation of the different branches of law that contribute to the multi-disciplinary nature of international criminal law and the reconciliation of divergent legal systems.

The Charter's Article 6(c) was intended to be the special part of that newly enunciated formulation of "crimes against humanity." In addition, Article 6 provided for the substantive inchoate offenses of conspiracy and attempt which were applicable

---

[22]   See CCL 10 and *infra* at 35.

[23]   The 1929 Geneva Convention provided for court martials conducted according to certain procedures to try the military personnel of belligerents who violated the provisions of the Convention. The Convention which governed the Allies and Germany did not allow for the various forms of prosecution which the Allies pursued. To some this was a question of form, but to others it was further evidence that the Allies relied on international law when it suited their purposes and disregarded it when it did not.

8

to all three Charter categories of crimes: "crimes against peace;" "war crimes;" and "crimes against humanity."

The general part for any of these crimes, as discussed in Chapter 9, was not, however, developed in the Charter, except with respect to two provisions: Article 7, which subjected all superiors including heads of state to individual criminal responsibility;[24] and, Article 8 which removed the defense of "obedience to superior orders."[25] Surely, no one can argue with the proposition that the general part of criminal law, consisting of the elements of criminal responsibility and conditions of exoneration thereof, was inadequately dealt with by the Charter.[26] Had the drafters been far-sighted enough and less troubled about anything German, they would have simply resolved the problem of the general part by applying the German Penal Code of 1871 which was in keeping with accepted theories of criminal law in the world's major criminal justice systems. To accomplish their intended result, the drafters would only have had to revoke the *Führerprinzip*, the defense of "obedience to superior orders," and, that of justification or excuse for having acted pursuant to Nazi laws passed after 1935. By adopting such an approach, the drafters would have avoided the claim of breach of the "principles of legality" with respect to general part issues.[27] This would have also reinforced the territorial application of criminal law with respect to offenses and offenders within German territory.[28] Such a solution to the problem of the proper applicable law would have also been consonant with generally accepted theories of conflict of laws or private international law rules.[29] Nevertheless, the drafters ignored

---

[24] *See* Chapter 5.

[25] *See* Chapter 10.

[26] *See* Chapter 9.

[27] *See* Chapter 3.

[28] *See* Blakesley, *Extraterritorial Jurisdiction*, in 2 BASSIOUNI ICL 3, 8-19; 1 M.C. BASSIOUNI, INTERNATIONAL EXTRADITION: UNITED STATES LAW & PRACTICE Ch. VI (2d rev. ed. 1987); H. DONNEDIEU DE VABRES, LES PRINCIPES MODERNES DU DROIT PÉNAL INTERNATIONAL Ch. 1 (1928). For a contemporary proposal regarding, *inter alia*, the jurisdiction of an international criminal court, *see, Draft Statute: International Criminal Tribunal, Presented to the Eighth United Nations Congress on Crime Prevention and The Treatment of Offenders* (Havana, Cuba, August-September 1990), A/Conf. 144/NGO 7, Item 5 (31 July 1990), *reprinted in* 15 NOVA L. Rev. 383 (1991); and Bassiouni, *The Time Has Come for an International Criminal Court*, 1 IND. INT'L & COMP. L. REV. 1, 25 (1991).

[29] *See generally* F. WHARTON, A TREATISE ON THE CONFLICT OF LAWS (2d. ed. 1881); J. BEALE, A TREATISE ON THE CONFLICT OF LAW (1935); A. KUHN, COMPARATIVE COMMENTARIES ON PRIVATE INTERNATIONAL LAW OR CONFLICT OF LAWS (1937); E. RABEL, THE CONFLICT OF LAWS: A COMPARATIVE

that better rule approach.[30] Another approach could have been the one argued by the three dissenting judges at the IMTFE, Judge Röling of the Netherlands, Judge Bernard of France, and Judge Pal of India. They argued that the creation of the Tribunal was valid, but that the Tribunal should have looked into the consistency of the Charter, in that case the Tokyo Charter, with customary international law. Such a position, however, had been rejected by the drafters of the London Charter who were quite certain about wanting their definitions and interpretations of law applied by the IMT without the possibility for anyone, including the Judges, to question the validity of the Charter, its contents, and its compliance with international law.

The Allies recognized the importance of the "principles of legality" and indeed passed legislation to uphold it. Acting through the Control Council the Allies provided, in Article IV, ordinance No. 7 of the Law No. 1 of the Military Government for the very principle from which they were deviating:

No charge shall be proffered, no sentence imposed or punishment inflicted for an act, unless such act is expressly made punishable by law in force at the time of its commission. Punishment for offences determined by analogy or in accordance with the alleged "sound instincts of the people" (gesundes Volksempfinden) is prohibited.[31]

The very valid purpose of this law was to repeal the provision in the Third Reich's Penal Code of 1935 which declared punishable a person who:

... commits an act, which either the statute declares punishable, or which deserves punishment according to the basic principles of a criminal statute or according to the sound instincts of the people. If no criminal statute can be applied directly to the

---

STUDY (1945); O. KAHN-FREUND, GENERAL PROBLEMS OF PRIVATE INTERNATIONAL LAW (1976); G. CHEVALIER CHESHIRE AND NORTH, PRIVATE INTERNATIONAL LAW (10th ed. 1979); F. VON SAVIGNY, A TREATISE ON THE CONFLICT OF LAWS (W. Guthrie trans. 1869, 2d. rev. ed. 1980); W.L.M. REESE, M. ROSENBERG, AND P. HAY, CONFLICT OF LAWS 753-777 (9th ed. 1990).

[30] See Leflar, Choice-Influencing Considerations in Conflict of Laws, 41 N.Y.U.L. REV. 267 (1966). See also R. LEFLAR, L. MCDOUGAL & R. FELIX, AMERICAN CONFLICTS LAW 279 et seq. (4th ed. 1986).

[31] Military Government-Germany, United States Zone, Ordinance No. 7, 18 October 1946 (Organization and Powers of Certain Military Tribunals) reprinted in 2 FRIEDMAN 913. See Document Section C.6.

10

act, the act will be punished according to that statute, whose underlying principle comes closest to it. (emphasis added)

In addition to these general part questions others pertaining to the special part also left much to be desired. The definitial contents of the special part defined in Article 6(c), discussed in Chapter 7, was a result of several considerations. Chief among them were: (1) the definition was tailored to the misdeeds that had been committed; (2) the Charter was intended for immediate application; (3) the Charter was deemed legally sufficient legislation; and, (4) conceptual and doctrinal legal differences were avoided; (5) nothing could be allowed in the Charter that might be used to defeat its legitimacy; (6) technical legal considerations could not be allowed in the Charter that would cause the proceedings to get out of the control of the Tribunal; and, (7) the fairness of the Tribunal should be preserved by allowing certain procedural safeguards to the accused without unduly burdening the proceedings with excessive legalism. Thus, the drafters produced a text that was decisively designed to serve as rules for adjudicating the conduct of those who would be accused as opposed to being framed as rules of conduct which prospectively place people on notice of what is prohibited.

The drafters were confronted with technical legal difficulties that had widely different solutions in the three legal systems represented in the process, and none of the eminent jurists had the time to devote to these technical legal difficulties, particularly because they also had to deal with other problems, and with two other crimes: "crimes against peace" and "war crimes." As most of them were men whose careers were spent in the application of the law, they focused more on the problems of establishing the process and settling the numerous questions of procedure and evidence than on substantive legal issues. Admittedly these issues were dealt with so differently in the Common Law and French Civilist legal systems, at the contrasting ends of legality-based systems, and the Soviet system which was not. The USSR delegates had no regard for what they considered as the excessive legalism of the two other systems' exponents. Thus, a reconciliation of these systems would have been impossible. The representatives of the Common Law and French Civilist traditions argued their differences with a view to reconcile them in order to achieve the fairest possible process under the circumstances. But the Russian representatives saw these discussions as wasteful, unnecessarily time consuming and unjustifiably providing the accused with too many rights and privileges. Thus, on many issues, when after much discussion, an agreement was reached or about to be reached between the Common Law and French Civilist participants, the Russian delegates frequently raised their opposition on the grounds stated above, and the negotiating process stalled. All of that took place while the political clock was ticking to get the prosecutions under way. To explain these difficulties, however, does not diminish the problematic outcome of the Charter's general part, as discussed in Chapters 9 and 10, and its special part, as discussed in Chapters 7 and 8.

The policies underlying the Charter and subsequent international prosecutions in the European Theater were, as stated above, articulated in the American Memorandum Presented at San Francisco, 30 April 1945. Its understanding is important in evaluating the legislative history of the Charter.[32] It is particularly relevant because the United States policy as articulated below was the one that was followed by the Allies:

MEMORANDUM OF PROPOSALS FOR THE PROSECUTION AND PUNISHMENT OF CERTAIN WAR CRIMINALS AND OTHER OFFENDERS[33]
30 April 1945

I. The Moscow Declaration Did Not Cover the Whole Problem of the Trial and Punishment of War Criminals.

In the statement jointly issued by President Roosevelt, Premier Stalin and Prime Minister Churchill on 1 November 1943, usually referred to as the Moscow Declaration, it was announced that those members of the Hitlerite forces who have been responsible for, or have taken a consenting part in, atrocities and war crimes in territory occupied by the Axis forces, would be sent back to the countries in which their abominable deeds were done in order that they may be judged according to the laws of those countries. It is assumed for the purposes of this memorandum that the four principal Allies will cooperate in carrying out this policy set out in the Moscow Declaration and also that the several Allies will cooperate fully in arranging for the trial and punishment by the United Nations concerned (or before an Allied military tribunal) of those Hitlerite nationals who have committed war offenses anywhere against the civilians or soldiers of any United Nation.

---

[32] *See* Document Section G.1.

[33] JACKSON'S REPORT 28-35. *See also* B.F. SMITH, THE AMERICAN ROAD TO NUREMBERG: THE DOCUMENTARY RECORD 1944-1945, 162 (1982). Professor A.N. Trainin was probably the first author whose work on the prosecution of German decision-makers for "crimes against peace," shaped the position of Stalin on that question and consequently of Roosevelt and Churchill. Stalin made a speech on November 6, 1943, in which he announced the policy that was later to be adopted in the Moscow Declaration (Moscow Conference). *See* J. STALIN, ON THE GREAT PATRIOTIC WAR OF THE SOVIET UNION (1945).

No policy, however, was fixed in the Moscow Declaration covering:

a. the punishment of the major war criminals whose offenses have no particular geographical localization, beyond the announcement that they would be punished by joint decision of the Governments of the Allies; or

b. the methods of punishment of those members of the principal Nazi organizations, such as the Gestapo and S.S., who voluntarily engaged in carrying out the ruthless policies of the Nazi regime but who cannot readily be proved to have participated personally in the execution of specific atrocities.

* * *

Proposed Policy

1. The Axis leaders should be tried before Allied military tribunals composed of officers of the four principal Allies. Their guilt and punishment should be determined by *judicial* action of a military tribunal and not by political action of the Allied Governments.

* * *

III.   The Trial and Punishment of the Hitlerite Leaders and the Major Hitlerite Organization Should be Based upon Their Voluntary Participation in a Common Criminal Enterprise of which the Axis Atrocities and War Crimes were an Integral Part and the Probable Consequence.

A. Method of Determining Guilt:

After Germany's defeat or unconditional surrender, the Allies by joint action, pursuant to treaty or otherwise, could probably agree to put to death the most notorious Nazi criminal without trial. Such action, however, would be violative of concepts of justice, which the freedom loving United Nations accept and, on that account, would be distasteful and inappropriate. For reasons more fully stated in Part IV of this memorandum, it is felt that all reasonable efforts should be made to avoid such a purely political disposition of the Nazi leaders. Instead, it should be possible to determine upon a suitable judicial process more in accord with the common traditions of the principal United Nations.

* * *

B. Punishment for Crime Should Only Follow a Judicial Trial:

No principle of justice is so fundamental in most men's minds as the rule that punishment will be inflicted by judicial action. Judicial punishment is imposed only after notice to the accused of the charges against him, establishment of the facts upon which the charges rest, and an opportunity to defend against the charges with the advice of counsel. The form in which proof is presented varies from nation to nation. So does the precise extent of the opportunity to defend, the nature of the hearing, and the incidence of the burden of proof. This principle is applied in greater or lesser degree by all nations, and historically its recognition is the first step in the approach to the democratic standard of liberty under law.

C. Punishment of War Criminals Is Designed as a Deterrent and to Raise International Standards of Conduct:

Punishment of war criminals should be motivated primarily by its deterrent effect, by the impetus which it gives to improved standards of international conduct and, if the theory of punishment is broad enough, by the implicit condemnation of ruthlessness and unlawful force as instruments of attaining national ends. The satisfaction of instincts of revenge and retribution for the sake of retribution are obviously the least sound basis of punishment. If punishment is to lead to progress, it must be carried out in a manner which world opinion will regard as progressive and as consistent with the fundamental morality of the Allied case. A purely political disposition of the Axis leaders without trial, however disguised, may be regarded eventually, and probably immediately, as adoption of the methods of the Axis itself. It will retard progress towards a new concept of international obligations simply because those who have sought in this war to preserve democracy will have made their most spectacular dealing with the vanquished a negation of democratic principles of justice. They will have adopted methods repugnant alike to Anglo-American and Continental traditions.

D. The Method of Punishment Adopted must not Detract from the Moral Force Behind the Allied Cause:

The preservation of the moral force behind the Allied cause is important. That force, born from the exigencies of self defense, has brought freedom-loving peoples together and can keep them together. If we lose it in the matter of punishing war criminals, we sacrifice a part of something very precious. Only the most imperative reasons could conceivably justify such action.

E. The Verdict of History Upon the Fairness of the Disposition of War Criminals Has Practical Significance:

A further highly important reason for adopting a fair judicial method of bringing war criminals to justice is that such methods are more likely than any others to commend themselves to the judgment of history. What future generations think of the Allied action on war criminals may have a profound effect upon the preservation of peace in years to come. That action certainly will set the tone of the Allied occupation of Germany by showing that a government of laws and not of men has begun. A political disposition of the Axis leaders, on the other hand, would look like, and would be, a continuation of totalitarian practices. One has only to remember the confusing propaganda interpretations of the Versailles Treaty to realize what might be the disastrous results of action dictated by politics and not by fundamental principles of law and justice. If Allied actions are soundly conceived, however, there exists an opportunity to mark up an important step in the obtaining of future world security. Punishment following a judicial determination, in which a number of nations participate, to the effect that the alleged violations of international law have occurred, will certainly induce future government leaders to think before they act in similar fashion. It will serve also to bring home the truth to those Germans who remain incredulous about the infamies of the Nazi regime.

The Aide-Mémoire from the United Kingdom, April 23, 1945 also adds an important policy goal as it states:

4. There is a further consideration which, in the view of H.M.G. needs to be very carefully weighed. If the method of public trial were adopted, the comment

must be expected from the very start to be that the whole thing is a "put-up job" designed by the Allies to justify a punishment they have already resolved on. Hitler and his advisers -- if they decide to take part and to challenge what is alleged -- may be expected to be very much alive to any opportunity of turning the tables. Public opinion as the trial goes on is likely to weary at the length of the process. It is difficult to think that anybody would in the course of time look on Hitler as an injured man, but it is by no means unlikely that a long trial will result in a change of public feeling as to the justification of trying Hitler at all. Will not some people begin to say "The man should be shot out of hand?" And if in the complicated and novel procedure which such a trial is bound to adopt -- for Russian, American and British ideas must in some way be amalgamated -- the defense secured some unexpected point, is there not a danger of the trial being denounced as a farce?[34]

At the San Francisco meeting between 2-10 May, 1945, the various delegations focussed on policy questions and presumably on questions of methodology, though there is no record of it. Experience teaches us that such an endeavor is replete with political considerations of all types and necessarily requires compromises that may not be legally sound or effective. It was necessary, for example, to have multiple tribunals to satisfy the exigencies of the nineteen Allied countries and to allow national military courts and national criminal courts to operate co-extensively. Discretionary considerations as to the type of adjudicating forum the Allies chose had to be conceded for obvious political reasons and that prevented uniformity. The legal process had to be fair but swift, the defense should be given some opportunities for legal arguments, but no technical legal argument could be allowed to prevail and result in dismissal of the charges or acquittal. The facts were to drive the law and the proceedings would be based on the facts, rejecting legalistic considerations. Lastly, the process had to clearly be for the defeated only and it could not be allowed to turn into one in which the victors could be accused of the same crimes. Thus, whenever a defendant raised arguments concerning reprisals and *tu quoque* they were summarily rejected, as discussed in Chapter 10. Finally, this new legal process had to have all the appearance of legality and fairness, even though it was designed to insure a pre-ordained result, and at the same time, to serve as a valid legal precedent for the future. These goals were difficult to reconcile and the ultimate outcome reflected it.

---

[34]   *See* JACKSON'S REPORT 19.

The primary goal of Stalin, Churchill and Roosevelt was to punish aggression, and their representatives who drafted the Charter found that there was hardly any solid legal basis to rely on with respect to this crime. Thus, they devoted much of their time, effort and ingenuity to defining it and finding a valid legal basis to support it. The four delegations did not, however, have a similar problem with war crimes because this category of crimes was well established in international law. But as they reviewed the facts, it was clear that certain atrocities did not fall within the traditional meaning of war crimes. In the course of their deliberations they gradually came to the realization that a third separate category was needed, and by July they settled for the heading "crimes against humanity." This third category thus grew out of "war crimes" but it was also viewed by some of the delegates as linked to the aggressive scheme criminalized as "crimes against peace."

There is no indication in Jackson's record as to how the heading "Crimes Against Humanity" came to be chosen. It appears, however, to have been Justice Jackson's choice, as were so many others, after a discussion he had with Professor Hersh Lauterpacht in London during the negotiations. The choice of terms, however, is most appropriate and is the progeny of the terms used in the Preamble of the 1907 Hague Convention: the "laws of humanity."[35]

Why there was not a more ample record of the discussions on this crime as there was for the two others is an intriguing question. Surely, the seriousness of the acts committed and the fact that there was a need to establish a solid legal foundation for this newly elaborated crime would have justified it. This writer suspects that what may have, in part, accounted for this lack of commentary, is that these atrocities were committed over a long period of time during which the Allies have disregarded them until near the end of the war. Indeed, some believe that had the Allies been more sensitive to these occurrences, they could have stopped them or at the very least minimized them. The indifference mentioned above and the history of anti-semitism in Europe, and in some respect in the United States, must have weighed heavily in the minds of the delegates, as did the political climate of that time. In addition, they surely must have remembered the post- World War I refusal to prosecute Turkish officials for violations of the "laws of humanity" against the Armenians, as discussed in Chapter 4. The United States must have felt that if it had not objected in 1919 to the inclusion of such a crime in the Versailles Peace Treaty, the task of including "crimes against humanity" in the Charter would have surely been easier. Interestingly, none of these,

---

[35]   *See* Document Section D.5.

or for that matter other political considerations, ever appear in the record of these long negotiations. The JACKSON REPORT is as antiseptic as it can be.

The apparent policy of "the less said the better" seemed to also have been extended to a variety of legal problems. One has the feeling that these learned jurists only sidestepped certain questions like the "principles of legality" in the hope that the questions would become less noticeable. Politically, they may have been right, but the legal legacy they left was weaker than if they would have confronted those issues and attempted to solve them in a more defensible legal manner. Had they done so the task of the prosecution would have surely been arduous but the precedent would have been more valid.

The policies articulated by the United States and the United Kingdom were a combination of contradictory goals as they combined principal and pragmatism, procedural fairness and technical legal laxity, establishing an *ad hoc* system of justice and hoping to lay the foundation for an eventual permanent one. But in so doing, they affirmed the primacy of international criminal law over national law and the direct international criminal responsibility of individuals irrespective of the dictates of national law. In that experience, as in others throughout the history of law, expedience was not conducive to sound and validly lasting outcomes, but expedience was needed to establish the new international legal process.

The Legislative History of Article 6(C)

In London, between June 26 and August 8, 1945, the four teams negotiated the contents of the Agreement and the annexed Charter.[36] The participants brought to the negotiations their own legal conceptions and the experiences of their respective legal systems: the Common Law as it had evolved differently in England and in the United States; the Marxist conceptions of "legality;" and, the French Civilist tradition. Considering the diversity of these conceptions of law and justice, as well as the different historical experiences of these systems, it can well be assumed that only the joint political decisions of the four respective governments bound the negotiators to

---

[36] *See* JACKSON'S REPORT. It is noteworthy that the drafters of the Charter, its legislators, also acted in different capacities thereafter. Jackson and Fyfe were prosecutors respectively for the United States and the United Kingdom, while Nikitchenko and Falco became judges at the IMT, one representing the USSR, the other was the alternate judge representing France. The cumulative roles of legislators turned prosecutors and judges threatened the impartiality and fairness of the subsequent legal process.

produce the intended outcome. In substance, it was the will of Roosevelt, Stalin and Churchill that the drafters executed, with Robert Jackson being the only one whose role was more significant than that of a negotiator. He was Roosevelt's advisor, and in those days, the weight of the United States was determining.

Justice Jackson, in the *Preface* to his REPORT containing a summary of the Charter's negotiating history, reported on the legal divergences as follows:

The four nations whose delegates sat down at London to reconcile their conflicting views represented the maximum divergence in legal concepts and traditions likely to be found among occidental nations. Great Britain and the United States, of course, are known as common-law countries but, with differences between their procedures. Together they exemplify the system of law peculiar to English-speaking peoples. On the other hand, France and the Soviet Union both used variations of what generally may be called the Continental system. But the differences between French and Soviet practice were significant. It was to be expected that differences in origin, tradition, and philosophy among these legal systems would beget different approaches to the novel task of dealing with an international criminal prosecution through a newly developed judicial process.

A fundamental irritant, which persisted throughout the negotiations, was caused by the difference between the Soviet practice, under which a judicial inquiry is carried on chiefly by the court and not by the parties, and the Anglo-American theory of a criminal trial, which the Soviet jurist rejected and which they called the "contest" trial approach. The Soviets rely on the diligence of the tribunal rather than on the zeal and self-interest of adversaries to develop the facts. Another fundamental opposition concerns the function of a judiciary. The Soviets view a court as "one of the organs of government power, a weapon in the hands of the ruling class for the purpose of safeguarding its interests." It is not strange that those trained in that view should find it difficult to accept or to understand the Anglo-American idea of a court as an independent agency responsible only before the law. It would not be difficult to trace in the deliberations of the Conference the influence of these antagonistic concepts. While the Soviet authorities accept the reality and binding force of international law in general, they do not submit themselves to the general mass of customary law deduced from the practice of western states. With dissimilar backgrounds in both penal law and international law it is less surprising that clashes developed at the Conference than that they could be reconciled.

19

That these discords were stubborn and deep, the minutes of conferences adequately disclose. They do not and cannot disclose all the efforts at conciliation, for there were many personal conversations between members of the different delegations, outside the formal meetings, which aimed to gain knowledge of each other's viewpoints and clear up misunderstandings.

And much of the exposition of rival legal systems is too cryptic and general to be satisfying to the student of comparative law. How much of the obvious difficulty in reaching a real meeting of minds was due to the barrier of language and how much to underlying differences in juristic principles and concepts was not always easy to estimate. But when difference was evident, from whatever source, we insisted with tedious perseverance that it be reconciled as far as possible in the closed conferences and not be glossed over only to flare up again in the public trials.[37]

The Charter that emerged from these long and difficult negotiations was a legal compromise, though it was heavily weighted in favor of the Common Law approach. As such it departed in many ways from the conceptions of law and justice as well as the procedures and practices of the other interested parties' legal systems, and of Germany's legal system where the IMT sat and judged German citizens.

The drafters were confronted with many substantive and procedural issues, some inherent to the very legislative process which was being undertaken, others relating to the diversity of the legal conceptions and systems that needed to be reconciled. The most notable example in the area of substantive law was described by Justice Jackson as follows:

Another point on which there was a significant difference of viewpoint concerned the principles of conspiracy as developed in Anglo-American law, which are not fully followed nor always well regarded by Continental jurists. Continental law recognizes the criminality of aiding and abetting but not all the aspects of the crime of conspiracy as we know it. But the French and Soviet Delegations agreed to its inclusion as appropriate to the kind of offenses the charter was designed to deal with. However, the language which expressed this agreement seems not to have conveyed to the minds of the judges the intention clearly expressed by the framers

---

[37]   *Id.* at v-vi.

20

of the charter in conference, for, while the legal concept of conspiracy was accepted by the Tribunal, it was given a very limited construction in the judgment.[38]

As to procedural questions, Justice Jackson stated:

The only problem was that a procedure that is acceptable as a fair trial in countries accustomed to the Continental system of law may not be regarded as a fair trial in common-law countries. What is even harder for Americans to recognize is that trials which we regard as fair trial in countries accustomed to the Continental system of law may not be regarded as a fair trial in common-law countries. What is even harder for Americans to recognize is that trials which we regard as fair and just may be regarded in Continental countries as not only inadequate to protect society but also as inadequate to protect the accused individual. However, features of both systems were amalgamated to safeguard both the rights of the defendants and the interests of society.

While it obviously was indispensable to provide for an expeditious hearing of the issues, for prevention of all attempts at unreasonable delay and for elimination of every kind of irrelevancy, these necessary measures were balanced by other provisions which assured to the defendants the fundamentals of procedural "due process of law." Although this famous phrase of the American Constitution bears an occasionally unfamiliar implication abroad, the Continental countries joined us in enacting its essence -- guaranties securing the defendants every reasonable opportunity to make a full and free defense. Thus the charter gives the defendant the right to counsel, to present evidence, and to cross-examine prosecution witnesses. It requires the indictment to include full particulars specifying the charges in detail -- more fully than in our own practice. It gives the defendant the right to make any explanation relevant to the charge against him and to have all proceedings conducted in or translated into his own language.
At least one of the procedural divergences among the conferring nations worked to the advantage of defendants. The Anglo-American system gives a defendant the right, which the Continental system usually does not grant, to give evidence in his own behalf under oath. However, Continental procedure allows a defendant the right, not accorded him under our practice, to make a final unsworn statement

---

[38] *Id.* at vii.

to the tribunal at the conclusion of all testimony and after summation by lawyers for both sides without subjecting himself to cross-examination. The charter resolved these differences by giving defendants both privileges, permitting them not only to testify in their own defense but also to make the final statement to the court.[39]

It should be noted, that the IMT's procedures were as fair as can be expected, and surely much more so than the procedures in many countries of the world at that time. Regrettably, the same cannot be said for the IMTFE and other Far-East prosecutions, as discussed in Chapter 5.

The initial methodological question, discussed by the drafters of the London Charter, was whether to have a generic definition or a listing of specific acts constituting international crimes, or a combination of the two. The listing of specific acts or crimes would have been the more precise approach, but it would have risked overlooking certain acts which might be uncovered later, while the choice of a generic definition risked being too broad, thus violating the "principles of legality."[40] As with all similar legislative exercises the drafters, as evident from the chronology of drafts listed in Document G.1, combined the generic with specific listings.

The United States revised its original American Draft in a new Proposed Agreement of June 14, 1945 which, in Article 12, referred to "Atrocities and Offenses against Persons or Property Constituting Violations of International Law, Including the Laws, Rules and Customs of Land and Naval Warfare" (Paragraph A). To some extent, it

---

[39] *Id.* at x-xi. *See also* Murphy, *Crimes Against Peace at Trial: Prosecution, Defense, Judgment*, in THE NUREMBERG TRIAL AND INTERNATIONAL LAW 141, 143-149 (G. Ginsburg and V.N. Kudriavtsev eds. 1990).

[40] For example, the San Francisco draft in Article 6 stated some specific crimes and then added: "This declaration shall also include the right to charge and try defendants under this Agreement for violations of law other than those recited above, including but not limited to atrocities and crimes committed in violation of the domestic law of any Axis Power or satellite or any of the United Nations." JACKSON'S REPORT 24. B.F. SMITH, REACHING JUDGMENT AT NUREMBERG 214 (1977), comments upon that language stated: "This remarkable statement would, among other things, have empowered the prosecutors to rummage through the law codes of some fifty-odd Allied nations in search of offenses that could be charged against the Nazi leaders. Obviously defendants in any international trial would have stood no chance if handfuls of accusations drawn from the statute books of a group of states could have been thrown onto the scales of justice by the prosecution." For the formulation of the definition on aggression, for example, *see* Bassiouni, *A Definition of Aggression in International Law: The Crime Against Peace*, 1 BASSIOUNI AND NANDA TREATISE 159.

22

could be said that the reference to "Violations of International Law" was broad enough to permit some form of judicial interpretation of what international law was at the time and thus avoid the need for including a specific reference or listing of violations. These words echo the Martens clause of the 1907 Hague Convention "laws of humanity," which incorporates "general principles of law recognized by civilized nations."[41] However, such a definition would be in conflict with the "principles of legality," as discussed in Chapter 3, which require more specificity than the generality of the Martens clause definitional approach. Furthermore, that formulation would have left unspecified the types of crimes that would be the object of indictment and would have given the judges of the Tribunal excessive discretion.

In response to the amended American proposal, the British amended Article 12 and proposed to "declare" what the drafters concluded would constitute criminal violations of international law. This categorical approach, they thought, would resolve the divergent views presented. The British proceeded from the assumption that the victorious powers possessed all the authority they needed by virtue of their triumphant position. Consequently, they believed that the drafters should only concern themselves with declaring what they concluded the law to be. The United States was more concerned with legitimacy and legality and sought a general definition incorporating by reference international law and leaving broad judicial discretion to the IMT. The U.S.S.R. and the French sought to focus on specific crimes as they believed them to suit the facts, but the French had a more pronounced penchant for legal technicality and they sought to link the post-World War I developments to the effort at hand.

The British changes of June 28, 1945 were included in amended Article 12(e) which stated: "[a]trocities and persecutions and deportations on political, racial, or religious grounds, in pursuance of the common plan or enterprise referred to in subparagraph (d) hereof, whether or not in violation of the domestic law of the country where perpetrated."[42] The British purpose was essentially to avoid discussions at the trial of what constituted a violation of international law by settling the question at what they deemed to be the legislative stage. But the French delegation sought more. On July 19, 1945,

---

[41] *See generally* Bassiouni, *A Functional Approach to General Principles of International Law*, 11 MICH. J. INT'L L. 968 (1990); B. CHENG, GENERAL PRINCIPLES OF LAW AS APPLIED BY INTERNATIONAL COURTS AND TRIBUNALS (1987); F. KALSHOVEN, P. KUYPER AND J. LAMMERS, ESSAYS ON THE DEVELOPMENT OF THE INTERNATIONAL LEGAL ORDER (1980); Friedman, *The Uses of 'General Principles' in the Development of International Law*, 57 AJIL 279 (1963); and McNair, *The General Principles of Law Recognized by Civilized Nations*, 33 BRIT. Y.B. INT'L L. 1 (1957).

[42] JACKSON'S REPORT 87.

it submitted a draft which would have given the future tribunal jurisdiction over acts constituting "the policy of atrocities and persecutions against civilian populations ... [and over those who are] responsible for the violations of international law, the laws of humanity, dictates of the public conscience, committed by the armed forces and civilian authorities in the service of those enemy Powers."[43] Clearly, that text indicated its strong attachment to the implied substance of the preamble of the 1907 Hague Convention, as well as the recommendations of the 1919 Commission concerning violations of the "laws of humanity."[44] France, in 1919, was the principal advocate of reliance on the "laws of humanity" proviso to prosecute Turkish officials but the United States, as stated above, opposed it. This may be the reason why the proposed French language was not adopted in London as it was too reminiscent of what had been rejected in 1919. Maybe the United States and Great Britain delegations thought that to incorporate terms that had been rejected, while paradoxically relying on that tenuous a precedent, would have appeared too incongruous.

Atrocities against civilian population, which were at the heart of the final formulation of Article 6(c), were based on identical factual manifestations of conduct falling within the traditional meaning of war crimes, but they extended to the civilian population of the country that had committed these violations. This explains why "crimes against humanity" as a category of crimes was linked to the other crimes within the jurisdiction of the Tribunal, namely "crimes against peace" and "war crimes." That may also explain the debate over the semicolon issue which was the object of the Protocol of October 6, 1945.[45] As signed on August 8, 1945, the English text of Article 6(c), contained a semicolon after the word "war," separating it from the following words, "or persecutions on political, racial or religious grounds in execution of or in connection with any crime within the jurisdiction of the Tribunal, whether or not in violation of the domestic law of the country where perpetrated." The Russians, however, insisted on the removal of the semicolon, replacing it with a comma, ostensibly to have the three languages of the text conform identically. But the legal implications of that seemingly minor change are so significant that it is inconceivable to have made it by virtue of an amending Protocol without having taken these implications into consideration. Since no transcript of these discussions exists, it will

---

[43] Jackson's Report 293.

[44] *See* Document Section A.2.

[45] *See* Document Section C.3.

24

remain a matter of speculation, but Professor Egon Schwelb, who followed these negotiations closely, stated in 1946:

> Under the original English and French texts, which contained the division of paragraph 6(c) by a semicolon, it could be said that this provision applied only to the words following the semicolon, i.e. to persecutions on political, racial, or religious grounds. This interpretation would have led to somewhat absurd results. Through the Berlin Protocol of 6 October 1945, and its replacement of the semicolon by a comma, it seems to be quite clear that the principle of the irrelevancy of the *lex loci* applies to both kinds of crimes against humanity and that it is no defence that the act alleged to be a crime against humanity was lawful under the domestic law of the country where it was perpetrated. This is made particularly clear by the new French text of Article 6(c), which expressly says "if such acts or persecutions, whether they have or have not constituted a violation of the internal law of the country where they were perpetrated, were committed ..." (*lorsque ces actes ou persécutions, qu'ils aient constitué ou non une violation du droit interne du pays où ils ont été perpétrés*). The exclusion of this plea is closely connected with the provisions of the Charter (Art. 8) regarding the defence of superior orders. Just as a defendant cannot free himself from responsibility because he acted pursuant to an order of his government or of a superior, in the same way it avails him nothing that the inhumane act was lawful under municipal law. The close connection between these two provisions emerges particularly clearly if one realizes that the persons to be tried under the Charter were members of a very small circle in whom legislative powers were vested under the Nazi régime.

(k) The words "in connection with or in execution of any crime within the jurisdiction of the Tribunal" are of particular importance for the problem here discussed. In the first instance, it is necessary to determine whether these words relate only to the second part of paragraph (c) or to the whole of it, in other words, whether they qualify only "persecutions" or both "persecutions" and what has been called in this Article "crimes of the murder type." The first interpretation would mean that crimes of the murder type, committed against any civilian population at any time, are crimes against humanity subject to the Tribunal's jurisdiction, irrespective of whether or not they are connected with the crime against peace or a war crime proper, while persecutions on political, racial, or religious grounds come within the definition only if they are so connected. Under this interpretation, "any crime within the jurisdiction of the Tribunal" would mean either a crime against peace, a war crime, or a crime against humanity of the murder type. The second interpretation would amount to the proposition that not only persecutions, but also crimes of the murder type, are outside the notion of crimes against humanity, unless it is established that they were connected with a crime against peace or a war crime. In order to arrive at an opinion on this vital question, it will be useful to recall the wording of the original English text of Article 6(c), as it was quoted *supra*, and to add the original French text which, in the Agreement dated 8 August 1945, reads as follows:

(c)   *Les Crimes Contre L'Humanité: c'est-à-dire l'assassinat, l'extermination, la réduction en esclavage, la déportation, et tout autre acte inhumain commis contre toutes populations civiles, avant ou pendant la guerre; ou bien les persécutions pour des motifs politiques, raciaux ou religieux, commises à la suite de tout crime rentrant dans la compétence du Tribunal International ou s'y rattachant, que ces persécutions aient constitué ou non une violation du droit interne du pays où elles ont été perpétrées.*

The reader of the English text will, by simple grammatical interpretation, arrive at the conclusion that "in execution of or in connection with any crime within the jurisdiction of the Tribunal" refers to "persecutions" and to "persecutions" only, and if the English text left any doubt, recourse to the equally authentic French text would show that *commises à la suite de tout crime rentrant dans la compétence du Tribunal International ou s'y rattachant* determines *les persécutions* and that, being the feminine form, it does not refer to the words from *l'assassinat* to *autre acte inhumain*.

By the Berlin Protocol of 6 October 1945 the semicolon dividing Article 6(c) has been replaced by a comma in both the English and French texts. It is submitted that the change of punctuation marks in itself would not bring about a fundamental alteration in the law if regard were not had to the circumstances attending this alteration. If we consider, however, that the four Great Powers went out of their way to negotiate an international protocol and to have it drawn up and signed on behalf of their respective governments, it is quite clear that the intention must have been to alter the law such as it appeared to be laid down in the English and French texts of the Charter in a significant manner. Even quite apart from the obvious grammatical conclusions arising from the original French text, the comma, followed by "or," would, in normal circumstances, have sufficed to divide the paragraph of the English text into two parts with the consequence that the words "in execution of or in connection with any crime within the jurisdiction of the Tribunal" would have related only to persecutions and not to crimes of the murder type. In view of the Preamble and the operative text of the Protocol, however, it is obvious that it has been the intention of the Contracting Parties to remove a certain barrier which, in the original texts, appeared to exist between the first and second parts of the paragraph. Any possible doubt about the consequence of the Berlin Protocol has, however, been removed by the alteration made in the French text, which, by virtue of the Berlin Protocol, now reads as follows:

(c)   *Les Crimes Contre L'Humanitée: c'est-à-dire l'assassinat, l'extermination, la réduction en esclavage, la déportation, et tout autre acte inhumain commis contre toutes populations civiles, avant ou pendant la guerre, ou bien les persécutions pour des motifs politiques, raciaux ou religieux, lorsque ces actes ou persécutions, qu'ils aient constitué ou non une violation du droit interne du pays où ils ont été perpétrés, ont été commis à la suite de tout crime rentrant dans la compétence du Tribunal, ou en liaison avec ce crime.*

Instead of containing the words *commises à la suite de tout crime rentrant dans la compétence du Tribunal International ou s'y rattachant*, determining *les persécutions* and severed from the preceding part of the paragraph by a semicolon, the new text, in addition to abolishing the semicolon, expressly speaks of *ces actes ou persécutions, ces actes* being *l'assassinat, l'extermination, la réduction en esclavage, la déportation, et tout autre acte inhumain*, or, in other words, the crimes against humanity of the murder type. The new French wording of Article 6(c) is the more important and decisive in view of the fact that it is contained not only in the French, but also in the English and Russian, texts of the Berlin Protocol, so that it is clear that all four Contracting parties have agreed that the text, as it is declared in the amended French wording, correctly reproduces the meaning of the Agreement and the intention of all four Parties.

Having regard to the English and French texts as they now stand, and to the Russian text as it has read from the beginning, it is now beyond doubt that the qualification "in execution of or in connection with any crime within the jurisdiction of the Tribunal" undoubtedly applies to the whole context of the paragraph and constitutes a very important restriction on the scope of the concept of crimes against humanity. This is the opinion which was hinted at in the Indictment, which was extensively

27

elaborated in the speeches of the Chief Prosecutors at the close of the case against the individual defendants, and which was finally adopted by the Judgment of the International Military Tribunal.[46]

More recently, Professor Clark commented:

The semi-colon following "war" was arguably of great substantive significance. A literal reading of the language prior to the semi-colon would include within the Tribunal's jurisdiction such acts as murder of the Jews within Germany, before or during the war, with no requirement that the prosecution show any connection between those acts and a crime against peace, or a war crime as that term was used in the Charter. Only "persecutions" (presumably something short of violent death or deportation when read in context) would require a connection with war crimes or crimes against peace. In short, the semi-colon would permit, even require, an expansive application of the Charter -- unless the preparatory work which has just been discussed could be relied upon to reach another result. And, of course, the preparatory work does suggest that the drafters intended to narrow the scope of crimes against humanity within the jurisdiction of the tribunal to those closely associated with an aggressive war. On the other hand, if the semi-colon were replaced by a comma, it would not be necessary to rely on the preparatory work. Now it could be argued that the words "in execution of or in connection with any crime within the jurisdiction of the Tribunal" should be read (as the Tribunal would later read them) so as to modify not only "persecutions" and the words following it, but also the words "murder, extermination" and their following material. This latter course of interpretation -- consistent with the apparent general aim of the drafters -- was facilitated by a Protocol to the original text, signed on 6 October, in Berlin by the four Chief prosecutors, which in fact replaced the semi-colon punctuation in the English text with a comma and made corresponding alterations to the French text.

The origin of the semi-colon is mysterious. It did not appear in the U.S. revision of Definition of "Crimes" which was submitted to the London Conference on 31 July 1945 and which was the re-draft substantially appearing in the final text as agreed upon in London. There is, indeed, no discussion of it in Justice Jackson's record of

---

[46]   Schwelb, *Crimes Against Humanity*, 23 BRIT. Y.B. INT'L L. 178, 192-195 (1946).

the London Conference. This history, and the rest of the drafting history which has just been discussed, would suggest that the usual bunch of incompetents struck -- an error was simply made. This at least is consistent with the position asserted in the Protocol. In its second preambular paragraph the document asserts that "a discrepancy has been found to exist between the originals of Article 6, paragraph (c), of the Charter in the Russian language, on the one hand, and the originals in the English and French languages, on the other, to wit, the semi-colon in Article 6, paragraph (c), of the Charter between the words "war" and "or," as carried in the English and French texts, is a comma in the Russian text." The operative paragraph of the Protocol goes on to say that the parties have agreed that "the Russian text is correct, and that the meaning and intention of the Agreement and Charter require that the said semi-colon in the English text should be changed to a comma, and that the French text should be amended ...." I have not been able to locate any information which suggests that this statement should be taken other than at face value. Someone made a mechanical mistake in London which arguably upset the narrow definition of crimes against humanity within the jurisdiction of the Tribunal intended by the drafters; the error was corrected in the October Protocol. Yet the nagging doubt remains that something more substantive was going on and that there had been a change of position.[47]

---

[47] Clark, *Crimes Against Humanity at Nuremberg,* in THE NUREMBERG TRIAL AND INTERNATIONAL LAW 177, 190-192 (G. Ginsburgs & V.N. Kudriavtsev eds. 1990). Even though Professor Clark indicates that he found no reference in the JACKSON REPORT on the semi-colon/comma controversy, the following statement by Professor Gros at the July 24, 1945 meeting indicates that a discussion on the separation of persecution from the other crimes may have taken place, though unreported. Gros states:

I have nothing to say on the material. It seems to me everything has been discussed. Now, as to drafting, naturally it is a question of general approach to the problem of drafting for an international conference. I don't know whether, when you put in for example, "murder and ill-treatment of civilians" it helps the difficulty. The fact that you are obliged to say "including *inter alia*" proves that it is only an illustration, and it makes the test a little heavy. But it is only a question of drafting. I do accept it with one or two verbal amendments.

I have one remark on (b), *where we appear as wanting to prosecute because of racial or religious treatments only because they were connected with the war. I know it was very clearly explained at the last session by Mr. Justice Jackson that we are in fact prosecuting those crimes only for that reason, but for the last century there have been many interventions for humanitarian* reasons. All countries have interfered in affairs of other countries to defend minorities who were being persecuted. *Perhaps it is only a question of wording* -- perhaps if we could avoid to appear as making the principle that those interventions are only justified because of the connection with aggressive war, it would not change your

This writer believes that the war connection was always intended by the drafters and that the change from the semicolon to the comma was to strengthen the link between "crimes against humanity" and "crimes against peace" and particularly with "war crimes," in order to avoid the criticism that Article 6(c) crimes were entirely new to international criminal law.[48] The trade-off which resulted by limiting the scope of Article 6(c), was the exclusion of all Nazi crimes before 1939,[49] in order to strengthen the validity of the crime in light of the requirements of the "principles of legality." The IMT Judgment thus stated:

> With regard to crimes against humanity, there is no doubt whatever that political opponents were murdered in Germany before the war, and that many of them were kept in concentration camps in circumstances of great horror and cruelty. The policy of terror was certainly carried out on a vast scale, and in many cases was organized and systematic. The policy of persecution, repression, and murder of civilians in Germany before the war of 1939, who were likely to be hostile to the Government, was most ruthlessly carried out. The persecution of the Jews during the same period is established beyond all doubt. To constitute Crimes against Humanity, the acts relied on before the outbreak of war must have been in execution of, or in connection with, any crime within the jurisdiction of the Tribunal. The Tribunal is of the opinion that revolting and horrible as many of these crimes were, it has not been satisfactorily proved that they were done in execution of, or in connection with,

---

intention, Mr. Justice Jackson, and it would not be so exclusive of the other intervention that has taken place in the last century. (emphasis added)

JACKSON REPORT at 360.

[48]   *See* Chapters 1 and 4.

[49]   *See* L. DAVIDOWICZ, THE WAR AGAINST THE JEWS 1933-1945 (1975) in which the author documents Nazi crimes against German, Polish, Czech and Hungarian Jews between 1933-39 which are similar to those committed between 1939-45 (though less in harmful intensity and results), but which, because of the war connecting element in Article 6(c) were not prosecuted, though they were prosecuted under CCL 10 and under the Criminal Laws of the Federal Republic of Germany after the IMT concluded its proceedings at Nuremberg. In the case of only four individuals (Frick, Goering, Streicher and Funk) the IMT referred to events prior to 1939 and while the respective individual judgments found that these activities were illegal by Charter standards, they did not make findings of guilt as to these pre-1939 events, nor did they take these events into consideration for purposes of sentencing for post-1939 events. *See* JUDGMENT at 60-64. *See also* Clark, *supra* note 47, at 185. It is to be noted that only Streicher and Van Schirah were charged with "crimes against humanity" and not with "war crimes." *See also* N. LEVIN, THE HOLOCAUST: THE DESTRUCTION OF EUROPEAN JEWRY, 1933-1945 (1973).

any such crime. The Tribunal therefore cannot make a general declaration that the acts before 1939 were Crimes against Humanity within the meaning of the Charter, but from the beginning of the war in 1939 War Crimes were committed on a vast scale, which were also Crimes against Humanity; and insofar as the inhuman acts charged in the Indictment, and committed after the beginning of the war, did not constitute War Crimes, they were committed in execution of, or in connection with, the aggressive war, and therefore constituted crimes against humanity.[50]

The Allies, however, did not feel compelled by these very considerations when they formulated CCL 10, which, as discussed below, removed the connection between "crimes against humanity" and the two other crimes.

During the course of the submission of the different drafts by the four delega-tions,[51] it is quite interesting to note that the recorded discussions on the subject of "crimes against humanity," as stated above, were extremely limited. The debates that Article 6(c) generated in the course of the IMT prosecutions, and subsequently in the legal literature, either did not take place in London or were not reported. In fact, it appears from the very scant record of the negotiating process that, between April 30 and August 8, the subject of "crimes against humanity" only appeared as an outgrowth of war crimes without much debate as to its compliance with the "principles of legality," its legal elements and the other legal issues that were subsequently so extensively debated in the literature on this subject. Surely, the issues created by the Charter's formulation were foreseeable by the drafters, which gives rise to speculation as to their reasons and motives. This writer's suspicion is that the debate took place but was not recorded for the same reasons that the scant record was not made public until after the IMT rendered its judgment. Thus, the defense was never able to discover the intent of the drafters as to any of the three Article 6 crimes during the course of the proceedings and therefore the defense could not use any arguments which the drafters considered might favor the defense. It is logical to assume that an extended record of discussions on the legal problems of the Article 6(c) formulation would have been beneficial to the defense, *ergo*, the absence of any record that would have supported the defense's contentions in any way, even after the proceedings. If, indeed, there were reservations in the drafters' minds about any aspects of that formulation, it would have reinforced the claims of those who considered "crimes against humanity" under Article

---

[50] 22 IMT 498.

[51] *See* Document Section G.1.

6(c) as violative of the "principles of legality" and that would have weakened the moral authority of the Judgment.

The legal rigor we have come to expect from national criminal legislation with respect to its adherence to "principles of legality" is certainly not evident in the formulation of this international criminal category. And what may be mitigated by the nature and scope of World War II crimes and the exigencies of that time, cannot be regarded as valid excuses for the failure to have cured these defects during almost half a century, as discussed in Chapters 11 and 12.

While the arguments presented in this Chapter, as well as other Chapters in this book, may at times seem overly technical, and pale in relationship to the crimes covered by Article 6(c), they are an important part of the legal baggage which forms the international "Rule of Law." Indeed, without an international "Rule of Law," the judgments of might would always prevail over those of right. Still the formulation of Article 6(c) constitutes a valid precedent, even though the weaknesses of the definition exist and have not been cured by the passage of time.[52]

Formulations Subsequent to Article 6(c)

The evolution of "crimes against humanity" as an international crime under positive international criminal law can be divided into three phases. The first one led up to and culminated in the Charter's Article 6(c) which first established this crime in conventional international criminal law. The second phase involved two post-Charter formulations namely the 1946 Tokyo Charter and CCL 10. The third phase dealt with other Post-Charter Legal Developments during which several relevant international

---

[52]   Professor Clark reaching the same conclusion stated: "The Nuremberg Charter and Judgment firmly established the basic concept of a crime against humanity as a crime under international law. Beyond that, however, they left the precise contours of the crime vague and largely overlapping with that of war crimes. This lack of substantive clarity was compounded by the apparent limitations in the jurisdiction of the Nuremberg Tribunal which prevented it from delving deeply into Nazi crimes, especially before September 1939, since those could not be directly connected with the waging of aggressive war.

"To my mind, the most significant contribution of the establishment of the doctrine of crimes against humanity was not the creation of that doctrine in itself but that -- along with the reiteration of the criminality of war crimes and the establishment of the criminality of waging aggressive war -- it paved the way for subsequent development of other offenses of international concern. It led directly to the definitions of genocide and the crime of *apartheid* and less directly to the development of a whole package of international crimes. It led also to the so far abortive efforts to devise a code of offenses against the peace and security of mankind." Clark, *supra* note 47, at 198-199. *See also* Chapter 11.

instruments were developed.[53] Only one of the instruments dealt with "crimes against humanity" in the Charter's sense, the 1950 International Law Commission's Report on the Nuremberg Principles.[54] All the other international instruments developed since 1947 cover narrower aspects pertaining to "crimes against humanity" and have different legally binding authority.[55] The various formulations of the ILC's Draft Code of Offences Against the Peace and Security of Mankind, until its adoption in 1954, include provisions on "crimes against humanity." Since 1987, after it was renamed Draft Code of Crimes aainst the Peace and Security of Mankind, its provisions have also included "crimes against humanity," as discussed in Chapter 11. But they are unrelated to the Charter and constitute, particularly the 1991 formulation, something different from Article 6(c), and a complete departure from the ILC's 1950 Report on the Nuremberg Principles, as discussed in Chapter 11.

After the London Charter, discussed above, the second phase, which consists of the Tokyo Charter and CCL 10, is discussed below. An additional section of this Chapter deals with the 1950 ILC formulation of the Nuremberg Principles which tracks the London Charter's formulation and purports to codify the principles arising out of the Charter and prosecutions. Historically, the 1950 ILC Report falls into the Post-Charter Legal Developments phase discussed in Chapter 11, but its direct relevance to Article 6(c) requires its inclusion in this Chapter.

The Tokyo Charter

The Tokyo Charter was appended to a promulgation by General Douglas McArthur made in his capacity as Supreme Allied Commander for the Pacific Theater. Unlike the London Charter, it was not part of a treaty or agreement between the Allies. But the Tokyo Charter was substantially the same as the London Charter, save for some exceptions. A major exception was the exclusion of Emperor Hirohito's personal responsibility. But of interest to this study is the slight difference in the definition of "crimes against humanity."

---

[53] *See* Chapter 11.

[54] *See infra* at 39, and Document Section C.12.

[55] *See* Chapter 11 and Jescheck, *Codification, Development and Future Prospects*, in 1 BASSIOUNI ICL 83 (1986).

33

The Tokyo Charter stated:

Article 5. Jurisdiction over Persons and Offences. The Tribunal shall have the power to try and punish Far Eastern War Criminals who as individuals or as members of organizations are charged with offences which include crimes against peace. The following acts, or any of them, are crimes coming within the jurisdiction of the Tribunal for which there shall be individual responsibility: ...

c. Crimes against Humanity: namely, murder, extermination, enslavement, deportation, and other inhumane acts committed before or during the war, or persecutions on political or racial grounds in execution of or in connection with any crime within the jurisdiction of the Tribunal, whether or not in violation of the domestic law of the country where perpetrated. *Leaders, organizers, instigators and accomplices participating in the formulation or execution of a common plan or conspiracy to commit any of the foregoing crimes are responsible for all acts performed by any person in execution of such plan.* [The italicized language is not included in Article 6(c).]

There is no available record of the deliberations and discussions leading to the promulgation of this text by General Douglas McArthur which is substantially similar to Article 6(c) of the Charter. The Tokyo Charter differs from The London Charter, however, in two ways. The Tokyo Charter adds the categories of persons to be held responsible (italicized in the quoted text), and it does not make "persecution" subject to "religious" grounds. The first variance is only in the drafting of Article 5(c) since the same responsibility basis exists in the Charter though not in Article 6(c). The second variance is due to the fact that the Nazi crimes against Jews did not have a counterpart in the Asian conflict.

The London and Tokyo Charters were applicable only to major criminals, leaving other criminals to be tried by the Allies. In Germany, the Allies acted pursuant to CCL 10 in their respective zones of occupation. But they also relied on their military and national tribunals, where they applied their own laws. There was no counterpart in Japan to CCL 10 because the United States was the sole occupying power of Japan, whereas Germany was occupied by the four major Allies.

The same legal issues pertaining to Article 6(c) also apply to Article 5(c).

Control Council Law No. 10

This Law, unlike the London and Tokyo Charters, was made pursuant to the supreme legislative authority of the Allies over Germany in view of that country's unconditional surrender on May 8, 1945. It was not intended to be an international instrument but national legislation. CCL 10 defines "crimes against humanity" as follows:

Article II

(c) Crimes against Humanity: *Atrocities and offences, including but not limited to* murder, extermination, enslavement, deportation, *imprisonment,* torture, *rape,* or other inhumane acts committed against any civilian population, or persecutions on political, racial or religious grounds, whether or not in violation of the domestic laws of the country where perpetrated.

[The italicized language is not included in Article 6(c).]

The obvious differences between Article II(c) and Articles 6(c) and 5(c) respectively of the London and Tokyo Charters are:

1 - The heading for Article II(c) defining "crimes against humanity," as "Atrocities and Offences;"
2 - It includes the overly broad terms, "included but not limited to;"
3 - The addition of the terms "imprisonment" and "rape," even though both are subsumed within the words "or other inhumane acts" contained in all three texts provided, however, that the "imprisonment" is unlawful; and,
4 - The removal of any connection between the specific crimes listed in Article II(c) and "crimes against peace" or "war crimes."

Article II(c) clearly overreaches in its definition of this category of crimes by removing the necessary connection with any of the two other crimes as do Articles 6(c) and 5(c). Consequently, it strains the "principles of legality," far more than do Articles 6(c) and 5(c).

It could be argued that CCL 10 is, however, distinguishable from Article 6(c) of the Charter and 5(c) of the Tokyo counterpart on the grounds that it is not an international instrument, but a national one. As stated in its Preamble, CCL 10 was intended to be the Allies' legal basis for criminal prosecutions in Germany.[56] It was therefore applied only territorially. Yet, that law incorporated by reference two international instruments, the Moscow Declaration of 1943 and the London Charter which were deemed to constitute an integral part thereof. The inconsistency is obvious, since it was purported to be a national law applicable only territorially but its source deriving from international law, and its formulation and enactment was by the victorious Allies acting pursuant to their supreme authority over Germany by virtue of that country's unconditional surrender. This inconsistency was dealt with in *The Justice Case* as follows:

> The Nuernberg Tribunals are not German courts. They are not enforcing German Law. The charges are not based on violations by the defendants of German law. On the contrary, the jurisdiction of this Tribunal rests on international authority. It enforces the law as declared by the IMT Charter and C.C.Law 10, and within the limitations on the power conferred, it enforces international law as superior in authority to any German statute or decree.[57]

Such a legal construction is clearly strained. The reasoning makes the law and the tribunal that applied it a strange hybrid of international and national law. Furthermore, this legal confusion was compounded by the fact that the Allies in their respective zones of occupation also applied their military laws instead of CCL 10 which was to be the uniform legal basis for prosecutions in Germany.[58] Thus, persons who were

---

[56] *See* A. VON KNIEREM, THE NUREMBERG TRIALS (1959), in particular Part III.

[57] *The Justice Case* at 1213.

[58] A. VON KNIERIEM, *supra* note 56, who states:

English and Australian courts, on the other hand, have applied punishment under their own law of war regardless of the place where the act was committed and the nationality of the actor or of the person injured. Field Marshall Kesselring and Generals v. Mackensen and Malezer were sentenced by a British court for acts committed in Italy against Italians. Australian courts sentenced Japanese nationals for acts committed outside of Australia against Indians or Chinese people. Lord Wright stressed the fact that such punishment could be explained only as an application of the principle of world law.

The strong objections that can be raised against extending this principle beyond the special cases to which it has traditionally been applied appeared to be shared by the continental countries, none of which after World War II seems to have punished any foreign national for an act which would not have been punishable under its criminal laws as applied in accordance with the principles of territoriality.

36

accused of the same crime could find themselves prosecuted pursuant to CCL 10 or in accordance the military laws of any of the Allies. And, in addition to having separate applicable substantive laws, the procedures of these tribunals were also different.

In a lonely dissenting opinion on the question of whether CCL 10 derived from or was premised on international law, or if it was deemed German national criminal law because it was promulgated by the sole governing authority which represented foreign occupiers, Judge Blair (from Iowa) stated in *The Justice Case*:

The Judgment states at one place --

"International law is not the product of statute. Its content is not static. The absence from the world of any governmental body authorized to enact substantive rules of international law has not prevented the progressive development of the law. After the manner of the English common law, it has grown to meet the exigencies of changing conditions."

The Judgment recites at another point --

"Since the Charter and CCL 10 are the product of legislative action by an international authority, it follows, of necessity, that there is no national constitution of any one State which could be invoked to invalidate the substantive provisions of such international legislation."

At still another place, the Judgment recites --

"In its aspect as a statute defining crime and providing punishment the limited purpose of CC Law 10 is clearly set forth. It is an exercise of supreme legislative power in and for Germany. It does not purport to establish by legislative act any new crimes of international applicability."

Still at another place in the Judgment, it is declared that --

---

It should be noted that Article 43 of the 1907 Hague Conventions states: "The authority of the legitimate power having in fact passed into the hands of the occupant, the latter shall take all the measures in his power to restore, and ensure, as far as possible, public order and safety, while respecting, unless absolutely prevented, the laws in force in the country." *Id.* at 82-83.

"Only by giving consideration to the extraordinary and temporary situation in Germany can the procedure here be harmonized with established principles of national sovereignty. In Germany an international body (the Control Council) has assumed and exercised the power to establish judicial machinery for the punishment of those who have violated the rules of the common international law, a power which no international authority without consent could assume or exercise within a State having a national government presently in the exercise of its sovereign powers."

Thus, in the first quotation, the judgment states that there has never been an international legislature and that, therefore, international law is not the product of statute; whereas, in the second quotation, it is contended that Control Council Law No. 10 is "the product of legislative action by an international authority." The third recitation is that Control Council Law No. 10 is "the product of legislative action by an international authority." The third recitation is that Control Council Law No. 10 "is an exercise of supreme legislative power in and for Germany."

The fourth quotation doubts the legality of our procedure unless the international body in Germany (the Allied Control Council) has assumed and exercised the power to establish judicial machinery for punishment of crimes in violation of international law ....

With these conflicting conclusions as to the source of authority of Control Council Law No. 10, I must respectfully disagree.[59] (emphasis added)

Comparing the formulations of the Nuremberg Charter, the Tokyo Charter and CCL 10, the UNWCC offered these conclusions:

(a) There were two types of crimes against humanity, those of the "murder type" (murder, extermination, enslavement, deportation and the like), and those of the "persecution type" committed on racial, political or religious grounds.

(b) Crimes against humanity of the murder type were offences committed against the civilian population. Offences committed against members of the armed forces

---

[59]   Separate Opinion of Judge Blair, *The Justice Case.*

were outside the scope of this type, and probably also outside the scope of the persecution type.

(c)   Isolated offences did not fall within the notion of crimes against humanity. As a rule systematic mass action, particularly if it was authoritative, was necessary to transform a common crime, punishable only under municipal law, into a crime against humanity, which thus became also the concern of international law. Only crimes which either by their magnitude and savagery or by their large number or by the fact that a similar pattern was applied at different times and places, endangered the international community or shocked the conscience of mankind, warranted intervention by States other than that on whose territory the crimes had been committed, or whose subjects had become their victims.

(d)   It was irrelevant whether a crime against humanity had been committed before or during the war.

(e)   The nationality of the victims was likewise irrelevant.

(f)   Not only the ringleaders, but also the actual perpetrators of crimes against humanity were criminally responsible.

(g)   It was irrelevant whether or not a crime against humanity had been committed in violation of the *lex loci*.

(h)   A crime against humanity may be committed by enacting legislation which orders or permits crimes against humanity, e.g. unjustified killing, deportations, racial discrimination, suppression of civil liberties, etc.[60]

The 1950 ILC Report

The ILC report was made pursuant to a mandate by the General Assembly. Its heading was: *Principles of International Law Recognized by the Charter of the Nuremberg Tribunal and the Judgement of the Tribunal.* Thus it was based solely on

---

[60]   UNWCC at 178-179. *See also* Document Section B.2.

the Charter and the IMT Judgment, excluding the Tokyo Charter and its tribunal's judgment as well as all other subsequent proceedings.

The ILC's formulation is as follows:

Principle VI. The crimes hereinafter set out are punishable as crimes under international law:

...

c. Crimes Against Humanity:

Murder, extermination, enslavement, deportation and other inhuman acts done against any civilian population, or persecutions on political, racial or religious grounds, when such acts are done or such persecutions are carried on in execution of or in connexion with any crime against peace or any war crime.

Principle VII. Complicity in the commission of a crime against peace, a war crime, or a crime against humanity as set forth in Principle VI is a crime under international law.[61]

This formulation departs from the Charter's Article 6(c) in that it removes the war connection with respect to the specific crimes of "murder, extermination, enslavement, deportation and other inhumane acts," thus extending such violations to peaceful contexts. But it retains the connection to crimes against peace and war crimes for "persecution on political, racial, or religious grounds." Commenting on the Principle II definition of "crimes against humanity," the ILC Report states:

120. Article 6(c) of the Charter of the Nürnberg Tribunal distinguished two categories of punishable acts, to wit: first, murder, extermination, enslavement, deportation and other inhuman acts committed against any civilian population, before or during the war, and second, persecution on political, racial or religious grounds. Acts within these categories, according to the Charter, constituted international crimes only when committed "in execution of or in connexion with any crimes

---

[61] *See* Document Section C.12.

40

within the jurisdiction of the Tribunal." The crimes referred to as falling within the jurisdiction of the Tribunal were crimes against peace and war crimes.

121. Though it found that "political opponents were murdered in Germany before the war, and that many of them were kept in concentration camps in circumstances of great horror and cruelty," that "the policy of persecution, repression and murder of civilians in Germany before the war of 1939, who were likely to be hostile to the Government, was most ruthlessly carried out," and that "the persecution of Jews during the same period is established beyond all doubt," the Tribunal considered that it had not been satisfactorily proved that before the outbreak of war these acts had been committed in execution of, or in connexion with, any crime within the jurisdiction of the Tribunal. For this reason the Tribunal declared itself unable to "make a general declaration that the acts before 1939 were crimes against humanity within the meaning of the Charter." [TRIAL OF THE MAJOR WAR CRIMINALS BEFORE THE INTERNATIONAL MILITARY TRIBUNAL, Vol. I, Nürnberg 1947.]

122. The Tribunal did not, however, thereby exclude the possibility that crimes against humanity might be committed also before a war.

123. In its definition of crimes against humanity the Commission has omitted the phrase "before or during the war" contained in article 6(c) of the Charter of the Nürnberg Tribunal because this phrase referred to a particular war, the war of 1939. The omission of the phrase does not mean that the Commission considers that crimes against humanity can be committed only during a war. On the contrary, the Commission is of the opinion that such crimes may take place also before a war in connexion with crimes against peace.

124. In accordance with article 6(c) of the Charter, the above formulation characterizes as crimes against humanity murder, extermination, enslavement, etc., committed against "any" civilian population. This means that these acts may be crimes against humanity even if they are committed by the perpetrator against his own population.[62]

---

[62] *See* Nuremberg Principles at 238, 239.

Commenting upon Principle VII which complements Principle VI, the ILC Report states:

125. The only provision in the Charter of the Nürnberg Tribunal regarding responsibility for complicity was that of the last paragraph of article 6 which reads as follows: "Leaders, organizers, instigators and accomplices participating in the formulation or execution of a common plan or conspiracy to commit any of the foregoing crimes are responsible for all acts performed by any persons in execution of such a plan."

126. The Tribunal, commenting on this provision in connexion with its discussion of count one of the indictment, which charged certain defendants with conspiracy to commit aggressive war, war crimes and crimes against humanity, said that, in its opinion, the provision did not "add a new and separate crime to those already listed." In the view of the Tribunal, the provision was designed to "establish the responsibility of persons participating in a common plan" [TRIAL OF THE MAJOR WAR CRIMINALS BEFORE THE INTERNATIONAL MILITARY TRIBUNAL, vol. I, Nürnberg 1947, p. 226.] "to prepare, initiate and wage aggressive war." Interpreted literally, this statement would seem to imply that the complicity rule did not apply to crimes perpetrated by individual action.

127. On the other hand, the Tribunal convicted several of the defendants of war crimes and crimes against humanity because they gave orders resulting in atrocious and criminal acts which they did not commit themselves. In practice, therefore, the Tribunal seems to have applied general principles of criminal law regarding complicity. This view is corroborated by expressions used by the Tribunal in assessing the guilt of particular defendants. [*Ibid.*, pages 281, 287, 295, 298, 306, 314, 319, 320, 321, 330.]

The ILC, following the mandate of the General Assembly, simply reformulated the prescriptions of the Charter in a fashion that could be deemed a "general principle," and sought to reconcile the sometimes confusing or otherwise unclear opinions in the IMT judgment. In an interesting disclaimer, the ILC stated:

Formulation of the Nurnberg Principles
by the International Law Commission

35.   The International Law Commission dealt with the question of the formulation of the principles of international law recognized in the Charter of the Nürnberg Tribunal and in the judgment of the Tribunal during its first session at its meetings of 9, 23, 24, 25, 26, 27, 31 May and 1, 3, 7 June 1949. The Commission had before it a memorandum submitted by the Secretary-General entitled "The Charter and Judgment of the Nürnberg Tribunal; History and Analysis." [U.N. Pub. Sales No. 1949, V. 7.]

36.   The Commission began its work by discussing its task in this matter. One of the main questions in this connexion was whether or not the Commission had to ascertain to what extent the principles contained in the Charter and judgment constitute principles of international law. The conclusion of the Commission was that, since the Nürnberg principles had been affirmed by the General Assembly in its resolution 95 (I) of 11 December 1946, *it was not the task of the Commission to examine whether these principles were or were not principles of international law. The Commission had merely to formulate them.*[63] (emphasis added)

The ILC's position led Professor Jescheck, a critic of the Law of the Charter, to comment that such an outcome cannot be considered as part of binding international criminal law:

The judgment of the International Military Tribunal of 1 October 1946, by virtue of which the majority of the accused were sentenced to death or other severe punishments for crimes against peace, war crimes and crimes against humanity, rested upon the four Allied Powers' London Agreement of 8 August 1945, to which was annexed a Charter establishing the Tribunal. Nineteen other states subsequently acceded to the Agreement. The attempts of the United Nations to incorporate "en bloc" those norms of the Charter and the Nuremberg judgment that relate to criminal responsibility for crimes against peace, war crimes and crimes against humanity as part of generally accepted international law have remained unsuccessful. Admittedly, the General Assembly of the United Nations adopted a Resolution on 11 December

---

[63]   *See* 2 Y.B. INT'L L. COMM'N 189 (1950).

1946 affirming the "principles of international law recognized by the Charter of the Nürnberg Tribunal and the judgment of the Tribunal." However, this Resolution merely recognized the action taken by the four Allied Powers against the former German leadership as being in harmony with criminal law corresponding to historical justice and whose application was appropriate in the circumstances. Furthermore, the Resolution confirmed the General Assembly's desire to see this criminal law of the victorious powers generally applied in the future. Nevertheless, the criminal law of the Nuremberg Charter did not, by virtue of this Resolution, become generally binding; in accordance with the United Nations Charter, the General Assembly was not a legally competent body to create new international law, even if it so desired, which cannot be inferred from the context and tone of the Resolution itself. The second Resolution of 21 November 1947 did not even embody a reaffirmation of the Nuremberg legal principles; it merely consigned their formulation and also the elaboration of a draft Code of Offenses against the Peace and Security of Mankind to the newly created International Law Commission. In 1950, the Commission submitted its formulation of the law of Nuremberg in the form of seven legal principles. In 1954, the Code of Offenses against the Peace and Security of Mankind was completed and accepted by the Commission in draft form. Neither of these texts has, however, ever been accepted definitively by the General Assembly or any state, whether a member of the United Nations or not.... Consequently, a comprehensive regulation of crimes against peace, war crimes and crimes against humanity, based on the London Charter and the Nuremberg judgment, has not yet been evolved. Under present conditions, where violence is used as a means of international politics by states -- whether great or small -- such a development is hardly to be expected. For this reason, we must give separate consideration to the further development of each of these three crimes since Nuremberg.[64]

The question is not so much the authoritativeness of the ILC's Principles but their legally binding effect. The ILC's reported principles are not binding, but are part of the customary law baggage of international criminal law. As further evidence of this proposition is the fact that the very ILC which formulated the Nuremberg Principles did not consider itself bound by that formulation in connection with the subsequent definition of "crimes against humanity" in the 1954 Draft Code of Offences. That was

---

[64] Jescheck, *supra* note 55, at 84, 85. *See also* Jescheck, *Etat actuel et perspectives d'avenir des projets dans le domaine du droit international pénal*, 35 RIDP 83, 92 (1964).

evident in the deliberations of the ILC and its adopted 1954 Draft Code of Offences which it submitted that year to the General Assembly. When the ILC resumed work on the Draft Code between 1980-1991 (see Chapter 11 for a discussion of the ILC's codification efforts), it disregarded its own earlier formulation of the Nuremberg Principles, as well as its earlier 1954 Draft Code. The ILC did so because it felt that the General Assembly's mandate for the formulation of the Nuremberg Principles was different from the mandate regarding the contents of the Draft Code of Offences, which it renamed in 1987 the Draft Code of Crimes against the Peace and Security of Mankind.

International Criminalization Policy

International crimes have evolved over the course of time and have been embodied in a number of multilateral conventions. Between 1815 and 1989, 315 multilateral instruments have been developed. These instruments fall within twenty-two categories of international crimes.[65] This evolutionary process is characterized by unevenness and lack of systematization; "crimes against humanity" is not, therefore, an exception.

The questions of what constitutes an international crime, and why, have long been debated and continue to be at issue.[66] Whether "crimes against humanity" should have been established as a separate international criminal category does not only depend on what it encompasses, but also on whether it corresponds to recognized criteria for international criminalization. One way of answering these two questions is the deductive approach based on the empirical identification of international crimes on the basis of that which is recognized in accordance with the sources of international law. Since conventions are the international law source *par excellence*, they are the starting point in this inquiry,[67] but this does not exclude reliance on other sources such as customary international law[68] and "general principles of law."[69]

---

[65] *See e.g.* BASSIOUNI DIGEST and BASSIOUNI DRAFT CODE.

[66] *See* Chapter 3.

[67] *See* Chapter 3.

[68] *See generally* Chapter 3.

[69] *See generally* Chapter 7, and particularly Chapter 3 for the limitations imposed by the "principles of legality."

An analysis of the twenty-two categories of crimes reveals the following characteristics which reflect the social interest sought to be protected.[70] They are:

(a) The prohibited conduct affects a significant international interest;

(b) The prohibited conduct constitutes an egregious conduct deemed offensive to the commonly shared values of the world community;

(c) The prohibited conduct involves more than one state in its planning, preparation or commission, either through the diversity of nationality of its perpetrators or victims, or because the means employed transcend national boundaries; or

(d) The effects of the conduct bear upon an internationally protected interest that is not sufficient to fall into either (a) or (b) above, but requires international criminalization in order to ensure its prevention, control and suppression because it is predicated on "state action or policy" without which it could not be performed, as discussed in Chapter 6.

On the basis of these characteristics and on the basis of the nature and scope of all 315 multilateral instruments, it can be concluded that each of the twenty-two categories of crime reflects the existence of any one or a combination of the following elements:

1. International:

(a) Conduct constituting a threat to the peace and security of the international community, whether directly or indirectly; or,

(b) Conduct recognized by commonly shared world community values as shocking to the collective conscience of the world community.

2. Transnational:

(a) Conduct affecting the public safety and economic interests of more than one state whose commission transcends national boundaries; or,

---

[70] *See* BASSIOUNI DRAFT CODE 45.

(b) Conduct involving citizens of more than one state (either as victims or perpetrators) or conduct performed across national boundaries.

3. State Action or Policy:

Conduct containing in part any one of the first two elements but whose prevention, control and suppression necessitates international cooperation because it is predicated on "state action or state policy" without which the conduct in question could not be performed.[71]

On the basis of the characteristics and elements identified above, a proposed definition for an international crime is:

An international offense is conduct internationally proscribed for which there is an international duty for states to criminalize the said conduct, prosecute or extradite the accused and punish the transgressor, and to cooperate internationally for the effective implementation of these obligations.[72]

"Crimes against humanity" is a category of international crimes that satisfies the third criteria for international criminalization, as further discussed in Chapter 6. But certainly Nazi Germany's World War II conduct equally satisfies the first and second criteria. That conduct was shocking to the commonly shared values of the world community, and it did disrupt the peace and security of humankind. It was, above all, conduct which was predicated on "state action or policy," as discussed in Chapter 6, that could not have been prevented, controlled or suppressed without international criminalization and international enforcement.

The drafters of the London Charter were, therefore, entirely correct in formulating "crimes against humanity" as a new international category of crimes under positive international criminal law.

---

[71]   *Id.* at 36, and *also* Chapter 6.

[72]   *Id.* at 55.

CHAPTER 2

THRESHOLD ISSUES OF LEGAL PHILOSOPHY

non autoritas sed veritas lex facit

Introduction

The Charter's legal validity as controlling the responsibility of those accused of "crimes against humanity" irrespective of prior national positive law depends on the choice of a given legal philosophical premise. Rigid positivism and absolutist naturalism stand at the two extremes, with each theory spawning several different doctrinal perspectives. Thus, some naturalists recognize and rely on some aspects of positivism, while some proponents of positivism also borrow from naturalism. A wide range of pragmatic and utilitarian philosophies are positioned between these parameters and borrow from positivism and from naturalism. Since this study is only marginally concerned with the intricacies of legal philosophy, this Chapter will only deal with limited aspects of that branch of the law.

The basic substantive legal issues arising out of the Charter, which call into question various philosophies of law can be summarized as follows:

1 - What constitutes an international crime;

2 - Does international criminal law have primacy over national law;

3 - Before the Charter, was there an international crime that could be labelled "crimes against humanity," and if so,

    a) what was its legal source (or sources),
    b) what were the contents and legal elements of this crime;
    c) what were the bases for criminal responsibility; and,
    d) what legal exoneration factors existed;

4 - In its definition of "crimes against humanity," did Article 6(c) conform in whole or in part to pre-existing international law, as discussed in Chapter 4;

5 - Did the Charter satisfy all or some of the "principles of legality" in international criminal law, as discussed in Chapter 3.

In order to better consider these questions, some threshold issues of legal philosophy must be addressed. They are:

1 - Whether a higher source of law can override and invalidate positive law;

2 - Whether international law can override and invalidate national law; and,

3 - Whether the progressive codification of international law, particularly in cases where it embodies a moral or ethical content, permits a different threshold of legality than as otherwise required by positive law.[1]

The answers to these issues will depend upon the choice of a theory of legal philosophy. Therefore, in order to assess the validity of the normative aspects of "crimes against humanity," it is necessary to examine the different doctrines of legal philosophy which bear upon the interpretation of the sources, scope and content of international criminal law.

How to reconcile these legal issues with the different legal philosophical perspectives identified below was a challenge that the drafters of the Charter avoided, as discussed in Chapters 1 and 3, thus leaving it open to future legal question.

Historical Perspective

Legal philosophers who have benefitted civilization with their thoughts throughout the course of history have reflected in their teachings the moral values and political ideas of their times, as well as their individual learned experiences. Their writings can be divided into general theory of philosophy, including philosophy of law; legal philosophy applied to certain branches of the law; or a combination of general theory and selected applications to one or more branches of the law. It is important, therefore, to distinguish between general postulates of legal philosophy and those that have been advanced by their proponents as applicable to a certain branch of the law and which are not necessarily transferable to other branches of the law. Thus, the relevance of certain philosophical doctrines will depend on whether they were formulated exclusively or substantially for a specific application, or whether they were formulated

---

[1] *See also* Chapter 3.

as general postulates capable of application to various aspects of the law. For example, Plato, Aristotle, Cicero and Aquinas were general philosophers, as were Kant, Hegel and Hobbes. Their works, however, covered several aspects of law and justice, and occasionally the examples they used, and the applications they made of their theories, touched upon different branches of the law. Others like Vittoria, Suarez, Ayala, Gentili, Grotius, Puffendorf, Thomasius and de Vattel were essentially publicists, and their writings focused on the law of nations, which Roman law called *jus gentium*. Of these, Grotius was the one who ventured the farthest into international criminal law. Other writers who are not considered general philosophers or even specialists in a given branch of law, like Beccaria, contributed to international criminal law through their views on criminal justice.

Roman Law, from which the European legal systems descended, was in part positivistic, but it was influenced by natural law, which also inspired other legal philosophies, in particular, social contract theories as evidenced in the writings of Montesquieu, Voltaire and Rousseau. The ideas of these writers in turn provided political idealogies with philosophical and legal content, as was the case with the French and American ideologies of freedom and justice, which spurred their revolutions. Moreover, these ideologies, founded on a certain legal philosophy, inspired the winds of political and social changes which swept Europe during the eighteenth and nineteenth centuries.[2] Later, their influence extended to other political systems throughout the world. In turn, the transformation of European political thought during these two centuries brought about significant changes in legal philosophy, which resulted in the transformation of many legal systems. It is this historical process that ripened into what is now called the "Rule of Law."

Due to the intricate connections between political philosophy and legal philosophy, and between philosophical doctrines and legal disciplines, Europe's major legal systems evolved differently during the critical two centuries between the late 1600's and the late 1800's. The changes that occurred early in this period have had a far-reaching impact that has been felt up to contemporary times. During this period, European legal thought evolved significantly, transforming itself as it went through different phases. This historical evolutionary process engendered diverse approaches and techniques of law-making and legal interpretation. For example, the Germanic legal system moved away from the naturalist tradition and adopted a positivist approach. Some of the English

---

[2] *See* F.L. BAUMER, MODERN EUROPEAN THOUGHT: CONTINUITY AND CHANGE IN IDEAS 1600-1950, 218-236 (1977).

Common Law philosophers, like Austin,[3] did the same, while others, like Blackstone, continued to adhere to a natural law tradition.[4] Still others, like Bentham, developed a utilitarian philosophy as an alternative to both naturalism and positivism.[5] The French Civilist system, largely influenced by Roman Law, reflected natural law values but relied on positivist techniques in law-making and judicial interpretation because of its adherence to codification. By the 1800's, however, the three families of European legal systems, Common Law, Germanic and French Civilist, had developed a number of similar characteristics; the relevant one for this inquiry was the requirement of certain "principles of legality" for penal legislation, discussed in Chapter 3, and certain criteria for the establishment of criminal responsibility, discussed in Chapters 9 and 10. The drafters of the Charter, however, did not take notice of these legal-philosophical considerations, as did subsequent commentators on the Law of Charter, who relied on different legal philosophies and doctrines to support their respective views.

The problem of sorting out the different schools of jurisprudence, in this brief inquiry into the threshold questions regarding the legal validity of the Charter, is compounded by the multi-disciplinary nature of international criminal law. This multi-disciplinary nature compels us to drift in and out of the boundaries of different branches of the law: public international law and national criminal law in its comparative aspects being the two principal ones, but also others like jurisprudence, comparative criminal procedure, comparative military law, national conflict of laws and private international law.[6] The multi-disciplinary nature of international criminal law makes the inquiry into the various legal issues presented by the Charter and Post-Charter Legal Developments, as discussed in Chapter 11, more difficult than if that discipline were an historically well established and homogeneous branch of the law.

---

[3] *See* J. AUSTIN, THE PROVINCE OF JURISPRUDENCE DETERMINED (B. Franklin ed. *reprinted in* 1970). Austin was inspired by David Hume who was opposed to naturalism; *see* D. HUME, TREATISE ON HUMAN NATURE (1739-40); and D. HUME, INQUIRY CONCERNING THE PRINCIPLES OF MORALS (1751).

[4] *See* W. BLACKSTONE, COMMENTARIES ON THE LAWS OF ENGLAND (First American ed. 1771).

[5] THE COLLECTED WORKS OF JEREMY BENTHAM (Bowring ed. 1859). *See* in particular J. BENTHAM, THE THEORY OF LEGISLATION (P. Hildreth trans., Oceana ed., 1975), THE UTILITARIANS: AN INTRODUCTION TO PRINCIPLES OF MORALS AND LEGISLATION (Dolphn Books ed., 1961), and INTRODUCTION TO MORALS AND LEGISLATION (6th printing, Hafner ed., 1948). Bentham was a scholar of legislation, of what or how the law might be and not what it ought to be. J. AUSTIN *supra* note 3, was a scholar of Jurisprudence, his main concern was with the law as it is, and not as it should be. *See also* for these distinctions in earlier legal systems, H. MAINE, EARLY HISTORY OF INSTITUTIONS 343-44 (3d ed. 1880).

[6] *See* 1 BASSIOUNI ICL 1-80.

It is not this writer's intention to discuss the wide range of differences among legal philosophies and the variety of applications of these views to the various branches of the law,[7] but rather, to raise issues unresolved by international criminal law doctrine and to propose some answers thereto with reference to "crimes against humanity."

Philosophical Underpinnings

Throughout legal history, it has been evident that legal norms, including international ones, embody certain values.[8] Hence, one of the important differences between legal systems and the various legal disciplines they contain is whether these values derive from religious, moral-ethical or social-policy sources.

The notion that written law is positive law derives from Roman Law and subsequently found its application in the Civilist and Germanic legal traditions.[9] Positivism rests on the notion that law is law and must be obeyed because it is law. But such a rigid view has been tempered by relative positivists who condition the validity of the law on certain assumptions. Naturalists also recognize positive law and give it the same enforceable status provided it is not incompatible with a higher law. The difference thus being whether a given law can be challenged or not and on what basis. The divergence of these views is particularly evident in criminal law doctrine and particularly with respect to the "principles of legality," the latter appears to be a corollary to positivism.

---

[7] *See generally* READINGS IN JURISPRUDENCE (J. Hall ed. 1938); C.J. FRIEDRICH, THE PHILOSOPHY OF LAW IN HISTORICAL PERSPECTIVE (2d ed. 1963); W. FRIEDMANN, LEGAL THEORY (5th ed. 1967); and PHILOSOPHY OF LAW (J. Feinberg & H. Gross eds. 3rd ed. 1986).

[8] *See* BONNARD, *Les idèes de L. Duguit sur les Valeures Sociales*, ARCHIVES DE PHILOSOPHIE DU DROIT ET DE SOCIOLOGIE JURIDIQUE 7 (1932). For a contemporary view of universally shared values, *see* PERLMAN, *Justice and Justification*, 16 NAT. L.F. 6 (1965). For a search into common values and language of the law, *see* Ehrenzweig, *Psychoanalytical Jurisprudence: A Common Language of Babylon*, 65 COLO. L. REV. 1331 (1965).

[9] This Compilation of Roman Law was ordered by the Byzantine Emperor Justinian I (whose reign was from 527-567), which earned this codification the name of Justinian Code. The most authoritative commentators on the criminal laws of the Middle-Ages, retracing them to their historical origins, were Benedict Carpzov (1595-1666), Guilio Claro (1525-1575) and Prospero Farinacci (1544-1618). For a survey of Roman Law *see* H.J. WOLFF, ROMAN LAW 3-7, 177-226 (1st ed. 1951); and Yntema, *Roman Law and Its Influence on Western Civilization*, 35 CORNELL L.Q. 77 (1949); *see also* P. VINOGRADOFF, ROMAN LAW IN MEDIEVAL EUROPE (2nd. ed. 1929).

The evolution of positivism, since the 1600's, favored a more rigid application of criminal law evidenced by the growing requirements of specificity which ultimately lead to the "principles of legality." This historical process was a direct outgrowth of the struggle for the secularization of criminal law and the limitations of the sovereign's powers. But the limitations of absolute sovereign power by means of establishing the supremacy of the "Rule of Law" was supported by some general legal positivists, pragmatists, utilitarianists and naturalists. This is reflected in the writings of Grotius, Helvetius, Beccaria, Puffendorf, Voltaire, Montesquieu, Rousseau, Bluntschli, Hobbes, Locke and Bentham, all of whom relied on different philosophical premises to frequently arrive at the same conclusions with respect to their support for the "principles of legality."[10] These and other social contract theorists are essentially pragmatists (in the common usage of the term). They all share the view that in some way the acknowledged power of the sovereign should be upheld, yet limited to avoid arbitrariness and injustice. Each, however, rests his views upon different philosophical foundations and relies on a particular method, legal theory and legal reasoning to reach a significantly similar conclusion requiring legality. But then, they also differ as to its origin, meaning, content, and application, because of the value-oriented outcomes of their respective philosophies. Thus, naturalists rely on a higher law though they arrive at the same conclusion with respect to "principles of legality," when there is no conflict between positive law and the higher law. Qualified positivists, however, condition the existence and validity of the law as a compelling fact to any or all of the following factors: legitimacy of the law-maker; legality of the law-making process; legitimacy of the purpose, goal, content or outcome of the law; and thus, rejoin naturalists on these limited grounds. Some pragmatists and utilitarians also accept a legitimacy premise.

Until the nineteenth century, European legal positivism stemmed in large part from notions of sovereignty and thus did not necessarily hold that "principles of legality" are basic to the validity of the law which is proclaimed by the sovereign. By then, criminal law positivistic doctrines, which were predicated on conceptions of fairness and justice, rejected *ex post facto* laws and upheld the principles of *nullum crimen sine lege, nulla poena sine lege*, but with different applications, were essentially limitations on the sovereign's arbitrariness and the judges who applied the law, but whose independence from the sovereign was not presupposed.[11] One should, therefore, distinguish between general legal positivism, in its various doctrinal expressions, from the legal positivism

---

[10]   *See* C.J. FRIEDRICH, *supra* note 7, who examines the legal philosophies of most of these authors.

[11]   *See* Chapter 3.

that gave rise to and relied upon "principles of legality." The latter must also, however, be distinguished on the basis of these philosophical premises and of their different applications in the world's major criminal justice systems, as discussed in Chapter 3.

International legal positivism is different from national criminal law positivism. The latter developed in Europe in the late 1800's. Its basic tenet was that only the written criminal law was applicable, but it also provided for a certain latitude in punishing those who were deemed to manifest social dangerousness, irrespective of the specificity of the written law.[12] At that time, national criminal law doctrine in the Civilist and Germanic legal traditions had evolved certain requirements for the "principles of legality," though with some distinctions, within the laws of the different countries belonging to these two families of legal systems. These requirements, however, were unmatched in the Common Law and other systems, such as the Islamic system.[13]

All legal philosophies, except naturalism, distinguish between the law as it is and the law as it ought to be.[14] The former is deemed valid because it is a legal fact which

---

[12] This theory was developed by Enrico Ferri in the late 1800's. *See* E. FERRI, SOCIOLOGIA CRIMINALE (1898); and R. GAROFALO, LA CRIMINOLOGIA (1815). Ferri followed the thoughts of Franz von Liszt of Austria, one of the founders of the *"Junge Neue Kriminalschuhle."* *See* Groenhüjsen & Van der Landen, *L'Union Internationale de Droit Pénal, dans la Zone de Tension Entre les Notions de Droit Classiques et les Conceptions Juridiques Modernes*, 61 RIDP 143, 159-163 (1990). This school sought to balance the dual need to protect society from crime and the accused from abuse of power through the "principles of legality." But the protection of society had to be achieved through a criminological (viz. sociological and psychological) approach to punishment that required less rigidity than the strict general legal positivists would require. This approach is also evident in the writings of Beccaria. In the late 1800's a new catchy label emerged -- that of "social defence," which was made into a school of thought, though it is an extension of the "Kriminalpolitik" described above. With the advent of internationally protected human rights, a new terminology entered the vocabulary of criminal sciences and also a new balance between society's and the individual's rights in criminal processes; that evolution led to MARC ANCEL'S, LA DEFENCE SOCIALE NOUVELLE (3d Rev. ed. 1981). For a survey of these and other criminological doctrines, *see* Jenkins, *Varieties of Enlightenment Criminology*, 24 BRIT. J. OF CRIMINOLOGY 112 (1984). The International Union of Pénal Law, founded in 1889 by Franz von Liszt, Gerard van Hamel and Adolphe Prins, was the predecessor of the International Association of Penal Law (1924). *See* Bassiouni, *A Century of Dedication to Criminal Justice and Human Rights: The International Association of Penal Law and the Institute of Higher Studies in Criminal Sciences*, 39 DEPAUL L. REV. 899 (1989), and *Un Siécle de Service Consacré à la Justice Criminelle et aux Droits de l'Homme: L'Association Internationale de Droit Pénale et l'Institut Superieur International des Sciences Criminelles*, 61 RIDP 29 (1990).

[13] *See* Chapter 3.

[14] *See* J. AUSTIN, *supra* note 3; J. BENTHAM, *supra* note 5; and Hart, *Positivism and the Separation of Law and Morals*, 71 HARV. L. REV. 593 (1958). Hart states:

compels obedience,[15] the latter is deemed to be a *desideratum* because it does not

---

No one has ever combined, with such even-minded sanity as the Utilitarians, the passion for reform with respect for law together with a due recognition of the need to control the abuse of power even when power is in the hands of reformers. One by one in Bentham's works you can identify the elements of the *Rechtstaat* and all the principles for the defense of which the terminology of natural law has in our day been revived. Here are liberty of speech, and of press, the right of association, the need that laws should be published and made widely known before they are enforced, the need to control administrative agencies, the insistence that there should be no criminal liability without fault, and the importance of the principle of legality, *nulla poena sine lege. Id.* at 595-96.

Hart's positivism rejects *ex post facto* laws, *see* H.L.A. HART, THE CONCEPT OF LAW 55-56 (1961). In that respect, he rejoins Fuller's naturalist view, *see* Fuller, *Positivism and Fidelity to Law - A Reply to Professor Hart*, 71 HARV. L. REV. 630, 661 (1958).

It is noteworthy that the command theory of positive law, though supported by international legal positivists, is difficult to reconcile with one of the basic tenets of the international legal obligations, namely *pacta sunt servanda*, which lacks authoritative sanction and does not command performance but directs it and indeed has achieved the status of being binding upon the parties to a treaty even without the power to enforce it. Such a practice indeed had existed in many early legal systems and it was reported by Grotius as customary binding international law. As stated by W. Friedmann   ". . . agreements made between states merge into an objective body of conventions which states are then no longer free to repudiate." W. FRIEDMAN, *supra* note 7, at 575 citing ANZILOTTI, CORSO DI DIRITTO INTERNAZIONALE (3d ed. 1928); O. DEL VECCHIO, LEHRBUCH DER RECHTSPHILOSOPHIE (German ed. 1937); and TRIXEL, VÖLKERRECHT UND LANDESRECHT (1899). For contemporary views, *see* M. McDOUGAL, H. LASSWELL AND J. MILLER, THE INTERPRETATION OF AGREEMENTS AND WORLD PUBLIC ORDER (1967); and Schacter, *Towards a Theory of International Obligations*, 8 VA. J. INT'L L. 300 (1968).

[15]   J. AUSTIN, *supra* note 3, at 6, posits that:

Command and duty are, therefore, correlative terms: the meaning denoted by each being implied or supposed by the other. Or (changing the expression) wherever a duty lies, a command has been signified; and whenever a command is signified, a duty is imposed.

Concisely expressed, the meaning of the correlative expressions is this: He who will inflict an evil in case his desire be disregarded, utters a command by expressing or intimating his desire: He who is liable to the evil in case he disregard the desire, is bound or obliged by the command.

The evil which will probably be incurred in case a command be disobeyed, or (to use an equivalent expression) in case a duty be broken, is frequently called a *sanction*, or an *enforcement of obedience*. Or (varying the phrase) the command or the duty is said to be *sanctioned* or *enforced* by the chance of incurring the evil. (Emphasis in original.)

Locke, whose views also inspired Austin, emphasized the requirement of promulgation of the law as a cornerstone of its legal validity, which, when combined with its legitimate authoritative source constitute its compelling and commanding force. *See* J. LOCKE, TREATISE ON CIVIL GOVERNMENT (1696). Kant, however,

exist as a compelling legal fact. Many philosophical approaches, except for naturalism, reject the notion that the legitimacy of the law as a legal reality can be challenged on the basis of its content, or because of what it ought to be. But for some positivists, pragmatists and utilitarianists, the inarticulated premise of legitimacy of the law-making process can be a basis for challenging the existence or legal validity of a given law. For some of these philosophies, however, considerations of premised legitimacy are not a sufficient basis for voiding the law of its legality, but could constitute a valid basis for resisting the law. Thus, the choice is to disobey the law and face the consequences until the law is repealed or changed.[16] For other positivists, however, the absence of the premise of legitimacy deprives the law of its existence as a compelling legal fact, thus rendering it legally unenforceable. Still, for some rigid positivists, the law can neither be challenged nor disobeyed so long as it is law. The difference between most doctrines of legal positivism rests on whether the premises of legitimacy enunciated above constitute a valid basis for challenging a given positive law.

No matter what the doctrinal differences may be among legal positivists, it is incorrect to believe that legal positivism is devoid of moral-ethical values.[17] The rejection by some positivists of the notion that the content of positive law must

---

viewed promulgation as the only necessary formal requirement, because power was the essential compelling legitimizing element of law. *See* I. KANT, THE CATEGORICAL IMPERATIVE (1797); and T. HOBBES, LEVIATHAN (A.R. Waller ed. 1904). While Hobbes acknowledges natural rights, he deprives them of sanction. Locke, however, opposed Hobbes' absolutism theory since he argued for the emancipation of the individual and saw absolutism as impeding that goal.

These positions are contradicted by naturalists, see *e.g.*, L. FULLER, THE MORALITY OF LAW (rev. ed. 1969); and utilitarianists, *see* W. FRIEDMANN, *supra* note 7, at 351-54.

Natural law also means the discovery of law by an empirical generalization or particularization of certain facts discovered in the history of societal human behavior.

Thus Montesquieu in arguing for natural law over positivism logically asked whether justice did not exist before positive law? He answers by saying:

"To say that there is nothing just or unjust but what is commanded or forbidden by positive laws, is the same as saying that before the describing of a circle all the radii were not equal."

L'ESPRIT DES LOIS (T. Nugent trans. 1748).

[16] For positivists, the proper moral response to an invalid law is resistance. *See* J. LOCKE and T. HOBBES, *supra* note 15; J. AUSTIN, *supra* note 3; J. BENTHAM, WORKS (Bowering ed. 1859); and H.L.A. HART, *supra* note 14. For resistance to invalid laws *see* J.D. LEWIS AND O. JASZI, AGAINST THE TYRANT: THE TRADITION AND THEORY OF TYRANNICIDE (1957); M.D. THOREAU, RESISTANCE TO CIVIL GOVERNMENT (1849); and Cohn, *The Right and Duty of Resistance*, 1 HUM. RTS. J. INT'L & COMP. L. 491 (1968); *see also e.g.*, THE LAW OF DISSENT AND RIOTS (M.C. Bassiouni ed. 1971).

[17] *See supra* notes 14-15 and accompanying text.

conform to, or be subject to a higher natural law, whether within the meaning of deistic or ethicistic naturalists, does not void legal positivism of moral-ethical content. Indeed, to most positivists, the very purpose of legal positivism is to insure adherence to a "Rule of Law" which reflects the belief that certainty of the law, deriving from a given lawful process, is a higher value deserving of protection over the unbridled discretionary powers of human-made and human-applied laws. As of the nineteenth century, positivists do not reject constitutional control over law-making and legal content. What they reject is the notion that interpreters of the law, or those who apply the law, can give it a different content or reject it altogether on the grounds of an unspecified and undefined higher law. Such an approach, however, falls short of what Karl Llwellyn succinctly referred to as "beyond rules lie effects."[18] To stop at the rules and ignore their effects, whether intended or unintended, does not separate law from morals, but draws an artificial line between the technique of the law and the functions of the law.[19]

Positivists, particularly in the Germanic tradition and some in the Common Law tradition, accept the notion that "law is law" because it derives from the law-maker's power or, because of the more absolutist doctrine, that law must be obeyed since it commands it. They reject any considerations relating to the inner content of the law or its outcome. Thus, for Hobbes, it is not rightness but authority that makes law, *non veritas sed autoritas facit legem.*[20] This positivistic conception derives from the dual notions of power and order and is based on the reasoning that law is the product of power and designed to produce order. Consequently, to obey power without question produces order, which is a positive value in and of itself. The logic is as follows: Power begets order, order begets good and good and order are attained by obeying the positive law. But since positive law derives from power, the argument is tautological and both self-justifying and self-fulfilling. Hobbes, however, would probably agree with this writer's reformulation of his postulate that *non autoritas sed veritas facit lex* because he, like other positivists, distinguishes between "law," *lex,* and "the law," *legem* -- the latter is what positivists deem to be the product of authority and therefore

---

[18] K. LLWELLYN, JURISPRUDENCE 42 (1962); *see also e.g.*, Radin, *Legal Realism*, 31 COLO. L. REV. 824 (1931). As Graham Hughes states it, "every legal system is a purposeful entreprise." Hughes, *The Existence of a Legal System*, 35 N.Y.U. L. REV. 1001 (1960).

[19] *See* R. POUND, AN INTRODUCTION TO THE PHILOSOPHY OF LAW 25-48 (rev. ed. 1954).

[20] Hobbes' utilitarianism recognized natural law as "rules of prudence," and he would have surely condemned Nazi laws and practices because they violate these "rules of prudence." T. HOBBES, *supra* note 15.

compelling. And it is essentially that dichotomy or separation of what is part of the same *continuum* that sets apart rigid positivism from other theories about the law, and techniques of interpretation and application of the law.

Naturalists, whether deists or ethicists, argue that a higher universal law exists even though it may yet have to be discovered by positive law and, therefore, not yet embodied in a written text. These views ensure not only control of the law's content, but stimulate the evolution of law beyond its positive stage. A parallel result is reached by some pragmatists and utilitarianists who argue that the evolutionary nature of law is a blend between what is and what ought to be and that historic circumstances bring about the necessary change.

Naturalists, since Plato and Aristotle, have subordinated the legitimacy of the laws of man to the higher laws of nature which, even if transcendental in their source, are nevertheless adduced by human reason.[21] Cicero described this process as "*Lex est*

---

[21] For Plato and Aristotle, the *nomai* (laws) are essential for the good order of the *polis* and should be obeyed unless they are contrary to the "higher law" or the law of reason, or enacted by the arbitrary command of a tyrant. As Aristotle proclaims:

I mean that law is either particular or universal; by "particular" law I mean that which an individual community lays down for itself (a law partly unwritten, partly written); and by "universal" law I mean the law of nature. For there is a natural and universal notion of right and wrong, one that all men instinctively apprehend, even when they have no mutual intercourse nor any compact.

THE RHETORIC OF ARISTOTLE 73 (L. Cooper trans. 1932); *see also* E. BARKER, THE POLITICAL THOUGHT OF PLATO AND ARISTOTLE (1906).

Similarly, Cicero in his DE REPUBLICA (Book III, XII) asserts that:

True law is right reason in agreement with nature; it is of universal application, unchanging and everlasting; it summons to duty by its commands, and averts from wrongdoing by its prohibitions. And it does not lay its commands or prohibitions upon good men in vain, though neither have any effect on the wicked. It is a sin to try to alter this law, nor is it allowable to attempt to repeal any part of it, and it is impossible to abolish it entirely. We cannot be freed from its obligations by senate or people, and we need not look outside ourselves for an expounder or interpreter of it. And there will not be different laws at Rome and at Athens, or different laws now and in the future, but one eternal and unchangeable law will be valid for all nations and all times, and there will be one master and ruler, that is, God, over us all, for he is the author of this law, its promulgator, and its enforcing judge. Whoever is disobedient is fleeing from himself and denying his human nature, and by reason of this very fact he will suffer the worst penalties, even if he escapes what is commonly considered punishment.

CICERO, DE REPUBLICA, DE LEGIBUS 211 (C.W. Keyes trans. 1928).

58

ratio summa insita in natura, quae iubet ea, quae facienda sunt, prohibetque contraria" (Law is the highest reason, implanted in nature, which commands what ought be done and forbids the opposite).[22] He also referred to natural law as "something eternal which rules the whole universe by its wisdom in command and prohibition."[23] Transcendental deists since St. Augustine and St. Thomas Aquinas have subordinated the legitimacy of the laws of man to "The Laws of God" as recognized through reason.[24] For all naturalists, good is at the center of the law and that good is achieved

---

But naturalists do not reject law as a historical fact, or as a command from the temporal sovereign which must be obeyed, and in that respect they are qualified positivists, *see* in particular, T. HOBBES, *supra* note 15; and C.L. MONTESQUIEU, DE L'ESPRIT DES LOIS (1748); SAMUEL PUFFENDORF, ELEMENTORUM JURISPRUDENTIAE UNIVERSALIS (1660); and DE JURE NATURALAE ET GENTIUM LIBRI OCTO (1676); and JEAN BODIN, DE REPUBLICA LIBRI SIX (1576). Sir William Blackstone posits that:

This law of nature, being co-eval with mankind and dictated by God himself, is of course superior in obligation to any other. It is binding over all the globe, in all countries, and at all times: no human laws are of any validity, if contrary to this; and such of them as are valid derive all their force, and all their authority, mediately or immediately, from this original. W. BLACKSTONE, *supra* note 4, at 41.

But see J. Austin, who comments upon the substance of Blackstone's proposition:

If he had said that a human law which conflicts with the law of God, ought not to be imposed, he would have said truly. For a human law which conflicts with that ultimate test, and a human law which ought not to be imposed, are one and the same object denoted by different phrases.
But to say that a human law which conflicts with the law of God, is therefore not binding, or not valid, is to talk stark nonsense. J. AUSTIN, *supra* note 3, at 234.

[22] CICERO, *supra* note 21, at 316-317.

[23] *Id.* at 381.

[24] As Aquinas stated:

But in order that the volition of what is commanded may have the nature of law, it needs to be in accord with some rule of reason. And in this sense is to be understood the saying that the will of the sovereign has the force of law; or otherwise the sovereign's will would savour of lawlessness rather than of law.

ST. THOMAS AQUINAS, TREATISE ON LAW (SUMMA THEOLOGICA, Questions 90-97) 4 (Gateway ed. 1970). For an insightful analysis of St. Augustine's thoughts, *see* H.A. DEANE, THE POLITICAL AND SOCIAL IDEAS OF ST. AUGUSTINE (1963); and ST. THOMAS, SUMMA THEOLOGICA, THE BASIC WRITINGS OF SAINT THOMAS AQUINAS Vol. II, 742-53, 773-80, 784-85, 791-95 (A.C. Pegis ed. 1945). Aquinas, Cicero and the Stoics follow Plato and Aristotle's view that law is an emanation of the *ratio* and should be the "right reason." *See generally* THE STOICS AND EPICUREAN PHILOSOPHERS (W.J. Oates ed. 1940).

by the law when it produces justice, individual and collective, retributive and distributive; and justice is achieved when the greater good for all concerned is served by the law. Deist naturalists, however, do not confuse crime and sin as necessarily deriving from the same original legal source, and in that respect they draw a further distinction between law and morality. For deists, the higher law punishes sins, and to the extent that sins also constitute violations of positive law they are crimes. This position is expressed by Talmudic and *Shari'a* scholars. But Christian theologians admit that, even though a sin may be a crime in the eyes of God, it does not necessarily have to be a crime under positive law. Indeed for the Christian naturalists the function of positive law is societal, and its basic purpose is to better society. Thus, as stated in the Roman Law maxim *ubis societas ibi ius*, law presupposes a societal function. Consequently, moral experience is essentially a matter for the individual's conscience, while legal experience is tied to a social community.[25]

Roman Law conceived of positive law as the rule of the *regnum res publica*. Nonetheless, it reflected natural law, largely as a result of the works of Cicero and the Stoics, which were based on the prior works of Plato, Socrates and Aristotle. This is evidenced by the Justinian codification *Corpus Iuris Civilis*, whose DIGEST (*Pandects*) portion contains many references by Ulpian and others to those higher values described by Plato and Aristotle.[26] In Liber I, titulus 1, *De iustitia et iure*, the DIGEST refers to law as both a science and an art. The former is the accumulated knowledge and experience of things human and divine, *divinarum atque humanarum rerum notitia*, on which a theory of right and wrong is built. The latter is the furtherance of good (also meaning justice) and equity, *arns boni et acqui*.[27] Such Roman Law equity and some of its maxims found their way into the Common Law[28] and also into international law, as evidenced in part by Article 38 of the statutes of the PCIJ and the ICJ, whereby states who are parties to a dispute before the court can agree to the application of *ex acquo et bono* as an alternative source of international law. Law and justice, however, are different in that one is the means for the attainment of the other. Law and justice

---

[25] *See* A. D'ENTRÉVES, NATURAL LAW 84 (2d ed. 1952).

[26] *See* H.J. WOLFF, *supra* note 9, at 166-67. The standard edition of CORPUS IURIS CIVILIS is that of P. KRUGER, R. SCHOELL, and G. KROLL, CORPUS IURIS CIVILIS, EDITIO STEREOTYPICA. For a critical edition of the DIGEST, *see* P. BONFANTE, C. FADDA, C. FERRINI, S. RICCOBONO, AND V. SCIALOJA, DIGESTA IUSTINIANI AUGUSTI (2 Vols. 1908).

[27] *See* H. MAINE, ANCIENT LAW 42-69 (3d American ed. 1885); and *infra* note 60.

[28] *See infra* notes 59 and 60 and accompanying text.

are correlative, but while law is tentative, justice is constant and perpetual, *iustitia est constans et perpetua.*[29]

For Plato, a good government is one that acts as a servant of the law and not its ruler. As he stated: "[W]here [law] is sovereign over the authorities and they its humble servants, I discern the presence of salvation and every blessing Heaven sends on society."[30] Thus, clearly no positive law enacted by a ruler can be above the higher law of nature, as adduced by reason to accomplish the greater good for all in human society. In addition to Plato's general dogma that law is above the ruler, Aquinas posits that since positive law serves human behavior so as to achieve happiness, meaning also justice, it follows that the positive law must be directed to that goal which can only be attained when the positive law is aimed at attaining the common good for all members of the human society.[31]

---

[29]   The maxim has been relied upon by naturalists including Aristotle and St. Thomas.

[30]   PLATO, THE LAWS 99-100 (A.E. Taylor trans. 1960). A telling early English case is *The Case of the College of Physicians*, commonly called *Bonham's Case* (1610). *See* 8 COOK'S INSTITUTES 114, discussed in Plunknett, *Bonham's Case and Judicial Review*, 40 HARV. L. REV. 30 (1926). Edward Cook said in that case: ". . . it appears in our books that in many cases the common law will control acts of parliament and sometimes adjudge them to be utterly void . . . for when an Act of Parliament is against the common right or repugnant or impossible to be performed, the common law will control it and adjudge such act to be void." 8 COOK'S INSTITUTES 118; and PLUNKNETT, *infra* 60 at 34.

William Blackstone followed Cook's position: "Lastly, acts of Parliament that are impossible to be performed are of no validity; and if there arise out of them collaterally any absurd consequences, manifestly contradictory to common reason, they are, with regard to those collateral consequences void. I lay down the rule with these restrictions; though I know it is generally laid down more largely, that acts of parliament contrary to reason are void." W. BLACKSTONE, *supra* note 4, at 91. To a large extent this reasoned approach to the common law's hierarchical control of the legitimacy of positive laws enacted by King and Parliament derive from a naturalist approach. *See* F. Pollock, *History of the Law of Nature*, in ESSAYS IN THE LAW 157 (1922).

Lastly, Robert Jackson quoted Coke:

The Charter of this Tribunal evidences a faith that the law is not only to govern the conduct of little men, but that even rulers are, as Lord Chief Justice Coke put it to King James, "under God and the law." The United States believed that the law long has afforded standards by which a juridical hearing could be conducted to make sure that we punish only the right men and for the right reasons.

See R.H. JACKSON, THE NÜRNBERG CASE 80 (1947, 2d printing 1971).

[31]   *See supra* notes 21-24, and 30 and accompanying text.

One of the difficulties with natural law generalities lies in the translation between abstractions to functional norms in the context of a given legal system. As one legal realist notes:

Even if sometimes bewildered by technical detail, plagued by woodenness of administration, or outraged by cynical lawyer's trading on the fact that a given matter turns "not on justice, but on law," no man can wrestle long with the things of law without becoming aware that under the very things which sometimes bewilder, plague or outrage him there pulses an urge for right, or decency, or justice: a drive toward an ideal attribute which men may well conceive as a proper and indeed the proper ultimate objective of all law and of all legal institutions. The concept of Natural Law seems to me an expression of this urge: an expression informed by the urge, and directed to its greater realization; yet an expression only partially effective, because baffled in part as it moves toward realization, baffled by the very legal technique which its objective is to criticize and remedy.

In saying this I am conscious of departing from one solid tradition in regard to the use of the term. "Natural Law" has been used as the designation of a body of principle for the right ordering of any human society; principle which for that reason is so broad as to require perplexing labor to give it any application concrete enough to be of service in practical legal work. To me principle as broad as that appears to be not a lawyer's Natural Law, nor Natural Law in a lawyer's sense. A lawyer, or indeed a jurist, has as one major function, the dealing with detailed principle and rule applicable to a given going society, in terms accurate .. ..[32]

The application of these doctrinal views differs in international law and national criminal law because of the very nature of these two branches of law, whose subjects and enforcement modalities are not the same. Some writers, like Grotius and Beccaria in particular, applied their conceptions of crime and justice in the same way to the international and national realms of the law. Grotius, for example, argued that kings:

have the right of demanding punishment not only on account of injuries committed against themselves or their subjects, but also on account of injuries

---

[32]   K. LLWELLYN, *supra* note 18, at 111-112.

which do not directly affect them but excessively violate the law of nature or of nations in regard to any person whatsoever.[33]

Similar views also are reflected in the international and national law theories providing for redress in cases of denial of justice, under the Common Law tradition, and in the *abus de droit* theory, which is a form of denial of justice in the French-Civilist tradition, and which found its way into international law.[34]

The French Civilist-Germanic and Common Law systems have, as stated above, their antecedents in Roman Law.[35] All of these legal systems, and others such as the Islamic one,[36] rely in some way on positivism, but they all differ as to its meaning and application. Above all, they differ as to the rules of legal interpretation which produce different outcomes, even when the basic legal norm stems from the same values. It is, therefore, noteworthy that all legal systems distinguish between the "law" as a concept and "a law" as a given norm. The Common Law distinguishes between "the law" as a concept and "a law," which refers to a singular norm. So too do the Civilist and Germanic systems, which respectively distinguish between *droit* and *loi*, and between *recht* and *Gesetz*.[37] But the difference between these legal systems lies

---

[33] H. GROTIUS, DE JURE BELLI AC PACIS LIBRI TRES Ch. XX, § XL (1646) (F. Kelsey, Trans. 1925); *see also* S. MOCCIA, CARPZOV E GROZIO: DALLA CONCEZIONE TEOCRATICA ALLA CONCEZIONE LAICA DEL DIRITTO (1979), where the author compares the theocratic and lay concepts of criminal law in the views of Benedikt Carpzov (Theocratic), who was the most influential German scholar of the time. His principal work is PRACTICA NOVA IMPERIALIS SAXONICA RERUM CRIMINALUM (1635), which is more like a common law compendium of law and practice, and Hugo Grotius, whose views though theocratically inspired were deemed to be laicized with respect to criminal law. The Christian-Lutheran conception of divinity influenced the thinking of both; Carpzov as a penalist and Grotius as a publicist dealing also with penal matters (in those days Jurists were not compartmentalized in specialties as has since become the case). The difference was that Carpzov distinguished crime and sin while Grotius saw crime as the product of social policy though subject to what we today call the constitutionality of natural law. For a contemporary utilitarian view founded on naturalism *see* D'Amato, *State Responsibility for the Exportation of Nuclear Power Technology*, 74 VA. L. REV. 101, 102-106 (1988); and Green, *International Criminal Law and the Protection of Human Rights*, in CONTEMPORARY PROBLEMS OF INTERNATIONAL LAW 116 (B. Cheng & E.O. Brown eds. 1988).

[34] For the international law application of this theory, *see* Politis, *Le Problême des Limitations de la Souveraineté et la Théorie de l'Abus de Droit dans les Rapports Internationaux*, RECEUIL 1-121 (1925); and Gutteridge, The Abuse of Rights 5 CAMB. L. Y. 22 (1935).

[35] *See supra* note 9 and 27, *infra* notes 59 and 60 and accompanying text.

[36] *See e.g.*, M.C. BASSIOUNI, THE ISLAMIC CRIMINAL JUSTICE SYSTEM (1982).

[37] *See* Dworkin, *The Model of Rules*, 35 U. CHI. L. REV. 14 (1967); *see also* Williams, *Language and*

63

in the meaning they give to these concepts and its consequences, particularly with respect to judicial discretion in the interpretation and application of the law. The Common Law judge, for example, has a wider latitude of discretion than the French Civilist and Germanic tradition judge,[38] and therefore, the Common Law judge is closer to what D'Entréves calls the "point of intersection between law and morals."[39] It was for this reason that the Common Law framers of the Charter had less difficulty with the "principles of legality" than the French-Civilist ones. As Justice Jackson said in his opening statement: "The refuge of the defendants can be only their hope that International Law will lag so far behind the moral sense of mankind that conduct which is crime in the moral sense must be regarded as innocent in law."[40] But with respect to "crimes against humanity," the issue was whether the laws under which these crimes, positively defined by the Charter after the fact, were only the positive embodiment of pre-existing unwritten law, and thus legally valid, or simply an exercise in *ex post facto* victor's vengeance, which would be legally invalid. If one adopts a naturalist view, it would be undisputable that a higher law existed which prohibited what occurred. Consequently, the Charter would be valid positive law embodying the higher law which always overrides any contrary positive law, in this case the laws of Germany, under which the conduct was performed and which would shield the perpetrators from responsibility and punishment. Such a naturalist view could also find support in some positive law, namely the 1907 Hague Convention which posits the prohibition of the conduct which is contrary to "laws of humanity," even though it does not specify its contents, as discussed in Chapter 4. If that legal basis is deemed sufficient, then the question would no longer be one of legal philosophy but of compliance with the "principles of legality," as discussed in Chapter 3.

The Law, 61 L.Q. REV. 71 (1941); and Williams, *International Law and the Controversy concerning the Word Law*, 22 BRIT. Y.B. INT'L L. 148 (1945), where he expands on his analysis of the "emotive" function of words particularly such terms as "rule of law" whose ambiguity fosters its emotive impact. "To define 'The Law' or 'law' in its generality may therefore be a futile endeavor as it would never be specific enough to avoid the type of ambiguity inherent in Humpty Dumpty's answer to Alice in Wonderland's question 'Whether you can make words mean different things,' namely, 'the question is which is to be master -- that's all'." This is a simplification of the premises of legal positivism.

[38]   *See e.g.*, Freund, *Interpretation of Statutes*, 65 U. PA. L. REV. 207 (1917); and Gutteridge, *A Comparative View of the Interpretation of Statute Law*, 8 TUL. L. REV. 1 (1933).

[39]   A. D'ENTRÉVES, *supra* note 25, at 116.

[40]   *See* R.H. JACKSON, *supra* note 30, at 94.

The Philosophy of International Law and the Law of the Charter

International law has, throughout its post-eighteenth century history, reflected the legal philosophies of the western world's legal systems with emphasis on legal positivism, because it is essentially a consensual body of norms regulating state conduct.[41] Thus, a substantial portion of all international legal norms is predicated on the narrow ground that states are only bound by those norms and rules to which they consent. This historically narrow consensual basis of international law engendered a rigid positivistic approach to the making, interpretation and application of its norms and rules of conduct. Gradually, however, this rigid positivistic approach gave way to a more flexible one that permitted the growth and evolution of this discipline, as evidenced by the broadened interpretation of customary international law[42] and by the expanded reliance on "general principles" as a source of international law.[43] Commenting insightfully on the relationship between natural principles and customs, the French philosopher-poet Pascal said, *"J'ai grand peur que cette nature ne soit elle-même qu'une première coutume, comme la coutume est une seconde nature."*[44] Indeed nature may well be but a first custom and custom a second nature. International law owes its evolution to these expanding sources of customary law and "general principles," even though the determination of their scope and content remains a subject of continued debate.[45]

---

[41]   *See generally* A. NUSSBAUM, A CONCISE HISTORY OF THE LAW OF NATIONS (rev. ed. 1954).

[42]   *See* A. D'AMATO, THE CONCEPT OF CUSTOM IN INTERNATIONAL LAW (1971); *see also* Ferrari-Bravo, *Methodes de Recherche de la Coutume Internationale dans la Pratique des Etats*, 192 RECEUIL 246 (1986); and Paust, *Customary International Law: Its Nature, Sources and Status as Law of the United States*, 12 MICH. J. INT'L L. 59 (1990).

[43]   *See* Bassiouni, *A Functional Approach to 'General Principles of International Law'*, 11 MICH. J. INT'L L. 768 (1991).

[44]   B. PASCAL, PENSÉES Chapter II, No. 93. For the English translation *see* B. PASCAL PENSÉES: THE PROVINCIAL LETTERS 36 (W.F. Trotter trans. 1941) ("I am much afraid that nature is itself only a first custom, as custom is a second nature.").

[45]   *See e.g.*, Christenson, *Jus Cogens: Guarding Interests Fundamental to International Society*, 28 VA. J. INT'L L. 585 (1988); L. HANNIKAINEN, PEREMPTORY NORMS (*JUS COGENS*) IN INTERNATIONAL LAW (1988); and M. JANIS, AN INTRODUCTION TO INTERNATIONAL LAW (1988). *See Contra* D'Amato, *It's A Bird, It's A Plane, It's Jus Cogens!* 6 CONN. J. INT'L L. 1 (1990).

International legal positivism, prior to World War II, derived from an absolutist conception of sovereignty which reflected the political thought of its time. It was this approach that hampered the growth of international law.[46] Furthermore, because international law evolved out of consensus, it trailed, as opposed to anticipated, international legal needs. As a result of this *a posteriori* process of development, when the need arose to codify "crimes against humanity," the facts had largely preceded the articulation of the norm, though the concepts underlying the norm had pre-existed its formulation and the dilemma of the Charter's drafters: to override traditional positivism with naturalism or to find a pragmatic compromise.

The legal nature of international law, until 1945, was sharply divided between those that saw international law as standing above national law and those who saw it as the inherent product of the states' will. The latter position simply translated into the proposition that states were only bound by those obligations they freely and voluntarily assumed, and which they could also discard subject to certain limitations. The relationship between international law and national law was thus divided between supporters of dualism and monism.[47] Dualists viewed international law as intrinsically different from national law in that it only regulated conduct between sovereign states thus excluding individuals. National law is that body of law applicable to individuals and all other matters within the States' territories and which are subject to state sovereignty. Thus, under this view, international law applied nationally only where and when national law specifically recognized it. Monism on the other hand, recognizes the binding effect of international law upon national law and its eventual application to individuals. For some, like Kelsen, national law derived in part from international law.[48] Whether international law has primacy over national law whenever the latter is in violation of the former and in what manner such primacy manifested itself and applied to the national context are among the questions of international legal philosophy

---

[46]   *See* A. NUSSBAUM, *supra* note 41, at 77; and 1 J.H.W. VERZIJL, HISTORY OF INTERNATIONAL LAW 256 *et seq.* (1968).

[47]   *See* Borchard, *The Relation Between International Law and Municipal Law*, 27 VA. L. REV. 137 (1940); Sinha, *The Position of the Individual in an International Criminal Law* in BASSIOUNI AND NANDA TREATISE 122; I. BROWNLIE, PRINCIPLES OF PUBLIC INTERNATIONAL LAW (4th ed. 1990); L. OPPENHEIM, INTERNATIONAL LAW VOLUME I (H. Lauterpacht ed.) (8th ed. 1955).

[48]   Kelsen, *Collective and Individual Responsibility in International Law with Particular Regard to the Punishment of War Criminals*, 31 CA. L. REV. 530, 538 (1943).

that have long been debated.[49] Thus, it became inevitable that the individual would become a subject of international law capable of benefitting directly from these provisions developed for his benefit. The implications of a philosophical legal choice of hierarchy of legal norms and the relationship between international and national law is a threshhold issue of international legal philosophy. That choice was clear when the Charter promulgated its decision-rules applicable directly to individuals irrespective of the otherwise applicable German national law.

The drafters of the Charter were mindful of this important threshhold question. They dealt with it implicitly rather than explicitly by relying on existing international legal norms, principles and standards which prescribed and proscribed some of the conduct they intended to submit to adjudication. The argument was, in a sense, tautological as the drafters implicitly relied on some existing international law to be the predicate of their legislative exercise. This predicate presumed that international law not only superseded national law, but that it incorporated some portions of international

---

[49]   By the late eighteenth century, the view of such naturalist writers as SAMUEL PUFFENDORF *supra* note 21, and EMMERICH DE VATTEL, LE DROIT DES GENS (1758); along with emerging humanistic philosophies of the post-enlightenment era, gave rise to the notion of the individual as a subject of international law. But it was not until after World War I, with the advent of the Treaty of Versailles, which granted individuals certain specific rights and privileges, that collective and individual human rights emerged in international law. Because these rights emerged under international law, they necessarily implied that the individual was a subject of such a body of law. But the scholarly debate continued as to whether the conferral of rights upon individuals is necessarily the recognition that he is a subject of that body of law. Such a view held that states could confer such rights under the doctrine of stipulation for the benefit of a third party which did not imply that the third party, the individual, could claim the standing of a subject imply by reason of conferral of rights of privilege. The debate thus moved from substantive to procedural. As one author notes:

> The agony of theorizing ... about the status of relationship of the individual to international law has been a result of the individual's assertiveness in the international legal system. Unlike early stages of international law when the legal attributes of the individual on the international plane were practically nonexistent, this century witnesses a steady growth of his contact with this legal system through the creation of his rights, duties, right to petition, procedural ability, and procedural amenability. Thus, in addition to enjoying rights and privileges as a diplomatic envoy, a head of state, or a member of military forces abroad, or through the operation of a rule of the international minimum standard of justice for the treatment of aliens, the individual has gained international rights through minority treaties, trusteeship system of the United Nations, International Labor Organization, and the Office of the United Nations High Commissioner for Refugees.

Sinha, *The Position of the Individual in an International Criminal Law* in BASSIOUNI AND NANDA TREATISE 122, 132.

law and that when the two systems conflicted, the latter prevailed. While this may be the case in the post-World War II era, due in part to the doctrine of preemptory norms of *jus cogens*, as discussed in Chapter 11, it was nonetheless a very questionable assertion in 1945. In the post-World War II era, that debate lost some of its acuteness as the shield of national sovereignty was pierced by the direct imposition of individual criminal responsibility under international criminal law irrespective of the dictates of national law. Nevertheless, it is equally undeniable that the thrust of international law at that time was in the direction it ultimately reached. Thus, the Charter gave international law an impetus that one can fairly label as progressive development, which Justice Jackson referred to as "declarative."[50] Like other progressive or declarative aspects of international law, the Charter was probably more solidly grounded in the international legal doctrine of the time whose future development was clearly foreseeable.[51] There is, however, a difference between foreseeable developments of legal philosophical premise of international law's supremacy over national law and the direct applicability of international law by means of its penetration into national law in a monistic sense, which was the inarticulated premise of the Charter.

A further distinction exists between the doctrine of international law's direct penetration of national law and two other basic questions, namely: what specific aspects of the international law so apply; and, how? Even today these questions are unsettled as we do not have supranational legal institutions to enforce international criminal law, particularly because of the absence of an international criminal code and of an international criminal court. If it is valid to ask the question today: what portion of international law directly applies to individuals irrespective of national law and how is that to be enforced, then it was surely a more valid question in 1945.

---

[50] *See* Chapters 1 and 12. This declarative aspect is the consequence of a legal discipline based on custom and which, as such, is necessarily evolutionary. As Donnedieu de Vabres recognized, the essence of international law is customary as he stated in his incisive analysis of the Nuremberg Trial: *"Il est de l'essence du droit international d'etre, en facte, un droit costumier." See* H. DONNEDIEU DE VABRES, *Le Processe de Nuremberg du Droit Penal International*, 70 RECUEIL DES COURS 481 at 575 (1947). Thus, every evolutionary stage necessarily results in some recognition of the refined customary rule and at times it is done by declarative methods. Thus, the issue is not whether international law recognizes the declarative method of its otherwise emerging norms, but whether these declared norms satisfy the requirements of legality under international criminal law.

[51] N. POLITIS, LES TENDENCES MODERNES DU DROIT INTERNATIONAL (1927) discusses how between World War I and the date of the book, the individual has become both an active and passive subject of international criminal law. *See also* G. SCELLE, MANUEL ELEMENTAIRE DE DROIT INTERNATIONAL 430 *et seq.* (1943).

Assuming, however, that the principle of supremacy of international law is accepted, its penetration of national law recognized and its capability of creating individual international criminal responsibility acknowledged, there nevertheless remains the question of what specific obligation international law creates that individuals must be deemed knowledgeable of consequences accounting for any violations thereof.[52] Thus, even if we resolve the threshhold philosophical question, a substantive issue remains with respect to its contents[53] which need to satisfy the requirements of legality, as discussed in Chapter 3.

The Charter's Dilemma: Between Law and Morality

Naturalists, pragmatists, utilitarianists as well as some relative positivists find invalid, but for different reasons, the post-1935 Nazi laws under which Article 6(c) crimes were committed. They, therefore, hold the perpetrators of such conduct criminally accountable. But the question they differ on is: under what law? One approach that the drafters of the Charter and the legislators of CCL 10 could have followed was to apply the pre-existing German Criminal Code of 1871 without the subsequent changes made to it after 1935. But they did not. Yet curiously, the Allies after adopting the Charter passed an ordinance declaring all such Nazi laws null and void.[54] The question, therefore, was whether it was proper to apply the Charter instead of the original version of the 1871 German Criminal Code. The latter would have provided natural legality to German accuseds whether tried before a special tribunal, as were the IMT and subsequent Nuremberg proceedings, or before ordinary criminal courts, as has been the case in Germany since 1950.

One should also recall that Section 2 of the German Criminal Code of 1871 provides: "No punishment can be inflicted unless such punishment was legally defined before the act was committed. If the law is changed between the time at which the act was committed and the sentence is pronounced, the milder of the laws should be applied."[55] This norm derived from a principle contained in the Weimar Constitution, which provided in Article 116: "Punishment can be inflicted for only such acts as the

---

[52] *See* Chapter 9 at 359.

[53] *See* Chapters 7 and 8.

[54] CCL 7. *See* Document Section.

[55] *Cited in* A. VON KNIEREM, THE NUREMBERG TRIALS 7 (1959).

law had declared punishable before the act was committed."[56] Whether that provision may have deterred the drafters from resorting to pre-1935 German criminal law or not is purely speculative. In this writer's judgment, a new law was needed to express the wrath and anger of the world at the Nazi regime that caused so much pain and suffering to so many for so long. Like any adjudication process, the one to be devised, as discussed in Chapter 1, had to strike a delicate balance between just retribution and a fair legal process. The latter, however, presented no particular difficulties, and both the Charter and the IMT Proceedings are evidence of a substantially fair process.

The basic moral dilemma in 1945 was whether the extension of international criminal responsibility to perpetrators of Article 6(c) "crimes against humanity" -- which constituted a breach of strict legal positivism -- was a greater or lesser breach than to allow such perpetrators to go unpunished. To uphold the first would be to give greater weight to a given legal theory over the substantive harmful outcome deriving from an undeniable gross abuse of power, which, even according to positivists, begot neither good nor order. The law of the Charter, however, violated the "principles of legality" as applied under then existing French Civilist and Germanic legal traditions, though not necessarily under the views of some Common Law exponents, as discussed in Chapter 3. But to deny legitimacy to the Charter would enable the perpetrators to escape criminal accountability for their misdeeds. Interestingly, this very dilemma was addressed by Grotius, three hundred years earlier when he asserted *crimen grave non potest non essere punibile*.[57] Without reference to Grotius, but certainly moved by the

---

[56]   *Id. see also* the 1919 Weimar Constitution *reprinted in* R. BRUNET, THE GERMAN CONSTITUTION (J. Gollomb trans. 1922).

[57]   H. GROTIUS, *supra* note 33, at Chap. XX, § II, 3. Grotius defines natural law as the "dictate of right reasons which points out that a given act, because of its opposition to or conformity with man's rational nature, is either morally wrong or morally necessary, and accordingly forbidden or commanded by God, the author of nature." *Id.* That definition is similar to that of AQUINAS, *supra* note 24; and of Aristotle, *see generally* ETHICS, I AND POLITICS, I (Gateway ed. 1954); *see also* E. WOLF, GROTIUS, PUFFENDORF, THOMASIUS (1927), where the author retraces the links between the three and their approaches to natural law. But *see* H. KELSEN, THE PURE THEORY OF LAW 214 (1967), where he states:

If we replace the concept of reality (as effectiveness of the legal order) by the concept of power, then the problem of the relation between validity and effectiveness of the legal order coincides with the more familiar problem of the relationship between law and power or right and might. And then, the solution attempted here is merely the scientifically exact formulation of the old truism that right cannot exist without might and yet is not identical with might. Right, (the law), according to the theory here developed, is a certain order (or organization) of might.

same philosophical conception, the Nuremberg Tribunal in its Judgment, with respect to one of the defendants, concluded as follows: "[S]o far from it being unjust to punish him, it would be unjust if his wrongs were allowed to go unpunished."[58] Certain basic truths thus remain immutable throughout the course of time, and spring naturally to the minds of rational and thoughtful persons.

It is noteworthy, that such an articulation calls into question justice, in accordance with certain values, but it also implicitly relies on what could be deemed an equity principle to reach this outcome. In fact, many of the protagonists and antagonists of the Charter resort to equity principles without specifically referring to them in order to reach their legal conclusions. Those of the Common Law tradition, including positivists could easily rely on equity principles, but to transcend the Common Law's distinction between cases at law and matters of equity and their respective processes by freely merging them as was the case in the above-quoted portion of the judgment is a big leap.[59]

The equity principle reflected in the formulation of the Charter derives in part from the Roman Law maxim of *ex injuria ius non oritur*. The rationale of this equity principle is as follows: can one who participated in the subversion of the law benefit from it, or as the equity maxim would have it, those with unclean hands cannot seek the benefits of equity.

Principles of equity existed in Roman law and were absorbed into the Common Law[60] but they did not quite find their way in the French Civilist and Germanic legal systems because their codified systems reflected a positivistic approach and their

---

Kelsen, however, held that the principle of *ex post facto* would not apply to war crimes where the morality of punishment supercedes the legal formality of positivism. *See* P. CORBETT, MORALS, LAW AND POWER IN INTERNATIONAL RELATIONS (1956); and H. KELSEN, PEACE THROUGH LAW 87-88 (1944); *see also* H. KELSEN, PRINCIPLES OF INTERNATIONAL LAW 128 *et seq.* (1959).

[58]   *See* 22 IMT 444.

[59]   *See generally* Z. CHAFEE JR., SOME PROBLEMS OF EQUITY (1950); and Cook, *The Powers of Courts of Equity*, 15 COLUM. L. REV. 37 (1915). On English approaches to equity, *see* 1 HOLDSWORTH, HISTORY OF ENGLISH LAW 395-476 (7th ed. 1956); and Holmes, *Early English Equity*, 1 L. Q. REV. 162 (1885).

[60]   *See* Re, *The Roman Contribution to the Common Law*, 29 FORDHAM L. REV. 447, 477-484 (1961). Equity derives from the Roman Law's aequitas which was applied by the *praetor peregrinus* when outside the scope of the *ius civile*. It has its origins in the Aristotelian concept of *epieikeia*. St. Thomas Aquinas also recognized the need for law to be tempered by reasoned equity. *See* Re *id.* at 480-81, particularly notes 158-160; *see also* T. PLUNKNETT, A CONCISE HISTORY OF THE COMMON LAW (2d. ed. 1939).

techniques of legal interpretation were also positivist. But once again the Common Law as espoused by Justice Jackson prevailed.

In his opening statement at Nuremberg, he indirectly referred to this principle when he exclaimed about the defendants in the dock:

It may be said that this is new law, not authoritatively declared at the time they did the acts it condemns, and that this declaration of the law has taken them by surprise.

I cannot, of course, deny that these men are surprised that this is the law; they really are surprised that there is any such thing as law. These defendants did not rely on any law at all. Their program ignored and defied all law.

German law, any law at all was to these men simply a propaganda devise to be invoked when it helped and to be ignored when it would condemn what they wanted to do. That men may be protected in relying upon the law at the time they act is the reason we find laws of retrospective operation unjust. But these men cannot bring themselves within the reason of the rule which in some systems of jurisprudence prohibits *ex post facto* laws. They cannot show that they ever relied upon International Law in any state or paid it the slightest regard.[61]

A corollary to that position is another equity maxim, that those who seek equity must do equity. Those who shaped the laws that permitted them to do their misdeeds should not, therefore, be able to claim the protection of legal defenses that they established for their benefit prior to the commission of their misdeeds.

Equity, as stated above, is not a stranger to international law. Indeed, it is recognized as an alternative source of international law under Articles 38 of the Statute of the PCIJ and of the ICJ.[62] Consequently, the drafters of the Charter and the IMT judges could have specifically relied on equity doctrine in support of certain propositions -- but they did not. The Common Law drafters of the Charter and the IMT judges who applied it did not articulate their legal arguments in equitable terms, though they surely relied on it, probably because it would have been so alien to the other legal systems represented in the process. Instead, they reflected a laicized naturalist

---

[61] R.H. JACKSON, *supra* note 30, at 81-82 (1971).

[62] Lapidoth, *Equity in International Law*, 22 ISRAEL L. REV. 161 (1987).

philosophy in the Grotian tradition, which they developed with more concern for pragmatism than doctrinal purity. The architect of this approach in the drafting of the Charter was Justice Robert Jackson, who best reflected American legal realism in this episode.[63]

Naturalists, relative positivists, pragmatists and utilitarians all found common ground albeit from different vantage points in upholding the legitimacy of the Charter, even though most acknowledged its technical legal deficiencies. The enormity of the human harm had helped to overcome concerns for legal imperfections.[64] Thus, the facts shaped the outcome of the law.

For some pragmatists and utilitarians, the fundamental tenets of natural law, which assert the existence of a higher and immutable law, do not hold true. In their view, law is mutable, dynamic and progressive. Thus, legal pragmatists and utilitarianists support the Law of Charter, as do naturalists, but for different reasons. The former relies on relativism, empiricism and realism, while the latter relies on metaphysical essences and transcendental beliefs.[65]

---

[63] Oliver Wendel Holmes best expressed it when he stated "The Life of the law has not been logic: it has been experience." O.W. HOLMES, THE COMMON LAW 1 (1881, 44th printing 1951). Experience as he meant it is the ability of the Common Law judge to interpret the law as he applied it to new and different contexts; *see also* O.W. Holmes, *The Path of the Law*, 10 HARV. L. REV. 457 (1897), where he states "The rational study of law is still to a large extent the study of history." *Id.*; H.L. POHLMAN, JUSTICE OLIVER WENDELL HOLMES AND UTILITARIAN JURISPRUDENCE (1984). Another influential American jurist was Benjamin Cardozo. *See* B. CARDOZO, THE NATURE OF THE JUDICIAL PROCESS (1921).

[64] A. VON KNIEREM in, *supra* note 55, took a critical view of the entire legal process on the basis of legal positivism. *See also* Harris, *Review of Nuremberg Trials by August Von Knierem*, 54 AJIL 444 (1960). Other critical views are found in W.E. BENTON AND G. GRIMM, NUREMBERG: GERMAN VIEWS OF WAR TRIALS (1955); and H.H. JESCHECK, DIE VERANTWORTLICHKEIT DER STAATSORGAN NACH VOLKERSTRA-FRECHT (1952). Four of the defense lawyers at Nuremberg expressed such sentiments: Krause (Chief Counsel for Schacht), *The Nuremberg Trials of the Major War Criminals: Reflections After Seventeen Years*, 13 DEPAUL L. REV. 233 (1964); Haensel (Chief Counsel for the S.S. and S.D.), *The Nuremberg Trial Revisited*, 13 DEPAUL L. REV. 298 (1964); Kranzbuhler (Chief Counsel for Donitz), *Nuremberg Eighteen Years Afterwards*, 14 DEPAUL L. REV. 333 (1965); Pannenbecker (Chief Counsel for Flick), *The Nuremberg War Crimes Trial*, 14 DEPAUL L. REV. 398 (1965). *See also* B.V.A. Roling, *The Nuremberg and Tokyo Trials in Retrospect* in 1 BASSIOUNI ICL 590; de Zayas, *Der Nürnberger Prozess vor dem Internationalen Militär Tribunal (1945-1954)* in MACHT UND RECHT 249 (H. von Alexander ed. 1990). *See also* Pappe, *On the Validity of Judicial Decisions in the Nazi Era*, 23 MOD. L. REV. 260 (1960); and Bodenheimer, *Significant Developments in German Legal Philosophy since 1945*, 3 AM. J. COMP. L. 379 (1954).

[65] For these different perspectives, *see* Kelsen, *Collective and Individual Responsibility in International Law with Particular Regard to the Punishment of War Criminals*, 31 CALIF. L. REV. 530 (1943); Lauterpacht, *The Law of Nations and the Punishment of War Crimes*, 21 BRIT. Y.B. INT'L L. 58

Some relative legal positivists rejoin these two schools of thought because the premises of legitimacy of the positive law under which these acts were committed were absent. As Radbruch stated in his famous FÜNF MINUTEN RECHTSPHILOSOPHIE:

"An order is an order," the soldier is told. "A law is a law," says the jurist. The soldier, however, is required neither by duty nor by law to obey an order that he knows to have been issued with a felony or misdemeanor in mind, while the jurists, since the last of the natural law theorists among them disappeared a hundred years ago, have recognized no such exceptions to the validity of a law or to the requirement of obedience by those subject to it. A law is valid because it is a law, and it is a law if in the general run of cases it has the power to prevail.

This view of the nature of a law and of its validity (we call it the positivistic theory) has rendered the jurist as well as the people defenseless against laws, however arbitrary, cruel, or criminal they may be. In the end, the positivistic theory equates the law with power; there is law only where there is power ....

If laws consciously deny the will to justice, if, for example, they grant and deny human rights arbitrarily, then these laws lack validity, the people owe them no obedience, and even the jurists must find the courage to deny their legal character ...

There are, therefore, principles of law that are stronger than any statute, so that a law conflicting with these principles is devoid of validity. One calls these principles the natural law or the law of reason. To be sure, their details remain somewhat doubtful, but the work of centuries has established a solid core of them and they have come to enjoy such a far-reaching consensus in the declarations of human and civil rights that only the deliberate skeptic can still entertain doubts about some of them.

(1944); S. GLUECK, WAR CRIMINALS, THEIR PROSECUTION AND PUNISHMENT (1944); Goodhart, *The Legality of the Nuremberg Trials*, 56 JURID. REV. 1 (1946); Glueck & Finch, *The Nuremberg Trial in International Law*, 41 AJIL 27 (1947); Schwarzenberger, *The Judgment at Nuremberg*, 21 TUL. L. REV. 328 (1947); Wright, *Legal Positivism and the Nuremberg Judgment*, 42 AJIL 405 (1948); J. KEENAN & B. BROWN, CRIMES AGAINST INTERNATIONAL LAW (1950); R. WOETZEL, THE NUREMBERG TRIALS IN INTERNATIONAL LAW (1960); 2 G. SCHWARZENBERGER, INTERNATIONAL LAW AS APPLIED BY INTERNATIONAL COURTS AND TRIBUNALS (1968); and A. TUSA AND J. TUSA, THE NUREMBERG TRIAL (1983).

In religious language the same thoughts have been recorded in two biblical passages. On the one hand it is written that you are to obey the authorities who have power over you. But then on the other, it is also written that you are to obey God before man -- and this is not simply a pious wish, but a valid proposition of law. The tension between these two directives cannot, however, be relieved by appealing to a third -- say, to the maxim: Render unto Caesar the things that are Caesar's and unto God the things that are God's. For this directive too, leaves the boundary in doubt. Rather, it leaves the solution to the voice of God, which speaks to the conscience of the individual only in the exceptional case.[66]

Thus, while naturalists and some pragmatists and utilitarians could agree -- for different reasons -- that the Law of the Charter was justified, rigid positivists could not share this position.[67]

Pragmatists and utilitarians saw in the Law of the Charter the triumph of social policy, which holds that empiricism produces the law that better serves humankind.[68] Naturalists saw in it the application of a higher metaphysical law that supercedes positive law, the triumph of good over evil, which is always distinguishable, positive law notwithstanding.[69] Moreover, positivists, who do not accept the Kantian-

---

[66]   G. RADBRUCH, RECHTSPHILOSOPHIE 327-329 (E. Wolff and H.P. Schneider eds. 1973).

[67]   *See* W.J. BOSCH, JUDGMENT ON NUREMBERG 40-66 (1970). In an incisive comment, Professor Wright states:

> The favorable or unfavorable character of comments upon events related to international law often depends less upon the nature of the events than upon the theory of international law assumed by the commentator.

Wright, *supra* note 65, at 405.

For a contemporary policy-oriented approach, *see generally* M. MCDOUGAL AND F.'FELICIANO, LAW AND MINIMUM WORLD PUBLIC ORDER (1961).

[68]   *See generally* P.E. CORBETT, THE STUDY OF INTERNATIONAL LAW (1955); and A. NUSSBAUM, *supra* note 41, at 114. For a contemporary view *see e.g.*, J. RAWLS, A THEORY OF JUSTICE (1971).

[69]   *See* Fuller, *supra* note 14, at 660. Fuller asserts:

> To me there is nothing shocking in saying that a dictatorship which clothes itself with a tinsel of legal form can so far depart from the morality of order, from the inner morality of law itself, that it ceases to be a legal system. When a system calling itself law is predicated upon a general disregard by judges

Hegelian-Austinian power concept from which positive law derives its absolute legitimacy, saw an opportunity to reassert the prerequisite of legitimacy of the legal order and of the legal process before the positive law can be held to apply more or less absolutely.

Paradoxically, Kantian-Hegelian-Austinian positivists might find validity in the Law of the Charter on the same grounds as they found validity for those who obeyed prior laws, because for them "law is law." But then they would argue that to prosecute and punish such persons still would be unjust because of their opposition to the retroactivity of criminal laws as violating one of the "principles of legality," namely the prohibition against *ex post facto* laws.

The two opposing views of naturalism and strict positivism rely on opposing morality arguments in their respective support and criticism of the Charter's legal validity. The naturalists arguing morality as an end, and the strict positivists advancing morality as a means. For the naturalists, society must prosecute and punish "crimes against humanity" for moral reasons. For the positivists, to prosecute and punish those who acted pursuant to the then existing national positive law, which was not explicitly prohibited by positive international law, would be an immoral as well as illegal violation. Obviously, a judgment was necessary, and in this case, the facts were certainly as significant in the choice as were the competing values. Thus, the facts were the inexorable driving force behind the logic leading to that choice.[70] In this context, the words of Saint Thomas Aquinas echoing those of Saint Augustine have a powerful appeal:

> As Augustine says, *that which is not just seems to be no law at all*:
> wherefore the force of a law depends on the extent of its justice. Now in human affairs a thing is said to be just from being right, according to the rule of reason. But the first rule of reason is the law of nature, as is clear from what has been

---

of the terms of the laws they purport to enforce, when this system habitually cures its legal irregularities, even the grossest, by retroactive statutes, when it has only to resort to forays of terror in the streets, which no one dares challenge, in order to escape even those scant restraints imposed by the pretence of legality -- when all these things have become true of a dictatorship, it is not hard for me, at least, to deny to it the name of law. *Id.*

See also D'Amato, *Lon Fuller and Substantive Natural Law*, 26 AM. J. JURIS. 202 (1981); and P. DEVLIN, THE ENFORCEMENT OF MORALS (1965).

[70] *See generally* G. GOTTLIEB, THE LOGIC OF CHOICE (1968); and P. COFFEY, THE SCIENCE OF LOGIC (1912).

stated above. Consequently, every human law has just so much of the nature of law, as it is derived from the law of nature. But if in any point it departs from the law of nature, it is no longer a law but a perversion of law.[71]

There is something perverse in rejecting the validity of the Law of the Charter, even though it violates the strict positivist view that "law is law," because such rejection would legitimize the legal order under which "crimes against humanity" were committed, and would sanction the notion that might makes right.[72] This is exactly what naturalists of all tendencies reject the most, and in this case so do many relative positivists, pragmatists and utilitarians.

The Law of the Charter can, however, also be described as the embodiment of might makes right because it enacted a new law based on the power derived from victory. Thus, conflicting legal approaches are not only a consequence of different legal techniques but of different philosophical perspectives embodying different values.

Professor Friedman summarized these issues as follows:

> The first possible approach is that of transcendental or "supernatural" ethics, which corresponds to the orthodox natural law approach in legal philosophy. This approach would regard the type of decrees that led to Auschwitz and Belsen as contrary to a natural law of respect for human dignity, as an emanation either of the law of God or of universal reason. It would conclude that a law clearly offending against these elementary principles was void and therefore not binding. From this premise flows the right to punish those who offended the higher law by

---

[71] *See* ST. THOMAS AQUINAS, *supra* note 24, at 78. (Emphasis added.).

[72] Duguit, *The Law and the State*, 31 HARV. L. REV. 1, 8 (F.J. de Sloovere trans. 1917). Duguit asserts:

> ... There is no will of the State; there are only individual wills of those governing. When they act they are not the mandataries or the subordinate parts of a supposed collective person, or an assumed personality, the State, whose will they express and execute. They express and carry out their own wills; there is no other. Any other conception of the State is fantastic.

See also Duguit, *Objective Law*, 20 COLUM, L. REV. 817 (1920), and 21 COLUM. L. REV. 17 (1921). Without reference to Duguit, and probably for most of the Charter's drafters without even knowledge of his thoughts, the concept of individual criminal responsibility was established and the artificial shield of state sovereignty was removed. This stripped those accused of the traditional defence of "Act of State." *See* Chapter 10.

obeying the positive law. In technical terms, this means that a subsequent legal order such as that expressed by the Nuremberg Charter or by postwar German legislation is made applicable retroactively.

A second approach would be that of the intuitionist ethics. The rightness or wrongness of a conduct would be determined by an objectively but intuitively known feeling of right or wrong, a *Rechtsgeful* or a *sentimento giuridico*. The difficulty with this approach is that an intuitive evaluation can lead the individual concerned to very different decisions. He may intuitively feel the wrongness of an extermination decree, and derive from this his duty to disobey it, or he may on the contrary accept the injunction of the Nazi law of 1935 which empowered judges to inflict punishment "in accordance with the sound instincts of the people," interpreting such sound instincts as dictating the persecution and even extermination of Jews, Slavs, and other inferior races. Or he may be inspired by the feeling: "Right or wrong, my Country." Intuition may help to inspire marginal decisions in the sense indicated by Gény, but if asked to guide in the basic choice of values it yields nothing.

Third, there are various relativistic approaches. One of these, that of Dewey, would be based on a pragmatic "logic of enquiry, directed to the exploration of a given value." Such an approach would tentatively appraise the Nazi laws that "legalized" racial oppression, degradation of the human personality, and mass murder, as evil. It would, however, study the question of subsequent punishment of those who obeyed the Nazi laws in the light of feasibility. Such a study might show that a complete implementation of the goal of punishing everybody who participated in the making and execution of such laws was simply not feasible. The result of such a pragmatic enquiry might be that a more modest goal, *i.e.*, the selection for punishment or other sanctions of those prominently associated with the Nazi regime through their high position or known deeds, would implement more adequately the objective of disapproval of the Nazi values, and of treating equals equally.

While pragmatic ethics are compatible with a relativistic approach, the basic attitude of relativistic ethics would be that whether to obey or disobey the Nazi laws was essentially a question of choice between the religious, humanistic, hedonistic, and other values relevant to the problem. One possible value -- which indeed was chosen by the great majority of Germans -- was that of obeying the positive authority of the State, at the expense of the principles of human dignity, compassion, and charity. The rationalistic ethics that are usually combined with the relativistic approach would demand a careful study of the means by which the different values would have to be implemented. It would show, for example, that the necessary implication of legal discrimination between "Aryans" and Jews would lead not only to the undermining of the family but also to a profound modification of the principles of equality, in contract, in criminal law, and in other fields. Such clarification of the goals might at least articulate and underline the severity of the choice between values.

"Noncognitivist" ethics would dismiss the entire problem as beyond the reach of rational discussion. It would regard the punishment of Nazi criminals, or their non-punishment, as expressions of conflicting emotions, be they the retribution imposed by an outraged humanity, a sophisticated version of the traditional exercise of the rights of victors over the vanquished, or on the other hand a skeptical or even cynical acquiescence in the man's cowardice.

The solution suggested later in this book for these problems is predicated on the belief that no legally compelling solution can be found for this type of problem. Whatever the technical device, a subsequent and differing set of values has to be substituted for the values governing the offensive action.[73]

The Charter was viewed by many as the product of a historical legal ripening process, even though positivists, opposing that view, pointed to the absence of specific norms pre-existing the facts. Naturalists on the other hand, viewed the Charter as the legally valid embodiment of a compelling higher law. Some pragmatists and utilitarians, recognizing the evolutionary nature of international law, saw the Charter as the enunciation of a positive norm that was grounded in a variety of historical legal precedents whose evolution was justified by moral-ethical considerations and by legal policy.

The question of whether, at the time the Charter was enacted, this ripening process had reached the appropriate level of legal sufficiency under some legal theory remained to be legally demonstrated. The basic line drawn between supporters and critics of the Charter is, therefore, whether it is grounded in prior law, and thus declarative, or whether it is essentially innovative. For strict positivists, the absence of specific pre-existing positive law remained an insurmountable obstacle to the legality of the Charter. Justice Jackson best expressed these divergent positions as follows:

---

[73] W. FRIEDMAN, *supra* note 7, at 40-42.

The principles of the charter, no less than its wide acceptance, establish its significance as a step in the evolution of a law-governed society of nations. The charter is something of a landmark, both as a substantive code defining crimes against the international community and also as an instrument establishing a procedure for prosecution and trial of such crimes before an international court. It carries the conception of crime against the society of nations far beyond its former state and to a point which probably will be exceeded, either through revision in principle or through restatement, in the foreseeable future. There is debate as to whether its provisions introduce innovations or whether they merely make explicit and unambiguous what was previously implicit in international law. But whether the London Conference merely codified existing but inchoate principles of law, or whether it originated new doctrine, the charter, followed by the international trial, conviction, and punishment of the German leaders at Nürnberg, marks a transition in international law which calls for a full exposition of the negotiations which brought it forth.[74]

Proponents and opponents of the Law of the Charter claimed moral, ethical and equitable considerations, but few of them dealt systematically with the variety of legal issues arising under international law.[75]   Keenan and Brown note:

It is the authors' contention that the Tokyo and Nürnberg war crimes trials were a manifestation of an intellectual and moral revolution which will have a profound and far-reaching influence upon the future of world society .... They maintain that the international moral order must be regarded as the cause, not the effect, of positive law; that such law does not derive its essence from physical power, and that any attempt to isolate such law from morals is a symptom   of juridical schizophrenia caused by the separation of the brain of the lawyer from that of the human being.[76]

Corbett also espoused these views by stating:

---

[74]   JACKSON'S REPORT at viii.

[75]   Two works are notable exceptions, those of A. VON KNIEREM, *supra* note 55; and R. WOETZEL, *supra* note 65.

[76]   J. KEENAN & B. BROWN, *supra* note 65, at v-vi.

Even if such justification is of moral rather than strictly legal significance, it is of great importance; for, in the last analysis, international morality is the soil which fosters the growth of international law. It is international morality which determines the general direction of the development of international law. Whatever is considered "just" in the sense of international morality has at least a tendency of becoming international "law."[77]

Lastly, Quincy Wright maintains:

[R]egularly enforced world criminal law applicable to individuals necessarily makes inroads upon national sovereignty and tends to change the foundations of the international community from a balance of power among sovereign states to a universal federation directly controlling individuals in all countries on matters covered by international law.[78]

The fact that criminal law has been held to apply territorially is nothing more than that discipline's reflection of the concept of sovereignty.[79] As sovereignty erodes, and states partake more in extra-territorial interests, and are affected more by extra-territorial activity, they share more common interests that need to be safeguarded irrespective of territorial limitations. Thus, the territoriality of criminal law loses some of its relevance and at times becomes a burden and a limitation to the needs and interests of states.[80]

Principles of justice are necessarily unbound by space and time, even though for reasons of policy or opportunity territorial and time limitations are placed on most criminal laws.[81] In practice, it is the policy or opportunity that brings about the outcome of that choice, not the substance of the right or the duty. Crimes do not disappear merely in time, or through a lack of prosecution -- these are prosecutorial and punishment policy decisions which arise after the criminal fact. Above all, they have

---

[77]   P.E. CORBETT, *supra* note 68, at 16; and *see also* H. KELSEN, LAW AND PEACE IN INTERNATIONAL RELATIONS 37-38 (1948).

[78]   Wright, *The Law of the Nuremberg Trial*, 41 AJIL 38, 47 (1941).

[79]   H. DONNEDIEU DE VABRES, LES PRINCIPES MODERNES DU DROIT PÉNAL INTERNATIONAL (1928).

[80]   *See* Chapter 11 at 509.

[81]   *See* Chapter 11 at 507.

no bearing on the harmful results and victimization produced by the crime, even when for policy reasons they may no longer be prosecutable or punishable.

The emergence of individual responsibility under international criminal law, as discussed in Chapter 5, and of individual rights under international protection of human rights, has evidenced a breakdown in the shield of national sovereignty.[82] Thus, one notes the current trend towards establishing the universality of individual rights and duties. This entitlement necessarily results in individual responsibility for those who breach international rules irrespective of national law.

Pragmatism Prevails

Only rigid positivists would uphold the validity of these Nazi German laws according to which "crimes against humanity" had been committed. All other philosophical views would invalidate the national laws of Nazi Germany which mandated or permitted the commission of those acts falling within the meaning of Article 6(c). But the logical conclusion to the rejection of such post-1935 Nazi laws would have been to apply German criminal law as it existed before the Nazi changes instead of the Law of the Charter, which enacted an alternative normative basis for the accountability of those charged with "crimes against humanity." But the drafters of the Charter did not pursue this arduous path. Instead, they simply relied on their delegated powers by the respective Allies to engage in their legislative exercise. In a sense their premise was equivalent to that of the rigid positivists who viewed law as the outcome of power. Yet the drafters believed that theirs was not a pure exercise in power, but the redress of a legal imbalance produced by prior abuse of power. Mindful of these considerations, Jackson stated in his opening statement: "That four great nations, flushed with victory and stung with injury stay the hand of vengeance and voluntarily submit their captive enemies to the judgment of the law is one of the most significant tributes that power ever has paid to reason."[83]

Some authors, like Schwarzenberger, believed that the Nuremberg and Tokyo Charters were not declarative of international law at the time, but were merely meant

---

[82] *See* Bassiouni, *The Proscribing Function of International Criminal Law in the Protection of Human Rights*, 9 YALE J. WORLD PUB. ORD. 193 (1982).

[83] R.H. JACKSON, *supra* note 30, at 31.

to punish the atrocious behavior of the Nazi and Japanese regimes because their deeds could not go unpunished. Thus, he stated:

> [the] limited and qualified character of the rule on crimes against humanity as formulated in the Charters of the Nuremberg and Tokyo Tribunals militates against the rule being accepted as one declaratory of international customary law. This rudimentary legal system [of international law] does not know of distinctions as subtle as those between crimes against humanity which are connected with other types of war crime and, therefore, are to be treated as analogous to war crimes in the strict sense and other types of inhumane acts which are not so linked and, therefore, are beyond the pale of international law. The Four-Power Protocol of October 6, 1945, offers even more decisive evidence of the anxiety of the Contracting Parties to avoid any misinterpretation of their intentions as having codified a generally applicable rule of international customary law.[84]

He concluded that what the Four Powers intended to do, under the heading of "crimes against humanity," was to deal retrospectively with the particularly "ugly facets of the relapse of two formerly civilized nations into a state of barbarism."[85] But that position was not generally shared by most of his contemporaries.[86] Indeed, even the rigid legal positivism expressed in the narrow interpretation expounded by critics of the Charter[87] stops short of reaching a contrary logical legal conclusion, namely: If a deed is recognized as deserving punishment where does that recognition stem from; would such recognition merely be another form of atavistic and vindictive expression, or is it based on the existence of an inarticulated premise that certain "general principles" exist which make such deeds deserving of punishment. If so, then how can a principle that recognizes the need for punishability not be based, at least implicitly, on some existing prescription? This is essentially a question that regards the meaning, content and application of the "principles of legality" as they arise in the different national legal systems.[88] Considering, however, that the conventional and customary regulations of armed conflicts refer to and rely upon basic "laws of humanity" as

---

[84] Schwarzenberger, *supra* note 65, at 499.

[85] *Id.*

[86] *See* Chapter 4, note 144.

[87] *See e.g.*, Schwarzenberger *supra* note 65, at 479, 483; and Lauterpacht, *supra* note 65.

[88] *See* Chapter 3.

specifically expressed in the Preamble of Hague IV, then the conclusion is inescapable that an inarticulated legal premise does exist. In this perspective the criticism of legal positivists appears to be more a question of form than one of substance. As Professor D'Amato aptly stated:

> Not only do positivists insist upon separating law from morality, but they also appear to be unable to deal with moral questions raised by law once the two are separated. This inability stems, I believe, from their simultaneous attempt to assert and to prove that law and morality are separate; the argument reduces to a vicious circle.[89]

The observations made in this Chapter denote the everlasting tension between the law as: given and made; science and art; coercion and acceptance; form and content; technique and outcome; is and ought; objective and subjective; evolving and rigid; and, growing of its own and dependent on external power. None of these issues were addressed by the framers of the Charter, nor did they even appear to surface in their deliberations, although they surely must have weighed on their thoughts. This tension is reflected by a prescient statement made by Jackson in his opening statement: "We must never forget that the record on which we judge these defendants is the record on which history will judge us tomorrow."[90] That is why it should be remembered that the post-World War II prosecutions suffered from a moral flaw: they applied only to the vanquished. This lack of impartiality taints the IMT and Subsequent Proceedings under CCL 10, the Tokyo trials, and other post-World War II trials with the one-sidedness of victor's law.[91] The very moral-ethical premises of the legality of these

---

[89]   D'Amato, *The Moral Dilemma of Positivism*, 20 VALP. L. REV. 43 (1985). *See also* A. D'AMATO, JURISPRUDENCE: A DESCRIPTIVE AND NORMATIVE ANALYSIS OF LAW 294-302 (1984); *Contra* Hart, *Positivism and the Separation of Law and Morals*, 71 HARV. L. REV. 593, 624-29 (1958).

[90]   *See* R.H. JACKSON, *supra* note 30, at 33-34.

[91]   *See* M. BELGION, EPITAPH ON NÜRNBERG 1947. Another author noted:

"the might of the victors is not law. Success in war does not imply a tribunal for law and truth. Such a tribunal could not possibly objectively investigate and judge war guilt and war crimes. Such a court must necessarily be partisan. Also a court even of neutrals would be partial, since the neutrals are powerless and, in fact, in the party of the victors. Only a court backed by a power able to enforce the decision on both contending parties could judge impartially.

The objection to this trial as pseudo-justice continues: after every war the guilt of it is laid to the loser. He is forced to the admission of his guilt. The economic exploitation following the war is

proceedings were compelling on all of those who violate the same law to equally stand trial for their deeds, but that did not occur.[92] In fact, even among the Axis powers, the same principles did not equally apply to all accused. The UNWCC listed some 750 Italians as accused war criminals, but they were never prosecuted. The requests for surrender of some of these offenders by Yugoslavia and Ethiopia were never granted by either the Allies occupying Italy, or by the subsequent Provisional Italian Government, despite the clear mandate of the Italian Armistice Agreement.[93]

Pragmatic considerations guided the decisions and choices of the Charter's drafters, as discussed in Chapter 1, but the legacy they left remained affected by certain imperfections.

---

disguised as a reparation for guilt. Pillaging is falsely put forth as an act of justice. If there can be no impartial justice, then there might better be open force. That would be at least honest and also easier to bear."

Karl Jaspers, *The Significance of the Nurnberg Trial for Germany and The World*, 22 NOTRE DAME LAW'Y. 150, 155 (1946). He went on to state:

"The pseudo-justice of the court, according to this objection, shows itself finally in the fact that the acts declared criminal are judged by the court only when they have been committed by the vanquished nations. These same acts committed by sovereign or victorious nations are passed over in silence and are not even discussed, let alone punished.

Against all this it should be said that might and brutal force are, as a matter of fact, a decisive reality in the world of men. However, they are not the sole decisive reality. The predominance of this reality abolishes every reliable relationship between men. As long as it predominates no agreement is possible. As Hitler has stated it: 'Treaties last only as long as they correspond to self interest.' And he has acted accordingly. But over against this stands the will, which despite the admission of the reality of might and that nihilistic concept, considers it something which should not exist and which must therefore be by all means opposed.

For in human affairs reality does not necessarily mean truth. To this reality a rather different reality is to be opposed. And whether this other reality is to be effected depends upon the will of men. Each one must honestly know where he stands and what he wishes.

From this point of view, it must then be said that the trial, as a new attempt to promote order in the world, does not lose its meaning even if it cannot yet base itself upon a legal world order, but is still necessarily handicapped by political considerations. It does not yet take place as does a court trial within an orderly state."

Id. at 156.

[92]   *Id.* and *also* A.M. DE ZAYAS, THE WEHRMACHT WAR CRIMES BUREAU 1939-1945 (1989), where the author reveals German documentation of Allied war crimes.

[93]   *See* Chapter 5.

The framing of the Charter, its value-bases, and the articulation of its norms were based on classical legal structuralism. But the drafters were selective. When consistency stood in the way of their intended purpose, they disregarded the very structuralism they relied upon without the slightest concern for their deviations. In this respect, however, they exercised what contemporary critical legal studies commentators call the reversability of legal arguments and the determinacy of application whose ultimate goals are self-validation. The end seemed to justify the means, and if the sacrifice to be made was legal consistency and coherence, it was probably felt to be a minor one in exchange for the larger gains of advancing the international rule of law (*sic*).

The drafters of the Charter, who in their representative capacity, were also the judges and prosecutors, employed the same technique as all legal systems throughout history--they separated rules of conduct from rules of decision. The Charter was essentially a set of decision rules which in Professor Dan-Cohen's terms maintained a legitimized "accoustical separation" from the pre-existing conduct rules.

CHAPTER 3

PRINCIPLES OF LEGALITY

> *Poena non irrogatur nisi quae quaque lege vel quo alio iure specialiter huic delicto imposita est.*
> CORPUS IURIS CIVILIS (PANDECTS, D.50.16.131.)

Introduction

As a consequence of the changes in European political thought and legal philosophy in the age of enlightenment, as discussed in Chapter 2, the principles *nullum crimen sine lege* and *nulla peona sine lege* have become, since the late 1800's, fundamental principles of criminal law in the world's major criminal justice systems.[1] They include such derivative principles as *nullum crimen sine lege praevia* and *nullum crimen sine poena legali*. Another fundamental principle is the prohibition against *ex post facto* criminal laws and its derivative rule of non-retroactive application of criminal laws and criminal sanctions. A corollary to these principles is the requirement of specificity and the prohibition of ambiguity in criminal legislation.

---

[1]   Though the principles of legality can be found in several legal systems, their modern European origin is attributed to Anselm Fueurbach who first articulated them in his 1801 LEHRBUCH DES PEINLICHEN RECHTS. This period was the height of intellectual liberalism and revolutionary liberalism in Europe, which also coincided with the highest point of modern western classicism. For a survey of these "principles of legality" *see* Vassalli, *Nullum Crimen Sine Lege*, APPENDICE DEL NUOVISSIMO DIGESTO ITALIANO 292, Vol. 5 (1984); Glaser, *Le Principe de la Légalité en Matière Pénale, Notamament en Droit Codifié, et en Droit Coutumier*, 46 REVUE DE DROIT PÉNAL ET DE CRIMINOLOGIE 889 (1966); Hall, *Nullum Crimen Sine Lege*, 47 YALE L.J. 165 (1937); Vassalli, *Nullum Crimen Sine Lege*, 8 NUOVO DIGESTO ITALIANO 1173 (1939); and J. DE LA MORANDIÈRE, DE LA RÈGLE NULLA POENA SINE LEGE (1910). For national approaches, *see* R. MERLE and A. VITU, TRAITÉ DE DROIT CRIMINAL 108 *et seq.* (1967), which documents the historical right of the judge in the French criminal justice system to interpret principles of law, and which, at 113, acknowledges the decline in the 20th century of the rigid positivist approach to "principles of legality;" Nuvolone, *Le principe de legalité, et les principes de la defence Sociale*, in REVUE DE SCIENCE CRIMINELLE ET DE DROIT COMPARÉ 231 (1956); Soyer, *La Formulation actuelle du principe nullum crimen*, REVUE DE SCIENCE CRIMINELLES 11 *et seq.* (1952); Ancel, *La règle nulla poena sine lege, dans les legislations modernes*, in ANNALES DE L'INSTITUT DE DROIT COMPARÉ 245 (1936); and *infra* notes 2, 18 and 19.

Though the "principles of legality" are essentially legislative constraints, they are also rules of judicial interpretation. In that context, the basic rule of interpretation embodying the "principles of legality" is the prohibition or limitation on the use of analogy in judicial interpretation. But legal systems differ as to their treatment of analogy and they can be loosely divided into three categories.[2]

The first category is when a legislative enactment permits the use of interpretative analogy to permit judicially created crimes. Some legal systems allow it for foreseeably analogous crimes, thus excluding unforeseeable ones, while most modern systems disallow it entirely, particularly for serious offenses. Those that permit it, condition analogy to crimes which closely resemble those which are legislatively defined. The assumption being that such an analogy is predicated on the general expectation that the judicially defined analogous crime is within the foreseeable scope of the legislative prohibition. The second category is when a legislative enactment is not sufficiently clear or fails to articulate with enough specificity one of the elements of the crime or does not completely list the instrumentalities of the material. Most legal systems allow for some narrow judicial discretion in the interpretation of such legislative enactments. This is particularly the case when the given law is otherwise specific but provides, for example, a non-exhaustive list of the prohibited methods or instruments with which the crime can be committed. The third category applies to penalties which are not legislatively defined, or which allow judicial discretion for their determination in individual cases. Most legal systems allow for some discretion within established legislative parameters but only a few permit resorting to analogy outside legislatively enacted penalties. Even legal systems which have a rigid positivistic approach to "principles of legality" permit discretionary sentencing within legislatively established

---

[2]   *See e.g.* F. MANTOVANI, DIRITTO PENALE 105 (1988); Jimenez de Asua, *L'Analogie en Droit pénal*, REVUE DE SCIENCE CRIMINELLES 187, 189 (1949); JIMENEZ DE ASUA, TRATADO DE DERECHO PENAL 477 *et seq.* (2d ed. 1949); N. BOBBIO, L'ANALOGIA NELLA LOGICA DEL DIRITTO (1938); Palazzo, *L'Analogie en Droit Pénal*, 14 RIDP 308 (1937); F. BELLAVISTA, L'INTERPRETAZIONE DELLA LEGGE PENALE (1936). For a classical German perspective *see* B. ACKERMAN, DAS ANALOGIEVERBOT IM GELTENDEN UND ZUKÜNFTIGEN STRAFRECHT (1934); Schem, *Die Analogie im Strafrecht in ihrer geschichtlichen Entwicklung und Heutigen Bedeutung*, STRAFRECHT ABDHANLUNGEN (Fasc. 369, 1936); SAX, DAS STRAFRECHTLI ANALOGIEVERBOT (1953); and *infra* note 18. For the Austrian approach *see* F. VON LISZT *infra* note 19. For a classical French approach *see* R. GARRAUD, TRAITÉ THÉORIQUE ET PRATIQUE DE DROIT PÉNAL FRANÇAIS (3d ed. 1913); 1 V. MOLINIER, TRAITÉ THÉORIQUE ET PRATIQUE DE DROIT PÉNAL (1893); A. NORMAND, TRAITÉ ELÉMENTAIRE DE DROIT CRIMINEL (1896); and DONNEDIEU DE VABRES *infra* note 16. For the history of the Common Law of Crimes and judicially created crimes *see infra* notes 25 and 27. In the United States on the Prohibition of *ex post facto see* U.S. Const. art. 1, and *infra* notes 25 and 29.

guidelines. It is noteworthy that among the systems that apply the "principles of legality" most rigidly, and thus totally forbid recourse to analogy, there remains an exception, and that is the rule *favor reo*.

The purposes of the "principles of legality" are to enhance the certainty of the law, provide justice and fairness for the accused, achieve the effective fulfillment of the deterrent function of the criminal sanction, prevent abuse of power and strengthen the application of the "Rule of Law."

For some, these goals can only be attained by a rigid formalistic approach inspired by legal positivism, while for others the substantive purposes of these principles should not be defeated by adherence to rigid formal requirements. The latter view was expressed by Professor Hans Kelsen with respect to the Law of the Charter, as follows:

The principle forbidding the enactment of norms with retroactive force as a rule of positive national law is not without many exceptions. Its basis is the moral idea that it is not just to make an individual responsible for an act if he, when performing the act, did not and could not know that his act constituted a wrong. If, however, the act was at the moment of its performance morally, although not legally wrong, a law attaching *ex post facto* a sanction to the act is retroactive only from a legal, not from a moral point of view. Such a law is not contrary to the moral idea which is at the basis of the principle in question. This is in particular true of an international treaty by which individuals are made responsible for having violated, in their capacity as organs of a State, international law. Morally they were responsible for the violation of international law at the moment when they performed the acts constituting a wrong not only from a moral but also from a legal point of view. The treaty only transforms their moral into a legal responsibility. The principle forbidding *ex post facto* laws is--in all reason--not applicable to such a treaty.[3]

Although Kelsen is a relative positivist, in this case he took a position similar to that of naturalists and some utilitarianists. Naturalists consider these principles as procedural and not substantive and, therefore, they would not uphold them over what they would deem to be the higher substance of the law.   Positivists, at the other end of the spectrum, consider these principles as substantive and thus, non-derogable. These divergent views evidence the fact that the recognition and interpretation of the

---

[3]   Kelsen, *Collective and Individual Responsibility in International Law with Particular Regard to the Punishment of War Criminals*, 31 CALIF. L. REV. 530, 544 (1943).

"principles of legality" and their corollary prohibition of analogy are dependent upon the choice of a given theory of legal philosophy, as discussed in Chapter 2.

The questions of whether and in what way "principles of legality" apply to international criminal legislation never arose before the Charter. Regrettably, since then, these questions have not been dealt with in international criminal law other than by reference to post-World War II crimes and their prosecutions. The reason may well be that international criminal law has thus far developed with a view to its indirect application, as opposed to the direct application that was the case with respect to the London Charter, the Tokyo Charter and under CCL 10, even though the Allies deemed such a law to be domestic, as discussed in Chapters 4 and 5.

International criminal law relies, for its enforcement, on the indirect approach whereby states embody international proscriptions in their national laws and enforce them through their national criminal justice system. This is evident from the provisions contained in the international criminal law conventions which establish duties to prosecute or extradite.[4] Consequently, the applicable "principles of legality" are those of the enforcing state. But in the case of direct enforcement by an international criminal court, the question of legality arises with respect to the general and special parts of the applicable international criminal law.[5] One approach is to adduce these principles from the various national legal systems in accordance with the methodology established for ascertaining the "general principles of law recognized by civilized nations."[6] Thus, an examination of the world's major criminal justice systems is necessary in order to ascertain the standards of legality which are to be applied to "crimes against humanity," as formulated in Article 6(c) of the London Charter, the first international formulation of this crime in positive international criminal law, and which was the basis for the Tokyo Charter's Article 5(c) and CCL 10 Article II(c). But an analysis of the world's

---

[4]   See Document Section G.4.

[5]   See e.g. BASSIOUNI DRAFT CODE and the work of the ILC since 1947 in its efforts to develop a Code of Offences Against the Peace and Security of Mankind; and see YEARBOOK OF THE ILC for annual reports on this question between 1950-54 and 1978-1991. See also Williams, The Draft Code of Offenses Against the Peace and Security of Mankind, in 1 BASSIOUNI ICL 109; Gross, The Draft Code of Offenses Against the Peace and Security of Mankind, 15 ISRAEL Y.B. H.R. 224 (1985); and [1991] Report of the ILC, U.N. GAOR Supp. No. 10 (1/46/10).

[6]   Bassiouni, A Functional Approach to 'General Principles of International Law', 11 MICH. J. INT'L L. 768 (1990); B. CHENG, GENERAL PRINCIPLES OF LAW AS APPLIED BY INTERNATIONAL COURTS AND TRIBUNALS (1987); and Chapter 7 describing the methodology of ascertaining "general principles."

90

major criminal justice systems needs also to be complemented by an appraisal of the international customary practices of states.

Lastly, it should be noted that no matter what the issues of legality were in 1945, they may be said to have been partly cured since then, as discussed in the concluding section of this Chapter and in Chapter 11. But because "crimes against humanity" have not yet been codified since the Charters of Nuremberg and Tokyo and CCL 10, some problems of legality still remain, particularly from the positivist's perspective and also in light of evolving standards of legality in the world's major criminal justice systems.

Principles of Legality in the World's Major Criminal Justice Systems

Since World War II, "principles of legality" have been recognized in all the world's major criminal justice systems.[7] Their content and application, however, vary in the world's major legal systems and also in particular national systems. In this context, it is important to bear in mind the historic evolution of the "principles of legality," and particularly how and why they have been recognized, applied, rejected or circumvented in the world's major criminal justice systems.

The doctrinal debate in legal literature throughout the historical evolution and application of these principles in the various national criminal justice systems centers essentially on whether the essence of these principles is substantive or formalistic. While that debate reflects the different schools of legal philosophy, as discussed in Chapter 1, it also reflects the struggle between protagonists of various forms of governmental tyranny and those seeking to uphold the "Rule of Law."

Eighteenth century continental European positivism tended toward a more rigid application of these principles than did the English Common Law. This was probably due to the codification approach of continental European legal systems rooted in the Roman Law tradition. Indeed, there does not appear to be any precedent for these principles in the so-called primitive European criminal laws of the Visigoths (410-585), the Franks and the Merovingians (481-768), and the Carolingians and the Ostrogoths (493-555). But while the Roman Law tradition can be credited for western Europe's reliance on the "principles of legality," the post-1800 emergence of these principles is essentially due to the political struggles in Europe where "principles of legality" became the means by which to limit the absolute power of monarchial regimes and to curb

---

[7] *See supra* notes 1 and 2.

abuse of power. This explains why the principal social contract theorists, Voltaire, Montesquieu, Rousseau and Beccaria, argued for the application of "principles of legality" with respect to judicial and administrative interpretation of the law.

In 1748, Montesquieu in L'ESPRIT DES LOIS stated:

Les juges de la nation ne sont que la bouche qui prononce les paroles de la loi, des êtres inanimés qui ne peuvent ni en addressé la force ni la rigeur.[8]

For him, judges were only those through whose mouth the law spoke, and they could neither address the law's force or rigor.

His works and those of Voltaire and Rousseau inspired many others, notably Beccaria, who in 1764 wrote on the "Interpretation of the Law" in his famous DEI DELITTI E DELLE POENE,[9]

There is a fourth consequence: the authority to interpret penal law can scarcely rest with criminal judges for the good reason that they are not lawmakers. Judges have not received laws from our forefathers as a family tradition or a legacy which leaves to posterity only the task of obeying; they receive them, rather, from a living society or from the sovereign who represents it and who is the depository of the current will of all citizens. Judges do not receive laws as obligations arising from an ancient oath. Such an oath would be void, for the wills currently bound did not exist when the oath was sworn, and it would be unjust, for it would reduce men from a social condition to the condition of a herd. On the contrary, judges receive laws as the result of a tacit or express oath that the united wills of living subjects have sworn to the sovereign, as bonds necessary to restrain and rule the internal ferment of private interests. This is the solid and true authority of the laws. Who, then, will be the legitimate interpreter of the laws? Will it be the sovereign, in other words, the depository of the actual wills of all the people, or will it be the judge, whose only charge is merely to examine whether or not a certain man has committed an action contrary to the laws?

In every criminal case, the judge should come to a perfect syllogism: the major premise should be the general law; the minor premise, the act which does or does

---

[8]   MONTESQUIEU, L'ESPRIT DES LOIS, Livre XI Ch. III, 127, also Ch. VI (1748).

[9]   *See* C. BECCARIA, ON CRIMES AND PUNISHMENT, 10-12 (D. Young trans. 1986).

not conform to the law; and the conclusion, acquittal or condemnation. If the judge were constrained to form even two syllogisms, or if he were to choose to do so, then the door to uncertainty would be opened.

... Nothing is more dangerous than the common axiom that one must consult the spirit of the law. This is a dike that is readily breached by the torrent of opinion. This truth, though it appears a paradox to uneducated minds that are struck more by a trifling contemporary disorder than by the harmful but remote consequences that follow from a false principle rooted in a nation, appears to me to be well established. "Our perceptions and all our ideas are linked together; the more complicated they are, the more numerous are the routes that lead to and from them. Everybody has his own point of view, and everybody has a different one at different times ...." The spirit of the law, then, would be dependent on the good and bad logic of a judge, on a sound or unhealthy digestion, on the violence of his passions, on the infirmities he suffers, on his relations with the victim, and on all the slight forces that change the appearance of every object in the fickle human mind. Thus we see the fate of a citizen change several times in going from one court to another, and we see that the lives of poor wretches are at the mercy of false reasonings or the momentary churning of a judge's humors. The judge deems all this confused series of notions which affect his mind to be a legitimate interpretation. Thus we see the same court punish the same crime in different ways at different times because it consulted the erroneous instability of interpretations rather than the firm and constant voice of the law.

Any confusion arising from the rigorous observation of the letter of the law cannot be compared with the disorders that spring from interpretation.

Such a temporary inconvenience is a motive for making the simple and necessary correction in the words of the law which give rise to any uncertainty, but it puts a stop to the fatal license of arguing, which is the cause of arbitrary and venal controversies. When a fixed legal code that must be observed to the letter leaves the judge no other task than to examine a citizen's actions and to determine whether or not they conform to the written law, when the standard of justice and injustice that must guide the actions of the ignorant as well as the philosophic citizen is not a matter of controversy but of fact, then subjects are not exposed to the petty tyrannies of many men. Such tyrannies are all the more cruel when there is a smaller distance between the oppressor and the oppressed. They are more ruinous than the tyranny of one person, for the despotism of many can be remedied only by the despotism of a single man, and the cruelty of a despot is not proportional to his strength, but to the obstacles he encounters. With fixed and immutable laws, then, citizens acquire personal security. This is just because it is the goal of society, and it is useful because it enables them to calculate precisely the ill consequences of a misdeed. It is just as true that they will acquire a spirit of independence, but this will not be to shake off the laws and resist the supreme magistrates; rather, they will resist those who have dared to claim the sacred name of virtue for their weakness in yielding to their private interests or capricious opinions. These principles will displease those who have assumed the right to pass on to their inferiors the tyrannical blows that they have received from their superiors. I should have everything to fear if the spirit of tyranny went hand-in-hand with a taste for reading.

In an equally prescient observation Beccaria wrote on the "Obscurity of Laws:"

If the interpretation of laws is an evil, their obscurity, which necessarily entails interpretation, is obviously another evil, one that will be all the greater if the laws are written in a language that is foreign to the common people. This places them at the mercy of a handful of men, for they cannot judge for themselves the prospect of their own liberty or that of others. A language of this sort transforms a solemn official book into one that is virtually private and domestic. What must we think of mankind when we consider that such is the ingrained custom of a good part of cultured and enlightened Europe! The greater the number of people who understand the sacred law code and who have it in their hands, the less frequent crimes will be, for there is no doubt that ignorance and uncertainty concerning punishments aid the eloquence of the passions.

One consequence of these last thoughts is that, without written texts, society will never assume a fixed form of government in which power derives from the whole rather than the parts and in which the laws, which cannot be altered save by the general will, are not corrupted as they move through the crush of private interests. Experience and reason have shown us that the probability and certainty of human traditions decline the farther removed they are from their source. If there is no lasting memorial of the social contract, how will the laws resist the inevitable force of time and the passions?[10]

The works of these social contract theorists inspired the French 1789 Declaration of the Rights of Man which quickly became Europe's and America's model charter of freedom. Many of its enunciated principles found their way into national constitutions and criminal codes. Thus, the French Declaration of the Rights of Man of 1789, stated in Article 7:

Nul homme ne peut-être accusé, arrêté, ni detenu que dans les cas determinés par la loi, et selon les formes qu'elle a prescrites. (No man can be accused, arrested or detained except in those cases determined by the law, and in accordance with the forms it prescribes.)

The French Constitution of 1791 embodied that principle and the CODE PÉNAL of 1791 stated in Article 4:

Nulle contravention, nul délit, nul crime ne prevent être punis de peines qui n'étaient pas prononcées par la loi avant qu'ils fussent commis. (No contravention, delict or crime can be punished by sanctions not established by the law before they were committed.)

The French Penal Code of 1810 retained this same Article 4, and it is still the law of France.

The most comprehensive comparative analysis of the recognition and application of the principle *nullum crimen sine lege*, as well as the limits on the resort to analogy was made by Professor Guiliano Vassalli in 1939.[11] The timing of that publication was no accident. Nazi Germany's laws were passed in 1935 which overturned the "principles of legality" that were enshrined in the Weimar Constitution of 1919, and which were already part of its 1871 Criminal Code, Article 2, para 1.[12] Yet, Italy's

---

[10] *Id.* at 12-13.

[11] *See* Vassalli, *supra* note 1; and for an earlier comprehensive study, *see* J. DE LA MORANDIÈRE, *supra* note 1.

[12] *See* Siegert, *Nulla Poena Sine Lege, Kritische Bermerkungen zü den Varshlägender Amtlichen Strafrechts Kommission*, DEUTSCHES STRAFRECHT 378 (1934).

Criminal Code of 1931, though promulgated under the fascist regime, had preserved in Article 1, the "principles of legality," which can be retraced to Roman Law.[13] Vassalli's seminal 1939 study showed inferentially how far the Nazi laws of 1935 had strayed from the historical German context, and also how they constituted a departure from other European criminal justice systems,[14] except for Denmark which specifically permitted analogy in the application and interpretation of its penal laws.[15] His study conclusively documents and supports the assertion that "principles of legality" were recognized and applied with significant similarity in late 19th century European criminal justice systems, but it also showed that analogy was recognized and applied in many legal systems, particularly with respect to judicial interpretation of minor

---

[13] *See* T. MOMMSSEN, RÖMISCHES STRAFRECHT 35 *et. seq.* (Vol. I, 1899) referring to Ulpiano whose commentaries in the first book of the DIGEST are: *"Multa guidem ex arbitrio eim venit qui multam dicit, poena non irrogatur nisi quae quaque lege velquo alio iure specialites huic delicto imposita est."* Also quoted in U. BRASIELLO, LA REPRESSIONE PENALE IN DIRITTO ROMANO 142 (2d. ed. 1937). Another DIGEST statement is *"Poena non irrogatur, nisi quae quaque lege vel quo alio jure specialiter huic delicto imposita est."* D. 50.16.131 *quoted in* 12 S.P. SCOTT, THE CIVIL LAW 278 (1932) ("a penalty is not inflicted unless it is expressly imposed by law, or by some other authority."). *See also* D.50.16.244. "... an appeal cannot be taken from a penalty, for where anyone is convicted of an offense, the penalty for it is fixed, and must be paid at once."

"Hence, the differences between these things becomes apparent, because certain penalties are prescribed for certain illegal acts; but this is not the case with fines, as the judge has power to impose any fine he pleases, unless the amount which he may impose is fixed by law." *See* 11 S.P. Scott, *supra* at 296.

But with the proliferation of criminal laws, and the extension of the empire, Roman law resorted to analogy for penalties and for minor offenses. J.L. Stracham-Davidson discusses these problems, *see* J.L. STRACHAM-DAVIDSON, 2 PROBLEMS OF THE ROMAN CRIMINAL LAW, Chap. 14 (1912). *See e.g.* C. FERRINI, DIRITTO PENALE ROMANO - PARTE GENERALE (1899); N. LANDUCCI, STORIA DEL DIRITTO ROMANO (2d ed. 1898).

Vassalli, *supra* note 1, at P. 20-25 holds that the principles *nullum crimen sine lege, nulla poena sine lege* only existed briefly in the procedure known as *questiones* and probably only for the rule of Scycla 100 A.C., other than that Roman law recognized complete latitude to the ruler and even to the judges for crimes and penalties by analogy.

See also infra note 41.

[14] *Supra* note 1; *see also* H. DONNEDIEU DE VABRES, LA POLITIQUE CRIMINELLE DES ETATS AUTORITAIRES (1938); G. SCHWARZENBERG, INTERNATIONAL LAW AND TOTALITARIANISM (1943); and *infra* note 22.

[15] Denmark Code of 1866 and 1930, Article II, Section 1, *see* Vassalli, *supra* note 1, at 81-82 with references.

offenses and for the determination of penalties. Indeed, the notion of judicial discretionary sentencing started to make its impact on European criminal law in the late 1800's, as a consequence of the rehabilitative doctrines of punishment which had emerged in European criminal law doctrine[16] The idea that penalties should fit the offender and not the offense was not new, and it had its roots in canon criminal law, which expressly permitted analogy in the imposition of penalties. Furthermore, it should be noted that many legal systems permitted and still permit resort to analogies with respect to juvenile proceedings, minor offenses and special proceedings such as extradition, where the universally accepted requirement of "double criminality" is predicated on analogy.[17]

The German legal system has the oldest and most consistent tradition of recognizing and applying the "principles of legality," though not without exceptions. It is reported that the Teutonic tribes (919-1493) included in their laws the principle of non-retroactivity of penal laws, and that of no punishment without law. This historical background and the inspiration of Roman Law were the basis of the Germanic legal system's adherence to the "principles of legality" until 1935 when Nazi Germany briefly interrupted this long-standing legal tradition.

The history of German codified criminal law is best expressed in the *Constitutio Criminalis* of 1532 promulgated by Charles V. The model for this codification was the earlier Bambergensis Code of 1507, whose Articles 104-105 included the principle of *nullum crimen sine lege* but also recognized the validity of analogy. The *Constitutio Criminalis* contained the same provisions in Articles 125-26 which used almost the same language as the Bambergensis Code. Likewise, the principle of judicial analogy in interpreting the laws was recognized. But prior to the unification of Germany in 1870, newer codifications did not prohibit analogy. The Prussian Code of 1721 provided that with respect to offenses or other matters not contained in the respective codes, the judge could resort to *ex acquo alquo et bono*, while the Bavarian Code of 1751 allowed resort to *ex acquitate et analogia juris*.[18] In 1794, the Prussian Criminal

---

[16] *See e.g.,* H. DONNEDIEU DE VABRES, TRAITÉ ELÉMENTAIRE DE DROIT CRIMINEL ET DE LEGISLATION PÉNALE COMPARÉ 433 *et. seq.* (1937); R. GAROFALO, CRIMINOLOGIA 278 *et. seq.* (2d ed. 1891).

[17] M.C. BASSIOUNI, INTERNATIONAL EXTRADITION IN UNITED STATES LAW AND PRACTICE 319-359 (2d rev. ed. 1987).

[18] For a German historical perspective *see* B. CARPZOW, PRACTICA NOVA IMPERIALIS SAXONICA RERUM CRIMINALIUM, Pars III, questio 133 (*de arbitraris sen extraordinarüs poenis*) (Frankfort ed. 1758). For a post-1800 perspective, *see* A.V. FUERBACH, LEHRBUCH DES GEMEINEN IN DEUTSCHLAND GÜLTIGEN

Code, which borrowed from the Austrian Code of 1787, was the first to establish the prohibition against analogy. Franz Von Liszt, who was one of the major influences on Austrian criminal law, proclaimed that the principle *"nullum crimen* [was the], *Magna Charta Libertatum* [of the offender]."[19] But it should be noted that the preceding Austrian Code of 1769 permitted resort to analogy though it limited analogy to its application in accordance with the principles laid down in the Code.

The German Criminal Code of 1871, however, contained in Article 2 a rigid norm on the "principles of legality" which prohibited the application of legalistive and judicial analogy. It stated:

No Punishment can be inflicted unless such punishment was legally defined before the act was committed. If the law is changed between the time at which the act was committed and the sentence is pronounced, the milder of the laws should be applied.[20]

Later the 1919 Weimar Constitution enshrined these principles in Article 116 which stated:

Punishment can be inflicted for only such acts as the law had declared punishable before the act was committed.[21]

The drafters of the Nazi law of June 28, 1935, which repealed Article 2 of the 1871 Code, were mindful of Germany's legal attachment to the "principles of legality" and

---

PEINLICHEN RECHTS (14th ed., Mittermaier ed. 1847); K. SIEGERT, GRUNDZÜGE DES STRAFRECHTS IN NEUEN STAATE (1934); H. HENKEL, STRAFRECHTES UND GESETZ IM NEUEN STAATE (1934); Goetzeler, *Der Grundsatz nulla poena sine lege*, 104 GERICHTSSAAL 343 (1934); GUERTNER-FREISLER, DAS NEUE STRAFRECHT (1936); Schinnerer, *Analogie und Rechtsschäpfreng*, 55 ZSTW 75 (1936); B. ACKERMAN and SCHEM, *supra* note 2.

[19] F. VON LISZT, LEHRBUCH DES STRAFRECHT 110 (1891); *Die Deterministischen Gegner des Zweckstrafen*, 13 ZSTW (1893).

[20] *Translated and Reprinted in* A. VON KNIEREM, THE NUREMBERG TRIALS 7 (E.D. Schmitt trans. 1959). The full text of German Criminal Code can be found in G. DRAGE, THE CRIMINAL CODE OF THE GERMAN EMPIRE (1885).

[21] *See also* 1919 Weimar Constitution, Article 116 *reprinted in* R. BRUNET, THE GERMAN CONSTITUTION 324 (J. Gollomb trans. 1922).

thus sought to articulate their law repealing the principles in terms of an extension of the rule of analogy by stating:

> Whoever commits an action which the law declares punishable or which is deserving of punishment according to the fundamental idea of a penal law and the sound perception of the people, shall be punished, if no determinable penal law is directly applicable to the crime, it shall be punished according to the law, the basic idea of which fits it best.[22]

Thus, analogy was permissible if the judicially created crime was within the scope of the penal law and foreseeable because based on the "sound perception of the people."[23] German Criminal Law literature between 1932-1936 extensively debated the nature of the new legal order, i.e. *regierungrecht* or *staatsrecht*, *Führerrecht*, *Völkstaatsrecht*,[24] and inevitably the division of opinion reflected different philosophical perceptions of the law and the state, thus highlighting the political implications of the "principles of legality" and its corollary prohibition in whole or in part of judicial analogy.

The Common Law of England, which was never based on a constitution, did not develop its crimes on the basis of codes, and did not formally recognize the "principles of legality." But there is evidence that judicial decisions interpreting the Common Law of Crimes relied on these principles and recognized them even in the absence of specific legal requirements to do so.[25]

---

[22]   See Preuss, *Punishment by Analogy in National Socialist States*, 26 J. OF CRIM. L. & CRIMINLOGY 847 (1936); and Bennett, *Notes on the German Legal and Penal System*, 37 J. CRIM. L. AND CRIMINOLOGY 368, 372-373 (1946). *See also* M. MARX, GOVERNMENT IN THE THIRD REICH (2d ed. 1937); F. EARMARTH, THE NEW GERMANY: NATIONAL SOCIALIST GOVERNMENT IN THEORY AND PRACTICE (1936); I. MÜLLER, HITLER'S JUSTICE (1991); and *e.g.* Steiner, *The Fascist Conception of Law*, 36 CALIF. L. REV. 1267 (1936); Hoefer, *The Nazi Penal System*, 35 J. CRIM. L. AND CRIMINOLOGY 385 (1945); Campbell, *Fascism and Legality*, 62 L.Q. REV. 141 (1946); Hughes, Book Review, 24 VAND. J. OF TRANSNATIONAL L. 845 (1991) (reviewing I. MÜLLER, HITLER'S JUSTICE (1991)).

[23]   The approach is no different than what the drafters of the Charter did in extending, by analogy, conduct prohibited as war crimes to "crimes against humanity," in reliance upon the higher "principles of humanity," *see* Chapter 4.

[24]   *See e.g., supra* notes 18 and 22.

[25]   *See* J. STEPHEN, DIGEST OF CRIMINAL LAW § 160 (1877); F. WHARTON, A TREATISE ON CRIMINAL LAW (8th ed. 1880); J. STEPHEN, A HISTORY OF THE CRIMINAL LAW OF ENGLAND 359 et seq. (1883); 5 L. RADZINOWICZ, A HISTORY OF ENGLISH CRIMINAL LAW AND ITS ADMINISTRATION (1948). *See also* J.

One reason why the "principles of legality" were not at issue in England may be that the political struggle for the "Rule of Law" in the Common Law tradition had achieved its first great victory at Runnymead in 1215 with the promulgation of the *Magna Carta*, which in Article 39 stated:

> No freeman shall be seized, or imprisoned, or dispossessed, or outlawed, or in any way destroyed; nor will we condemn him, nor will we commit him to prison, excepting by the legal judgment of his peers or by the laws of the land.[26]

By the 1600's, the Common Law had asserted its primacy over some of the King's powers through the concept of "due process of law," and that affected the way in which the goals of the "principles of legality" were achieved. The emphasis was on the application of Common Law and its rules of interpretation and on procedural safeguards. The result was that the Common Law of Crimes became less susceptible to the abuses of the rulers' arbitrary powers than was the case in other legal systems. Penal statutes promulgated by Parliament were interpreted in a manner consistent with the Common Law of Crimes by a judiciary whose admittedly wide latitude in statutory interpretation provided paradoxically more, rather than less, guarantees of fairness for

---

BENTHAM, 1 COLLECTED WORKS OF JEREMIAH BENTHAM Pt 3, Ch. 20, 576 (Bowering ed. 1843) (urged strict adherence to statutory interpretation "Principles of Penal Law"). In Midland Railway Co. v. Pye, 142 Eng. Rep. 419 (1861), Chief Justice Erle said, "It manifestly shocks one's sense of justice that an act legal at the time of doing it should be made unlawful by some new enactment. Modern legislation has almost entirely removed that blemish from the law" *id*. at 424. In 1941, Director of Public Prosecutions v. Lamb, 2 K.B.89, held that a law can be interpreted retroactively if that is the intention of Parliament. Almost one hundred years earlier in *Ex parte* Clinton, 6 State Trials, N.S. 1107, (1845) the Court held "It cannot be said that to give *ex post facto* operation to an enactment is hostile to the spirit of English law." In Phillips v. Eyre, 6 Q.B. 1 (1870), the Court held "A retrospective law is *prima facie* questionable but not contrary to natural justice" *id*. at 23. In Joyce v. Director of Public Prosecutions [1946] all E.R. 186 the House of Lords held: "It is not an extension of a penal law to apply its principles to circumstances unforeseen at the time of its enactment, so long as the case is fairly brought within its language." *id,* at 189. Lord Jowitt who wrote the opinion in this case was also the British representative at the London Conference who succeeded Sir David Maxwell Fyfe, *see* Chapter 2 n. 3. Later for analogy in misdemeanors, *see* Shaw v. Director of Public Prosecutions [1962] A.C. 220 (1960). For an insightful comment upon the Common Law's interpretation by analogy in misdemeanors, *see* Jackson, *Common Law Misdemeanors*, 6 CAMBRIDGE L. J. 193 (1937); and Stallybrass, *Public Mischief*, 49 L.Q. REV. 183 (1933) commenting on Rex v. Manley [1933] K.B. 529 (1932).

[26] R. STRINGHAM, MAGNA CARTA: FOUNTAINHEAD OF FREEDOM 235 (1966). *See however* The Constitution of Clarendon 1164 where the principle first appeared.

the accused. Analogy was particularly used with respect to misdemeanors and such offenses as those *contra bonos mores*.[27] But the customary and popularized understanding of common law crimes reduced the likelihood of interpretations that would go beyond the scope of the crimes, while remaining within foreseeable expectations. In fact, the legal standard for analogy was the foreseeability of the ordinary reasonable person that the given conduct would fall within the law's prohibition. Appellate review courts had, therefore, a legal standard by which to review lower court decisions, including jury trials whenever instructions on the law were not in conformity with the legal standard. Judicial interpretation by analogy was not only permissible but it was the basis for the development and evolution of the Common Law. This led many jurists to conclude that there is a fundamental difference between codified and case law based legal systems with respect to the recognition and application of "principles of legality," particularly with respect to the recognition of analogy in case-law based systems.

The United States followed the English Common Law approach but was more rigid in its recognition of the "principles of legality." It provided, in its Constitution, a specific prohibition against *ex post facto*[28] and Bills of Attainder.[29] With respect to statutory interpretation, the United States maintained some analogy,[30] but the "due process" clauses of the Fifth and Fourteenth amendments to the Constitution operate

---

[27] *See* 4 W. HOLDSWORTH, HISTORY OF ENGLISH LAW 492 (1924); 4 W. BLACKSTONE, COMMENTARIES 65 (6th ed. 1775); W. HAWKINS, A TREATISE OF PLEAS OF THE CROWN (8th ed. 1824) c.5, § 4; 1 E. EAST, PLEAS OF THE CROWN cc. 1, 3, 4 (1806); STEPHEN, A DIGEST OF THE CRIMINAL LAW 106, 107 (1878); Stallybrass, *supra* note 25; and Jackson, *supra* note 25.

[28] Art. 1, § 8(3); *see also* Calder v. Bull, (3 Dall) 3 U.S. 386 (1878); Note, *Ex Post Facto Limitations on Legislative Power*, 73 MICH L. REV. 491 (1975); and Crosskey, *The True Meaning of the Constitutional Prohibition of Ex Post Facto Laws*, 14 U. CHI. L. REV. 439, 558-66 (1947). The prohibition against *ex post facto* was not, however, held to apply to the lessening of statutory penalties, to statutory changes in rules of evidence and procedural changes. *See* M.C. BASSIOUNI, SUBSTANTIVE CRIMINAL LAW 31 (1978). *See also* Allen, *The Erosion of Legality in American Criminal Justice: Some Latter-Day Adventures of the 'Nulla Poena Principle,'* 29 ARIZ. L. REV. 385 (1987).

[29] Art. 1, § 9 and § 10; and J. STORY, COMMENTARIES ON THE CONSTITUTION § 1344 (Bigelow ed. 1891). The three landmark cases on this question are Fletcher v. Peck, 6 Cranch 87, 136 (1810); U.S. v. Lovett, 328 U.S. 303, 66 S. Ct. 1037 (1946); Groppie v. Leslie, 404 U.S. 496, 92 S. Ct. 584 (1972). *See also* Wormuth, *Legislative Disqualifications as Bills of Attainder*, 4 VAND. L. REV. 603 (1951); and Comment, *The Constitutional Prohibition of Bills of Attainder: A Waning Guaranty of Judicial Trial*, 63 YALE L. J. 844 (1954).

[30] *See* Freund, *Interpretation of Statutes*, 65 U. PA. L. REV. 207 at 226, 227, 230 (1917). *See also* Goodhart, *Precedent in English and Continental Jurisprudence*, 50 L.Q. REV. 40 (1943).

as a limitation against vagueness and ambiguity which also limit the use of judicial analogy. As to the retroactivity of substantive criminal laws, the United States provided against it since the early colonies,[31] but retroactivity of procedural and evidentiary rules are permitted, as are some particular *sui generis* criminal proceedings like extradition where treaties making certain offenses extraditable can be applied retroactively.[32]

The Islamic criminal justice system recognizes the "principles of legality" but applies them in a differentiated manner. The *Qu'ràn* and the *Sunna* mandate the application of "principles of legality" to criminal legislation and judicial interpretation.[33] But it does so with some differentiation as between three categories of crimes: *Hudud*, crimes which are codified in the *Qu'ràn*, require a rigid application of the "principles of legality;"[34] *Quesas* crimes, which are also stated in the *Qu'ràn*, permit some analogy for the different types of physical injuries and their compensation;[35] and, *Ta'azir* crimes, for which there are no stated prescriptions in the *Qu'ràn*, but which include either that which positive law may establish or that which the judge can find by analogy or in reliance on general principles found in the *Shari'à*. The application of the principles of legality in *Hudud* crimes is parallel to the one followed in the positivist Romanist-Civilist-Germanic systems, while in *Quesas* and *Ta'azir* crimes the application parallels the approach followed by the Common Law of Crimes, the latter being even more flexible.

In the Twentieth Century, the advent of Marxist-Socialism in the USSR in 1917, which after 1945 was imposed on Eastern and Central Europe, resulted until recently in the negation of these principles. These national legal systems permitted broad legislative prescriptions and even broader judicial interpretation including resort to

---

[31]   *See* Cummings v. Missouri, 71 U.S. 277 (1866); *Ex Parte Garland*, 71 U.S. 333 (1866). *See also* Smead, *The Rule Against Retroactive Legislation: A Basic Principle of Jurisprudence*, 20 MINN. L. REV. 775 (1936).

[32]   *See* M.C. BASSIOUNI, INTERNATIONAL EXTRADITION IN UNITED STATES LAW AND PRACTICE 465 (2d. rev. ed. 1987).

[33]   *See* Bassiouni, *Sources of Islamic Law and the Protection of Human Rights in the Islamic Criminal Justice System*, in ISLAMIC CRIMINAL JUSTICE 3, 24-26 (M.C. Bassiouni ed. 1982), citing SURAT AL-ISRAA (XVII:15), SURAT AL-NISSAA (IV:165); Kamel, *The Principle of Legality and Its Application in Islamic Criminal Justice, id.* at 149.

[34]   *See* Mansour, *Hudud* Crimes, *id.* at 195.

[35]   *See* Bassiouni, *Quesas* Crimes, *id.* at 203.

analogy so as to fulfill "socialist justice." The first Soviet Criminal Code of 1922 provided for analogy in Articles 9 and 10, and the Supreme Soviet of the USSR rejected the principles *nullum crimen sine lege, nulla poena sine lege* and *nulla poena sine judicio* in a decree promulgated December 25, 1958. Moreover, the Penal Code of October 27, 1960 provides for, in Articles 1 and 3, the principle of legislative and judicial analogy for conduct deemed "socially dangerous," even when not provided by law, and included the application of appropriate penalties not provided by law.[36] But the 1976 changes in the constitution of the USSR revived the application of the "principles of legality."[37] Since 1989, that country and all other eastern and central European countries have embarked on a reform of their criminal laws and procedures, and all of them have included in their reform projects a return to the "principles of legality" as applied in the contemporary western European legal systems.

One can thus conclude that, by 1945, the "principles of legality" had become part of "general principles of law" in western Europe, but were not yet universally accepted nor were they uniformly applied. They existed in part in the English Common Law and in the Islamic criminal justice system. They also existed in those Latin-American legal systems, which borrowed from Spanish law, where that principle had been established the late 1800's. They did not, however, exist in indigenous Asian and African legal systems except where the colonial laws of a western European country applied.

Nevertheless, there was, in 1945, some similarity between the world's major criminal justice systems, which has increased substantially. The conclusion can therefore be summarized as follows:

1 - All the families of legal systems prohibit *ex post facto* criminal laws, but not all of them extend it to an absolute non-retroactive application of some penal aspects.

2 - The principle of no crime without criminal law is widely recognized, and while in some systems it prohibits reliance on judicial analogy (i.e., the Romanist-Civilist-Germanic systems), in others it permits it (i.e., the Common Law, Islamic and Marxist-Socialist systems). But even in those families of systems which reject analogy in judicial interpretation, there still are some

---

[36] *See e.g.*, H. BERMAN, JUSTICE IN THE USSR (1963); H. BERMAN, SOVIET CRIMINAL LAW AND PROCEDURE (1966) discussing the Soviet Criminal Code of 1953.

[37] For a reaffirmation of the "principle of legality" after 1979, *see* THE CRIMINAL JUSTICE OF THE USSR 139 (M.C. Bassiouni & V.M. Savitski eds. 1979).

exceptions in certain national systems. Other national systems which profess to reject analogy altogether still make some exceptions.

3 - The principle of no penalty without law is probably the one that is applied with the greatest diversity. In some systems judicial discretion is wide and includes indeterminate and alternative sentencing, while in others the judge can apply a sentence by analogy to another similar crime.

The Law of the Charter implicitly relied on what was concluded above, but there is little evidence in the drafting history of the Charter, as discussed in Chapter 1, that such research was undertaken. But it can be assumed that such learned jurists relied on their personal knowledge and beliefs in their determination of the issue. There is no question, in this writer's mind, that they all knew that this was the weakness of the entire undertaking. Indeed, the IMT and IMTFE judgments and the Subsequent Proceedings under CCL 10 indicate that this question was consistently raised, but these judgments dealt with it only superficially, except for the dissents of Judges Pal and Röling, as discussed below.

Before Nuremberg and Tokyo, the question of legality arose only once in the history of the PCIJ in the *Advisory Opinion on the Consistency of Certain Dansig Legislative Decrees with the Constitution of the Free City, December 4, 1935.*[38] It never came before the ICJ.

In the PCIJ opinion, the Court held:

... before proceeding to the examination of the decrees from the constitutional point of view, it may be well to note the changes which they have introduced in the criminal law of Danzig.

The Penal Code in force in Danzig prior to the promulgation of the decrees, in its Article 2, paragraph I, provided: "An act is only punishable if the penalty applicable to it was already prescribed by a law in force before the commission of the act." This provision gives expression to the well-known two-fold maxim: *Nullum crimen sine lege*, and *Nulla poena sine lege*. The law alone determines and defines an offence. The law alone decrees the penalty. A penalty cannot be inflicted in a given case if it is not decreed by the law in respect of that case. A penalty decreed by the

---

[38]   3 PCIJ Series A/B No. 65, at 514, Dec. 4, 1935.

law for a particular case cannot be inflicted in another case. In other words, criminal laws may not be applied by analogy.

The first decree modifying the Penal Code lays down the rule that an act is punishable:

(1) where it is declared by law to be punishable, and
(2) where, according to the fundamental idea of a penal law and according to sound popular feeling, it deserves punishment. Where there is no particular penal law applicable to the act, it shall be punished in virtue of the law whose fundamental conception applies most nearly.

No. 1 requires no comment. No. 2 is an innovation which deserves careful examination. Where there is no legal provision expressly applicable, a person may, according to the new penal provision, be punished provided that two conditions are fulfilled: (a) the act must deserve punishment according to the fundamental idea of a penal law; and (b) the act must deserve punishment according to sound popular feeling.

[52] The procedure for applying this rule is laid down in the second decree, in which the two conditions are prescribed in the reverse order. That is to say, the Public Prosecutor (Art. 170a) and the tribunal (Art. 267a), in the case of an act not declared punishable by law, must first apply the criterion of sound popular feeling, and, if it is found that the act deserves punishment, must then examine whether the fundamental idea of a penal law also requires that it should be punished.

The object of these new provisions is stated to be to enable the judge to create law to fill up gaps in the penal legislation. This may be seen from the title of Article I of the first decree: "Creation of law [Rechtsschöfung] by the application of penal laws by analogy," and of Article I of the second decree: "Wider latitude accorded to judges. I. Creation of law [Rechtsschöpfung] by the application of penal laws by analogy."

The Agent for the Free City contends that, according to the new conception of penal law, real justice will take the place of formal justice, and that henceforth the rule will be Nullum crimen sine poena instead of Nullum crimen sine lege and Nulla poena sine lege. Detailed explanations have been given on behalf of the

Senate of the Free City concerning the advantages of the new phrenological idea over the old. With this the Court is not concerned. The sole question for it is whether the two decrees violate any of the provisions or principles of the Constitution.[39]

The PCIJ also stated:

The rule that a law is required in order to restrict the liberties provided for in the Constitution therefore involves the consequence that the law itself must define the conditions in which such restrictions of liberties are imposed. If this were not so, i.e., if a law could simply give a judge power to deprive a person of his liberty, without defining the circumstances in which his liberty might be forfeited, it could render entirely nugatory a provision such as that contained in Article 74 of the Constitution. But, as the Court has already explained, the decrees of August 29th, 1935, so far from supplying any such definition, empower a judge to deprive a person of his liberty even for an act not prohibited by the law, provided that he relies on the fundamental idea of a penal law and on sound popular feeling. These decrees therefore transfer to the judge an important function which, owing to its intrinsic character, the Constitution intended to reserve to the law so as to safeguard individual liberty from any arbitrary encroachment on the part of the authorities of the State.

It is true that a criminal law does not always regulate all details. By employing a system of general definition, it sometimes leaves the judge not only to interpret it, but also to determine how to apply it. The question as to the point beyond which this method comes in conflict with the principle that fundamental rights may not be restricted except by law may not be easy to solve. But there are some cases in which the discretionary power left to the judge is too wide to allow of any doubt but that it exceeds these limits. It is such a case which confronts the Court in the present proceedings.

The problem of the repression of crime may be approached from two different standpoints, that of the individual and that of the community. From the former standpoint, the object [57] is to protect the individual against the State: this object

---

[39]   *Id.* at 524-525.

finds its expression in the maxim *Nulla poena sine lege*. From the second standpoint, the object is to protect the community against the criminal, the basic principle being the notion *Nullum crimen sine poena*. The decrees of August 29th, 1935, are based on the second of these conceptions; the Danzig Constitution is based upon the former. For this Constitution takes as its starting-point the fundamental rights of the individual; these rights may indeed be restricted, as already pointed out, in the general public interest, but only in virtue of a law which must itself specify the conditions of such restriction, and, in particular, determine the limit beyond which an act can no longer be justified as an exercise of a fundamental liberty and becomes a punishable offense. It must be possible for the individual to know, beforehand, whether his acts are lawful or liable to punishment.

To sum up, the Court holds that the decrees of August 29th, 1935, are not consistent with the guarantees which Part II of the Danzig Constitution provides for fundamental rights; and in particular they are not consistent with Articles 74, 75 and 79. Furthermore, the Court holds that the decrees violate the principles on which, as already explained, Part II of the Constitution is founded.

For these reasons, the Court, by nine votes to three, is of opinion that the two decrees of August 29th, 1935, are not consistent with the Constitution of the Free City of Danzig, and that they violate certain provisions and certain principles thereof.[40]

That opinion applies only to the facts, as is the rule for PCIJ and ICJ rulings, and does not constitute a binding legal precedent. But it evidences the existence of recognition of the "princples of legality" in some legal systems.

Principles of Legality in International Criminal Law

In addition to reconciling the diversity among the world's major criminal justice systems in their recognition and application of the "principles of legality," as discussed above, it is necessary to explore whether similar principles have also emerged from international legal practice, separate and apart from the existence of said principles in

---

[40] *Id.* at 529-530.

national legal systems. In this respect it is noteworthy that the evolution of international law resembles more that of the Common Law than that of the Romanist-Civilist-Germanic systems. In Roman Law, *jus gentium*, a term that evolved into what has become international law, allowed for and indeed incorporated customary law, and recognized analogy as a rule of interpretation.[41]

International law originated as a product of the customs and practices of states, but it also derived from certain basic national principles,[42] and these in time became a separate source of international law known as "General Principles."[43] Thus, it would be more consonant with the nature of international law to reconcile the "principles of legality" as they emerge from national legal systems with the customary practices of states in international law. In this case, it would be the customary practices of states with respect to international criminal law, noting that such customary practices are strongly evidenced by conventional law.[44]

Distinguishing between national and international "principles of legality," Professor Stefan Glaser stated:

> *Or, en ce qui concerne le droit international pénal, il faut constater que l'interprétation du principe de la légalité des délits ainsi que des manifestations qu'il entraîne, s'écarte de l'interprétation qu'on admet en droit pénal interne.*

---

[41] *See supra* note 13; and *e.g.* D. BONFANTE, ISTITUZIONI DI DIRITTO ROMANO (10th ed. 1934); P. COLLINET AND A. GIFFORD, PRÉCIS DE DROIT ROMAIN (1927), on delicts 130-165. The Codification of Roman Law started with Augustus' JULIAN LAWS followed by Hadrian's reform, JULIAN'S DIGESTA of 90 volumes containing a systematic arrangement of civil and praetorian law followed by Justinian's INSTITUTES and Justinian's CODES. *See also e.g.* R. WORMSER, THE STORY OF THE LAW AND THE MEN WHO MADE IT 113-149 (1962).

[42] L.L. LE FUR, PRECIS DE DROIT INTERNATIONAL PUBLIC 204 *et seq.* (4th ed. 1939); A. VERDROSS, VÖLKERRECHT 84 *et seq.* (4th ed. 1954); and *e.g.* G. SCELLE, PRECIS DU DROIT DES GENS: PRINCIPES ET SYSTEMATIQUE (1st ed. 1932).

[43] *See supra* note 6.

[44] *See* Akehurst, *Custom as a Source of International Law*, 47 BRIT. Y.B. INT'L L. 1 (1974); A. D'AMATO, THE CONCEPT OF CUSTOM IN INTERNATIONAL LAW (1971); and Seferiadis, *Apercus sur la Coutume Internationale*, REVUE GENERALE DE DROIT INTERNATIONAL PUBLIC (No. 2), 129 (1936). *See also*, Trimble, *A Revisionist view of Customary International Law*, 33 UCLA L. REV. 665 (1986). *See also* Paust, *Customary International Law: Its Nature, Sources and Status as Law of the United States*, 12 MICH. J. INT'L L. 59 (1990).

108

Il est évident que le principe de la légalité des délits qui enseigne qu'il « n'y a pas d'infraction sans loi », ne peut pas être appliqué, au sens strict de ces termes, en droit international pénal, car celui-ci en tant droit coutumier, est dépourvu de « lois ».

En effet, on sait que le droit international pénal, de même que le droit international public en général, n'est pas jusqu'à présent un droit écrit, c'est-à-dire codifié.

Comme le droit international, de même le droit international pénal trouve son origine dans la conscience universelle du droit et de la justice. Il est fondé sur la conviction que ses régles sont conformes à l'idée de justice et de morale et qu'elles s'imposent pour la sauvegarde de l'ordre social international, en d'autres termes, des intérêts fondamentaux de la communauté internationale ("opinio juris vel necessitatis"). C'est ainsi qu'on dit parfois que le droit international en général n'est « qu'une expression graduelle, cas après cas, des jugements moraux du monde civilisé ».

Il en résulte que le droit international pénal, contrairement au droit pénal interne, n'est pas un « Tatbestandsrecht », c'est-à-dire un droit des « états de fait » précis et codifiés. Provenant de la coutume -- qui constitue aussi sa source principale -- il n'est pas une oeuvre ou une création juridico-technique. Il en est ainsi également dans le case où ses régles ou ses notions se trouvent incorporées dans le droit conventionnel (conventions, traités), donc où elles sont formulées par écrit.

Le droit conventionnel a donc, dans une certaine mesure, un caractère dérivatif: son bien-fondé et sa force obligatoire dépendent de sa conformité avec la coutume.

Or, il résulte forcément de ce fait, à savoir que le droit international pénal est un droit coutumier et non pas un droit codifié, qu'en matière d'infractions internationales on ne peut pas exiger que ces infractions soient incriminées au moment de leur accomplissement par une loi. D'ailleurs, on sait que même en droit interne là, où ce droit repose sur la coutume, comme c'est encore le cas en partie dans le pays anglo-saxons, le principe « Nullum crimen sine lege » au sens strict de ces termes, n'est pas valable.[45]

Glaser concludes that the principle *nullum crimen sine lege*, which exists in some national legal systems, is not applicable in the same strict sense in international criminal law because of the peculiarities of the discipline. Further narrowing the distinction in international criminal law, Professor H. Donnedieu de Vabres, quoting Samuel Puffendorf, asserted that when:

hostis humani generi [commit acts of brigandage and piracy] it is permissible to everyone to extract some vengeance [but that] the law of war which is different, permits the infliction of penalties (author's translation).[46]

This proposition highlights the importance of distinguishing the various international crimes, presumably because their goals are different. But there is also another distinction to be made, and that is between the techniques of international criminal law and national criminalization processes. International criminal law, with the exception of piracy and certain aspects of the regulation of armed conflicts, is conventional as evidenced by the 315 instruments elaborated between 1815-1988.[47] Most of these instruments were developed by international organizations and all of them were the

---

[45]   *See* Glaser, *La Méthode d'Interpretation en Droit International Penal*, 9 RIVISTA ITALIANA DI DIRITTO E PROCEDURA PENALE 757, 762-764 (1966). *See also* Glaser, *Nullum Crimen Sine Lege*, 24 THE JOURNAL OF COMPARATIVE LEGISLATION AND INTERNATIONAL LAW 29 (1942).

[46]   H. DONNEDIEU DE VABRES, INTRODUCTION À L'ETUDE DU DROIT PÉNAL INTERNATIONAL 345 (1922) citing SAMUEL PUFFENDORF, LE DROIT DE LA NATURE DES GENS (trans. 1771) Vol. II, Book III, Chapter III, 465. *See also* A. RUBIN, THE LAW OF PIRACY (1988). For the evolutionary history of piracy in England, *see* C. COLOMBOS, THE INTERNATIONAL LAW OF THE SEA 406 (5th ed. 1962). The first statute on Piracy is reported as dating 1535, *see* Sundberg, *Piracy* in 1 BASSIOUNI ICL 441.

[47]   *See* BASSIOUNI DIGEST which refers to 312 Instruments between 1815-1985 but in the meantime there have been three new international instruments in the areas of hijacking, crimes on board vessels and drugs. They are: Protocol for the Suppression of Unlawful Acts of Violence at Airports Serving International Civil Aviation, adopted by the International Civil Aviation Organization at Montreal, in 24 February 1988, *reprinted in* 27 ILM 628 (1988); Convention and Protocol on the Suppression of Unlawful Acts Against the Safety of Maritime Navigation, adopted by the International Maritime Organization at Rome, 10 March 1988, in 27 ILM 628 (1988); United Nations: Convention Against Illicit Traffic in Narcotic Drugs and Psychotropic Substances, adopted at Vienna, 19 December 1988, E/CONF. 82/15, *reprinted in* 28 ILM 497 (1989).

product of political circumstances. This process has been devoid of a consistent policy and of a uniform drafting technique. As a result, most of these conventions do not meet the test of legality under contemporary standards of western European legal systems. The reason for this may be the lack of attention given by those entrusted with the drafting of international conventions to the requirements of legality in the formulation of these instruments. This situation may be due to the fact that the drafters of these instruments are mostly diplomats who are seldom experts in international criminal law, and for that matter they are also seldom experts in comparative criminal law. But perhaps the more significant reason is that the international legislative process relies on the assumption that its textual formulations are not intended to apply directly to individuals through an international criminal court, but that they are intended as obligations upon states to reformulate these proscriptions and embody them in their respective national legal systems. Thus, each state should presumably reformulate international proscriptions in accordance with its own standards of legality before embodying these proscriptions in their national legislation. Consequently, to expect the same technical legal rigor from the international process as from national legislative bodies, may have been deemed unnecessary. Thus, the results of this international legislative process have regrettably been tentative and imprecise. International crimes have been frequently defined in broad general terms without regard for the enunciation of the elements of the international crime, and also without the inclusion of specific provisions on elements of responsibility and exoneration which are found in the general part of all national criminal laws. Furthermore, none of the 315 international criminal law instruments include penalties.[48] Consequently, customary international law practice does not include the principle *nulla poena sine lege*, which is found in most national legal systems.[49] Insofar as international criminal law penalties are concerned, they are

---

[48] *Id.*

[49] The ILC in the 1954 Draft Code of Offences provided in Article 5:

The penalty for any offence defined in this Code shall be determined by the tribunal exercising jurisdiction over the individual accused, taking into account the gravity of the offence.

This article provides for the punishment of the offences defined in the Code. Such a provision is considered desirable in view of the generally accepted principle *nulla poena sine lege*. However, as it is not deemed practicable to prescribe a definite penalty for each offence, it is left to the competent tribunal to determine the penalty, taking into consideration the gravity of the offence committed.

inherently left to national legal systems which promulgate them by analogy to similar national crimes. In addition, international criminal law permits a state having jurisdiction to enforce international proscriptions by analogy to similar offenses in that state's national laws. This is evidenced by the practice of states in international criminal prosecutions for war crimes and piracy, as discussed in Chapter 5.

It is obvious from this brief discussion that the "principles of legality" in international criminal law are different from their counterparts in the national legal systems with respect to their standards and application. They are necessarily *sui generis* because they must balance between the preservation of justice and fairness for the accused and the preservation of world order, taking into account the nature of international law, the absence of international legislative policies and standards, the *ad hoc* processes of technical drafting and the basic assumption that international criminal law norms will be embodied into the national criminal law of the various states.

It is this writer's conclusion that in the absence of the codification of international criminal law, as this writer and others have advocated for years,[50] the most appropriate articulation of international criminal law's counterpart to *nullum crimen sine lege* is *nullum crimen sine iure*.[51] That there cannot be a crime without law is, therefore, the core of the "principles of legality" in international criminal law, as evidenced by conventional international criminal law, which is also the clearest manifestation of states' customary practices.

International criminal law as it is now, and certainly as it was in 1945, requires the existence of a legal prohibition arising under conventional or customary international law, which is deemed to have primacy over national law, and which defines a certain conduct as criminal, punishable or prosecutable, or violative of international law. This minimum standard of legality permits the resort to the rule *ejusdem generis* with respect to analogous conduct, and also permits the application of penalties by analogy to similar crimes and penalties in the national criminal laws of the prosecuting state having proper jurisdiction.

Article V was first incorporated in the Draft Code of Offences in 1951. *See* 2 Y.B. INT'L L. COMM'N 137 (1951). It has been maintained since. Earlier, however, the 1919 Commission had recommended "it is desirable for the future that penal sanctions should be provided for such grave outrages against the elementary principles of international law," *see* 14 AJIL 95, 127 (1920). But that advice was never heeded, and international criminal law still suffers from the absence of an international criminal code which would satisfy the requirements of the "principles of legality," including that of *nulla poena sine lege*.

[50] *See* BASSIOUNI DRAFT CODE particularly at 3.

[51] *See* Glaser, *supra* note 45, at 766.

Depending upon one's legal philosophical premise, the difference between this international criminal law standard and national approaches may be one of degree and not of substantive difference. But of greater significance is the question of knowledge of international criminal law that can be attributed to the world's population to persons belonging to specific categories or groups.[52]

It is a well established truism in international law that if a given conduct is permitted by general or particular international law, that permissibility deprives the conduct of its criminal character under international criminal law.[53] But if a given conduct is prohibited by general or particular international law it does not mean that it is criminal *ipso iure*. The problem thus lies in distinguishing between prohibited conduct which falls within the legally defined criminal category and that which does not. Furthermore, there are many types of conduct that are neither permitted nor prohibited under general or particular international law, and the question arises as to what, why and when such conduct can be deemed internationally criminal. The last two questions can be answered rather simply: It is whenever a non-prohibited conduct is analogous to that which is deemed an international crime, or when injurious conduct produces the same harm as that of an international crime. But this, of course, leaves open the following questions:

1. From what sources of law will the analogy be made;
2. To what extent can analogy be applied; and
3. What legal standards and tests should be used.

It is, therefore, inevitable that we must turn to "general principles" to answer these questions, positivism notwithstanding. This exigency is indeed part of the nature of international law as well as a consequence thereof. Nevertheless, one thing is certain and that is the existence of a basic rule of international law prohibiting retroactivity. As Professor Charles Rousseau stated:

---

[52]   *See* Chapter 9 at 359.

[53]   A distinction exists between different violations of international law. As Kelsen puts it "not every act which constitutes a violation of law is a punishable crime," H. KELSEN, PEACE THROUGH LAW 116 (1944); and G. DAHM, ZUR PROBLEMATIK DES VÖLKERSTRAFRECHTS 49 (1956). The punishability of international crimes rests on the fact that such acts injure the international community in whole or in part and its prevention, control and repression is not based on the individual victim but on the international community as a whole. *See also* 1 OPPENHEIM'S INTERNATIONAL LAW 192 (Lauterpacht 7th ed. 1955).

International Law appears to be determined by the principle of non-retroactivity. This principle is the result of both the treaties and the diplomatic and judicial practice.[54]

This explains why the question of *ex post facto* was so pervasive in connection with the Law of the Charter, and why it was so difficult to address by the Charter's drafters and the judges at the various post-World War II judicial proceedings. The outcome, however, was far from satisfactory. One reason may well be that with respect to "crimes against humanity," the conduct was so abhorrent that technical legal rigor was swept aside by emotional reactions. But even so, one would have thought that such distinguished jurists as the Charter's drafters and the Judges at Nuremberg, Tokyo, and at the Subsequent CCL 10 Proceedings could have, and should have addressed this question in a more scholarly way or at least in a more convincing one. Instead, as is discussed below, they seem to have brushed these arguments aside and relied on their inner sense of justice and for some on their unbridled power to decide the outcome irrespective of the fundamental techniques of the criminal law. Their inarticulated premise must have been reliance on a higher law. In so doing, they reinforced the point frequently made by positivists' arguments that reliance on an inarticulated higher law is *per se* arbitrary, because one man's higher law is another's crime. Indeed, as argued by many defendants before the IMT and Subsequent Proceedings, their "higher law" was obedience to the *Führer*, and for them that could never be a crime. But their conduct was deemed criminal by reference to other legal standards, as discussed in Chapter 4 and 5.

The Charter and the Post-World War II Prosecution's Treatment of the Question

The drafters of the Charter, in this writer's opinion, purposely sidestepped the question of the "principles of legality," as discussed in Chapter 1, in order to avoid providing an opportunity for the defense to challenge the Charter's validity. During the deliberations on the formulation of the Charter,[55] the participants were particularly

---

[54] C. ROUSSEAU, 1 PRINCIPLES GÉNÉRAUX DU DROIT INTERNATIONAL PUBLIC 486 (1944).

[55] *See* Herbert Wechsler in B. SMITH, THE AMERICAN ROAD TO NUREMBERG: THE DOCUMENTARY RECORD 86 (1982).

concerned with defining the unprecedented "crimes against peace," which presented the most difficult challenge from the perspective of the "principles of legality." The legislative approach they developed for that crime was also in part applied to the other two categories of crimes and that approach was simply to establish that what the drafters had agreed upon would be deemed to constitute an international crime. In short, they relied on their power to legislate. That position is illustrated by a comment of one of the drafters at the London Conference, Sir David Maxwell Fyfe, who stated:

I think that my points are largely points of clarification. But there is one fundamental point that I want to see whether we are agreed on. I think we are. *I want to make clear in this document what are the things for which the Tribunal can punish the defendants. I don't want it to be left to the Tribunal to interpret what are the principles of international law that it should apply.* I should like to know where there is general agreement on that, clearly stated -- for what things the Tribunal can punish the defendants. *It should not be left to the Tribunal to say what is or is not a violation of international law.* That is why I wanted in the English draft the words "convict and sentence after trial" -- that is, the Tribunal should have the power to "try, convict and sentence." Developing the same point, I am a little worried by the inclusion in a) of "in violation of the principles of international law and treaties," because I would be afraid that that would start a discussion before the Tribunal as to what were the principles of international law. I should prefer it to be simply "in violation of treaties, agreements, and assurances." Now b) and c) -- paragraph b) deals with the civilian population and c) deals with the actual waging of war. I'm not clear why the draft includes at the end of b) "and other violations of the laws and customs of warfare," because the draft seems to cover that so explicitly in c). But I should have preferred to leave it "ill-treatment of civilians" -- stop at "slave labour." "And other violations of the laws and customs of warfare" seems to limit it.[56] [emphasis added]

It may be [suggested] that any treaty definition which goes beyond the laws of war would have retroactive application in violation of the principle *nullum crimen sine lege*, a principle that the Nazis rejected in Germany but that would ordinarily weigh with us. I think it a sufficient answer that the crime charged involves so many elements of criminality under the accepted laws of war and the penal laws of all civilized states that the incorporation of the additional factors in question does not offer the type of threat to innocence which the prohibition of *ex post facto* laws is designed to prevent.

See also Chapter 2.

[56] *See* JACKSON'S REPORT 328, 329.

He further stated:

I should like, greatly daring, to try to achieve a compromise between Mr. Justice Jackson and Professor Trainin, because on a first hearing there is nothing in what Professor Trainin has said with which I disagree at all. It seems to me that this is the first point: Mr. Justice Jackson says, "I want these acts defined as crimes;" Professor Trainin has said, "It is quite true that the American draft is quite precise in that it states these are the violations." It seems to me that on that point in the introductory paragraph there is really substantial agreement except for the argument against "ex post facto" legislation which Professor Gros put forward.

I put this point to Professor Gros: The drafting committee's draft says that "The following acts shall be considered criminal violations of International Law ...." Our usual word in English statutes is "deemed," but there is no difference. It is a common word with us. Doesn't that meet Professor Gros' point that *we are not declaring the law as it was but the law as we agree on it for this purpose?*[57] [emphasis added]

Responding to the *ex post facto* debate, Mr. Justice Jackson argues:

... I think it is entirely proper that these four powers, in view of the disputed state of the law of nations, should settle by agreement what the law is as the basis of this proceeding; ...[58]

The position of Sir David Maxwell Fyfe prevailed:

... *What we want to abolish at the trial is a discussion as to whether the acts are violations of international law or not. We declare what the international law is so that there won't be any discussion on whether it is international law or not ...*[59] [emphasis added]

Later in his opening statement at the IMT, Jackson affirmed:

---

[57] *Id.* at 334.

[58] *Id.* at 329.

[59] *Id.* at 99.

116

The validity of the provisions of the Charter is conclusive upon us all whether we have accepted the duty of judging or of prosecuting under it, as well as upon the defendants, who can point to no other law which gives them a right to be heard at all. My able and experienced colleagues believe, as do I, that it will contribute to the expedition and clarity of this trial if I expound briefly the application of the legal philosophy of the Charter to the facts I have recited.

While this declaration of the law by the Charter is final, it may be contended that the prisoners on trial are entitled to have it applied to their conduct only most charitably if at all. *It may be said that this is new law, not authoritatively declared at the time they did the acts it condemns, and that this declaration of the law has taken them by surprise.*

I cannot, of course, deny that these men are surprised that this is the law; they really are surprised that there is any such thing as law. These defendants did not rely on any law at all. Their program ignored and defied all law. That this is so will appear from many acts and statements, of which I cite but a few. In the Führer's speech to all military commanders on November 23, 1939, he reminded them that at the moment Germany had a pact with Russia, but declared, "Agreements are to be kept only as long as they serve a certain purpose."[60] [emphasis added]

But since some of the drafters were also the prosecutors and judges at the IMT, they were subsequently able to control the judicial outcome of the issue of legality; which is the advantage of being both law-maker and interpreter of that very law.[61]

The answers, though unsatisfactory, to the problems raised by the "principles of legality" are found in the IMT Proceedings and Judgment, in the Subsequent CCL 10 Proceedings and in the Tokyo Proceedings and Judgment. These answers were essentially based on four arguments:

---

[60] 2 IMT 143, 144; *see also* JACKSON, THE NÜREMBERG CASE 81 (1947, 2d printing 1971).

[61] Professor Donnedieu de Vabres, an IMT judge, only one year after the Judgment said: *"Le statut, s'il exprime, en principe, la valente des Etats contractrants est en fait l'oeuvre de quelques techniciciens dont plusieus se sont retrouvès parim les membres du Tribunal Militaire International."* Donnedieu de Vabres, *Le Procès de Nuremberg Devant les Principes Modernes du Droit Pènal International,* 70 RECUEIL DES COURS 481 at 556 (1947); *see also* note 1, at 556 wherein he notes the involvement of three of the Charter's members, two were judges (Nikitchenko for the U.S.S.R., Faleo as alternate judge for France), and one, Robert Jackson was Chief Prosecutor for the United States.

117

1. The Tribunal was bound by its law and could not inquire into its own validity or the legality of its law;
2. "Crimes against humanity" was an extension of "war crimes" and as such Article 6(c) did not violate the "principles of legality;"
3. The Charter was declarative of international law, and international law prohibited that conduct; and,
4. "Principles of legality" are non-binding principles of national criminal justice.

The first of these arguments, the Tribunal was bound by its law and could not inquire into its own validity or the legality of its law, is clearly tautological and self-serving. The second, "crimes against humanity" were an extension of "war crimes" and as such Article 6(c) did not violate the "principles of legality," and the third, the Charter was declarative of international law, have substantial validity, as discussed in Chapters 1 and 4. The fourth, "principles of legality" are non-binding principles of national criminal justice, is not entirely well founded, though as discussed above, it has some validity.

As to the first argument, it was advanced by Mr. Alderman, alternate prosecutor for Britain, who stated in Britain's opening statement:

> The International Military Tribunal was established for the trial and punishment of major war criminals on the basis of the London Agreement, dated 8 August 1945, signed by the four countries acting in the interests of all freedom-loving nations. Being an integral part of this agreement, the Charter of the International Military Tribunal is to be considered an unquestionable and sufficient legislative act, defining and determining the basis and the procedure for the trial and punishment of major war criminals. Provoked by fear of responsibility or, at best, by insufficient knowledge of the organic nature of international justice, the references to the principle *nullum crimen sine lege*, or to the principle that "a statute cannot have retroactive power," are not applicable because of the following fundamental, decisive fact: The Charter of the Tribunal is in force and in operation and all its provisions possess absolute and binding force.[62]

---

[62]   3 IMT 148.

The same position was also stated by General Rudenko, Chief Prosecutor for the USSR, though more vigorously, when he said in his closing statement:

> In the speeches of the Defense a number of legal questions were again raised on the importance of the principle *Nullum crimen sine lege*; ...

> I therefore consider it necessary to return again to some legal questions in order to answer the attempts of the Defense to confuse clear and simple statements and to change the legal argumentation into a kind of "smoke screen" in an effort to conceal from the Tribunal the gruesome reality of the fascist crimes.

> a) Principle *Nullum crimen sine lege*.

> The Defense attempted to deny the accusation by proving that at the time the defendants were perpetrating the offenses with which they were charged, the latter had not been foreseen by existing laws, and that therefore the defendants cannot bear criminal responsibility for them.

> I could simply pass over the principle *Nullum crimen sine lege*, as the Charter of the International Military Tribunal, which is an immutable law and is unconditionally to be carried out, provides that this Tribunal "shall have the power to try and punish all persons, who acting in the interest of an European Axis countries, whether as individuals or as members of organization or group," committed any of the crimes enumerated in Article 6 of the Charter.

> Therefore, from the legal point of view, sentences can be pronounced and carried out without requiring that the deeds which incriminate the defendants be foreseen by the criminal law at the time of their perpetration. Nevertheless, there is no doubt that the deeds of the defendants, at the time when they were being committed, were actual criminal acts from the standpoint of the then existing criminal law.

> The principles of criminal law contained in the Charter of the International Military Tribunal are the expression of the principles contained in a number of international agreements, enumerated in my opening statement of 8 February 1946 and in the criminal law of all civilized countries. The law of all civilized countries provides criminal responsibility for murder, torture, violence, plunder,

et cetera. The fact that those crimes have been initiated by the defendants on a scale surpassing all human imagination and bear the marks of unheard-of sadistic cruelty does not, of course, exclude but rather increases the responsibility of the defendants. If the defendants had committed the crimes on the territory and against the citizens of any one country, then in accordance with the declaration of the heads of the governments of the USSR, of Great Britain and the United States of America, published on 2 November 1943, and in full agreement with the universally accepted principles of criminal law, they would be tried in that country and according to that country's laws.[63]

The argument that Article 6 of the Charter -- which was "decisive and binding upon the Tribunal"[64]--makes it clear that individuals are responsible for acts defined as criminal therein. Thus, the IMT concluded:

The jurisdiction of the Tribunal is defined in the Agreement and Charter, and the crimes coming within the jurisdiction of the Tribunal, for which there shall be individual responsibility, are set out in Article 6. The law of the Charter is decisive, and binding upon the Tribunal.

The making of the Charter was the exercise of the sovereign legislative power by the countries to which the German Reich unconditionally surrendered; and the undoubted right of these countries to legislate for the occupied territories has been recognized by the civilized world. The Charter is not an arbitrary exercise of power on the part of the victorious nations, but in the view of the Tribunal, as will be shown, it is the expression of international law existing at the time of its creation; and to that extent is itself a contribution to international law.

The Signatory Powers created this Tribunal, defined the law it was to administer, and made regulations for the proper conduct of the Trial. In doing so, they have done together what any one of them might have done singly; for it is not to be doubted that any nation has the right thus to set up special courts to administer law.

---

[63]   19 IMT 575-576.

[64]   1 IMT 218.

120

With regard to the constitution of the Court, all that the defendants are entitled to ask is to receive a fair trial on the facts and law.[65]

Such a postulate also seems to rely on the doctrine of *la compétence de la compétence*, whereby the international tribunal can determine its own authority.[66] But whereas this doctrine applies with respect to jurisdiction, it can hardly be applied to the judicial creation of international criminal law.

The argument that "crimes against humanity" did not violate the standards of legality in international criminal law because it is merely a jurisdictional extension of war crimes may be valid for many, except to strict positivists. As discussed in Chapter 4, "crimes against humanity" were an outgrowth of war crimes and international law prohibited such crimes, and therefore, the international criminal law standard of legality, *nullum crimen sine iure*, was satisfied. But that, of course, required a connection between "crimes against humanity" and war or war crimes as required by Article 6(c) of the London Charter and Article 5(c) of the Tokyo Charter, as discussed in Chapter 1. This was not, however, the case with respect to CCL 10 Article II(c), which departed from that connecting requirement, as discussed in Chapter 1. Strict adherents of the "principles of legality" who are usually positivists, maintain, however, that Articles 6(c), 5(c), and II(c) nonetheless violated the "principle of legality" prohibiting *ex post facto* criminal legislation, as discussed earlier in this chapter.

The Charter's drafters and the IMT Judgment added another justification, namely that the specific crimes which are contained in Article 6(c), which are substantially the same in 5(c) and II(c)[67] are also crimes in "general principles of law recognized by civilized nations." There are two problems with this rationalization. The first is that not all the specific crimes listed in Articles 6(c), 5(c) and II(c) are universally or substantially found in the world's major criminal justice systems, as discussed in Chapter 7. The second is that international criminal law has never relied on "general principles" as a source for international criminalization. If it had, then simple murder would be an international crime because it is included in the criminal law of all national legal systems. But to rely on "general principles" may also be a way of begging the whole question of legality since "general principles" are more likely to

---

[65]   22 IMT 461.

[66]   *See* I. SHIHATA, THE POWER OF THE INTERNATIONAL COURT TO DETERMINE ITS OWN JURISDICTION; COMPÉTENCE DE LA COMPÉTENCE (1965).

[67]   *See* Chapter 1 at 32.

121

produce generality than specificity. Consequently, "general principles" as used in this context, is a tenuous argument without adding more to it. It is, however, valid insofar as it can be used to interpret international law and to fill gaps in the application of existing law, as discussed in Chapter 7.

The third argument, namely that the Charter was declarative of international law, is conclusionary, but has substantial validity for the reasons discussed in Chapter 4.

The fourth argument is that "principles of legality" are non-binding principles of national criminal justice. This argument is only partially valid for the reasons discussed above, that "principles of legality" existed in part in the world's major legal systems though they varied in their degree of recognition and manner of application. The IMT, however, peremptorily concluded:

> It was urged on behalf of the defendants that a fundamental principle of all law --- international and domestic -- is that there can be no punishment of crime without a pre-existing law. *Nullum crimen sine lege, nulla poena sine lege.* It was submitted that *ex post facto* punishment is abhorrent to the law of all civilized nations, that no sovereign power had made aggressive war a crime at the time that the alleged criminal acts were committed, that no statute had defined aggressive war, that no penalty had been fixed for its commission, and no court had been created to try and punish offenders.

> In the first place, it is to be observed that the maxim *nullum crimen sine lege* is not a limitation of sovereignty, but is in general a principle of justice. To assert that it is unjust to punish those who in defiance of treaties and assurances have attacked neighboring states without warning is obviously untrue, for in such circumstances the attacker must know that he is doing wrong, and so far from it being unjust to punish him, it would be unjust if his wrong were allowed to go unpunished. Occupying the positions they did in the Government of Germany, the defendants, or at least some of them, must have known of the treaties signed by Germany, outlawing recourse to war for the settlement of international disputes; they must have known that they were acting in defiance of all international law when in complete deliberation they carried out their designs of invasion and aggression. On this view of the case alone, it would appear that the maxim has no application to the present facts.[68]

---

[68]   22 IMT 461-462.

One author supporting the Tribunal's conclusion found it necessary to show how these principles existed in the world's major legal systems, but that they were applied in a way that did not make them binding principles:

The advocates of this point of view base themselves on the famous maxim *nullum crimen sine lege, nulla poena sine lege praevia,* which means that there is no crime without pre-existing law. This rule was already recognized in ancient Roman times, and it has been affirmed at various times in history. It was not until the seventeenth and eighteenth centuries, however, that it was introduced as a fundamental principle of justice into the continental European system of law. The modern formulation of the rule is attributed to Anselm Feuerbach. In England, too, great jurists like Blackstone demanded protection against retroactive legislation.

But the *nulla poena* rule was never adopted there as a binding general principle. British courts decided that laws should not be applied retroactively unless there was special provision to that effect.

This opinion has been severely criticized on various grounds. Some writers maintain that the maxim *nullum crimen sine lege, nulla poena sine lege* is a procedural safeguard against injustice, an accepted moral principle, and an ideal of lawyers and judges. But it is not a rule of law. Since it is an ethical principle rather than a rule of law, it may be set aside if considerations of justice demand it. The principle of *Rechtssicherheit* must yield to *Gerechtigkeit.*[69]

Such a position is questionable since "principles of legality" existed in the European criminal justice systems, as discussed above, and thus may be said to be a regionally binding principle of law. But the question is not the existence of the principle, rather it is the contents and applications of the principles which are at issue. The existence, meaning, contents and applications of these principles in the world's major criminal

---

[69]   R. WOETZEL, THE NUREMBERG TRIALS IN INTERNATIONAL LAW 111-112 (1962); and Biddle, *The Nuremberg Trial,* 33 VA. L. REV. 679 (1947). *Contra see* Ehard, *The Nuremberg Trial Against the Major War Criminals and International Law,* 43 AJIL 223 (1949); Mignone, *After Nuremberg, Tokyo,* 25 TEX. L. REV. 475-490 (1947); and Ireland, *Ex Post Facto From Rome to Tokyo,* 21 TEMPLE L. Q. 27 (1947); Jaspers, *The Significance of the Nurnberg Trials for Germany and the World,* 22 NOTRE DAME LAW'Y. 150 (1946). Professor Schwarzenberger also raised similar concerns in *The Judgment of Nuremberg,* 21 TUL. L. REV. 329 (1947).

justice systems vary and their counterparts in international criminal law are also different. But to dismiss them as non-binding *desiderata* is unfounded.

The Charter and the IMT Judgment considered "crimes against humanity" an extension of war crimes, and as such the "principles of legality" were not violated in spirit and certainly not according to those legal systems which permit analogy to similar foreseeable crimes. There is, therefore, a valid legal foundation which pre-existed the Charter to support this position, as discussed in Chapter 4. Furthermore, the specific conduct deemed violative under Article 6(c) constituted a crime in the world's major criminal justice systems except for "persecution," as discussed in Chapter 7. And even though the position of this writer differs from that of the Charter's drafters and the IMT Judgment that "general principles" cannot create international crimes because the lack of specificity in "general principles" would violate minimum standards of legality, "general principles" are nonetheless relevant in defining the content of legal terms such as the term "laws of humanity" embodied in the 1899 and 1907 Hague Conventions, as discussed in Chapter 4.

With respect to the issue of retroactivity, Lord Hartley Shawcross, as British chief prosecutor, stated in his opening statement at the IMT:

There is thus no substantial retroactivity in the provisions of the Charter. It merely fixes the responsibility for a crime already clearly established as such by positive law upon its actual perpetrators. It fills a gap in international criminal procedure. There is all the difference between saying to a man, "You will now be punished for what was not a crime at all at the time you committed it," and in saying to him, "You will now pay the penalty for conduct which was contrary to law and a crime when you executed it, although, owing to the imperfection of the international machinery, there was at that time no court competent to pronounce judgment against you." It is that latter course which we adopt, and if that be retroactivity, we proclaim it to be most fully consistent with that higher justice which, in the practice of civilized states, has set a definite limit to the retroactive operation of laws. Let the defendants and their protagonists complain that the Charter is in this matter an *ex parte fiat* of the victors. These victors, composing, as they do, the overwhelming majority of the nations of the world, represent also the world's sense of justice, which would be outraged if the crime of war, after this second world conflict, were to remain unpunished. In thus interpreting, declaring, and supplementing the existing law, these states are content to be judged by the verdict of history. *Securus judicat orbis terrarum.* Insofar as the Charter of this Tribunal introduces new law, its authors have established when the Charter was adopted. It is only by way of corruption of language that it can be described as a retroactive law.[70]

In the subsequent proceedings under CCL 10, the question of *ex post facto* and *nulla crimen sine lege* was also raised by the defendants, and in this writer's opinion with much more validity, because CCL 10 removed the war connection from "crimes against humanity," as discussed below and in Chapter 2. In these judgments, the rationale for concluding that "principles of legality" did not apply was conflicting and weak. In *The Justice Case*,[71] the judgment concluded that *ex post facto* is not specifically prohibited in international law, particularly where the law is said to develop by cases as opposed to being exclusively statutory. But that judgment went on to add another reason, namely that the actors in this case were bound to know that what they were doing was wrong. Presumably, what the Tribunal was trying to articulate was that interpretation by analogy of similar foreseeable crimes is permissible particularly when the accused knew of the wrongful nature or potential wrongful nature of the conduct. In *The "Einsatzgruppen" Case*,[72] the Tribunal instead relied on the argument already propounded by the IMT that the Charter was not an arbitrary exercise of power of the victorious nations, but the embodiment of international law as it existed at the time of Charter, though never posited in written law.[73] In *The Krupp Case*,[74] the Tribunal simply concluded that it did not adjudge as criminal an act that was not criminal when it was committed. As self-serving as that statement was, the Tribunal made no effort to advance any specific reason to support its conclusion. To a large extent, *The Farben Case* [75] took the same approach by concluding that CCL 10, under which the

---

[70] 3 IMT 106. *See also* Forbes, *Some Legal Aspects of the Nuremberg Trials*, 24 CAN. B. REV. 584, 596 (1946); Goodhart, *The Legality of the Nuremberg Trials*, 58 JURIDICAL REVIEW 1, 17 (1946).

[71] *See e.g. The Justice Case* at 23.

[72] *See e.g. The "Einsatzgruppen" Case* at 15.

[73] *See* Chapter 2.

[74] *The Krupp Case* at 1331 states:

The Tribunal has not given and does not give any *ex post facto* application to Control Council Law No. 10. It is administered as a statement of international law which previously was at least partly uncodified. This Tribunal adjudges no act criminal which was not criminal under international law as it existed when the act was committed.

[75] *The Farben Case* at 58-59 states:

prosecution was conducted, only made punishable what was punishable before. In *The Flick Case*,[76] the Tribunal relied on the declaratory and binding effect of CCL 10 and on the linkage between "crimes against humanity" and other crimes.[77] All of the CCL 10 cases ultimately relied on the argument that the sovereign legislative power that was previously exercised by the Third Reich had become vested in the four allied powers by virtue of the unconditional surrender of Germany, and therefore, the applicable law of these cases, namely CCL 10, was valid. Some cases, as stated above, sought to articulate other reasons, but none of them can be said to be legally satisfactory even though they could have made a valid argument that "crimes against humanity" are an outgrowth of war crimes and that by applying a narrowly construed rule of analogy based on *ejusdem generis* their conclusion would have been valid under a number of legal philosophies except for positivism.

At the Tokyo trials under Article 5(c) "crimes against humanity," the defendants also raised the "principles of legality" and in this judgment, save for the dissenting opinion of Judges Pal and Röling, the Tribunal concluded along the same lines as the IMT judgment even though it also held that it was not bound by the IMT judgment as a precedent.

The IMTFE, which had dismissed the defense motions that the "principles of legality" were violated, basically relied on the IMT's judgment. The IMT's judgment was:

> The maxim *nullum crimen sine lege* is not a limitation of sovereignty but is in general a principle of justice. To assert that it is unjust to punish those who in defiance of treaties and assurances have attacked neighbouring states without

---

The acts and conduct of the defendants set forth in this count were committed unlawfully, willfully, and knowingly, and constitute violations of international conventions, particularly of Articles 3, 4, 5, 6, 7, 14, 18, 23, 43, 46 and 52 of the Hague Regulations, 1907, and of Articles 2, 3, 4, 6, 9-15, 23, 27-34, 46-48, 50, 51, 54, 56, 57, 60, 63, 65-68, and 76 of the Prisoner-of-War Convention (Geneva, 1929), of the laws and customs of war, of the general principles of criminal law as derived from the criminal laws of all civilized nations, of the internal penal laws of the countries in which such crimes were committed, and of Article II of Control Council Law No. 10.

[76] *See e.g., The Flick Case* at 1187.

[77] *Id.* For a discussion of the linkage *see* Chapters 2, 4 and 7. Flick appealed the CCL 10 Tribunal decision to the U.S. Court of Appeals for the District of Columbia, United States v. Flick, 174 F.2d 983 (D.C.), *cert denied*, 338 U.S. 879 (1949), which affirmed on the basis that Germany had surrendered unconditionally to the Allies and that the Allies, having acquired sovereignty over Germany, could exercise their supreme governing authority through the Control Council.

warning is obviously untrue for in such circumstances the attacker must know that he is doing wrong, and so far from it being unjust to punish him, it would be unjust if his wrong were allowed to go unpunished.[78]

The Tokyo Tribunal relied upon and quoted that portion of the IMT judgment and further added that:

> With the foregoing opinions of the Nuremberg Tribunal and the reasoning by which they are reached this Tribunal is in complete accord.[79]

In his dissenting opinion, Judge Pal (India), considered three (3) material questions of law. The second was stated by him as follows:

> 2.   (a) Whether wars of the alleged character became criminal in international law during the period in question in the indictment.
>
> If not, (b) Whether any *ex post facto* law could be and was enacted making such wars criminal so as to affect the legal character of the acts alleged in the indictment.[80]

He answered the second material question as follows:

> Before proceeding to examine the provisions of the Charter in relation to the question now under consideration, I would like to dispose of one branch of the arguments of the defense in this connection, based, I am inclined to believe, on a misconception of a well-recognized rule of construction of statutes arising from the principle of non-retroactivity of law. The defense wanted to say that the definitions, if any, in the Charter would be void on this principle.

---

[78]   1 B. FERENCZ, DEFINING INTERNATIONAL AGGRESSION 539, 546 (2 vols. 1975).

[79]   *Id.*

[80]   2 THE TOKYO JUDGMENTS: THE INTERNATIONAL TRIBUNAL FOR THE FAR EAST (IMTFE) 530 (B. Röling and C. Rüter, eds. 1977) (Judgment of the Member from India, Opinion of the Member from the Netherlands). *See also* B.F. BROWN, THE CRIMINAL CONSPIRACY IN THE JAPANESE WAR CRIME TRIALS (1948) where he discusses legality on the basis of a higher law.

The rule denying retroactivity to a law is not that law cannot be made retroactive by its promulgator, but that it should not ordinarily be made so and that if such retroactive operation can be avoided courts should always do that.

The Charter here is clearly intended to provide a court for the trial of offenses, if any, in respect of past acts. There cannot be any doubt as to this scope of the Charter and consequently it is difficult for us to read into its provisions any non-retroactivity.

Nor can it be denied that if the promulgator of the Charter was at all invested with any authority to promulgate a law, his authority was in respect of acts which are all matters of the past and already completed.[81]

He went on to re-phrase the issue:

The real questions that arise for our consideration are:

1. Whether the Charter has defined the crime in question; if so,
2. Whether it was in the competence of its author so to define the crime;
3. Whether it is within our competence to question his authority in this respect.[82]

Lastly, it should be recalled that there were many prosecutions before military and other national tribunals of the Allies after World War II.[83] These prosecutions were conducted pursuant to the jurisdiction of that particular country, whether exercised by its military authorities, by special tribunals, or by its ordinary criminal courts. Numerically, the largest number of cases were prosecuted by military tribunals set up by the Allies in their respective zones of occupation.[84] The charges were mostly in the nature of war crimes in accordance with the military laws of the prosecuting country, including "crimes against humanity" as defined by the London and Tokyo Charters' Articles 6(c) and 5(c), though in some cases they followed the CCL 10

---

[81]   THE TOKYO JUDGMENTS *id.* at 538.

[82]   THE TOKYO JUDGMENTS *id.* at 539.

[83]   *See* H. MEYROWITZ, LES CRIMINELS DE GUERRE DEVANT LES TRIBUNAUX ALLIÉS (1960).

[84]   *See* Chapter 5.

formulation which removed the war connection from "crimes against humanity." As such, the same issues discussed above with respect to Nuremberg, Tokyo and Subsequent CCL 10 Proceedings apply to all other legal proceedings which relied on Articles 6(c), 5(c) and II(c).

Assessing the Arguments of Legality in the Law of the Charter

By using the rule *ejusdem generis* it can be shown that pre-existing prohibitions under the international regulation of armed conflicts are analogous to Article 6(c).[85] Consequently, there was no violation under the international criminal law of the "principle of legality" *nullum crimen sine iure*. But under the principle *nullum crimen sine lege*, as interpreted by positivism, Articles 6(c) and 5(c) are new positive law, and therefore violate the principle prohibiting *ex post facto* as applied in the western European legal systems. But it must be noted that these "principles of legality" were not recognized and applied in Japan and other Asian legal systems before 1945.

The absence of specific penalties in the London and Tokyo Charters and in CCL 10 does not, however, *ipso iure*, violate international criminal law legality, since it has not, so far, been included in any international criminal law instrument. Thus, its absence confirms a customary rule of international law practice that penalties by analogy are valid.

It is evident that international criminal law legality, unlike many national criminal justice systems, relies more heavily on analogy. In the national criminal law of most legal systems, opposition to analogy stems essentially from the fears of abuse of power though the arguments relied upon are frequently of a criminological nature. The resort to analogy in some instances can be unfair, particularly where there is no reasonable expectation of the applicable analogy. Notice, also an element of deterrence, is an important component of fairness though some, like Professor Glanville Williams, maintain that limitations on punishment through a rigid application of *nulla poena sine*

---

[85]   *See* Chapters 4 and 6. In *The Hostage Case*, decided under CCL 10, the court held:

It is not essential that a crime be specifically defined and charged in accordance with a particular ordinance, statute or treaty if it is made a crime by international convention, recognised customs, and usages of war, or the general principles of criminal justice common to civilised nations generally.

11 CCL Trials 1239 (1948); *see also* R. WOETZEL, *supra* note 69, at 116.

lege is not only superfluous but does not necessarily advance individual protections.[86] Others emphasize deterrence as the expectation of what the law proclaims as notice for the consequences of its violation. One author, commenting on the deterrence element of the Charter, stated: "The Nazis certainly would not have been checked by the precedent of legal sanctions if such a trial as Nuremberg had occurred before their advent to power. German and Japanese leaders knew that failure most likely would mean death, but they accepted this possibility."[87] This is certainly true of the policy-makers and principal executors of Nazi and Japanese war crimes and their extension by analogy to "crimes against humanity." But that certainty, however, diminishes as the accused perpetrator is far removed from decision-making capability. If the legal notions of fairness and foreseeability are accepted as a basis for the validity of analogy in international criminal law legality, then clearly its application should be based on the reasonableness test so as to preclude unfair results. It is perhaps in this connection that one has to consider the defense of "obedience to superior orders,"[88] and the significance of its removal by Article 8 of the London Charter and Article 6 of the Tokyo Charter for the "principles of legality" under international criminal law. The complete removal of this defense, which existed in the German and Japanese national legal systems before 1945, and in international law, is probably the more serious violation of legality because of its *ex post facto* nature. But it should be noted that German military law, after 1935, excluded the defense if the order was unlawful. Thus, the question exists as to whether the orders that lead to the commission of "crimes against humanity" were unlawful under the reasonableness test.

The notion of fairness should be the proper guide in determining the appropriateness of analogy in a given case of legal interpretation, and it should be based on the objective standard of reasonable expectation that a court in resorting to analogy would reach a predictable outcome. Surely if that outcome were to be favorable to the accused no one would argue against it. As one author stated, there had to be a reasonable expectation of punishment including death for the major war criminals at Nuremberg and Tokyo.[89]

---

[86] G. WILLIAMS, CRIMINAL LAW: THE GENERAL PART 464 (1953).

[87] W.J. BOSCH, JUDGMENT ON NUREMBERG 48 (1970).

[88] *See* Chapter 10.

[89] *See* W.J. BOSCH, *supra* note 87; P.E. CORBETT, THE STUDY OF INTERNATIONAL LAW 34-36 (1955); and B.F. SMITH, REACHING JUDGMENT AT NUREMBERG 48 (1977).

130

Critics of the Charter charge that Articles 6(c), 5(c) and II(c) were a retroactive application of newly developed law for which there were no pre-established penalties, that the IMT and IMTFE were engaging in an unreasonable application of analogy, and that CCL 10 Article II(c) was definitely in violation of international standards of legality because it removed the connection to war and war crimes from "crimes against humanity." But nowhere in the proceedings of the Nuremberg and post-Nuremberg trials is there any convincing evidence presented by the defense that the European national systems did not in some way apply analogy in judicial interpretation of broad legislative textual language. Nor was there a convincing argument to explain why Article 6(c) and CCL 10 Article II(c) were different from what the German legal system under the Third Reich recognized and applied.[90] It is noteworthy, as stated earlier, that a Third Reich law, promulgated June 28, 1935, specifically abrogated Section 2 of the German Penal Code of 1871, which provided for the principle *nullum crimen sine lege* and substituted the 1871 code provision with a new Section 2 and added subsections 2a and 2b (with entry into affect September 1, 1935), which repudiated the principle and established instead the principle of legislative and judicial analogy.[91] The 1935 law was abrogated by a decree of the Control Council in 1945, which restored Germany's prior standard of legality.[92] The same argument applies to

---

[90] *See supra* note 22; and also G. AVERNA, IL PROGGETTO DEL CODICE PENALE DELLA GERMANIA SOCIAL-NAZIONALISTA 9 (1936).

[91] German Act of June 28, 1935 quoted in Zupanàc, *On Legal Formalism: The Principle of Legality in Criminal Law*, 27 LOY. L. REV. 369, 411 n. 99 (1981); and Preuss, *supra* note 22.

[92] CCL No. 7, Article IV. *See also* Ryu and Silving, *International Criminal Law -- A Search for Meaning*, in 1 BASSIOUNI AND NANDA TREATISE 29 wherein at footnote 23 the authors stated:

Prosecution of National Socialist criminals in Germany simply charged crimes as defined in the GERMAN PENAL CODE, which was never formally amended to authorize or condone the atrocities of the National Socialist era. Thus, *e.g.*, one of the most celebrated cases decided by the Bundesgerichtshof, 2 BGH ST. 234 (1952) (I. Strafsenat, Jan. 29, 1952, g. K. u.a.), involved charges within the terms of § 239 of the Penal Code, defining "wrongful deprivation of liberty." The defense argued that the deportations of Jews in which defendants participated were ordered by the authorities in power and were thus not known by the defendants to have been "wrongful" or "illegal." The Supreme Court reversed acceptance of this defense by the Court below, stating that an authorization or condonation of such nature conflicted with basic principles recognized by all civilized nations. Said the Supreme Court with reference to the "retroactivity" argument (*supra* at 239):

This does not mean that the conduct of the defendants is being measured by standards which did not acquire general validity until after the events, and it is not being claimed that defendants should have

131

the Tokyo Charter's Article 5(c) since the Japanese system permitted analogy.[93] Thus, the defense arguments that Nuremberg and Tokyo prosecutions violated the "principles of legality" were technically correct from a positivist perspective. But such arguments could not be reconciled with the subversion of German law by the operators of the regime who manipulated the law in order to "legitimize" their otherwise criminal conduct. This regime violated the very principles with which its perpetrators were trying to shield themselves. This in essence is what happens when "state action or policy" subverts the law and the legal process, as discussed in Chapter 6, and this is why such a situation requires international criminalization.[94]

Equity compelled the rejection of the perpetrators claims at Nuremberg, Tokyo and subsequent trials arising out of the World War II tragedy,[95] even though rigid positivistic application of the "principles of legality" as understood in the post-1800 Continental European positivist legal tradition gave validity to this argument.[96] Indeed, until 1945 "crimes against humanity" had not been promulgated under positive

---

answered the question of right or wrong according to principles which were not or which were no longer in force at the time. That they should have ignored the few principles which are essential to men's life in a community and which belong to the inviolable essence and fundamental core of law, as is alive in the legal consciousness of all civilized nations, or that they should have failed to realize the binding force of these principles independently of any recognition by the state, cannot be accepted, particularly in the light of the fact that they had received the impressions in which such persuasions are formed at a time before National Socialism could spread its confusing and poisonous propaganda.

[93] Dando, *Basic Concepts in Temporal and Territorial limits on the Applicability of the Penal Law of Japan*, 9 N.Y.L.SCH. J. INT'L L. COMP. L. 237 (1988). Justice Dando focuses on the principle of legality in post World War II Japan, but refers also to the previous period under the Meiji Constitution which allowed broad statutory and administrative penalties to be promulgated by the cabinet, *id*. at 238. The Meiji Constitution did not forbid the retroactivity of penal legislation, *id*. at 249.

[94] *See* Chapter 1 at 45 and Chapter 6.

[95] For the equitable argument *see* Chapter 2 at 71. In 1946 Justice Jackson who was a proponent of this argument stated:

That men may be protected in relying upon the law at the time they act is the reason we find laws of retroactive operation unjust. But these men cannot bring themselves within the reason of the rule which in some systems of jurisprudence prohibits *ex post facto* laws.

Cited in Forbes, *supra* note 70, at 596.

[96] *See* Von Liszt, *Die Deterministischen Gegner der Zwechstrafe*, 13 ZSTW 356, 357 (1893); and LEHRBUCH DES STRAFRECHTS § 18 (1890).

international criminal law. The failed efforts to include this type of conduct in the post-World War I peace treaties were also a factor.[97] Thus, the omissions of past failures came to haunt the post-World War II proceedings.

The law of the Charter viewed "crimes against humanity" as within the context of the law of war and not as part of the law of peace. That distinction was meaningful at the time and it explains the reluctance of the Charters' drafters to extend Articles 6(c) and 5(c) beyond its war related context.[98] The opposition to an expanded meaning of "crimes against humanity" to the same type of criminal conduct unrelated to war was also reflected in the earlier position of the United States after World War I, as discussed in Chapter 4. At that time the United States objected to the prosecution of Turkish citizens for a separate crime against "the laws of humanity" since, as the United States believed then, there was little recognition of this offense in conventional or customary international law.[99] As one author stated -- what can be called the obvious: "The diplomats' past reluctance to codify international law resulted in Nuremberg's applying retroactive law."[100]

The conflict between the views of the Tribunal and those of its critics regarding the question of legality stems from differing views as to the sources and functions of international law. International positivists hold that the principle source of international law is treaties, and therefore, that which is not agreed upon by a given state cannot bind it. Similarly, for positivists, if acquiescence in a general custom is not evidenced by consistent practice, then that given custom is also not binding upon that state. International positivists also exclude "general principles of law recognized by civilized nations" as a binding source of international criminal law, in the absence of some explicit agreement to it and some specific definitional content of the purported violation. Assuming the validity of this positivist perspective, then the criticism of the Charter's "crimes against humanity" is valid. But as discussed above and in Chapter 3, this is not the exclusive perspective on international law.

If the assertion of this writer is accepted, that "principles of legality" under international criminal law are embodied in the maxim *nullum crimen sine iure* and that *nulla poena sine lege* does not apply except by analogy, then it follows that the London and Tokyo Charters' formulation of Article 6(c) and 5(c) are substantially valid because

---

[97] *See* 1919 Commission Report and discussion thereof in Chapters 1 and 4.

[98] *See* discussion of semi-colon in Chapter 1 at 24.

[99] *See* Chapter 4; and 1919 Commission Report, Annex II, dissent of the American members.

[100] *See* W.J. BOSCH, *supra* note 87, at 49.

they are premised on the analogy to the norms, rules and principles of international regulation of armed conflicts viewed in the totality of their historical development and in the context of the values they embody and the protections they seek to achieve, as discussed in Chapter 4. There can be no doubt that at the very least some law existed prior to the Charter and that such law prohibited the conduct described as "crimes against humanity." Furthermore, there can be no question that the conduct described in Article 6(c) and 5(c) was clearly *mala in se* and was criminal in the world's major criminal justice systems in 1945, as evidenced in the comparative research presented in Chapter 7. What was missing, according to a strict positivist approach, is a pre-existing law that specifically provided what the London and Tokyo Charters stated in Articles 6(c) and 5(c). Considering, however, that the goals and values of the "principles of legality" are, *inter alia*, to provide notice, maximize compliance, avoid individual injustice, curtail arbitrary powers and enhance social justice, then these values and goals are not violated by the Charter's formulation, but only with respect to those offenders who knew or could reasonably foresee that their conduct constituted a violation of international criminal law if it were not for the special national legislation which purported to legalize it. In short, we are looking to the postulate of whether the substantive law or the form of the law prevails.

It should be said that the question of knowledge of the law[101] may be deemed a premise upon which "principles of legality" are founded, and that the absence of promulgation with some degree of specificity by international law of Articles 6(c) and 5(c) crimes prior to their commission denies the assumption of knowledge and thus deprives the applicable law of an important component of legality. Furthermore, the fact that the London Charter overrode other aspects of German criminal law also raises a question about legality. The genuine issues of legality, however, which are distinguishable from whether "crimes against humanity" existed in international criminal law, are those issues relating to the basis of imputability and culpability under international criminal law,[102] including, but not limited to, such factors as: conditions of criminal responsibility; exonerating defenses; excusable circumstances, such as

---

[101] As discussed earlier in this Chapter and in Chapter 10.

[102] *See* Vassalli, *Colpevolezza*, 1 ENCICLOPEDIA GIURIDICA TRECCANI,1-24 (Vol. 6, 1988), containing a comparative survey of national legal systems and reflecting the different meanings of culpability and imputability in various continental legal systems; and S. GLASER, INFRACTION INTERNATIONALE (1957) for elements of international crimes and the basis of responsibility.

"obedience to superior orders;" and necessity and coercion.[103] All of these, and other factors, known in almost every national system of criminal justice, are nonetheless perceived, applied and interpreted differently. Thus, necessarily, "principles of legality" in international criminal law are a composite of what emerges from national legal systems but adapted to the context and exigencies of international criminal law. The combined effect of the Law of the Charter and subsequent legal developments surely establishes that "crimes against humanity" is an international crime, *delicto jus gentium*, whose commission is by *hosti humani generi* which must be prosecuted[104] without statutory limitations[105] in whatever jurisdiction.[106]

Highlighting the conflict between law and morality, Professor Kelsen stated:

The objection most frequently put forward -- although not the weightiest one -- is that the law applied by the judgment of Nuremberg is an *ex post facto* law. There can be little doubt that the London Agreement provides individual punishment for acts which, at the time they were performed were not punishable, either under international or under any national law. The rule against retroactive legislation has certainly not been respected by the London Agreement. However, this rule is not valid within national law only with important exceptions. The rule excluding retroactive legislation is based on the more general principle that no law should be applied to a person who did not know the law at the moment he behaved contrarily to it. But there is another generally accepted principle, opposite to the former, that ignorance of the law is no excuse. If knowledge of a non-retroactive law is actually impossible -- which is sometimes the case since the assumption that everybody knows the existing law is a fiction -- then there is, psychologically, no difference between the application of this non-retroactive law and the application of a retroactive law which is considered to be objectionable because it applies to persons who did not and could not know it. In such a case the law applied to the delinquent

---

[103]   *See* Chapter 10; and Y. DINSTEIN, THE DEFENCE OF "OBEDIENCE TO SUPERIOR ORDERS" IN INTERNATIONAL LAW (1965); E. MÜLLER-RAPPARD, L'ORDRE SUPÉRIEUR MILITAIRE ET LA RESPONSABILITÉ PÉNALE DU SUBORDONNÉ (1965); L.C. GREEN, SUPERIOR ORDERS IN NATIONAL AND INTERNATIONAL LAW (1976); N. KEIJZER, MILITARY OBEDIENCE (1978). *Contra* Vogler, *The Defense of 'Superior Orders' in International Criminal Law*, 1 BASSIOUNI AND NANDA TREATISE 619.

[104]   *See* Chapters 5 and 11.

[105]   *See* Chapter 11 at 507.

[106]   *See* Chapter 11 at 509.

has actually retroactive effect although it was legally in force at the time the delict has been committed.

The rule excluding retroactive legislation is restricted to penal law and does not apply if the new law is in favour of the accused person. It does not apply to customary law and to law created by a precedent, for such law is necessarily retroactive in respect to the first case to which it is applied.

A retroactive law providing individual punishment for acts which were illegal though not criminal at the time they were committed, seems also to be an exception to the rule against *ex post facto* laws. The London Agreement is such a law. It is retroactive only in so far as it established individual criminal responsibility for acts which at the time they were committed constituted violations of existing international law, but for which this law has provided only collective responsibility. The rule against retroactive legislation is a principle of justice. Individual criminal responsibility represents certainly a higher degree of justice than collective responsibility, the typical technique of primitive law. Since the internationally illegal acts for which the London Agreement established individual criminal responsibility were certainly also morally most objectionable, and the persons who committed these acts were certainly aware of their immoral character, the retroactivity of the law applied to them can hardly be considered as absolutely incompatible with justice. Justice required the punishment of these men, in spite of the fact that under positive law they were not punishable at the time they performed the acts made punishable with retroactive force. In case two postulates of justice are in conflict with each other, the higher one prevails; and to punish those who were morally responsible for the international crime of the second World War may certainly be considered as more important than to comply with the rather relative rule against *ex post facto* laws, open to so many exceptions.[107]

In a foretelling comment that admits to the innovative aspects of the Charter's law, the British Chief Prosecutor, Lord Hartley Shawcross, said in a statement before the IMT:

---

[107]   Kelsen, *Will the Judgment in the Nuremberg Trial Constitute a Precedent in International Law?*, 1 INT'L. L. Q. 164, 165 (1947). *See also* Kelsen, *The Rule Against Ex Post Facto Law and the Prosecution of the Axis War Criminals*, 2 THE JUDGE ADVOCATE JOURNAL, 8 (1945); *contra* Ehard, *supra* note 69; Mignones, *supra* note 69; Ireland, *supra* note 69; and A. VON KNIEREM, *supra* note 20.

Insofar as the Charter of this Tribunal introduces new law, its authors have established a precedent for the future -- a precedent operative against all, including themselves ....[108]

In contrast, Professor Kelsen stated:

The judgment rendered by the International Military Tribunal in the Nuremberg Trial cannot constitute a true precedent because it did not establish a new rule of law, but merely applied preexisting rules of law laid down by the International Agreement concluded on August 8, 1945, in London for the Prosecution of European Axis War Criminals by the Government of Great Britain, the United States of America, France, and the Soviet Union. The rules created by this Treaty and applied by the Nuremberg Trial, but not created by it, represent certainly a new law ....[109]

The same conclusions were never reached between whether 1.) the London and Tokyo Charters are new or old law, 2.) the self-declarative nature of these Charters are just that or more, and 3.) the "principles of legality" existed or not, and if so whether they were wholly, substantially or only partially satisfied.

Jackson, who admitted to the validity of *nulla poena sine lege* presented an equitable argument to counter it:

But these men cannot bring themselves within the reason of the rule which in some systems of jurisprudence prohibits *ex post facto* laws. They cannot show that they ever relied upon international law in any state or paid it the slightest regard.[110]

---

[108]   3 IMT 124.

[109]   *See supra* note 107.

[110]   2 IMT 70. The French prosecutor François de Menthan stated at the IMT: "Has not the juridical doctrine of National-Socialism admitted that in domestic criminal law even the judge can and must supplement the law? The written law no longer constituted the Magna Carta of the delinquent. The Judge could punish when, in the absence of a provision for punishment, the National-Socialist sense was gravely offended," 5 IMT 372. The conclusion was therefore that because National-Socialist Germany had abandoned the principles of legality, the accused could not claim these principles as a defense. This argument was in the nature of an equitable estoppel, but it was also in the nature of *tu quoque*, namely that since the Nazi law set aside legality, so could the Allies. Interestingly, when the accused raised the defense of *tu quoque* in connection with the charges of war crimes, the Tribunal rejected it out of hand.

Following upon this equitable approach to the "principles of legality" but adding to it a moral dimension, Kelsen stated:

> The infliction of an evil, if not carried out as a reaction against a wrong, is a wrong itself. The non-application of the rule against *ex post facto* law is a first sanction inflicted upon those who have violated this rule and hence have forfeited the privilege to be protected by it.[111]

Another author concluded:

> It would not be a violation of the *nullum crimen, nulla poena* rule, therefore, if a legal principle was applied to an act unforeseen, so long as the act was clearly of the kind affected by the principle.

> It seems clear that in international law the maxim *nullum crimen, nulla poena* has much the same significance as it does in common law countries rather than in those states which operate only by statutory law, since international law develops more like common law, i.e., from case to case on the customary as well as judicial level, than like statutory law. It, therefore, cannot be considered a limitation upon the sovereignty of a prosecuting state, but a general principle of justice. It is intended to guard against abuses of justice through retroactive legislation. But if no injustice is worked, then there is no violation of the principle.[112]

Every act of punishment involves the exercise of power whether by a legitimate or illegitimate authority. But the legitimacy of the punishing authority is not sufficient by itself to make the punishment legal. What is needed is a legitimate law that places people on notice of the prohibition and the due process of law to determine individual responsibility. As Lord Aldersen Wright, Chairman of the UNWCC, said:

---

[111] Kelsen, *supra* note 107, at 165.

[112] *See* R. WOETZEL, *supra* note 69, at 115. The same argument was also made in the case of The Attorney General of the Government of Israel v. Adolf, the son of Karl Adolf Eichmann, District Court of Jerusalem, Criminal Case No. 40/61, *appeal dismissed* by the Supreme Court of Israel, Decision No. 336/61. Eichmann was third under the Israeli law called "The Nazi and the Nazi Collaborators (Punishment) Law" (1950). *See also* Green, *Legal Issues of the Eichmann Trial*, 37 TUL. L. REV. 669 (1962).

138

To punish without law is to exercise an act of power divorced from law ... but if it is not based on law it may be morally just, but it is not a manifestation of justice according to law, though some seem to think that if the justice and morality are incontrovertible, it may serve as a precedent for similar acts in the future and thus establish a rule of International Law.[113]

Similarly, writers and Commentators on the post-World War II prosecution differed as to these questions.

The crimes committed during World War II which fall within the meaning of "crimes against humanity" were unprecedented in history. Not because the violations were unknown, but because the scale and manner of their perpetration was until then unknown to humankind. To that extent they are the first of a kind. The absence of positive law foreseeing such crimes was, therefore, inevitable, just as the killing of Cain by Abel was inevitably a first. But from that point on, it became a crime based on that precedent. The custom grew out of the practice, the practice developed from an initial case, and that initial case became the precedent.

Post-Charter Legal Developments

In its summary of the "Nuremberg Principles," the ILC, in 1950, concluded:

Another question of equally general importance arose at the beginning of the proceedings. It concerns the doubt of the defense as to whether certain provisions of the Charter were consistent with international law. The court dismissed a motion of the defence expressing doubts as to the consistency with international law of certain provisions of the Charter and requesting that an opinion regarding the legal basis of the trial should be obtained from recognized authorities on international law. (TRIAL OF THE MAJOR WAR CRIMINALS, RECORD OF PROCEEDINGS, published by the International Military Tribunal, vol. I, 1947, p. 168.) "The law of the Charter," said the Court, "is decisive and binding upon the Tribunal." (NAZI CONSPIRACY AND AGGRESSION, OPINION AND JUDGEMENT, p. 48.) The same view is expressed in another passage of the findings in connexion with the question of the validity of Article 6 of the Charter. "These provisions" said the Court, "are

---

[113] Wright, *War Crimes Under International Law*, 62 L.Q. REV. 40, 49-50 (1946).

binding upon the Tribunal as the law to be applied to the case." (*Ibid.*, p. 4.) However, the above motion of the defence was disallowed only in so far as it constituted a plea to the jurisdiction of the Court. The Court declared itself ready to hear any argument of the parties as to the compatibility of the Charter with international law. It is characteristic of the attitude of the Court that the Court itself on various occasions examined this problem when discussing the interpretation and application of provisions of the Charter. Thus, for instance, the Court, commenting on the plea of the defence that Article 6 of the Charter, which enumerates the crimes for which the major war criminals were to be punished, constitutes an *ex post facto* law, conflicting with the principle *nullum crimen sine lege, nulla poena sine lege*, said:

"It is to be observed that the maxim *nullum crimen sine lege* is not a limitation of sovereignty, but is in general a principle of justice. To assert that it is unjust to punish those who in defiance of treaties and assurances have attacked neighbouring States without warning is obviously untrue, for in such circumstances the attacker must know that he is doing wrong, and so far from it being unjust to punish him, it would be unjust if his wrong were allowed to go unpunished. Occupying the positions they did in the government of Germany, the defendants, or at least some of them must have known of the treaties signed by Germany, outlawing recourse to war for the settlement of international disputes; they must have known that they were acting in defiance of all international law when in complete deliberation they carried out their designs of invasion and aggression. On this view of the case alone, it would appear that the maxim has no application to the present facts."

As already stated, a considerable part of the findings consists of comments on the interpretation and application of Articles 6 to 8 of the Charter, which contain the substantive principles of international law of the Charter. The ideas expressed in the comments which have particular importance for the formulation of the principles of international law recognized by the Charter and the judgment, are mentioned in Part IV of the present report since they may serve as an analysis of the principles enumerated therein.[114]

---

[114]   2 Y.B. INT'L L. COMM'N. 187-88 (1950).

The ILC did not add anything in its summary restatement of what the IMT's judgment may be deemed to have concluded. Even so, the ILC was, by its shortness, misleading, particularly because it failed to state the inconsistencies and weaknesses in the opinions expressed by the Charter's drafters, the prosecutors and judges at the IMT, IMTFE and those of the Subsequent CCL 10 Proceedings. Thus, it must be regrettably concluded that the ILC's formulation is of little scholarly value.

"Principles of legality" in international criminal law progressed inferentially through the new substantive instruments developed after 1946, which contained more specificity.[115] But nothing was added to "crimes against humanity," which were left in a legal limbo, hanging between the problematic precedents of Nuremberg, Tokyo and the Subsequent CCL 10 Proceedings, and the sketchy summary which the ILC made in the form of the Nuremberg Principles and whose legally binding nature is highly questionable. But the "principles of legality" gained independent recognition in a number of other international instruments. The first of these was the Universal Declaration of Human Rights of 1948, which states in Article II, para. 2:

> No one shall be held guilty of any penal offence on account of any act or omission which did not constitute a penal offence, under national or international law, at the time when it was committed. Nor shall a heavier penalty be imposed than the one that was applicable at the time the penal offence was committed.[116]

The "principles of legality" were later reaffirmed in the International Covenant on Civil and Political Rights, which states in Article 15:

> 1. No one shall be held guilty of any criminal offence on account of any act or omission which did not constitute a criminal offence, under national or international law, at the time when it was committed. Nor shall a heavier penalty be imposed than the one that was applicable at the time when the criminal offence was committed. If, subsequent to the commission of the Offence, provision is made by law for the imposition of the lighter penalty, the offender shall benefit thereby.
>
> 2. Nothing in this article shall prejudice the trial and punishment of any person for any act or omission which, at the time when it was committed, was criminal

---

115 *See* BASSIOUNI DIGEST.

116 Universal Declaration.

according to the general principles of law recognized by the community of nations.[117]

But in this formulation, the Covenant recognized "general principles of law" as susceptible of creating crimes, a postulate which, in the opinion of this writer, is contrary to the "principles of legality" because "general principles of law" can seldom satisfy the minimum standards of specificity that legality requires.

In the area of the international regulation of armed conflicts, the Third Geneva Convention of August 12, 1949 states in Article 99:

> No prisoner of war may be tried or sentenced for an act which is not forbidden by the law of the Detaining Power or by International Law, in force at the time the said act was committed.[118]

In the Protocols additional to the Geneva Conventions of 12 August 1949, Protocol I, Article 2(c) states that:

> No one shall be accused or convicted of a criminal offence on account of any act or omission which did not constitute a criminal offence under the national or international law to which he was subject at the time when it was committed; nor shall a heavier penalty be imposed than that which was applicable at the time when the criminal offence was committed; if, after the commission of the offence, provision is made by law for the imposition of a lighter penalty, the offender shall benefit thereby.[119]

Protocol II, Article 6(c) - Penal Prosecutions, further prohibits prosecution under an *ex post facto* or retroactive law:

> No one shall be held guilty of any criminal offence on account of any act or omission which did not constitute a criminal offence, under the law, at the time when it was committed; nor shall a heavier penalty be imposed than that which was applicable at the time when the criminal offence was committed; if, after the

---

[117]   U.N. Covenant.

[118]   *See* Third Geneva Convention, Article 99.

[119]   1977 Additional Protocols, Protocol I (Article 2(c)).

142

commission of the offence, provision is made by law for the imposition of a lighter penalty, the offender shall benefit thereby.[120]

The 1991 version of the Draft Code of Crimes asserts the principle of non-retroactivity in article 10.[121] In addition, article 1 specifies that: "the crimes [under international law] defined in this code constitute crimes against the peace and security of mankind."[122] The implication is that crimes must be defined, even though, as discussed in Chapter 11, the present stage of codification substantially violates contemporary standards of legality, which is surprising since it has been in the making since 1947. Ironically, however, the ILC's 1991 report contains extensive discussion on penalities[123] which criticize the 1954 Draft Code of Crimes because it did not contain penalties, noting that such a gap is "in total disregard of the *nulla poena sine lege* rule."[124] Consequently, a very questionable proposed draft article "Z" was inserted into the 1991 ILC report,[125] but it was not acted upon. Suffice it to say that it proposed "community service" as one of the penalties for "crimes against humanity."

Presumably, one has to assume that the ILC considers the inclusion of specific penalties in international criminal law as indispensable to satisfying the "principles of legality." But it also appears that the ILC's conception of legality is limited to the statement of a given proposition, as opposed to providing specificity of content and meaning, in order that such a provision be specific enough to provide knowledge to the ordinarily reasonable person, even one belonging to a particular category to which a higher degree of knowledge may be attributed.[126] It is difficult to see how otherwise the "principles of legality" can be upheld if rules of conduct are not clearly and sufficiently spelled out. The mere statement of a given legal proposition irrespective of its extrinsic merit is not enough to satisfy minimum standards of legality, as discussed above. If that were the case, criticism levied against the Charter would be equally valid against the 1991 Draft Code of Crimes. But what may have been justified

---

[120] 1977 Additional Protocols, Protocol II (Article 6(c)).

[121] *See* 1991 Draft Code of Crimes at 242.

[122] *Id.* at 238.

[123] *Id.* at 202-213.

[124] *Id.* at 212.

[125] *Id.* at 213-14 n. 298.

[126] Such as military personnel and government officials. *See* Chapter 9 at 359.

143

in 1945 is inexcusable in 1991. Moreover, vagueness can only engender arbitrariness. Thus, in addition to a failed attempt in providing legally sufficient rules of conduct, the 1991 Draft Code of Crimes provides an opportunity for abuse of power by those who may selectively rely upon it and enforce it in whatever way they may deem appropriate, against whatever person they may wish. That is certainly not what is expected from this learned body after so many years of deliberation, as discussed in Chapter 11.

Since the Nuremberg, Tokyo, Subsequent CCL 10 Proceedings and other prosecutions by the victorious Allies in their respective zones of occupation and before national tribunals, as discussed in Chapters 1 and 5, several states have passed national criminal legislation to prosecute "crimes against humanity."[127] Israel prosecuted Adolf Eichmann in 1960,[128] France prosecuted Klaus Barbie in 1988[129] and Canada prosecuted Imre Finta in 1989.[130] In these and other similar cases, the plea of violation of the "principles of legality" was rejected in reliance upon the Law of Charter and no new arguments were presented in support of that conclusion. Recently the issue of *ex post facto* as it relates to the Law of the Charter arose in connection

---

[127] *See* Chapter 11.

[128] *See supra* note 112.

[129] *See* Matter of Barbie, Gaz. Pal. Jur. 710 (France Cass. Crim. Oct. 6, 1983). *See also* Le Gunehec, *Affaire Barbie*, GAZETTE DU PALAIS, No. 127-128, *106e année, Mercredi 7-Jeudi 8 Mai*, 1985; and Angevin, *Ensignements de L'Affaire Barbie en Matière de Crimes Contre l'humanité*, LA SEMAIRE JURIDIQUE, 62 e année, No. 5, 14 Dec. 1988, 2149; Doman, *Aftermath of Nuremberg: The Trial of Klaus Barbie*, 60 COLO. L. REV. 449 (1989).

[130] *See* Regina v. Finta, 50 C.C.C. (3d.) 247; 61 D.L.R. 85 (4th 1989). *See also* Jacquart, *La notion de crime contre l'humanité en droit international contemporain et en droit canadien*, 21 REVUE GÉNÉRALE DE DROIT 607 (1990); Green, *Canadian Law, War Crimes and Crimes Against Humanity*, 59 BRIT. Y.B. INT'L L. 217 (1988); Green, *Canadian Law and the Punishment of War Crimes*, 28 CHITTY'S LAW J. 249 (1980).

with Israel's request for the extradition of Demjanjuk from the United States.[131] The Court in that case held:

[13]   The Israeli statute merely provides Israeli courts with jurisdiction to try persons accused of certain crimes committed extraterritorially and establishes judicial procedures and applicable penalties. *See Calder v. Bull*, 3 Dall. (U.S.) 386, 390-93, 1 L.Ed. 648 (1797) (discussion of *ex post facto* laws, as prohibited in the United States Constitution); Cook v. United States, 138 U.S. 157, 183, 11 S.Ct. 268, 275, 34 L.Ed. 906 (1891). Similarly, the Nuremberg International Military Tribunal provided a new forum in which to prosecute persons accused of war crimes committed during World War II pursuant to an agreement of the wartime Allies, *see The Nurnberg Tribunal*, 6 F.R.D. 69. That tribunal consistently rejected defendants' claims that they were being tried under *ex post facto* laws. *Id.; see also United States v. Waldeck; United States v. Otto; United States v. Brust.* The statute is not retroactive because it is jurisdictional and does not create a new crime. Thus, Israel has not violated any prohibition against the *ex post facto* applications of criminal laws which may exist in international law.[132]

Thus, the question of *ex post facto* was simply dealt with in reliance on the IMT's judgment that the Charter was declarative of international law and was not new law,

---

[131]   Matter of Extradition of Demjanjuk, 612 F. Supp. 544 (D.C.), *aff'd* 776 F.2d 571 (6th Cir. 1985), *cert. denied* 475 U.S. 1016 (1986).

Respondent's argument that the Israeli statute violates the United States Constitution's prohibition against *ex post facto* law is misplaced. This Court does not have jurisdiction to determine whether Israeli criminal procedure extends to respondent all of the constitutional rights of a defendant in an American court. Due process rights in extradition proceedings cannot be extended extraterritorially. Neely v. Henkel, 180 U.S. 109, 21 S.Ct. 302, 45 L.Ed. 448 (1901); Kamrin v. United States, 725 F.2d 1225, 1228 (9th Cir. 1984), *cert. denied*, 469 U.S. 817, 105 S.Ct. 85, 83 L.Ed. 2d 32 (1984). This Court is "bound by the existence of an extradition treaty to assume that the trial will be fair." Glucksman v. Henkel, 221 U.S. 508, 512, 31 S.Ct. 704, 55 L.Ed. 830 (1911) (J. Holmes). As the Second Circuit held in Rosado v. Civiletti, 621 F.2d 1179, (2d Cir. 1980),

"Even where the treaty fails to secure to those who are extradited to another country the same constitutional safeguards they would enjoy in an American criminal trial, it does not run afoul of the Constitution." *Id.* at 1193.

[132]   *See* Matter of Extradition of Demjanjuk, *Id.* at 567-568.

nor *ex post facto* law.[133] In fact, all national prosecutions undertaken after 1946 took the same position, and none reopened the question as if the accumulation of time and precedents relying on the IMT's judgments had cured all possible legal defects. This leads to the legally incongruous conclusion that reiteration of the same argument confirms its validity. Such an approach would surely be valid for facts occurring after 1945, but it can hardly be said, from a jurisprudential point of view, that a precedent like the IMT's judgment on the question of *ex post facto* can be validated with respect to itself only by the subsequent reaffirmation of others. Surely a better legal case could have been made by the IMT, and subsequent decisions could have at least attempted to cure its defects by buttressing the arguments in suport of legality with stronger and more convincing arguments.

---

[133]   *See supra* at 118.

CHAPTER 4

HISTORICAL LEGAL FOUNDATIONS: INTERNATIONAL HUMANITARIAN LAW AND THE REGULATION OF ARMED CONFLICTS

> *Le droit des gens est naturellement fondé sur ce principe que les diverses nations doivent se faire dans la paix le plus de bien et dans la guerre le moins de mal qu'il est possible, sans nuire à leurs véritables intérêts*
> C.L. MONTESQUIEU, DE L'ESPRIT DES LOIS, Livre I, c.3, 1748 (La Pléiade ed. 1974).

Introduction

The Charter's Article 6(c) formulation was the first instance in positive international criminal law that the specific terms "crimes against humanity" were used. It was also the first time that this international criminal category was defined, though it should be noted that the notion of protecting civilians in time of war is historically well established in the international regulation of armed conflicts and precedes the Charter. The international regulation of armed conflicts provided for similar protections to civilians as did the Charter, though not in the same manner, scope and application as formulated by the Charter. It also provided for the principle of individual criminal responsibility for violations of these and other norms regulating armed conflicts though that principle was not frequently, nor consistently applied. Thus, while the Charter was the first international instrument to specify the contents of "crimes against humanity," it did not create a new principle of international law because the notion of offenses against the law of nations, *delicti jus gentium*, pre-existed the Charter by centuries.[1]

---

[1] As stated by Professor L.C. Green: "It has often been assumed that the campaign for the trial and punishment of war criminals is a modern innovation, based on feelings of revenge and political ideology rather than on legal considerations. In fact, it can be traced back to the code of chivalry that prevailed in the Middle Ages among the orders of knighthood, while in the early part of the sixteenth century Vitoria was asserting that 'a prince who has on hand a just war is *ipso jure* the judge of his enemies and can inflict a legal punishment on them, according to the scale of wrongdoing'." Green, *Canadian Law, War Crimes and Crimes Against Humanity*, 59 BRIT. Y. INT'L L. 217 (1988). *See also* Green, *The Law of Armed Conflict and the Enforcement of International Criminal Law*, 27 ANNUAIRE CANADIEN DE DROIT INTERNATIONAL 4 (1984); Green, *Human Rights and the Law of Armed Conflict*, 10 ISRAEL Y.B. H.R. 9 (1980) wherein he cites

In addition, the Charter did not innovate the principle of individual criminal responsibility because the notion of punishing *hostis humani generi*, had also pre-existed the Charter by centuries.[2]

Apart from the more or less specific norms prohibiting certain types of conduct in the course of war a separate humanitarian basis existed which prohibited certain human depredations in broader humanistic terms. This concept found its way into the Preamble of the 1907 Hague Convention under the rubrique "the laws of humanity."[3] The Preamble of the 1907 Hague Convention, like that of its 1899 predecessor, states:

> Until a more complete code of the laws of war has been issued, the High Contracting Parties deem it expedient to declare that, in cases not included in the Regulations adopted by them, the inhabitants and the belligerents remain under the protection and the *rule of the principles of the law of nations, as they result from the usages established among civilized peoples, from the laws of humanity, and the dictates of the public conscience.* (emphasis added)

Thus, the philosophical origin of "crimes against humanity" lies in humanistic and humanitarian values, while its normative origin rests in the evolution of the international regulation of armed conflicts.

For a time, it was argued that *jus in bello* was divided between the Hague rules (1907) as being humanitarian and the Geneva rules (1929) as being the normative regulations. The Charter merged these two conceptions and relied on the humanitarian basis to interpret the normative provisions of the regulation of armed conflicts through the use of "general principles," as discussed in Chapter 7. Seventy years later, Protocols I and II in fact used language similar to that of the 1907 Hague Convention, thus confirming the merger of what is now conclusively called "humanitarian law of armed conflict." Protocol I states in Article 1-2:

> In cases not covered by this Protocol or by other international agreements, civilians and combatants remain under the protection and authority of the principles of international law derived from established custom, from the principles of humanity and from the dictates of public conscience.

Belli (1563), Ayala (1582), Gentili (1612), Grotius (1625) *id.* at 7.

[2]   Discussed throughout this Chapter. *See also* Chapters 5 and 10.

[3]   *See infra* notes 62-67 and accompanying text.

Protocol II states in its Preamble:

Recalling that the humanitarian principles enshrined in Article 3 common to the Geneva Conventions of 12 August 1949, constitute the foundation of respect for the human person in cases of armed conflict not of an international character.

Recalling furthermore that international instruments relating to human rights offer a basic protection to the human person.

Emphasizing the need to ensure a better protection for the victims of those armed conflicts,

Recalling that, *in cases not covered by the law in force, the human person remains under the protection of the principles of humanity and the dictates of the public conscience,* (emphasis added)

The Charter established a generic criminal category labelled "crimes against humanity" to fit the unforeseen and unforeseeable depredations that only the unbridled nefarious imagination of evil and banal men could have actuated. Indeed, the facts that gave rise to "crimes against humanity" were too barbarous to foresee and thus, no specific positive law existed that covered all of the misdeeds committed. It was simply a case where the facts exceeded positive law only because of their nature, magnitude and consequences, and not because of absence of any applicable law, as discussed throughout this Chapter.

The legal nature of this category of crimes is still debated since it partakes of general humanitarian law and particular international regulation of armed conflicts. The first is akin to what is called human rights law, and the second arises out of the conventional and customary international law pertaining to the regulation of armed conflicts. Though such a distinction is as *dépassé* as is the distinction between the international law of peace and the international law of war, it was relevant at the time of the Charter. This is why the drafters of the Charter, as discussed in Chapter 1, had to take this distinction into account in order to anchor the new international criminal category of "crimes against humanity" to the established one of war crimes. That is also the reason why the Charter linked "crimes against humanity" to the initiation or conduct of war, as discussed below and in Chapter 1.

In addition, the drafters had to develop particular characteristics to this international category of crimes in order to set it apart from what would otherwise be deemed national common crimes. These particular international characteristics, discussed in Chapters 1 and 6, are woven into the war connecting link discussed in this Chapter and in Chapter 1.

Historical Evolution

The paradox in regulating the conduct of armed conflicts is best expressed in the contrasting views of Montesquieu and Clausewitz. Montesquieu, whose quote appears at this Chapter's opening is the humanistic perspective -- the parties to an armed conflict (war) should inflict on each other the least possible harm. The opposing view is represented by Karl Von Clausewitz who in his celebrated book VOM KRIEG (ON WAR) (1832) affirms that in war the party seeking to win should inflict upon his enemy as much harm as is necessary to insure swift and decisive victory. In time, Montesquieu's view prevailed even though the practices of states do not always prove to be consistent with it. Symbolically, however, in recent times the anachronistic term "law of war" has been dropped in favor of the "humanitarian law of armed conflicts."

For over seven thousand years, humanitarian principles regulating armed conflicts evolved gradually in different civilizations.[4] In time, these humanitarian principles formed a protective fabric of norms and rules designed to prevent certain forms of physical harm and hardships from befalling innocent civilian non-combatants, as well as certain categories of combatants such as the sick, wounded, shipwrecked and prisoners of war.[5] As the protective scheme of prescriptions contained in conventional and customary international law increased both qualitatively and quantitatively,[6] its

---

[4]   For a recent survey *see* Draper, *The Development of International Humanitarian Law*, in INTERNATIONAL DIMENSIONS OF HUMANITARIAN LAW 67 (UNESCO 1988). *See also* Jacquart, *La Notion du Crime contre l'Humanité en Droit International Contemporain et, en Droit Canadien*, 21 REVUE GÉNÉRALE de Droit 607 (1990) wherein the author also makes the distinction made earlier by this writer between the humanitarian or humanistic foundation for "crimes against humanity" and its normative legal foundation in the international regulation of armed conflicts. *See also e.g.* Sherman, *The Civilization of Military Law*, 22 ME. L. REV. 3 (1970); H. McCOUBREY, *Humanitarianism in the Laws of Armed Conflict*, INTERNATIONAL HUMANITARIAN LAW, 1-21 (1990); J. PICTET, DEVELOPMENT AND PRINCIPLES OF INTERNATIONAL HUMANITARIAN LAW (1985); G. BEST, HUMANITY IN WARFARE (1983).

[5]   *See generally* H. LEVIE, THE CODE OF INTERNATIONAL ARMED CONFLICT (1986); Schindler/Toman; Friedman.

[6]   *See* BASSIOUNI DIGEST.

more serious breaches were criminalized.[7] But, the processes of normative development and criminalization of international criminal law have never been part of a consistent or cohesive international policy.[8] Instead, international crimes have evolved by virtue of a haphazard mixture of conventions, customs, general principles, the writings of scholars[9] and the efforts of non-governmental organizations. Among these, the writings of "the most distinguished publicists" have significantly contributed to the advancement of world community values and expectations.[10] This advancement was

---

[7] *See* Bassiouni, *The Proscribing Function of International Criminal Law in the Protection of Human Rights*, 9 YALE J. WORLD PUB. ORD. 193, 196-198 (1982); Lillich, *Can the Criminal Process Be Used to Help Enforce Human Rights Law?* in INTERNATIONAL HUMAN RIGHTS: PROBLEMS OF LAW, POLICY AND PRACTICE, (War Crimes Genocide, *Apartheid*, Terrorism and Torture) 864 (1991); J. DONNELLY, UNIVERSAL HUMAN RIGHTS IN THEORY AND PRACTICE (1989); United Nations Centre for Human Rights Fact Sheet No. 13: INTERNATIONAL HUMANITARIAN LAW AND HUMAN RIGHTS (July, 1991).

[8] *See generally* BASSIOUNI DRAFT CODE. *See* Lillich, *supra* note 7 at 766, *Respect for Human Rights in Armed Conflict, Civil Strife and States of Emergency (Human Rights in Extremes)*.

[9] *See* Article 38, Charter of the United Nations, Statute of the International Court of Justice, signed at San Francisco, 26 June 1945, 59 Stat. 1031, T.S. No. 993, and PCIJ Statute, art. 38, para. 3 (listing the sources of international law). For an early work on the subject, *see generally* Pollock, *The Sources of International Law*, 2 COLUM. L. REV. 511 (1902).

[10] *See inter alia* the following major texts: A. HEGLER, PRINZIPEN DES INTERNATIONALEN STRAFRECHTS (1906); F. MELLI, LEHRBRUCH DES INTERNATIONALEN STRAFRECHTS UND STRAFPROCESSRECHTS (1910); H. DONNEDIEU DE VABRES, INTRODUCTION A L'ETUDE DU DROIT PÉNAL INTERNATIONAL (1922); V.V. PELLA, LA CODIFICATION DU DROIT PÉNAL INTERNATIONAL (1922); M.TRAVERS, LE DROIT PÉNAL INTERNATIONAL ET SA MISE EN EOUVRE EN TEMPS DE PAIX ET EN TEMPS DE GUERRE (5 VOLS. 1920-1922); H. DONNEDIEU DE VABRES, LES PRINCIPLES MODERNES DU DROIT PÉNAL INTERNATIONAL (1928); N. LEVI, DIRITTO PENALE INTERNAZIONALE (1944); H.H. JESCHECK, DIE VORANTWORTLICHKEIT DER STAATSORGANE NACH VOLKERSTRAFRECHT (1952); S. GLASER, INTRODUCTION A L'ETUDE DU DROIT INTERNATIONAL PÉNAL (1954); A. QUINTANO-RIPOLES, TRATADO DE DERECHO PENAL INTERNACIONAL Y INTERNACIONAL PENAL (2 vols. 1955-1957); S. GLASER, LES INFRACTIONS INTERNATIONALES (1957); INTERNATIONAL CRIMINAL LAW (G.O.W. Mueller & E.M. Wise eds. 1965); O. TRIFFTERER, DOGMATISCHE UNTERSUCHUGEN ZUR ENTWICKLUNG DES MATERIELLEN VOLKERSTRAFRECHTS SEIT NURNBERG (1966); S. PLAWSKI, ETUDE DES PRINCIPES FONDAMENTEAUX DU DROIT INTERNATIONAL PENAL (1972); 1 BASSIOUNI AND NANDA TREATISE; LA BELGIQUE ET LE DROIT INTERNATIONAL PÉNAL (B. DeSchutter ed. 1975); S. GLASER, LE DROIT PENAL INTERNATIONAL CONVENTIONEL (2 vols. 1977-79); G. FIERRO, LA LEY PENAL Y EL DERECHO INTERNACIONAL (1977-79); C. LOMBOIS, DROIT PÉNAL INTERNATIONAL (2D ED. 1979); H. EBEID, AL-GARIMA AL-DAWLIA (THE INTERNATIONAL CRIME) (1979); D. OEHLER, INTERNATIONALES STRAFRECHT (2d ed. 1983); BASSIOUNI DIGEST (Vols. 1 and 2); BASSIOUNI DRAFT CODE; F. MALEKIAN, INTERNATIONAL CRIMINAL LAW (2 Vols. 1991). *See also inter alia* the following major articles: Radin, *International Crimes*, 32 IOWA L. REV. 33 (1946); Wise, *Prolegomenan to the Principles of International Criminal Law*, 16 N.Y. L. F. 562 (1970); Schwarzenberger, *The Problem of*

indispensable to the development of positive international criminal law, which frequently occurred in spite of the politically oriented authoritative processes of international law-making.[11]

One of the categories of these international crimes which has suffered from the difficulties of the international legal process is known as "crimes against humanity," which originated as an extension of war crimes and by analogy thereto. Acts, such as those committed during World War II, were so offensive to basic principles of humanity that they could not go unpunished merely because of the absence of their inclusion in the narrow scope of war crimes and the exclusive application of the latter to the context of international armed conflicts and to certain categories of protected persons.[12] Thus, the Charter's extension of certain prohibited conduct in positive international criminal law by analogy to war crimes was a logical, predictable and necessary step. No one, in fact, ever questioned the merits of prohibiting such conduct as defined by the Charter. But whether the newly formulated crime could be made to

---

an *International Criminal Law*, 3 CURRENT LEGAL PROB. 263 (1950); Dinstein, *International Criminal Crimes*, 5 ISRAEL Y.B. H. R. 55 (1975); Wright, *The Scope of International Criminal Law: A Conceptual Framework*, 15 VA. J. INT'L L. 562 (1975); Wise, *War Crimes and Criminal Law*, in STUDIES IN COMPARATIVE LAW 35 (E. Wise and G.O.W. Mueller eds. 1975); Green, *An International Criminal Code Now?*, 3 DALHOUSIE L.J. 560 (1976); Mueller, *International Criminal Law: Civitas Maxima*, 15 CASE W. RES. J. INT'L L. 1 (1983); Friedlander, *The Foundations of International Criminal Law: A Present Day Inquiry*, 15 CASE W. RES. J. INT'L L. 13 (1983); Dinstein, *International Criminal Law*, 20 ISRAEL L. REV. 206 (1985); Schindler, *Crimes Against the Law of Nations*, 8 ENCYCLOPEDIA OF PUB. INT'L L. 109 (1985); Wise, *Terrorism and the Problems of an International Criminal Law*, 19 CONN. L. REV. 799 (1987); Green, *International Criminal Law and the Protection of Human Rights* in CONTEMPORARY PROBLEMS OF INTERNATIONAL LAW: ESSAYS IN HONOR OF GEORG SCHWARZENBERGER 116 (B. Cheng and E. Brown eds. 1988); Clark, *Offenses of International Concern: Multilateral State Treaty Practice in the Forty Years Since Nuremberg*, 57 NORDIC J. INT'L L. 49 (1988); Wise, *International Crimes and Domestic Criminal Law*, 38 DEPAUL L. REV. 923 (1989). *Also* 52 RIDP, Nos. 3-4 (1981), symposium issue on a Draft International Criminal Code; Bouzat, *Introduction* 331; Jescheck, *Development, Present State and Future Prospects of International Law* 377; Decker, *A Critique of the Draft International Criminal Code* 373; Ottenhof, *Considerations sur la Forme le Style, et la Methode d'Elaboration du Project de Code Penal International*, 385; Friedlander, *Some Observations Relating to the Draft International Criminal Code Project* 393; Oehler, *Perspectives on the Contents of the Special Part of the Draft International Criminal Code* 407; Nanda, *International Crimes under the Draft Criminal Code* at 627. *See also* the Draft Code of Offenses and since 1987 the Draft Code of Crimes which have been in the process of revision since 1977; *Symposium Issue on International Criminal Law*, 15 NOVA L. REV. 343 *et seq.* (1991); Annual Reports of the ILC on the Work of its Thirty-Second Session, (1984), up to its Forty Third Session (1991).

[11] *See generally* M. MCDOUGAL & F. FELICIANO, LAW AND MINIMUM WORLD PUBLIC ORDER (1960).

[12] *See* G. Draper, *supra* note 4.

apply after the fact and only to the vanquished, as discussed in Chapter 3, were among the most persistent questions and they have yet to be satisfactorily answered.

The historical legal origins of "crimes against humanity" are evidenced in the evolutionary development of the international regulation of armed conflicts. Thus, the drafters of the Charter found it necessary to establish a link between war and "crimes against humanity" in order to meet the minimum requirements of the "principles of legality."[13] Hence, the evolution of humanitarian law and the international regulation of armed conflicts is the indispensable philosophical and normative framework within which to view "crimes against humanity," as articulated in the Nuremberg and Tokyo Charters and CCL 10, and as applied by the IMT at Nuremberg and the IMTFE at Tokyo and in the Subsequent Proceedings under CCL 10; their separate and collective weaknesses notwithstanding.

An historical review of the humanization and regulation of armed conflicts clearly reveals that various civilizations, dating back several thousand years, have either specifically prohibited or at least condemned unnecessary use of force and violence against civilians. This historical process, spanning several millennia, reveals the convergence of basic human values in diverse civilizations frequently without any link between them. At first, certain principles emerged restricting what a belligerent can do during the conduct of war. Thereafter, through consensus and custom, specific norms were agreed upon which proscribed certain types of conduct. As Grotius stated:

[Consider] both those who wage war and on what grounds war may be waged. It follows that we should determine what is permissible in war, also to what extent, and in what ways, it is permissible. What is permissible in war is viewed either absolutely or in relation to a previous premise. It is viewed absolutely, first from the standpoint of the law of nature, and then from that of the law of nations.[14]

In ancient Greece, there was an awareness that certain acts were contrary "to traditional usages and principles spontaneously enforced by human conscience."[15]

---

[13]   See Chapter 3.

[14]   H. GROTIUS, DE JURE BELLI AC PACIS (Libri Tres) (1625), *reported in* 3 CLASSICS OF INTERNATIONAL LAW 599 (F.W. Kelsey trans. 1925).

[15]   1 C. PHILLIPSON, THE INTERNATIONAL LAW AND CUSTOM OF ANCIENT GREECE AND ROME 59 (1911) wherein the author states that many rulers of ancient Greece were conscious of the need to observe "traditional usages and principles spontaneously enforced by human conscience" *id.* at 50.

Herodotus recounts that as early as the fifth century B.C. certain conduct was prohibited:

[T]he slaughter of the Persian envoys by the Athenians and Spartans was confessedly a transgression of the [laws of men], as a law of the human race generally, and not merely as a law applicable exclusively to the barbarians. And Xerxes recognized and submitted to such general law, when he answered on suggestions being made to him that he should resort to similar retaliation, that he would not be like Lacedaemonians, for they had violated the law of all nations, by murdering his heralds, and that he would not do the very thing which he blamed in them.[16]

Similarly, but relating to war, the Chinese scholar Sun Tzu asserted in the same century, though continents apart, that it is important to "treat the captives well, and care for them."[17]

In Western Civilization, the writings of Aristotle, Cicero, St. Augustine and St. Thomas Aquinas have set forth the philosophical premises for the conditions of legitimacy of war, so as to distinguish between the just and the unjust war.[18] But, Western Civilization also developed principles and norms limiting the means and consequences of the conduct of war. St. Thomas Aquinas, in his *Summa Theologica* frequently quoting St. Augustine, refers to these basic laws of humanity in the treatment of civilian non-combatants, the sick, wounded and prisoners of war as follows: "these rules belong to the *jus gentium* which are deduced from natural law as conclusion principles."[19] He called it "positive human law," not because it was codified, but because citizens of civilized nations agreed to it.[20] This positive natural

---

[16]   *Id.* PHILLIPSON at 60, *citing* HERODOTUS, HISTORY.

[17]   SUN TZU, THE ART OF WAR 76 (S.B. Griffith trans. 1971).

[18]   The distillation of these writings is found in H. GROTIUS, *supra* note 14, which is considered to be one of the foundations of Western international law; *see also* S. PUFFENDORF, DE JURE NATURAE ET GENTIUM LIBRI Octo 8, III (1672), in 2 CLASSICS OF INTERNATIONAL LAW, (W.A. Oldfather trans. 1934); E. DE VATTEL, LE DROIT DES GENS (1758), in 2 CLASSICS OF INTERNATIONAL LAW, (C. Fenwick trans. 1916). *See also e.g.* A. NUSSBAUM, A CONCISE HISTORY OF THE LAW OF NATIONS (1954); Von Elbe, *The Evolution of the Concept of 'Just War' in International Law*, 33 AJIL 665 (1939).

[19]   2 ac, Q. 95 art. 4. For an English translation of ST. THOMAS AQUINAS', SUMMA THEOLOGICA, *see* the first complete American edition, published by Benziger Bros. Inc. (1947).

[20]   *Supra* note 19, Conclusion.

154

law which Plato and Aristotle posited long before St. Thomas was also the supreme law of the Romans who divided the *jus positivum* into *jus gentium* and *jus civile*. In this connection, H.M. Keen, a scholar on the law of war in the Middle Ages, stated:

> [T]he "Roman people" meant not only the man of the empire but those of the independent *regna* and *civitates* also, and so a law which was common to it, was genuinely a "law of nations." To the *jus genitum* in its broader sense of the natural law of all men, these two laws added for those within Christendom a further series of positive rules, for "beyond doubt the canon and civil laws add something further in the matter of war over and above the dictates of reason." Once again there was no question of any conflict of laws, for the equity of the canon and civil laws was just the same as that of the *jus gentium*. They too derived their ultimate authority from natural reason. The canon law was derived from natural law because it was derived from Holy Writ, and "The divine laws operate in nature." The civil law was founded in natural law, because it was the accepted definition of civil laws that they were derived "from the law of nature, by means of specific rulings on particulars." For the Roman people these two laws expanded the *jus naturale* and the *jus gentium* with a further series of specific rules, binding on all its members, but on them only. In dealings with *extranei*, as Tartars, Greeks and Saracens, only the rules of the *jus gentium* proper were binding.[21]

These views are echoed in the eighteenth century by the international law scholar, G.F. Martens who stated:

> ... but our right to wound and kill being founded on self-defence, or on the resistance opposed to us, we can, with justice wound or take the life of none except those who take an active part in the war. So that, children, old men, women, and in general all of those who cannot carry arms, or who ought not to do it, are safe under the protection of the law of nations, unless they have exercised violence against the enemy.[22]

---

[21]   M.H. KEEN, THE LAWS OF WAR IN THE LATE MIDDLE AGES 14-15 (1965) wherein he relies upon the medieval work of HONORÉ BONET, TREE OF BATTLES, *id.* at 21; and *see* A. FITZGERALD, PEACE AND WAR IN ANTIQUITY (1931). For an earlier seminal work *see* PHILIPPE CONTAMINE, WAR IN THE MIDDLE AGES (M. Jones trans. 1984). Interestingly the rules of war until well into the 1800's were with respect to Christians applicable only to wars in Christendom.

[22]   G.F. MARTENS, SUMMARY OF THE LAW OF NATIONS 282 (1788) (W. Cobbett trans. 1795).

The values embodied in these moral and legal positions are not only found in Western civilization. They also existed in other civilizations such as the Chinese,[23] Hindu,[24] Egyptian and Assyrian-Babylonian, which likewise devised principles of legitimacy for resorting to war and particular rules for its conduct.[25]

The Islamic civilization, based on the *Qu'ràn*, set forth specific rules as to the legitimacy of war and its conduct.[26] In 634 A.D., Caliph Abu Bakr charged the Muslim Arab army invading Syria:

> Do not commit treachery, nor depart from the right path. You must not mutilate, neither kill a child or aged man or woman. Do not destroy a palm tree, nor burn it with fire and do not cut any fruitful tree. You must not slay any of the flock or the herds or the camels, save for your subsistence. You are likely to pass by people who have devoted their lives to monastic services; leave them to that which they have devoted their lives.[27]

---

[23] See SUN-TZU, *supra* note 17, at 76.

[24] THE BOOK OF MANU: MANUSMURTI discussed in detail by Nagendra Singh in *Armed Conflicts and Humanitarian Laws of Ancient India*, ETUDES ET ESSAIS SUR LE DROIT INTERNATIONAL HUMANITAIRE ET SUR LES PRINCIPES DE LA CROIX-ROUGE EN L'HONNEUR DE JEAN PICTET (C. Swinarski ed. 1984); and COMMENTARIES: THE LAWS OF MAN (G. Bühler trans. 1967).

[25] For a description of some of the practices of war in these civilizations *see e.g.*, 1 A. AYMARD AND J. AUBOYER, L'ORIENT ET LA GRÈCE ANTIQUE 293-99 (1953); P. ROUSSEL, P. CLOCHE & R. GROUSSET, LA GRÈCE ET L'ORIENT DES GUERRES MEDIQUES À LA CONQUÊTE ROMAINE (2d. ed. 1938); and M. GRANT, ARMY OF THE CAESARS (1974).

[26] The cases and practices of Muslim conduct in war were taught by Al-Shaybani in the eighth century and were written in a Digest by el-Shahristani. The first known publication was published in HAIDERABAD in 1335-1336, translated by M. Khadduri in WAR AND PEACE IN THE LAW OF ISLAM. *See also* Algase, *Protection of Civilian Lives in Warfare: A Comparison Between Islamic Law and Modern International Law Concerning the Conduct of Hostilities*, 16 REVUE DE DROIT PÉNAL MILITAIRE ET DU DROIT DE LA GUERRE 246 (1977); Bassiouni, *Islam: Concept, Law and World Habeas Corpus*, 1 RUT.-CAM. L.J. 160 (1969); *see also e.g.*, A. MAHMASSANI, THE PRINCIPLES OF INTERNATIONAL LAW IN LIGHT OF ISLAMIC DOCTRINE (1966); M. KHADDURI, THE ISLAMIC LAW OF NATIONS (1966); S. RAMADAN, ISLAMIC LAW, ITS SCOPE AND EQUITY (1961); H. HAMIDULLAH, MUSLIM CONDUCT OF STATE (1961); Draz, *Le Droit International Public de l'Islam*, 5 REV. EGYPTIENNE DE DROIT INT'L 17 (1949); Reshid, *L'Islam et le Droit de Gens*, 56 RECEUIL DES COURS DE L'ACADEMIE DE DROIT INTERNATIONAL DE LA HAYE 4 (1937); A. ARMANAZI, L'ISLAM ET LE DROIT INTERNATIONAL (1929); Majid, *The Moslem International Law*, 28 L.Q. REV. 89 (1912).

[27] *Cited in* M. KHADDURI, WAR AND PEACE IN THE LAW OF ISLAM 102 (1955); and Solf, *Protection of Civilians Against the Effects of Hostilities Under Customary International Law and under Protocol I*, 1

156

Abu Bakr's mandate was based on the *Qu'rán* and the *Sunna*, the tradition of the Prophet Muhammad, which is a source of the *Shari'a*, the Islamic law. These Muslim principles, rules and practices also influenced the development of Western legal thought. This occurred through Islam's contacts during the Middle Ages with Western civilization particularly in Spain, Southern France and Southern Italy when these areas were under Muslim control, and also as a result of the Crusades. This influence clearly appears in the writings of certain Canonists.[28] That the three monotheistic faiths of Judaism, Christianity and Islam join in the affirmation of the same humanitarian principles is inescapable. The similarity between the admonitions of the *Qu'rán* and those of the old Testament are best expressed in the second Book of Kings:

> ... the King of Israel ... said to Eli'sha, "My Father shall I slay them?" ... He answered, "You shall not slay them. Would you slay those whom you have taken captive with your sword and bow? Set bread and water before them, that they may eat and drink and go to their master."[29]

Jews honor the Sabbath and other holy days like *Yom Kippur* and no warlike activities can be conducted on those days, as does Islam on the various days of the *Eid*. Similarly, in Medieval times, the Catholic Church specifically proscribed the conduct of war on particular days. In fact, as the Archbishop of Arles exclaimed in 1035, there was to be a "Truce of God" from "vespers on Wednesday to sunrise on Monday."[30]

AM. U.J. INT'L L. & POL'Y 117, 118 (1986). *See also* H. MCCOUBREY *supra* note 4, at 9 referring to the humanitarian practices of Abu-Bakr and Salah el-Din el Ayyubi in the fourth Crusade.

[28] *See* F. Vitoria (1483-1546), *De Indis et de Iure Belli Reflectiones*, in CLASSICS OF INTERNATIONAL LAW (J. Scott ed. 1917); F. Suarez (1548-1584), *On War*, in 2 CLASSICS OF INTERNATIONAL LAW (J. Scott ed. 1944); B. Ayala (1548-1617), *Three Books on the Law of War*, in 2 CLASSICS OF INTERNATIONAL LAW (J. Bates trans. 1912); A. Gentili (1552-1608), *De Jure Belli Libre Tres* in CLASSICS OF INTERNATIONAL LAW (J. Scott ed. 1933). For a recent account of Islamic influence on canonist writers and consequently on Hugo Grotius who relied on their works, *see* C. RHYNE, INTERNATIONAL LAW 23 (1971). Ayala, Gentili, Suarez, and Grotius all wrote that women and those unable to bear arms should always be spared, though as Ayala reported the practice was seldom followed.

[29] 2 Kings, 6:21, 22.

[30] *See* Trooboff, *Introduction* to LAW AND RESPONSIBILITY IN WARFARE 7 (P.D. Trooboff ed. 1975). *See also* L.C. GREEN, INTERNATIONAL CRIMINAL LAW AND THE PROTECTION OF HUMAN RIGHTS: CONTEMPORARY PROBLEMS OF INTERNATIONAL LAW 116-137 (B. Cheng and R. Brown eds. 1988) where the author refers to many valuable historical precedents, *id.* 116-129.

As the laws of chivalry developed during the Middle Ages in Western Europe, so did rules limiting the means and manner of conducting war.[31] Heraldic courts developed a code of chivalry that regulated a knight's conduct in battle and which Christian princes enforced in their courts.[32] The goal of all these principles, norms and rules was to protect non-combatants, innocent civilians and those who were *hors de combat* from unnecessary harm. As Keen informs us about the siege of Limoges in 1370:

Three French knights, who defended themselves gallantly, seeing at length no alternative to surrender, threw themselves on the mercy of John of Gaunt and the Earl of Cambridge. "My Lords," they cried, "we are yours: you have vanquished us. Act therefore to the law of arms." John of Gaunt acceded to their request, and they were taken prisoner on the understanding that their lives would be protected.[33]

On the march to Agincourt in 1415, Shakespeare quotes Henry V giving his army the following instructions:

. . . We give express charge that in our marches through the country there be nothing compelled from the villages, nothing taken but paid for, none of the French upbraided or abused in disdainful language; For when levity and cruelty play for a kingdom, the gentler gamester is the soonest winner.[34]

---

[31] *See* M.H. KEEN, *supra* note 21, and A. FITZGERALD, *supra* note 21. *See also* Bastid, *Le Droit de la Guerre dans les Documents Judiciares Francais du XIVe Siede*, 8 ANNUAIRE FRANCAIS DE DROIT INTERNATIONAL 181 (1962) referring to the records of the Hundred Years War (1337-1469) which reveal the existence of rules of warfare protection of non-combatants and prisoners of war, as well as the prosecution of violators of these rules; A. DALEGNANO, TRACTABUS DE BELLA, DE REPRESALIIS ET DE DUELLO (1477); H. BONET, THE TREE OF BATTLES (CA. 1387)(G. Coupland ed. 1949)(trans. of Nys 1883) and PEDRO LOPEZ D'AYALA, CRONICLES DE LOS REYES DE CASTILLA TOME I (1779-1780) describing several trials for violations of the laws of war; G.F. MARTENS, *supra* note 22; C. FENWICK, DIGEST OF INTERNATIONAL LAW 7 (1965); and H. MAINE, INTERNATIONAL LAW 138-140 (2d ed. 1894).

[32] M.H. KEEN *supra* note 21, at 7.

[33] M.H. KEEN, *supra* note 21, at 1, *citing* LES OEUVRES DE FROISSART 43 (K. de Leffenhove ed. 1869).

[34] W. SHAKESPEARE, THE LIFE OF HENRY THE FIFTH, Act III, sc. vi (1599), THE COMPLETE WORKS OF SHAKESPEARE 835 (G. Kittredge ed. 1971).

158

Referring to the battle of Agincourt (1415), when King Henry V of England felt compelled to execute his French prisoners held in his besieged base camp, Shakespeare has the King's Captain Fluellen exclaim: "Kill the poys and the luggage! 'tis expressly against the law of arms: 'tis as arrant a piece of knavery ... as can be offer'd."[35]

After the Middle Ages, additional norms and rules were developed thereby strengthening these basic principles of humanity on which they were based. This historical phase was also founded upon the emerging shared values of the world community to limit the resort to war and regulate its conduct in order to minimize its harmful human consequences. Thereafter, bilateral and multilateral treaties, particularly after the Treaty of Westphalia in 1648, sought to regulate relations among states for the prevention and conduct of war and were a tangible expression of these values and concerns.[36] Thus, with regard to the care of wounded in the field, Professor Green states:

> In 1679 a convention was signed between the Elector of Brandenburg, for the League of Augsburg, and the Count of Asfield, who commanded the French forces [providing] for a mutual respect towards both hospitals and wounded .... [A] convention [of] 1743 between Lord Stair on behalf of the Pragmatic army and the Marshall Noailles for the French during the Dettingen campaign bound both sides to treat hospitals and wounded with consideration. Noailles, when he thought that his operations might cause alarm to the inmates at the hospitals at Tachenheim, went so far as to send word that they should rest tranquil as they would not be disturbed. A fuller, and more highly developed type of agreement, was that signed at L'Ecluse in 1759 by the Marshal de Brail, who commanded the French, and Major General Conway the British general officer commanding. The hospital staff, chaplains, doctors, surgeons and apothecaries were not ... to be taken prisoners; and, if they should happen to be apprehended within the lines of the enemy, they were to be sent back immediately. The wounded of the enemy who should fall into the hands of their opponents were to be cared for, and their food and medicine should in due course be paid for. They were not to be made prisoner and might stay in hospital

---

[35] *Id.* at Act IV, sc. vii. *See* Meron, *Shakespeare's Henry the Fifth and the Law of War*, 86 AJIL 1 (1992).

[36] *See* MAJOR PEACE TREATIES OF MODERN HISTORY 1698-1967 (F. Israel and E. Chile eds. with an introduction by A. Toynbee, 1967). *See e.g.*, Gross, *The Peace of Westphalia*, 1648-1948, 42 AJIL 20 (1948).

safely under guard. Surgeons and servants might be sent to them under the general's passports. Finally, on their discharge, they were themselves to travel under the same authority and were to travel by the shortest route.[37]

During the Age of Enlightenment, that development continued, but the emphasis was on the pragmatism of regulating the conduct of war. Thus, Jean-Jacques Rousseau argued in his seminal work LE CONTRAT SOCIAL that:

> Since the aim of war is to subdue a hostile State, a combatant has the right to kill the defenders of that state while they are armed; but as soon as they lay down their arms and surrender, they cease to be either enemies or instruments of the enemy; they become simply men once more, and no one has any longer the right to take their lives. It is sometimes possible to destroy a state without killing their lives. It is sometimes possible to destroy a state without killing a single one of its members, and war gives no right to inflict any more destruction than is necessary for victory. These principles were not invented by Grotius, nor are they founded on the authority of the poets; they are derived from the nature of things; they are based on reason.[38]

In many respects, the evolution of humanitarianism in armed conflicts came to fruition in the middle of the nineteenth century, more specifically after the battle of Solferino in June of 1859 where France defeated Austria-Hungary.[39] Henry Dunant, a Swiss businessman who happened to be in the vicinity of the battlefield, was deeply moved by the sight of the many wounded men who were left to suffer and die for lack of medical attention. Dunant organized medical relief in the field. Thereafter, he published a booklet entitled SOUVENIRS DE SOLFERINO (1862) in which he proposed the establishment of voluntary relief agencies to aid the battlefield wounded and for an

---

[37] *See* L.C. GREEN, ESSAYS ON THE MODERN LAW OF WAR 86 (1985), *citing* G.G. BUTLER AND MACCOBY, THE DEVELOPMENT OF INTERNATIONAL LAW 149-50 (1928). J. PICTET, *supra* at note 4 recounts that prior to the battle of Fontenoy in 1747, Louis XV of France declared in advance of the battle that the wounded be treated like his own men because as wounded they were no longer enemies. They were *hors de combat.*

[38] J.J. ROUSSEAU, THE SOCIAL CONTRACT AND DISCOURSES 171 (G. Cole trans. 1973). Rousseau also argued that "War then is not a relation between men, but between states, in war individuals are enemies wholly by chance, not as men, not even as citizens, but only as soldiers, not as members of their country, but also as its defenders." *Id.*

[39] *See* H. MCCOUBREY, INTERNATIONAL HUMANITARIAN LAW 6, 10-11 (1990).

160

international agreement on the humane treatment of the sick and injured of war.[40] Dunant's proposals became a reality on August 22, 1864 with the Geneva Convention for the Amelioration of the Condition of the Wounded of Armies in the Field.

Between 1854 and 1977, 59 international instruments on the regulation of armed conflicts were developed.[41] Their purposes are to humanize armed conflicts by prohibiting the use of certain weapons which inflict unnecessary harm and to protect non-combatants, prisoners, the sick, wounded, shipwrecked, and also to protect cultural monuments and property, and more recently the 1977 Protocol I to the Geneva Conventions added the protection of the environment.

The notion of protecting combatants from unnecessary pain and suffering was not, however, a product of modern international law. It derived from a doctrine developed by the Second Lateran Council (1139) which prohibited the use of the cross-bow and the harquebus. Today, this doctrine is the philosophical foundation for the prohibition of chemical and bacteriological weapons, and in the opinion of this writer, it also extends to nuclear weapons. The modern international instruments inspired by such premises include: the Declaration of Paris of 1856;[42] the Geneva (Red Cross) Convention of 1864;[43] the St. Petersburg Declaration of 1868;[44] the Declaration of

---

[40]   Henry Dunant's proposals stirred great interest and received widespread attention. Following the publication of Dunant's booklet, Gustave Moynier, President of the Geneva Public Welfare Society, organized a committee of five (all Swiss, including Dunant) to examine the practical possibilities for implementing the proposals -- that committee was the forerunner of the International Committee of the Red Cross.

[41]   *See* 1 BASSIOUNI DIGEST 143. There also exist 34 other international instruments containing relevant provisions from 1868 to 1981, which are classified under other categories of crimes. *Id. See also*, BIBLIOGRAPHY OF INTERNATIONAL HUMANITARIAN LAW APPLICABLE IN ARMED CONFLICTS (2nd Ed. Revised & Updated, International Committee of the Red Cross and Henry Dunant Institute, Geneva, 1987); Sanduz, *Penal Aspects of International Humanitarian Law*, 1 BASSIOUNI ICL 209; Levie, *Criminality in the Law of War*, 1 BASSIOUNI ICL 233.

[42]   Declaration Respecting Maritime Law, Paris, 16 April 1856, 15 Martens 791; 115 Parry's 1; *reprinted in* 1 AJIL 89 (1907) (Supp.).

[43]   Geneva Convention for the Amelioration of the Condition of the Wounded in Armies in the Field, Geneva, 22 August 1864, 18 Martens 440; 22 Stat. 940; T.S. No. 377, 55 Brit. & For. St. Papers 43; *reprinted in* 1 AJIL 90 (1907) (Supp.).

[44]   Declaration Renouncing the Use, in Time of War, of Explosive Projectiles Under 400 Grammes Weight (St. Petersburg Declaration), signed at St. Petersburg, 11 December 1868, 18 Martens 474; 138 Parry's 297; *reprinted in* 1 AJIL 95 (1907) (Supp.).

CRIMES AGAINST HUMANITY

Brussels of 1874;[45] the Hague Conventions of 1899[46] and 1907[47] (including the

---

[45]   Project of an International Declaration Concerning the Laws and Customs of War (Declaration of Brussels) [Brussels Conference on the Laws and Customs of War, No. 18], adopted at Brussels, 27 August 1874, 4 Martens (2d) 219 and 226, 148 Parry's 133, *reprinted in* 1 AJIL 96 (1907) (Supp.).

[46]   Convention for the Peaceful Adjustment of International Disputes (First Hague, I), The Hague, 29 July 1899, 26 Martens (2d) 920, 32 Stat. 1779, T.S. No. 392, *reprinted in* 1 AJIL 107 (1907); 1899 Hague Convention; Convention for the Adaptation to Maritime Warfare of the Principles of the Geneva Convention of 22 August 1864 (First Hague, III), signed at The Hague, 29 July 1899, 26 Martens (2d) 979, 32 Stat. 1827, T.S. No. 396, *reprinted in* 1 AJIL 159 (1907); Declaration Concerning the Prohibition, for the Term of Five Years, of the Launching of Projectiles and Explosives from Balloons or Other New Methods of a Similar Nature (First Hague, IV, 1), signed at The Hague, 29 July 1899, 26 Martens (2d) 994, 32 Stat. 1839, T.S. No. 393, *reprinted in* 1 AJIL 153 (1907); Declaration Concerning the Prohibition of the Use of Projectiles Diffusing Asphyxiating Gases (First Hague, IV, 2), signed at The Hague, 29 July 1899, 26 Martens (2d) 998, 187 Parry's 453, *reprinted in* 1 AJIL 157 (1907); Declaration Concerning the Prohibition of the Use of Expanding Bullets (First Hague, IV, 3), signed at The Hague, 29 July 1899, 26 Martens (2d) 1002, 187 Parry's 459, *reprinted in* 1 AJIL 155 (1907) (Supp.).

[47]   Convention for the Pacific Settlement of International Disputes (Second Hague, I), signed at The Hague, 18 October 1907, 3 Martens (3d) 360, 36 Stat. 2199, T.S. No. 536, *reprinted in* 2 AJIL 43 (1908); Convention Respecting the Limitation of the Employment of Force for the Recovery of Contract Debts (Second Hague, II), signed at The Hague, 18 October 1907, 3 Martens, (3d) 414, 36 Stat. 2259, T.S. No. 537, *reprinted in* 2 AJIL 81 (1908); Convention Relative to the Opening of Hostilities (Second Hague, III), signed at The Hague, 18 October 1907, 3 Martens (3d) 437, 36 Stat. 2259, T.S. No. 538, *reprinted in* 2 AJIL 85 (1908); Convention Respecting the Rights and Duties of Neutral Powers and Persons in Case of War on Land (Second Hague, V) signed at The Hague, 18 October 1907, 3 Martens (3d) 504, 36 Stat. 2310, T.S. No. 540, *reprinted in* 2 AJIL 117 (1908); Convention Relative to the Status of Enemy Merchant Ships at the Outbreak of Hostilities (Second Hague, VI), signed at The Hague, 18 October 1907, 3 Martens (3d) 533, *reprinted in* 2 AJIL 127 (1908); Convention Relative to the Conversion of Merchant Ships into Warships (Second Hague, VII), signed at The Hague, 18 October 1907, 3 Martens (3d) 557, *reprinted in* 2 AJIL 133 (1908); Convention Relative to the Laying of Automatic Submarine Contact Mines (Second Hague, VIII), signed at The Hague, 18 October 1907, 3 Martens (3d) 580, 36 Stat. 2332, T.S. No. 541, *reprinted in* 2 AJIL 138 (1908); Convention Concerning Bombardment by Naval Forces in Time of War (Second Hague, IX), signed at The Hague, 18 October 1907, 3 Martens (3d) 604, 36 Stat. 2351, T.S. No. 542, *reprinted in* 2 AJIL 146 (1908); Convention for the Adaptation of the Principles of the Geneva Convention to Maritime Warfare (Second Hague, X), signed at The Hague, 18 October 1907, 3 Martens (3d) 630, 36 Stat. 2371, T.S. No. 543, *reprinted in* 2 AJIL 153 (1908); Convention Relative to Certain Restrictions with Regard to the Exercise of the Right of Capture in Naval War (Second Hague, XI), signed at The Hague, 18 October 1907, 3 Martens (3d) 663, 36 Stat. 2396, T.S. No. 544, *reprinted in* 2 AJIL 167 (1908); Convention Relative to the Establishment of an International Prize Court (Second Hague, XII), signed at The Hague, 18 October 1907, 3 Martens (3d) 688, *reprinted in* 2 AJIL 174 (1908); Convention Concerning the Rights and Duties of Neutral Powers in Naval War (Second Hague, XIII), signed at The Hague, 18 October 1907, 3 Martens (3d) 713, 36 Stat. 2415, T.S. No. 545, *reprinted in* 2 AJIL 202 (1908); Declaration Relative to Prohibiting the

162

Annex on the Laws and Customs of Land Warfare); the 1925 Protocol for the Prohibition of the Use in War of Asphyxiating, Poisonous or other Gases and Bacteriological Methods of Warfare;[48] the Geneva Convention of 1929;[49] the Four Geneva Conventions of 1949;[50] and the two 1977 Additional Protocols to the 1949 Geneva Conventions.[51] This great collection of international instruments embodies principles, norms and rules developed over centuries of tragic human experience.

The evolution of international regulations on armed conflicts was also parallelled in national laws and regulations.[52] Among these national regulations are those which

---

Discharge of Projectiles and Explosives from Balloons (Second Hague, XIV), signed at The Hague, 18 October 1907, 3 Martens (3d) 745, 36 Stat. 2439, T.S. No. 546, *reprinted in* 2 AJIL 216 (1908).

[48] 1925 Protocol for the Prohibition of the Use in War of Asphyxiating, Poisonous, or other Gases and Bacteriological Methods of Warfare, signed at Geneva, 17 June 1925, 94 L.N.T.S. 65, 26 U.S.T. 571, T.I.A.S. No. 8061, *reprinted in* 25 AJIL 94 (1931).

[49] Geneva Convention for the Amelioration of the Condition of the Wounded and Sick of Armies in the Field, (Red Cross Convention) 27 July 1929. For relevant provisions, *see* Document Section.

[50] For relevant provisions of the 1949 Geneva Conventions, *see* Document Section. *See also* J. PICTET, COMMENTARIES ON THE FOURTH GENEVA CONVENTION (1956).

[51] For relevant provisions of the 1977 Geneva Protocols, *see* Document Section. *See also* COMMENTARY ON THE ADDITIONAL PROTOCOLS 583-1124 (eds. Y. Sandoz, C. Swinarski, B. Zimmermann 1987); and NEW RULES FOR VICTIMS OF ARMED CONFLICTS 273-489 (M. Bothe, K.J. Partsch, W.A. Solf eds. 1982). *See also* Solf, *Protection of Civilians Against the Effects of Hostilities Under Customary International Law and Under Protocol I*, 1 AM. U. J. INT'L L. & POL'Y 117 (1986); Solf & Cummings, *A Survey of Penal Sanctions Under Protocol I to the Geneva Conventions of August 12, 1949*, 9 CASE W. RES. J. INT'L L. 205 (1977).

[52] For the national military regulations *see* Lieber Code. Promulgated as: *Instruction for the Government of the United States in the Field by Order of the Secretary of War*, in Washington D.C., 24 April 1863 and approved by President Lincoln. For other similar rules of the United States of America, *see* RULES OF LAND WARFARE, War Dept. Doc. No. 467, Office of the Chief of Staff, approved 25 April 1914 (G.P.O. 1917); and Army Field Manual 27-10, RULES OF LAND WARFARE (1956). *See also* G. DAVIS, A TREATISE ON THE MILITARY LAW OF THE UNITED STATES (3rd rev. ed. 1918) (which traces the history of the first Articles of War of 1775); and W. DeHART, OBSERVATIONS ON MILITARY LAW, AND THE CONSTITUTION, AND PRACTICE OF COURTS MARTIAL (1846). *See also* W. WINTHROP, MILITARY LAW AND PRECEDENTS (1896). The BRITISH MANUAL OF MILITARY LAW (1929 revised in 1940); GERMAN ARMY REGULATIONS (1902, revised in 1911, revised in 1935) to which the 1907 Hague Convention was appended as Annex II, quoted in Lauterpacht, *The Law of Nations and the Punishment of War Crimes*, 21 BRIT. Y.B. INT'L L. 58 (1944); and the 1935 version; and the OXFORD MANUAL ON THE LAWS AND CUSTOMS OF WAR ON LAND (Institute of International Law 1880). *See also, Regolamento di Servizio in Guera*, in 3 LEGGI E DECRETI DEL REGNO D'ITALIA, 3184 (1896). For commentaries on these laws and regulations by distinguished publicists, *see* BLUNTSCHLI, DROIT INTERNATIONAL § 531-32 (5th ed. 1895); 4 C. CALVO, LE DROIT

Gustavus Adolphus of Sweden promulgated in 1621 in the "Articles of Military Laws to be Observed in the Wars." They provided in the general article that "no Colonel or Captain shall command his soldiers to do any unlawful thing; which who so does, shall be punished according to the discretion of the Judge."[53] In the United States, the first Articles of War, promulgated in 1775, contained explicit provision for the punishment of officers who failed to keep "good order" among the troops, which included a number of prescriptions for the protection of civilians, prisoners of war, and the sick and injured in the field. This provision was retained and strengthened in the Articles of War of 1806[54] and served as the basis for prosecutions for conduct against the law of nations.[55] The most noteworthy national regulations are the United States Lieber Code of 1863,[56] the 1880 Oxford Manual,[57] Great-Britain's war office Manual of Military Law of 1929,[58] and the German General Staff *Kriegsbrauch im Landkriege* (Regulations of War) of 1902.[59] These are only some examples of national military regulations protecting, *inter alia*, civilian populations. Consequently, there can be no question that national laws also prohibited the same conduct which was prohibited under international law. Presently, over 155 countries have included in their military

---

INTERNATIONAL THEORIQUE ET PRATIQUE § 2034-35 (5th ed. 1896); 7 MOORE, DIGEST OF INTERNATIONAL LAW, § 1109 (1906); 2 HYDE, INTERNATIONAL LAW § 653-54 (1922); 2 L. OPPENHEIM, INTERNATIONAL LAW § 107 (6th ed. 1940).

[53]   G. ADOLPHUS, ARTICLES OF MILITARY LAWS TO BE OBSERVED IN THE WARS (1621), cited in Gross, *The Punishment of War Criminals*, 11 NETH. INT'L L. REV. 356 (1955). Adolphus' rules served as a source for the British Articles of War, which, in turn, served as the source for the first American Articles of War (1775). *See* Sherman, *The Civilization of Military Law*, 22 ME. L. REV. 3 (1970).

[54]   Articles of War, Article IX (1775); re-enacted with modifications, Articles of War, Article IX (1776); Articles of War, Article 32 (1806). This provision survives in weakened form in the *Uniform Code of Military Justice*, art. 138, 10 U.S.C. para. 1038. *See also* DAVIS, DEHART and WINTHROP *supra* note 52.

[55]   *Henfield's Case*, 11 F. Cas. 1099 (Case No. 6,360) (C.C. Pa. 1793) (violation of principles of neutrality by civilian).

[56]   *See supra* note 52 and excerpts in Document Section D. 1.

[57]   *See* OXFORD MANUAL, *supra* note 52.

[58]   *See* BRITISH MANUAL OF MILITARY LAW, *supra* note 52. The first manual was developed under the title of LAWES AND ORDINANCES OF WARRE, *see* CLADE, I MILITARY FORCES OF THE CROWN, App. VI (1869), *quoted* by Green in *The Law of Armed Conflict and the Enforcement of International Criminal Law*, *supra* note 1, at 7.

[59]   *See* GERMAN ARMY REGULATIONS, *supra* note 52. These regulations were amended in 1935 but they preserved the same rules referred to in note 52 and accompanying text.

laws or military regulations provisions on the protection and treatment of civilians during armed conflicts, prisoners of war, the sick, injured and the shipwrecked and other limitations. These national laws and regulations are largely the result of the Geneva Conventions of 12 August, 1949,[60] which require the introduction of such norms in the national laws of the contracting parties, and which also require the dissemination of these rules to military personnel in order to insure compliance and to avoid claims of ignorance of the law.

The cumulative effect of these historical experiences and precedents demonstrates the universality of humanitarian principles governing the conduct of war. Indeed, as illustratively shown above, these humanitarian principles, norms and rules regulating armed conflict developed over several millennia, spanning many civilizations continents apart, and covering a wide range of conduct. Each succeeding generation added another layer of principles, norms and rules which reinforced the preceding ones. Their culmination came to be described in the Preamble of the 1907 Hague Convention as the basic "laws of humanity."

This evolution can be seen in its spatial and temporal dimensions as part and parcel of the processes of humankind's history.[61] It is this cumulative historical baggage which constitutes the foundation upon which "crimes against humanity" are premised.

Crimes Against Humanity as an Outgrowth of War Crimes

The seeds of the Charter's "crimes against humanity" provision were planted in the First Hague Convention of 1899 on the Laws and Customs of War and the Fourth Hague Convention of 1907, and in their annexed Regulations Respecting the Laws and Customs of War on Land. The Preamble of the two conventions used the term "laws

---

[60] *See* 1949 Geneva Conventions and excerpts in Document Section D. 9-12.

[61] Arnold Toynbee refers to some 34 civilizations between 3500 B.C. and our century whose evolution he chronicles in his 12 volumes entitled A STUDY OF HISTORY (1939-1962); *See also* the abridged one volume version: A. TOYNBEE, A STUDY OF HISTORY 72 (1972). More specifically in a case involving the law of war *Ex Parte Quirin*, 317 U.S. (1942) the United States Supreme Court held: "The Law of war, like civil law, has a great *lex non scripta*, its own common law. This common law of war is a centuries old body of largely unwritten rules and principles of international law which governs the behavior of both soldiers and civilians during time of war. W. WINTHROP, MILITARY LAW AND PRECEDENTS (1920), 17, 41, 42, 773. *Id.* at 13-14.

of humanity" and they based their normative prescriptions on these unarticulated values.[62]

Prior to the Charter, the words used in the Preamble of the two Hague Conventions are the only references in conventional international law which approach the term "crimes against humanity."[63] Though the Hague Conventions concerned "war crimes" in a narrow and specific sense, they derived from the larger meaning of violations of "the laws of humanity."[64] Thus, these words were intended to provide an overarching concept to protect against unspecified violations whose identification in positive international law was left to future normative development.

As the predecessor to the 1907 Hague Convention, the 1899 Hague Convention was the first comprehensive international instrument to develop rules derived from the customary practices of states in time of war.[65] At the time, it went even further when it stated that in cases not covered by specific regulations:

> populations and belligerents remain under the protection and empire of the principles of international law, as they result from the usages established between civilized nations, from the laws of humanity, and the requirements of the public conscience.[66]

---

[62]   *See* 1899 Hague Convention and 1907 Hague Convention. For relevant excerpts, *see* Document Section D. 3-6.

[63]   The 1907 Hague Convention provides that:

the inhabitants and the belligerents shall remain under the protection and the rule of principles of the laws of nations, as they result from the usages established among civilized peoples, from the laws of humanity, and the dictates of the public conscience.

1907 Hague Convention, preamble (emphasis added); *reprinted in* 2 AJIL 90, 92 (1908). The preamble of the 1899 Hague Convention employs similar phrasing. *See infra* note 66 and accompanying text.

[64]   *See* Schwelb, *Crimes Against Humanity*, 23 BRIT. Y.B. INT'L L. 178, 180 (1946). Professor Schwelb's article is probably the most reliable scholarly article on the interpretation of Article 6(c).

[65]   The 1874 Declaration of Brussels also developed rules derived from the customary laws of war, but it never entered into force. Project of an International Declaration Concerning the Laws and Customs of War (Declaration of Brussels), Brussels Conference on the Laws and Customs of War, 27 August 1874; *see supra* note 45.

[66]   1899 Hague Convention, para. 9 of the Preamble.

The basis for such protection of the principles of international law was then reinforced in the Preamble to the 1907 Hague Convention which states:

It has not been found possible at present to concert regulations covering all the circumstances which arise in practice.

On the other hand, the High Contracting Parties clearly do not intend that unforeseen cases should, in the absence of a written undertaking, be left to the arbitrary judgment of military commanders.

Until a more complete code of the laws of war has been issued, the High Contracting Parties deem it expedient to declare that, in cases not included in the Regulations adopted by them, the inhabitants and the belligerents remain under the protection and the rule of the principles of the law of nations, as they result from the usages established among civilized peoples, from the laws of humanity, and the dictates of the public conscience.[67]

This language embodies the well-known Martens clause[68] which permits the resort to "general principles" as a means of interpreting provisions in international instruments and to fill gaps in conventional textual language.[69]

The same formulation of the Hague Conventions has been used in the latest international instrument on the humanitarian law of armed conflicts, Protocol I of the 1977 Protocols Additional to the Geneva Conventions of August 12, 1949 whose Article 1 states:

In cases not covered by this Protocol or by other international agreements, civilians and combatants remain under the protection and authority of the principles of

---

[67]   1907 Hague Convention, paras. 6-8 of the Preamble.

[68]   The Martens Clause is named after Fyodor Martens, the Russian diplomat and jurist who drafted it. A similar formula appears in each of the 1949 Geneva Conventions and in the 1977 Protocols. *See* First Geneva Convention of 1949 at art. 63(4); Second Geneva Convention of 1949 Art. 62(4); Third Geneva Convention of 1949 at Art. 142(4); Fourth Geneva Convention of 1949 at Art. 158(4); Protocol I at Art. 1(2); Protocol II at preamble.

[69]   *See* Bassiouni, *A Functional Approach to General Principles of International Law*, 11 MICH J. INT'L L. 768 (1990).

international law derived from established custom, from the principles of humanity and from the dictates of public conscience.[70]

Article 22 of the Hague Regulations in the 1899 and 1907 Conventions also provided the general norm that "the right of belligerents to adopt means of injuring the enemy is not unlimited." The continuity of that principle is evidenced in its inclusion in the 1977 Protocol I, Article 35(1) which states "in any armed conflict, the right of the parties to the conflict to choose methods or means of warfare is not unlimited."

Earlier in 1776, Thomas Paine, in his famous book COMMON SENSE, urged the new United States of America to follow this principle, stating: "The laying of a country desolate with fire and sword, declaring war against the national rights of all mankind, and extirpating the defenders from the face of the Earth is the concern of every man ...."[71]

This historical evolution demonstrates that what became known as "crimes against humanity" existed as part of "general principles of law recognized by civilized nations" long before the Charter's formulation in 1945.

Justice Robert H. Jackson, in his capacity as Chief Counsel for the United States in the Nuremberg prosecution, relied on such principles as he wrote in his Report to the President of the United States on June 6, 1945: "These principles [crimes against humanity] have been assimilated as a part of International Law at least since 1907."[72] Thus, the Charter's recognition of "crimes against humanity" as constituting violations of already existing conventional and customary international law, as well as "general principles of law," is evidenced by previous efforts of the international community to prohibit conduct proscribed by Article 6(c) of the Charter, as discussed below.[73]

The origin of the term "crimes against humanity" as the label for a category of international crimes goes back to 1915 when the governments of France, Great Britain, and Russia issued a joint declaration on May 28 denouncing the Ottoman Government's massacre of the Armenian population in Turkey as constituting "crimes against civilization and humanity" for which all members of the Turkish Government would

---

[70] 1977 Geneva Protocols (I), art. 1. *See also* Solf, *supra* note 51, *Protection of Civilians Against the Effects of Hostilities Under Customary International Law and Under Protocol I.*

[71] T. PAINE, COMMON SENSE *Introduction* (Feb. 14, 1776), *reprinted in* THE ESSENTIAL THOMAS PAINE 23-4 (S. Hook ed. 1969).

[72] Jackson's Report 50.

[73] *See also* Chapter 8.

be held responsible together with its agents implicated in the massacres.[74] However, the Treaty of Versailles (1919) did not include such a crime. It only contained provisions for prosecuting German military personnel for war crimes (Article 228). Regrettably, it excluded what the *1919 Report of the Commission on the Responsibilities of the Authors of War and on Enforcement of Penalties for Violations of the Laws and Customs of War* termed as "crimes against civilization and humanity."[75] This was

---

[74] This statement is quoted in the Armenian Memorandum presented by the Greek delegation to the 1919 Commission on March 14, 1919, as reproduced in Schwelb, *supra* note 64 at 181. *See also* J.F. WILLIS, PROLOGUE TO NUREMBERG: THE POLITICS AND DIPLOMACY OF PUNISHING WAR CRIMINALS OF THE FIRST WORLD WAR 27 (1982), *citing* H. MORGENTHAU, AMBASSADOR MORGENTHAU'S STORY 359. For a thorough examination of the Armenian genocide *see* Dadrian, *Genocide as a Problem of National and International Law: The World War I Armenian Case and Its Contemporary Legal Ramifications*, 14 YALE J. INT'L L. 221 (1989); Of all the conflicting and contradictory literature on the subject, including many Turkish publications denying, justifying or explaining what happened, Dadrian's article is the most legally convincing and from other accounts, the closest to historical accuracy with such debated facts.

[75] *See* excerpts in Document Section A 1-2. In the texts of the Treaty of Versailles, arts. 228-230, as well as the Treaty of Peace Between the Allied and Associated Powers and Austria (Treaty of St. Germain-en-Laye), 10 September 1919, arts. 118-120, 11 Martens (3d) 691, 226 Parry's 8, *reprinted in* 14 AJIL 1 (1920); Treaty of Peace Between the Allied and Associated Powers and Bulgaria (Treaty of Neuilly-sur-Seine), 27 Nov. 1919, 226 Parry's 332, *reprinted in* 14 AJIL 185 (1920), the phrase "laws of humanity" does not appear; those Treaties dealt only with acts committed in violation of the laws and customs of war. However, the Treaty of Sèvres, signed on 10 August 1920, *infra* note 90, contained, in addition to the provisions of its Articles 226-8, which corresponded to Articles 228-30 of the Treaty of Versailles, and Article 229 which regulated the position of the territories that ceased to be parts of the Turkish Empire, Article 230 which states:

The Turkish Government undertakes to hand over to the Allied Powers the persons whose surrender may be required by the latter as being responsible for the massacres committed during the continuance of the state of war on territory which formed part of the Turkish Empire on the 1st August, 1914.

The Allied Powers reserve to themselves the right to designate the Tribunal which shall try the persons so accused, and the Turkish Government undertakes to recognize such Tribunal. In the event of the League of Nations having created in sufficient time a Tribunal competent to deal with the said massacres, the Allied Powers reserve to themselves the right to bring the accused persons mentioned above before such Tribunal, and the Turkish Government undertakes equally to recognize such Tribunal.

This is in conformity with the Allied note of 1919 (*see supra* note 74, and accompanying text), expressing their intent to bring justice to persons who, during the war, had committed on Turkish territory crimes against persons of Turkish citizenship of Armenian or Greek ethnic background, a clear example of "crimes against humanity" as understood in the 1945 Charter. The Treaty of Sèvres was, however, not ratified and did not come into force. It was replaced by the Treaty of Lausanne, *infra* note 94, which did not contain provisions

due to the United States' position that the juridical content of "the laws of humanity" could not be defined.[76] Nevertheless, the 1919 Commission whose purpose was to report on the violations of international law, repeatedly used such words as "laws of humanity," "offences against the laws of humanity," and "breach of the laws of humanity."[77] Generally, the Commission (whose participating states were the United States, the United Kingdom, France, Italy, Belgium, Greece, Poland, Romania, Serbia and Japan) concluded that "[t]he war was carried on by the Central Empires together with their allies, Turkey and Bulgaria, by barbarous or illegitimate methods in violation of the established laws and customs of war and the elementary laws of humanity."[78] Regarding individual criminal responsibility, the Commission concluded that:

> [A]ll persons belonging to enemy countries, however high their position may have been, without distinction of rank, including Chiefs of State, who have been guilty of offences against the laws and customs of war or *the laws of humanity*, are liable to criminal prosecution.[79] (emphasis added)

The Commission also concluded that such individual criminal responsibility had no limits of rank or position: "[T]he degree of responsibility for these offences attaching to particular members of the enemy forces, including members of the General Staffs and other individuals, however highly placed."[80]

To prosecute war criminals for their offenses, the Commission called for the establishment of a High Tribunal. The Commission also identified "[t]wo classes of culpable acts"[81] for which the Tribunal could try accused war criminals:

(a)   Acts which provoked the world war and accompanied its inception.

---

respecting the punishment of war crimes, but was accompanied by a "Declaration of Amnesty" for all offenses committed between 1914 and 1922.

[76]   *See* Schwelb, *supra* note 64, at 182.

[77]   *See* 1919 Commission Report 58.

[78]   1919 Commission Report at 19. Thus, the warning issued to the Turkish government four years earlier by the Triple Entente, that those responsible for the Armenian massacre would be held accountable, was acted upon by the 1919 Commission.

[79]   *Id.* at 20.

[80]   *Id.* at 19.

[81]   *Id.* at 21.

170

(b) Violations of the laws and customs of war and the laws of humanity.[82]

Moreover, the Report found four categories of charges:

(a) Against persons belonging to enemy countries who have committed outrages against a number of civilians and soldiers of several Allied nations, such as outrages committed in prison camps where prisoners of war of several nations were congregated or the crime of forced labour in mines where prisoners of more than one nationality were forced to work;

(b) Against persons of authority, belonging to enemy countries, whose orders were executed not only in one area or on one battle front, but whose orders affected the conduct of operations against several of the Allied armies;

(c) Against all authorities, civil or military, belonging to enemy countries, however high their position may have been, without distinction of rank, including the heads of States, who ordered, or, with knowledge thereof and with power to intervene, abstained from preventing or taking measures to prevent, putting an end to or repressing, violations of the laws or customs of war (it being understood that no such abstention should constitute a defence for the actual perpetrators);

(d) Against such other persons belonging to enemy countries as, having regard to the character of the offence or the law of any belligerent country, it may be considered advisable not to proceed before a court other than the High Tribunal hereafter referred to.[83]

The Commission also recommended that the law applied by this High Tribunal ought to be "*the principles of the law of nations as they result from the usages established among civilized peoples, from the laws of humanity and from the dictates of public conscience.*"[84] (emphasis added)

The two members of the Commission from the United States dissented from the Report's use of "laws of humanity" on the ground that the legal concept of "offences against the laws of humanity" was too vague to support prosecutions, and they pointed

---

[82] *Id.*

[83] *Id.* at 23-24.

[84] *Id.* at 24.

out the difficulty of determining a universal standard for humanity.[85] Specifically, the American position was expressed as follows:

> The duty of the Commission was ... to determine whether the facts found were violations of the laws and customs of war. It was not asked whether these facts were violations of the laws or of the principles of humanity. Nevertheless, the report of the Commission does not, as in the opinion of the American Representatives it should, confine itself to the ascertainment of the facts and to their violation of the laws and customs of war, but, going beyond the terms of the mandate, declares that the facts found and acts committed were in violation of the laws of the elementary principles of humanity. The laws and customs of war are a standard certain, to be found in books of authority and in the practice of nations. The laws and principles of humanity vary with the individual, which, if for no other reason, should exclude them from consideration in a court of justice, especially one charged with the administration of criminal law. The American Representatives, therefore, objected to the references to the laws and principles of humanity, to be found in the report, in what they believed was meant to be a judicial proceeding, as, in their opinion, the facts found were to be violations or breaches of the laws and customs of war, and the persons singled out for trial and punishment for acts committed during the war were only to be those persons guilty of acts which should have been committed in violation of the laws and customs of war.[86]

---

[85]   *Id.*, Annex II, Memorandum of Reservations presented by the Representatives of the United States to the Report of the Commission on Responsibilities. Wright, *War Crimes Under International Law*, 62 L.Q. REV. 40 (1946), replied to this claim by pointing out that in the common law the principles of negligence and equity are equally uncertain legal concepts, but nonetheless they are established parts of our legal system. *Id.* at 48-49. As he states: "If these elastic standards are of as wide utility as they have proved to be, there is no reason why the doctrine of crimes against humanity should not be equally valid and valuable in International Law." *Id.* at 49.

[86]   1919 Commission Report 63-64. Twenty-five years later, the Chairman of the United Nations War Crimes Commission criticizing the 1919 United States position, stated:

> They said there was no fixed and universal standard of humanity .... They referred to the place of equity in the Anglo-American legal system and to John Seldon's definition of equity as a roguish thing. But, ... equity has established itself as a regular branch of [the American] legal system. Equally, it might be said that the negligence is too indeterminate to constitute a legal head of liability, but ... in the Anglo-American law of tort it has become one of the widest and most comprehensive and most important categories of liability.

Moreover, the United States delegates concluded that "[a] judicial tribunal only deals with existing law and only administers existing law, leaving to another forum infractions of the moral law and actions contrary to the laws and principles of humanity."[87]

Despite the American dissent, the Report clearly expressed recognition for the fact that "laws of humanity" did exist, could be ascertained, and could be breached, and that such breaches constituted "offences" which were punishable.[88] Nevertheless, there were no prosecutions for violations of "laws of humanity" but only for "war crimes." Twenty-six years later, it was found that some of these acts committed during World War II were of the same type and violated the same principles as those which occurred during World War I and the term "crimes against humanity" was coined.[89] But, the timidity of certain governments prevented the forging of another important link in the historical chain of humanitarian law and that missed opportunity was a proven weakness when the world was faced with the events of World War II.

If these elastic standards are of as wide utility as they have proved to be there is no reason why the doctrine of crimes against humanity should not be equally valid and valuable in [i]nternational [l]aw. That law deals with large concepts and not with the meticulous distinctions of [m]unicipal [l]aw.

Wright, *supra* note 85, at 48-49.

[87]   1919 Commission Report at 73.

[88]   Indeed, similar words have been used since the 18th century and attached to more general violations of the law of nations. *See e.g.*, 1 OP. ATT'Y GEN. 509, 513 (1821) ("crimes against mankind") (citing Hugo Grotius); *id.* at 515 ("enemies of the whole human family"); E. DE VATTEL, LAW OF NATIONS 464-65 (J. Chitty ed. 1883) ("Crime against mankind;" in 1758); *Republica v. De Longchamps*, 1 U.S. (1 Dall.) 108, 116 (Pa. 1784) ("crime against the whole world"); *Henfield's Case*, 11 F. Cas. 1099, 1107 (C.C.D. Pa. 1793) (No. 6,360) (criminally sanctionable "duties of humanity," "duty of humanity"). *See generally* Paust, *Federal Jurisdiction Over Extraterritorial Acts of Terrorism and Non-immunity for Foreign Violators of International Law Under the FSIA and the Act of State Doctrine*, 23 VA. J. INT'L L. 191, 211-214 (1983). During the 1915 massacre of Armenians in Turkey, the governments of Great Britain, France and Russia had condemned the massacres as "crimes against humanity and civilization," *see* A. WRIGHT, HISTORY OF THE UNITED NATIONS WAR CRIMES COMMISSION (1948). Later, a former United States Secretary of State wrote that the slave trade had become a "crime against humanity." Lansing, *Notes on World Sovereignty*, 15 AJIL 13, 25 (1921). But Lansing who represented the U.S. at the 1919 Commission dissented from the Commission's Report on "crimes against the laws of humanity," *see* notes 84-86 and accompanying text. *See also* Kunz, *La Primauté du Droit des Gens*, in REVUE DE DROIT INTERNATIONAL ET DE LEGISLATION COMPARÉ 556 (1925); Garner, *Punishment of Offenders Against the Laws and Customs of War*, 14 AJIL 70 (1926); and Lauterpacht, *supra* note 52.

[89]   *Id.*

The influence of the United States opposing prosecution for "offences against the laws of humanity" after World War I was also evident in other respects. In the original peace treaty with Turkey, the Treaty of Sèvres signed August 10, 1920,[90] the Allied Powers inserted several provisions which called for the trial and punishment of those responsible for the Armenian genocide.[91] Specifically, Article 226 stipulated that the Turkish government recognized the Allied Powers' right to try and punish the perpetrators "notwithstanding any proceedings or prosecutions before a Tribunal in Turkey." Article 230 of the Treaty also obligated Turkey to:

... hand over to the Allied Powers the persons whose surrender may be required by the latter as being responsible for the massacres committed during the continuance of the state of war on territory which formed part of the Turkish Empire on August 1, 1914. The Allied powers reserve to themselves the right to designate the tribunal which shall try the persons so accused, and the Turkish Government undertakes to recognize such tribunal. The provisions of Article 228 apply to the cases dealt with in this Article.[92]

---

[90] The Treaty of Peace Between the Allied Powers and Turkey (Treaty of Sèvres), 10 August 1920, 15 AJIL 179 (1921) (Supp.). Twenty Countries other than Turkey signed the Treaty. The United States, however, was not a party. For further elaboration of the Treaty of Sèvres, *see* Matas, *Prosecuting Crimes Against Humanity: The Lessons of World War I*, 13 FORDHAM INT'L L.J. 86 (1990).

[91] Treaty of Sèvres, *supra* note 90. Of course, the Treaty of Sèvres was never put into effect, but rather was replaced by the Treaty of Lausanne, *infra* note 94, which did not contain such provisions.

[92] In early 1919, at the direction of the Allied Powers, the Turkish government began to arrest and detain a number of war criminals. The custody of the offenders was very unpopular in Turkey and created serious problems. As one author writes, there was an imminent danger of "storming the Bekiraga military prison in the style of the Bastille raid." (B. SIMSIR, MALTA SÜRGÜNLERI (The Malta Exiles) 113 (1976)). In personal correspondence of November 17, 1989 received from Professor Dadrian, he stated that while the Turkish Military Tribunal did prosecute and convict a number of offenders, between April 1919 and July 1920, thirty-four offenders were convicted, fifteen sentenced to death. Of the fifteen sentenced to death, only three were actually executed, eleven received the sentence in absentia and one escaped. The remaining 19 received sentences of: five to 15 years, three to 10 years, one to 6 years and 3 months, one to 5 years and 4 months, two to 2 years, one to 1 year, six to less than a year. Public opinion forced the Ottoman Grand Vezir to release forty-one prisoners. (B. Simsir, *supra*, at 113.) This prompted Great Britain to request the transfer of the remaining detainees to British custody. The Turkish government objected claiming that such a transfer:

... would be in direct contradiction with its sovereign rights in view of the fact that by international law each State has [the] right to try its own tribunals. Moreover, His Britannic Majesty having by conclusion

Thus, the parties to the Treaty of Sèvres intended to bring to justice those who committed "crimes against humanity" as that crime was later defined in the Charter.[93] The Treaty of Sèvres, however, was never ratified and its replacement, the Treaty of Lausanne, did not include provisions for the prosecution of Turkish nationals for these "crimes against civilization and humanity."[94] The obvious reason for this omission is found in the "Declaration of Amnesty" for all offenses committed between 1914-1922, which the Allies gave Turkey as part of the Treaty of Lausanne's political package.[95] As such, the potential prosecution of those charged with violations of the "laws of humanity" for crimes against the Armenians of Turkey was removed. Such a clearly politically motivated decision did not, however, alter the fact that criminal responsibility had been recognized, though actual prosecution of individual offenders was subsequently foregone.[96] Moreover, it is noteworthy that an "amnesty" can only

---

of an armistice with the Ottoman Empire recognized [the] latter as a *de facto* and *de jure* sovereign State, it is incontestably evident that the Imperial Government possesses all the prerogatives for freely exercising [the] principles inherent in its sovereignty. [FO 608/244/3749 (folio 315)].

Reprinted in Dadrian, *supra* note 74, at 285.

In May 1919, the British seized sixty-seven detainees from the military prison. Twelve of them -- mostly ex-ministers -- were sent to the island of Mudos and later sent to Malta where the other Turks were imprisoned. By August 1920, the British had detained 118 Turks at Malta.

However, none of these detainees were prosecuted. Political considerations aimed at winning the favor of the new Turkish government provided a major roadblock to the prosecutions. The British eventually succumbed to political expediency rather than pursue justice. *Id.*

[93] *See* Schwelb, *supra* note 64, at 182.

[94] *See* the Treaty of Peace Between the Allied Powers and Turkey (Treaty of Lausanne), 24 July 1923, 28 L.N.T.S., 11, 18 AJIL 1 (1924) (Supp.).

[95] *See* E. Schwelb, *supra* note 64, at 182.

[96] *See* J.F. WILLIS, *supra* note 74, at 158, citing Robert Vasittart Report to Lord Curzon, 12 January 1920, in DOCUMENTS ON BRITISH FOREIGN POLICY, first series, 4:1016-25: "Delays in making peace also undermined the war crimes project. During the two years between the armistice of Madros and the signing of the Treaty of Sèvres, the Turkish Nationalist movement grew into a major force, and the Allied coalition virtually dissolved. By 1920, most of the victors no longer included among their aims the punishment of Turkish war criminals ... the American government, which had never declared war on the Ottoman Empire, took no part in drawing up the Treaty of Sèvres." And at 163, citing the footnote to dispatch of Rumbold to Curzon, 24 April 1922, in DOCUMENTS ON BRITISH FOREIGN POLICY, first series, 17:791-92, regarding the capitulation to Turkish Nationalists with the Treaty of Lausanne, "Later, Curzon had regrets and wrote:

be for a crime. Clearly, the fact that a crime is not prosecuted does not negate its legal existence. Indeed, what other reason would there have been to provide amnesty if there was not a crime whose prosecution was waived. Consequently, in 1945, no precedent existed for the international criminalization and international prosecution for "crimes against humanity," but the implications of certain historical backgrounds could be relied upon to sustain the "declarative" nature of the Charter.

The pre-1945 historical record of the world community's efforts to ban war and humanize its conduct by progressively limiting means and methods of waging war is impressive. But, it is neither consistent nor cohesive. Viewed in the context of its sporadic manifestations, it is tenuous. However, viewed in its totality, it is compelling. Thus, if we compressed the time span during which humanitarian law and the regulation of armed conflicts developed and if we ignored the different contexts from which it emerged, we have an impressive record that cannot be ignored.

The Connection Between War Crimes and Crimes Against Humanity

The Charter expanded the narrow traditional scope of war crimes punishable under international law to include "crimes against humanity." The basis for this expanded jurisdictional scope was existing conventions, other international instruments, customs and "general principles of law." It included, but was not limited to: the particulars of the 1899 and 1907 Hague Conventions; experiences and practices in the aftermath of World War I; and, the Allied declarations during World War II. But, these precedents must also be viewed in the historical context of the humanization and regulation of armed conflicts and the concomitant efforts of the world community to prohibit such

---

'I think we made a great mistake in ever letting these people [the Turks] out. I had to yield at the time to a pressure which I always felt to be mistaken'." For a comprehensive survey of the Armenian legal issues, *see* Dadrian, *supra* note 74. Willis advances that the failure to prosecute Turkish officials may well have encouraged Hitler to conduct his policies against the Jews. Hitler is quoted to have said concerning the Armenian Massacre: "Our strength lies in our quickness and in our brutality; Genghis Khan has sent millions of women and children into death knowingly and with a light heart. History sees in him only the great founder of States... [a]nd so for the present only in the East I have put my death-head formations in place with the command relentlessly and without compassion to send into death many women and children of Polish origin and language. Only thus we can gain the living space we need. Who after all is today speaking about the destruction of the Armenians?" J.F. WILLIS, *supra* note 74, at 173, citing G. Ogilvie-Forkes to Kirkpatrick, 25 August 1939, with enclosures of Hitler's speech to Chief Commanders and Commanding Generals, 22 August 1939, Great Britain, Foreign Office, 7 DOCUMENTS ON BRITISH FOREIGN POLICY, 1919-1939, 258 (third series, ed. E.L. Woodward, et al., 9 vols. 1949-55).

conduct and punish its perpetrators.[97] The Charter's Article 6(c) was, therefore, the final evolutionary stage which declared with some particularity that these war crimes punishable under international law include "murder," "extermination," "enslavement" and "other inhumane acts" when committed in time of war against civilians extended to all civilians irrespective of their nationality.[98] As such, the Charter was the final step of a steady progressive historical development and evolution of international criminal responsibility for harmful conduct committed against civilian populations irrespective of nationality, but subject to the condition that it be linked to the initiation and conduct of war. Subsequently, however, this connection to war was removed in CCL 10.[99]

It must be emphasized that, "murder, extermination, enslavement, deportation, and other inhumane acts committed against any civilian population," as stated in Article 6(c) of the Charter, if committed during an armed conflict by the belligerent forces of

---

[97] This is evident by the discussion and authorities cited in this Chapter.

[98] *See* 2 G. SCHWARZENBERGER, INTERNATIONAL LAW AS APPLIED BY INTERNATIONAL COURTS AND TRIBUNALS 498 (1968), he quotes COMMAND PAPERS 6964 64 (1946) [*sic* 1964], and states, "'The Tribunal is, of course, bound by the Charter, in the definition which it gives both of war crimes and crimes against humanity. With respect to war crimes, however, as has already been pointed out, the crimes defined by Article 6, Section (b), of the Charter were already recognized as war crimes under international law.' It would be hard to miss the argument *a contrario* implied in this statement ... [a]ctually, the limited and qualified character of the rule on crimes against humanity as formulated in the Charters of the Nuremberg and Tokyo Tribunals militates against the rule being accepted as one declaratory of international customary law." Schwarzenberger also states that, "This view of the matter closely corresponded to that prevalent among the draftsmen of the Charter at the London Four-Power Conference in the Summer of 1945. Lord Kilmuir (Sir David Maxwell Fyfe, as he then was), the Chairman of the London Conference, stated his view, from which none of those present dissented, in plain words: 'What we want to abolish at the trial is a discussion as to whether the acts are violations of international law or not. We declare what the international law is so that there won't be any discussion on whether it is international law or not. We hope that is in line with Professor Trainin's book'." [A.N. TRAININ, HITLERITE RESPONSIBILITY UNDER CRIMINAL LAW (A.Y. Vishinsky ed. 1944 and A. Rothstein trans. 1945).] *Id.* at 479, citing the Jackson Report. *See also* LORD KILMUIR, POLITICAL ADVENTURE 78 and 329 *et seq.* (1964), cited by Schwarzenberger. The Nuremberg and Tokyo Tribunals themselves took this view of their verdicts, "The Charter is not an arbitrary exercise of power on the part of the victorious nations, but in the view of the Tribunal ... it is the expression of international law existing at the time of its creation; and to that extent is itself a contribution to international law." *Id.* at 483, quoting COMMAND PAPERS 6964 at 38 (1946).

[99] *See* CCL 10, *reprinted in* Document Section C.5, and see discussion of this question in Chapter 1.

one state against the nationals of another state constitute war crimes.[100] Similarly, "persecutions on political, racial or religious grounds in execution of or in connection with war"[101] would also constitute war crimes if committed in time of war against the civilian population of another belligerent power.[102] The prohibitions contained in Article 6(c) are clearly contained in the regulation of armed conflicts and can be found in the 1863 Lieber Code,[103] the 1899 Hague Convention,[104] the 1907 Hague Convention[105] (acknowledged to be custom at Nuremberg), and the 1864 and 1929 Geneva Conventions[106] (also acknowledged to be custom at Nuremberg). Such prohibitions appear in the "List of War Crimes" prepared at the Paris Peace Conference of 1919 by the Commission on the Responsibilities of the Authors of War and on Enforcement of Penalties for Violations of the Laws and Customs of War.[107] Numerous texts also document the existence of such prohibitions under customary international law.[108] Justice Robert Jackson referred to these texts in his 1945 report to the President of the United States: "[t]hese principles ... result from the usages established among civilized peoples, from the laws of humanity and the dictates of the

---

[100]   *See* Paust, *The Universality and the Responsibility to Enforce International Criminal Law: No U.S. Sanctuary for Alleged Nazi War Criminals,* 11 HOUS. J. INT'L L. 337 (1989); Cowles, *Universality of Jurisdiction Over War Crimes,* 33 CALIF. L. REV. 177 (1945). *See also* Abramson, *Reflections on the Unthinkable: Standards Relating to the Denaturalization and Deportation of Nazis and Those Who Collaborated with the Nazis During World War II,* 57 CINC. L. REV. 1311 (1989); and discussion of "Universal Jurisdiction" in Chapter 11.

[101]   *See* Schwelb, *supra* note 64.

[102]   *See* Paust, *supra* note 100.

[103]   *See* Lieber Code, *supra* note 52.

[104]   *See* 1899 Hague Convention.

[105]   *See* 1907 Hague Convention.

[106]   *See supra* notes 43 and 49.

[107]   *See* 1919 Commission Report.

[108]   *See* W. WINTHROP, MILITARY LAW AND PRECEDENTS 778, 796 (2 ed. 1920); Paust, *After My Lai: Norms, Myths and Leader Responsibility,* 57 MIL. L. REV. 99, 108-116, 130-33, 143-46 (1972), and references cited; Paust, *Aggression Against Authority: The Crime of Oppression, Politicide and Other Crimes Against Human Rights,* 18 CASE W. RES. J. INT'L L. 283, 283-284, 295-296 (1986); Paust and Blaustein, *War Crimes Jurisdiction and Due Process: the Bangladesh Experience,* 11 VAND. J. TRANSNAT'L. L. 1 (1978), also quoting BLUNTSCHLI, ON THE LAW OF WAR AND NEUTRALITY, and adding: "[t]here is ample evidence of a customary, inherited expectation that genocide was actually prohibited as a violation of the customary international law of war." *Id.* at 22.

public conscience."[109]   Thus, the Charter's definition of "crimes against humanity" did not substantively add to what was well established under war crimes.

The essential difference between acts deemed war crimes and those deemed "crimes against humanity" is that the former are acts committed in time of war against nationals of another state, while the latter are acts committed against nationals of the same state as that of the perpetrators. Thus, the Charter took a step forward in the form of a jurisdictional extension when it provided that the victims of the same types of conduct that constitute war crimes were protected without the requirement that they be of a different nationality than that of the perpetrators.

This jurisdictional extension from war crimes to "crimes against humanity" through the linkage to war developed gradually as the horrors of World War II became known. This gradualism is evident in the drafting process leading to the adoption of the Charter, as discussed in Chapter 1. The first step toward the formulation of Article 6(c) was taken by the London International Assembly, an unofficial body comprised of distinguished jurists representing the fledgling United Nations, and which began its work on the crimes of Nazi Germany in the autumn of 1941.[110] The LIA bitterly referred to the lessons of World War I -- "[t]he punishment of the war criminals of World War I was a complete failure"[111] -- and noted that its primary objective was the trial and conviction of all war criminals. Among the most important of the recommendations submitted by the LIA was that "a comprehensive view should be taken [of war crimes], including not only the customary violations of the laws of war ... but any other serious crime against the local law committed in time of war, the perpetrator of which has not been visited by appropriate punishment ...."[112]

The LIA paid particular attention to the extermination of the Jews, including German Jews, and stated that "[i]n respect of the extermination of Jews, it was recommended that punishment should be imposed not only when victims were Allied Jews, but even when the crimes had been committed against stateless Jews or any other Jews, in Germany or elsewhere."[113]   In prosecutions of this type, the "criminal policies concern humanity as a whole, and [the] condemnation should be pronounced, not by

---

[109]   Jackson's Report 51.

[110]   *See* THE PUNISHMENT OF WAR CRIMINALS: RECOMMENDATIONS OF THE LONDON INTERNATIONAL ASSEMBLY (REPORT OF COMMISSION I). *See also* Document Section B.1.

[111]   *Id.* at 3.

[112]   *Id.* at 7. (emphasis in original)

[113]   *Id.* at 7.

one individual country, but by the United Nations, in the name of mankind."[114] This type of prosecution, the LIA believed, would simply be a "matter of recognition of the fundamental principles the upholding of which is the concern of mankind, because they are necessary to the very existence of humanity."[115]

After the work of the LIA, the United Nations War Crimes Commission added its contribution to the evolution of "crimes against humanity." As set forth in the London and Tokyo Charters, the term "crimes against humanity" was not meant, in the words of the UNWCC, to be limited to war crimes in the "traditional and narrow sense, that is violations of the laws and customs of war, perpetrated on Allied territory or against Allied citizens, but that atrocities committed on Axis territory and against persons of other than Allied nationality should also be punished."[116] The UNWCC went even further when it held that international law may sanction individuals for "crimes against humanity" committed not only during war but also during peace. It held that:

[There exists] a system of international law under which individuals are responsible to the community of nations for violations of rules of international criminal law, and according to which attacks on the fundamental liberties and constitutional rights of people and individual persons, that is inhuman acts, constitute international crimes not only in time of war, but also, in certain circumstances, in time of peace.[117]

Notice of this position was expressed in the Allied Declaration of December 17, 1942, denouncing the barbaric treatment of the Jews and emphasizing the Allies' solemn resolve to visit retribution on the perpetrators of "these crimes,"[118] even though many of the Nazi atrocities were not war crimes in the traditional sense. It was also expressed by the Moscow Declaration of 1943 as follows:

The United Kingdom, the United States and the Soviet Union have received from many quarters evidence of atrocities, massacres and cold-blooded mass executions which are being perpetrated by the Hitlerite forces in the many countries they have overrun and from which they are now being steadily expelled. The brutalities of

---

114   *Id.* at 8.

115   *Id.* at 9.

116   UNWCC at 191.

117   *Id.* at 192-193.

118   *Quoted in* Schwelb, *supra* note 64, at 183.

180

Hitlerite domination are no new thing and all the peoples or territories in their grip have suffered from the worst form of government by terror. What is new is that many of these territories are now being redeemed by the advancing armies of the liberating Powers and that in their desperation, the recoiling Hitlerite Huns are redoubling their ruthless cruelties. This is now evidenced with particular clearness by monstrous crimes of the Hitlerites on the territory of the Soviet Union which is being liberated from the Hitlerites, and on French and Italian territory.[119]

Such notice was also subsequently expressed in 1943-44 by the LIA, who voiced an authoritative position on extending Allied punishment beyond the traditional narrow scope of war crimes. The Assembly urged that:

punishment should be imposed not only when the victims were Allied Jews, but even where the crimes had been committed against stateless Jews or any other Jews in Germany or elsewhere.[120]

Additionally, in 1943, the UNWCC recommended that Allied retribution should extend beyond the traditional reach of the laws of war to encompass Nazi crimes committed not only against Allied combatants, but also to the civilian populations of the occupied countries and of the Axis countries themselves. Finally, Article 29 of the Instrument of the Surrender of Italy, signed on September 29, 1943,[121] foreshadowed the Charter's codification of "crimes against humanity" by imposing on Italy the obligation to apprehend and surrender into the hands of the United Nations persons suspected of both traditional war crimes and "analogous offenses," an expression suggesting what the Charter would classify as "crimes against humanity" two years later. Thus, the jurisdictional barrier which shielded those who committed crimes against their own civilian population was held inapplicable to crimes against "the laws of humanity" or "crimes against humanity."

---

[119] *Reprinted in* The Moscow Declaration, *see* Document Section B.3.

[120] *Quoted in* Schwelb, *supra* note 64, at 184.

[121] Instrument of Surrender of Italy, 29 September 1943, 61 Stat. 2742, T.I.A.S. No. 1604. DOCUMENTS RELATING TO THE CONDITIONS OF AN ARMISTICE WITH ITALY, COMMAND PAPERS 6693, 8. Article 29 referred to the perpetrators of "War Crimes" and also to persons suspected of "Analogous Offences," an expression clearly indicating what subsequently became known as "crimes against humanity."

Before the London Charter was promulgated in 1945, the pronouncements and declarations of the Allies' between 1942-44[122] revealed a consensus that many Nazi atrocities, including the "deportation" of civilians to concentration camps and their "enslavement," constituted "crimes against humanity" under "general principles of law," and that these crimes were punishable on the basis of the same rationale as war crimes. The logic of that jurisdictional extension is clear: conduct which constitutes punishable war crimes when victims and violators are not of the same nationality cannot be deemed lawful only because the nationality of victims and violators is the same. To claim that such a jurisdictional legal fiction is a bar to criminal responsibility in light of the contrary positions expressed by so many civilizations over such a long period of time would empty international law of its value content.[123]

The analogy between war crimes and "crimes against humanity" is evident in the similarity between types of acts described in Article 6(c), which when committed by a belligerent against the nationals of another state constitute war crimes, and when committed by the agents of a given state against its own nationals are deemed "crimes against humanity." As Professor Schwelb stated:

Crimes against humanity can be committed against a civilian population both of territories to which the provisions of Section 3 of The Hague Regulations annexed to the Fourth Hague Convention of 1907 respecting military authority over the territory of the hostile state apply, and of such territories to which they do not apply. This means that a crime against humanity under Article 6(c) of the Charter may or may not simultaneously be a violation of the laws and customs of war and therefore a war crime in the narrower sense, coming under Article 6(b) of the Charter. It follows that the term "crimes against humanity" on the one hand, and "war crimes" or "violations of the laws and customs of war" on the other, overlap. Many crimes against humanity are also violations of the laws and customs of war; many, though not all, war crimes are simultaneously crimes against humanity. In so far as these crimes (viz. crimes against humanity) constitute violations of the laws of war there is no juristic problem because they are merely the same crimes as those set forth in Count Three [of the *Violations of the Laws and Customs of War*] under a different

---

[122]   For excerpts of these declarations, *see* Document Section.

[123]   The contrary argument, at least until 1945, was two-fold: 1) only States are subjects of international law; and 2) States are only obligated by those duties they specifically agree to assume.

name, but novel considerations arise when the acts charged cannot be brought within this category.[124]

Professor Goodhart, on the same subject, noted that:

> ... where "war crimes" and "crimes against humanity" overlap, no independent legal problems arise. It was natural that the notion of crimes against humanity had to be examined by the International Military Tribunal particularly in such cases where it was alleged that facts which did not simultaneously constitute violations of the laws of war constituted "Crimes Against Humanity."[125]

Sir Hartley Shawcross, as Chief Prosecutor for the United Kingdom, in his closing arguments delivered on the 26th and 27th of July 1946 before the International Military Tribunal at Nuremberg, stated the general theory on which the Nuremberg Indictment was based with respect to the charge of "crimes against humanity:"

> So the crime against the Jews, insofar as it is a Crime Against Humanity and not a War Crime, is one which we indict because of its association with the Crime Against the Peace. That is, of course, a very important qualification, and is not always appreciated by those who have questioned the exercise of this jurisdiction. But, subject to that qualification, we have thought it right to deal with matters which the Criminal Law of all countries would normally stigmatize as crimes: murder, extermination, enslavement, persecution on political, racial or economic grounds. These things done against belligerent nationals, or, for that matter, done against German nationals in belligerent occupied territory, would be ordinary War Crimes, the prosecution of which would form no novelty. Done against others they would be crimes against Municipal Law except in so far as German law, departing from all the canons of civilized procedure, may have authorized them to be done by the State or by persons acting on behalf of the State. Although to do so does not in any way place those defendants in greater jeopardy than they would otherwise be, the nations adhering to the Charter of this Tribunal have felt it proper and necessary in the interest of civilization to say that those things, even if done in accordance with the laws of the German State, as created and ruled by these men and their

---

[124]   See Schwelb, *supra* note 64, at 189.

[125]   See Goodhart, *The Legality of the Nuremberg Trials*, 58 JURID. REV. 1, 15 (1946).

ringleader, were, when committed with the intention of affecting the international community -- that is in connection with the other crimes charged -- not mere matters of domestic concern but crimes against the Laws of Nations. I do not minimize the significance for the future of the political and jurisprudential doctrine which is here implied. Normally International Law concedes that it is for the State to decide how it shall treat its own nationals; it is a matter of domestic jurisdiction. And although the Social and Economic Council of the United Nations Organization is seeking to formulate a Charter of the Rights of Man, the Covenant of the League of Nations and the Charter of the United Nations Organization does recognize that general position. Yet International Law has in the past made some claim that there is a limit to the omnipotence of the State and that the individual human being, the ultimate unit of all law, is not disentitled to the protection of mankind when the State tramples upon his rights in a manner which outrages the conscience of mankind.[126]

Professor Schwelb commenting upon Shawcross' closing argument stated:

> After quoting Grotius, who affirmed, with reference to atrocities committed by tyrants against their subjects, that intervention is justified for "the right of social connection is not cut off in such a case," and the expression of the same idea by John Westlake, Sir Hartley Shawcross went on to say: "The same view was acted upon by the European Powers which in time past intervened in order to protect the Christian subjects of Turkey against cruel persecution. The fact is that the right of humanitarian intervention by war is not a novelty in international law -- can intervention by judicial process then be illegal? The Charter of this Tribunal embodies a beneficent principle -- much more limited than some would like it to be -- and it gives warning for the future -- I say, and repeat again, gives warning for the future, to dictators and tyrants masquerading as a State that if, in order to strengthen or further their crimes against the community of nations they debase the sanctity of man in their own countries, they act at their peril, for they affront the international law of mankind."[127]

---

[126] *See* SPEECHES OF THE CHIEF PROSECUTORS AT THE CLOSE OF THE CASE AGAINST THE INDIVIDUAL DEFENDANTS, (published under the authority of H.M. Attorney-General by H.M. Stationery Office) (COMMAND PAPERS 6964), 63, *cited by* Schwelb, *supra* note 64, at 198.

[127] *See* E. Schwelb, *supra* note 64, at 198-199. Supporting this proposition *see* Jescheck, *Development and Future Prospects of International Criminal Law*, in 1 BASSIOUNI ICL 83. Professor Jescheck is, however, a critic of Nuremberg's approach with respect to the defense of "obedience to superior

The conclusion is clear that "crimes against humanity" are analogous to war crimes and are an extension thereof, and that they are based on the same moral and legal principles which have long existed and which are the underpinning of principles, norms and rules of the humanization and regulation of armed conflicts.

But, as George Schwarzenberger, a sometime critic of certain aspects of the Nuremberg Charter and prosecutions, noted:

> [I]n Article 6(c) of the Charter of the Nuremberg International Military Tribunal, as modified by the Four-Power Protocol of October 6, 1945, crimes against humanity are defined as "murder, extermination, enslavement, deportation, and other inhumane acts committed against any civil population, before or during the war, or persecutions on political, racial or religious grounds in execution of or in connection with any crime within the jurisdiction of the Tribunal, whether or not in violation of the domestic law of the country where perpetrated."

> In the original versions of the United States, United Kingdom and French texts of the London Agreement of August 8, 1945, the two parts of the definition had been separated by a semicolon after the word "war." Thus, it was possible to argue that any inhumane act against any civilian population amounts to a crime under the Charter, irrespective of its date of commission before or after the outbreak of the Second World War.[128]

Schwarzenberger went on to state:

> [A]ccording to Article 7 of the Four-Power Agreement of August 8, 1945, each of the four texts was to have equal authority. With the solemnity of a Protocol, the United States, United Kingdom and French texts were adjusted to the Russian version, and further modifications were introduced in the French version of the clause on crimes against humanity to adjust it to the other three texts. Thus, beyond any shadow of doubt, the Contracting Parties clarified their intention. Unless the qualifications made in Article 6(c) applied, they did not intend crimes against

orders," and its *ex post facto* application, *see* H.H. JESCHECK, DIE VERANTWORLISHKEIT DER STAATSORGAN NACH VÖLKERSTRAFRECHT (1952).

[128]   G. SCHWARZENBERGER, *supra* note 98, at 496.

humanity under the Nuremberg Charter to cover inhumane acts against civilian populations in time of peace.[129]

Indeed, the Nuremberg Tribunal interpreted "crimes against humanity" as meaning crimes committed in connection with war, that is after 1939, in accordance with the adopted version of Article 6(c) of the Charter. The Tribunal also found that Nazi atrocities constituted pre-Charter "crimes against humanity," but refused to apply that notion to acts which occurred before 1939, when the war began, because of the language of the Charter which was binding upon it.[130] One reason for this cut-off date was the fact that the London Agreement of 8 August 1945 contained some discrepancies in its official languages (English, French and Russian) whose texts were to have equal weight, as discussed in Chapter 1. The Russian text specifically stated that "inhumane acts fell under the Tribunal's jurisdiction only if committed in the execution of, or in connection with, war crimes in the strict sense and crimes against peace,"[131] thus including the limiting connection to war. That connection, in the opinion of this writer, was probably motivated by a desire of the Charter's drafters to strengthen its legality by connecting it to the more established notion of war crimes. Thus, by foregoing prosecution for crimes committed between 1933 and the advent of war in 1939, the framers of the Charter most likely believed that it would strengthen the prosecution's legal case for post-1939 criminalization.[132] That limitation was, however, removed in CCL 10, as discussed in Chapter 1, which was the basis for Allied prosecutions in their respective zones of occupation.[133]

Recently, Professor Clark explained that the IMT did not provide a concise clarification of the analogy between "crimes against humanity" and war crimes, and generally lacked a clear analysis of the distinctions between these two categories of crimes. He stated:

> When it came to discussing the offenses as they applied to particular defendants, the Tribunal continued its practice of simply jumbling up the discussion of both war

---

[129]   *Id.* at 497.

[130]   For a discussion of this issue, *see* Chapter 6; *see also* C. LOMBOIS, DROIT PÉNAL INTERNATIONAL 156 (1979); and L. DAWIDOWICZ, THE WAR AGAINST THE JEWS 1933-1945 (1975).

[131]   *See* Chapter 1; and G. SCHWARZENBERGER, *supra* note 98, at 496-497.

[132]   *See* Chapter 3.

[133]   *See* CCL 10.

crimes and crimes against humanity -- except in the cases of Streicher and von Schirach who were charged with crimes against humanity but not with war crimes and who were both convicted. In its discussion of the deeds of particular individuals, the Tribunal did not make any systematic use of its sub-headings of categories of offenses. Nonetheless, an examination of the Tribunal's discussion in particular cases suggests an approach which uses the general framework of those headings as a basis of analysis. Depending on the particular facts, the Tribunal discussed in a quite unsystematic fashion:

> "offenses against prisoners of war; murder and ill-treatment of civilian populations, including terrorism, shooting hostages, use of economic resources for Germany, concentration camps, deportations, unnecessary damage to homes, Germanization, exterminations -- of Jews, of those thought likely to mount opposition, of political commissars, of intellectuals, of the insane and the old -- and deciding that the Hague Rules did not apply in the occupied East; pillage of public and private property; the slave labor policy; persecution of the Jews, including the passage of laws aimed at excluding them from economic life and from the protection of the law."

Fourteen of the defendants were convicted of both types of offense -- war crimes and crimes against humanity -- after discussions which often seemed applicable mainly to war crimes. Occasionally, there appear to be some distinctions drawn. Seyss-Inquart, for example, was active both in Austria and later in Poland and the Netherlands. The Tribunal regarded his activities in Austria as occurring within Germany and analyzed them as crimes against humanity. His activities in the Netherlands and Poland were treated primarily as war crimes.

The cases of the two defendants charged with crimes against humanity but not war crimes are, perhaps, instructive. The gravamen of the finding of guilt in the case of Streicher, "Jew Baiter Number One," lay in his advocacy of "persecution" on political and racial grounds -- persecution which included murder and extermination. Von Schirach, as a senior official in Vienna, was involved in the use of forced labor under disgraceful conditions in that city and in continuing the deportation of the Jews therefrom. His activities ran the gamut of the definition of crimes against humanity in the Charter. Again, Austria was treated as part of Germany and von Schirach was duly convicted of crimes against humanity.

All in all, though, it is fair to say that crimes against humanity did not play a prominent part in the analysis of the Tribunal or in its disposition of particular cases. The two officials convicted of crimes against humanity but not war crimes were not at the forefront of the Tribunal's discussion. That said, one should note that nonetheless one of them was sentenced to death and the other to a lengthy term of imprisonment solely on the basis of the commission of crimes against humanity. Notwithstanding the relative paucity of discussion and its failure always to distinguish the offense carefully from war crimes, the Tribunal obviously took crimes against humanity seriously.[134]

One important post-Nuremberg case which contains a weighty analysis of the origins of "crimes against humanity" is *United States v. Altstoetter*, et al. (*The Justice Case*), where the Tribunal noted that:

CCL 10 is not limited to the punishment of persons guilty of violating the laws and customs of war in the narrow sense; furthermore, it can no longer be said that violations of the laws and customs of war are the only offenses recognized by common international law. The force of circumstance, the grim fact of worldwide interdependence, and the moral pressure of public opinion have resulted in international recognition that certain crimes against humanity committed by Nazi authority against German nationals constituted violations not alone of statute but also of common international law.[135]

Based on this rationale, CCL 10 did not contain the same limitation as did the London Charter in Article 6(c), that is that "crimes against humanity" be limited to those acts connected to the "initiation or conduct of war." Indeed, as discussed in Chapter 1, logic would require that a crime against "common international law" not be limited in its application to a given context such as war. As stated above, the war connecting limitation established by the Charter should be viewed as a precaution by the drafters to avoid the argument that "crimes against humanity" violated the "principles of legality," known in some way to most national legal systems.[136]

---

[134] Clark, *Crimes Against Humanity at Nuremberg*, in THE NUREMBERG TRIALS AND INTERNATIONAL LAW 177, 196-198 (G. Ginsburgs and V.N. Kudriavtsev eds. 1990).

[135] *The Justice Case.*

[136] *See* Chapter 3.

Despite the IMT's lack of clarity, it can be stated that while "crimes against humanity" overlap with war crimes in the strict sense, at the time of the Charter they were intended to constitute an auxiliary category as long as the required connection between "crimes against humanity" and the other two types of crimes under the Charter, i.e., "crimes against peace" and "war crimes," existed. The Tribunal's jurisdiction regarding "crimes against humanity" thus extended to crimes committed against German nationals, other nationals and stateless persons under German control, irrespective of whether such acts were lawful under any particular local law, so long as the connection to war existed.[137]

Some authors, like Schwarzenberger, reject these arguments and hold that the Nuremberg and Tokyo Charters were not declarative of international law at the time but were merely meant to punish the atrocious behavior of the Nazi and Japanese regimes because their deeds could not go unpunished. Thus, he stated:

> [The] limited and qualified character of the rule on crimes against humanity as formulated in the Charters of the Nuremberg and Tokyo Tribunals militates against the rule being accepted as one declaratory of international customary law. This rudimentary legal system [of international law] does not know of distinctions as subtle as those between crimes against humanity which are connected with other types of war crime and, therefore, are to be treated as analogous to war crimes in the strict sense and other types of inhumane acts which are not so linked and, therefore, are beyond the pale of international law. The Four-Power Protocol of October 6, 1945, offers even more decisive evidence of the anxiety of the Contracting Parties to avoid any misinterpretation of their intentions as having codified a generally applicable rule of international customary law.[138]

He concluded that what the Four Powers intended to do under the heading of "crimes against humanity" was to deal retrospectively with the particularly "ugly facets of the relapse of two formerly civilized nations into a state of barbarism."[139]

---

[137]   *See* G. SCHWARZENBERGER, *supra* note 98, at 497. The Charter also excluded the applicability of national laws by reason of the fact that such laws provided the national legal basis to justify such acts, in disregard of international conventional, and customary law, and in disregard of "general principles of law." That exclusion of national laws was valid under the existing principles and norms of international regulation of armed conflicts. *Id.* at 498.

[138]   *Id.*

[139]   *Id.* at 499.

However, that position was not generally shared by most of his non-German contemporaries.[140] Indeed, even the rigid legal positivism expressed in the narrow interpretation expounded by critics of the Charter[141] stops short of reaching a contrary logical legal conclusion, namely that, if a deed is recognized as deserving punishment, from where does that recognition stem? Would such recognition merely be another form of atavistic or vindictive expression, or is it based on the existence of an unarticulated premise that certain "general principles" exist which make such deeds deserving of punishment? If so, how can a principle that recognizes the need for punishability not be based, at least implicitly, on some existing prescription? This is essentially a question of legal philosophy, as discussed in Chapter 2, and second of legality, as discussed in Chapter 3.[142] Considering, however, that the conventional and customary regulations of armed conflicts refer to and rely upon basic "laws of humanity" as

---

[140]   For this writer, it is only a logical premise that if something is recognized as deserving of punishment it must necessarily rest on a violation of a legal principle. The logic of this legal reasoning also finds support in M. HALE, PREFACE TO ROLLE'S ABRIDGEMENT (1668), *cited in* WAMBAUGH, THE STUDY OF CASES 90-93 (1894), and *reprinted in* J. HALL, READINGS ON JURISPRUDENCE 342 (1938), where Lord Hale states: "The Wisdom of laws, especially of England, is to determine general notions of just and honest by particular rules, applications and constitutions found out and continued by great wisdom, experience and time ... "; *See also e.g.*, Cohen, *The Place of Logic in the Law*, 29 HARV. L. REV. 622 (1916); Dewey, *Logical Method and Law*, 10 CORNELL L. Q. 17 (1924). Such reasoning is certainly part of the Common Law. *See e.g.*, J. SALMOND, JURISPRUDENCE (1862) (10th ed. 1947); T.E. HOLLAND, THE ELEMENTS OF JURISPRUDENCE (1924); F. POLLOCK, A FIRST BOOK OF JURISPRUDENCE (1929). With respect to authors supporting the contrary view to Lauterpacht's, *see* among many others: Schwelb, *Crimes Against Humanity*, 23 BRIT. Y.B. INT'L L. 178 (1946); Aroneanu, *Le Crime Contre l'Humanité*, NOUVELLE REVUE DE DROIT INTERNATIONAL PRIVÉ 369 (1946); Dautricourt, *La Definition du Crime Contre l'Humanité*, 25 REVUE DE DROIT INTERNATIONAL 294 (1947); Aroneanu, *Naissance et Application de la loi Internationale Réprimant le Crime Contre l'Humanité*, REVUE DE DROIT PÉNAL ET DE CRIMINOLOGIE 876 (1947); Herzog, *Contribution A L'Etude de la Definition du Crime Contre l'Humanité*, 18 RIDP 155 (1947); Boissarie, *La Répression des Crimes Nazis Contre l'Humanité et la Protection des Libertés Démocratiques (Raport Général Présenté au Congrés International du Mouvement National Judiciaire)*, 18 RIDP 11 (1947); Aroneanu, *Responsabilités pénales pour crime contra l'humanité*, REVUE DE DROIT INTERNATIONAL, DE SCIENCES DIPLOMATIQUES ET POLITIQUES 144 (1948); Brand, *Crimes Against Humanity and the Nüremberg Trials*, 28 OR. L. REV. 93 (1949); Graven, *Les Crimes Contre l'Humanité* 76 RECEIUL DES COURS 433 (1950); P. DROST, THE CRIME OF STATE (2 vols. 1959); E. ARONEANU, LE CRIME CONTRE L'HUMANITÉ (1961); Bassiouni, *International Criminal Law and the Holocaust*, 9 CALIF. W. INT'L L.J. 202 (1979).

[141]   *See e.g.*, G. SCHWARZENBERGER, *supra* note 98, at 479, 483; and Lauterpacht, *supra* note 52.

[142]   Particularly the meaning, content and application of the "principles of legality," as discussed in Chapter 3.

specifically stated in the Preamble of Hague Conventions,[143] then the conclusion is inescapable that an unarticulated legal premise does exist. In this perspective, the criticism of legal positivists, as discussed in Chapters 2 and 3, could appear to be more a question of form than one of substance. As aptly stated by Professor D'Amato:

> Not only do positivists insist upon separating law from morality, but they also appear to be unable to deal with moral questions raised by law once the two are separated. This inability stems, I believe, from their simultaneous attempt to assert and to prove that law and morality are separate; the argument reduces to a vicious circle.[144]

The analogy to war crimes and the linkage of "crimes against humanity" to war are relevant only to the context of the London and Tokyo Charters, their related prosecutions and CCL 10 since these instruments encompassed the protection of civilians as a jurisdictional extension by analogy to the violations contained in the international regulation of armed conflicts. But, the analogy to war crimes and the connection to war are no longer necessary for acts committed subsequent to the Charter since the Charter became the legal basis for criminalization under positive international criminal law.[145] Indeed, after 1945, international instruments reaffirmed the category of "crimes against humanity" independent of its original Charter context.[146] Consequently, events that occurred after 1945 need not be linked to war. Also, since 1945, "crimes against humanity" have a separate and autonomous legal basis in positive international criminal law, as discussed in Chapter 11. Indeed, none of the Post-Charter legal instruments link the prescribed violations they contain to war. This is the case with the Genocide and *Apartheid* Conventions, the 1954 Draft Code of Offences and its successor, the 1991 Draft Code of Crimes.

---

[143]   See *supra* notes 62-67 and accompanying text.

[144]   D'Amato, *The Moral Dilemma of Positivism*, 20 VAL. U. L. REV. 43 (1985). *See also* A. D'AMATO, JURISPRUDENCE: A DESCRIPTIVE AND NORMATIVE ANALYSIS OF LAW 294-302 (1984); *Contra* Hart, *Positivism and the Separation of Law and Morals*, 71 HARV. L. REV. 593, 624-29 (1958); and Chapter 3.

[145]   See Chapter 11.

[146]   *Id.*

CHAPTER 5

INDIVIDUAL CRIMINAL RESPONSIBILITY
AND INTERNATIONAL PROSECUTIONS

"Justice without force is important. Force without justice is tyrannical. Justice without force is infringed because there is always the mean. One must, therefore, combine justice and force, and, therefore, make strong what is right, and make right what is wrong."

B. PASCAL, PENSÉES: THE PROVINCIAL LETTERS (W.F. Trotter, trans. 1941).

Introduction

The evolution of international humanitarian law and the international regulation of armed conflicts, as discussed in Chapter 4, establishes individual criminal responsibility and reveals the basis for prosecutions of their violations. And just as the international criminalization of violations of some of the principles, norms and regulations regarding the conduct of war evolved gradually, so did the international prosecution of violators of such norms.

The history of such prosecutions can be divided into internationally defined war crimes before international and national tribunals and national trials for nationally defined crimes of international significance. Only internationally defined "war crimes," *largo senso*, are within the scope of this survey regardless of the tribunal's composition.

It is noteworthy that in all war and war crimes related prosecutions, the charges were brought against individuals for violations of norms arising out of the sources of law discussed in Chapter 4. The accused were charged on the basis of individual responsibility for having participated in the decision or carrying out, in whole or in part, those acts deemed violative of these principles, norms and rules. Some were also charged with having failed to prevent their occurrence, when as commanders they had a duty which they intentionally, knowingly or recklessly disregarded.

The subject matter of those prosecutions covered the initiation or participation in aggressive war and the violation of the laws of war. In the post-World War II trials, they were expanded to include "crimes against humanity."

192

Understandably, as the world community achieves higher levels of perceived interdependence, it tends towards greater actualization of international cooperation in penal matters. This, in part, contributes to the elimination of traditional sovereignty barriers which stand in the way of international adjudication and international prosecution of international criminal law violations. But international prosecutions of individuals for internatioanl criminal law violations had only occurred rarely before the conclusion of World War I.

The post-World War II prosecutions have been the principal examples and basic precedents for international individual criminal accountability before internationally constituted tribunals. But, these tribunals were for a limited purpose and time, for specific crimes, and for a limited category of offenders. The criticisms of these prosecutions reaffirm the need for a permanent international criminal tribunal. And though the idea of establishing such a tribunal has progressed since the 1919 Versailles Treaty, it has yet to be achieved.

The various historical examples of international and national prosecutions for some international crimes, as described in this Chapter, are nonetheless important precedents. In all of these, the principle of individual criminal responsibility has been reaffirmed in much the same terms as it is with respect to criminal responsibility in the national criminal justice systems of every country in the world -- the difference being that the source of applicable law is international as opposed to national law.

The relevance of this Chapter to the thesis of this book is that the application of international legal norms to individuals and their subjection to criminal responsibility for "crimes against humanity" has been established under international law and in the practice of several states. Such practices reinforce the international principles of international individual responsibility and for the international prosecution of "crimes against humanity," whether by an international criminal tribunal or by national tribunals, irrespective of whether the latter directly apply international legal norms or national ones which derive from an international source.

Pre-World War I

Prior to the late 1800's, the applicability of international criminal law to individuals was limited to piracy, slavery and certain violations of the regulations of armed conflicts. Notwithstanding the history of the international regulation of armed conflicts, as discussed in Chapter 4, piracy seems to have a more widely recognized historical starting point in the 1500's as a customary international crime.[1]

Evidence of piracy as an international crime for which there was individual criminal responsibility can be found as early as 1511 when King Henry VIII commissioned John Hopton to:

> seize and subdue all pirates wherever they shall from time to time be found; and if they cannot otherwise be seized, to destroy them, and to bring all and singular of them, who are captured, into one of our ports, and to hand over and deliver them...to our commissioners.[2]

Pierino Belli wrote, evidencing further the notion of individual criminal responsibility, in regard to pirates, in 1563, that "...people whose hand is against every man should expect a like return from all men, and it should be permissible for any one to attack them."[3] A reason for the early recognition of individual criminal responsibility of pirates is that piracy involves conduct which effects state interests. As one author noted:

> ...It is right to make war on pirates...for they violate the common law of nations. And if war against pirates justly calls all men to arms because of love of our neighbors and the desire to live in peace, so also does the general violation of the common law of humanity and a wrong done to mankind. Piracy is contrary to the law of nations and the league of human society....[4]

Piracy, as a customary international crime, was formulated in two international instruments in 1937[5]. In addition, there are four other instruments containing

---

[1]   See A. RUBIN, THE LAW OF PIRACY (1988); Sundberg, *The Crime of Piracy*, in 1 BASSIOUNI ICL 441.

[2]   A. RUBIN, *supra* note 1 at 100 *citing* MARSDEN, DOCUMENTS RELATING TO THE LAW AND CUSTOM OF THE SEA 146-147.

[3]   BELLI, DE RE MILITARI ET BELLO TRACTATUS 83 (H.S. Nutting trans. 1936), *quoted in* A. RUBIN, *supra* note 1 at 18.

[4]   Green, *International Criminal Law and the Protection of Human Rights*, in BASSIOUNI ICL 116, 119, *citing* A. DE GENTILLI, DE IURE BELLI (1612), Bk. I, Chap. XXV, 124 (Carnegie trans. 1933).

[5]   See 2 BASSIOUNI DIGEST at 31-37. The Nyon Arrangement, Nyon, 14 September 1937, 181

provisions applicable to piracy dating from 1841.[6] Piracy emerged as a conventional international crime under the 1958 Geneva Convention on the High Seas[7] and the 1982 U.N. Convention on the Law of the Sea.[8] These conventions were the product of a number of efforts, dating back to the League of Nations, to arrive at an international conventional regulation of piracy.[9]

Slavery, throughout the ages, was thought to be morally repugnant by many societies, and it has evolved from a "moral" offense to an international crime.[10] As one commentator noted: "As circumstances changed, what was legally and morally legitimate gradually became condemned. The Church [of England] again took the lead and the law reluctantly followed."[11] Due to the widespread economic benefit of the slave trade, many countries found it difficult to condemn it. France abolished slavery in 1791 and England did the same in 1833, although both allowed the practice to continue in some of their colonies.[12] Sweden abolished slavery in 1846, Denmark in 1848, Portugal in 1856, Holland in 1860, Brazil in 1884 and 1890, and the United States in 1862.[13]

The prohibition of slavery emerged in the 1800's, as a conventional international crime, as a result of attempts by European powers who recognized its evil nature and gradually established duties to prohibit, prevent, prosecute and punish those engaged

---

L.N.T.S. 135; Agreement Supplementary to the Nyon Agreement, Geneva, 17 September 1937, 181 L.N.T.S. 149. Subsequent to the Charter two more international agreements criminalized piracy. These agreements are the Convention on the High Seas (Geneva Convention on the Law of the Sea), Geneva, 29 April 1958, 450 U.N.T.S. 82, 13 U.S.T. 2313, T.I.A.S. No. 5200; and the Convention on the Law of the Sea (Montego Bay Convention) Montego Bay, 10 December 1982, U.N. Doc. A/CONF. 62/122.

[6] See 2 BASSIOUNI ICL at 41. Subsequent to the Charter, four more instruments contained provisions applicable to piracy. These instruments are: 1954 Draft Code of Offenses; Convention on the High Seas, *Id.*; Convention on the Law of the Sea, *Id.*; 1991 Draft Code of Crimes.

[7] See Geneva Convention on the Law of the Sea, *supra* note 5.

[8] See Montego Bay Convention, *supra* note 5.

[9] See Sundberg, *supra* note 1 at 442.

[10] Bassiouni, *Enslavement as an International Crime*, 23 N.Y.U.J. INT'L L. 445, 450 (1991).

[11] Umozurike, *The African Slave Trade and the Attitudes of International Law Towards It*, 16 HOW. L.J. 334, 341 (1971), *cited in* Bassiouni, *supra* note 10.

[12] See Bassiouni, *supra* note 10 at 451.

[13] *Id.* at 451-52.

in the slave trade.[14] By making slavery an international crime, states were allowed to search and detain vessels thought to be carrying slaves.[15] The goal was to eliminate slavery by obligating each state to make it a crime and by creating universal jurisdiction over the crime.[16] For example, under Article 5 of The 1890 Convention Relative to the Slave-Trade and Importation into Africa of Firearms, Ammunition, Spirituous Liquors (General Act of Brussels Conference),[17] the contracting parties obligated themselves to enact or introduce penal legislation to punish serious offenses against individuals.[18] Those responsible for mutilating male adults and children, and anyone participating in the capture of slaves by force, were to be punished.[19] Those guilty of such crimes were to be brought to justice in the place where they were found, thus establishing universal jurisdiction for those violating terms of the Treaty.[20] In all seventy-nine separate international instruments and documents have addressed the issue of slavery, the slave trade, slave related practices, forced labor, and their respective institutions.[21]

In the area of international regulation of armed conflicts, the historical evolution described in Chapter 4 was a slow process, but its manifestations pre-dated all other efforts of international criminalization of certain violations and placed responsibility on individual offenders. There were even a few war crimes prosecutions inflicting individual criminal responsibility on violators of international law as far back as ancient Greece.[22] But, the first documented prosecution for initiating an unjust war is reported

---

[14]   *See* Bassiouni, *supra* note 10 at 454, *see also* 42 MARTENS NOUVEAU RECUEIL 432, *reprinted in* 63 PARRY'S T.S. 473 (1969).

[15]   *Id.*

[16]   *Id.*

[17]   27 Stat. 886, T.S. No. 383, *reprinted in* 1 Bevans 134.

[18]   *See* Bassiouni, *supra* note 10, at 463.

[19]   *Id.*

[20]   *Id.*

[21]   *Id.* at 454.

[22]   *See* R.K. WOETZEL, THE NUREMBERG TRIALS IN INTERNATIONAL LAW WITH A POSTLUDE ON THE EICHMANN CASE 17-18 (1962). Woetzel refers to a lecture by Professor George S. Maridakis (and citing to Maridakis, *Un précédent du Procès de Nuremberg tiré de l'histoire de la Grèce ancienne*, 5 REV. HELLÉNIQUE DE DROIT INT'LE 1 (1952)) who makes reference to a kind of court, established in 405 B.C. after the destruction of the Athenian fleet at Aegospotamos, which examined evidence and heard witnesses before it passed judgment and sentenced to death all but one Athenian prisoner.

to have been in Naples in 1268 and Conradin von Hohenstafen was put to death for that reason.[23] The first reported international prosecution, however, was in 1474 in Breisach, Germany, of Peter von Hagenbach for war crimes.[24] Von Hagenbach was tried before a tribunal of twenty-eight judges from the allied states of the Holy Roman Empire. He was stripped of his knighthood by this international tribunal, which found him guilty of murder, rape, perjury, and other crimes against the "laws of God and man" in the execution of a military occupation.[25] Later for the same reasons in 1689, James II of England, although then in exile, relieved one Count Rosen of all further military duties, not for the failure of his mission, but rather because his siege of Londonderry was so outrageous and included the murder of innocent civilians.[26]

Other than the courts of chivalry in the middle-ages, there are practically no instances of national prosecutions for violating internationally accepted principles, norms and rules regulating the conduct of armed conflicts.

As one author states:

> Insofar as the written law of war is concerned, nothing has appeared concerning the trial of individual offenders save in national military codes. Thus, by the time of the establishment of the Commonwealth, England had promulgated its Lawwes and Ordinances of Warre regulating the behaviour of the armed forces, forbidding, marauding of the countryside, individual acts against the enemy without authorization from a superior, private taking of booty, or private detention of an enemy prisoner.[27]

Individual criminal responsibility for violations of the regulations of armed conflict as customary international law can further be evidenced by the regulations of

---

[23] Reported by Bierzanek, *The Prosecution of War Crimes*, in I BASSIOUNI AND NANDA TREATISE at 559-60 (1973). The original source is likely to be E. DE VATTEL, LE DROIT DES GENS, bk III (1887).

[24] *See* 2 G. SCHWARZENBERGER, INTERNATIONAL LAW AS APPLIED BY INTERNATIONAL COURTS AND TRIBUNALS 462-466 (1968); A.G. DE BARRANTE, HISTOIRE DES DUCS DE BOURGOGNE, vols. 9, 10 (1837); JOHANNIS KNEBEL CAPPELLANI, ECCLESIAE BASITIENSIS DIARIUM, Sept. 1473-Jan. 1476, p. 1 *et. seq.* BASLER CHRONIKEN (Vol. II - 1880 ed. by W. Vischer and H. Boos).

[25] *See* 10 A.G. DE BARRANTE, *supra* note 24, at 15 and H. BRAUER-GRAMM, DER LANDVOGT PETER VON HAGENBACH 235, 282-84 (1957).

[26] *Reported in* W.H. Parks, *Command Responsibility for War Crimes*, 62 MIL. L. REV. 1, 5 (1973). *See also* Colby, *War Crimes*, 23 MICH. L. REV. 482 (1925).

[27] Green, *supra* note 4 at 6. *See also* CLODE, I MILITARY FORCES OF THE CROWN, 1869, App. VI.

individual nations. In 1863, the United States stated its intentions in the Lieber Code, enacted as Instructions for the Government of Armies of the United States in the Field:

> A prisoner of war remains answerable for his crime against the captors' army or people, committed before he was captured, and for which he has not been punished by his own authorities.[28]

The Lieber Code also provides:

> Whoever intentionally inflicts additional wounds on or encourages soldiers to do so, shall suffer death, if duly convicted, whether he belongs to the Army of the United States, or is an enemy captured after having committed his misdeed.[29]

A similar position was adopted by the Institute of International Law of the Oxford Manual of Laws of War of 1880, which stated:

> In case the preceding rules are violated, the perpetrator shall, after a due process of law, be punished by the belligerent in whose power he is.[30]

It was under the Lieber Code, however, that the United States tried and sentenced to death Confederate Major Henry Wirz, a prisoner of war camp commandant, for his role in the death of several thousand Union prisoners in the Andersonville prison.[31] The United States prosecuted him under Article 59 of the Lieber Code which held prisoners of war liable to prosecution for violations of war conducted prior to their imprisonment. The tribunal found him guilty, despite his plea of "obedience to superior orders," and sentenced him to death. The United States also convened war crimes tribunals after the Spanish-American War and the occupation of the Philippines.[32]

---

[28]   Lieber Code, art. 59.

[29]   Lieber Code, art. 71.

[30]   OXFORD MANUAL ON THE LAWS AND CUSTOMS OF WAR ON LAND, art. 84 (Institute of International Law 1880).

[31]   8 AMERICAN STATE TRIALS 666 (J.D. Lawson ed. 1918). The proceedings of the Military Commission were published in 8 HOUSE EXECUTIVE DOCUMENTS, No. 23, serial No. 1381, 40th Cong. 2d Sess., 764 (1868). *See also* A. ROACH, THE PRISONERS OF WAR AND HOW THEY WERE TREATED (1865).

[32]   *See, Court Martial of General Jacob H. Smith*, Manila, P.I., April 1902, S. Doc. 213, 57th Cong.

After the Boer War, British tribunals prosecuted prisoners of war for crimes they had committed prior to their imprisonment.[33] But, the record of history is sparse on this subject. It nonetheless evidences a growing awareness and even recognition that certain violations should subject their perpetrators to individual criminal responsibility and to international prosecution. The principle of individual criminal responsibility under the laws of war was also recognized in the Weimar Constitution of 1919 and included in German military law. The German Ordinance "Usage in Land Warfare" enumerated the violations contained in the aforementioned 1907 Hague Convention and held that:

> Any person who violates these prohibitions shall be held responsible by his own state. If he is taken prisoner, he shall be punished according to the laws of war.[34]

Post-World War I

In 1919, the Treaty of Versailles contained provisions for prosecuting German military personnel for war crimes. Article 228 provided:

> The German Government recognizes the right of the Allied and Associated Powers to bring before military tribunals persons accused of having committed acts in violation of the laws and customs of war.[35]

Article 227 of the Treaty established the individual responsibility of the Kaiser. It also provided for the Allies' right to establish national war crimes tribunals to try Germans (Article 229).[36] But no war crimes tribunals were established because Germany did

---

2d Sess. at 5-17; *Court Martial of Lt. Preston Brown*, Manila, P.I., June 1902, S. Doc. 213, 57th Cong., 2d Sess. at 48-62.

[33] *See* H.H. JESCHECK, DER VERANTWORTLICHKEIT DER STAATSORGANE NACH VÖLKERSTRAFRECHT 36 (1952). *See also* Berenton, *The Administration of Justice Among Prisoners of War by Military Courts*, 1 PROCEEDINGS OF THE AUSTRALIAN AND NEW ZEALAND SOCIETY OF INTERNATIONAL LAW 143 (1935).

[34] Weimar Constitution of 1919.

[35] Treaty of Versailles, art. 228.

[36] *See* Treaty of Versailles, arts. 228-230. Also, the Treaty stipulated the prosecution of Kaiser Wilhelm II by an international tribunal, *id.*, art. 227, for the "supreme offence against international morality and the sanctity of treaties," *i.e.*, the neutrality of Belgium, however, the Kaiser was never tried because he sought refuge in Holland which refused to extradite him on the grounds that the crime with which he was

not extradite its own nationals. Also, since the conventional and customary law of armed conflicts required the repatriation of prisoners of war after the end of the conflict, some legalistic arguments were raised about the eventual invalidity of prosecuting prisoners of war after the cessation of hostilities. But, in the final analysis, it was a question of opportunity and political judgment that led the Allies to forego international and national prosecution and to allow Germany to prosecute its own nationals before its national court in Leipzig.[37]

Perhaps the greatest development for its time in the area of individual responsibility under international criminal law was the *1919 Report of the Commission on the Responsibilities of the Authors of War and Enforcement of Penalties for Violations of the Laws and Customs of War*.[38] This report established an elaborate scheme of international crimes and individual responsibility, but was not accepted by the United States.[39]

In the report prepared by the Commission on the Responsibility of the Authors of the War and Enforcement of Penalties,[40] the Allies submitted 895 names of alleged war criminals to Germany. However, for mostly political reasons and because of Germany's reluctance to hand over accused war criminals, that list dwindled and only 45 cases were selected for prosecution. Moreover, the Allies consented, as stated above, to let Germany prosecute the alleged war criminals; a concession which the Allies would subsequently regret. Of the short list of 45 selected for actual prosecution (from

---

charged was a "political offense" exempt from extradition. *See* Wright, *The Legality of the Kaiser*, 8 AM. POL. SCI. REV. 121 (1919). For an earlier precedent, *see also* the decision of the Congress of Aix-La-Chapelle of 1810 on the detention of Napoleon for waging wars which disturbed the peace of the world.

[37] Toward the end of World War II, one commentator called upon the United Nations to learn lessons from Versailles and Leipzig. Specifically, this commentator denounced the Leipzig trials:

> Thus ended the tragi-comedy of the Leipzig trials, beginning with the German manipulation of the Allied statesmen for two and a half years, while the evidence of atrocities grew cold, accused and witnesses disappeared, and chauvinistic public opinion was whipped up inside Germany; and ending with the patriotic cooperation of those conveniently negligent bloodhounds.

Glueck, *War Criminals - Their Prosecution and Punishment*, 5 LAW GUILD REV. 1, 9 (1945).

[38] *See* 1 BASSIOUNI, INTERNATIONAL EXTRADITION IN U.S. LAW AND PRACTICE 187-246 (2nd rev. ed. 1987).

[39] *Id.*

[40] *See* 1919 Commission Report.

the 895), Germany only tried 12 before its Supreme Court sitting in Leipzig and six of these 12 were acquitted.[41]

The Allies and Germany had agreed that any of the Allied nations could initiate a prosecution before the Leipzig Court by providing to the German Prosecutor General complete details and evidence of the acts of which a person was accused. To avoid the problem of who had ultimate control of deciding whether or not to initiate a prosecution, a procedure was established whereby if the German Prosecutor General did not believe that the facts justified an indictment, he was nonetheless under the obligation to request a mini-trial, in the nature of a preliminary hearing, to judicially ascertain the facts on a preliminary basis and decide whether to continue with the prosecution.[42]

A number of cases were brought by Great Britain, France and Belgium. The British Government initiated and pursued six prosecutions.[43] Three men, Sergeant Karl Heynen, Captain Emil Muller and Private Robert Neumann, were charged and convicted for brutalizing prisoners of war. Two naval officers, First Lieutenants Ludwig Ditman and John Boldt, were found guilty in *The Llandovery Castle Case* for the sinking of life boats carrying survivors of a hospital ship they had just sunk. Another naval officer, Lieutenant-Captain Karl Newmann, was acquitted for his part in the sinking of the *Dover Castle*, also a hospital ship like the *Llandovery Castle*. His defense was "obedience to superior orders;" the German Admiralty had issued the order to torpedo hospital ships on the assumption that the British had violated the Red Cross insignia and concealed war ships as hospital ships. Belgium and France each brought cases mainly regarding the maltreatment of prisoners of war and wounded in the field. Belgium initiated prosecution against Max Randohr, but he was not convicted. France pursued the prosecutions of Lieutenant-General Karl Stenger, Major Benn Crusius, First

---

[41] Glueck, *supra* note 37, at 7 (1945). The two major prosecutions, which also involved the issue of defense to superior orders, were *The Dover Castle*, 16 AJIL 704 (1922); and the *Llandovery Castle*, 16 AJIL 708 (1922). *See also* C. MULLINS, THE LEIPZIG TRIALS 35 (1921). Mullins *id.* and J.F. WILLIS PROLOGUE TO NUREMBERG: THE POLITICS AND DIPLOMACY OF PUNISHING WAR CRIMINALS OF THE FIRST WORLD WAR (1982) are the two most authoritative works on that episode. *See also* Garver, *Punishment of Offenders Against the Laws and Customs of War*, 14 AJIL 70 (1926). The court which tried the German War Criminals was known as the Criminal Senate of the Imperial Court of Justice. In December 1919, Germany's Parliament passed a special law to carry out the provisions of the agreement with the Allies. This new law was supplemented by two subsequent acts, March, 1920 and May, 1921. These laws gave the Imperial Court of Justice special jurisdiction to conduct the prosecutions.

[42] *See* C. MULLINS, *supra* note 41 at 35-36.

[43] *Id.* at 51-67.

Lieutenant Adolph Laule, Lieutenant-General Hans von Schack, and Major-General Benno Kruska. Only Major Crusius was convicted.[44]

The trials at Leipzig were held between May 23 and July 16, 1921 and the Armistice had been signed on November 11, 1918. Therefore, it was almost three years after the Armistice that the proceedings ended. The delay between the Armistice and the end of the trials played a critical role in determining the number of prosecutions and in some respects the low number of convictions obtained. In the Allied countries a public opinion shift against prosecuting German war criminals became noticeable and that reduced an already shaky German resolve to do so. German public opinion, as may be expected, favored the accused officers and enlisted men who were brought to trial. Later, the UNWCC noted, "the German public showed indignation that German judges could be found to sentence the [German] war criminals and the press brought all possible pressure to the court."[45] Consequently, the Allies were dissatisfied with the result and decided not to submit any further defendants to the German court and to conduct their own trials according to Article 229 of the Versailles Treaty. The Allies, however, did not request the extradition of any accused German and only Belgium and France held a few *in absentia* trials.[46] Thus, the Leipzig Trials, affected by the *realpolitik* exercised by the Allied Powers and the impact of German public opinion, resulted in few prosecutions and even fewer convictions.

While the Leipzig Trials may be viewed essentially as failures and examples of the difficulty in achieving effective punishment of war criminals through national prosecutions, especially prosecutions by the national courts of the very vanquished belligerent, they nevertheless serve as important markers in the history of war crimes trials. It is obvious that the Leipzig prosecutions convicted only a small fraction of the number accused, but the value of these trials lies not with their prosecutorial success but with the principle they helped to establish. As Mullins, the author of one of the most authoritative texts on the Leipzig trials, states; "great principles are often established by minor events .... [These trials] undoubtedly established the principle that

---

[44] For the facts described above, *see* C. MULLINS, *supra* note 41 at 67-189.

[45] The UNWCC at 51-52.

[46] *See* R. WOETZEL, *supra* note 22, at 34. *See also* 1921 J. DE DROIT INT'L 781-782, 1076-1077; and *e.g.* Garner, *Punishment of Offenders Against the Laws and Customs of War*, 14 AJIL 70 (1926).

individual atrocities committed during a war may be punished when the war is over."[47] Therefore, Mullins further asserts:

> In my view, the object of the War Criminals' Trials at Leipzig was to establish a principle, to put on record before history that might is not right, and that men whose sole conception of the duty they owe to their country is to inflict torture upon others, may be put on trial.[48]

Taking into consideration all of the pre-World War II prosecutions, it can be concluded, as does one author:

> ... that there is no exact precedent for the IMT at Nuremberg. Nevertheless, it is evident that the development in international law ... provided many of the prerequisites for the action taken by the Allies at the London Conference of 1945. The idea of an international tribunal was clearly contained in the punitive provisions of the Versailles Peace Treaty. The principle of individual responsibility for violations of the laws of war had been accepted in the First World War, and was extended to other crimes in the period between the two great wars. Both these conceptions are fundamental to the Charter of the IMT.[49]

Along with these prosecutions of individuals under the regulations of armed conflicts and individual criminal responsibility under piracy and slavery, there is further evidence of individual criminal responsibility in other areas of international law prior to the Law

---

[47] C. MULLINS, *supra* note 41, at 224. In this connection, Mullins quotes Tennison: "And finding that of fifty seeds/She often brings one to bear." *Id.* at 231.

[48] *Id.* at 231. Similarly, Professor Bert Röling, who was a judge at Tokyo, commenting upon the Nuremberg trials states:

> The purpose was not to punish all cases of criminal guilt, but to give expression to the abhorrence of what had happened. The exemplary punishments served the purpose of restoring the legal order, that is of reassuring the whole community that what they had witnessed for so many years was criminal behavior.

Röling, *Aspects of Criminal Responsibility for Violations of the Laws of War*, in THE NEW HUMANITARIAN LAW 199, 206 (A. Cassese ed. 1979). *See also* Röling, *The Nuremberg and Tokyo Trials in Retrospect*, I BASSIOUNI AND NANDA TREATISE at 590.

[49] R. WOETZEL, *supra* note 22, at 38.

of the Charter. In 1884, the International Convention for the Protection of Submarine Telegraph Cables[50] established individual responsibility. Article II of the Convention provides:

> The breaking or injury of a submarine cable, done willfully or through culpable negligence, and resulting in the total or partial interruption or embarrassment of telegraphic communication, shall be a punishable offense, but the punishment inflicted shall be no bar to a civil action for damages.[51]

Articles I, II and III of the Agreement for the Suppression of the Circulation of Obscene Publications,[52] signed in 1910, establish a duty or right to cooperate in prosecution and punishment, including judicial assistance.[53] Similar provisions could be found in the International Convention for the Suppression of the Circulation of and Traffic in Obscene Publications[54] which entered into force in 1924.[55] Drug trafficking was another area in which individual responsibility had been established. Seven documents, prior to the Charter, criminalized the conduct and established a duty or right to prohibit, prevent, prosecute, punish, or the like.[56] The International Conven-

---

[50]   11 Martens, 24 Stat. 989, T.S. No. 380. *Reprinted in* 163 Parry's 391; 1 Bevans 89.

[51]   *Id.* at art. II.

[52]   7 Martens (3d) 266, 37 Stat. 1511, T.S. No. 559. *Reprinted in* 211 Parry's 54; 5 AJIL 167 (1911); 1 Bevans 748.

[53]   2 BASSIOUNI DIGEST 170.

[54]   27 L.N.T.S. 213. *Reprinted in* 7 Martens (3d) 266, 20 AJIL 178 (1926); 2 HUDSON 1051.

[55]   *See* 2 BASSIOUNI DIGEST 171-174.

[56]   *See* 2 BASSIOUNI DIGEST 99-120. These documents are: International Opium Convention, The Hague 23 January 1912, 8 L.N.T.S. 187, 38 Stat. 1912, T.S. No. 612, *reprinted in* 215 Parry's 297; 6 AJIL 177 (1912); 1 Bevans 855; 1914 FOR. REL. 938. Agreement Concerning the Suppression of the Manufacturing of Internal Trade in and Use of, Prepared Opium, Geneva, 11 February 1925, 51 L.N.T.S. 337, *reprinted in* 3 HUDSON 1580. International Opium Convention, Geneva, 19 February 1925, 81 L.N.T.S. 317, *reprinted in* 23 AJIL 135 (1929); 3 HUDSON 1589. Protocol to the International Opium Convention, Geneva, 19 February 1925, 81 L.N.T.S. 356, *reprinted in* 23 AJIL 155; 3 HUDSON 1614. Convention for Limiting the Manufacture and Regulating the Distribution of Narcotic Drugs, Geneva, 13 July 1931, 139 L.N.T.S. 301, 48 Stat. 1543, T.S. No. 863, *reprinted in* 28 AJIL 21 (1934); 3 Bevans 1; 5 HUDSON 1048. Agreement Concerning the Suppression of Opium-Smoking, Bangkok, 27 November 1931, 177 L.N.T.S. 373, *reprinted in* 5 HUDSON 1149. Convention for the Suppression of the Illicit Traffic in Dangerous Drugs, Geneva, 26 June 1936, 198 L.N.T.S. 299, *reprinted in* 7 HUDSON 359.

tion for the Suppression of Counterfeiting Currency[57] signed in 1929 established individual responsibility as well.[58]

Therefore, by the time of the Charter, individual criminal responsibility in international law was a generally accepted principle. The practice of holding an individual criminally responsible, however, was limited because the notions and perceptions of nations were such that it would not work without a victor's power as there was no international enforcement mechanism other than war. After the Leipzig trials, some private associations, such as the *Association Internationale de Droit Pénal*, urged the establishment of an international criminal court to administer international criminal law.[59] However, such efforts were not supported by many governments. For the most part, the period between World War I and World War II witnessed a lull in the development of international regulation concerning the laws of war because of the belief that the so-called "Great War," as it was called, was indeed going to "end all wars," as the saying went at that time. Furthermore, most people believed that the newly founded League of Nations was to usher in a new period of world peace based on a new world order, a concept that seems to emerge recurringly after each major conflict but which has yet to achieve a meaningful impact on the advancement of the international "Rule of Law."

Post-World War II: The Charters of Nuremberg and Tokyo

World War II was unleashed against all hopes and efforts of civilized humankind. During its conduct, it became apparent, particularly after the tide of the war came to favor the Allies and after the discovery of untold horrors, that those who initiated the aggressive war, carried it out, and committed war crimes and other atrocities -- which were later labeled "crimes against humanity" -- would be prosecuted and punished. After the war, the victors had a choice between summary punishment and the establishment of a legal process by which to advance law and justice. The first clear Allied indication came in the Moscow Declaration of 30 October 1943 which called for

---

[57]   122 L.N.T.S. 371, *reprinted in* 4 HUDSON 2692.

[58]   *See* 2 BASSIOUNI DIGEST 416-418.

[59]   For the history of the AIDP's efforts *see* BASSIOUNI DRAFT CODE at 3 *et seq.* and 468-470. *See also* Principles of the Nuremberg Tribunal at 11-14, *infra* note 117. For a recent survey of international criminal responsibility and international prosecutions *see* Lippman, *Nuremberg Forty-Five Years Later*, 7 CONN. J. INT'L. L. 1 (1991).

the prosecution and punishment of those responsible for the "atrocities" conducted during the war.[60] It was followed by the Agreement for the Prosecution and Punishment of the Major War Criminals of the European Axis (the London Charter of 8 August 1945) which established at Nuremberg the first of modern history's international military tribunals. The second such tribunal, at Tokyo, was based on a separate statute promulgated as a General Order issued by General Douglas MacArthur in 1946.

The Nuremberg and Tokyo Charters were effective tools for individual enforcement of international criminal law. Their credibility, however, was undermined by the selective enforcement of their provisions and by not applying the same standards to those Allied personnel that committed some of the same atrocities.[61] Further damage was done by the subsequent Nuremberg proceedings which under CCL 10 stretched the limit of the "principles of legality."[62]

The basic premise of the London and Tokyo Charters and all prosecutions arising out of World War II was that of direct individual criminal accountability under international law, as discussed in Chapter 4. Indeed, the Charter makes clear that the three categories of crimes listed in Article 6 *"are crimes coming within the jurisdiction of the Tribunal for which there shall be individual responsibility."* (emphasis added)[63] Along with the principle of individual responsibility, Article 6 establishes the principles of individual responsibility regardless of national law, individual responsibility all the

---

[60] Moscow Declaration; The Cairo Declaration (Conferences at Cairo and Tehran), 1 December 1943, 1943 FOR. REL. 448; and Potsdam Conference. It should be noted that, in 1943 and 1944, the Soviet Union conducted the first trials involving atrocities committed by the Germans (and their accomplices) during World War II. These prosecutions resulted from Nazi actions in the Eastern USSR, where an estimated 10,000 people were exterminated during a six month period. While the organizers and directors of these atrocities (the Nazis themselves) could not be brought to justice, eleven Soviet citizens were convicted for treason because they assisted the Nazis, and some minor Nazi war criminals were prosecuted for engaging in mass executions and employing gas vans to murder the inhabitants of the Kharkov region. *See* Lediakh, *The Application of the Nuremberg Principles by Other Military Tribunals and National Courts*, in THE NUREMBERG TRIAL AND INTERNATIONAL LAW at 263-265 (G. Ginsburgs and V.N. Kudriavtsev eds. 1990).

[61] *See* Chapter 1.

[62] *See* Chapter 3.

[63] Charter, Art. 6. The Tokyo Charter in Art. 5 states that the "Tribunal shall have the power to try and punish Far Eastern war criminals who as individuals or as members of organizations are charged with offenses...." CCL 10, at Art. II, para. 2, provides that "[a]ny person without regard to nationality or capacity in which he acted, is deemed to have committed a crime ... if ...."

way up to and including heads of state and precludes the defense of "obedience to superior orders."[64] In its Judgment, the IMT stated:

The Jurisdiction of the Tribunal is defined in the Agreement and Charter, and the crimes coming within the jurisdiction of the Tribunal, for which there shall be individual responsibility, are set out in Article 6. The law of the Charter is decisive and binding upon the tribunal.[65]

Also, the Tribunal noted that:

...individuals can be punished for violations of international law. Crimes against international law are committed by men, not by abstract entities, and only by punishing individuals who commit such crimes can the provisions of international law be enforced.[66]

The Tribunal further stated:

The very essence of the Charter is that individuals have international duties which transcend the national obligations of obedience imposed by the individual state.[67]

Moreover, in the words of the IMT, "[t]hat international law imposes duties and liabilities upon individuals as well as upon states has long been recognized."[68] Thus, the IMT accepted the view of Justice Jackson, who in his opening statement asserted:

---

[64]   *See* Charter, Art. 6.

[65]   IMT 38, *quoted in* R. Baxter, *The Effects of Ill-Conceived Codification and Development of International Law*, in RECEUIL D'ETUDES DE DROIT INTERNATIONAL EN HOMAGE A PAUL GUGGENHEIM 146, 149 (1952).

[66]   22 IMT 466.

[67]   *Id.*

[68]   22 IMT 465. Similarly, Lord Shawcross asserted: "Nor is the principle of individual international responsibility for offenses against the law of nations altogether new. It has been applied not only to pirates. The entire law relating to war crimes, as distinct from the crime of war, is based upon the principle distinct from the crime of war, is based upon the principle responsibility." 3 IMT 106. *See also Ex parte Quirin* 317 U.S. 1, 27-28, (1942), which the IMT quoted, at 22 IMT 465: "From the very beginning of its history this Court has applied the law of war as including that part of the law of nations which proscribes for the conduct of war, the status, rights, and duties of enemy nations as well as enemy individuals."

The charter also recognizes individual responsibility on the part of those who commit acts defined as crimes, or who incite others to do so, or who join a common plan with other persons, groups or organizations to bring about their commission. The principle of individual responsibility for piracy and brigandage, which have long been recognized as crimes punishable under International Law, is old and well established. That is what illegal warfare is. This principle of personal liability is a necessary as well as logical one if International Law is to render real help to the maintenance of peace. An International Law which operates only on states can be enforced only by war because the most practicable method of coercing a state is warfare.... Only sanctions which reach individuals can peacefully and effectively be enforced. Hence, the principle of the criminality of aggressive war is implemented by the Charter with the principle of personal responsibility.

Of course, the idea that a state, any more than a corporation, commits crimes is a fiction. Crimes always are committed only by persons. While it is quite proper to employ the fiction of responsibility of a state or a corporation for the purpose of imposing a collective liability, it is quite intolerable to let such a legalism become the basis of personal immunity.[69]

In his report to the President, Jackson stated:

The Charter also enacts the principle that individuals rather than states are responsible for criminal violations of international law and applies to such lawbreakers the principle of conspiracy by which one who joins in a common plan to commit crime becomes responsible for the acts of any other conspirator in executing the plan. In prohibiting the plea of "acts of state" as freeing defendants from legal responsibility, the charter refuses to recognize the immunity once enjoyed by criminal statesmanship.[70]

The purpose of the International Military Tribunal sitting at Nuremberg was to try the "major" German war criminals.[71] The tribunal had eight members: a senior and

---

[69]   R.H. JACKSON, THE NÜRNBERG CASE 88 (1947, 2d printing 1971).

[70]   Jackson's Report at ix.

[71]   *See e.g.*, A TUSA & J. TUSA, THE NUREMBERG TRIAL (1984); R.E. CONOT, JUSTICE AT NUREMBERG (1983); B.F. SMITH, REACHING JUDGMENT AT NUREMBERG (1977); E. DAVIDSON, THE TRIAL

an alternate member from each of the four signatory Powers (Francis Biddle and Judge John J. Parker of the United States; Lord Justice Geoffrey Lawrence and Justice Norman Birkett of Great Britain; Professor H. Donnendieu de Vabres and Judge R. Falco from France; and Major General I.T. Nikitchenko and Lieutenant Colonel A.F. Volchkov of the Soviet Union). These men would mold together different approaches to criminal law and procedure, as discussed in Chapter 1. The process of the Tribunal's work was set in motion in October of 1945, when, after much negotiation and compromise,[72] the Committee of Chief Counsels of the four signatories to the London Agreement (Justice Robert H. Jackson of the United States, Sir Hartley Shawcross of Great Britain, General Roman A. Rudenko of the Soviet Union, and François de Menthon and Auguste Champetier de Ribes of France) signed and filed an indictment setting forth the crimes charged against twenty-four high-ranking individuals, as well as of the organizations to which they belonged.[73] The indictment charged the defendants with four counts: (1) "common plan or conspiracy;" (2) "crimes against peace;" (3) "war crimes;" and, (4) "crimes against humanity."[74] The IMT held its first session at Nuremberg on November 14, 1945, worked 216 days, and held its last session on August 31, 1946. It held 403 open sessions and heard evidence from thirty-three witnesses for the prosecution and eighty for the defense, nineteen of whom were the defendants themselves. Most of the evidence presented to the Tribunal was documentary (as was particularly true of the evidence presented by the American prosecution team) and it consisted of official German documents. The Germans' meticulous way of recording things was the principal reason for the availability of such a documentary record which insured the success of the prosecution, something that is

---

OF THE GERMANS (1969). Moreover, N.E. TUTOROW, WAR CRIMES, WAR CRIMINALS, AND WAR CRIMES TRIALS (1986) provides, at 283-342, a comprehensive bibliography of works that examine Nuremberg.

[72] *See* Chapter 1 and B. SMITH, *supra* note 71, at 67-73.

[73] Of the original twenty-four defendants, charges were dropped against Gustav Krupp, and Robert Ley committed suicide, and Martin Bormann, who has never been found, was tried *in absentia*. An interesting historical footnote concerning Gustav Krupp. At the trial, the senile old man was found *non compos mentis*. The prosecutors had earlier realized that the Krupp they wanted was Alfried, the son of Gustav, who ran the factories with the Nazis and supplied slave labor. That realization came shortly after the trial began, and the prosecutors tried to substitute Alfried for Gustav. To its credit, the IMT refused. It should be noted further that during the course of the Nuremberg trials, the possibility of a second international military tribunal was considered but the United States felt that the British were not too keen on it and that the Russians were more interested in the propaganda value of the ongoing proceedings than on their own judicial significance.

[74] *See* Indictment.

unlikely to occur in other cultures. The prosecution also relied heavily on affidavits, a practice unknown to all but the Common Law system. But, even in that system, it is subject to certain defense rights of confrontation and cross-examination of the affiant, which were made available to the defendants but which they seldom requested. At times when they did and the affiant was unavailable, the court did not rule the affidavit inadmissible and relied upon it. In general, the trials were fair and offered the defendants an opportunity to adequately defend themselves, though not in accordance with the full panoply of rights that the Common Law systems of England and the United States would have offered.[75]

The Tribunal handed down twelve death sentences, seven prison terms (three for life, two for twenty years, one for fifteen years, and one for ten years) and three acquittals.[76] More specifically, the Tribunal reached these verdicts for those convicted of "crimes against humanity" -- i.e., Count 4 - after describing the conduct for which they were held responsible.[77] The disposition of the defendants is in the Document Section C.4.

Of the eighteen defendants who were indicted for "crimes against humanity," only Hess and Fritzsche were found not guilty. Also, of these eighteen, only two defendants

---

[75] Most commentators agree, see Robinson, *The International Military Tribunal and the Holocaust: Some Legal Reflections*, 7 ISRAEL L. REV. 1 (1972); but see contra the position of four of the defense lawyers at Nuremberg: H. Kraus (Chief Counsel for Schacht), *The Nuremberg Trials of the Major War Criminals: Reflections after Seventeen Years*, 13 DE PAUL L. REV. 233 (1964); C. Haensel (Chief Counsel for the S.S. and S.D.), *The Nuremberg Trial Revisited*, 13 DE PAUL L. REV. 248 (1964); O. Kranzbuhler (Chief Counsel for Donitz), *Nuremberg Eighteen Years Afterwards*, 14 DE PAUL L. REV. 333 (1965); O. Pannenbecker (Chief Counsel for Frick), *The Nuremberg War Crimes Trial*, 14 DE PAUL L. REV. 348 (1965); and Chapter 3, footnote 67 for other authors questioning the legality of the proceedings. Another critique of the Nuremberg and Tokyo proceedings and in the Subsequent Proceedings, seldom discussed in the literature, is whether it was valid to prosecute prisoners of war in such *fora* because of the requirements of Article 63 of the 1929 Geneva Convention which requires that prisoners of war shall be tried by the same court and according to the same procedure as in the case of persons belonging to the armed forces of the detaining powers. Also, Article 60 required notification to the Protecting Power which was not given by the Allies. Thus, these proceedings could have been in violation of the 1929 Geneva Convention whose Article 82 binds its High Contracting Parties to respect and observance. See, COMITÉ INTERNATIONAL DE LA CROIX ROUGE: ACTES DE LA CONFÈRENCE DIPLOMATIQUE DE GENÈVE (Des Gouttes ed. 1929); and RASMUSSEN, CODE DES PRISONIERS DE GUERRE (1931), particularly pages 70-75.

[76] The three acquitted were later tried by German denazification courts and were found guilty of war crimes. See E. DAVIDSON, *supra* note 71, at 29.

[77] The information which follows is included in almost every book on the subject, including those cited above at note 71, but see B. SMITH, *supra* note 71 at 194-226.

were charged with "crimes against humanity" but not war crimes: Streicher and Schirach.

The Tokyo Charter has language similar to the London Charter on the subject of individual criminal responsibility. Article 5 states:

> The following acts, or any of them, are crimes coming within the jurisdiction of the Tribunal for which there shall be individual responsibility...[78]

CCL 10 similarly created individual criminal responsibility for war criminals other than those tried at Nuremberg.

At the Tokyo Tribunal,[79] Allied prosecutors representing eleven nations (Australia, Canada, China, France, Great Britain, India, the Netherlands, New Zealand, the Philippines, the Soviet Union and the United States) acted through a single Chief Counsel for the prosecution as opposed to the IMT where four co-equal prosecutors acted with respect to each defendant. The Tokyo prosecutors filed a joint indictment against twenty-eight Japanese on April 29, 1946. The document consisted of fifty-five counts divided into three sections: "crimes against peace" (counts 1-36); "murder" (counts 37-52); "other conventional war crimes and crimes against humanity" (counts 53-55).[80] Thus, the heading of the charges differed in Tokyo from those of Nuremberg. The register of defendants included four prime ministers, four foreign ministers, five war ministers, two navy ministers, a lord keeper of the privy seal and four ambassadors.[81] However, Emperor Hirohito was not indicted, primarily for

---

[78]   Tokyo Charter, art. 5.

[79]   The literature on the Tokyo trial is small by comparison to the one on Nuremberg. *See e.g.*, A.C. BRACKMAN, THE OTHER NUREMBERG: THE UNTOLD STORY OF THE TOKYO WAR CRIMES TRIALS (1987); THE TOKYO WAR CRIMES TRIAL (C. Hosoya, N. Audà, Y. Onuma, R. Minear eds. 1986); THE TOKYO WAR CRIMES TRIAL: THE COMPLETE TRANSCRIPTS OF THE PROCEEDINGS OF THE INTERNATIONAL MILITARY TRIBUNAL FOR THE FAR-EAST (22 Vols. and 5 suppl. vols. R. John Pritchard and Sonia M. Zaide eds. 1981); P.R. PICCIGALLO, THE JAPANESE ON TRIAL (1979); THE TOKYO JUDGMENT (B.V.A. Röling and C.F. Rüter eds. 1977); R.H. MINEAR, VICTOR'S JUSTICE: THE TOKYO WAR CRIMES TRIAL (1971). For a bibliographic listing *see also* N.E. TUTOROW, *supra* note 71, at 259-282.

[80]   *See* P. PICCIGALLO, *supra* note 79, at 14 (1979). Originally, the suspected war criminals were divided into three categories: Class A -- those who allegedly had planned, initiated, or waged war " in violation of international treaties;" Class B -- those who had violated "the laws and customs of war;" Class C -- those who had carried out the tortures and murders ordered by superiors. A.C. BRACKMAN, *supra* note 79 at 46 (1987).

[81]   P. PICCIGALLO, *supra* note 79, at 14.

political reasons.[82] The IMTFE formally convened in Tokyo on May 3, 1946 and pronounced judgment on November 4, 1948. The tribunal heard testimony from no less than 419 witnesses and examined 779 affidavits and depositions which were admitted into evidence.[83] All the defendants were found guilty, with seven receiving death sentences, sixteen receiving life imprisonment, one a sentence of twenty years and another of seven years.[84] The defendants and verdicts are in the Document Section C.10.[85]

A comparison of these two post-War II Tribunals and their respective Charters reveals some differences, as discussed in Chapter 1. The procedural differences were, however, more marked. For example, while at Nuremberg, each signatory of the Charter had the right to appoint a Chief Prosecutor. On the other hand, at Tokyo the Supreme Commander of the Allied Powers (General MacArthur) appointed the Chief of Counsel, who was solely responsible for the prosecution of the trials. Also, whereas at Nuremberg criminal organizations were indicted, no Japanese organizations were indicted. Additionally, the proceedings at Tokyo left much to be desired in terms of fairness, whereas the Nuremberg proceedings were substantially fair. And the judgment at Nuremberg was, with few exceptions, substantially fair, whereas the Tokyo judgment was substantially unfair to a number of defendants.[86]

In the final analysis, both stood for the principle of individual criminal responsibility for international crimes, rejecting immunities and defenses such as "obedience to superior orders," upholding command responsibility. More importantly for the purposes of this book, they recognized the existence of "crimes against humanity" as pre-Charter crimes on the legal bases discussed in Chapter 4.

---

[82] However, as Joseph Keenan, the chief prosecutor at Tokyo, conceded, from a strict legal standpoint, the Emperor could have been convicted as a war criminal. *Id.* at 16.

[83] *See* A.C. BRACKMAN, *supra* note 79, at 18, who notes that the witnesses ranged from "buck privates to the last emperor of China." *Id.*

[84] *Id.* at 378-382. Two defendants died during the trial and one was not able to plead.

[85] This information is found in almost every book on the Tokyo Trials, including the authors cited at note 79, *but see* A.C. BRACKMAN, *id.* at 406-413.

[86] The authors cited in note 79 support this conclusion, particularly those in THE TOKYO WAR CRIMES TRIAL, *id.* Among them *see* Pritchard, *An Overview of the Historical Importance of the Tokyo War Trial*, *id.* at 89, and Judge Röling's *Introduction* at 15. *See also supra* note 48. RICHARD MINEAR, VICTORS' JUSTICE: THE TOKYO WAR CRIMES TRIAL (1971) which is particularly scathing.

INDIVIDUAL CRIMINAL RESPONSIBILITY

Post-World War II: Subsequent Proceedings

In addition to these two internationally constituted military tribunals, a number of other tribunals were formed to conduct war crimes trials.[87] Of particular note, the Allies established military tribunals in their respective zones of occupation under CCL 10 of 20 December 1945, which provided that each occupying power could try lower-level German officials.[88] These tribunals, especially those of the United States, relied heavily on the Charter and the IMT's judgment.[89] These and other tribunals picked up where Nuremberg and Tokyo left off and tried the "lesser" war criminals. They included, among others, the following:[90]

For the United States: the Military Tribunal at Nuremberg; the United States Military Commissions, sitting at various places in Europe and Asia; the General Military Government Court and Intermediate Military Government Court of the American Zone of Germany; the U.S. Court of Appeals and The United States Supreme Court;

For the United Kingdom: British Military Courts, sitting at various places in Europe and Asia;

For France: the Permanent Military Tribunal; the French Court of Appeal;

---

[87] *See* A. MAUNOIR, LA REPRESSION DES CRIMES DE GUERRE DEVANT LES TRIBUNAUX FRANCAIS ET ALLIÉS (1956); Cowles, *Trial of War Criminals (Non-Nuremberg)*, 41 AJIL 299 (1948). *See also* H. MEYROVITZ, LA REPRESSION PAR LES TRIBUN AUX ALLEMADUOES DES CRIMES CONTRE L'HUMANITÉ ET DE L'APPARTENANCE À LEURS ORGANIZATION CRIMINELLE (1960).

[88] *See* CCL 10 and CCL Trials. Since this Law was passed on the basis that Germany had become *debellatio* and had unconditionally surrendered to the Allies, the legal status of Germany is relevant. *See* Rheinstein, *The Legal Status of Occupied Germany*, 47 MICH. L. REV. 23 (1948).

[89] *See* T. TAYLOR, FINAL REPORT TO THE SECRETARY OF THE ARMY ON THE NÜRNBERG WAR CRIMES TRIALS UNDER CONTROL COUNCIL LAW NO. 10, (1949); and F.M. BUSCHER, THE U.S. WAR CRIMES TRIAL PROGRAM IN GERMANY, 1946-1955 (1989). *See also* Basak, *The Influence of the Nuremberg Judgment on the Practice of the Allied Courts in Germany*, 9 POLISH Y.B. INT'L L. 161 (1977-78) (who studies the influence of the factual determinations of the Nuremberg Tribunal, and, the Tribunal's legal views regarding the foundations of jurisdiction and the interpretation of existing law).

[90] R. WOETZEL, *supra* note 22 at 219.

213

For Australia: the Australian Military Court;

For Canada: the Canadian Military Court;

For the Netherlands: the Netherlands Court-Martial and Special Courts;

For Norway: the Norwegian Court of Appeal and Supreme Court of Norway;

For Denmark: the Danish Military Courts and the Danish Appellate and Supreme Court;

For China: the Chinese War Crimes Court;

For Poland: the Supreme National Tribunal of Poland;

For the USSR: Various summary military courts.

During and after the Nuremberg Trials, it is reported that the United States convicted 1,814 (450 executed) in its occupation zone; Great Britain 1,085 (240 executed), France 2,107 (109 executed), and the USSR an unestimable number of persons tried and executed in addition to countless German POW's held long after the cessation of hostilities and treated in violation of existing norms, rules and practices of international law.

The United States denominated "War Crimes Trial Program" in Germany was based on the Charter and CCL 10.[91] Two types of proceedings were established under United States Military Government Ordinance No. 7, 18 October 1946. One was the establishment of 12 tribunals which convened at Nuremberg after the conclusion of the IMT proceedings and which prosecuted 195 persons charged with offenses arising under the three crimes embodied in CCL 10 but deriving from the Charter.[92] They were commonly called the Nuremberg Subsequent Proceedings because the twelve cases were heard before tribunals which sat at Nuremberg, the venue of the IMT.[93]

---

[91] See F. BUSCHER, supra note 89.

[92] See 15 CCL Trials 22-25; and T. TAYLOR, supra note 89.

[93] The (subsequent) Nuremberg proceedings involved 12 trials and 195 defendants: (1) The Krupp Case, (2) The Ministries Case, (3) The Hostage Case, (4) The Justice Case, (5) The High Command Case,

These proceedings targeted high ranking persons in organizations such as the SS, the German High Command, the *Einztsgruppen* (mobile death squads), the Foreign Ministry, the Justice Ministry, Industrialists (I.G. Farben, Krupp) and others. The subsequent prosecutions were conducted under the guidance of Brigadier Telford Taylor who followed Justice Robert Jackson as the United States Chief of Counsel for War Crimes. Some criticism of these trials emerged and appeals and petitions for writs of *habeas corpus* were filed with United States courts, including the Supreme Court, but none succeeded.[94]

The other U.S. military proceedings involved offenders who perpetrated crimes against American military personnel. These were conducted at Dachau between 1944-47 where some 1,672 persons were prosecuted by the Deputy Judge Advocate for War Crimes, European Command, who had opened 3,887 cases of which 1,416 were convicted. By 1951, 50% of all war criminals had been released and only 659 remained in U.S., French and U.K. custody. By 1950, two clemency boards were established, one to review the subsequent proceedings (at Nuremberg) and the other to review the 489 trials at Dachau. Their recommendations respectively to the High Commissioner for Germany and to the Commander of European Forces resulted in wholesale clemency.[95]

In addition, military trials were established for "violation of the laws of war" under the jurisdiction of the respective United States military theater commanders. These trials by United States military courts, were conducted pursuant to United States legal authority though in reliance upon the Charter and CCL 10.

An important distinction between the Subsequent Nuremberg and Dachau trials was that the former included the charges of "crimes against peace" and "crimes against humanity" while the latter was only based on "violations of laws of war" as established by conventional and customary international regulation of armed conflicts. Thus, the

---

(6) The Medical Case, (7) The Milch Case, (8) The Rusha Case, (9) The Flick Case, (10) The Pohl Case, (11) The "Einsatzgruppen" Case, (12) I.G. Farben Case.

[94] *See e.g.*, Milch v. U.S., 332 U.S. 789 (1947); Brandt v. U.S., 333 U.S. 836 (1948).

[95] For example, in the *Einsatzgruppen* trial, of the 21 charged with the murder of approximately two million persons, 14 received the death sentence but only four were executed. By 1955, only 55 prisoners were left in custody, they were at the Landsberg prison. The last one was released in 1958. For a critical appraisal of this policy, *see* F. BUSCHER, *supra* note 89, at 46-68; and Mendelssohn, *War Crimes Trials and Clemency in Germany and Japan*, in AMERICANS AS PROCONSULS: UNITED STATES MILITARY GOVERNMENT IN GERMANY AND JAPAN, 1944-1952, 226, 259 (R. Wolfe ed. 1984). Mendelssohn is the editor of the encyclopedic work THE HOLOCAUST (18 vols. 1982).

Dachau proceedings did not have the problems relating to the "principles of legality" that the Subsequent Nuremberg ones had. Nevertheless some of the Dachau proceedings were criticized for unfair prosecutorial conduct.[96] A political uproar developed in the United States over these proceedings mostly due to the demagogical tactics of Senator Joseph McCarthy.[97]

In addition, several Allied nationals were prosecuted for collaboration with the enemy and for commission of war crimes and "crimes against humanity" in their respective countries.[98]

In the Far East, the United States set up special Military Commissions in the Philippines to try Japanese officers for war crimes.[99] Most notable of these trials were those of General Yamashita and General Homma. Both were found guilty of war crimes and sentenced to death. The cases were appealed to the United States Supreme Court -- by the defense petitioning for a writ of "habeas corpus" -- but the Supreme Court denied both petitions.[100] The trial, conviction and execution of General Yamashita was fraught with misconduct and the misapplication of an improper legal standard of "command responsibility" discussed in Chapter 9. It remains a blot on the history of American justice.

In addition, the U.S. military tribunals located in Yokohama, headquarters of the Eighth Army, convicted 854 Japanese, 51 of whom were executed, while other nations also prosecuted Japanese war criminals: Nationalist Chinese courts convicted 504; the British, 811; the Dutch, 969; the French, 198; and the Australians, 644.[101]

The Subsequent Proceedings, as well as the proceedings under the Nuremberg and Tokyo Charters, not only intended to hold individuals criminally responsible for their

---

[96] See e.g., J.F. WEINGARTNER, CROSSROAD OF DEATH: THE STORY OF THE MALMEDY MASSACRE AND TRIAL (1979).

[97] See F. BUSCHER, supra note 89 at 89.

[98] See A. MAUNOIR, supra note 87; and Cowles, supra note 87.

[99] See generally P.R. PICCIGALLO, supra note 79 at 49-67.

[100] In re Yamashita, 327 U.S. 1 (1946); and Homma v. United States, 327 U.S. 759 (1946). Both cases were criticized because they established unprecedented criteria for command responsibility; namely that the two commanding generals in question should have known and should have prevented the war crimes committed by soldiers under their command. In the Yamashita Case, id., Justices Rutledge and Murphy wrote scathing dissents, id. at 26 et seq. See A.F. REEL, THE CASE OF GENERAL YAMASHITA (1949). Reel as a JAG captain defended Yamashita in the Philippines and before the Supreme Court.

[101] A.C. BRACKMAN, supra note 79 at 52-53.

216

actions, but they also intended that individuals could be held responsible regardless of national law. The defendants in the IMT and subsequent proceedings had raised, *inter alia*, the argument that under Article 4 of the Constitution of Weimar, "... any German statute or any norm similar to a statute took precedence over international law as transformed into national law."[102]

The High Command Case, in two relevant statements, answered that argument as follows:

> International law operates as a restriction and limitation on the sovereignty of nations. It may also limit the obligations which individuals owe to their states, and create for them international obligations which are binding upon them to an extent that they must be carried out even if to do so violates a positive law or directive of the state.[103]

> [I]t is undoubtedly true that international common law in case of conflict with state law takes precedence over it.[104]

These statements echo that of Francis Biddle, a member of the Nuremberg Tribunal from the United States, who stated: "It seems to me that the domestic law cannot be permitted to stand in face of the higher international law just as with us, the State statute which conflicts with the Federal Constitution is invalid. If any other result were achieved, international law, by definition, would become meaningless."[105] Similarly, Doman, a prosecutor at Nuremberg, noted that if national law were supreme, then "instigators of international crimes could fashion their own laws in such a way as to exclude their criminal acts from the applicability of the national penal law. Then there would be no international nor national law under which even the most horrendous crimes and mass murders could be punished."[106]

---

[102]   A. VON KNIERIEM, THE NUREMBERG TRIALS 36-37 (1959).

[103]   *The High Command Case* at 489.

[104]   *Id.* at 487.

[105]   *Reprinted in* The Fifth Report on the Draft Code of Offenses Against the Peace and Security of Mankind, 17 March 1987, A/CN.4/404 at 5, para. (3).

[106]   N.R. Doman, *The Nuremberg Trials Revisited*, 47 A.B.A.J. 260, 261 (1961). *See also* J. APPLEMAN, MILITARY TRIBUNALS AND INTERNATIONAL CRIMES 77 (1954).

There was uncertainty in some of the decisions rendered by the IMT and in subsequent proceedings over whether "crimes against humanity" constituted a pre-existing international crime creating an international legal obligation on all states to prohibit such conduct, or at least an obligation not to legalize it. There was further uncertainty as to whether individual criminal responsibility for such conduct arose under international law, irrespective of its inclusion into national law.

The following relevant statements of some of these decisions are indicative of this uncertainty or confusion. The IMT in its Judgment held:

...the very essence of the Charter is that individuals have international duties which transcend the national obligations of obedience imposed by the individual state. He who violates the laws of war cannot obtain immunity while acting in pursuance of authority of the state, if the state in authorizing action moves outside its competence under international law.[107]

In *The Justice Case*, the court stated:

The force of circumstance, the grim fact of world-wide interdependence, and the moral pressure of public opinion have resulted in international recognition that certain crimes against humanity committed by Nazi authority against German nationals constituted violations not alone of statute but also of common international law.[108]

In *The Flick Case*, the court stated:

It cannot longer be successfully maintained that international law is concerned only with the actions of sovereign states and provides no punishment for individuals.[109]

In *The High Command Case*, the court stated:

For the first time in history individuals are called upon to answer criminally for certain violations of international law. Individual criminal responsibility has been

---

[107]   22 IMT 466.

[108]   *The Justice Case* at 979.

[109]   *The Flick Case* at 1191.

known, accepted, and applied heretofore as to certain offenses against international law, but the Nuremberg trials have extended that individual responsibility beyond those specific and somewhat limited fields.[110]

In *The Farben Case*, it was stated:

It can no longer be questioned that the criminal sanctions of international law are applicable to private individuals. The judgment of Military Tribunal IV, *United States v. Flick* (Case 5) held:

"The question of the responsibility of individuals for such breaches of international law as constitute crimes has been widely discussed and is settled in part by the Judgment of the IMT. It can not longer be successfully maintained that international law is concerned only with the actions of sovereign states and provides no punishment for individuals."

We quote further:

"Acts adjudged criminal when done by an officer of the government are criminal also when done by a private individual. The guilt differs only in magnitude, not in quality. The offender in either case is charged with personal wrong and punishment falls on the offender in *propria persona*. The application of international law to individuals is no novelty."[111]

In the internationally constituted tribunals, as well as in related or similar national prosecutions, as discussed below, the basic principle of accountability was that of individual criminal responsibility stemming from international legal obligations. The absolute defense of "obedience to superior orders" was rejected.[112]

The prosecutions occurring after World War I were also based on individual criminal responsibility for:

---

[110]   *The High Command Case* at 509-510.

[111]   *The Farben Case* at 1136.

[112]   *See* Chapter 10 at 398.

(1) violations of laws and customs of war as established in customary international law and codified in the Hague Conventions.[113]

By contrast, the prosecutions occurring after World War II were based on individual criminal responsibility, command responsibility, and vicarious responsibility for:

(1) conspiracy, initiation and waging of aggressive war in violation of customary and conventional international law;

(2) violation of laws and customs of war; and,

(3) "crimes against humanity."

In the World War I and World War II prosecutions, two principal arguments were raised by the defendants:

(1) the unenforcibility of certain crimes because they violated the "principles of legality;"[114] and,

(2) the defense of "obedience to superior orders."[115]

As to the first argument, it was advanced that there was no positive international law constituting normative proscriptions of a criminal nature against the initiation of war and against "crimes against humanity." Thus, it was argued that such prosecutions and punishment violated the principles of *nulla poena sine lege* and *ex post facto,* as discussed in Chapter 3. During the prosecutions stemming from World War II, the arguments of *ex post facto* and *nulla poena sine lege* were consistently raised and were

---

[113]   *See* C. MULLINS, *supra* note 41. "The principle that the individual Soldier who commits acts in violation of the laws of war, when these acts are at the same time offenses against the general criminal law, should be liable to trial and punishment, not only by the courts of his own State, but also by the Courts of the injured adversary in case he falls into the hands of the authorities thereof, has long been maintained ...." 2 J.W. GARNER, INTERNATIONAL LAW AND THE WORLD WAR (1920). *See also* Garner, *Punishment of Offenders Against the Laws and Customs of War*, 14 AJIL 70 (1920); Levy, *Criminal Responsibility of Individuals and International Law*, 12 U. CHI. L. REV. 313 (1945); and Glaser, *Culpabilité en Droit International Pénal*, 99 RECUEIL DES COURS 473 (1960).

[114]   *See* Chapter 3.

[115]   *See* Chapter 3 and *also* Chapter 10 at 398.

220

valid from a national criminal law point of view but not entirely applicable under international law.[116]

To avoid such difficulties, there was an effort after World War II to codify some of the norms and principles which had been challenged at the time so as to avoid the recurrence of these arguments if subsequent prosecutions were to take place, as discussed in Chapter 11. Thus, in 1946, the General Assembly of the United Nations adopted a resolution entitled Affirmation of the Principles of International Law Recognized by the Charter of the Nuremberg Tribunal. It was followed by a report of the International Law Commission in 1950 bearing the same title which summarized the "Nuremberg Principles" as follows:[117]

PRINCIPLES OF INTERNATIONAL LAW RECOGNIZED IN THE CHARTER OF THE NUREMBERG TRIBUNAL AND IN THE JUDGMENT OF THE TRIBUNAL

PRINCIPLE I

Any person who commits an act which constitutes a crime under international law is responsible therefor and liable to punishment.

98. This principle is based on the first paragraph of article 6 of the Charter of the Nuremberg Tribunal which established the competence of the Tribunal to try and punish persons who, acting in the interests of the European Axis countries, whether as individuals or as members of organizations, committed any of the crimes defined in sub-paragraphs (a), (b) and (c) of article 6. The text of the Charter declared punishable

---

[116] Referring to the nature of international criminal law as to the legality of the Nuremberg Charter and in particular with respect to the issue of *ex post facto* concerning "crimes against humanity," *see* W.J. Ganshof Van der Meersch who holds that International Criminal Law is a branch of international law and a customary type of law which evolves even though its basis is in conventional international law, Ganshof Van der Meersch, *Justice et Droit International Pénal*, 76 REVUE DE DROIT PÉNAL ET DE CRIMINOLOGIE 3, 31 (1961). He also cites in support of the proposition that the Nuremberg formulation does not violate the principles of legality in international criminal law.

[117] Principles of the Nuremberg Tribunal at 11-14.

only persons "acting in the interests of the European Axis countries' but, as a matter of course, Principle I is now formulated in general terms.

99. The general rule underlying Principle I is that international law may impose duties on individuals directly without interposition of internal law. The findings of the Tribunal were very definite on the questions whether rules of international law may apply to individuals. "That international law imposes duties and liabilities upon individuals as well as upon States," said the judgment of the Tribunal, "Has long been recognized." (TRIAL OF THE MAJOR WAR CRIMINALS BEFORE THE INTERNATIONAL MILITARY TRIBUNAL, vol. I, Nuremberg 1947, page 223.) It added: "Crimes against international law are committed by men, not by abstract entities, and only by punishing individuals who commit such crimes can the provision of international law be enforced." (*Ibid.*)

PRINCIPLE II

The fact that international law does not impose a penalty for an act which constitutes a crime under international law does not relieve the person who committed the act from responsibility under international law.

100. This principle is a corollary to Principle I. Once it is admitted that individuals are responsible for crimes under international law, it is obvious that they are not relieved from their international responsibility by the fact that their acts are not held to be crimes under the law of any particular country.

101. The Charter of the Nuremberg Tribunal referred, in express terms, to this relation between international and national responsibility only with respect to crimes against humanity. Sub-paragraph (c) of article 6 of the Charter defined as crimes against humanity certain acts "whether or not [committed] in violation of the domestic law of the country where perpetrated." The Commission has formulated Principle II in general terms.

102. The principle that a person who has committed an international crime is responsible therefor and liable to punishment under international law, independently of the provisions of internal law, implies what is commonly called the "supremacy" of international law over national law. The Tribunal considered that international law can bind individuals even if national law does not direct them to observe the rules of

international law, as shown by the following statement of the judgement: "...the very essence of the Charter is that individuals have international duties which transcend the national obligations of obedience imposed by the individual State." (TRIAL OF THE MAJOR WAR CRIMINALS BEFORE THE INTERNATIONAL MILITARY TRIBUNAL, Vol. I, Nuremberg 1947, page 223.)

PRINCIPLE III

The fact that a person who committed an act which constitutes a crime under international law acted as Head of State or responsible Government official does not relieve him from responsibility under international law.

103. This principle is based in article 7 of the Charter of the Nürnberg Tribunal. According to the Charter and the Judgment, the fact than an individual acted as a Head of State or responsible official did not relieve him from international responsibility. "The principle of international law which, under certain circumstances, protects the representatives of a State," said the Tribunal, "cannot be applied to acts which are condemned as criminal by international law. The authors of these acts cannot shelter themselves behind their official position in order to be freed from punishment..." (*Ibid.*) The same idea was also expressed in the following passage of the findings: "He who violates the laws of war cannot obtain immunity while acting in pursuance of the authority of the State if the State in authorizing action moves outside its competence under international law." (*Ibid.*)

104. This last phrase of article 7 of the Charter, "or mitigating punishment," has not been retained in this formulation of Principle III. The Commission considered that the question of mitigating punishment is a matter for the competent Court to decide.

PRINCIPLE IV

The fact that a person acted pursuant to an order of his Government or of a superior does not relieve him from responsibility under international law, provided a moral choice was in fact possible to him.

105. This text is based on the principle contained in article 8 of the Charter of the Nürnberg Tribunal as interpreted in the judgement. The idea expressed in Principle IV is that superior orders are not a defence provided a moral choice was possible to

223

the accused. In conformity with this conception, the Tribunal rejected the argument of the defence that there could not be any responsibility since most of the defendants acted under the orders of Hitler. The Tribunal declared: "The provisions of this article [article 8] are in conformity with the law of all nations. That a soldier was ordered to kill or torture in violation of the international law of war has never been recognized as a defence to such acts of brutality, though, as the Charter here provides, the order may be urged in mitigation of the punishment. The true test, which is found in varying degrees in the criminal law of most nations, is not the existence of the order, but whether moral choice was in fact possible." (*Ibid.*, page 224).

106.   The last phrase of article 8 of the Charter, "but may be considered in mitigation of punishment, if the Tribunal determines that justice so requires," has not been retained for the reason stated under Principle III, in paragraph 104 above.

Since World War II, many documents have included individual responsibility for international criminal law violations. The 1949 Geneva Conventions impose direct obligations on individuals and sanctions for the breach of any of them. In the common articles of the four Conventions, it states:

> The High Contracting Parties undertake to enact any legislation necessary to provide effective penal sanctions for persons committing, or ordering to be committed, any of the grave breaches of the present Convention defined in the following Article.[118]

Subsequently, 1954 Draft Code of Offenses[119] stated in Article 1, "Offenses against the peace and security of mankind, as defined in this code, are crimes under international law, for which the responsible individual shall be punished."[120]

As for other international crimes, the Genocide Convention[121] provides for individual criminal responsibility in Article IV, which states:

---

[118]   Geneva I, art. 49, *see also* arts. 50, 53. Geneva II, art. 50, *see also* art. 51. Geneva III, art. 129, *see also* art. 130. Geneva IV, art. 146, *see also* art. 147.

[119]   1954 Draft Code of Offenses at 11. *See* Document Section F.4.

[120]   *Id.* at art. 1.

[121]   Genocide Convention. *See* Document Section F.1.

Persons committing genocide...shall be punished, whether they are constitutionally responsible rulers, public officials, or private individuals.[122]

Also, the *Apartheid* Convention[123] in Article III provides that "Individual criminal responsibility shall apply ... to individuals, members of organizations and institutions and representatives of the State..."[124]

Protocol I provides that "no one shall be convicted of an offence except on the basis of individual penal responsibility."[125] Moreover, the Contracting Parties "in order to avoid any doubt concerning the prosecution and trial of persons accused of war crimes and crimes against humanity" are called upon to submit such persons "for the purpose of prosecution and trial in accordance with the applicable rules of international law."[126] Of particular importance with regard to "crimes against humanity" is the Convention on the Non-Applicability of Statutory Limitations to War Crimes and Crimes Against Humanity,[127] which in Article II states that "the provisions of this Convention shall apply to representatives of the state authority and private individuals...."[128]

The 1991 Draft Code of Crimes also speaks to individual criminal responsibility. In Article 3, the Code states: "An individual who commits a crime against the peace and security of mankind is responsible therefor and is liable to punishment."[129] The 1991 Draft Code, in Article 6, establishes a state's obligation to try or extradite an individual who committed a crime against peace and security of mankind, if the individual is in that state's territory.[130]

---

[122] *Id.* art. IV.

[123] *Apartheid* Convention, *See* Document Section F.2.

[124] *Id.* art. III.

[125] 1977 Geneva Protocol I, art. 75(4) (b).

[126] *Id.* art. 75(7) (a).

[127] *See* Non-applicability of Statutory Limitations to War Crimes, *see* Document Section E.3.

[128] *Id.* art. II.

[129] 1991 Draft Code of Crimes, art. 3. *See* Document Section F.5.

[130] *Id.* at art. 6.

National Prosecutions: Post-World War II

Since 1946, the Federal Republic of Germany has taken on the task of prosecuting war criminals in its national courts and between 1947-1990 some 60,000 such prosecutions have been reported. The three landmark cases prosecuted outside the Federal Republic of Germany after 1945 were the *Eichmann*[131] and *Demjanjuk*[132] cases by Israel, and *The Barbie Case*[133] by France. The first two were for crimes not committed on the territory of the prosecuting state, while the third prosecution was for crimes committed within the territory of the prosecuting state.

It is noteworthy that the only case brought against one of the World War II Allies for war crimes was brought by Japanese citizens for the use by the United States of atomic weapons against Japan. In Hiroshima and Nagasaki, the use of atomic weapons killed and injured an estimated 225,000 innocent civilians.[134] The case was rejected by the Supreme Court of Japan on technical jurisdictional grounds.[135]

In 1989, Canada prosecuted the first case under a 1987 statute that permits retrospective application of international law. The case of *R. v. Finta*[136] for "crimes

---

[131]   *See* Attorney General of Israel v. Eichmann (Israel Dist. Court of Jerusalem, 1961), 36 I.L.R. 5 (1962), (Supreme Court of Israel 1962), 36 I.L.R. 277 (1962). *See also e.g.* G. HAUSER, JUSTICE IN JERUSALEM (1966).

[132]   *See* Demjanjuk v. Petrovsky, 776 F.2d 571 (6th Cir. 1985), *cert. denied* 475 U.S. 1016 (1986).

[133]   *See* Matter of Barbie, Gaz. Pal. Jur. 710 (France Cass. Crim. Oct. 6, 1983). *See also* Le Gunehec, *Affaire Barbie* GAZETTE DU PALAIS, No. 127-128, 106e année, Mercredi 7-Jeudi 8 Mai, 1985; i Angevin, *Enseignements de L'Affaire Barbie en Matière de Crimes Contre l'Humanité,* LA SEMAINE JURIDIQUE, 62e année, No. 5, 14 Dec. 1988, 2149; Ponceler, *L'Humanité, une victime peu présentable,* 1991--No. 34 1987 REVUE DES SCIENCES CRIMINELLES, 275; and Massé , 1989 REVUE DES SCIENCES CRIMINELLES 798. *See also* Doman, *Aftermath of Nuremberg: The Trial of Klaus Barbie,* 60 COLO. L. REV. 449 (1989).

[134]   29 THE NEW ENCYCLOPEDIA BRITANICA 1022 (1990).

[135]   Shimoda v. The State, 355 Hanrel Jiho (Supreme Court of Japan 7 December 1963); also quoted in part in 2 Friedman at 1688. *See also* R.A. Falk, *The Shimoda Case: A Legal Appraisal of the Atomic Attacks Upon Hiroshima and Nagasaki,* 59 AJIL 759 (1965). The claim in that case was against the United States of America for dropping atomic bombs on Nagasaki and Hiroshima in violation of the laws and customs of war.

[136]   50 C.C.C. (3d.) 247; 61 D.L.R. 85 (4th 1989). *See also,* Green, *Canadian Law, War Crimes and Crimes Against Humanity,* 59 BRIT. Y.B. INT'L L. 217 (1988); Jacquart, *La notion de crime contre l'humanité en droit international contemporaraire et en droit Canadian,* 21 REVUE GÉNÉRAL DE DROIT 607 (1990). *See also* Dubner, *The Law of International Sea Piracy,* 11 N.Y.U. J. INT'L L & POLITICS 471 (1979). *See also, Report of the Commission of Inquiry on War Criminals* (J. Deschênes, ed. 1986).

against humanity," at which this writer served as Canada's chief legal expert in testifying on what constitutes "crimes against humanity" before 1945, resulted in the acquittal of Hungarian Gendarmerie Captain Finta on the facts, but the judgment recognized the existence of "crimes against humanity" under international law before 1945.

Selective Enforcement

While this century has seen some individuals held responsible under international criminal law, there have been all too many instances where prosecution did not occur. In some instances, such as Stalin's purges of the 1950's and the mass killings in Cambodia in the 1980's, no efforts were made toward prosecuting the violators of these atrocities. In other instances, such as after the Bangladesh war of independence and the Iraqui occupation of Kuwait prosecution was considered, but then dropped.

Among the most notable examples of selective enforcement was the case of accused Italian war criminals of the 1930's and 1940's and the accused Pakistani war criminals of the 1971 Cessation War between East and West Pakistan which produced India's intervention and resulted in Bangladesh's independence.

As for the first instance, the UNWCC listed 750 Italian war criminals accusing them of using poison and mustard gas against the ethiopians during that aggressive war in 1936 in violation of the 1925 Protocol for the Prohibition of the Use in War of Asphyxiating, Poisonous or other Gases, and of Bacteriological Methods of Warfare,[137] killing prisoners of war, bombarding hospitals and committing other violations of the customary law of armed conflicts.[138] Also during World War II, several war crime violations were documented by Yugoslavia and Greece against their Italian occupiers relating to the mistreatment of prisoners of war, the killing of innocent civilians and the destruction of civilian property.[139] Lybia also advanced similar claims during Italy's occupation of that country. The 1943 Moscow Declaration provided that countries in which such violations were committed had the right to prosecute offenders. The Instrument of Surrender of Italy,[140] Article 45, provided that

---

[137]   94 L.N.T.S. 65, 26 U.S.T. 571, T.I.A.S. No. 8061, Geneva, 17 June 1925.

[138]   *See* UNWCC at 51-52.

[139]   *Id.* at 179.

[140]   4 Bevans 311, at 326 (1970).

227

Italy had a duty to extradite anyone of its nationals charged with war crimes. Yugoslavia, Ethiopia and Greece repeatedly requested extradition of a number of Italian war criminals, which included Marshall Badoglio and General Graziani, for war crimes committed in Ethiopia and Generals Roata and Ambrosio, for crimes committed in the Balkans. Lybia also asked for Badoglio and Graziani, but Italy turned a deaf ear with United States and British assent and never surrendered anyone accused of war crimes.

The UNWCC specifically referred to the use of prohibited gas in Ethiopia and to the bombardment of Red Cross hospitals by troops under the commands of Badoglio and Graziani, as well as eight other officers. At first, the United States and the United Kingdom, being the Allies in control of Italy, ignored the extradition requests of Yugoslavia, Greece and Ethiopia and also ignored their repeated protests. Subsequently, as stated above, the Italian Government also refused their extradition. Thus, the United States and the United Kingdom violated the terms of the 1943 Moscow Declaration and the provisions of the Italian Armistice Agreement. Subsequently, these two countries formally renounced their rights to try Italian war criminals under Article 45 of the said Armistice Agreement. Italian Governments since 1946 have also refused extradition to these same requesting countries. Only one Italian officer was prosecuted for war crimes committed outside of Italy; it was General Bellomo who was convicted and sentenced to death. Interestingly, he was a non-fascist. None of the fascist generals were ever prosecuted for war crimes committed outside of Italy. It is commonly assumed that this benign attitude towards Italian fascist war criminals was due to the fact that, in 1943, Marshall Badoglio headed a provisional government for Italy while it was still occupied by Germany. He made a separate Armistice with the Allies who were particularly eager to neutralize the Italian navy in the Mediterranean and who wanted to attract as many as possible from the Italian military to fight alongside the Allies against Germany. Thereafter, it was the belief of United States and United Kingdom senior officials that the future stability of Italy required the co-option of the fascists into the democratic process to oppose what they feared was a communist onslaught in that country.

Prosecution was also forsaken after the war for Bangladesh's independence. In 1971, Pakistan experienced a civil war in East Pakistan, resulting in the independence of that region which became Bangladesh. During the course of that conflict, West Pakistan troops reportedly killed approximately one million East Pakistanis and caused ten million to flee into India.[141] On November 21, 1971, India militarily intervened on the basis of the international law doctrine of humanitarian intervention. Three weeks

---

[141] *See* Case Concerning Trial of Pakistani Prisoners of War (Pakistan v. India), ICJ Pleadings, 3-7. *See also* MacDermot, *Crimes Against Humanity in Bangladesh*, 7 INT'L LAW. 476 (1973).

later, the Pakistani army's eastern command surrendered to the Indian armed forces, with both parties agreeing to the application of the 1949 Geneva Convention relative to the Treatment of Prisoners of War. At that time, India had detained over 92,000 Pakistanis, both military personnel and civilians.[142]

In 1972, the President of Bangladesh issued an order which established special tribunals to prosecute Bangladeshi citizens who had collaborated with the Pakistani armed forces during 1971. Thereafter, India and Bangladesh agreed to bring criminal charges against certain Pakistani prisoners of war held by India. In anticipation of these trials, Bangladesh published Act No. XIX of 1973,[143] which was entitled "An Act to provide for the detention, prosecution and punishment of persons for genocide, crimes against humanity, war crimes and other crimes under international law." The Act contains a provision which follows to some extent Article 6 of the Charter. In particular, the provision on "crimes against humanity" declares:

> The following acts or any of them are crimes within the jurisdiction of a Tribunal for which there shall be individual responsibility, namely:
>
> (a) Crimes against Humanity: namely, murder, extermination, enslavement, deportation, imprisonment, abduction, confinement, torture, rape or other inhumane acts committed against any civilian population or persecutions on political, racial, ethnic or religious grounds, whether or not in violation of the domestic law of the country where perpetrated;[144]

As Bangladesh prepared for the prosecution, Pakistan filed an action before the International Court of Justice.[145] The basis of Pakistan's action against India was predicated on the grounds that India detained 92,000 Pakistani prisoners of war and civilian internees in violation of the third and fourth Geneva Conventions of 1949.

---

[142] ICJ Pleadings, *supra* note 141, at 6. Levie, *The Indo-Pakistani Agreement of August 28, 1973*, 68 AJIL 95 (1974). Levie breaks down the figure to 82,000 prisoners of war and some 10,000 civilian internees.

[143] THE BANGLADESH GAZETTE 5987 (July 20, 1973). *See also* Paust & Blaustein, *War Crimes Jurisdiction and Due Process: The Bangladesh Experience*, 11 VAND. J. TRANS. L. 1 (1978).

[144] THE BANGLADESH GAZETTE, *supra* note 143, at 5988.

[145] Trial of Pakistani Prisoners of War, ICJ Reports 1973, 347. *See* Levie, *Legal Aspects of the Continued Detention of the Pakistani Prisoners of War by India*, 67 AJIL 512 (1973).

Pakistan claimed that pursuant to these conventions India had the duty to repatriate these persons at the conclusion of the conflict which had indeed ceased on December 21, 1971. However, India did not continue the repatriation of detainees which it had begun in 1972 because it claimed that it had agreed with Bangladesh to surrender to that country those persons whose number exceeded ten thousand, and who were to be charged with genocide or other international crimes. By 1973, the exact number was fixed at 195.

Pakistan maintained that pursuant to Article VI of the Genocide Convention, there could be no "competent tribunal" in Bangladesh because of the "extreme emotionally charged situation that prevails there."[146] Pakistan further claimed that it had jurisdiction to try the 195 persons accused of genocide in its own tribunals.

With regard to these events, it is interesting to note that India and Bangladesh focused more specifically on genocide than on war crimes or "crimes against humanity." Also, Pakistan was particularly opposed to the notion of war crimes since it considered the conflict an internal one. In a sense, Pakistan could politically accept -- at that time -- a charge of individual atrocities, but it could not accept the legitimacy of East Pakistan's insurrection and of India's intervention.

The dispute finally ended in 1973 as the parties came to a political agreement[147] and the ICJ, by consent of the parties, removed the case from its docket. Notwithstanding the enormous victimization and the apparent efforts of Bangladesh, abetted by India, to prosecute such violations, political considerations prevailed and Bangladesh did not carry out its intentions. It did so in exchange for political recognition by Pakistan and once this recognition was given, India returned the Pakistani detainees and accused war criminals who thus escaped individual criminal responsibility.

It will not escape the reader that the aggressive occupation of Kuwait by Iraq as of August 3, 1990, was accompanied by the commission of war crimes against Kuwaiti and non-Kuwaiti citizens during the occupation, the holding by Iraq of civilian hostages of different nationalities as "human shields," and environmental damage resulting from an oil spill and the setting afire of Kuwaiti oil-fields. All of these acts constituted war crimes and the coalition forces, including Kuwait, had proclaimed that Iraqi President Saddam Hussein and those in the military and occupation forces who committed such crimes would be prosecuted.[148] Instead, Kuwait shamelessly prosecuted what it called

---

[146]   ICJ Pleadings, *supra* note 141, at 6-7.

[147]   *See generally*, Levie, *supra* note 142.

[148]   These violations have been reported by the world media and in a report by Amnesty International

"collaborators" in special courts which lacked every semblance of justice and which meted out disproportionate and unjust sentences.[149] No prosecution of Iraqis ensued as of the date of publication of this book. Furthermore, the coalition forces, mostly the United States, engaged in some indiscriminate bombing of civilian targets and protected targets leading to the conclusion that investigation of these bombings could have produced evidence of war crimes. But, none took place. Once again, political considerations prevailed over considerations of justice.

The proposition that a person accused of an international crime should answer the accusation and stand trial if reasonable evidence exists is the notion of *aut dedere aut iudicare*, as discussed in Chapter 11. The use of the word *iudicare* removes the implication that the concept is purely retributive. Furthermore, the concept upholds the principle of equal and impartial application of the law, reinforces the effectiveness of general deterrence, provides general prevention, vindicates victim's rights and permits the accused to atone for his crime. Above all, it confirms the will of the international community to uphold the international "Rule of Law." In respect of the above stated goals, this concept is merely the extension of national criminal justice to the international level.

It will surely escape no one that the precedents discussed above all involve prosecutions of the defeated by the victorious. Thus, when Nuremberg, Tokyo, and Subsequent Proceedings are referred to as "victor's vengeance," it is not without merit if it means one-sided justice. These prosecutions were, nevertheless, justified. The fact that only a few prosecutions of personnel belonging to victorious powers occurred (mostly by their own courts martial), does not diminish the legal validity of the prosecutions that did take place. But one-sided justice reveals the unfairness of the international legal system. Germany, during World War I and World War II, had records of Allied violations of the very laws and rules with which the Allies charged Germany of violating.[150] The German documentation of World War I Allies'

(October 1989). Other human rights organizations like Human Rights Watch have issued several reports. *See* Hearings Before the Committee on the Judiciary, United States House of Representatives, 102nd Congress (1st Session) March 13, 1991, (Serial No. 3, 1991) and in particular the testimony and prepared statement of M. Cherif Bassiouni pp. 21-44.

[149] These trials have been widely reported by the world media and by human rights organizations like Amnesty International and Human Rights Watch.

[150] *See* A.M. DE ZAYAS, THE WHERMACHT WAR CRIMES BUREAU, 1939-1945 (1989). Earlier in 1941 Germany had filed with the International Committee of the Red Cross a Report entitled, "Russian Crimes Against the Laws of War and Humanity," in which they documented such violations. At the IMT

violations against Germany even escaped public attention and no significant trace of World War II Allied violations against Germany and against Germans and others appears in the recollection of world public opinion. Some exceptions, however, exist, such as the dreadful fire-bombing of Dresden during World War II that remains in the world's consciousness as a symbol of the terrible sufferance that befell the civilian German population between 1943-45. It is shocking that the wholesale violations of conventional and customary rules of war against German prisoners of war by the USSR, has escaped international public attention. The same inattention applies to the Allies' violations against the Japanese, the worst example of which is the World community's approval of the use of two atomic bombs in 1945 against the cities of Hiroshima and Nagasaki, killing and injuring hundreds of thousands of civilians. Had Japan or Germany so bombed an Allied power, there is no doubt that its perpetrators, from the decision-makers to the crews of the planes that dropped the bombs, would have been tried and convicted of war crimes. These horrible events deserve the same equally forceful condemnation as that visited upon the perpetrators of similar acts performed by the defeated.

What will also not escape the reader is the fact that since World War II many regional and national conflicts have occurred. Korea, Vietnam, Palestine, Pakistan-Bangladesh-India, Cyprus, Lebanon, and the Gulf are among the regional armed conflicts with an international character, while Biafra and Cambodia are among those national conflicts which have engulfed the entire population. In all of these conflicts, there have been violations which constitute war crimes and/or "crimes against humanity," but in no case were the perpetrators prosecuted. Only Bangladesh, as discussed above, considered setting up a war crimes tribunal to prosecute Pakistan's military personnel, but then dropped the initiative for a variety of political and diplomatic considerations.

Germany lost both World War I and World War II and some of its officials were prosecuted. The same was true for Japan after World War II. But not Italy, which was part of the Axis. Turkey, who was an Ally of Germany in World War I and whose officials were accused of killing an estimated one million Armenians and of deporting a large number of non-Turkish nationals and other minorities, particularly Greeks, never incurred that fate, though it came close to it with the Treaty of Sèvres. The USSR,

---

the report was presented on behalf of the defense. *See* IX PROCEEDINGS at 684-88. It is noteworthy that in this 1941 Report, Germany had acknowledged the applicability of 1907 Hague Convention provisions on the "laws of humanity," but at the IMT the prosecution did not seem to have caught the importance of that fact as an argument to oppose the defense's argument that crimes against the "laws of humanity" did not exist.

whose troops committed war crimes in World War II, some of which it falsely charged Germany with -- such as the Katyn massacre of some 14,700 Polish prisoners of war[151] -- was never even officially reproached for such war crimes. And in the 1950's, the Stalinist purges resulted in an estimable number of millions of persons killed, but no prosecutions arose out of these and other mass killing incidents. These and other national conflicts evidence the need to reformulate the concept of "crimes against humanity" to include such violations that fall within the cracks of the Article 6(c) definition, and which are not covered by the Genocide Convention.

In the midst of two cities in ruins by Allied hands, Nuremberg and Tokyo, Allied Tribunals sat in legal, moral and ethical judgment. These prosecutions and judgments were to be a beacon of higher values, standards and rules of conduct for those entrusted with the power to harm others. Lamentably, the light it produced was not that of a beacon which spreads widely and evenly. Instead, the light that came out was narrow, like that which comes out of a tunnel. It was also uneven. The moral tunnel condemned the Germans and the Japanese, but ignored Italian and Allied violations.[152] Nuremberg and Tokyo, like the Leipzig trials after World War I, left many unanswered questions and provided only partial answers. To be sure, the post-World War I and II prosecutions were not unjust, nor were the prosecutions, in the main, unfair, considering the crimes committed and the legal standards of the time. It is more the missed opportunities to advance a more permanent and a more universal Rule of Law that one cannot help but deeply regret.

Since World War I, the World Community has hoped for a permanent international criminal court which could be relied upon to fairly apply international criminal law based on an international criminal code but the lack of political consensus by the world's major

---

[151]   *See* J. ZAWODNY, DEATH IN THE FOREST: THE STORY OF THE KATYN FOREST MASSACRE (1962).

[152]   B.F. SMITH, *supra* note 71, at 1-73.

powers have prevented its occurrence.[153] Time and again the opportunity arose, but it was never seized. Politics prevailed over justice.

---

[153] For a comprehensive, historical survey of the subject *see* Ferencz, and more recently Bassiouni, *The Time Has Come for an International Criminal Court*, 1 IND. INT'L. & COMP. L. REV. 1 (1991). *See also* 52 RIDP, Nos. 3-4 (1984), symposium issue on Draft International Criminal Court; Bouzat, *Introduction*, 331; Jescheck, *Development, Present State and Future Prospects of International Law*, 377; Decker, *A Critique of the Draft International Criminal Code*, 365; Shupilov, *General Comments on the Draft International Criminal Code*, 373; Ottenhof, *Considerations sur la Forme le Style, et la Methode d'Elaboration du Projet de Code Pénal International*, 385; Friedlander, *Some Observations Relating to the Draft International Criminal Code Project*, 393; Oehler, *Perspectives on the Contents of the Special Part of the Draft International Criminal Code*, 407. *Draft Statute for an International Commission of Criminal Inquiry and a Draft Statute for an International Criminal Court*, International Law Association, 60th Conference, Montreal, August 29-September 4, 1982, in REPORT OF THE 60TH CONFERENCE OF THE INTERNATIONAL LAW ASSOCIATION (1983). For other works *see* Dautricourt, *The Concept of International Criminal Jurisdiction-- Definition and Limitations of the Subject*, in *supra* note 2, at 636; Kos-Rabcewicz-Zubkowski, *The Creation of an International Criminal Court*, in INTERNATIONAL TERRORISM AND POLITICAL CRIMES 519 (M.C. Bassiouni ed. 1975); BASSIOUNI DRAFT CODE; *Draft Statute for an International Criminal Court*, WORK PAPER, ABIDJAN WORLD CONFERENCE ON WORLD PEACE THROUGH LAW, AUGUST 26-31, (1973); *Draft Statute for an International Criminal Court*, Foundation for the Establishment of an International Criminal Court (Wingspread Conference, September 1971); J. STONE AND R. WOETZEL, TOWARDS A FEASIBLE INTERNATIONAL CRIMINAL COURT (1970); Klein and Wilkes, *United Nations Draft Statute for an International Criminal Court: An American Evaluation*, in G.O.W. MUELLER AND E. WISE, INTERNATIONAL CRIMINAL LAW, 573 (1965); P. CARJEU, PROJECT D'UNE JURISDICTION PENALE INTERNATIONALE (1953); A. SOTTILE, THE PROBLEM OF THE CREATION OF A PERMANENT INTERNATIONAL CRIMINAL COURT (1951); *Project for the Establishment of a Convention for the Creation of a United Nations Tribunal for War Crimes*, established by the United Nations War Crimes Commission, 1944, *see* UNWCC, *supra* note 16; L'UNION INTERPARLIAMENTAIRE. COMPTE RENDU DE LA XXVII CONFERENCE TENUE À ROME EN 1948, (1949); *Projet d'une Cour Criminelle Internationale*, adopted by the International Law Association at its 34th Conference in Vienna, August, 1926, THE INTERNATIONAL LAW ASSOCIATION, REPORT OF THE 34TH CONFERENCE, VIENNA, AUGUST 5-11, 1926 (1927); Project of the International Association of Penal Law, in ACTES DU PREMIER CONGRES INTERNATIONAL DE DROIT PÉNAL, BRUXELLES, 26-29 JUNE 1926 (1927); *Projet de Statut pour la Creation d'une Chambre Criminelle au Sein de la Cour Permanente de Justice Internationale*, presented by the International Association of Penal Law to the League of Nations in 1927, 5 RIDP (1928); *Constitution et Procedure D'un Tribunal Approprié pour Juger de la Responsabilite des Auteurs des Crime de Guerre*, presenté à la Conference Preliminaires de Paix par la Commission des Responsabilitiés des Auteurs de la Guerre et Sanctions, III, LA PAIX DE VERSAILLES (1930); and *see* V.V. Pella the Inter-Parliamentary Union, XXII Conference, held in Berne and Geneva, 1924, in L'UNION INTERPARLIAMENTAIRE. COMPTE RENDU DE LA XXII CONFERENCE TENUE À BERNE ET A GENÈVE EN 1924, PUBLIÉ PAR LE BUREAU INTERPARLIAMENTAIRE. COMPTE RENDU DE LA XXIII CONFERENCE TENUE À WASHINGTON ET À OTTOWA EN 1925 (1926).

The IMT at Nuremberg with Court on the right and defendants on the left. (Reprinted with permission from U.S. National Archives)

The judges of the IMT. (Reprinted with permission from U.S. National Archives)

The U.S. and U.S.S.R. prosecution teams at the IMT. Justice Robert Jackson in center. (Reprinted with permission from U.S. National Archives)

The IMTFE at Tokyo, a view of the bench. (Reprinted with permission from U.S. National Archives)

IMTFE at Tokyo, a view of the defendants, prosecution, and defense teams. (Reprinted with permission from U.S. National Archives)

The Hall of Mirros, Palace of Versailles where the 1919 Peace Treaty was signed. (Reprinted with permission from U.S. National Archives)

CHAPTER 6

PREREQUISITE LEGAL ELEMENTS:
PUBLIC LAW CONNECTION AND INTERNATIONAL COGNIZABLE HARM

> "Power is never the property of an individual, it belongs to a group and remains in existence only so long as the group stays together"
>
> HANNA ARENDT, ON VIOLENCE 44 (1969).

Introduction

Legal abstractions deemed to have a juridical personality, like states and organizations, do not have the capacity of engaging in conduct. But, human beings that direct such entities perform conduct which is legally cognizable. Thus, from a factual as well as a legal policy perspective, it is individual conduct that needs to be deterred in order to prevent harmful results. Deterrence, however, as the history of criminal law teaches us, depends on the existence of a punitive system capable of inducing the belief that reasonably prompt and fairly certain punishment is the likely outcome of a transgression of the law.[1] Consequently, the less likely the processes of criminal justice produce this outcome, the less effective the criminal law is in deterring, and thus, preventing unlawful conduct.

Unlike national systems which have their own enforcement machinery, the international system does not have machinery for direct enforcement and it, therefore, depends on the voluntary cooperation of States.[2] Contemporary national justice systems, however, suffer from a decrease in effectiveness and as a result, so does the international one. The consequences include the inability of the international and national systems to control individual action which is the outcome of "state action or policy."

National legal systems have mechanisms designed to control errant behavior by those entrusted with operating the organs of state. Therefore, public officials who violate, by commission or omission, their public duties are subject to the sanctions of their national law, provided that its administration is sufficiently independent of

---

[1]   *See* Chapter 11 for the concept *aut dedere aut judicare.*

[2]   *See e.g.* BASSIOUNI DRAFT CODE and 3 BASSIOUNI ICL.

political control or influence to effectively enforce such legal norms. The problem, therefore, is whether persons in authority who violate or abuse the law become above the law or beyond the reach of the law.[3]

The international legal system developed principles by which to determine state responsibility[4] on the basis of customary norms and standards for the imputability of individual conduct to the State. But the question arises as to whether the same approach can apply *mutatis mutandi* to "state action or policy" for an individual's conduct. The relevance of these principles, norms and standards for imputability of individual conduct to the state, and the determination that such conduct represents "state action or policy" is particularly relevant to "crimes against humanity" and to all other international crimes which require "state action or policy" as an element of international criminalization.[5] "State action or policy" is the essential characteristic of "crimes against humanity," without which such a category of crimes could not be deemed international. Thus, the meaning and content of this characteristic as it relates to "crimes against humanity" requires specific identification. Furthermore, the specifics of "state action or policy" are pre-requisite legal elements which need to be established as any other legal element pertaining to this international category of crimes.

Imputability of Individual Responsibility to the State

As stated above, individual conduct can be imputed to the state, and "state action or policy" can be attributed to the individual. But, while the customary rules of international law have been well established for the former, they have not been for the latter.

---

[3] This was one of the subjects of the Sixth United Nations Congress on Crime Prevention and the Treatment of Offenders, *infra* note 94.

[4] *See* Draft Principles of State Responsibility elaborated by the ILC in the annual reports of the ILC from 1979 to 1991 and also in the YEARBOOK OF THE ILC. *See also* I. BROWNLIE, STATE RESPONSIBILITY (2 Vols. 1983). For the criminal responsibility of states, *see* Article 19 of Draft Principles of State Responsibility, and the Draft Code of Crimes against the Peace and Security of Mankind, particularly the version contained in the Report of the ILC on the work of its forty-third session, 29 April - 19 July 1991, G.A.O.R. 46th Sess. Supp. No. 10 (A/46/10). *See also* F. MALEKIAN, INTERNATIONAL CRIMINAL RESPONSIBILITY OF STATES (1985).

[5] *See e.g.* Chapter 5 on individual criminal responsibility and international prosecutions which reveal that concepts of state imputablity and state responsibility have not been applied in such international prosecutions.

The existence or absence of "state action or policy" as a factor controlling or shaping individual conduct has historically been viewed as a question of imputability or attributability of an agent's conduct to the state. For some, like Kelsen, the consequence of such imputability is a sufficient basis for the individual's exoneration.[6] Such a position, which was also shared by Hersh Lauterpacht at least until 1940, necessarily meant that individuals acting for or on behalf of their state or acting pursuant to "superior orders" would be exonerated from any criminal responsibility.[7] This position has been repudiated since the Law of the Charter with respect to war crimes and "crimes against humanity".[8]

Decisions of international tribunals and the writings of scholars agree that imputing responsibility of an individual's conduct to a state is neither based on nationality, nor on the official representativeness or authoritative capacity of the individual deemed to be an agent of the State.[9] In this regard Bin Cheng states:

As regards the imputability of the acts of each particular officer, it will be seen that, in the last analysis, this also is a question of fact, namely whether the officer occupies a position in which he exercises the authority, or a fraction of the authority, possessed by the Government as a whole. His acts, in the exercise of that fraction of state authority, constituted a manifestation of the State's will and are imputable to the State, whatever may be his nationality, his function, his rank, or whether he has acted in error, in disobedience to instructions, or in contravention of municipal law.[10]

---

[6] *See* Kelsen, *Collective and Individual Responsibility in International Law with Particular Regard to the Punishment of War Criminals*, 31 CALIF. L. REV. 530 (1943).

[7] *See* OPPENHEIM, INTERNATIONAL LAW, (6th ed. 1940); which was changed; and Chapter 10 at 400.

[8] *See* Chapter 10 at 431.

[9] *See e.g.*, B. CHENG, GENERAL PRINCIPLES OF LAW AS APPLIED BY INTERNATIONAL COURTS AND TRIBUNALS (1987); and G. VATTEL, LE DROIT DES GENS (1887); Anzilotti, *Teoria Generale Della Responsabilita Dello Stato Nel Diritto Internazionale*, in D. ANZILOTTI, CORSO DI DIRITTO INTERNAZIONALE (1928); 3 K. STRUPP, HANDBUCH DES VÖLKERRECHTS - DAS VÖLLKERRECHTLICHE DELIKT (1920); C. DE-VISSCHER, LA RESPONSABILITE DES ETATS (1924); C. EAGLETON, THE RESPONSIBILITY OF STATES IN INTERNATIONAL LAW (1928); J. PERSONNAZ, LA REPARATION DU PREJUDICE EN DROIT INTERNATIONAL PUBLIC (1939). For a more recent view, *see* F. MALEKIAN, *supra* note 4.

[10] *Id.* at 192-193.

By analogy it can be concluded that nationality, rank and function of the individual are not outcome determinative of the question of individual criminal responsibility, even though they are relevant to the question of assessing the degree of that individual's responsibility and the appropriate punishment.

Concepts which are relevant with respect to imputability of the acts of an individual to a state for purposes of determining whether state responsibility exists are separate from those of individual criminal responsibility; though they may be relevant with respect to exoneration from criminal responsibility and for purposes of mitigation of punishment. Consequently, responsibility applies irrespective of whether a person acted on behalf of a state, or pursuant to "superior orders."[11]

Individual criminal responsibility is an axiomatic principle of international criminal law, as discussed in Chapter 5. It is also a basic principle of criminal responsibility in every national legal system, save for some primitive tribal legal systems, which extend the conduct of one to the entire group.[12]

Bin Cheng further states:

This principle that everyone should only be responsible for his own acts or those of his agents may be called the *principle of individual responsibility*.[13] (emphasis added)

The Permanent Court of International Arbitration succinctly referred to this principle of individual responsibility as the "juridical essence of the notion of responsibility in the very nature of law."[14] Such a principle is part of those "general principles" which Professor Hersch Lauterpacht described as:

[T]hose principles of law, private and public, which contemplation of the legal experience of civilized nations leads one to regard as obvious maxims of jurisprudence of general and fundamental character.[15]

---

[11]   *See* Chapter 10 at 398.

[12]   *See e.g.* H. MAINE, ANCIENT LAW: ITS CONNECTION WITH THE EARLY HISTORY OF SOCIETY AND RELATION TO MODERN IDEAS (15th ed. 1894).

[13]   *Id.* at 208.

[14]   Russian Indemnity Case, 1 H.C.R., 532, 541 (1912).

[15]   1 INTERNATIONAL LAW: THE COLLECTED PAPERS OF HERSCH LAUTERPACHT 69 (E. Lauterpacht ed. 1970).

Conditions of imputability of an individual agent's conduct to a state should not, however, be confused with the elements of individual responsibility under the general part of international criminal law, as discussed in Chapter 9. The legal reasoning here is the same as with respect to the laws of agency applicable to civil responsibility and those of responsibility for the conduct of another applicable to criminal responsibility.

Thus, if a person is not a national of a given state but acted at the behest of that state, his acts may be imputed to that state under principles of state responsibility because the nationality of the actor is irrelevant. That principle was relied upon in the *Damas-Hainah Case*,[16] decided by the mixed Franco-German Arbitral Tribunal, where the issue was whether the acts of German nationals working for the Turkish Government would be imputed to Germany or Turkey. The Tribunal held:

> One could not object that Von Kress, as well as Dickmann, are both of German Nationality, it being clear that, in this case, they acted in their capacity as officials of the Turkish government, on behalf of this government.[17]

In 1923, the PCIJ held that: "States can act only by and through their agents and representatives."[18]
Principles of state responsibility can be applied by analogy to international criminal law and as such they give rise to two separate but related principles: imputability of an agent's conduct to a state and individual criminal responsibility.

Justice Robert Jackson, in his opening statement at the Nuremberg trials stated:

> While it is quite proper to employ the fiction of responsibility of a state or corporation for the purpose of imposing a collective liability, it is quite intolerable to let such a legalism become the basis of personal immunity. The Charter recognizes that one who has committed criminal acts may not take refuge in superior orders nor in the doctrine that his crimes were acts of states .... The Charter also recognizes a vicarious liability, which responsibility is recognized by most modern systems of law, for acts committed by others in carrying out a common plan or

---

[16] Damas-Hainah, 4 T.A.M. 801 (1924).

[17] *Id.* at 804, *also cited* in B. CHENG *supra* note 9, at 193.

[18] *German Settlers in Poland*, PCIJ No. 6, at 22 (1923). *See also* the decision of the ICJ in *Reparations for Injuries Suffered in the Service of the United Nations*, (Advisory Opinion), ICJ, 174, 177 (1949).

conspiracy to which a defendant has become a party .... [M]en are convicted for acts that they did not personally commit but for which they were held responsible because of membership in illegal combinations or plans or conspiracies.[19]

The Law of the Charter, however, commingled the principle of individual responsibility with that of collective responsibility and with that of attribution of group or institutional conduct to the individual.[20] There is no doubt that some confusion existed in the minds of the IMT judges, and later among protagonists and critics of the Charter, with respect to the question of imputability or attributability of the acts of an agent to the state for purposes of state responsibility as distinguished from individual criminal responsibility for acts which are outside the realm of legality under international law even when committed for or on behalf of a state. The former shields the individual from civil and criminal responsibility while the latter is outside the scope of such a legal shield, though subject to certain conditions pertaining to individual criminal responsibility.[21]

The historical record of prosecutions for international crimes *delicti jus gentium,* as discussed in Chapter 5, clearly shows that the responsibility of those who act in violation of international law is individual, whether based on responsibility for one's own conduct or for the conduct of another, and that such persons are deemed *hostis humani generi.*[22] This position, however, does not exclude the civil or even criminal responsibility of the state under customary international law or "general principles of law."

The Public Law Connection Between Individual Conduct and "State Action or Policy"

The notion of "state action or policy" is essentially that all or some of a state's public personnel, using public power and resources, acting through public institutions, or with the color of public authority, develop a policy for others to follow, or engage

---

[19]   R. JACKSON, THE NÜRNBERG CASE at 88-89 (reprinted 1971).

[20]   *See* Chapter 9, at 350.

[21]   *See* 2 IMT 150 (1949). *See also* 1919 Commission Report.

[22]   *See* A. RUBIN, THE LAW OF PIRACY (1988); and Sundberg, *The Crime of Piracy* in 1 BASSIOUNI ICL 441.

in conduct designed to carry out policies, or perform acts in furtherance thereof which, if committed by another person, would be criminal. Such policy or action can be carried out by a few individuals, small groups or a collective that administers a totalitarian government, which is the most drastic form of political oppression.[23] The former can be the practices of a guard unit in a prison which engages in torture knowing that those in the higher echelons of their hierarchy will neither seek to discover nor prevent their activity. The latter is government by a combination of ideology and terror.[24] Between these two extremes there is a wide range of collective behavior ranging from those at the highest levels of decision-making, involving most segments of the government's structures, resources and personnel, to those at the lowest levels of governmental hierarchy.

"Crimes against humanity" by virtue of their nature and scale require the use of governmental institutions, structures, resources and personnel acting in reliance upon arbitrary power uncontrolled by law. All too frequently, however, governments have managed to co-opt the legal process which produces positive law, thereby claiming "legitimacy" or "lawfulness" for that which would otherwise be illegitimate or unlawful. By sustaining an absolutist positivist approach to law, totalitarian governments claim the legitimacy and authority of the positive law, which they are able to fashion as they please in order to provide apparent "lawfulness" to their otherwise unlawful conduct.[25] Thus, "state action or policy" frequently relies on positive law to carry out its otherwise violative conduct, rejecting any claim of discrepancy between law as an instrument of their ideology or power-system, and legitimacy of the law as understood in any of its meanings other than that which strict positivists attribute to it.[26]

It is interesting to note that throughout the twentieth century most "state action or policy" resulting in mass killings and other mass human rights violations have been committed in reliance on three interactive factors: ideology, terror, and positive law.

---

[23] *See* H. ARENDT, TOTALITARIANISM at 158 (1968). In the Klaus Barbie case, the Chambre Criminelle defined "crimes against humanity" as follows: "*Les actes inhumain et les persécutions qui, au norm d'un état pratiquant une politique d'hégémonie ideologique*, ont été commis d'une façon systematique, non seulemont des personnes en raison de leur appartenance à une collectivité raciale ou religieuse, mais aussi contre les adversaires de cette politique, quelle que soit la forme de leur opposition" (emphasis added) BULLETIN CRIMINEL No. 407, 20 December 1985. *See also*, Poncela, *L'humainté, une victime peu présentable*, 1991, RECUEIL DALLOZ-SIREY No. 34, 229, 17 October 1991.

[24] *Id.* at 158-177.

[25] For a discussion of positivism, *see* Chapter 2.

[26] *Id.*

The latter being the instrument of the other two. With few exceptions in this century, totalitarianism, dictatorship, tyranny, and other forms of government relying on arbitrary power have enacted or declared it to be "the law" which protects the ideology and terror-inspiring strategies and tactics of that regime.[27] Thus, positive laws are either specifically enacted to provide measures designed to protect whatever that regime's ideology espouses, or else positive law is used through general and broad provisions to protect "public order," "the best interest of society" and other similar terms designed to falsely convey an impression of legitimacy and lawfulness. The Nazis spoke of the "sound instinct of the people" as a basis for their discriminatory and terror-inspiring strategies and tactics.[28] They also referred to their racial supremacist "laws" as the "law of nature," in order to convey a perception of legitimacy and lawfulness for their otherwise unlawful conduct.[29] Marxism, for example, relied on "the law of history" to fashion the theory of class-struggle, which is at the heart of that ideology.[30] These totalitarian ideologies relied on the authority of positive law to govern through terror. And that is why the "principles of legality" have sought increased specificity in penal norms, in order to prevent such abuses of power.[31]

In totalitarianism and similar regimes, law is transformed from being the embodiment of legitimate *consensus iuris* to an instrument of socio-political change devoid of historical legitimacy and legal validity. Such type of "law" fluctuates without certainty, predictability or boundary as it follows the motions of the power it serves. And just like that power which never ceases its motion in quest of constant expansion, that type of "law" which serves it is also in a constant state of flux. As Hannah Arendt describes it:

> Whether the driving force of this development was called nature or history is relatively secondary. In these ideologies, the term "law" itself changed its meaning:

---

[27] *See* Bassiouni, *A Policy-Oriented Inquiry into the Different Forms and Manifestations of 'International Terrorism,'* in LEGAL RESPONSES TO INTERNATIONAL TERRORISM XV, XXXV-XL (M.C. Bassiouni ed. 1988).

[28] *See* Chapter 3 at 98.

[29] *See e.g.* A. HITLER, MEIN KAMPF (1930).

[30] *See e.g.* F. ENGELS, *Introduction*, THE COMMUNIST MANIFESTO (1890). *See also* V.I. LENNIN, STATE AND REVOLUTION (1918).

[31] *See* Chapter 3.

from expressing the framework of stability within which actions and motions can take place, it became the expression of the motion itself.[32]

Thus nothing remains fixed, certainly nothing remains immutable, as everything becomes a state of flux in order to serve the vagueries of totalitarian ideology. The accumulated verity of experiences of such societies, as well as the time-tested and honored basic values and truths are rejected.[33]

Every regime which combines ideology and terror as a form of government starts with the proposition that an initial state of flux is necessary, *voire*, indispensable, in order to achieve the ultimate goal which invariably promises all or some of man's perennial hopes and expectations such as peace, justice, order, stability and happiness. As the goals appear valid only the means appear different and only for a brief transitional phase. Afterwards all good is predicted. Such ideologies, to paraphrase Karl Marx's description of religion, are the "opium of the people." The seductive slogans are indispensable in order to convey the notion that the terror is only temporary, exceptional and discriminating as it befalls only the few errants, thus excluding the believers, and those who are willing to accept a passive role.

---

[32] *See* H. ARENDT, *supra* note 23 at 162.

[33] Hannah Arendt perspicaciously states:

Terror is lawfulness, if law is the law of the movement of some suprahuman force, Nature or History.

Terror as the execution of a law of movement whose ultimate goal is not the welfare of men or the interest of one man but the fabrication of mankind, eliminates individuals for the sake of the species, sacrifices the "parts" for the sake of the "whole." The suprahuman force of Nature or History has its own beginning and its own end, so that it can be hindered only by the new beginning and the individual end which the life of each man actually is.

Positive laws in constitutional government are designed to erect boundaries and establish channels of communication between men whose community is continually endangered by the new men born into it. With each new birth, a new beginning is born into the world, a new world has potentially come into being. The stability of the laws corresponds to the constant motion of all human affairs, a motion which can never end as long as men are born and die. The laws hedge in each new beginning and at the same time assure its freedom of movement, the potentiality of something entirely new and unpredictable; the boundaries of positive laws are for the political existence of man what memory is for his historical existence: they guarantee the pre-existence of a common world, the reality of some continuity which transcends the individual life span of each generation, absorbs all new origins and is nourished by them.

Supra note 23 at 163.

As one looks at the pattern of behavior of such regimes there is invariably an apparent sense of order, at times even objectivity in the selection of the victims. This order is usually presented as a rationale for the strategies of "lawful" terror imposed in the name of the higher ideology and for the sake of its ultimate lofty goals. The higher good is invariably invoked, as is the best interest of the collectivity. All of that provides a basis of credibility for the believer, the profiteer, the gullible, and the faint of heart. An inexorable straight-jacket logic compels those who accept the ideological premises of such regimes to also accept the means of terror which they employ and its outcomes. Only when the vicious cycle is broken, does the twisted logic reveal itself in all its horror. But by then, the reality that it produced cannot be undone, much as the original reality that ideological terror sought to alter remains undone -- certain basic truths remain immutable. But few ever remember that throughout history such means have never produced collective good. The fall of Nazism and Bolshevism has proven this point, as have other similar forms of regimes which used ideological terror to victimize their societies. It is not only the scale on which these crimes are committed, but the process of subversion of society, its values and institutions. The engendered outcome is one where the sum total of human depredation exceeds its individual parts. Thus, crimes committed by virtue of "state action or policy" alter the nature and character of such crimes, and that is the essential characteristic of "crimes against humanity."

The International Element

With the exception of "aggression," every other international crime is a crime under the criminal laws of the world's major criminal justice systems.[34] The label and elements of these crimes may be different in the various national legal systems, but the same facts which support prosecution and punishment under international criminal law would also support prosecution and punishment under their counterpart or equivalent national criminal law.[35]

One of the logical consequences of this identity, or functional equivalent of international and national crimes, is that the basic constitutive legal elements of the

---

[34] *See* Chapter 7 for national crimes which correspond to "Crimes Against Humanity."

[35] *See e.g.* BASSIOUNI DIGEST and BASSIOUNI DRAFT CODE.

specific crimes arising out of these two sources of law are substantially similar.[36] But what distinguishes international from national crimes is the existence of an international element. Thus, international crimes have additional legal elements which are peculiar to these crimes.[37] Among these crimes are those which require "state action or policy" as defined in this chapter. The characteristics and components of "state action or policy," are, therefore, to be viewed as pre-requisite elements which are additional to those legal elements required by each of the specific crimes contained in "crimes against humanity."[38]

"Crimes against humanity," like war crimes, is a label for an entire category of specific crimes which are stated in Article 6(c) of the Charter and identified in Chapters 7 and 8. However, none of the specific crimes contained in Article 6(c) are defined in the Charter and, therefore, their definition and legal elements must be found elsewhere. This raises methodological questions as to the legal sources of their identification.[39] In addition, there are a number of other substantive legal issues, among them the one pertaining to "principles of legality."[40]

Some of the specific crimes referred to in Article 6(c), like "murder," "extermination" and "enslavement," are common crimes in the criminal laws of the major legal systems of the world, as discussed in Chapter 8. Other crimes like "deportation" and "persecution" are not usually found in the national criminal laws of the world's major legal systems under that label.[41] "Deportation," for example, may be part of the crime of kidnapping, while "persecution" may be implicit in a variety of national crimes whenever that practice violates established legal rights protected by criminal laws.[42] But, none of the national criminal legislators deem "persecution," *per se* to be a crime. As to the Charter's reference to "other inhumane acts," those crimes are, in reliance on the *ejusdem generis* rule of interpretation, similar to the earlier ones enumerated in

---

[36] Compare these elements as they are identified in Chapter 7 and BASSIOUNI DRAFT CODE.

[37] *See* BASSIOUNI DRAFT CODE.

[38] The general legal elements of criminal responsibility discussed in Chapter 9 are different from the specific legal elements of each and every crime as described in Chapters 7 and 8.

[39] For the sources arising under the international regulation of armed conflicts *see* Chapter 4 and for the national law sources under "General Principles" *see* Chapter 7, and for the combined national and international law sources of "General Principles" *see* Chapter 8.

[40] *See* Chapter 3.

[41] *See* Chapter 8.

[42] *Id.* at 317.

Article 6(c).[43] However, they also extend beyond those listed in Article 6(c), and in such a case, their identification and content must be established in a way that does not violate the "principles of legality."[44] Thus, all the crimes contained within the meaning of Article 6(c), except for "persecution" *per se*, exist in the criminal laws of the world's major justice systems under the labels (or their equivalent) of: murder, manslaughter, rape, slavery, assault, battery, kidnapping, forcible confinement, robbery and theft.[45] These findings derive from the use of "general principles of law" whose relevance in this context is to interpret and fill the gaps in conventional and customary international law, and in particular Article 6(c) of the Charter.[46] By relying on "general principles" it is possible in some respects to satisfy the requirements of specificity of the "principles of legality" with respect to the contents of Article 6(c), as discussed in Chapter 3. But this is not enough in and of itself to make these crimes international. That is why an added international element is needed.

It should be noted that international criminal responsibility is individual,[47] as it is in all national legal systems and it is necessary, therefore, to maintain the distinction between:

1.   the pre-requisite legal elements discussed in this chapter;
2.   the constitutive elements of each of the specific crimes under Article 6(c), which are discussed in Chapter 8;
3.   the elements of individual criminal responsibility discussed in Chapter 9; and
4.   the conditions of exoneration discussed in Chapter 10.

The specific crimes contained in Article 6(c), prescinding from their existence in conventional and customary international law, can be found, as stated above and is evidenced in Chapter 7, in the criminal laws of the world's major legal systems. The identification of these crimes in national criminal laws does not, however, make these national crimes *ipso iure* international crimes, but it makes the protected interest and

---

[43]   *Id.* at 320.

[44]   *Id.* and *also* Chapter 3.

[45]   *See* Chapter 7.

[46]   *Id.*

[47]   *See* Chapter 5.

prohibited conduct part of "general principles of law."[48] What makes the specific crimes contained in Article 6(c) part of the international crime category of "crimes against humanity" is their nexus to an international element. This element is the indispensable link that warrants inclusion in the international criminal category of that which would otherwise remain within the category of national crimes. And that international element is "state action or policy," the pre-requisite legal element for "crimes against humanity."

Implicit in the notion of "state action or policy" as the international element, is the realization that national legal systems are frequently incapable of reaching certain persons who, by virtue of their position, are beyond the reach of the law.[49] Thus, there is a necessity for international criminalization as discussed below under the heading Assessing The Relevance of the Pre-Requisite Legal Element.

The Charter in its definition of "crimes against humanity" appears, however, to have established two international elements. The first being the connection to war,[50] and the second being the use of the term "persecution" implying "state action or policy."[51] But some confusion appears to have existed as to these two international elements.[52] One interpretative approach has been to consider the specific crimes contained in Article 6(c) as falling into two separate and distinct categories, the crimes of "murder, extermination, enslavement, deportation and other inhumane acts" as one category, and "persecution" as the other. Another approach has been to consider that all the specific crimes contained in Article 6(c) must be connected to war. The latter was the approach followed by the IMT, IMTFE and the Subsequent Proceedings. Post-Charter Legal Developments, however, have removed the war connection as a precondition to the applicability of "crimes against humanity," but they have not specified the required international element, which is necessary to distinguish between the national and international nature of the specific offenses contained within "crimes against humanity." That international element is, in this writer's opinion, what is referred to as "state action or policy," as discussed in this Chapter.

---

[48] *See* Chapter 7.

[49] *See supra* note 3 and *infra* notes 73-75 and corresponding text.

[50] *See* Chapter 1 at 25.

[51] *Id.*

[52] *Id.*

The Contents of the Pre-Requisite Legal Element

The pre-requisite legal element of the "state action or policy" as applicable to "crimes against humanity" has the following characteristics. They are:

1. The specific crimes are committed as part of "state action or policy;"
2. The action or policy is based on discrimination-persecution against an identifiable group of persons;
3. The acts committed are otherwise crimes in the national criminal laws of that State;
4. They are committed by State officials or their agents in furtherance of "state action or policy;"
5. The specific crimes are connected to war under the Law of the Charter, but not under Post-Charter Legal Developments.

1. The Specific Crimes are Committed as Part of "State Action or Policy."

"Crimes against humanity" are collective crimes which cannot be committed unless they are part of a given state's policy because their commission requires the use of the state's institutions, personnel and resources in order to commit, or refrain from preventing the commission of, the specific crimes described in Article 6(c). But they do not alter the fact that the perpetrators of each specific crime, such as "murder" or "enslavement," are individually accountable for each one of these crimes perpetrated against each individual victim.

"State action or policy" can be based on a decision by the Head of State, or a common design agreed to by senior officials, who rely on the State's powers and resources, in whole or in part, to carry out such a decision, or when the conduct of low-ranking public officials relying on state powers and resources are committed with the connivance or knowledge of higher-ranking public officials, or when such higher-ranking officials fail to carry out their obligation to prevent the conduct in question or fail to punish the perpetrators when the conduct is discovered or reasonably discoverable.

As discussed above, the agency relationship between the individual and the state must also be found in accordance with the norms and standards of imputability. As a consequence of such "state action or policy," individuals who take part in the policy-making can be charged with the common law crime of conspiracy, or its equivalent in other legal systems, while those who also implement the policy can be additionally charged with the specific crime they commit (e.g., murder).

The rationale for this requisite of "state action or policy" is that "crimes against humanity," like other international crimes such as genocide[53] and *apartheid*,[54] cannot be committed without it because of the nature and scale of the crime. Thus, this element is not due to any exigency pertaining to each of the specific crimes (e.g. murder) contained within the meaning of this criminal category, but because the commission of such specific crimes against a large number of persons (i.e. "extermination," "persecution") cannot take place without pre-existing "state action or policy" requiring reliance on the powers of the State in order to be carried out.

The policy of extermination of Jews, gypsies, and the mentally ill established by Nazi Germany was clearly developed at the highest level of State decision-making, starting with the Head of State,[55] even though these decisions were also shared by government officials at various levels of the hierarchy. The execution of these policies involved several State organs and required substantial State personnel and State resources. As a corollary, and as a consequence, of the "state action or policy" requirement the traditional immunity for Heads of State and the "defense of obedience to superiors" had to be eliminated, in order to subject decision-makers and those who carried out such acts to individual criminal responsibility.[56] The combination of factors found in the case of Nazi Germany and Bolshevik USSR does not seem to appear in other State practices since World War II, even when these State practices resulted in mass killings.[57] Thus, the question arises as to whether the same characteristics as

---

[53]   *See* Bassiouni, *Introduction to the Genocide Convention*, in 1 BASSIOUNI ICL 281.

[54]   *See* Clark, *The Crime of Apartheid*, in 1 BASSIOUNI ICL 299.

[55]   In addition to the ample documentation that was revealed at the IMT, *The Justice Case*, which involved public officials, clearly reveals how State policy can subvert a system of Justice to produce what would otherwise be criminal, and what was still then criminal had it been carried against the non-targeted groups. *See also* H. DONNEDIEU DE VABRES, LA POLITIQUE CRIMINELLE DES ETATS AUTORITAIRES (1938); and H. ARENDT, ON VIOLENCE (1969); and H. ARENDT, *supra* note 23.

[56]   *See* Chapter 9 at 368.

[57]   This is true with respect to a number of situations arising out of internal political conflict in: Biafra, Nigeria; West Pakistan, now Bangladesh. *See* L. KUPER, GENOCIDE (1981). *See*, however, Dadrian, *Genocide as a Problem of National and International Law: The World War I Armenian Case and Its Contemporary Legal Ramifications*, 14 YALE J. INT'L L. 221 (1989) for events in Turkey between 1915-1919 which had some of the characteristics of a "state action or policy" directed against an entire group of persons, namely, Armenians. *See also* Matas, *Prosecuting Crimes Against Humanity: The Lessons of World War I*,

those that existed in these regimes need to be present in other situations resulting in the violations included within the meaning of Article 6(c). In that context, four issues remain open to further interpretation. They are:

1. The required scope of the "state action or policy;"
2. The level at which such "state action or policy" must be formulated;
3. The degree of participation of the various strata of the State power structure; and
4. The extent of utilization of State personnel and resources involved in carrying out the "state action or policy."

It is clear that the Nazi Germany precedent is the highest possible standard of "state action or policy" and its implementation. If this standard is to be held applicable in the future, it would be difficult to find, let alone to prove this pre-requisite element in many instances involving massive human rights depredations which would fall within the definition of "crimes against humanity." Consequently, certain State practiced policies of human rights depredations resulting in mass killings would not be deemed "crimes against humanity," and this would not be a desirable result.

Since the Law of the Charter is the conventional and customary law basis upon which to rely in identifying and applying this and other pre-requisite elements of this international category of crime, one has to deem this precedent as setting the highest standard, but not the exclusive standard. Thus, to find out what lesser legally acceptable standards might be, one has to rely on other conventional and customary international law sources.

Article 6(c) refers to "persecution," and a question arises as to whether the term is intended to create another specific crime or whether it is meant to evidence "state action or policy." In the opinion of this writer, it is more logically intended to refer to "state action or policy" and thus to be read in addition to the term discrimination as used below.[58] But that does not exclude consideration of "persecution" as a separate specific crime, whose contents in this case have to be identified with some degree of specificity in order to satisfy the "principles of legality."[59]

---

13 FORDHAM INT'L L. J. 86 (1990).

[58] See Chapter 1 at 25.

[59] See Chapter 3.

2. The Policy is Based on Discrimination-Persecution Against an Identifiable Group of Persons.

Article 6(c) linked "persecution" to the other two crimes of "crimes against peace" and "war crimes." The Charter referred to two specific discriminatory grounds: "political" and "religious." But the IMT and Subsequent Proceedings included the discriminatory categories of: race, religion, political belief and health conditions. Presumably this is broad enough to encompass contemporary international definitions of discrimination which have expanded the meaning of the term to include other factors such as color, sex and age, but that is not what the Law of the Charter postulates. Furthermore, all these groups have not been included within the meaning of genocide[60] or *apartheid*.[61]

Thus, the discriminatory categories included in the Law of the Charter's "crimes against humanity" are broader than in other international crimes, including genocide and *apartheid*. But no effort has been made in Post-Charter Legal Developments to clarify the uncertainty about the groups included within the protection of "crimes against humanity." Even the latest 1991 Report of the ILC on the Draft Code of Crimes against the Peace and Security of Mankind fails to cover this question, though it appears implicit in many provisions describing certain specific crimes.

Discrimination, as required in "crimes against humanity," is the exclusion, without valid legal justification, of a group of persons from the protection of criminal laws afforded to others, or the subjection of that identified group of persons to laws from which others are exempted, with the result that harm befalls the targeted group. In this respect it is inconceivable that any targeted group, no matter what its affinity may be, should be excluded. The element of discrimination evidences the collective nature of the crime and its scope should have no limits and no quantitative or numerical standards for the persons to be included in the discriminated group. Consequently, even a limited number of persons in a discriminated category, no matter how defined, should suffice. The criterion in this case should not be objective, but subjective, namely what was the intent of the policy as opposed to who or what specifically defined the target group. In other words, if the purpose is to protect victims, it should make no difference

---

[60]   *See supra* note 53.

[61]   *See supra* note 53. It is to be noted that the *Apartheid* Convention refers to that crime as a "crime against humanity," *see* Article I, and also to the practices of *apartheid* as "inhumane acts."

what objective group or category they belong to.[62] The intent of the policy of targeting the victims should be controlling. This is the approach followed by the Genocide Convention, whereby the killing of a single individual with the intent to "exterminate the group in whole or in part" suffices.[63]

Article 6(c) refers to "persecution" and that term, as stated above, can have two different applications: (1) "persecution" could be linked to a specific crime like "murder," "extermination," "enslavement," "deportation," and "other inhumane acts;" or, (2) it could be deemed a pre-requisite legal element to be read *in pari materia* with the discriminatory requirements based on political, racial or religious grounds.

The question about these two applications of the term "persecution" stems from the positioning of the words "persecution ... on political or religious grounds ..." in Article 6(c) which follows in sequence after the listing of specific crimes, "... and other inhumane acts committed against any civilian population, ...," but which is separated therefrom by a general qualifying requirement namely, "... before or during the war ...," and with the word "or" preceding persecution.[64] It, therefore, seems logical that "persecution" refers to the discriminatory requirement particularly because it would otherwise be impossible to distinguish discriminatory "state action or policy" which constitutes a violation of civil rights and those which constitute "crimes against humanity." Such a distinction would be relevant with respect to the national legislation of United States[65] and Canada[66] by virtue of which their citizens who were of Japanese origin were interned during World War II, and Nazi Germany interning its citizens who were Jews or Communists. In the first instance, the violation by the United States and Canada is of the civil rights of its citizens because, *inter alia*, it was not motivated by, nor seeking to result in, "persecution" of that group of persons even though it discriminated against an identifiable group.[67]

The IMT Judgment and the Judgments of the Subsequent Proceedings arising out of CCL 10 are not clear as to when "persecution" is exclusively a pre-requisite element

---

[62] *See* Bassiouni, *The Protection of 'Collective Victims' in International Law*, 2 HUMAN RIGHTS ANNUAL 239 (1985).

[63] *See supra* note 53.

[64] *See* Chapter 1.

[65] *See* Korematsu v. United States, 323 U.S. 214 (1944).

[66] *See* CANADIAN WAR ORDERS AND REGULATIONS, THE WAR MEASURES ACT R.S.C. (1927) Chap. 206; and PROCLAMATIONS AND ORDERS IN COUNCIL FOR THE INTERNMENT OF ENEMY ALIENS (1939).

[67] For the definition of the term "persecution," *see* Chapter 8 at 317.

and when it is a separate specific crime. Some cases deemed it a specific crime, much like "... other inhumane acts ..." but under both of these headings there has to be a finding that other crimes have been committed. A crime labelled "persecution" cannot be defined in itself without reference to other harmful conduct. Consequently, it can only be defined by reference to another common crime whereby the "persecution" is an additional characteristic that justifies giving the crime a different character thereby resulting in an increased penalty.

3. *The Acts Committed are International Crimes, or Crimes in the National Criminal Laws of that State if it were not for the Policy of Discrimination -- Persecution.*

This characteristic requires that the acts committed against the targeted group are: (a) criminal in the national criminal laws of that state if they were committed against anyone other than those belonging to the discriminated-persecuted group; (b) that the criminality of the conduct carried out against the targeted group is not enforced; or (c) the acts performed constitute a violation of international criminal law. In other words, the discriminatory-persecutional "state action or policy" makes permissible, with respect to the discriminated-persecuted category of persons; certain acts otherwise deemed criminal under national or international law; or, allows the crimes committed against such an identifiable group of persons to be unprevented or to go unpunished. The discriminatory-persecutional policy, therefore, denies the legal consequences of the revocation, alteration, waiver, or non-enforcement of the national criminal laws. The logical conclusion is that the criminal nature of the acts performed remains the same and the criminality of such acts survives any legislative measure that seeks to extinguish it on the sole basis of the discriminatory-persecutional policy. This conclusion is based on the analogy to non-enforcement of the law which does not extinguish the criminality of the act nor alter its criminal nature. Indeed, in the world's major criminal justice systems the non-application of the state's criminal laws does not extinguish the violation except in rare cases of *désuètude*, since such a policy relates only to enforcement.

Whenever the crime in question arises under international law, the state has the obligation to enforce it and to prevent its commission. Thus, whenever the state fails to enforce, it commits a breach of international law which gives rise to state responsibility.[68] The State's duty of prevention and enforcement is based on the reasonableness test and applies to national as well as to international crimes.

"General principles of law recognized by civilized nations" as evidenced by the inductive method of comparative analysis supports the proposition that such acts as "murder, extermination, enslavement, deportation and other inhumane acts" are crimes, whether known by that label or another, in the world's major legal systems.[69] As a consequence of the above, any specially enacted laws predicated on the intent to discriminate-persecute a given group which purport to revoke, alter, waive or render inapplicable criminal laws prohibiting the acts described in Article 6(c) would be void. The perpetrators of such acts would, therefore, be held criminally accountable notwithstanding special laws or practices which are intended to shield them from the consequences of acts which would otherwise be deemed criminal.

This characteristic is clearly designed to satisfy the requirements of the "principles of legality" because it is based on the pre-existing criminality of the acts performed.[70] But it does leave open the question of the perpetrator's intent with respect to his knowledge of the illegality of the conduct under international law in view of the fact that national law purports to make such conduct legal.[71] In that respect, one would have to resort to conventional, customary and "general principles of law" to demonstrate the illegality of the conduct permitted or condoned by special national legislation unenforced with respect to the discriminated-persecuted group of persons.

Another approach arises under the Common Law doctrine of *mala in se* crimes,[72] and that is to consider such crimes whenever they can be found in the world's major criminal justice systems as "general principles of law" which are not susceptible of waiver by special national legislation based on discrimination-persecution against a given group of people, provided, however, that the international element is also present.

---

[68]   *See supra* note 5.

[69]   *See* Chapter 7.

[70]   *See* Chapter 3.

[71]   *See* Chapter 9 at 359.

[72]   *See* Chapter 12 at 532.

4. The Acts are Committed by State Officials or Their Agents in Furtherance of the State's Discriminatory-Persecutional Action or Policy.

This characteristic requires that the acts committed in furtherance of the discriminatory-persecutional "state action or policy" would otherwise be deemed criminal if it were not for the revocation, waiver or unenforced criminal laws making such acts a common crime, must be performed by agents of the State.

This is the position taken by the Torture Convention which criminalizes, under international law, the conduct of public officials or their agents.[73] These agents may be military, para-military, police personnel, other public officials or private individuals acting under the orders of or at the behest of responsible public officials. In this respect, principles of agency relationship would apply in the same way as they do for purposes of imputability or attributability of an individual's conduct to the state for purposes of state responsibility, as discussed above. Consequently, this element excludes private conduct which is not commanded, aided, abetted, or condoned by public officials in furtherance of the "state action or policy," irrespective of the number of individuals involved in the commission of any of the specific crimes contained in Article 6(c). Thus, spontaneous or private action is excluded unless it is supported or encouraged by the State or by any official in an agency entrusted with the prevention of such action. This problem arose in Turkey between 1915-1919 with respect to popular action by private Turkish citizens acting as mobs, or organized groups, which resulted in the random killing of Armenians. In this situation, Turkish public officials at times only supported, encouraged, or condoned such action, or failed to prevent the violations, but that conduct was deemed attributable to them.[74]

A reasonable interpretation of this characteristic is to construe it in light of the duties of public officials under "general principles of law." Consequently, whenever such officials, with the intent that certain crimes be committed, fail to carry out their duties to enforce criminal laws equally and fairly and to equally protect people from criminal offenses, then such public officials are criminally accountable because the conduct of others is either imputed to them or because of their omissions in the face of legal duties established by national law or international law. Conduct by public officials must also

---

[73] *See* Bassiouni and Derby, *The Crime of Torture*, 1 BASSIOUNI ICL 363, *reprinted with* modifications from 48 RIDP 23-103 (1977); H. DANELIUS AND M. BURGERS, THE UNITED NATIONS CONVENTION AGAINST TORTURE: A HANDBOOK ON THE CONVENTION AGAINST TORTURE AND OTHER CRUEL, INHUMAN, OR DEGRADING TREATMENT OR PUNISHMENT (1988).

[74] *See* Dadrian, *supra* note 57 and Chapter 4 at notes 74-83 and accompanying text.

be in furtherance of the States' policy of discrimination and persecution, and not merely for the personal interests of the actors.

The relevance of this characteristic is that it links the acts committed by State officials or their Agents and discriminatory and persecutional "state action or policy." Thus, conduct by public officials which is unrelated to the "state action or policy" is not sufficient to satisfy this element, nor is the occasional conduct by some public officials acting independently of any "state action or policy."

Public officials acting in furtherance of "state action or policy" do not, however, need to know that they are part of an overall scheme or design, nor do they need to know the specifics of the overall scheme or design beyond their own role if they know that their conduct is illegal, or that the orders under which they are acting are manifestly illegal.[75] It would be harsh to propose a higher standard of responsibility for low-level executors of such "state action or policy." But it would be propitious as a matter of deterrence policy to place a higher standard on decision-makers and on those in the intermediate echelons of governmental hierarchy since their refusal to execute such "state action or policy" can prevent its execution.[76]

The inquiry into a public official's failure to act arises at two levels: (1) for purposes of imputing private conduct to "state action or policy;" and (2) with respect to individual criminal responsibility. The former is a pre-requisite element pertaining to this category of international crimes, while the latter pertains to individual criminal responsibility for one's own conduct, and for the conduct of another.[77]

Prior to the Law of the Charter, the doctrine of imputability of individual conduct to the State was deemed to be an exonerating factor. Thus, the individual perpetrator's conduct was covered by State Immunity. This position was in some respects similar to that of the defense of "obedience to superior orders" in military law, which before 1940, was argued by some to be absolute except for commanders.[78] But both doctrines were discredited and rejected under conventional and customary law since the Treaty of Versailles, as evidenced in part by the 1919 Commission Report and the Leipzig

---

[75] *See* Chapter 10 at 398.

[76] *See* Chapter 9 at 368.

[77] *See* Chapter 10 at 398.

[78] *See* Chapters 4 and 10.

trials.[79] They were also rejected by the Law of the Charter and that rejection was confirmed by Post-Charter Legal Developments.[80]

5. The Acts Committed are Connected to War.

At the time of the Charter, this element was the only connecting factor between crimes committed within the jurisdiction of a given State and an internationally regulated activity, namely war.[81] Thus, it provides an international element to that which would otherwise be an activity wholly within the context of the national criminal jurisdiction of states and that would, therefore, be immune from question under international law because of the doctrine of state sovereignty.

The post-United Nations Charter developments in the field of international protection of human rights do not, however, require the existence of a link between a state's human rights violations and other internationally regulated activity.[82] But these international human rights norms and standards do not *per se* criminalize violative conduct. Such international criminalization has always been developed by means of other specialized international conventions.[83]

A question, however, arises as to the war connecting element. Does it mean conduct by a given State which is at war, or a factual causal connection between the violative conduct and the actual conduct of war? Also, does the term war have a legal specificance requiring the existence of a state of war accompanied by an armed conflict between states. Since the Charter, the international regulation of armed conflicts under the Geneva Convention and customary international law no longer require such legal

---

[79] *See* Chapter 10.

[80] *See* Chapter 11.

[81] *See* Chapters 1 and 4.

[82] *See* Universal Declaration; U.N. Covenant; European Convention; European Protocols; Inter-American Human Rights Convention; Optional Protocol to the International Covenant of Civil and Political Rights, 16 December 1966, G.A. Res. 2200 A, 21 U.N. GAOR, Supp. (No. 16) 59; U.N. Doc. A/6316 (1966). *Reprinted in* UNITED NATIONS - HUMAN RIGHTS: A COMPILATION OF INTERNATIONAL INSTRUMENTS at 16, U.N. Doc ST/HR/1/Rev. Z., U.N. Sales No. #. 83. XIV. 1 (1983), Council of Europe, HUMAN RIGHTS IN INTERNATIONAL LAW (1985) at 49. *See also* R. LILLICH, INTERNATIONAL HUMAN RIGHTS: PROBLEMS OF LAW, POLICY, AND PRACTICE (2nd. ed. 1991).

[83] *See* Bassiouni, *The Proscribing Function of International Criminal Law in the Processes of International Protection of Human Rights*, 9 YALE J. WORLD PUB. ORD. 193 (1982).

or factual distinctions, and they apply to conflicts of an international as well as non-international character. But they apply to civil strife only under certain exceptions.[84]

Returning once again to the example of internment by the United States and Canada of its citizens of Japanese origin,[85] is the fact that these countries were at war with another country sufficient, or must there be a closer causal link between the domestic violative conduct and the actual conduct of aggressive war and war crimes? The IMT Judgment, as well as the judgments under CCL 10, indicate that the connection must be to the initiation and waging of aggressive war and the commission of war crimes.

The war connecting element was, however, useful for three reasons:

1.   It avoided violating the "principles of legality;"
2.   It allowed reliance on conventional and customary international law as sources of binding legal obligations; and
3.   It permitted resort to "general principles of law recognized by civilized nations" as a source of international law to interpret Article 6(c) and to eventually fill gaps in the textual language of this and other provisions.

At the time the Charter was enacted, the war connecting element was indispensable, to link "crimes against humanity" to pre-existing conventional and customary international law prohibiting such conduct in time of war.[86] Without such a connecting element, the Charter would have clearly been a violation of the "principles of legality."[87] But since the Charter, and particularly with the Post-Charter Legal Developments, "crimes against humanity" have been established in positive international criminal law, therefore, this connecting element is no longer necessary.

CCL 10 removed the war connecting element by virtue of the complete authoritative powers that the Council had at that time over Germany,[88] but since it applied to

---

[84]   *See* Protocol I; and for commentary, *see* THE INTERNATIONAL LAW OF CIVIL WAR (R. Falk ed., 1971); M. VEUTHEY, GUÈRILLA ET DROIT HUMMITAIRE (1983); M. BOTHE, K. PARTSCH, AND W. SOLF, NEW RULES FOR VICTIMS OF ARMED CONFLICTS at 37 n. 1 (1982); COMMENTARY ON THE ADDTIONAL PROTOCOLS OF 8 JUNE 1977 TO THE GENEVA CONVENTIONS OF 12 AUGUST 1949 (Y. Sandoz, C. Swinarski, and B. Zimmerman, eds., 1987).

[85]   *See supra* notes 65 and 66.

[86]   *See* Chapter 4.

[87]   *See* Chapter 3 at 121.

[88]   *See* Chapter 1.

conduct preceding its promulgation, it is of questionable legality and does not fall in the same category as prospective application subsequent to the Law of the Charter. Article 6(c) also contains a redundancy with reference to this war connecting element since it mentions the connection to war as well as the connection between the specific crimes enumerated and "... connection with any crime within the jurisdiction of the Tribunal ...," namely, "Crimes Against Peace" in Article 6(a) and "War Crimes" in Article 6(b) both of which are related to war.[89]

Post-World War II practices of States involving conduct falling within the definition of Article 6(c), and which occurred exclusively within the national context, were mostly without connection to war in the sense of an international conflict. Thus, if such a war connecting element is still required, the conduct in question could not be deemed part of "crimes against humanity" because of the absence of the war connecting element. If, however, one can rely on the IMT Judgment and CCL 10, the Genocide and *Apartheid* Conventions, all of which do not require such a war connecting element, then its removal as a pre-requisite element can be sustained for conduct subsequent to 1945. This approach de-couples "crimes against humanity" from war crimes and removes the war connecting element. Under this interpretation, "crimes against humanity" are linked to the broader scheme of international protection of human rights.[90] This is indeed the approach of the Genocide and *Apartheid* Conventions.

Assessing the Relevance of the Pre-Requisite Legal Element

As stated in the *Introduction* to the Chapter, not every harmful conduct can be internationally criminalized and certain criteria are required which make conduct that could be criminal under the national laws of a given state or all states also criminal under international law.

"Crimes against humanity" as defined in Article 6(c) are essentially committed within the national jurisdiction of a given state, and the question arises as to what makes this conduct, or can make it, an international crime. The essential features which distinguish this conduct from being exclusively criminal under the national jurisdiction of a given state, are:

---

[89]   *Id.*

[90]   *Id.* at 45.

1.   The characteristics of the pre-requisite legal element discussed in this Chapter which transform the conduct by virtue of its public law connection to "state action or policy" cognizable under international law;
2.   The collective victimization it produces; and,
3.   The impossibility of preventing, controlling or suppressing the conduct in question which necessitates its international criminalization.

It could be argued that conduct which falls within the meaning of Article 6(c) rises to a level which threatens the peace and security of humankind, and therefore, it fulfills one of the criteria of international criminalization.[91] Even if it did not, such conduct could be so shocking to the commonly shared values of the world community that it would satisfy this second criterion. And lastly, it can be said that even if the conduct did not rise to the level of threatening the peace and security of humankind, but only had the potential of doing so, or did not rise to the level of being so shocking to the values of the world community, but does so only partially; and, constitutes conduct which is the expression of "state action or policy," it would satisfy the third criterion because as a matter of fact it could not be prevented, controlled or suppressed without being internationally criminalized. Surely, "crimes against humanity" as they arose during World War II satisfied all three criteria. But it is important to underscore the separateness of these criteria and the pre-requisite legal elements discussed above which connect such conduct to internationally criminally cognizable conduct.

   In recent times, the world community faced with the continued horrors of torture resolved to prohibit it by virtue of an international convention adopted in 1984, which criminalizes such aberrant conduct. It is clear that torture is conduct performed entirely within a given state, that it does not essentially involve citizens of different countries, that it does not affect the peace and security of humankind (unless it arises in significantly high numbers), and while it is shocking to the commonly shared values of the world community, it does not usually arise in significantly high numbers to qualify for that criterion as it has been interpreted heretofore. Torture, however, partakes in part of the last two criteria. But what made it cognizable as an international crime is the added criteria of "state action or policy" and the inability to prevent, control or suppress such conduct without its international criminalization. It was my

---

[91]   *See* Chapter 1 at 45-47 for a discussion on the recognized criteria for international criminalization; and *see also supra* 248-259 for a discussion on the contents of the pre-requisite legal element.

partakes in part of the last two criteria. But what made it cognizable as an international crime is the added criteria of "state action or policy" and the inability to prevent, control or suppress such conduct without its international criminalization. It was my privilege to Co-chair, with Niall MacDermot, the Committee of Experts that prepared the first Draft of the Torture Convention which was presented to the United Nations by the International Association of Penal Law in 1978.[92] In that connection, I prepared a memorandum and commentary which justified the international criminalization of torture on the basis outlined above.[93] Since there is nothing in the negotiating history of the Torture Convention to indicate otherwise,[94] it can be assumed that this legal reasoning was accepted. This position was confirmed by the General Assembly's adoption of the 1980 Sixth United Nations Congress on Crime Prevention and the Treatment of Offenders on the question of offenders beyond the reach of the Law.[95]

The prerequisite legal element discussed above is, therefore, indispensable to the legal nature of "crimes against humanity," and must be established before such an international criminal charge can be brought against an alleged perpetrator. This becomes particularly important since Post-Charter Legal Developments have removed the connection between "crimes against humanity" and "crimes against peace" or "war crimes."[96] In the absence of such a link to an internationally prohibited conduct, "crimes against humanity" becomes less viable as an international crime unless another link joins it to the valid sphere of international criminalization.

The responsibility of those decision-makers who formulated "state action or policy" is much easier to determine than that of lower-level executors of some specific aspect of that "state action or policy." Such persons would likely raise the defenses of: lack of knowledge of the law, mistake of law, mistake of fact, lack of intent, and defense of "obedience to superior orders."[97] All of these defenses would also depend on the legal standards applied to determine whether in fact as well as in law they apply in a

---

[92] U.N. Doc. E/CN/4/NGO/213, 1 Feb. 1978.

[93] Bassiouni, *An Appraisal of Torture in International Law and Practice*, 48 RIDP 17 (1977).

[94] For a history of the Torture Convention *see supra* note 73.

[95] *See* Ottenhof, General Report of the International Association of Penal Law to the Sixth United Nations Congress on Crime Prevention and the Treatment of Offenders (Caracas, 1980, Venezuela, 25 August - 2 September, 1980) *Crime and the Abuse of Offenders Beyond the Reach of the Law. See also* RESOLUTIONS OF THE SIXTH CONGRESS, A/CONF./87/14/REV. (1981).

[96] *See* Chapter 11.

[97] *See* Chapter 10.

given case.[98] The application of different national legal standards, will necessarily produce different results which would not necessarily be unfair if they are applied to the nationals of the adjudicating system who have the expectations of their application.

Post-Charter events, referred to in Chapter 12, clearly reveal the importance of these pre-requisite legal elements to such events and the continued need to uphold the international criminal category of "crimes against humanity."

---

[98]   *See* Chapter 10 at 396.

CHAPTER 7

IDENTIFYING THE SPECIFIC CRIMES IN
"GENERAL PRINCIPLES OF LAW" AT THE TIME OF THE CHARTER

Law is the Right Reason.

Aristotle

Introduction

The codification of customary rules of international armed conflicts, as embodied in the 1899 Hague Convention on the Laws and Customs of War on Land, and then in the 1907 Hague Convention, included only some of the violations of the "Laws of Humanity."[1] The Preamble of the 1907 Convention states that the Contracting Parties:

Animated by the desire to serve, even in this extreme case, the interests of humanity and the ever progressive needs of civilization;

Until a more complete code of the laws of war has been issued, the High Contracting Parties deem it expedient to declare that, in cases not included in the Regulations adopted by them, the inhabitants and the belligerents remain under the protection and the rule of the principles of the law of nations, as they result from the usages established among civilized peoples, from the laws of humanity, and the dictates of the public conscience .... (emphasis added)[2]

---

[1] *See* Chapter 4.

[2] The Preamble of the 1899 Convention states that the Contracting Parties:

Inspired by these views which are enjoined at the present day, as they were twenty-five years ago at the time of the Brussels Conference in 1874, by a wise and generous foresight;
Have, in this spirit, adopted a great number of provisions, the object of which is to define and govern the usages of war on land.
In view of the High Contracting parties, these provisions, the working of which has been inspired by the desire to diminish the evils of war so far as military necessities permit, are destined to serve as general rules of conduct for belligerents in their relations with each other and with populations . . . .

Justice Jackson refers to these "laws of humanity" in his Report to the President: As he states with regard to:

263

Thus, conceptually, all violations of the "laws of humanity" are prohibited, but their specific contents are not all codified nor otherwise embodied in positive law. The question therefore arises as to the identification of the specific contents of those violations which are not included in specific norms. It is in this context that one can resort to "general principles."

It must be noted, however, that "general principles" are not relied upon to establish international crimes, but to identify certain protected interests, and on that basis to interpret the meaning of the terms "laws of humanity," which include unspecified violations deemed to be equivalent to war crimes. Thus, such violations, which have been extended to protected persons who had not, before the Charter, been specifically included within the narrow normative meaning of war crimes, are nonetheless protected by the jurisdictional extension provided by the Charter's "crimes against humanity," as discussed in Chapter 4, but subject to the limitations of the requirements of the "principles of legality," as discussed in Chapter 3.

The notion that "general principles" can be the source of international crimes is established under the provisions of the 1948 Universal Declaration of Human Rights, the 1966 International Covenant on Civil and Political Rights, the 1949 Geneva Conventions and the 1977 Protocols. However, in the opinion of this writer, they remain subject to the requirements of the "principles of legality" which are also a "general principle of law," as discussed in Chapter 3.

"General Principles of Law:" Meaning, Method and Function

"General Principles of Law" as a legal basis are a recognized source of international law.[3] The Statute of the PCIJ employed the terms "general principles of law

---

(b) Atrocities and offenses, including atrocities and persecutions on racial or religious grounds, committed since 1933. This is only to recognize the principles of criminal law as they are generally observed in civilized states. These principles have been assimilated as a part of International Law at least since 1907. The Fourth Hague Convention provided that inhabitants and belligerents shall remain under the protection and the rule of "*the principles of the law of nations, as they result from the usage established among civilized peoples, from the laws of humanity and the dictates of the public conscience.*"

Report to the President of the United States by Robert H. Jackson, Chief Counsel for the United States. Released for Publication by President Truman with His Approval on June 7, 1945, in R.H. JACKSON, THE NÜRNBERG CASE 13 (1947, 2d printing 1971) (emphasis added).

[3] *See* 1 L. OPPENHEIM, INTERNATIONAL LAW 29-30 (H. Lauterpacht ed. 8th ed. 1955). *See also* Bassiouni, *A Functional Approach to General Principles of International Law*, 11 MICH. J. INT'L L. 768

recognized by civilized nations," as did the Statute of the ICJ,[4] and both the PCIJ and the ICJ have relied upon "general principles" in their decisions.[5]

A number of the most distinguished publicists have put forth definitions of "general principles." For example, Professor Hersch Lauterpacht states:

> They are ... those principles of law, private and public, which contemplation of the legal experience of civilized nations leads one to regard as obvious maxims of jurisprudence of general and fundamental character ... a comparison, generalization and synthesis of rules of law in its various branches -- private and public, constitutional and administrative, procedural -- common to various systems of national law.[6]

To Bin Cheng, perhaps the most authoritative scholar on the subject, they are: "Cardinal principles of the legal system in the light of which international ... law is to be interpreted and applied."[7]

Professor Schlesinger refers to them as "a core of legal ideas which are common to all civilized legal systems."[8] Another distinguished scholar, Verzijl, states that they are "principles which are so fundamental to every well-ordered society that no reasonable form of co-existence is possible without their being generally recognized as valid."[9]

(1990) on which this section is predicated and borrows from the text of the article cited.

[4] PCIJ Statute Art. 38 para. I(3), and ICJ Statute, Art. 38 para. (1)(c).

[5] It should be noted that national courts also may rely upon General Principles, see B. CHENG, GENERAL PRINCIPLES OF LAW AS APPLIED BY INTERNATIONAL COURTS AND TRIBUNALS 400-408 (1953), which provides as an appendix *Municipal Codes Which Provide For the Application of the General Principles of Law, Equity or Natural Law.*

[6] 1 INTERNATIONAL LAW BEING THE COLLECTED PAPERS OF HERSCH LAUTERPACHT (THE GENERAL WORKS) 69, 74 (E. Lauterpacht ed. 1970).

[7] *See* Discussion of Bin Cheng, in *The Meaning and Scope of Article 38 (1)(c) of the Statute of the International Court of Justice*, 38 GROTIUS SOCIETY TRANSACTIONS FOR THE YEAR I, 125, at 132 (1952).

[8] R. Schlesinger, *Research on the General Principles of Law Recognized by Civilized Nations*, 51 AJIL 734, 739 (1957).

[9] 1 J.H.W. VERZIJL, INTERNATIONAL LAW IN HISTORICAL PERSPECTIVE 59 (1968), referring to VON DER HEYDTE, GLOSSEN ZU EINER THEORIE DER ALLGEMEINEN RECHTSGRUNDSATIE IN DIE FRIEDENSWARTE 289, *et seq.* (1933).

Jalet asserts a universalist formulation as he states, "principles that ... constitute that unformulated reservoir of basic legal concepts universal in application, which exist independently of the institutions of any particular country and form the irreducible essence of all legal systems."[10] As can be seen, the consensus of these scholarly definitions emphasizes the objective character of the term "principle."

As noted above, the PCIJ and ICJ, under Article 38(I)(3) and Article 38(1)(c) respectively, can and did in fact apply "general principles"[11] in a number of cases, even though the extent of the two Courts' reliance on "general principles" and the specificity with which the Courts utilized them varied from case to case.

One of the earliest references to "general principles" by the PCIJ is found in the *Mavrommatis Palestine Concessions Case.*[12] In his dissenting opinion, Judge John Basset Moore asserted that a court's requirement for jurisdiction is one of the principles common to all legal systems. He concluded that:

> There are certain elementary conceptions common to all systems of jurisprudence, and one of these is the principle that a court of justice is never justified in hearing and adjudging the merits of a cause of which it has no jurisdiction ....

> The requirement of jurisdiction, which is universally recognized in the national sphere, is not less fundamental and peremptory in the international.[13]

The *S.S. Lotus*[14] is a seminal PCIJ case which illustrates how the court may ascertain the existence of a given principle. The issue in this case was whether Turkey had acted in conflict with principles of international law when it assumed jurisdiction over an officer of a French ship which had collided with a Turkish vessel on the high seas.[15] The Court explained that:

---

[10]   Jalet, *The Quest for the General Principles of Law Recognized by Civilized Nations*, 10 U.C.L.A. L. REV. 1041, 1044 (1963).

[11]   *See supra* note 4.

[12]   Mavrommatis Palestine Concessions, 1924 P.C.I.J. (ser. A) No. 2, at 6.

[13]   *Id.* (Moore, Dissenting) at 57-59.

[14]   S.S. Lotus, 1927 P.C.I.J. (Ser. A) No. 10, at 4.

[15]   *Id.* at 21.

... in the fulfillment of its task of itself ascertaining what the international law is ... [the Court] has included in its researches all precedents, teachings and facts to which it had access and which might possibly have revealed the existence of one of the principles of international law ... the result of these researches has not been to establish the existence of any such principles.[16]

In *Chorzów Factory (Claim for Indemnity)*,[17] which involved the German government seeking damages for harm sustained by two of its companies and caused by the express acts of the Polish government, the PCIJ again articulated the basis of the general principle upon which it relied. The Court stated that:

The essential principle contained in the actual notion of an illegal act -- a principle which seems to be established by international practice and in particular by decisions of arbitral tribunals -- is that reparation must, as far as possible, wipe out all the consequences of the illegal act and reestablish the situation which would in all probability, have existed if that act had not been committed.[18]

The Court was not always so specific in articulating the basis of the general principle it found and relied upon. For example, in the Advisory Opinion concerning the *Greco-Bulgarian Communities*,[19] the issue arose as to which of two conflicting provisions -- a convention or a national law -- should be preferred. The PCIJ simply held that "it is a generally accepted principle of international law that in the relations between Powers who are contracting Parties to a treaty, the provisions of municipal law cannot prevail over those of the treaty."[20]

The PCIJ relied on general principles in a number of other cases;[21] though not

---

[16]   *Id.* at 31.

[17]   Chorzów Factory (Claim for Indemnity), 1928 P.C.I.J. (Ser. A) No. 17, at 4; *reprinted in* M.O. HUDSON, 1 WORLD COURT REPORTS 646 (1969).

[18]   *Id.* at 47.

[19]   Greco-Bulgarian Communities, 1930 P.C.I.J. (Ser. B) No. 17, at 4.

[20]   *Id.* at 32.

[21]   *See e.g.*, German Interests in Polish Upper Silesia, 1925 P.C.I.J. (Ser. A), No. 6, at 4, 19; Chorzów Factory (Judgment), 1927 P.C.I.J. (Ser. A) No. 9, at 4, 31; Serbian Loans (Judgment), 1929 P.C.I.J. (Ser. A) Nos. 20/21, at 39-40; Treatment of Polish Nationals in Danzig, 1932 P.C.I.J. (Ser. A/B) No. 44, at 4, 24; Legal Status of Eastern Greenland 1933 P.C.I.J. (Ser. A/B) No. 53, at 22, 68-69; Lighthouses (Judgment)

always clearly expressing how it identified them, it nonetheless resorted to "general principles" as a source of law in cases presented before it.

The ICJ continued the PCIJ's tradition of utilizing "general principles,"[22] and both courts used that source of law to fill gaps or *lacunae* in conventional and customary international law. These gaps arise where conventions and customs (whether general, particular, or regional) fail to address the issues in a particular legal dispute or fail to provide a solution to the dispute. For example, in the *South West Africa Cases,*[23] Judge Jessup's separate opinion relied on "general principles" to fill the gap in a treaty. In that case, South Africa had argued that the court lacked compulsory jurisdiction because no dispute existed pursuant to Article 7 of the League of Nations Mandate which triggered the Court's jurisdiction.[24] Jessup rejected South Africa's argument on the grounds that parties have a "legal interest" in a case in which the outcome of the case directly affects their financial and economic interest.[25] He thereby recognized the principle that a party may seek adjudication if it has a "legal interest" at stake and applied it to fill a *lacunae* on standing in the treaty in question.

The two Courts have also relied on "general principles" as a means of interpreting existing conventions by examining words not susceptible to an ordinary or common meaning or interpretation, or as a means for objectively ascertaining the intent of the parties. Judge Fernandes advocated this position in the *Right of Passage Case*:

> The priority given by Article 38 of the Statute of the Court to conventions and to custom in relation to the general principles of law in no way excludes a simultaneous application of those principles and of the first two sources of law. It frequently happens that a decision given on the basis of a particular or general

---

1934 P.C.I.J. (Ser. A/B) No. 62, at 4, 47; Electricity Company of Sophia and Bulgaria (Interim Protection) 1944 P.C.I.J. (Ser. A/B) No. 79, at 194, 199.

[22] *See e.g.*, International Status of South West Africa, Advisory Opinion (Sep. Op. McNair), 1950 I.C.J. 146, at 148-149; The Case Concerning the Temple of Preah Vihear (Cambodia v. Thailand) Merits, 1962 ICJ Reports 6, at 23; North Sea Continental Shelf (Judgment), (Sep. Op. Ammoun), 1969 I.C.J. 101, at 134; a number of ICJ Dissenting Opinions make reference to "General Principles." *See e.g.*, Columbian Peruvian Asylum Case (Judgment), (Castilla, J., dissenting) 1950 I.C.J. 359, at 369; *See* South West Africa Cases (Second Phase) (Tanaka, J., dissenting) 1966 I.C.J. 199; North Sea Continental Shelf, *supra* (Lachs, J., dissenting), at 229.

[23] South West Africa Cases, 1950 I.C.J. 128.

[24] *Id.* at 401.

[25] *Id.* at 425.

convention or of a custom requires recourse to the general principles .... A court will have recourse to those principles to fill gaps in the conventional rules, or to interpret them.[26]

In that case, two conflicting rights existed because Portugal had a sovereign claim over the enclaves while India claimed right of passage. Judge Wellington Koo resorted to "general principles" to determine if Portugal had a right of access to the Dadra enclaves. Based on the elementary principle of justice founded on logic and reason which is evidenced in international customary law, he concluded that a principle existed which dictated the proposition that states, as a necessity, have a right of passage in surrounding territories and suggested Portuguese sovereignty over the enclaves is subject to the control and regulation by India.[27]

"General principles" as a source of international law perform four functions.[28] First, they are a source of interpretation for conventional and customary international law and in this respect, they have been used to clarify and interpret international law. This interpretive function is the most widely recognized and applied. Second, they are a means for developing new norms of conventional and customary international law. This may be called the growth function because such an approach injects a dynamic element into international law, which is constantly evolving to meet the needs of this discipline. Third, they serve as a supplemental source to conventional and customary international law, thereby providing a norm or standard when a custom or treaty is inapplicable or nonexistent. The framers of Article 38 of the PCIJ Statute had this function in mind; as one Advisory Committee member pointed out, "[a] rule must be established to ... avoid the possibility of the court declaring itself incompetent through lack of an applicable rule."[29] Fourth, general principles may serve as a modifier of conventional and customary international law. Thus, "general principles" can be used to set aside or modify provisions of conventional or customary law in favor of a greater good. The argument that general principles in certain circumstances should be utilized to modify

---

[26] Right of Passage Over Indian Territory (Portugal v. India), (Fernandes, J., dissenting) 1960 I.C.J. 123, 140 (Apr. 12).

[27] *Id*. at 66-68.

[28] For further elaboration, see Bassiouni, *supra* note 3.

[29] *See* C. RHYNE, INTERNATIONAL LAW: THE SUBSTANCE, PROCESSES, PROCEDURES AND INSTITUTIONS FOR WORLD PEACE WITH JUSTICE 59 (1971).

conventional or customary law is at the heart of the *Jus Cogens* doctrine. Professor Gordon Christenson explains this as follows:

> Some principles of general international law are or ought to be so compelling that they might be recognized by the international community for the purposes of invalidating or forcing revision in ordinary norms of treaty or custom in conflict with them.[30]

In this respect, general principles which rise to the level of *jus cogens* are "peremptory" in that they modify or overturn, as the case may require, customary or conventional law.

The majority of scholars recognize that "general principles" under Article 38(I)(3) of the PCIJ Statute and Article 38(1)(c) of the ICJ Statute can be identified from two sources: national and international. Under the national source, a given principle must be objectively found in the national legal systems of the world's major legal systems. Under the international source it must be found in the practice of states or in the positive legal expressions of states.[31] This requires the identification of a given "principle" by means of inquiring into the various perfected and unperfected sources of international law, namely: treaties and conventions, customs and practices of states, writings of the most distinguished publicists, and decisions of international tribunals.[32]

---

[30]   Christenson, *Jus Cogens: Guarding Interests Fundamental to International Society*, 28 VA. J. INT'L L. 585, 586 (1988).

[31]   Not all scholars agree that general principles are found in both national legal systems and the international expression of states. *See* Lammers, *General Principles of Law Recognized by Civilized Nations*, in ESSAYS ON THE DEVELOPMENT OF THE INTERNATIONAL LEGAL ORDER 53 (F. Kalshoven, P.J. Kuyper & J.G. Lammers eds. 1980), where, at 57, he cites several authorities. The difference between those who claim that general principles are found only in national legal systems and those who advance the proposition that they are also found in the international legal system is based on two unarticulated premises: specificity and certainty. Principles embedded in national law will usually have undergone the test of time and experience and therefore are more easily ascertainable and also more reliable and more specific. Consequently, they are believed to be worthy of greater deference. By contrast, the international legal system may prove more tentative and thus less specific and more difficult to ascertain. This author nonetheless asserts that those principles deemed basic to international law may emerge in the international legal context without necessarily having a specific counterpart in national legal systems. The reason for this separate source of "General Principles" is found in the nature of international law as a discipline, which regulates international relations between States on the basis of consent of the parties, and voluntary acquiescence.

[32]   *Supra* note 3.

270

Furthermore, *opino juris*, policies and pronouncements of states as expressions of their national commitment are also relevant in evidencing the existence of a "general principle."

The application of this source of "general principles" reveals that "crimes against humanity" are prohibited by conventional and customary international law. The evidence for that proposition is found in the cumulative effect of the history of the international regulation of armed conflicts, as discussed in Chapter 4, and in the record of international and national prosecutions, discussed in Chapter 5. The writings of the most distinguished publicists and other sources of conventional and customary international law also support this conclusion.

The national law source of "general principles," as discussed below, also reveals that the specific violations contained within the meaning of "crimes against humanity," as defined in the Charter, are also crimes under the national criminal justice systems of all countries representing the world's major legal systems.

The combined and cumulative weight of these international and national sources of law evidences the existence of "general principles" which prohibit the commission of that which is included in the definition of "crimes against humanity." In time, such universal condemnation raised these principles to the level of *jus cogens*, as discussed in Chapter 11.[33]

The National Law Source of "General Principles": Identifying the Specific Crimes Contained in Article 6(c) and Their Counterparts in National Criminal Laws Prior to the Charter

"Crimes against humanity," as defined in Article 6(c) of the London Charter and Article 5(c) of the Tokyo Charter, include the same specific crimes of "murder, extermination, enslavement, deportation, and other inhumane acts," that constitute crimes in the criminal laws of the world's major legal systems prior to the promulgation of the Charter. To demonstrate this proposition, however, it is important to first establish the methodology used to arrive at this conclusion.

To identify "general principles" of law which arise from the various national legal systems, the inductive method of research is employed. By that method, one identifies

---

[33] J. BLUNTSCHLI, MODERN LAW OF NATIONS OF CIVILIZED STATES (1869) *cited in* M. MCDOUGAL, H. LASWELL, L. CHEN, HUMAN RIGHTS AND WORLD PUBLIC ORDER (1980) wherein he states that, "Treaties, the contents of which violate the generally recognized human rights ... are invalid." *Id.* at 341.

271

the existence of a legal principle in the world's major legal systems, or, more specifically, one searches for, under the national laws of different countries which represent the world's major legal systems, an identity or commonality that exists with respect to a given principle. Obviously, such an inductive method, which is both the most logical and simple approach to comparative research methodology, will have to be particularized with respect to each subject, or specific inquiry, for which the research is undertaken. Thus, if the principle which is being researched is one of great generality, it will more likely be easier to identify in the various major legal systems, and in specific national legal systems representing the world's major legal systems. If, however, the principle inquired of is narrow or specific, then the focus of the research will have to be on the more relevant or particularized sources of law within the various national legal systems representing the world's major legal systems.

It should be noted that this methodology is also recognized and relied upon in the identification of customary rules of international law.[34] Furthermore, the PCIJ used this methodology in the *Lotus Case*.[35] In that case both Turkey and France relied on inductive methodology to identify a principle of criminal jurisdiction in the various national legal systems. Turkey surveyed the various legal systems to identify their criminal jurisdiction norms and correlated them to derive the principle of territorial criminal jurisdiction and the Court relied on these findings.[36]

Professor Akehurst confirms in his research on customs that this methodology has been recognized and relied upon by international and national courts, and by policy-makers in different countries.[37] Among the countries he specifically cites are Great Britain and the United States.[38]

The British Foreign Office, as early as 1877, recognized the validity of this approach particularly with respect to criminal matters, and so instructed the British Minister in Rio de Janeiro as follows: "Her Majesty's Government ... would not be justified in

---

[34] *See e.g.*, A. D'AMATO, THE CONCEPT OF CUSTOM IN INTERNATIONAL LAW (1971); and Akehurst, *Custom As a Source of International Law*, 47 BRIT. Y.B. INT'L L. 1 (1974). The remaining portion of this methodological analysis is adapted from Bassiouni, *supra* note 3.

[35] *See* S.S. Lotus, *supra* note 14, at 21.

[36] *Id. See also* M. MAREK, 2 REPERTOIRES DES DECISIONS ET DES DOCUMENTS DE LA CPJI ET DE LA CIJ 864, 876-888 (1967).

[37] *See* Akehurst, *supra* note 34, at 8-12.

[38] *Id.* at 8.

protesting against a law extending the jurisdiction of Brazilian criminal courts because the law was similar to the laws of several other countries."[39]

The United States of America has also followed this position since the late 1800's.[40] The *Cutting Case* between the United States and Mexico is a landmark ruling on this point.[41] Both the United States and Mexico relied on the laws of different countries to establish the existence of a principle or custom or both. But of particular relevance in this case was the emphasis on the representativeness of the countries referred to and the sufficiency of their number.[42] The United States has relied on this approach in its national courts[43] as has Italy.[44]

The ICJ, like its predecessor the PCIJ, examined national legal systems to derive from them the existence of a custom or general principle. In both instances the methodology of empirical research was the same, though obviously the relevance of the laws discovered and their widespread similarity made for their inclusion in these two sources of international law. The ICJ in the *Nottenbohm Case*[45] comparatively examined national legal provisions on nationality law, and in the *North Sea Continental Shelf Case*,[46] the Court looked for relevant national laws on exploration of continental shelves.[47]

Akehurst concludes: "Obviously a law which is frequently applied carries greater weight than a law which is never or seldom applied; any kind of state practice carries greater weight if it involves an element of repetition."[48] Thus, the existence of the same legal prohibition in a number of legal systems evidences the existence of the

---

[39] A. McNair, 2 International Law Opinions 153 (1956).

[40] *See* 1887 Foreign Relations of the United States 859-867 (1888).

[41] The Cutting Case, 1887 Foreign Relations of the United States, 751 (1888).

[42] *Id.* at 754-55 and 781-817.

[43] *See, The Scotia*, 81 U.S. 170 (1871); and *The Paquete Habana*, 175 U.S. 677 (1899), *see* particularly 688-700.

[44] *See* Lagos v. Baggianini (1953), 22 ILR 533 (1955) (Tribunal of Rome). In determining diplomatic immunity, the court looked at custom and practice of states to determine "the generally accepted rule." *id.* at 534.

[45] Nottenbohm, 1955 ICJ 4, at 22.

[46] *See* North Sea Continental Shelf, *supra* note 22.

[47] *Id.* at 129, 175 and 228-29 containing the views of Judges Ammoun, Tanaka, Lachs.

[48] Akehurst, *supra* note 34, at 9.

principle embodied in the prohibition. Also, the more a given principle is reiterated the more it deserves deference.[49]

As mentioned above, the empirical methodology used herein for demonstrating the existence of "general principles" is the same for demonstrating the existence of a customary rule of international law, thus, giving additional legal support to the validity of this methodology. It must be pointed out that while this method can serve as a valid technique for identifying both a custom and a principle, the appraisal of the research will be different with respect to establishing the existence of a custom as compared to the identification of a given principle.[50]

The significance of this parallelism is that customs draw on principles to establish their existence and that principles can also derive from customs. Thus, "general principles" are a means to interpret and fill gaps in customary law.

"General principles" are, therefore, a valid source for the identification of the specific crimes contained in the meaning of Article 6(c) as they arise under the customary law of armed conflicts, including that portion of customary law which is incorporated in the conventional law of armed conflicts, namely the 1907 Hague Convention.

As stated above, the "general principles" identified hereinafter in the criminal laws of the world's major legal systems serve three functions:

1. To interpret and fill gaps in the conventional law of armed conflicts;
2. To interpret and fill gaps in the customary law of armed conflicts; and,
3. As a separate legal source of international law, which, when universally recognized, becomes a *jus cogens* principle.

The methodology employed is based on a four step approach: (a) identifying the world's major legal systems; (b) identifying representative national legal systems in the world's major legal systems; (c) correlating the principles identified within major legal

---

[49] Bleicher, *The Legal Significance of Re-citation of General Assembly Resolutions*, 63 AJIL 444 (1969).

[50] The difference will depend on the nature of the custom and the "principle" which in some cases could be the same. This is indeed an overlap between sources of international law. Professor D'AMATO, *supra* note 34, looks at treaties as evidence of custom and practice. Akehurst, *supra* note 34, and both the PCIJ and ICJ, *supra* notes 39, 45 and 46, use national laws as evidence of practice, while other PCIJ and ICJ cases cited in *supra* notes 21 and 22 use it to evidence General Principles.

systems; and (d) demonstrating the equivalence between the principles identified and the specific crimes enunciated in Article 6(c).

a. The World's Major Legal Systems

Scholars in comparative legal studies recognize the major legal systems of the world as:[51]

1. The Romanist-Civilist-Germanic Family of Legal Systems
2. The Common Law Family of Legal Systems
3. The Marxist-Socialist Family of Legal Systems
4. The Islamic Family of Legal Systems

b. Identifying Legal Principles

A distinction must be made between broad and narrow legal principles. For example, a broad legal principle may be whether there exists in the major legal systems of the world a right to life. A narrow legal principle may be whether the taking of the life of one person by another without legal justification constitutes a crime or, even more specifically, what crime it constitutes. The type of inquiry will determine the appropriateness of the choice of legal sources.

c. Correlation Between the Sources of Law to be Consulted and the Principle Sought to be Identified

The sources of law to be consulted with respect to narrow or specific legal principles are the relevant statutes, laws, or other normative sources. Thus, the inquiry of whether the killing of one person by another without legal justification constitutes murder,

---

[51] René David, who is recognized as the world's leading authority on comparative law, in his work LES GRANDS SYSTÈMES DE DROIT CONTEMPORAINES (5th ed. 1973) states that the major world systems are: 1. The Romanist-Germanic; 2. The Socialist; 3. The Common Law; 4. Islamic Law; 5. Asian Legal Systems. He refers to them as "famille" or families of law, at 22-32. For the most part, however, the legal systems of Asian countries which are not former colonies of the United Kingdom are considered part of the civil law system. *See* Parker and Neylon, *Jus Cogens: Compelling the Law of Human Rights*, 12 HASTINGS INT'L & COMP. L. REV. 411, 425 n. 71 (1989).

would necessarily entail consultation of the criminal laws of the countries representing the world's major legal systems with appropriate geographic representativeness, as identified below.

The quantitative factor as to the number of national legal systems that need to be consulted within the world's major legal systems will depend upon the type of inquiry and the degree of identity or similarity that may emerge from the research. Thus, the more obvious the similarity or sameness of the outcome of the research in the different legal systems, the more likely it is that adding more countries with the same general legal basis may not significantly add to the research. However, if there is only general similarity which is only vaguely equivalent, but not of such sufficient comparative equivalence to ensure a broad consensus, then it would appear that a larger number of national legal systems would have to be consulted.

It is obvious that no two national legal systems are alike and certainly the legal provisions of different countries, for example, on the definition of murder, are not likely to be identical. The question, therefore, is whether, by the notion of sameness, one intends: (i) identical normative formulation; (ii) identical legal elements; or (iii) substantial similarity, irrespective of the identical normative formulation or required elements. In short, the question is whether or not one has to seek sameness of normative provisions or comparative equivalence of normative provisions. The answer to that question will depend on whether the inquiry involves a broad "general principle," or not. By its very nature, a broad "general principle" does not require sameness in terms of its specific normative formulation, but a narrower or specific principle will require greater similarity.

In comparative criminal law research involving the determination of what constitutes a crime in different national legal systems, there is a substantial historical basis and national practice which provide a foundation for such an inquiry. This is embodied in the law of practice of international extradition which has been in existence for a substantial period of time throughout history and has been relied upon by almost all countries in the world. In that process, the search for comparative criminal legal provisions is referred to as the "principle of double criminality" or as the "principle of dual criminality."[52] Under this principle, the requested state in an extradition process

---

[52] *See* 1 M.C. BASSIOUNI, INTERNATIONAL EXTRADITION IN UNITED STATES LAW AND PRACTICE Chap. VII, 319-380 (2d rev. ed. 1987); and A. LAFOREST, INTERNATIONAL EXTRADITION TO AND FROM CANADA 52-56 (2d ed. 1970); at pages 54-55 the author notes that it is the position of the Canadian Government that "... an exact correspondence between offenses in two countries cannot be expected. It is, therefore, not necessary that the crime concerned bears the same name in both countries. It is sufficient if

examines the crime charged by the requesting state and seeks to determine whether that crime also constitutes a crime under the national criminal laws of the requested state. In the course of that inquiry there are two methods: the application of the *in concreto* and *in abstracto* approaches.[53] In the *in concreto* approach, whose use since the late 1800's has been gradually abandoned, the search is for whether or not the elements of the crime in the laws of the requested state are the same as the elements of the crime in the laws of the requesting state. In other words, the search is for greater specificity and sameness of incentive provisions. In the *in abstracto* application, which is now generally adopted by almost all states, the inquiry is whether or not the crime in the requested state is generally comparable to the crime in the requesting state. The modern trend is to examine the underlying facts of the criminal charge to determine whether or not these facts would give rise in the requested state to the same or to a comparable charge as the one in the requesting state.[54] Therefore, a person who is charged with

---

the acts constituting the offence in the demanding state also amount to a crime in the country from which the fugitive is sought to be extradited even though it may be called by a different name. As already mentioned, it is the essence of the offence that is important." *See also* LEGAL ASPECTS OF EXTRADITION AMONG EUROPEAN STATES (Council of Europe, European Committee on Crime Prevention, 1970); 6 M. WHITEMAN, DIGEST OF INTERNATIONAL LAW 773-779 (1968); I. SHEARER, EXTRADITION IN INTERNATIONAL LAW 132-149 (1971); Vieira, *L'Evolution Recent de l'Extradition dans le Continent Americain*, 185 RECUEIL DES COURS, ACADEMIE DE DROIT INTERNATIONAL 155 (1978); V.E.H. BOOTH, BRITISH EXTRADITION LAW AND PROCEDURE (1980); H.A. BOUKHRISS, LA COOPERATION PÉNALE INTERNATIONALE PAR VOI D'EXTRADITION AU MAROC (1986); O. LAGODNY, DIE RECHTSSTELLUNG DES AUSZULIEFERNDEN IN DER BUNDESREPUBLIK DEUTSCHLAND (1987).

[53] *See* 39 RIDP (1968) dedicated to national reports on extradition from: Austria, Belgium, Brazil, Chile, Czechoslovakia, Finland, France, Federal Republic of Germany, Greece, Hungary, Italy, Japan, Poland, Sweden, Switzerland, United States and Yugoslavia. All of these country reports indicate reliance on the principle of "double criminality," whether "in concreto" or "in abstracto."

[54] The principle of "double criminality" is also required in all modalities of international cooperation in penal matters. *See* E. MULLER-RAPPARD AND M.C. BASSIOUNI, EUROPEAN INTER-STATE COOPERATION IN CRIMINAL MATTERS, LA COOPERATION INTER-ETATIQUE EUROPÉENE EN MATIÈRE PENALE (3 vols. 1987). For different modalities of international cooperation in penal matters, *see* Muller-Rappard, Schutte, Epp, Poncet, Zagaris, *et al.*, in 2 BASSIOUNI ICL; Grutzner, *International Judicial Assistance and Cooperation in Criminal Matters*, in 2 BASSIOUNI AND NANDA TREATISE 189. For a survey of recent Mutual Legal Assistance Treaties between the United States and other countries *see* Nadelman, *Negotiations in Criminal Law Assistance Treaties*, 33 AM. J. COMP. L. 467 (1985); and Zagaris and Simonetti, *Judicial Assistance Under U.S. Bilateral Treaties*, in LEGAL RESPONSES TO INTERNATIONAL TERRORISM 219 (M.C. Bassiouni ed. 1988). For a Socialist perspective, *see* Krapac, *An Outline of the Recent Development of the Yugoslav Law of International Judicial Assistance and Cooperation in Criminal Matters*, 34 NETH. INT'L L. REV. 324 (1987); Gardocki, *The Socialist System of Judicial Assistance and Mutual Cooperation in Penal Matters*, in

the killing of another person without legal justification may be charged in different countries under different types of statutes involving criminal homicides. These homicide laws may have different labels, as well as distinctions as to either the different degrees or types of intentional killings and different elements required for each such offense. But all would have in common the same general elements: the material element of one person engaging in conduct which produced the death of another, the mental element of intention to commit the act, however described, and the causation between conduct and resulting death. If, as a result of the above, the fact that a person would be charged in one country with a crime called murder, whereas in another it is called intentional killing or voluntary manslaughter, would not be legally relevant to a finding that "dual criminality" exists. The reason is that the underlying facts would give rise to a similar though not necessarily identical charge in the requested state. The inquiry then focuses on the general characteristics of the crime charged in comparative analysis and not on the sameness or identity of the label of the crime, or the legal elements needed to prove it. It would be of no consequence to the requested state if the charge by the requesting State is murder or intentional killing or voluntary manslaughter or, for that matter, involuntary manslaughter, so long as the crime charged, irrespective of the specificity of its elements, generally corresponds to an equivalent counterpart crime in the requested state. The issue will, therefore, not turn on what type of mental element is required, for example, for the offense of murder or first degree murder or voluntary manslaughter or involuntary manslaughter, rather the inquiry will be whether the facts allegedly committed by the individual sought are such that they constitute the material element of the killing of one person by another accompanied by some type of mental state and that a death resulted. If these basic facts would constitute a homicidal offense in both the requested and requesting states, then extradition shall be granted.

By analogy to the above, one must therefore conclude, that in order to inquire into the specific crimes contained within the definition of "crimes against humanity," one should examine the criminal laws of the most representative countries of the world's major criminal justice systems. The number of countries to be researched will depend upon the degree of similarity or comparable equivalence that may arise as a result of the research.

---

2 BASSIOUNI ICL 133; Shupilov, *Legal Assistance in Criminal Cases and Some Important Questions of Extradition [in the USSR]*, 15 CASE W. RES. J. OF INT'L L. 127 (1983). *See also* DOUBLE CRIMINALITY STUDIES IN INTERNATIONAL CRIMINAL LAW (N. Jareborg ed. 1989).

The following 74 countries existed in 1944[55]: (1) **Afghànistan***; (2) **Albania***; (3) **Africa**, Union of South*; (4) **Arabia** [Saudi Arabia, Yemen, Muscat and Oman, Kuwait, The Trucial Sheikdoms, and Bahrain]; (5) **Argentina***; (6) **Australia***; (7) **Belgium*** [Belgian Congo, Rwanda and Urundi]; (8) **Bhutàn**; (9) **Bolivia***; (10) **Brazil**; (11) **British Empire*** [*Europe*: United Kingdom of Great Britain and Northern Ireland, Gibraltar, Malta; *Asia*: Aden, Borneo, Brune; and Sarawak, Ceylon, Cyprus, Hong Kong, India, Burma, Straits Settlements, Federated Malay States, Unfederated Malay States, and Palestine. Kenya, Uganda, Zanzibar, Mauritius and Dependencies, Nyasaland, St. Bechuanoland, Somiland, Basutoland, Southern Rhodesia, Northern Rhodesia, Swaziland, Nigeria, Gambia, Ghana (Gold Coast), Sierra Leone, Angle-Egyptian Sudan, Tanganyika Territory, S.W. Africa, Cameroon, and Togoland; *Americas*: Bermuda, Falkland Islands and South Georgia, British Guinea, British Honduras, Newfoundland and Labrador, Bahamas, Barbados, Jamaica (and other islands), Leeward Islands, Trinidad, and Windward Islands; *Australasia*: Australian Commonwealth, Papua, Fiji, Pacific Islands, Territory of New Guinea, Western Samoa, and Nauru.]; (12) **Bulgaria***; (13) **Burma**; (14) **Canada***; (15) **Chile**; (16) **China*** [Manchukuo (Manchuria), Tibet, Sing-Kiang, and Mongolia]; (17) **Columbia***; (18) **Costa Rica***; (19) **Cuba***; (20) **Czecho-Slovakia***; (21) **Denmark***: [*Europe*: Denmark (Continental); *Americas*: Greenland]; (22) **Dominican Republic***; (23) **Ecuador***; (24) **Egypt***; (25) **Estonia***; (26) **Ethiopia** (also referred to as Abyssinia)*; (27) **Finland***; (28) **France*** [*Europe*: France (Continental) and Andorra; *Asia*: French India, French Indo-China, Cochin-China, Annam, Cambodia, Tonring, Laos, and Kwang Chau Wan, Lebanon and Syria; *Africa*: Algeria, Cameroon, French Equatorial Africa, French Somaliland, Madagascar, Matotte and the Comoro Islands, Reunion, Togo, Tunis, West Africa and the Sahara Senegal, Guinea, Ivory Coast, Dahomey, French Sudan, Mauritania, Niger; *Americas*: Guadeloupe and Dependencies, Guiana, Martinique, St. Pierre and Miquelon; *Oceania*: New Caledonia and Dependencies, New Hebrides, French Establishments in Oceania, and French Possession in the Antarctic.];

---

[55] * Indicates Member of the League of Nations as of 1944. [The following states withdrew from the League of Nations: Brazil on June 12, 1935; Spain on September 8, 1930; Japan on March 27, 1933; Germany on October 21, 1933; Paraguay on February 24, 1935; Guatemala on May 13, 1933; Honduras on June 22, 1936; Nicaragua on June 26, 1936; Italy on December 11, 1937; Chile on June 2, 1938; Venezuela on July 11, 1938; San Salvador on August 10, 1938; Peru on April 8, 1939; Hungary on April 11, 1939; Albania on April 14, 1939; Rumania on July 11, 1940; France on April 19, 1940; and Haiti on April 8, 1942. On April 16, 1948, General DeGaulle, in agreement with General Giraud, repudiated the Vichy Government's withdrawal from the League and asked that France still be considered a member. On March 22, 1920, Spain resolved to continue as a member of the League, but again gave notice of withdrawal on May 9, 1939.]

279

(29) **Germany**; (30) **Greece***; (31) **Guatemala**; (32) **Holy See - Vatican**; (33) **Haiti***; (34) **Honduras**; (35) **Hungary**; (36) **Iceland**; (37) **Iran***; (38) **Iraq***; (39) **India***; (40) **Ireland***; (41) **Italy** [*Europe*: Italy (Continental and Islands); *Africa*: (Italian Colonial Empire, Libya, Italian East Africa, Eritrea, Italian Somaliland, Tientein (Concession of), and Saseno]; (42) **Japan** [Asian Territories]; (43) **Korea** [*Continental Asia and Pacific*: Formosa (Taiwan), Sakhalen, Kwantung, and Pacific Islands]; (44) **Latvia***; (45) **Liberia***; (46) **Liechtenstein**; (47) **Lithuania***; (48) **Luxembourg***; (49) **Mexico***; (50) **Monaco**; (51) **Morocco**; (52) **Nepál**; (53) **Netherlands** (The)* [*Europe*: Holland (Continental); *Americas*: Surinam and Netherlands West Indies; *Asia*: Dutch Guiana.]; (54) **New Zealand***; (55) **Nicaragua**; (56) **Norway*** [*Europe*: Scandinavian Norway, Spitsbergen, Jan Mayen Island, Bouvet Island, Peter I Island, and Antarctic Dependency.]; (57) **Panama***; (58) **Paraguay**; (59) **Peru**; (60) **Poland***; (61) **Portugal*** [*Europe*: Continental Portugal; *Africa*: Angola, Cape Verdé, and Mozambique]; (62) **Rumania**; (63) **El Salvador**; (64) **San Marino**; (65) **Spain** [including Canary Islands and Spanish Morocco]; (66) **Sweden***; (67) **Switzerland***; (68) **Thailand***; (69) **Turkey***; (70) **Uruguay***; (71) **Union of Soviet Socialist Republics**; (72) **United States of America** [*Americas*: Alaska, Panama Canal under U.S. Control, United States Virgin Islands; *Oceania*: Hawaii, the Phillipines, Guam and other Pacific Islands]; (73) **Venezuela**; (74) **Yugoslavia***.

The laws of 39 of these countries were researched.[56] These countries represent the world's major legal systems. The selection represents all the world's geographic

---

[56] The following 39 states were selected for specific empirical study because they are geo-politically representative of all the then existing countries of the world, and more importantly, because they represent the major criminal justice systems of the world. This selection reflects the methodology outlined above which is based on the representation of all families of legal systems. These countries are: Argentina; Arabian Peninsula; Australia; Austria; Belgium; Brazil; Chile; China; Columbia; Czecho-Slovakia; Denmark; Egypt; Ethiopia; Finland; France; Germany; Ghana (Gold Coast); Greece; Hungary; India; Italy; Japan; Liberia; Mexico; Netherlands; New Zealand; Poland; Portugal; South Africa; Spain; Sudan; Switzerland; Tunisia; Union of Soviet Socialist Republics; United Kingdom of Great Britain and Northern Ireland; United States of America; Venezuela; Yugoslavia.

regions.[57] The combination of these criteria thus provides the necessary objectivity for the basis and sampling of the research.

d. Corresponding Equivalence Between the Specific Crimes Identified in Article 6(c) and the National Criminal Laws

"Crimes against humanity" are defined in Article 6(c) of the London Charter and Article 5(c) of the Tokyo Charter as:

[M]urder, extermination, enslavement, deportation, and other inhumane acts committed against any civilian population before or during the war; or persecutions on political, racial, or religious grounds in execution of or in connection with any crime . . . . [58]

On its face, this definition includes a number of common crimes known to almost all the criminal laws of the world's major legal systems. As the IMT Indictment provided in "Count Four -- Crimes Against Humanity:" These methods and crimes constituted violations of . . . *the general principles of criminal law as derived from the criminal law of all civilized nations* . . . ."[59] (emphasis added) Thus, the specific terms employed in Articles 6(c) and 5(c) respectively are the same or equivalent to certain crimes which existed in all the world's major legal systems, with insubstantial variations from country to country as is demonstrated below.

---

[57] Geographic Distribution: North America--Mexico, United States of America; *Latin America*--Argentina, Brazil, Chile, Columbia, Venezuela; *Western Europe*--Austria, Belgium, France, Germany, Greece, Italy, Netherlands, Spain, Switzerland, United Kingdom of Great Britain and Northern Ireland; *Scandinavia*--Denmark, Finland, Sweden; *Eastern Europe*--Czecho-Slovakia, Poland, Hungary, Union of Soviet Socialist Republics, Yugoslavia; *Africa*--Ethiopia, Ghana (Gold Coast), Liberia, South Africa, Sudan; *Australasia*--Australia; *Far East*--China, India, Japan, New Zealand; *Middle East*--Arabian-Peninsula, Egypt, Tunisia.

[58] *See* London and Tokyo Charters.

[59] 1 IMT 65. Along the same lines, Professor Gros, in a conference leading to the Charter's formulation, stated that: "[I]f you define their crimes according to their practical results, if you show that the Germans have been breaking treaties and as a result of that have annexed populations, run concentration camps, and violated international law by criminal acts against people, what you will condemn are those acts which in fact are criminal in all legislation, and you will condemn them for having directed those acts. Minutes of Conference Session of July 19, 1945, Statement of Professor Gros, in Jackson's Report 297.

COMPARATIVE USE OF TERMS

Specific Charter	Plain Meaning (as Defined in the 1940 Oxford English Dictionary)	Equivalent Crimes in the World's Major Criminal Justice Systems in 1940
Murder	Unjustifiable Killing	Murder and Manslaughter
Extermination	To destroy the person	Murder and Manslaughter
Enslavement	To reduce to slavery, to subjugate and treat as a slave, to employ in servile or forced labour, to wear out by severe toil	Slavery, kidnapping, abduction, forcible confinement
Deportation	To carry away, remove into exile, to banish, forcible removal, forcible transportation	Kidnapping, abduction, forcible confinement
Persecution	Based on discrimination to: oppress, harass, impose mental or physical harm	Depending on the specific acts committed as part of the persecution there could be: murder, manslaughter, rape; assault; battery; theft; robbery; destruction of property and a variety of crimes related to unlawful interference with fundemental legal rights
Other Inhumane Acts	Brutality, barbarous or cruel conduct, conduct contrary to humane	In reliance on the *ejusdem generis* method of interpretation, it would cover all the crimes in type and nature to those identified above. Depending on the specific acts, it could include other forms of homicide, physical injury, mental suffering, deprivation of rights, such as murder; manslaughter; rape; assault; battery; theft; robbery; destruction of property; slavery; kidnapping; abduction; forcible confinement

SPECIFIC CRIMES IN GENERAL PRINCIPLES

At this point, the inquiry is whether all the specific crimes contained in Article 6(c) of the London Charter and Article 5(c) of the Tokyo Statute were crimes, in 1944, in the world's major criminal justice systems. This is evidenced by a sufficient and representative number of states which proscribe those specific crimes. If the outcome of the empirical research is such as to reveal universality or substantial similarity in the criminal proscription of these acts, then the conclusion would be that the human interests sought to be protected and the harm sought to be prevented are embodied in "general principles of law recognized by civilized nations."

The empirical research[60] undertaken was conducted, as indicated below, for 39

---

[60] This extensive research was done in connection with *R.J. Finta* and the author's testimony as the legal expert for the Canadian Government on international criminal law and particularly on "crimes against humanity." The author expresses appreciation to the Canadian Department of Justice for the opportunity to serve in the above-mentioned capacity and to have been able to conduct this research and present it to the Ontario Supreme Court. The research consisted in: (1) obtaining the texts of laws in 1944 from the 39 researched countries; (2) translating them into English; (3) obtaining an expert opinion from distinguished jurists in these countries to explain each crime and its required legal elements; (4) summarizing the texts of laws and the legal opinions; and, (5) correlating the data which is presented in the Chart that appears in the text.

The data was principally obtained through the assistance of Daniel Wade, International Law Librarian, Yale Law School and those distinguished experts whose names and titles follow:

1. Argentina: Raoul Zaffaroni, Professor of Criminal Law, The University of Buenos Aires; Judge, Court of Appeals of Buenos-Aires; Deputy Secretary-General, International Association of Penal Law (AIDP).
2. Austria: Otto Triffterer, Professor of Criminal Law, Procedure, and International Criminal Law, The University of Salzbourg.
3. Belgium: Paul de Cant, Retired Advocat General, Près de la Cour d'Appel de Bruxelles; Honorary Vice-President, International Association of Penal Law (AIDP).
4. Brazil: Jaoa Marcello de Arraujo, Professor of Criminal Law, The University of Rio de Janeiro; Member of the Conseil de Direction, International Association of Penal Law (AIDP).
5. Chile: Alfredo Etcheberry, Professor of Criminal Law, The National University of Chile; President, Chilean Bar Association; Member of the Conseil de Direction, International Association of Penal Law (AIDP).
6. Czechoslovakia: Bohumil Repik, Vice-President, Supreme Court of Czechoslavakia; Member of the Conseil de Direction, International Association of Penal Law (AIDP).
7. Egypt: Abdel Azim Wazir, Professor of Criminal Law and Vice Dean, The University of Mansourah, Egypt; Deputy Secretary-General, International Association of Penal Law (AIDP).
8. France: Reynald Ottenhof, Professor of Criminal Law; Director, Institute of Criminal Sciences, The University of Pau; Secretary-General, International Association of Penal Law (AIDP).

States representing the world's major legal systems. The following summary reveals that the acts contained in Article 6(c) are criminal in these national legal systems.

---

9.   Greece: Dionysios Spinellis, Professor of Criminal Law, The University of Athens; Consultant, Ministry of Justice of Greece; Member of the Conseil de Direction, International Association of Penal Law (AIDP).

10.   Italy: Ennio Amadio, Professor of Criminal Procedure and Comparative Criminal Law, The University of Milano.

11.   Japan: Ryuchi Hirano, Professor Criminal Law, The University of Tokyo; Former President, The University of Tokyo; Honorary Member of the Conseil de Direction, International Association of Penal Law (AIDP).

12.   Portugal: Jorge Figueredo Dias, Professor of Criminal Law, The University of Coimbra; Member of the Conseil de Direction, International Association of Penal Law (AIDP).

13.   Sudan: Abdel Azim Wazir, Professor of Criminal Law and Vice Dean, The University of Mansourah, Egypt; Deputy Secretary-General, International Association of Penal Law (AIDP).

14.   Switzerland: Stefan Trechsel, Professor of Criminal Law, The University of St. Gallen; Vice-Chairman, The European Commission on Human Rights; Member of the Conseil de Droit, International Association of Penal Law (AIDP).

15.   Tunisia: Abdel Azim Wazir, Professor of Criminal Law and Vice Dean, The University of Mansourah, Egypt; Deputy Secretary-General, International Association of Penal Law (AIDP).

16.   United Kingdom: Leonard Leigh, Professor of Criminal Law, The London School of Economics; Member of the Conseil de Direction, International Association of Penal Law (AIDP).

My research assistant George Gullo (J.D. DePaul 1991) assisted me in correlating the voluminous materials we received and from which we extracted the data presented in this Chapter.

284

WHICH CORRESPOND TO THE SPECIFIC CRIMES CONTAINED IN ARTICLE 6(C)

	Murder	Manslaughter	Torture[1]	Enslavement[2]	Kidnapping[3]	Forcible Confinement[4]	Assault/ Battery	Robbery	Deportation[5]
1. Argentina	‖	‖			‖	‖	‖	‖	‖
2. Arabian Peninsula (Islamic Law)	‖	‖	•	‖	‖	‖	‖	‖	•
3. Australia	‖	‖						‖	
4. Austria	‖	‖	•	‖	‖	‖	‖	‖	‖
5. Belgium	‖	‖	•	•	‖	‖	‖	‖	•
6. Brazil	‖	‖	‖		‖	‖		‖	•
7. Chile	‖	‖	•					‖	‖
8. China	‖	‖	‖		‖			‖	
9. Colombia	‖	‖	•	•	•			‖	•
10. Czechoslovakia	‖	‖		•				‖	
11. Denmark	‖	‖	‖	•	•	‖		‖	‖
12. Egypt	‖	‖	‖		‖	‖	‖	‖	
13. Ethiopia	‖	‖	•			‖		‖	•
14. Finland	‖	‖	‖	‖	‖	‖	‖	‖	‖
15. France	‖	‖	‖					‖	•
16. Germany	‖	‖		‖	‖	‖	‖	‖	‖
17. Ghana (Gold Coast)	‖	‖	‖					‖	•
18. Greece	‖	‖	‖	•				‖	•
19. Hungary	‖	‖	•		‖	‖	‖	‖	•

[1] Where indicated by a bullet, although not specifically provided for, Torture is subsumed under crimes against physical integrity, *i.e.*, Assault/Battery.

[2] Where indicated by a bullet, although not specifically provided for, Enslavement is subsumed under Kidnapping and/or Forcible Confinement.

[3] Where indicated by a bullet, although not specifically provided for, Kidnapping is subsumed under Forcible Confinement.

[4] Where indicated by a bullet, although not specifically provided for, Forcible Confinement is subsumed under Kidnapping.

[5] Where indicated by a bullet, although not specifically provided for, Deportation is subsumed under Kidnapping and/or Forcible Confinement.

285

	Murder	Manslaughter	Torture[1]	Enslavement[2]	Kidnapping[3]	Forcible Confinement[4]	Assault/ Battery	Robbery	Deportation[5]
20. India	■	■	■	■	■	■	■	■	■
21. Italy	■	■	•	■	■	■	■	■	•
22. Japan	■	■	•	•	■	■	■	■	•
23. Liberia	■	■	•	•	■	■	■	■	•
24. Mexico	■	■	•	■	•	■	■	■	■
25. Netherlands	■	■	•	■	■	■	■	■	•
26. New Zealand	■	■	•	■	•	•	■	■	■
27. Poland	■	■	■	•	■	■	■	■	•
28. Portugal	■	■	■	■	■	■	■	■	•
29. South Africa	■	■	•	•	■	■	■	■	■
30. Spain	■	■	•	•	■	■	■	■	•
31. Sweden	■	■	•	•	■	■	■	■	•
32. Switzerland	■	■	■	■	■	■	■	■	■
33. Tunisia	■	■	■	■	■	■	■	■	■
34. USSR	■	■	■	■	■	■	■	■	•
35. UK	■	■	•	•	■	■	■	■	•
36. USA	■	■	■	■	■	■	■	■	•
37. Venezuela	■	■	•	■	•	■	■	■	■
38. Yugoslavia	■	■	•	•	•	■	■	■	•

[1] Where indicated by a bullet, although not specifically provided for, Torture is subsumed under crimes against physical integrity, i.e., Assault/Battery.

[2] Where indicated by a bullet, although not specifically provided for, Enslavement is subsumed under Kidnapping and/or Forcible Confinement.

[3] Where indicated by a bullet, although not specifically provided for, Kidnapping is subsumed under Forcible Confinement.

[4] Where indicated by a bullet, although not specifically provided for, Forcible Confinement is subsumed under Kidnapping.

[5] Where indicated by a bullet, although not specifically provided for, Deportation is subsumed under Kidnapping and/or Forcible Confinement.

Conclusion

As has been established above, the specific crimes contained in the category of "crimes against humanity" were prohibited in the world's major criminal justice systems and, therefore, they constituted violations of "general principles of law recognized by civilized nations" well before the Charter was promulgated.

The legal consequences that derive from this conclusion are:

1. They can be used to interpret and fill the gaps in the 1907 Hague Convention, which refers to violations of the "Laws of Humanity;"
2. They can be relied upon to interpret and fill the gaps in customary international law between 1907 and 1945;
3. They negate the assertion that Article 6(c) posited new violations contrary to basic "principles of legality;"
4. They can be relied upon to define the terms of Article 6(c) and the contents of the specific crimes contained in this category of crimes to satisfy the requirements of the "principles of legality;"
5. They demonstrate that "superior orders" to carry out such acts are manifestly unlawful, thus negating the defense of "obedience to superior orders;"
6. They impose command responsibility;
7. They can be relied upon as an independent legal source for the prohibition of the acts included in Article 6(c).

The demonstration that a given crime, for example murder, exists in all legal systems, does not make murder an international crime. What is required, other than the existence of conventional or customary international law declaring it to be such, is the existence of an "international element" that takes such a national common crime out of the exclusive sphere of national criminal jurisdiction and moves it to that of international criminal law, as discussed in Chapter 6.

Chapter 8 will apply the findings of this Chapter to the specific crimes contained in Article 6(c).

CHAPTER 8

CONTENTS OF THE SPECIFIC CRIMES FROM THE CHARTER UNTIL NOW

> The timeless mosaic of the law is constantly enriched by experience; even by unmatching pieces of discordant colors.

Introduction to the Legal Bases

While the concept of "crimes against humanity" was well established in humanitarian international law and the regulation of armed conflicts before the Charter's promulgation, as discussed in Chapter 4, questions remained as to whether the contents of the specific crimes contained in Article 6(c) satisfied the "principles of legality," as discussed in Chapter 3. Admittedly, international criminal law is not as rigorous as some national legal systems with respect to the specificity required in the definitional contents of international crimes. There is nonetheless a minimum standard of specificity which must be met, as discussed in Chapter 3. This standard must be sufficient to place people on notice of the prohibited conduct, so that they can conform their actions to the requirements of international criminal law. It is also needed in order to determine the elements of a specific crime and the general elements of individual criminal responsibility and exoneration therefrom.

Article 6(c) crimes were not defined in the Charter and thus a *prima facie* argument could be made that they lacked sufficient specificity to satisfy the minimum standards of legality required by international criminal law. Thus, there is the need to resort to other legal sources to determine the specific contents and elements of these crimes.

The study of national criminal justice systems, described in Chapter 7, reveals that substantial similarity existed between the specific crimes contained in Article 6(c) and their counterparts in the national criminal laws of the world's major legal systems at the time of the Charter's promulgation. That study also reveals similarities between the legal elements required for Article 6(c) crimes and their counterparts in national criminal laws. But it is well established that national legal systems differ, *inter alia* as to: their conceptual approaches to criminal responsibility; the techniques they employ to define crimes; the general and specific elements they require for different crimes; and their legal requirements for criminal responsibility and exoneration therefrom. Thus, the methods of interpretation by analogy must be carefully defined. Some of the

288

Article 6(c) crimes can, however, be clearly identified by analogy to war crimes under the conventional and customary law of armed conflicts as interpreted by "general principles of law." But it is important to bear in mind that "general principles" are not, in this writer's opinion, capable in and of themselves, of creating international crimes.[1] To so hold would be a violation of the "principles of legality." The significance and role of "general principles" is, however, evident in the findings outlined in Chapter 7, and their functional use as a means of interpretation.

Before 1945, it would start with the 1907 Hague Convention's general prohibition against violations of the "laws of humanity" and the specific provisions, contained in articles 42-57, which protect civilian populations. After 1945, "general principles" would be used to interpret the provisions of the Fourth Geneva Convention and the Additional Protocols and to ascertain from other international law sources, either additional factors to interpret conventional and customary sources or to ascertain the existence of independent principles.

The same reasoning and methodological approach would apply to the identification of national principles, whether before or after that Charter's promulgation.

Certain Article 6(c) crimes are not, however, identifiable by analogy to war crimes. Thus, it is necessary in such cases to:

1.   identify Article 6(c) crimes under an appropriate source of international law, namely conventional and customary international law; and

2.   demonstrate the sufficiency of the definitional content of each of these crimes, and in this respect, in reliance upon "general principles."

An examination of each specific crime contained in Article 6(c) follows. It is made for purposes of identifying the specifity of Article 6(c) crimes and in order to determine their legal elements and contents prior to and subsequent to the Charter. The outcome of the analysis will determine whether Article 6(c) crimes satisfy the requirements of legality under international criminal law.

These specific crimes are discussed in the same order as they appear in the Charter's Article 6(c) definition but their analysis extends to Post-Charter Legal Developments.

---

[1]   *See* Chapter 7 at 264.

1. Murder and Extermination

Murder of civilian populations in time of war by a foreign occupier is prohibited by conventional and customary regulation of armed conflicts. Extermination is murder on a large scale. While the 1899 and 1907 Hague Conventions, which embody customary law, protect the "lives" of civilian populations,[2] they do not provide specific definitions as to the crime or crimes of taking the life of a civilian under occupation. The Fourth Geneva Convention and Protocol I also fail to define murder and the meaning of protection of life. Therefore, one must first resort to customary practices of states in time of war to ascertain the types of life-taking that would constitute a violation of the provision protecting the "lives" of the civilian population, and thereafter to "general principles of law."

The customary practice of states, evidenced in international and national military prosecutions, reveals that murder is intentional killing without lawful justification. Lawful justification refers to those legal justifications, excuses and defenses known to the world's major criminal justice systems, *e.g.*, self-defense, coercion, necessity and reasonable mistake of law or fact. But state practice also shows that under certain circumstances, the doctrines of "military necessity" and "obedience to superior orders" are exonerating or mitigating factors.[3]

The protection of life is a "general principle" because it is specifically enunciated in a variety of international instruments and in national legal instruments. It includes a prohibition against unjustified killing. Indeed, all the world's major criminal justice systems have crimes such as murder and manslaughter, no matter how they are defined or graded in the various national legal systems. But the fact that every legal system in the world criminalizes murder does not make murder an international crime. Thus, it is necessary to show the nexus between murder as understood in the world's major criminal justice systems and the international crime of murder and extermination under Article 6(c). Such a nexus can be established by the war connecting element that the Charter required, as discussed in Chapter 1, or by the fact that the conduct was part of "state action or policy," as discussed in Chapter 6. The same nexus or international element is required as all other Article 6(c) crimes.

The customary practice of states, evidenced by international and national military prosecutions, reveals that murder is not intended to mean only those specific intentional

---

[2]   1907 Hague Convention, Article 42.

[3]   *See* Chapter 10 at 398.

killings without lawful justification. Instead, state practice views murder in its *largo senso* meaning as including the creation of life endangering conditions likely to result in death according to reasonable human experience. This standard was used in war related cases involving mistreatment of prisoners of war and civilians.

The label, definition and elements of homicide differ among national criminal justice systems. This difference raises a problem with respect to defining murder as an Article 6(c) crime by analogy to the definition of murder in the world's major criminal justice systems. Combining the practice of states in national military prosecutions and the *in extenso* definition of murder in major systems, one can conclude that murder as intended under Article 6(c) includes a closely related form of unintentional but foreseeable death which the common law labels manslaughter. But that does not mean that all forms of unintended killings can be included in the extended meaning of "murder" under Article 6(c), otherwise a traffic accident resulting in death could become, under certain circumstances, an international crime.

The extension of murder to include unintended killing is particularly relevant to "extermination." The plain language and ordinary meaning of the word extermination implies both intentional and unintentional killing. The reason for the latter is that mass killing of a group of people involves planning and implementation by a number of persons who, though knowing and wanting the intended result, may not necessarily know their victims. Furthermore, such persons may not necessarily perform the *actus reus* which produced the deaths, nor have specific intent toward a particular victim. All of these are necessary elements of murder or its counterpart in the world's major criminal justice systems. Thus, the individual responsibility of each actor (whether direct, indirect, or vicarious) for a given killing cannot be predicated on the element of specific knowledge of the identity of the victim or personal knowledge of the specific act that was the direct cause of death of a given victim. It is, therefore, necessary in that type of group killing to extend the definitions of "murder" and particularly that of "extermination" to include other forms of intentional and unintentional killing.

Notwithstanding the technical differences in the definitions of various forms of intentional and unintentional killing in the world's major criminal justice systems, the widespread common understanding of the meaning of murder includes life-endangering conditions likely to result in death according to the known or foreseeable expectations of a reasonable person in the same circumstances. Admittedly, this definition includes what the Common Law considers to be voluntary and involuntary manslaughter, and the Romanist-Civilist-Germanic systems consider homicide with *dolus* and homicide with *culpa*. The latter systems, however, allow consideration of motive while the former does not. But in this case motive, or an extensive interpretation of intent to

291

include the ultimate purpose is particularly relevant because a link has to be established with the pre-requisite legal elements discussed in Chapter 6. The intent (or motive) of the perpetrator in "murder" and "extermination" must be linked to carrying out the "state action or policy."

Since the promulgation of the Charter, other sources of specificity for certain types of "murder" as a "crime against humanity" are found in several international instruments.

Common articles to the four 1949 Geneva Conventions, state: "[g]rave breaches . . . shall be those involving any of the following acts, if committed against persons or property protected by the Convention: *wilful killing* . . . . "[4] (emphasis added)

The Genocide Convention provides in Article II:

> [i]n the present Convention, genocide means any of the following acts committed with intent to destroy, in whole or in part, a national, ethnic, racial, or religious group, as such:
>
> (a) [k]illing members of the group;
> (b) [c]ausing serious bodily or mental harm to members of the group;
> (c) [d]eliberately inflicting on the group, conditions of life calculated to bring about its physical destruction in whole or in part;
> (d) [i]mposing measures intended to prevent births within the group;
> (e) [f]orcibly transferring children of the group to another group.[5]

The application of this broad definition of condition causing or leading to death is, however, limited, as it excludes (a) situations where the required intent does not exist, and (b) other groups not specifically identified for protection (*e.g.*, social or political groups). But this definition expands the meaning of murder and extermination as species of international crimes. The importance of the prohibition and its non-derogability was affirmed by the ICJ in its advisory opinion on *Reservations to the Convention on Genocide.*[6]

As Lemkin said nearly a half century ago, the word "genocide" is:

---

[4] 1949 Geneva Conventions; Geneva I, art. L; Geneva II, art. L I; Geneva III, art. CXXX; and Geneva IV, art. CXLVII.

[5] Genocide Convention, Article II.

[6] 1951 I.C.J. 15; *see also* 45 AJIL 13 (Supp. 1951); and Bassiouni, *infra* note 7, at 283-284.

intended to signify a coordinated plan of different actions aiming at the destruction of essential foundations of life of national groups . . . The objectives of such a plan would be the disintegration of the political and social institutions of culture, language, national feelings, religion, and the economical existence of national groups, and the destruction of personal security, liberty, health, dignity, and even lives of the individuals belonging to such groups.[7]

Lastly, a number of international human rights instruments assert a right to life,[8] and they explicitly or implicitly prohibit the unlawful taking of life. The generality of such rights does not, however, allow for their *ipso iure* conversion to criminal violations. As "general principles of law" they stand for the protecting of life, which is the same interest protected by the criminalization of murder and extermination as "crimes against humanity." Since the Charter, however, only the Genocide and *Apartheid* Conventions contain provisions making "murder" and "extermination" international crimes in certain contexts and subject to narrow legal requirements.

2. Enslavement

The international criminalization of certain types of "murder" and "extermination" in particular contexts began almost one century ago with the 1899 and 1907 Hague Conventions. The legal prohibition of slavery and slave-related practices, however, started earlier. In 1815, the Congress of Vienna Declaration, stated that slavery is "repugnant" to the values of the civilized international community. Since then, a succession of international instruments prohibited these practices and several criminalized some of its manifestations. Also, between 1820 and 1945, a number of countries criminalized slavery, slave-trade and slave-related practices.[9] Thus, slavery was clearly a violation of "general principles of law" under the national law source of

---

[7] R. LEMKIN, AXIS RULE IN OCCUPIED EUROPE 79 (1944); *see also* Bassiouni, *Introduction to the Genocide Convention*, in 1 BASSIOUNI ICL 281.

[8] *See e.g.* Universal Declaration on Human Rights; U.N. Covenant; European Convention; Inter-American Convention; and African Charter on Human and Peoples' Rights, Nairobi, June 1981, *reprinted from* HUMAN RIGHTS IN INTERNATIONAL LAW 208 (Council of Europe, 1985), arts. 4, 6.

[9] *See supra* Chapter 7 at 280, n.56 for the various representative countries of the world's major legal systems.

"general principles" and under its international law source before the Charter.[10] Since then international legal instruments have expanded the scope of the criminal violation, and all national laws prohibit it explicitly or implicitly. The prohibition is thus universal, but some of its specific contents, i.e., certain manifestations of slave-related practices, are not yet well established or well defined.

The Geneva Conventions deem slavery, slave-related practices and slave labor a war crime, as does the customary regulation of international armed conflicts when the practice is performed by the armed forces or occupying forces of one country against the civilian population or armed forces of another country in time of war. Pre-World War I use of forced labor in time of war was not, however, uncommon and was narrowly permitted by the 1899 and 1907 Hague Conventions.[11] But after World War

---

[10]   *See* Document Section G.2.

[11]   Both the Hague Convention of 1899 and the 1907 Convention, respecting the laws and customs of war, incorporated protections for both civilians and belligerents from enslavement and forced labor into the international regulation of armed conflict. Similar to that of the 1899 Convention, the preamble to the 1907 Convention asserts that: "[T]he inhabitants and the belligerents remain under the protection and the rule of the principles of the law of nations, as they result from the usages established among civilized peoples, from the laws of humanity, and the dictates of public conscience." Also, Article 52 of the 1907 Convention provides:

Requisitions in kind and services shall not be demanded from municipalities or inhabitants except for the needs of the army of occupation. They shall be in proportion to the resources of the country, and of such a nature as not to involve the inhabitants in the obligation of taking part in military operations against their own country.

Such requisitions and services shall only be demanded on the authority of the commander in the locality occupied.

Contributions in kind shall as far as possible be paid for in cash; if not, a receipt shall be given and the payment of the amount due shall be made as soon as possible.

Similarly, Article 52 of the 1899 Convention provides:

Neither requisitions in kind nor services can be demanded from communes or inhabitants except for the necessities of the army of occupation. They must be in proportion to the resources of the country, and of such a nature as not to involve the population in the obligation of taking part in military operations against their country.

These requisitions and services shall only be demanded on the authority of the Commander in the locality occupied.

I, it was prohibited for POW's under the 1929 Geneva Convention, and it was prohibited under customary international law as evidenced by the 1919 Commission Report and subsequent declarations and actions by the then Allies. It was also prohibited by the 1926 Slavery Convention, as discussed below.

The practice of using belligerent civilians and prisoners of war in forced labor began to a large extent during World War I. The need for increases in wide-based industrial support, coupled with the need to free millions of men for fighting, necessitated the utilization of the lucrative labor of belligerents, both civilian and prisoners of war. Frequently, the utilization of this free labor source required the transporting of civilian populations from their homes to the work-place, thus, also constituting "deportation." As one author notes, the "[d]eportation of civilian populations except in cases of extreme military necessity constitutes a war crime."[12] Furthermore, "[e]mployment of civilians as slave labor is also criminal."[13] Thus, he stated:

> lines of distinction must be carefully drawn. It is not illegal for an occupying power to require civilians to work in order to maintain their own existence of their internal economy. It is, however, improper to transport them from their own land, to place them in hazardous employment, to require them to work to aid the efforts of the aggressor in its belligerencies, or to require them to do any act demeaning disloyalty toward their own nation. If such persons are employed, they must receive adequate remuneration, and adequate housing, food, and clothing must be provided. It was not until clear violations of all of these requirements was shown that the term "slave labor" came into general use by these tribunals.[14]

The contributions in kind shall, as far as possible, be paid for in ready money; if not, their receipt shall be acknowledged.

See also Bassiouni, *The Proscribing Function of the International Criminal Law in the Process of International Protection of Human Rights*, 9 YALE J. WORLD PUB. ORD. 193 (1982); Bassiouni, *Enslavement as an International Crime*, 23 N.Y.U. J. INT'L. L. & POLITICS 445 (1991); Bassiouni & Nanda, *Slavery and Slave Trade: Steps Toward Eradication*, 12 SANTA CLARA L. REV. 424 (1972).

[12] *See* J. APPLEMAN, MILITARY TRIBUNALS AND INTERNATIONAL CRIMES 298 (1954).

[13] *Id.*

[14] *Id.*

As Oppenheim states far more succinctly: "there is no right to deport inhabitants to the country of the occupant for the purpose of compelling them to work there."[15]

One example was Germany's forced deportation of thousands of Belgian men to Germany to work in factories during World War I:

> Beginning [on] October 26, 1916, occupation authorities in Belgium began deporting civilians to Germany to use in a forced-labor program. During the next month, some 66,000 Belgians were arbitrarily conscripted and transported to Germany under the harshest conditions; as a result, 1,250 of the workers lost their lives . . . . There were worldwide protests . . . [and] only the [K]aiser's insistence kept Governor General von Bissing, who thought the actions violated Hague [C]onventions, from resigning.[16]

In a memorandum sent to the Secretary of State of the United States following the occupation of Belgium, the Belgian Government noted that the Germans put into effect a plan which called for the exploitation of the economic resources of the occupied countries to the benefit of Germany's war effort.[17] Germany deported Belgian men between the ages of 17 and 55. Working conditions apparently were atrocious. The deportees were required to work on trench construction and thus, indirectly aided the German war effort by freeing German men for fighting.[18] With regard to the deportation of Belgians to Germany, Oppenheim notes that "the whole civilized world stigmatized this practice as an outrage."[19]

Nothing, however, in the history of humankind approaches the magnitude and terrible hardship of Nazi Germany's World War II use of slavery, slave-related

---

[15] 2 L. OPPENHEIM'S INTERNATIONAL LAW 441 (H. Lauterpacht 7th ed. 1952).

[16] J. WILLIS, PROLOGUE TO NUREMBERG: THE POLITICS AND DIPLOMACY OF PUNISHING WAR CRIMINALS OF THE FIRST WORLD WAR 34-35 (1982).

[17] *See Violations of the Laws and Customs of War, Report of the Majority and Dissenting Reports of American and Japanese Members of the Commission on Responsibilities, Conference of Paris, 1919,* Carnegie Endowment for International Peace, Division of International Law, Pamphlet No. 32; 21, 23, 24-26, 64, and Annex I, *reprinted in* 14 AJIL 95, 112 (1920).

[18] *See 1919 Commission Report.* The authors cited the deportation of civilians and forced labor of civilians in connection with the military operations of the enemy as offenses deserving of punishment. *Id.*

[19] L. OPPENHEIM, *supra* note 15, at 441.

practices and forced labor. In what this writer considers an understatement, Schwarzenberger notes that:

> Germany developed questionable practices in earlier wars regarding the requisition of labor in occupied territories into a system, branded in the Nuremberg Judgment (1946) as "slave labor policy." The International Military Tribunal found that Germany had conceived this policy as an integral part of her war economy and planned and organized "this particular war crime" down to the last detail.

> "Blocked industries," that is, industries in the occupied territories which were employed exclusively for export to Germany, were one of the refinements of this policy. If workers liable to be dispatched to Germany consented to work in such industries, they escaped deportation. Yet, as the Nuremberg Tribunal observed, while this system was less inhumane than deportation to Germany, it was illegal.[20]

Attempts were made to recruit foreigners voluntarily for German labor. These were, however, for the most part unsuccessful, and Germany began to implement a program to use the concentration camps as a source for slave labor. As Schwarzenberger notes:

> As the German campaign for voluntary recruitment proved unsuccessful in obtaining anything like the number of workers required, pressure was exercised by withdrawing ration cards from workers who refused to go to Germany, discharging them from their jobs and denying them unemployment benefits or opportunities to work elsewhere. Workers and their families were also threatened with police action if they persisted in their refusal, "man-hunts took place in the streets, at motion picture houses, even at churches and at night in private houses. Houses were sometimes burnt down, and the families taken as hostages," practices which were described ... as having their origin "in the blackest periods of the slave trade."[21]

---

[20] *See* 2 G. SCHWARZENBERGER, INTERNATIONAL LAW: AS APPLIED BY INTERNATIONAL COURTS AND TRIBUNALS 225 (1968).

[21] *Id.* at 230.

The 1926 Slavery Convention clearly prohibits the practices of forced labor engaged in by Nazi Germany. But as Benjamin Ferencz so aptly states:

> The Jewish concentration camp workers were less than slaves. Slave masters care for their human property and try to preserve it; it was the Nazi plan and intention that the Jews would be used up and then burned. The term "slave" is used in this narrative only because our vocabulary has no precise word to describe the lowly status of unpaid workers who are earmarked for destruction.[22]

The Nazi practices in the area of slave-related practices and forced labor constituted violations of: conventional and customary regulation of armed conflict when its subjects were POW's, civilians of another belligerent or occupied power, and of conventional and customary international law when its subjects were the very citizens of the country engaging in such practices (and while there are some arguable loopholes in the 1926 Slavery Convention on the question of forced labor, it nonetheless clearly applies in the conditions that Schwarzenberger and Ferencz describe above, and which the IMT and the Subsequent Proceedings so graphically illustrated).

In addition to the prohibition of slavery, slave-related conditions, and forced labor, under conventional and customary regulation of armed conflicts, the same type of prohibition, though for wider application, developed through a number of international instruments. Like other internationally prohibited conduct, it has evolved gradually.[23] At first, the prohibition appeared in the nature of general condemnatory statements, followed by a succession of international instruments -- some dealing with particular or particularized aspects of these practices. Finally, specific criminal proscriptions were embodied in conventions.[24] This evolution of human rights protections through international criminal law is also evidenced in other areas of international human rights protected interests.[25]

The combination of national and international law sources of "general principles" confirms the prohibition of slavery and slave-related practices including forced labor.

---

[22] B. FERENCZ, LESS THAN SLAVES xvii (1979).

[23] See 1 BASSIOUNI DIGEST 499-512.

[24] See Bassiouni, *The Proscribing Function of International Law in the Processes of International Protection of Human Rights*, 9 YALE J. WORLD PUB. ORD. 193-214 (1982), *reprinted with modification in* 1 BASSIOUNI ICL at 15.

[25] *Id.*

Before 1945, there were 26 international instruments prohibiting slavery and slave-related practices including forced labor.[26] No one could doubt, therefore, that even before 1945, submitting a person to slavery or slave-related practices, including forced labor, constituted a violation of "general principles of law." Since 1945, there have been 45 instruments on the prohibition of these practices.

A description of 71 applicable international instruments and relevant provisions is provided in the Document Section,[27] particularly those of a penal nature. The cumulative effect of these instruments establishes that slavery, slave-related practices and forced labor, were before 1945, prohibited under conventional international law, and that the prohibition has been expanding ever since. These instruments also establish the customary international law basis for the prohibition of these practices and for their inclusion as part of "crimes against humanity."

Slavery is "the status or condition of a person over whom any of the powers attaching to the right of ownership are exercised."[28] Examples of slave-related institutions include debt bondage, serfdom, marital bondage, slave labor and sexual bondage or exploitation and traffic and exploitation of children.[29] Various acts of slavery occur when a person knowingly performs acts such as (1) placing a person in a condition of slavery, (2) exercising control over a person in a condition of slavery, and, (3) any other conduct which facilitates the continuation of slavery.[30] Though these prohibitions are covered in a number of international instruments, their definitions and elements should be stated more specifically in the codification of "crimes against humanity," particularly in the work of the ILC whose latest 1991 text on this question, as discussed in Chapter 11, has not adequately included the specifics of slave-related

---

[26] *See* Bassiouni, *Enslavement as an International Crime*, 23 N.Y.U. J. INT'L L. & POLITICS 445 (1991).

[27] *See* Document Section G.2.

[28] *See* Bassiouni, *supra* note 26 at 467.

[29] *See generally*, Richardson, *Debt Bondage of Children: A Slavery-like institution and the U.N. Convention on the Rights of the Child*, 62 RIDP 785 (1991); *see also*, Whittacher, *Child Bonded Labour*, 62 RIDP 769 (1991); Marietta Jaramillo de Marin, *Children's and Youth's Work*, in 62 RIDP 821 (1991); Nanda and Bassiouni, *The Crime of Slavery and Slave Trade*, 1 BASSIOUNI ICL 325; *United Nations Report on Continued Manifestations of Slavery and Slavery-Like Practices*, E/CN.4/Sub.2/1982/20/Rev. 1.; U.N. Doc. E/CN. 4/Sub. 2/1984/ 22, 22 June 1984.

[30] Supplementary Convention on the Abolition of Slavery, the Slave Trade, and Institutions and Practices Similar to Slavery, 7 September 1956, Articles 3 and 7, *see* Document Section G.2.

practices, forced labor, debt bondage and exploitation of women and children in labor and sexual matters, and the traffic of children for adoption.[31] The prospective

---

[31] BASSIOUNI DRAFT CODE at 146-150, defines slavery as follows:

Section 1. Definitions

1.1 "Slavery" is the status or condition of a person over whom any of the powers attaching to the right of ownership are exercised.

1.2 "Slavery-related institutions" include the institutions or practices of debt bondage, serfdom, marital bondage, slave labor and sexual bondage:

(a) "Debt bondage" is the status or condition arising from a pledge by a debtor of his or her freedom or services or the use of such services or those of a person under his or her control as security for a debt, if the value of such services is not applied toward the liquidation of the debt or the length and nature of such services are not limited and defined or no alternative mode of payment is permitted.

(b) "Serfdom" is the condition or status of a tenant who is by law, custom or agreement bound to live and labor on land belonging to another person and to render such determinate service to such other person, whether for reward or not, where such tenant is not free to change his or her status.

(c) "Marital bondage" consists of practices whereby:

(i) a person, without the right to refuse, is promised or given in marriage on payment of a consideration in money or in kind to her parents, guardian, family or any other person or group;

(ii) a person's spouse or the spouse's family or clan has the right to transfer that person, without his or her consent, to another person, whether for value received or otherwise;

(iii) a person upon the death of his or her spouse, is liable to be inherited by another person.

(d) "Slave labor" consists of:

(i) Child exploitation, whereby a child is transferred into the control of another person, with or without his or her consent, and whether for reward or not, with a view to the exploitation of that child's labor.
Child exploitation occurs when a child is:

(A) working without reasonable remuneration, or
(B) working or living under conditions detrimental to his or her physical or mental well-being.

codification should contain specific definitions of all these violations, identifying with clarity the elements of each offense.

3. Deportation and Population Transfer

The prohibition against deportation and population transfer has a shorter and less decisive historical development than that of slavery. Deportation is the forced removal of people from one country to another, while population transfer applies to compulsory movement of people from one area to another within the same state. Protection against

---

(ii) Forced or compulsory labor shall mean: all work or service which is exacted from any person under the menace of any penalty and for which the said person has not offered himself voluntarily, but, subject to applicable Human Rights Conventions, shall not include:

    (A) any work or service exacted in virtue of compulsory military service laws for work of a purely military character;

    (B) any work or service which forms part of the normal civic obligations of the citizens of a fully self-governing country;

    (C) any work or service exacted from any person as a consequence of a conviction in a court of law, provided that the said work or service is carried out under the supervision and control of a public authority, and that the said person is not hired to or placed at the disposal of private individuals, companies or associations;

    (D) any work or service exacted in cases of emergency, that is to say, in the event of war or of a calamity or threatened calamity, such as fire, flood, famine, earthquake, violent epidemic or epizootic diseases, invasion by animal, insect or vegetable pests, and in general any circumstance that would endanger the existence or the well-being of the whole or part of the population;

    (E) minor communal services of a kind which, being performed by the members of the community in the direct interest of normal civic obligations, are incumbent upon the members of the community, provided that the members of the community or their direct representatives shall have the right to be consulted in regard to the need for such services.

(e) "Sexual bondage" is an institution or practice whereby a person is forcibly transferred or held for the purpose of performing any sexual conduct whatsoever, whether for reward or not.

1.3 The "Status or condition of slavery" is that of a person subjected to slavery-related institutions or practices.

301

deportation is currently well embedded in international law though much less with respect to population transfer.

The 1899 Hague Convention and the 1907 Hague Convention provided for general and specific protections of civilian population against deportation. The general protection is found in Article 46, which is identical in both conventions and which states:

> Family honour and rights, the lives of persons and private property, as well as religious convictions and practices must be respected. Private property cannot be confiscated.

Presumably one can argue that such a general provision extends protection against deportation and transfer within the territory.

Articles 47-53, provide for other protections, all of which when read with Article 46, indicate by implication that civilian populations are to remain in place and not to be deported. Subsequently, the Fourth Geneva Convention of August 12, 1949 in Article 49 unequivocally prohibited deportation:

> Individual or mass forcible transfers, as well as deportations of protected persons from occupied territory to the territory of the Occupying Power or to that of any other country, occupied or not, are prohibited regardless of their motive.[32]

Deportation is a "grave breach" under Article 147 of the Fourth Geneva Convention, which calls for severe penal sanctions for such breaches.

The 1919 Report of the Commission on the Responsibilities of the Authors of the War and on the Enforcement of Penalties, included deportation as a prosecutable crime.

The list of war crimes and crimes against the "laws of humanity" prepared by the Commission included "deportation of civilians" and "internment of civilians under inhuman conditions."[33] Though deportation was deemed a crime against the "laws of humanity" and a war crime, it was not prosecuted as such for reasons discussed in Chapter 4, which weakens the precedent.

The specific incidents of deportations, set out in detail in Annex I to the Commission Report, include: (a) the deportation of more than 1 million Armenians by

---

[32]   See Geneva IV, at article 49.

[33]   See supra note 17.

302

Turkish authorities; (b) the deportation of 400,000 Greeks living in Thrace and the west coast of Asia Minor to Greece by Turkish authorities; and (c) 1 million Greek-speaking Turks deported from Turkey by Turkish and German authorities.[34] By virtue of this finding it is clear that even at the time of World War I, the deportation by a country of its own nationals was classified as an international crime even though no Turkish official was prosecuted for this crime. The Turks were not prosecuted, as discussed in Chapter 4, for two reasons: (1) The United States dissented from that portion of the Commission's Report concerning crimes "against the laws of humanity" because these were not specifically embodied in positive international law; (2) The Treaty of Sèvres between the Allies and Turkey, which was to establish the responsibility and prosecutability of certain Turkish officials, was never ratified, and its substitute the Treaty of Lausanne, gave these officials "amnesty."

The relevant findings of the 1919 Commission had been incorporated in the Treaty of Sèvres, signed by Turkey on August 10, 1920.[35] This Treaty provided for various acts of reparation by Turkey, including reparation to those who were deported or displaced. Specifically, Article 142 required Turkish authorities to assist "in the search for and deliverance of all persons, of whatever race or religion, who have disappeared, been carried off, interned or placed in captivity since November 1, 1914." In addition, Article 144 required the Turkish Government to "facilitate to the greatest possible extent the return to their homes and re-establishment in their business of the Turkish subjects of non-Turkish race who have been forcibly driven from their homes by fear of massacre or any other form of pressure since January 1, 1914."[36] The same article also provided for the establishment of an arbitral commission which could order "the removal of any person who, after inquiry, [was] recognized as having taken an active part in massacres or deportations or as having provoked them."[37] Article 226 provided for the right of the Allied powers to "bring before military tribunals persons accused of having committed acts in violation of the laws and customs of war."[38] Article 230 also provided that the Turkish Government would hand over to the Allied powers "the persons whose surrender may be required, by the latter, as being

---

[34]   1919 Commission Report at Annex I.

[35]   The Treaty of Peace Between the Allied Powers, and Turkey, 10 August 1920 (Treaty of Sèvres), British Treaty Series No. 11 (1920), *reprinted in* 15 AJIL 179 (Supp.) (1921).

[36]   *Id.* at art. 144.

[37]   *Id.*

[38]   *Id.* at art. 226.

responsible for the massacres committed during the continuance of the state of war on territory which formed part of the Turkish Empire on August 1, 1914."[39] The inclusion of this clause in the treaty originated in the 1919 Report of the Commission, which included deportations as part of the crimes committed by Turkey against its Armenian nationals on Turkish soil. One should note that the Commission's Report was based on Allied memoranda filed before the Commission. The majority of these memoranda included a reference to deportation as one of the atrocities or outrages committed by Germany or Turkey.[40] Deportations by Germany of non-German nationals were deemed war crimes and those committed by Turkey against Turkish nationals were deemed crimes "against the laws of humanity."[41]

In defining the term "massacres on Turkish territory" incorporated in the Treaty of Sèvres, numerous documents prepared by Greek and Armenian committees, as well as by independent observers of the activities in the areas, consistently cited deportation and expulsion as violations committed by Turkey.[42] Therefore, although the specific Treaty language refers only to the "massacre" based on the reports which formed the basis of the Commission Report and the subsequent Treaty of Sèvres provision, one can conclude that the term incorporated the mass deportations.

As stated above, the Treaty of Sèvres, however, was never ratified. Later, in 1923, the Treaty of Lausanne,[43] which was ratified, relieved the Turks from submitting to any prosecution for their acts committed against the civilian population during World War I. Thus, while deportation was classified as a crime, its prosecution was waived. But the Treaty of Lausanne also condoned the deportations. As one commentator writes: "The Lausanne Treaty made a very bad precedent in international law, in that it approved the first compulsory transplanting of peoples from lands where their ancestors had lived for many hundreds of years."[44]

---

[39]   *Id.* at art. 230.

[40]   *See supra* note 34.

[41]   The deportation of Turkish people living in Germany by Germany was a war crime because the act occurred between the peoples of two nations - Germany and Turkey. However, a war crime cannot arise between the citizens of one country and their government. Thus, the Turkish Government's deportation of Turkish nationals is considered a "crime against humanity."

[42]   *See supra* note 34.

[43]   The Treaty of Peace Between the Allied Powers and Turkey, 24 July 1923 (Treaty of Lausanne), 28 L.N.T.S. 11, *reprinted in* 18 AJIL 4 (official documents) (1924).

[44]   DeZayas, *International Law and Mass Population Transfers*, 16 HARV. INT'L L. J. 207, 223 (1975).

Germany also engaged in deportations during World War I prompting certain countries to protest the mass deportation of their nationals by Germany. Many formal condemnations appear in the Commission's Report. For example, France protested the deportation of women and girls from Lille, Roubaix and Tourcoing, by the Germans during the Spring of 1916.[45] The unanimous condemnation of the activity is reflected in Oppenheim's remark: "during the First World War the Germans deported to Germany several thousand Belgian and French men and women and compelled them to work there, the whole civilized world stigmatized this practice 'as an outrage.'"[46]

The condemnation of such practices may evidence that deportation of civilians in time of war was contrary to customary international law, but it is difficult to reconcile with the practice of States, including the Allies after World War I, who engaged in or condoned, mass deportation and population transfers, a practice in which the Allies freely engaged in after World War II while condemning Germany for doing the same. A significant difference must, however, be pointed out in that the German deportation and population transfers were for the purposes of subjecting the people to extermination, slavery, slave-related practices and forced labor. Thus, in the opinion of this writer, it is not so much the transfer of civilians within a country's national jurisdiction which constitutes the violation, but the transfer for the purposes of extermination, slavery, slave-related practices and slave labor. Deportation and population transfers of another belligerent state remain war crimes in and of themselves.

During World War II, there were numerous protests against German acts of deportation of civilians under occupation. Among other things, these protests assailed acts of deportation, which can be classified as both war crimes and "crimes against humanity" depending on the location and nationality of the deportees. If the deportees were non-nationals it would be a war crime, while if they were nationals it would be a "crime against humanity," but, as stated above, only if in connection with another crime.[47] On January 13, 1942, the Declaration of St. James issued by Belgium, Czechoslovakia, France, Greece, Luxembourg, Norway, the Netherlands, Poland and

---

[45] *See* 1919 Commission Report at Annex I, No. 7, (France).

[46] *See* L. OPPENHEIM, *supra* note 15, at 441 who cites documents in support of this proposition; *see also* PASSALACQUA, DEPORTATION ET TRAVAIL FORCÉ DES OUVRIERS ET DE LA POPULATION CIVILE DE LA BELGIQUE, 1916-1918 (1928); and SEVENAER, L'OCCUPATION ALLEMANDE PENDANT LA DERNIÈRE GUERRE MONDIALE (1946).

[47] For declarations made by Allied Leaders, *see e.g.*, Declaration of German Atrocities, 1 November 1943, 1943 FOR. REL. 749; and The Cairo Declaration, 1 December 1943, 1943 FOR. REL. 448.

Yugoslavia, stated: "Germany, since the beginning of the present conflict, which arose out of her policy of aggression has instituted in the occupied countries, a regime of terror characterized amongst other things by imprisonment, mass expulsions, the execution of hostages and massacres . . . ."[48]   While the document specifically makes reference to occupied territories, the speeches surrounding the issuance of the Declaration suggest that the Declaration was intended, in broader terms, as a condemnation of all the acts which had outraged the conscience of humanity and which had violated national and international law. The Declaration went far beyond the then existing status of international law.

On October 17, 1942, the Polish government in exile approved a Decree on the Punishment of German War Crimes Committed in Poland, which declared: "The punishment inflicted will be increased to life imprisonment or the death penalty will be imposed, if such actions caused death, special suffering, deportation, [or] transfers of population . . . ."[49]

On December 17, 1942, the governments of Belgium, Czechoslovakia, France, Greece, Luxembourg, the Netherlands, Norway, Poland, the USSR, the United Kingdom, the United States of America and Yugoslavia issued a Declaration in the United States, the Soviet Union and Britain.[50] The Declaration specifically condemned German actions against the Jews and resolved to ensure that those responsible for those crimes would not escape retribution. The text stated:

[T]he German authorities, not content with denying to persons of Jewish race in all the territories over which their barbarous rule has been extended the most elementary human rights, are now carrying into effect Hitler's oft-repeated intention to exterminate Jewish people in Europe. From all the occupied countries Jews are being transported in conditions of appalling horror and brutality to Eastern Europe. In Poland, which has been made the principle Nazi slaughterhouse, the ghettos established by the German invaders are being systematically emptied of all Jews except a few highly skilled workers required for war industries. None of those

---

[48]   For the full text of the Declaration of St. James, *see* PUNISHMENT FOR WAR CRIMES: THE INTER-ALLIED DECLARATION SIGNED AT ST. JAMES' PALACE, LONDON, ON 13TH JANUARY, 1942, AND RELATIVE DOCUMENTS (United Nations Information Office, New York, undated).

[49]   *See* 1 WAR AND PEACE AIMS OF THE UNITED NATIONS 480 (L. Holborn ed. 1943).

[50]   Declaration Regarding German Atrocities Against Jews in German Occupied Countries, issued 17 December 1942, VII BULLETIN Department of State, No. 182, Dec. 19, 1942, p. 1009, 385 H.C. DEB. (5th ser.) col. 2083.

taken away are ever heard of again. The able-bodied are slowly worked to death in labor camps. The infirm are left to die of exposure and starvation or are deliberately massacred in mass executions. The number of victims of these bloody cruelties is reckoned in many hundreds of thousands of entirely innocent men, women and children . . .[51]

The text continues to reaffirm the solemn resolution to ensure that those responsible for these crimes will not escape retribution.

Another further significant Declaration was issued on March 24, 1944 by the United States, on behalf of the United Nations. This Declaration stated:

> The United Nations are fighting to make a world in which tyranny and aggression cannot exist; a world based on freedom, equality and justice; a world in which all persons regardless of race, colour or creed may live in peace, honour and dignity . . . in one of the blackest crimes of all history -- begun by the Nazis in the day of peace and multiplied by them a hundred times in time of war -- the wholesale systematic murder of the Jews of Europe goes on unabated every hour. As a result of the events of the last few days, hundreds of thousands of Jews who, while living under persecution, have at least found a haven from death in Hungary and the Balkans, are now threatened by annihilation as Hitler's forces descend more heavily upon these lands. That these innocent people who have already survived a decade of Hitler's fury should perish, on the very eve of triumph over the barbarism which their persecution symbolizes, would be a major tragedy.
>
> It is therefore fitting that we should again proclaim our determination that no one who participates in these acts of savagery shall go unpunished. The United Nations have made it clear that they will pursue the guilty and deliver them up in order that Justice be done. That warning applies not only to the leaders but also to their functionaries and subordinates in Germany and in the satellite countries. All who knowingly take part in the deportation of Jews to their death in Poland or Norwegians and French to their death in Germany are equally guilty with the executioner. All who share that guilt shall share the punishment . . .[52]

---

[51] *Id.*

[52] Declaration referring to the *Systematic Torture and Murder of Civilians*, issued 24 March 1944, X BULLETIN DEPARTMENT OF STATE, No. 248, Mar. 25, 1944, p. 277.

This Declaration supports the position that deportation of the Hungarian Jews from Hungary to Germany, at that stage of the war, was recognized as a crime.

In addition to official protests during the war, the London International Assembly produced a report, in 1943, holding deportation as a punishable international offense.[53] The Assembly, created under the auspices of the League of Nations, was composed of representatives of fourteen countries including Britain, France, the United States and the USSR. In November of 1943, the Assembly recommended that the expression "war crimes" should be understood to cover not only war crimes proper, but also the preparation and the waging of aggressive war and crimes committed within or outside any Axis country for the purpose of racial or political extermination. The LIA specified the types of conduct which constituted "[v]iolations of the Laws of War," which included: "Acts whether or not directly connected with warfare . . . such as: . . . (2) Crimes ordered by or committed under order of or with approval of authorities: . . . (9) Mass deportations . . ."[54]

The Treaties, Declarations and Reports discussed above recognized deportation as a violation of the laws and customs of war and as a crime against the "laws of humanity" prior to the promulgation of Article 6(c). These sources, therefore, provide the historical legal foundation for the inclusion of deportation as a "crime against humanity" in Article 6(c) of the London Charter of August 8, 1945 and for its application by the IMT. Consequently, the IMT Indictment included the charge of "deportation." It stated:

> In certain occupied territories purportedly annexed to Germany, the defendants methodically and pursuant to plan endeavored to assimilate these territories politically, culturally, socially, and economically into the German Reich. They endeavored to obliterate the former national character of these territories. In pursuance of these plans, the defendants forcibly deported inhabitants who were predominantly non-German and replaced them by thousands of German colonists.[55]

---

[53] *See* THE PUNISHMENT OF WAR CRIMES: RECOMMENDATIONS OF THE LONDON INTERNATIONAL ASSEMBLY (1943). *See also* Document Section B.1.

[54] *Id.* at 17.

[55] 2 IMT 57, Count 3, § J.

On the first day of the trial, November 20, 1945, Pierre Mounier, Assistant Prosecutor for France, charged the defendants with mass deportations. He stated:

> These deportations were contrary to the international conventions, in particular to Article 46 of the Hague Regulations, 1907, the laws and customs of war, the general principles of criminal law as derived from the criminal laws of all civilized nations, the internal penal laws of the countries in which such crimes were committed . . .[56]

Another French prosecutor, Edgar Faure, on February 1, 1946, exclaimed that German activities of deportation in France, Belgium and Luxembourg were "a criminal undertaking against humanity."[57] Other such undertakings were described by L.N. Smirnour, Assistant Prosecutor for the Soviet Union, who on February 26, 1946, read from an official report:

> Such was the plan. The facts which were put into practice were the following:

> Locality after locality, village after village, hamlets and cities in the incorporated territories were cleared of the Polish inhabitants. This began in October 1939, when the locality of Orlov was cleared of all the Poles who lived and worked there. Then came the Polish port of Gdynia. In February 1940 about 40,000 persons were expelled from the city of Posen. They were replaced by 36,000 Baltic-Germans, families of soldiers and of German officials. The Polish population was expelled from the following towns: Gnesen, Kuln, Kostian, Neshkva, Inovrotzlav ... and, many other towns.[58]

The defense unsuccessfully attempted to explain these crimes away. Alfred Seidl, Defense Counsel for Hans Frank, tried to establish that the Allies engaged in the same types of practices by reading from a statement issued by German bishops which stated:

---

[56]   *Id.* at 49. Further into the trials, on January 17, 1946, the Chief French Prosecutor, M. de Menthon, described large-scale expulsions committed by the Nazis, of which he declared, "[t]his inhumane evacuation of entire populations . . . will remain one of the horrors of our century." *Id.* at 85.

[57]   6 IMT 427.

[58]   8 IMT 256.

Some weeks ago, we found occasion to comment on the outrageous happenings in the East of Germany, particularly in Silesia and the Sudentenland, where more than 10 million Germans have been driven from their ancestral homes in brutal fashion, no investigation having been made to ascertain whether or not there was any question of personal guilt. No pen can describe the unspeakable misery there imposed in contravention of all consideration of humanity and justice . . .[59]

Seidl asserted that the expulsions of millions of Germans from their ancestral lands was done "in accordance with a resolution taken at Potsdam on 2 August 1945 by President Truman, Generalismo Stalin and Prime Minister Attlee . . ."[60] This argument sought to equate German deportation with similar practices committed by the Allies. At this point in the Proceedings, the Chief Soviet Prosecutor, General Rudenko objected, stating "It seems to me that the legal considerations and the criticism of the decisions taken at Potsdam have no bearing on the present case."[61] The Tribunal sustained the objection and thus evaded the issue of the expulsions carried out as a consequence of the Potsdam political arrangement. Aside from the double-standard applied, the argument was legally relevant to demonstrate that the mere transfer of population was not contrary to customary international law since it was indeed practiced. The IMT also failed to establish a solid distinction between:

1. Deportation or transfer of population for purposes of "murder," "extermination," "enslavement," "other inhumane acts;"
2. Transfer of populations within the national jurisdiction of a state for valid purposes and in a lawful way;
3. Transfer of population by lawful means in connection with a treaty that places a given territory under the sovereignty of another state;
4. Deportation arising from transfer of territory to another state; and
5. Deportation and transfer of population exclusively on the basis of discrimination.

---

[59] 18 IMT 149.

[60] 18 IMT 149, 150.

[61] *Id.*

Customary and conventional international law had at the time evolved different rules and standards for each of these categories. Since then, the evolution of international law has not eliminated the legal relevance of these distinctions.

These distinctions may be illustrated by the Allies' deportation and population transfers during and after World War II in connection with territorial changes. Between 1944 and 1949, approximately 16 million Germans were expelled from their territory and their homes.[62] In a different category, the United States engaged in population transfers when it moved and interned thousands of its Japanese-American citizens for alleged security reasons, and the United States Supreme Court upheld the legality of these practices.[63] The distinction between United States transfer of population of its Japanese nationals to internment camps in the United States for a temporary period of time, a practice which Canada also engaged in, and Germany's transfer of population and deportation of Jews for extermination and for slave labor use is obvious. The first of these types of population transfers and internment were conducted as humanely as possible, under conditions of war and were later rescinded, even though they constituted violations of the civil rights of these citizens. They did not produce death and physical injury. The latter did. Thus they were war crimes with respect to non-nationals of Germany and "crimes against humanity" with respect to citizens of Germany.

As stated above, deportation and transfer of civilian population by the Allies after World War I and World War II took place in large numbers but essentially as a consequence of territorial changes and transfer of territory from one state to another. Such an instance of acknowledged compulsory transfer of populations occurred after World War I between Turkey and Greece,[64] and was the subject of the PCIJ Advisory Opinion in the case of the *Exchange of Greek and Turkish Populations*.[65] The Court describes how the transfer was effectuated:

---

[62] DeZayas, *supra* note 44, at 228.

[63] Korematsu v. United States, 323 U.S. 214 (1944). Recently, however, the United States Congress has passed a law to compensate these hapless victims.

[64] *See* A. DEVEDJI, L'ÉCHANGE OBLIGATOIRE DES MINORITÉS GRECQUES ET TURQUES (1929); de la Grotte, *La Cour permanente de Justice internationale en 1925*, 7 REV. DE DROIT INT'L. ET DE LÉGISLATION COMPARÉE 223 (1926); *Judgments and Advisory Opinions of the Permanent Court of International Justice*, 6 BRIT. Y.B. INT'L L. 198 (1925); S.P. LADAS, THE EXCHANGE OF MINORITIES, BULGARIA, GREECE AND TURKEY (1932).

[65] Exchange of Greek and Turkish Populations, 1925 P.C.I.J. (Ser. B), No. 11, at 6, *reprinted in* 1 WORLD COURT REPORTS 440 (M.O. Hudson ed. 1969).

In the course of negotiations for the establishment of peace with Turkey conducted at Lausanne during 1922 and 1923, amongst other diplomatic instruments, was concluded a Convention concerning the exchange of Greek and Turkish populations. This Convention, which was signed at Lausanne on January 30th, 1923, by the Greek and Turkish delegates, came into effect after the ratification by Greece and Turkey of the Peace Treaty of July 24th, 1923, viz. on August 6th, 1924.

Article II of this Convention provides for the setting up, within one month from its coming into force, of a Mixed Commission composed of four members representing each of the High Contracting Parties and three members chosen by the Council of the League of Nations from amongst nationals of Powers which did not take part in the war of 1914-1918 . . . .

The Mixed Commission's duties, under Article 12, were, amongst other things, to supervise and facilitate the emigration provided for in the Convention and to settle the methods to be followed. Generally speaking, it has full power to take the measures necessitated by the execution of the Convention and to decide all questions to which this Convention may give rise.

The principle governing the emigration in question is laid down in the first article of the Convention as follows:

> As from May 1st, 1923, there shall take place a compulsory exchange of Turkish nationals of the Greek Orthodox religion established in Turkish territory, and of Greek nationals of the Moslem religion established in Greek territory.

> These persons shall not return to live in Turkey or Greece respectively without the authorization of the Turkish Government or of the Greek Government respectively.[66]

---

[66] *Id.* at 9-10.

The Court was not asked to rule on the merits of the transfer, but simply to identify who was subject to such transfers,[67] thus implicitly admitting the legal validity of the transfer which was itself predicated on an international Convention. Therefore, the practice of states, including that of the Allies after World War I and World War II, can hardly be said to have been consistent with international law as they invoked it against Germany.

After World War II, however, a concerted effort was made to deal with these problems within the context of both war and peace. The Fourth Geneva Convention Relative to the Protection of Civilian Persons in Time of War, in Article 49, prohibits the deportation and transfer of civilians, although allowing temporary movements of persons where the security of the population or "imperative military reasons" require it. In Article 147, the Convention prohibits and deems a "grave breach" the unlawful deportation or transfer of civilians under occupation. As a "grave breach," the High Contracting Parties, pursuant to Article 146, are obligated to bring persons alleged to have committed such practices before its own courts, or "hand such persons over for trial to another High Contracting Power." The 1977 Protocols extended protection to the effects of hostilities and to armed conflicts which have the nature of organized civil war,[68] thus taking over in part, what "crimes against humanity" covered between 1945-1977.

In addition to these conventions prohibiting deportation and population transfer in time of war and organized civil war, several other conventions address deportation outside the context of armed conflicts. A number of specific and general instruments prohibit, although do not criminalize, deportation in time of peace. One of the earliest such instruments was the 1951 Convention relating to the Status of Refugees.[69] Article 32 (Expulsion) provides:

> 1. The Contracting States shall not expel a refugee lawfully in their territory save on grounds of national security or public order.

---

[67] *Id.* at 10, 25-26.

[68] *See* N. SINGH, ENFORCEMENT OF HUMAN RIGHTS 110-111 (1986).

[69] Adopted on 28 July 1951 by the United Nations Conference of Plenipotentiaries on the Status of Refugees and Stateless Persons convened under General Assembly Resolution 429 (V) of 14 December 1950, *reprinted in* HUMAN RIGHTS COMPILATION.

2. The expulsion of such a refugee shall be only in pursuance of a decision reached in accordance with due process of law. Except where compelling reasons of national security otherwise require, the refugee shall be allowed to submit evidence to clear himself, and to appeal to and be represented for the purpose before competent authority or a person or persons specially designated by the competent authority.

3. The Contracting States shall allow such a refugee a reasonable period within which to seek legal admission into another country. The Contracting States reserve the right to apply during that period such internal measures as they may deem necessary.[70]

Also, Article 33 on the Prohibition of Expulsion or Return ("Refoulement") states:

1. No Contracting State shall expel or return (*refouler*) a refugee in any manner whatsoever to the frontiers of territories where his life or freedom would be threatened on account of his race, religion, nationality, membership of a particular social group or political opinion.[71]

---

[70] Similarly, Article 31 of the Convention relating to the Status of Stateless Persons, adopted on 28 September 1954 by a Conference of Plenipotentiaries convened by Economic and Social Council Resolution 526A (XVII) of 26 April 1954, *reprinted in* HUMAN RIGHTS COMPILATION, at 93, 97 provides:

1. The Contracting States shall not expel a stateless person lawfully in their territory save on grounds of national security or public order.

2. The expulsion of such a stateless person shall be only in pursuance of a decision reached in accordance with due process of law. Except where compelling reasons of national security otherwise require, the stateless person shall be allowed to submit evidence to clear himself, and to appeal to and be represented for the purpose before competent authority or a person or persons specially designated by the competent authority.

3. The Contracting States shall allow such a stateless person a reasonable period within which to seek legal admission into another country. The Contracting States reserve the right to apply during that period such internal measures as they may deem necessary.

[71] *Id.*, art. 33.

314

The 1951 Convention also prohibits any Contracting State to make any reservations to Article 33. Thus, the right to *non-refoulement* is unconditional.[72] The 1951 Convention was expanded in 1967 by the Territorial Declaration on Asylum.

The 1967 Declaration on Territorial Asylum declares that:

> No person seeking asylum from persecution shall be subjected to measures such as rejection at the frontier or, if he has already entered the territory in which he seeks asylum, expulsion or compulsory return to any State where he may be subjected to persecution.[73]

This provision applies to any person seeking asylum, regardless of whether the person is legally within the territory of the host state. Exceptions are allowed "only for overriding reasons of national security or in order to safeguard the population, as in the case of a mass influx of people."[74]

The 1967 Protocol Amending the 1951 Refugee Convention eliminated the time and geographical constraints of the 1951 Convention and broadened the category of refugees entitled to the protection against *non-refoulement*.[75]

Other international instruments also prohibit deportation such as the Universal Declaration of Human Rights,[76] and the International Covenant on Civil and Political Rights.

Articles 13(2) and 14 of the Universal Declaration more directly address deportation prohibitions. By the terms of Article 13(2), persons have the right to leave any country, including their own, and return to their country. Article 14 guarantees that all persons have the right to seek and enjoy asylum in other countries to escape persecution arising from truly political acts.

---

[72] In order to utilize article 33, the person seeking protection must fall within the definition of "refugee" as stated in the 1951 Convention. This definition is limited to persons who became refugees due to events taking place in Europe prior to January 1, 1951.

[73] Resolution 2312 (XXII), adopted by the General Assembly of the United Nations on 14 December 1967, *reprinted in* HUMAN RIGHTS COMPILATION, at 109, 110, art. 3(1).

[74] *Id.* art 3(2). The 1967 Declaration does not cover refugees of "generalized violence," economic hardship or displaced persons. Currently scholars argue that the right of "non-refoulement" has created a new international norm - the right to temporary refuge. This new norm is an extension of "non-refoulement," and protects refugees from being returned to a country engaged in civil war until the violence ceases.

[75] *See supra* note 73.

[76] *See supra* note 8.

Article 12 of the 1966 International Covenant on Civil and Political Rights[77] provides that: (1) persons within a territory may move freely within the territory and choose their place of residence; (2) all persons are free to leave any country, including their own; (3) the aforementioned rights are unrestricted except as necessary to protect national security, public order, public health or the rights of others; and (4) no person shall be deprived of the right to enter his own country arbitrarily. Article 13 provides that an alien may be expelled from a country only after a decision reached in accordance with law by the competent authority, and that this right may only be limited as needed by matters of national security.

Regional human rights instruments also provide similar protections. The Fourth Protocol to the 1950 European Convention on Human Rights and Fundamental Freedoms,[78] explicitly addresses deportation in Article 2 which guarantees freedom of movement and choice of residence and the right to leave any country, but subject to the interests of national security, public order, and the protection of the rights of others. Article 4 prohibits the collective expulsion of aliens.[79] The Inter-American Convention provides the same in Article 22.[80]

The 1969 African Charter on Human and Peoples Rights,[81] provides that "the mass expulsion of non-nationals shall be prohibited. Mass expulsion shall be that which is aimed at national, racial, ethnic or religious groups.[82]

There are, of course, important distinctions which must be drawn between international and regional human rights instruments prohibiting deportation and transfer of population, and between instruments that criminalize such acts. In the first category of instruments, it should be noted that with respect to certain specific aspects of these protections they are not absolute and do not criminalize the violative conduct. In the second category, only those instruments that apply to the regulation of armed conflicts criminalize deportation and transfer of population. But with respect to population

---

[77] *Id.*

[78] *See supra* note 8.

[79] *Id. see* at arts. 2 and 4, *see also* article 3, which provides that a country's nationals may not be expelled, either individually or collectively, and a country's nationals may not be refused re-entry.

[80] *See supra* note 8.

[81] Nairobi, June 1981, as *reprinted in* HUMAN RIGHTS IN INTERNATIONAL LAW: BASIC TEXTS 207 (Council of Europe 1985), based on the text provided by the Division of Press and Information of the Organization of African Unity General Secretariat.

[82] *Id.* art. 12, para. 5.

transfers which are a consequence of territorial changes, there are no international instruments which criminalize them. Consequently, it is important for the future codification of "crimes against humanity" to integrate those two dimensions of international protection to avoid the confusion between protected rights which are and those which are not criminalized. Certainly one way to maintain a distinction between such acts is to apply the prerequisite legal elements, discussed in Chapter 7, which would allow the criminalization of deportation and population transfer when done as part of "state action or policy" in furtherance of a discriminatory policy.

4. Persecution

Throughout history, across many cultures and civilizations, the terms "persecute" and "persecution" have come to be understood to refer to discriminatory practices resulting in physical or mental harm, economic harm, or all of the above. The term persecution has a particular historical meaning in Western civilization as it has come to be associated with the Roman persecution of Christians. Since World War II, world public opinion has associated it with Nazi atrocities against Jews.

The words "persecute" and the act of "persecution" have come to acquire a universally accepted meaning for which a proposed definition is:

> State Action or Policy leading to the infliction upon an individual of harassment, torment, oppression, or discriminatory measures, designed to or likely to produce physical or mental suffering or economic harm, because of the victim's beliefs, views, or membership in a given identifiable group (religious, social, ethnic, linguistic etc.), or simply because the perpetrator sought to single out a given category of victims for reasons peculiar to the perpetrator.

To support the theory that the above composite definition reflects the common understanding of these terms prior to 1945, this writer turned to the most obvious source -- dictionaries. The languages researched are those reflected in the world's major criminal justice systems, as was the case with the research described in Chapter 7. They are: Arabic; Danish; Dutch; English; French; German; Greek; Hungarian; Italian; Japanese; Norwegian; Polish; Portuguese; Romanian; Russian; Spanish; Swedish; and

Turkish. They express the plain and common meaning of the term and to some extent its legal significance in these various cultures.[83]

Still, there is no crime known by the label "persecution" in the world's major criminal justice systems, nor is there an international instrument that criminalizes it, except for the *Apartheid* and the Genocide Conventions, provided that the "persecution" is coupled with other acts and with a specific intent on the part of the perpetrator.

The Nuremberg, Tokyo and CCL 10 prosecutions dealt with "persecution" in two ways: 1) as a pre-requisite legal element, as discussed in Chapters 1 and 6; and 2) as a specific crime. The former approach is both self-evident and reasonable, but the later is problematic because "persecution" is either the product of "state action or policy," or it is committed by a non-state supported group action which cannot be imputed to the state. It is the conclusion of this writer that "persecution" is neither a crime in the world's major legal systems, nor an international crime *per se* unless it is the basis for the commission of other crimes. Therefore, certain national crimes become international criminal violations as they are based on persecutorial policies of an identifiable group of persons. The same acts remain criminal even when national law permits them with regard to some people on the basis of discrimination. A reasonable nexus between the discriminatory policy and existing international crimes is needed.[84]

Since 1945, a number of international instruments prohibit and denounce the use of discriminatory practices or measures which result in the persecution or oppression of persons and groups though none of these criminalize their violations except the *Apartheid* Convention. They are:

1. Universal Declaration of Human Rights;
2. International Covenant on Civil and Political Rights;
3. International Covenant on Social, Economic and Cultural Rights;
4. Declaration on the Elimination of All Forms of Racial Discrimination;[85]
5. International Convention on the Elimination of Racial Discrimination;[86]

---

[83] *See* Document Section G.3.

[84] *See* Chapter 1 at 45 and Chapter 6 at 244.

[85] U.N.G.A. Res. 1904 (XVIII), 20 November 1963, *reprinted in* HUMAN RIGHTS COMPILATION, at 22.

[86] Adopted and opened for signature and ratification by General Assembly Resolution 2106A (XX) of 21 December 1965, *reprinted in* HUMAN RIGHTS COMPILATION, at 23.

318

6. International Convention on the Suppression and Punishment of the Crime of *Apartheid;*[87]
7. Declaration on the Elimination of Discrimination Against Women;[88]
8. Convention on the Elimination of All Forms of Discrimination Against Women;[89]
9. Declaration on the Elimination of All Forms of Intolerance and of Discrimination Based on Religion or Belief.[90]

In addition to these instruments,[91] the Genocide Convention bars and criminalizes discrimination, when it leads to certain consequences subject to certain legal requirements, but with limitations. The Genocide Convention is, however, particularly significant, as it outlines the manners in which persecution is achieved. It states that persecution involves the intentional attempt to destroy a national, ethnic, racial, or religious group by:

1. Killing members of the group;
2. Causing serious bodily or mental harm to members of the group;
3. Deliberately inflicting on the group, conditions of life calculated to bring about its physical destruction in whole or in part;
4. Imposing measures intended to prevent births within the group;
5. Forcibly transferring children of the group to another group.[92]

The *Apartheid* Convention, in Article II, is even more detailed and explicit than others with respect to the policies and practices of racial discrimination and oppression

---

[87] Adopted and opened for signature and ratification by General Assembly Resolution 3068 (XXVIII) of 30 November 1973, *reprinted in* HUMAN RIGHTS COMPILATION, at 29.

[88] U.N.G.A. Res. 2263 (XXII), 7 November 1967, *reprinted in* HUMAN RIGHTS COMPILATION, at 41.

[89] Adopted and opened for signature, ratification and accession by General Assembly resolution 34/180 of 18 December 1979, *reprinted in* HUMAN RIGHTS COMPILATION, at 43.

[90] U.N.G.A. Res. 36/55, 25 November 1981, *reprinted in* HUMAN RIGHTS COMPILATION, at 48.

[91] For other documents on the prevention of discrimination, *see* HUMAN RIGHTS COMPILATION, at 32-41, 50-55.

[92] Genocide Convention at article II. *See also* Beres, *Genocide and Genocide-like Crimes*, 1 BASSIOUNI ICL 271; *United Nations Report on the Study of the Prevention and Punishment of the Crime of Genocide*, E/CN/4/Sub. 1/416, 4 July 1978 at 1324.

in order to insure the racial superiority of one group over another. Unlike any other convention, it also specifies economic and labor practices which are employed as a means of preserving the dominance of one racial group over another.

The cumulative effect of these international instruments shows that persecution is not only an offence against human dignity, but also a violation of international law as evidenced in "general principles of law," and by analogy to genocide and *apartheid* it is a "crime against humanity."

5. Other Inhumane Acts

There is no crime by such a label under any source of international or national law. However, it seems as though the framers of the Charter, as discussed in Chapter 1, intended the phrase to extend by analogy the earlier Article 6(c) crimes to similar species. Thus, other similar crimes to "murder, extermination, enslavement" which are "inhumane" are also criminalized. This *ejusdem generis* interpretation may well be deemed a violation of the "principles of legality" if the interpretation by analogy is not carefully circumscribed.[93]

The international regulation of armed conflicts reveals that the following acts, *inter alia*, are prohibited because they are inhumane: infliction of physical harm upon innocent civilians; subjecting them to undue physical hardship; pillage, plunder, and deprivation of their personal property and means of livelihood; gravely affecting personal honor and dignity; the forceful removal of innocent civilians from their ordinary habitat or environment; breaking up families; desecrating religious symbols; and the seizure or destruction of public, religious and cultural property. These customary violations have been evidenced in national military laws and regulations, the conduct of states during hostilities, and the prosecution of violators by international and national tribunals and military bodies. These customary rules are embodied in the 1907 Hague Convention and subsequently they were codified in the Geneva Conventions. They have thus acquired a conventional law basis. In addition, a number of international and regional human rights instruments protect against "inhumane acts" or prohibit them. Three of these species are specifically discussed below. They are: torture, unlawful human experimentation and *apartheid*. In addition to these three specific crimes which exist under international law, other offenses similar to those

---

[93]   *See* Chapter 3.

enumerated in Article 6(c) can be identified in the national criminal laws of the world's major legal systems. As described in Chapter 7, certain crimes are universally prohibited under similar or comparable labels such as: assault, battery, rape, kidnapping, forcible detention, robbery and theft. But, once again, it must be noted that a given conduct is universally criminal in the national laws, does not make it an international crime. An international element is needed for this change in the character of the offense.[94]

Torture[95]

Torture was not always prohibited. In fact, for a long period of time, it was legal. The first traces of the practice of torture can be found in some of the earliest historical records left by Man.[96] In ancient Greece, both Aristotle and Demosthenes expressed the view that torture was the surest method for obtaining evidence. Slaves in Athens were frequently subjected to it.[97] Late Roman Law recognized the concept of torture as an aid to fact-finding in criminal investigations and trials.[98] However, this practice, and the abuses associated with it, met with disfavor from the Church, and in 384 A.D., its use was condemned. Eventually, torture was applied not only to establish the guilt

---

[94] See Chapter 7.

[95] See Bassiouni and Derby, An Appraisal of Torture in International Law and Practice: The Need for an International Convention for the Prevention and Suppression of Torture, 48 RIDP 17, 23-28 (Nos. 3 and 4, 1977); DE LA CIRESTA ARZAMEND, JOSÉ L., EL DELITO DE TORTURA: CONCEPTO BIEN JURIDICO Y ESTRUCTURA TÍPICA DEL ART. 204 BIS DEL CÓDIGO PENAL, (1990); see also D. MANNIX, THE HISTORY OF TORTURE, (1964); and J. HERMAN BURGERS AND HANS DANELIUS, THE UNITED NATIONS CONVENTION AGAINST TORTURE, A HANDBOOK ON THE CONVENTION AGAINST TORTURE AND OTHER CRUEL, INHUMANE, OR DEGRADING TREATMENT OR PUNISHMENT (1988).

[96] See Draper, The Judicial Aspects of Torture, at 1, presented to the International Institute on Humanitarian Law, 30 August - 1 September, 1977 San Remo, Italy.

[97] Keeton and Williams, Torture, ENCYCLOPEDIA BRITANNICA Vol. 22, 311 (1946).

[98] See e.g., LIPENIUS, BIBLIOTHECA REALIS JURIDICA, S.V. "TORTURA," (1679); K. KELBING, DIE TORTURE (1913); P. DE GALLINION, TRAITE DES INSTRUMENTS DE MARTYRS ET DES DIVERS MODES DE SUPPLICES EMPLOYÉS PAR LES PAIENS CONTRE LES CHRETIENS (1904); H. Gregoire, Les Persecutions dans l'Empire Romain, 46 MEMOIRE DE L'ACADEMIE ROYAL 1 (1951); G. DE LACAZE-DUTHIERS, LA TORTURE À TRAVERS LES AGES (1961); A. MELLOR, LA TORTURE, SON HISTOIRE (1949); J. MOREAU, LA PERSÉCUTION DU CHRISTIANISME DANS L'EMPIRE ROMAIN (1956); and G. SCOTT, THE HISTORY OF TORTURE THROUGHOUT THE AGES (1940).

of an accused, but also to obtain names of accomplices and other information useful to law enforcement authorities. In France, *torture prèparatoire*, which was applied before conviction in order to obtain proof, was accompanied by *torture préalable*, which followed conviction and concentrated on eliciting further useful information. In England, although the common law had made use of torture in obtaining criminal convictions, its other uses were not overlooked. Thus, the *peine forte et dure* was applied to coerce individuals who refused to plead at all, and thereby sought to avoid forfeit of their lands for felony convictions.[99] The oath *ex officio,* while it existed, legalized torture. Torture was also used in England without reference to the common law where the Star Chamber, or Crown Council found it expedient.[100]

At this point, mention must be made of the Inquisition, under which ecclesiastic courts came to interrogate accused heretics with the aid of torture. However, the subject of the Inquisition was not criminal justice, but rather orthodox religious thought, speech and behavior.

In medieval Japan, persons tried for theft were forced to hold a red hot iron, so that the presence or absence of a burn could be used to determine guilt or innocence respectively. In addition to this remnant of trial by ordeal, confessions were at times extracted by means of an adjustable boot of planks.[101] In the Chinese sphere, torture-obtained confessions were prescribed by the code of the Manchu Dynasty.[102] In other, non-Western civilizations, torture also flourished and was still in use when early Western travellers first visited these regions.[103]

The use of torture in connection with armed conflicts reflects the evolution of what used to be called the art of warfare. In many cultures and until the age of enlightenment, the defeated, whether former combatants or not, were subject to enslavement or any form of treatment expedient to the conquering forces. But the efforts to abolish torture in some or all situations also has long and well established historic roots.

---

[99]   Keeton and Williams *supra* note 97 at 74-77; *see* L. PARRY, THE HISTORY OF TORTURE IN ENGLAND (1933).

[100]   Keeton and Williams *supra* note 97, at 79-82.

[101]   Keeton and Williams, *supra* note 97, at 314.

[102]   *See e.g.*, TA'T SING LU LI, (G.T. Staunton, ed. 1810); and J. MURDOCK, HISOTRY OF JAPAN (1903).

[103]   *See* H. GROTIUS, DE JURE BELLI AC PACIS 649 (F. Kelsey ed. 1964).

CONTENTS OF SPECIFIC CRIMES

The prohibition of torture under all guises gradually entered into different national legal systems and slowly emerged at the international level. In the Orient, where sophistication came earlier to human civilizations, regulation of warfare to minimize incidental suffering was first expressed. Thus, by the fourth century B.C., the customs of war in China had been recorded by Sun Tzu, and among them were provisions for sparing the wounded and elderly.[104] At about the same period the BOOK OF MANU chronicled Hindu regulations for the conduct of war.[105] Other efforts to limit needless suffering in war were made in the Greek, Roman, Hebrew, Babylonian and Muslim civilizations.[106] But the first major efforts in the West aimed specifically at minimizing suffering of combatants were made in medieval Europe in the form of bans on such weapons as the harquebus, poison and the crossbow.[107]

Such a pattern was appropriate to the early nature of warfare. But with the development of feudal societies, warfare assumed a role more limited in scope, though just as frequent in occurrence, as a contest among princes rather than peoples. Under this formula, the general population participated only to a limited degree, so that it generally was spared some of the effects of defeat. During this period, the consequences of defeat for former combatants were subject to elaborate customs of which there were many local variations. Generally, treatment of vanquished combatants was tempered by principles of chivalry.[108] The practice of enslavement and, therefore, torture of conquered peoples receded.

At the international level, torture was barred under the 1899 and 1907 Hague Conventions. Then, the Geneva Conventions of 1949 proscribed torture in common Article 3 which deemed it a "grave breach." In addition, the 1977 Additional Protocols reinforced these prohibitions. Article 11 of Protocol I and Article 5, Paragraph 2(e) of Protocol II prohibit interference with the health or mental or physical integrity of

---

[104] SUN TZU, THE ART OF WAR 76 (S. Griffith transl. 1963).

[105] The BOOK OF MANU: MANUSMORTI discussed in detail by Nagendra Singh in *Armed Conflicts and Human Freedom Laws of Ancient India*, ETUDES ET ESSAIS SUR LE DROIT INTERNATIONAL HUMANITAIRE ET SUR LES PRINCIPES DE LA CROIX-ROGE L'HONNEUR DE JEAN PIETET (C. Swinarski ed. 1984); and COMMENTARY: THE LAWS OF MANU (G. Buhler trans. 1967).

[106] *See* A. AYMARD AND S. AUBOYER, L'ORIENT ET LA GRECE ANTIQUE 293-99 (1951); and C. FENWICK, INTERNATIONAL LAW 7-8 (4th ed. 1965).

[107] *See* C. FENWICK, *supra* note 106, at 667; and H. MAINE, INTERNATIONAL LAW 138-39 (2d ed. 1894).

[108] H. GROTIUS, *supra* note 103, at 723 *et seq.*

persons interned, detained or deprived of liberty. Articles 6 and 7 of Protocol II, governing penal prosecutions and protection and care respectively, are of particular note.[109]

Thus, in connection with an armed conflict, the Geneva Conventions and the Protocols prohibit any act constituting torture against any non-nationals, whether innocent civilians, prisoners of war, or persons acting on behalf of an opposing armed force not qualifying as prisoners of war, such as spies or saboteurs. This protection is extended under Protocol I to organized civil wars; thus, it applies in that context to persons of the same nationality.

With regard to instruments not limited to armed conflicts, the 1966 International Covenant on Civil and Political Rights, like the Universal Declaration, makes a strong statement against torture.[110] Article 7 states that: "No one shall be subjected to torture or to cruel, inhumane or degrading treatment or punishment. In particular, no one shall be subjected without his free consent to medical or scientific experimentation."[111]

Regional human rights instruments also prohibit torture. The European Convention[112] states in Article 3: "No one shall be subjected to torture or to inhumane or degrading treatment or punishment."[113] This prohibition is clearly binding on signatories. The American Convention on Human Rights,[114] prohibits torture in much the same language in its Article 5, Section 2: "No one shall be subjected to torture or to cruel, inhumane or degrading punishment or treatment. All persons deprived of their liberty shall be treated with respect for the inherent dignity of the human person."[115]

In addition, a number of General Assembly Resolutions denounce torture. Of particular note are five General Assembly resolutions, adopted between 1973-1976, relating to torture, against which not a single negative vote was cast. The first, entitled "Question of Torture and Other Cruel, Inhumane, or Degrading Treatment or

---

109 Protocol I, art. 11 and Protocol II, arts. 5, 6 and 7.

110 *See supra* note 8.

111 *Id.* at art. 7; *see also* the UNIVERSAL DECLARATION, *supra* note 8, at art. 5.

112 *See supra* note 8.

113 *See supra* note 8.

114 *See supra* note 8.

115 *See supra* note 8 at art. 5 § 2.

Punishment,"[116] "rejects" any form of such treatment. A year later, another resolution, "Torture and Other Cruel, Inhumane, or Degrading Treatment or Punishment in relation to Detention and Imprisonment,"[117] reaffirmed the rejection of torture. It requested the Fifth United Nations Congress on the Prevention of Crime and the Treatment of Offenders to include, in its elaboration of the Standard Minimum Rules for the Treatment of Prisoners,[118] which provides for "rules for the protection of all persons subjected to any form of detention or imprisonment against torture and other cruel, inhumane, or degrading treatment or punishment . . . "[119] In 1975, the "Declaration on the Protection of All Persons From Being Subjected to Torture and Other Cruel, Inhumane or Degrading Treatment or Punishment" was adopted.[120] This Declaration defined torture, characterizing it as an aggravated and deliberate form of cruel, inhumane or degrading treatment or punishment. It also condemned torture as negating the purposes of the Charter of the United Nations and as a violation of the Universal Declaration of Human Rights regardless of any threats to state security or public order.[121] In addition, the Declaration called on each state to take effective measures to prevent torture. In 1976, the General Assembly passed another resolution, which encouraged diligence in implementation of its earlier requests to sub-agencies, and which included torture in the provisional agenda for its thirty-second session. Finally, as this report was being compiled, the General Assembly approved a draft resolution based on a draft submitted October 28, 1977, calling on the Commission on Human Rights to draw up a convention against torture and other cruel, inhumane or degrading treatment or punishment.[122] This resolution was acted upon in 1980 with the drafting of the Draft Convention Against Torture and Other Cruel, Inhumane or Degrading Treatment or Punishment,[123] and in 1984 the Convention Against Torture and Other

---

[116] G.A. Res. 3059 (XXVIII), adopted unanimously, 2 November 1973.

[117] G.A. Res. 3218 (XXIX), adopted 6 November 1974.

[118] Adopted by the First United Nations Congress on the Prevention of Crime and the Treatment of Offenders (1955), reproduced in its report, U.N. publication, Sales No. 1956 IV. 4; approved by Resolution 663 (XXIV) of July 31, 1957 of the Economic and Social Council.

[119] *Id.*

[120] G.A. Res. 3552 (XXX), adopted 9 December 1975.

[121] *See supra* note 8.

[122] G.A. Res. 31/85, adopted 13 December 1976.

[123] ECOSOC Resolution, 6 March 1984, U.N. Doc. E/CN.4/1984/72/ Annex 1 (1980). *See* 23 ILM

Cruel, Inhumane or Degrading Treatment or Punishment was adopted. It clearly prohibits and criminalizes the infliction of torture under international law.

Article 1 provides a definition of torture:

> For the purposes of this Convention, the term "torture" means any act by which severe pain or suffering, whether physical or mental, is intentionally inflicted on a person for such purposes as obtaining from him or a third person information or a confession, punishing him for an act he or a third person has committed or is suspected of having committed, or intimidating or coercing him or a third person, or for any reason based on discrimination of any kind, when such pain or suffering is inflicted by or at the instigation of or with the consent or acquiescence of a public official or other person acting in an official capacity. It does not include pain or suffering arising only from, inherent in or incidental to lawful sanctions.[124]

Important procedural aspects with respect to acts of torture are set forth in Article 2, which obligates each State Party to take effective legislative, judicial and other measures to prevent torture within its territory. Article 2 clearly points out that torture may not be invoked as a justification under any circumstances (*e.g.*, state of war, internal political instability, etc.). Another important provision is found in Article 4, which obligates each State Party to proscribe torture under its criminal laws.

The status of international law prohibiting torture for belligerents has been well established since 1899-1907 and has grown in detail and specificity under the 1949 Geneva Conventions and the 1977 Protocols. It has been unequivocally criminalized in the 1984 Torture Convention, which makes no distinctions between war and peace, thus, it is presumably applicable, in addition to the customary and conventional regulation of armed conflicts, in time of war and organized civil war. Torture was also a crime under the national criminal laws of the world's major criminal justice systems even before the promulgation of the Charter, as evidenced by the research appearing in Chapter 7. Finally, it should be noted that every international regional human rights convention, and a number of United Nations and other international bodies, including judicial ones, like the European Court of Human Rights, condemn torture and similar

---

1027 (1984).

[124] U.N. G.A. Res. 39/46. *See* 24 ILM 535 (1985); and 23 ILM 1027 (1984), art. 1. *See also* BASSIOUNI DRAFT CODE, at 151-153.

practices. Thus, there is no doubt that torture is an international crime, and that it was a war crime before 1945.

Unlawful Human Experimentation[125]

As with torture, human experimentation was at first approved by many civilizations. Also like torture, the practice, in order to be internationally cognizable must be the product of "state action or policy," as discussed in Chapter 6. The history of human experimentation dates to some of the oldest writings on earth. Documents reflect that the ancient civilizations of China, Persia, India, Egypt, Greece and Rome all conducted human experimentation.[126] In Western societies, Galen stressed medical experimentation about 1800 years ago.[127] Harvey's dominance in the seventeenth century supplanted the earlier dominance of Galen.[128] Along with experimentation, records show that medical experts were concerned with the welfare of their patients.

Just as the origins of human experimentation have ancient roots, so too do the antecedents of society's burgeoning awareness that experimentation on man creates ethical problems. For example, Celsus, practicing in Alexandria in the third century B.C., spoke out against the dissection of living men.[129] The oath of Hippocrates in the fifth century B.C. has been viewed as giving advice on experimental diagnosis and therapy. Other documents such as Percival's code of 1803, Beaumont's code of 1833, and Claude Bernard's personal code of 1856 express concern about the ethical issues of human experimentation.[130]

Moreover, a number of traditions view the medical practitioner's role as a moral enterprise. For example, the inscription on the Asklepieon of the Acropolis exhorts

---

[125] The following discussion is adopted in part on Bassiouni, Baffes & Evrand, *An Appraisal of Human Experimentation in International Law and Practice: The Need for International Regulation of Human Experimentation*, 72 J. CRIM. L. & CRIMINOLOGY 1597, 1598-1599, 1601-1603, 1606-1607, 1639-1641 (1981).

[126] *See* Bollet, *Smallpox: The Biography of a Disease -- I*, RESIDENT AND STAFF PHYSICIAN, Aug. 1978, at 47, 48; and H. BEECHER, RESEARCH AND THE INDIVIDUAL: HUMAN STUDIES 5 (1970).

[127] *Id.* at 5-6.

[128] *Id.* at 6.

[129] *Id.* at 10.

[130] *Id.* at 12.

physicians to treat all men as brothers. The Hindu oath instructs physicians to assist all people as if they are relatives. The Chinese code of Sun Sumiao, 7th century A.D., affirms that all people are to be treated equally. And the prayer of Maimonides ends with a request that God support the physician in his task for the benefit of mankind.[131] The credo basic to these ethical statements is *primum non nocere*: "Above all do no harm." An ethical duty arises between the physician and the patient whereby the former is not morally free to exercise his skills in any manner he desires but rather, he is bound by the origin, nature and purpose of his enterprise to use them primarily for the patient's benefit.[132]

Governments have entered the arena of human experimentation by recognizing social and economic implications and devoting tax revenues toward its development.[133] Politicians and heads of state have utilized and exploited the popular appeal and potential for population control in human experimentation, and military strategists have sought to use experimentation to achieve victory.[134] Not surprisingly, the role of governments in this field of science evokes serious concerns. Novelists have expressed the fear of widespread government control of people's minds and behavior through experiments intended to perfect psychosurgical techniques, psychological conditioning and psychotropic drugs.[135] Others have objected to governmental approval of the coercive use of prisoners, orphans, and the insane.[136] Physicians reportedly have performed experiments on behalf of their governments in order to scientifically study the effects of torture.[137]

---

[131]   *See* Curran, *The Proper and Improper Concerns of Medical Law and Ethics*, 295 NEW ENGLAND J. MED. 1057 (1976); and Jonsen, *Do No Harm*, 88 ANNALS INTERNAL MED. 827 (1978).

[132]   Jonsen, *supra* note 131, at 828.

[133]   *See* Confrey, *PHS Grant-Supported Research with Human Subjects*, 83 PUB. HEALTH REP. 127, 130 (1968). In the Declaration on the Use of Scientific and Technological Progress in the Interests of Peace and for the Benefit of Mankind, G.A. Res. 3384 (XXX), 10 November 1975, the United Nations expressed concern that governments should use science and technology for the benefit of mankind.

[134]   *See* E. RUSSELL, THE SCOURGE OF THE SWASTIKA 214 (1954).

[135]   *See generally*, A. BURGESS, A CLOCKWORK ORANGE (1962); G. ORWELL, 1984 (1949); A. HUXLEY, BRAVE NEW WORLD (1932).

[136]   *See* Daube, *Legal Problems in Medical Advance*, 6 ISRAEL L. REV. 1, 8 (1971); *see also* Yeo, *Psychiatry, the Law and Dissent in the Soviet Union*, 14 REV. INT'L COMM. JUR. 34 (1975); Young-Anawaty, *International Human Rights Norms and Soviet Abuse of Psychiatry*, 10 CASE W. J. INT'L L. 785 (1978).

[137]   *See* Sagan & Jonsen, *Medical Ethics and Torture*, 294 NEW ENGLAND J. MED. 1427 (1976). The

328

Along with these concerns, however, state involvement in human experimentation has influenced the evolution of controls designed to limit it. Because the state has assumed an increasingly active role in the discovery of medical knowledge, its policies concerning citizens as subjects of experimentation is critical. Many of the current prohibitions against human experimentation are a reaction to the brutal Nazi state policy concerning medical experimentation. Nazi physicians committed atrocious crimes which first came to international attention at Nuremberg.[138] Nothing like that had ever occurred in history and thus neither conventional nor customary international law had provided any specific norms which could be relied upon in the post-World War II prosecutions.

With regard to World War II, the post-Nuremberg medical prosecutions[139] offer the scientific and legal communities important lessons regarding the dangers to individual safety inherent in human experimentation, and the controls needed to maintain a balance between advances in medical knowledge and the need to protect individuals. The principle of individual responsibility and the showing of moral delinquency emerged from the war crimes proceedings. The trials revealed the Nazi belief that humans could be used forcibly as experimental subjects for vague scientific investigations without regard to either therapeutic advantage or the pain and suffering inflicted upon such hapless victims. From the start, the Nazi experiments were in violation of existing German law and the code of ethics of the German medical community.[140] However, by degrees, the Nazi philosophy eroded the resistance of the

---

authors refer to a report in the Manchester Guardian of May 3, 1974, in which photos taken during interrogation appeared of prisoners in Portugal. These prisoners were made available to prison doctors who wanted to study the effects of torture. Medical experimentation can cross the line into torture when no useful scientific purpose is served and the subject is transformed into a suffering victim. *But see* Gellhorn, *Violations of Human Rights: Torture and the Medical Profession,* 299 NEW ENGLAND J. MED. 358 (1978) (discussing international medical seminar for purpose of preparing casebook on effects of torture for use when legal redress is possible.) *See generally* Bassiouni, *supra* note 95.

[138] *See* Enloe, *The German Medical War Crimes--Their Nature and Significance,* 30 RHODE ISLAND MED. J. 801 (1947); Ivy, *Nazi War Crimes of a Medical Nature,* 139 J.A.M.A. 131 (1949); Ivy, *The History and Ethics of the Use of Human Subjects in Medical Experiments,* 108 SCIENCE 1 (1948); Mellanby, *Nazi Experiments on Human Beings in Concentration Camps in Nazi Germany,* 1 BRIT. MED. J. 148 (1947); A. MITSCHERLICH & F. MIELKE, DOCTORS OF INFAMY: THE STORY OF THE NAZI MEDICAL CRIMES xi-xii (1949); and Mulford, *Human Experimentation,* 20 STAN. L. REV. 99 (1967); *see also* R.J. LIFTON, THE NAZI DOCTORS (1986).

[139] *See* J. APPLEMAN, *supra* note 12, at 142-143.

[140] *See* Weinschenk, *Nazis Before German Courts,* 10 INT'L LAW, 515, 518-519 (1976).

German medical profession until German law was ignored without legal effect or social opprobrium.[141] What perhaps began as well-intentioned scientific inquiry became distorted beyond all reasonable ethical and humane limits. Even though the defendant physicians at the Subsequent CCL 10 Proceedings argued that their studies led to useful information, this argument was rejected, both on its own terms and in light of the harm done to the victims.[142]

The Subsequent CCL 10 Proceedings' medical trials also suggest that the magnitude of the crimes committed would have been impossible without the involvement of the State. Thus, Nuremberg reflects that "crimes against humanity" needs state policy, sponsorship or condonation as a pre-requisite legal element.[143] Since these unlawful human experimentations essentially were conducted against Jews and Slavs, the elements of discrimination and persecution are also evident. German scientists were, in part, persuaded to engage in these experiments because of the knowledge that the subjects available were prisoners already scheduled for disposal by the state.[144] This practice hideously dramatizes the notion that the state is free to treat

---

[141]   See Ivy, Nazi War Crimes of a Medical Nature, supra note 138, at 131.   Another factor which has been attributed to the moral destruction of the German medical profession under Hitler is the notion that "the welfare of the armed forces was the supreme good and anything that helped the armed forces was right." Id. at 144; see also Enloe, supra note 138, at 804.

[142]   See Ivy, Nazi War Crimes of a Medical Nature, supra note 138, at 132.

[143]   See Chapter 7.

[144]   3 IMT 160-161 (1946). With Hitler's full knowledge, and at the instigation of Heinrich Himmler, Reichsführer of the S.S., and other members of the High Command, those experiments were carried out, under the direction or organization of the various physicians in positions of authority in the Nazi regime, upon unknown numbers of prisoners in the concentration camps. Though not an exhaustive list, some of the experiments and projects included the following: (1) immersion in tanks of cold water of varying temperatures for periods up to fourteen hours to develop technique for rapid and complete resuscitation of German pilots downed at sea; (2) simulation of high altitude atmospheric conditions in decompression chambers, with autopsies then performed to study the effect of sudden pressure changes on the body; (3) attempted mass sterilization through castration doses of x-rays, treated diet and intrauterine injections apparently of silver nitrate, (4) mutilation of prisoners as experimental surgical subjects for the training of German surgical students; (5) injection of virulent typhus into prisoners to ensure a ready supply of virus for typhus experiments; (6) infliction of bullet wounds and incisions and introduction of bacteria into the wounds to study and treat infections; (7) shooting of prisoners with poisonous aconite bullets to study the effects of aconite poisoning; (8) forced ingestion of seawater into prisoners to test desalinization processes; (9) experimental bone transplantation; (10) execution and dismemberment of prisoners to furnish "subhuman" skeletal specimens for an anthropological museum; (11) injection of malaria to test malaria immunity; and (12) injection of dye in the eyes to change its color. These human experiments were conducted on the

330

its nationals in the manner it chooses because it perceives itself as the source of all rights and, therefore, is beyond the reach of law.[145] This was one reason why the drafters of the London Charter formulated in Article 6(c) that national law which permits a practice otherwise unlawful cannot be interposed as a defense. The twenty-three defendants in *The Medical Case* of the Subsequent Proceedings at Nuremberg were tried under CCL 10. Of the sixteen defendants found guilty, fifteen were convicted of committing war crimes and "crimes against humanity."[146]

There is no doubt that such conduct is prohibited by the general provisions of the 1899 and 1907 Hague Conventions' "laws of humanity," and the specific provisions on the protection of the "lives and honour" of the civilian population. Nothing more needed to be added than the practices that developed during World War II that were unknown until recent history. But the legal prohibition was in existence against such practices, even though it did not specifically address the instrumentalities and methods developed subsequently.

It should be noted that some accounts exist of at least one of the Allies' similar practices against POW's during World War II. These accounts attribute to the USSR some forms of unlawful human experimentation.

The Four Geneva Conventions of August 12, 1949, provide the same basic protection against unlawful human experimentation during war as it does against torture. The Conventions expressly forbid the use of either protected military personnel

---

victims without anesthetic, and they received no subsequent treatment for their injuries. Thus, they suffered atrociously, and died in great pain and suffering.

[145] The atrocities reported at Nuremberg were only a few of many examples in political history of misappropriation of individual rights for public expediency. One of the earliest such events recorded concerns the sacrifice of youths to provide blood for Pope Innocent VIII, in a futile attempt to restore the aging pontiff to vigorous youth. *See* Beecher, *Scarce Resources and Medical Advancement*, in EXPERIMENTATION WITH HUMAN SUBJECTS, at 88. Another example was provided by Queen Caroline of England, who, before allowing her own children to be inoculated with cow pox, had the vaccine tested on prisoners and children of the poor. *See* Beecher, *Experimentation in Man*, 169 J.A.M.A. 461, 469 (1959). Ironically in Germany, the Nazi brutality presented a contradiction of Germany's greatest philosopher, Immanuel Kant, whose central theory of ethics held that people should never be treated as means but only as ends. *See* I. KANT, FOUNDATIONS OF THE METAPHYSICS OF MORALS 47 (L. Beck trans. 1959).

[146] Of the fifteen defendants guilty of War Crimes and "Crimes Against Humanity," seven were put to death, five were sentenced to life imprisonment, two were sentenced to twenty years imprisonment and one was sentenced to fifteen years imprisonment. *See* J. APPLEMAN, *supra* note 12 at 139-140.

or civilians for biological experimentation.[147] Moreover, common Article 3, which protects persons taking no active part in either international or non-international armed conflict, requires that all such persons be treated humanely. To this end, cruel, humiliating or degrading treatment is expressly prohibited. Article 12 of the First and Second Conventions, Article 12 of the Third, and Articles 16, 27 and 32 of the Fourth provide that protected persons be treated humanely. In particular, these articles provide that protected persons not be subject to ill treatment, biological, medical or scientific experiments regardless of their state of health, age or sex.[148]

These violations constitute "grave breaches" of Article 50 of the First Convention, Article 51 of the Second Convention, Article 130 of the Third Convention and Article 147 of the Fourth Convention.

The 1977 Protocols provide even more extended legal protection than do the 1949 Geneva Conventions. Article 11 of Protocol I prohibits medical or scientific experiments on protected persons even with their consent. Article 16(2) of Protocols I and II provide that medical personnel not be compelled to perform or refrain from performing medical activities "required by the rules of medical ethics." Article 12(1)-(2) of Protocol II provides that protected persons shall not be subjected to any medical

---

[147] *See generally*, J. PICTET, HUMANITARIAN LAW AND THE PROTECTION OF WAR VICTIMS (1975); and I COMMENTARY: THE GENEVA CONVENTIONS OF 12 AUGUST, 1949 370-72 (Pictet ed. 1952).

[148] With regard to the specific crime of the "inhumane act" of unlawful human experimentation, this author has defined it in BASSIOUNI DRAFT CODE as follows:

Section 1. Acts of Unlawful Human Experimentation

1.0   The crime of unlawful human experimentation consists of any physical and/or psychological alterations by means of either surgical operations, or injections, ingestion or inhalation of substances inflicted by or at the instigation of a public official, or for which a public official is responsible and to which the person subject to such experiment does not grant consent.

Section 2. Defence of Consent

2.1   For the purpose of this crime a person shall not be deemed to have consented to medical experimentation unless he or she has the capacity to consent and does so freely after being fully informed of the nature of the experiment and its possible consequences.

2.2   A person may withdraw his or her consent at any time and shall be deemed to have done so if he or she is not kept fully informed within a reasonable time of the progress of the experiment and any development concerning its possible consequences.

332

procedure, particularly a medical or scientific experiment, which is not necessary for their health or which is contrary to accepted medical standards.

These provisions of the Geneva Conventions and Protocols are predicated exclusively on humanitarian considerations and experimentation on human subjects committed during armed conflict.

Genocide is an international crime whether it is committed in time of war or peace.[149] In particular, genocide is committed by any individual who causes bodily or mental harm to members of a national, ethnic, racial or religious group or by anyone who imposes measures intended to prevent births within such groups.[150] Although it is reasonable to include unethical human experimentation within the criminal acts prohibited by these articles, the Genocide Convention is not sufficiently specific to adequately protect against unethical human experimentation. Furthermore, it does not extend to other persons who are within its protected group.

The Standard Minimum Rules for the Treatment of Prisoners,[151] set forth standards for adequate medical care of prisoners but are silent as to the use of prisoners as experimental subjects. Moreover, the Rules were passed as a United Nations resolution and consequently are only recommendatory.[152] Nonetheless, the Rules seek

---

[149]   Lopez-Rey, *Crime and Human Rights*, 42 FED. PROB. 10, 12 (1978). *See generally*, P. DROST, THE CRIME OF STATE 119-136 (1959).

[150]   Article II defines the protected groups as:

[i]n the present Convention, genocide means any of the following acts committed with intent to destroy, in whole or in part, a national, ethical, racial or religious group, as such:

(a)   Killing members of the group;
(b)   Causing serious bodily or mental harm to members of the group;
(c)   Deliberately inflicting on the group conditions of life calculated to bring about its physical destruction in whole or in part;
(d)   Imposing measures intended to prevent births within the group;
(e)   Forcibly transferring children of the group to another group.

[151]   E.S.C. Res. 663 C (XXIV), 31 July 1957; *see also* Note by the Secretary-General, The Range of Application and the Implementation of the Standard Minimum Rules for the Treatment of Prisoners, U.N. General Assembly Provisional Agenda, Item 6, E/AC. 57/28, 24 May, 1976; and Analytical Summary by the Secretary-General, Torture and Other Cruel, Inhuman or Degrading Treatment or Punishment in Relation to Detention and Imprisonment, U.N. General Assembly Provisional Agenda, Item 75, A/10158, 23 July, 1975.

[152]   J. BRIERLY, THE LAW OF NATIONS 380-96, 413-32 (1963); I. BROWNLIE, PRINCIPLES OF PUBLIC INTERNATIONAL LAW 14, 696 (1979).

to advance the principle of asserting individual interests over those of prison authorities who may be unduly oppressive in their efforts to maintain order.[153]

To the extent that unlawful human experimentation produces pain and suffering it is also torture, as discussed above. Thus, it is protected by the same provisions in international human rights law which prohibit all forms of "cruel, inhumane or degrading treatment or punishment," discussed above under torture. Unlawful human experimentation is an inhumane act within the meaning of "crimes against humanity" but it must be the product of "state action or policy," as discussed in Chapter 6.

Apartheid[154]

A third form of "inhumane acts" carries the infamous nomenclature of *apartheid*. The *Apartheid* Convention was opened for signature and ratification by the United Nations on November 30, 1973 and entered into effect on July 18, 1976.

The Convention refers to a variety of forms of human depredation based on racial discrimination in reliance upon the practices of the Union of South Africa and labels these practices "crimes against humanity." Other international instruments relevant to "crimes against humanity" also refer to *apartheid* as an "inhumane act" within the meaning of "crimes against humanity." These instruments are:

-the Convention on the Non-Applicability of Statutory Limitations to War Crimes and Crimes Against Humanity[155] in which "inhumane acts resulting from the policy of *apartheid* are condemned as a crime against humanity

-a number of resolutions of the General Assembly in which the policies and practices of *apartheid* are condemned as a "crime against humanity"[156]

---

[153]   *See supra* note 151, at art. 7.

[154]   *See generally* Clark, *The Crime of Apartheid*, in 1 BASSIOUNI ICL 299.

[155]   G.A. Res. 2391 (XXIII), 23 U.N. GAOR, Supp. No. 18 at 40, U.N. Doc. A/7218 (1968).

[156]   Notably, G.A. Res. 2202A (XXI), 21 U.N. GAOR, Supp. No. 16, U.N. Doc. A/6316 (1967); G.A. Res. 2671F (XXV)(25 U.N. GAOR, Supp. No. 28 at 33, U.N. Doc. A/8028 (1970). These resolutions had overwhelming support. Only South Africa and Portugal voted against and there were few abstentions.

-and Security Council resolutions in which the Council has emphasized that *apartheid* and its continued expansion seriously disturb and threaten international peace and security.[157]

The Preamble of the Convention is explicit about the criminal motive of the acts described in Article II that "would make it possible to take more effective measures at the international and national levels with a view to the suppression and punishment of the crime of *apartheid*.[158] Clark says with regard to criminalizing *apartheid* that "emphasizing the criminal nature of the deed symbolizes the heinous nature of it, as seen by the international community."[159]

The substantive part of the Convention is Article II, which lists six different kinds of "inhumane acts," which, if done with the necessary intent, constitute the crime of *apartheid*. These six acts include: (1) the denial to members of a racial group the right to life and liberty or person; (2) the deliberate imposition on racial groups living

---

[157]   *E.g.*, S.C. Res. 282, Resolutions and Decisions of the Security Council, 25 U.N. SCOR at 12 (1970); S.C. Res. 311, Resolutions and Decisions of the Security Council, 27 U.N. SCOR at 10 (1972); *see also* S.C. Res. 392, Resolutions and Decisions of the Security Council, 31 U.N. SCOR at 11, U.N. Doc. S/INF/32 (1976), adopted by consensus, which reaffirms that "the policy of *apartheid* is a crime against the conscience and dignity of mankind and seriously disturbs international peace and security."

Other formats include:

-the provisions of the Charter in which members of the organization pledge themselves to take joint and separate action on human rights matters,

-the promise in the Universal Declaration of Human Rights that all are entitled to their rights without distinctions such as race, colour or national origin,

-the Declaration on the Granting of Independence to Colonial Countries and Peoples with its promise of an end to colonialism and practices of segregation and discrimination associated therewith,

-the International Convention on the Elimination of All Forms of Racial Discrimination under which states particularly condemn racial segregation and *apartheid* and undertake to prevent, prohibit and eradicate all practices of this nature in territories under their jurisdiction; and

-the Convention on the Prevention and Punishment of the Crime of Genocide, in which certain acts, which may also be qualified as acts of *apartheid* constitute a crime under international law.

[158]   *See supra* note 155, at Preamble.

[159]   *See* Clark, *supra* note 154, at 301.

conditions calculated to cause their physical destruction; (3) any legislation calculated to prevent racial groups from participating in the political, social, economic, and cultural life of the country; (4) any measures designed to racially divide the population; (5) the exploitation of labor of racial groups, and, (6) persecution depriving racial groups of their fundamental rights and freedoms.[160]

---

[160] *See Apartheid* Convention article II. The full text of article II provides:

For the purpose of the present Convention, the term "the crime of *apartheid*," which shall include similar policies and practices of racial segregation and discrimination as practiced in southern Africa, shall apply to the following inhuman acts committed for the purpose of establishing and maintaining domination by one racial group of persons over any other racial group of persons and systematically oppressing them:

(a)   Denial to a member of members of a racial group or groups of the right to life and liberty of person:

  (i)   By murder of members of a racial group or groups;
  (ii) By the infliction upon the member of a racial group or groups of serious bodily or mental harm, by infringement of their freedom or dignity, or by subjecting them to torture or to cruel, inhuman or degrading treatment or punishment;
  (iii) By arbitrary arrest and illegal imprisonment of the members of a racial group or groups.

(b)   Deliberate imposition on a racial group or groups of living conditions calculated to cause its or their physical destruction in whole or in part;

(c)   Any legislative measures and other measures calculated to prevent a racial group or groups from participating in the political, social, economic and cultural life of the country and the deliberate creation of conditions preventing the full development of such a group or groups, in particular by denying to members of a racial group or groups basic human rights and freedoms, including the right to work, the right to form recognized trade unions, the right to educate, the right to leave and return to their country, the right to a nationality, the right to freedom of movement and residence, the right to freedom of opinion and expression, the right to freedom of peaceful assembly and association;

(d)   Any measures, including legislative measures, designed to divide the population along racial lines by the creation of separate reserves and ghettos for the members of a racial group or groups, the prohibition of mixed marriage among members of various racial groups, the expropriation of landed property belonging to a racial group or groups or to members thereof;

(e)   Exploitation of the labour of the members of a racial group or groups, in particular by submitting them to forced labour;

Article I to the Convention declares:

[A]*partheid* is a crime against humanity and that inhuman acts resulting from the policies and practices of *apartheid* and similar policies and practices of racial segregation and discrimination, as defined in article II of the Convention, are crimes violating the principles of international law, in particular the purposes and principles of the Charter of the United Nations, and constituting a serious threat to international peace and security.[161]

Thus, *apartheid* is an inhumane act, along with torture and unlawful human experimentation. All three are, therefore, "crimes against humanity."

Assessment

The general contents of the specific crimes included within the meaning of Article 6(c) of the Charter are fairly easy to ascertain. But beyond such a broad brush approach it is difficult to ascertain the applicable source of law, its binding legal effects and upon which parties, the applicable context, and the parties subject to the protection and of the prohibition, the specificity of each crime and its elements. For a penalist requiring some specifity it is a very arduous task to sort out all of these distinctions. This is why positivists, whether publicists or penalists, find it impossible. If poetic license is permitted, the analogy would be like the weaving of a tapestry with uneven size, shape and color of cloth and thread expecting to come out with a cohesive and harmonious product. Instead the product would be of uncertain design with differing shapes and contrasting colors. Nevertheless, a definite commonality exists between all these pieces of cloth and thread, and the product may still ultimately reveal an overall harmony. But, if it were not for the determination of the weavers at Nuremberg, the final product would not have been achieved. In addition to the Charter's drafters, the prosecutors and judges, who, for all practical purposes were part of the same team, also greatly contributed to this undertaking.[162] Surely one can find support for the proposition that

---

(f)   Persecution of organization and persons by depriving them of fundamental rights and freedoms, because they oppose *apartheid*.

[161]   *Id.* at art. I.

[162]   *See* Chapter 1 at 18.

the specific crimes listed in Article 6(c), with the exception of "persecution" *per se,* existed before 1945 in the world's major criminal justice systems, as evidenced in Chapter 7. It can also be shown that these acts were prohibited in whole or in part under one of the sources of international law. But only some were criminalized and only as to some of their aspects, with application to certain limited contexts, and also, only to certain parties.

Since 1945, the overall situation has not changed significantly with respect to the specificity of Article 6(c) crimes. No comprehensive convention was adopted, even though so many others in the field of international criminal law have been adopted. Certainly it cannot be argued that the legal needs evidenced by the Charter and its ensuing prosecutions have not been readily apparent. Nor can it be argued that similar acts have ceased, as discussed in Chapter 12. Thus, the unexplainable void fills the concerned with justifiable perplexity, and frustration.

CHAPTER 9

ELEMENTS OF CRIMINAL RESPONSIBILITY

> In the law, it is not the obvious that needs to be specified, but the ambiguous that must be clarified.

Problems in Identifying the General Part

International criminal law, prior to the Charter, was a nascent discipline in its early stages. It consisted of some conventional and customary international law, mostly concerning piracy, slavery, and the regulation of armed conflicts, and some legal doctrine by a few specialists.[1] It did not, however, have a counterpart to national criminal law's general part. Few, if any, of the conventional international criminal law instruments, prior to 1945, contained provisions on the general part. As to the customary practice of states, it was simply to apply the law of the enforcing state, though there was a body of domestic jurisprudence and private international law doctrine on questions of conflicts between different national criminal jurisdictions.[2]

The Charter's Article 6(c) defines the substantive contents of "crimes against humanity," as discussed in Chapters 1, 7 and 8, but it does not contain the elements of criminal responsibility and exonerating factors which are usually found in the general part of criminal law in the world's major criminal justice systems,[3] except for: 1) the notion of accomplice responsibility and conspiracy; and, 2) the removal of the absolute defence of "obedience to superior orders" and the immunity of heads of State, as discussed in Chapter 10.[4] It can be assumed that the Charter's drafters wanted to avoid

---

[1] *See* note 10 in Chapter 4.

[2] *See* among them: H. DONNEDIEU DE VABRES, LES PRINCIPLES MODERNES DU DROIT PÉNAL INTERNATIONAL (1928); and INTRODUCTION À L'ETUDE DU DROIT PÉNAL INTERNATIONAL (1922); F. MELLI, LEHRBURH DES INTERNATIONALEN STRAFRECHTS UND STRAFPROCESSRECHTS (1910); A. HEGLER, PRINZIPEN DES INTERNATIONALES STRAFRECTHS (1906).

[3] The Charter, however, contains a provision on conspiracy, "common design," in Article 6. This charge came out of a specific common law substantive crime which was, and still is, unknown to other legal systems. Since it was used in the Law of the Charter as a specific crime, it cannot be viewed as referring to a form of imputed criminal responsibility.

[4] *See* Charter Articles 7 and 8.

the difficulties inherent in reconciling the different legal conceptions in the four legal systems represented by the negotiators.[5] Surely they were not oblivious to these questions as evidenced by the fact that they specifically dealt with one of them, namely the defense of "obedience to superior orders."[6]

International criminal law instruments, even after 1945, seldom contain provisions relating to a general part question. The specific elements of the twenty-two categories of international crimes, whenever they are found in the 315 international instruments applicable to these crimes,[7] usually identify the objective or material element of the crime, but seldom do they identify the subjective or mental element of the offense. The causation element is rarely identified and the result is occasionally found in these instruments though more frequently by implication only. And with the exception of this writer's *Draft International Criminal Code*,[8] there is no source for the general part of international criminal law, whether for all or part of it, except for the scholarly writings on some aspects of the general part, notably those of the late Professor Stefan Glaser.[9]

In the absence of any legislative provisions in the Charter, and in the absence of any general source of international criminal law, two sources must be relied upon to identify these general part questions: 1) the indictments and judgments of the IMT, IMTFE and Subsequent Proceedings; and 2) "general principles of law recognized by civilized nations."

The Law of the Charter

In general, the IMT, IMTFE and the Subsequent Proceedings, indictments and judgments, as well as the record of these proceedings do not particularly deal with general part questions. For example, the charges before the IMT against Alfred Krupp

---

[5] *See* Chapter 1 at 18.

[6] *See* Charter Article 8.

[7] *See, e.g.* BASSIOUNI DIGEST and BASSIOUNI DRAFT CODE 115-178.

[8] *See* BASSIOUNI DRAFT CODE 81-114.

[9] *See* S. GLASER, INFRACTION INTERNATIONALE: LES ELEMENTS CONSTITUTIFS ET LES ASPECTS JURIDIQUES (1957). The late Professor Glaser has also published numerous articles on international criminal law and some of them dealt with the general part, like *L'élément moral des infractions de commission par omission en droit international pénal*, 73 REVUE PÉNAL SUISSE 263 (1958); and *Culpabilité en Droit International Pénal*, 99 RECEUIL DES COURS 473 (1960).

were dismissed because he was deemed *non compos mentis*, and the charges against "criminal organizations," like the SS and SD, were deemed not to constitute *ipso iure* or *ipso facto* criminal responsibility for its individual members. Various judgments hold that "crimes against humanity" are international crimes, but without stating the elements of such a crime. Others state the proposition that the mental element of "knowingly and intentionally" is required, or is found to exist in a particular case, but do not explain or discuss the requirements of the mental element, its legal standards and tests. Other related questions of intent such as knowledge, mistake of law and facts are superficially addressed in the IMT judgment, but more so in the Subsequent Proceedings. The IMTFE judgment on these questions was the worst.

"Command responsibility," as a basis for imputed criminal responsibility and the defenses of "obedience to superior orders" and "military necessity" were, however, frequently raised and broadly discussed in all the proceedings and in the judgments. While other general part questions were hardly addressed.

As is evident from the record of the Proceedings, the attitude of the IMT and IMTFE judges and prosecutors were overwhelmingly negative to the defenses' raising of general part issues. It can almost be surmised from these attitudes and from the tribunals' rulings that there was a tacit agreement between judges and prosecutors not to let the proceedings get out of control by allowing the defendants to effectively use such legal arguments to override factual arguments on which criminal responsibility was to be assessed.[10] Consequently, rather than deal with them, the tribunals ignored these cumbersome and complicated legal issues as much as they could. This can be explained in several ways, but the three most likely hypotheses are:

---

[10]   One Noted scholar said:

"Il s'aigssait en effet de trouver les règles juridiques preciser permettant de frapper, tous les coupables. Il fallait eviter deux eceuils opposes: d'un Côtè une extension illimité du cercle des personnes considérées comme responsables; de l'autre côtè la dilution de la culpabilitè par l'admission des causes justificatives ou de non-imputabilité tirées de l'ordre juridique nazi. H. MEYROVITZ, LA REPRESSION PER LES TRIBUNAUX ALLEMANDS DES CRIMES CONTRE L'HUMANITÉ ET DE L'APPARTENANCE À LEURS ORGANIZATIONS CRIMINELLES 290 (1960). *See also* Donnedieu de Vabres, *Le Procès de Nuremberg Devant les Principes Modernes du Droit Pènal International*, 70 RECUEIL DES COURS 480 (1947), who took the same position as Meyrovitz, *id.*

1)   The defendants were selected for having been part of the highest echelons of decision-makers and executors of the crimes charged,[11]

2)   The law was driven by the facts because of the enormity of the human harm which occurred; and,

3)   The tangible evidence, at least at the IMT overwhelmingly showed that almost all the defendants at these trials committed or ordered these crimes or allowed them to occur when they presumably could have prevented them.[12]

Other than arguments about the "principles of legality," as discussed in Chapter 3, the following general part issues were recurring throughout the post-World War II proceedings: 1) knowledge of the law; 2) consciousness of wrongdoing; 3) individual responsibility for: participation in a criminal organization; as an accessory to a crime; and conspiracy; 4) command responsibility, 5) the defense of "obedience to superior orders;" 6) compulsion (necessity) 7) reprisals; and 8) *tu quoque*. The first four arguments are discussed in this Chapter, the other four are discussed in Chapter 10.

Theoretically, responsibility under international criminal law presents the same issues as those arising under national criminal law. But since there is no codified, customary or case-law general part for international criminal law, except for a few rules, it cannot be conclusively stated what these legal requirements are unless one resorts to "general principles of law."

Criminal Responsibility in International and Comparative Criminal Law

The finding that a given "general principle" exists requires substantial similarity as to any given issue in the world's major criminal justice systems, as discussed in Chapter 7. And that is very difficult to obtain in comparative criminal law, particularly

---

[11]   *See* Document Section C. 4 and C. 10. Some of the defendants before the IMTFE were not the actual decision-makers, and some of the cases brought before the United States Military Commission in the Philippines, particularly in the Yamashita case, discussed below under "Command Responsibility" and in Chapter 5, were a miscarriage of justice. *See infra* notes 73 to 87.

[12]   With the reservations expressed *supra* in note 5.

as to the general part, as discussed below.[13] Consequently,the identification of the general part of international criminal law is, in the absence of codification, an almost impossible task to accomplish. And that is probably the best reason why the drafters of the Charter did not address these questions. It also explains why the judgments of the IMT, IMTFE, and Subsequent Proceedings touched upon most of these issues in a superficial way.

The Charter did, however, establish unequivacably, the principle of individual criminal responsibility under international criminal law, as discussed in Chapter 5, irrespective of any mandates under national law, and irrespective of the doctrine of Act of State and other immunities, and the defense of "obedience to superior orders."

In the opening statement before the IMT, Justice Jackson eloquently stated:

> Of course, it was under the law of all civilized peoples a crime for one man with his bare knuckles to assault another. How did it come that multiplying this crime by a million, and adding firearms to bare knuckles, made a legally innocent act? The doctrine was that one could not be regarded as criminal for committing the usual violent acts in the conduct of legitimate warfare.... An International Law which operates only on states can be enforced only by war because the most practicable method of coercing a state is warfare... the only answer to recalcitrance was impotence of war.... Of course, the idea that a state, any more than a corporation, commits crimes is a fiction. While it is quite proper to employ the fiction of responsibility of a state or corporation for the purpose of imposing a collective liability, it is quite intolerable to let such a legalism become the basis of personal immunity. The Charter recognizes that one who has committed criminal acts may not take refuge in superior orders nor in the doctrine that his crimes were

---

[13]   *See* Glaser, *Culpabité en Droit International Pénal*, 99 RECUEIL DES COURS 473 (1960). Glaser also states at 525 *"...en matière de culpabilité le droit international pénal emprunte les idées et les constructions juridiques au droit intern contre." Id.* at 482. *See* also in support of this position, Graven, *Les Crimes Contre l'Humanité*, 76 RECEUIL DES COURS 433 (1950); and Donnedieu de Vabres, *supra* note 10. Indeed so long as international criminal law is not codified, it must rely on the domestic general part of criminal law. This can be easily accomplished by applying the general part of the criminal law of the state where the crime occured. To attempt the development of a general part for international criminal law from "general principles" of the world's major criminal justice systems, is in the absence of codification, a very arduous task. Professors Donnedieu de Vabres, Graven and Glaser, while generally supporting this view, nevertheless felt that "general principles" are more easily identifiable than does this writer. They probably reached this conclusion because, at that time, the French-civilist system was dominant in the world and the identification of similar principles was easier to make. But the topography of legal systems has changed significantly since the 1960's and the diversity that now exists is much more difficult to reconcile.

acts of states.... The Charter also recognizes a vicarious liability, which responsibility is recognized by most modern systems of law, for acts committed by others in carrying out a common plan or conspiracy to which a defendant has become a party.... [M]en are convicted for acts that they did not personally commit but for which they were held responsible because of membership in illegal combinations or plans or conspiracies.[14]

National criminal law systems vary as to the types and degrees of direct responsibility, participatory responsibility and imputed responsibility, and as to the legal techniques employed to determine their application.[15] There are also wide ranging diversities in national criminal law systems pertaining to conditions which: constitute a bar to criminal responsibility, or justify or excuse the conduct; or, which reduce the level of responsibility; or, mitigate the punishment.[16] In some national legal systems

---

[14]   R. JACKSON, THE NURENBERG CASE AS PRESENTED BY ROBERT H. JACKSON, CHIEF OF COUNSEL FOR THE UNITED STATES 82-83, 88-89 (1971).

Hugo Grotius, who advocated individual criminal responsibility, was, however, contrary to punishing one person for the wrongs of another, thus implicitly he was contrary to various forms of imputed criminal responsibility for the conduct of another. H. GROTIUS, DE JUR E BELLI AC PACIS, Bk. III, Chapt. iv, 643-48 (Carnegie endowment ed. 1925). Grotius also stated: "That no one who was innocent of wrong may be punished for the wrong done by another." id. at 539. He also cites VITTORIA'S, DE JURE BELLI in support of that position. Id. at 723. Gentili was also contrary to collective punishment, see DE JURE BELLI, Bk. III, Ch. viii, pp. 322-27 (Carnegie Endowment ed. 1933).

[15]   For the German system see H.-H. JESCHECK, LEHRBUCH DES STRAFRECHT at 365 et. seq. (4th ed. 1988). For the French system, see G. STAFANI, G. LEVASSEUR, B. BOULOC, DROIT PÈNAL GÈNÈRAL 241 et. seq. (12th ed. 1984) wherein the authors state "...l'intention criminelle réside dans la connaissance ou la conscience chez l'agent qu'il accomplit un acte illicit" ed. at 241; see also R. MERLE AND A. VITU, TRAITE DE DROIT CRIMINEL, at 425 et. seq. (1967); and H. DONNEDIEU DE VABRES, TRAITÈ DE DROIT CRIMINEL ET DE LEGISLATION COMPARÈ (3rd ed. 1947). For the Italian system, see F. MANTOVANI, DIRITTO PENALE: PARTE GENERALE at 303 et. seq. (1988). For the United States system see M.C. BASSIOUNI, SUBSTANTIVE CRIMINAL LAW at 158 et. seq. (1978); H. SILVING, THE CONSTITUENT ELEMENTS OF CRIME (1967); J. HALL, GENERAL PRINCIPLES OF CRIMINAL LAW (2d ed. 1960). For a critical appraisal of the United States system, see G. FLETCHER, RETHINKING CRIMINAL LAW (1978). For a contemporary English Common Law perspective, see H.L.A. HART, PUNISHMENT AND RESPONSIBILITY 187 et. seq. (1968). For a survey of different national conceptions of culpability see Vassalli, Copevolezza, ENCYCLOPEDIA GUIRIDICA TRECCANI, 1-24 (Vol. 6, 1988).

[16]   See JUSTIFICATION AND EXCUSE (A. Eser and G. Fletcher eds. 1987); P.H. ROBINSON, CRIMINAL LAW DEFENSES (4 Vols. 1984); J. HALL, GENERAL PRINCIPLES OF CRIMINAL LAW 360-588 (2d. ed. 1960); and see H.L.A. HART, supra note 15.

the questions of individual, participatory or imputed responsibility, and exonerating factors, are deemed part of the concept of culpability, while in other systems they may be deemed part of the elements or conditions of responsibility. These differences have certain consequences bearing on the criteria for criminal responsibility to be applied to those charged with "crimes against humanity."

Furthermore, national military laws and regulations applicable to military personnel, whether in time of war or peace, differ in some respects from their criminal law counterpart applicable to civilians. This is particularly true with respect to the question of "obedience to superior orders," which is treated differently in the various national military and criminal laws.[17]

Because of discipline's critical importance to a military system, a subordinate is dutybound to obey a superior's orders. A logical corollary of the duty to obey is therefore the defense of "obedience to superior orders." To remove or reduce the defense implicitly removes or reduces the duty to obey. But to maintain the duty to obey requires the imposition of "command responsibility," as discussed below. Thus, military regulations struggle with the extent of the duty to obey and the limits of the defense and also with the legal standards and tests to be applied to "command responsibility" and to the defense of "obedience to superior orders."

Criminal responsibility for "crimes against humanity," by those who do not personally carry out the specific acts, centers on the role of a given person in the chain of events ranging from the highest levels of the decision-making process to any conduct performed before, during, or after the commission of any crime in whole or in part, or conduct, which in some way aided or abetted the commission in whole or in part of any crime. Persons who are part of a collective decision-making body or group are also individually responsible for the group's collective decisions, subsequent actions by all or some of those who carry out decisions to commit specific crimes, and for the harmful results caused by such collective decision-making groups. That responsibility persists even when the accused dissented or opposed the crime or withdrew from the group but did nothing to oppose the wrongful decision or prevent the harm from occuring. Thus, the closer a person is involved in the decision-making process and the less he does to oppose or prevent the decision, or fails to dissociate himself from it, the more likely that person's criminal responsibility will be at stake.

National criminal justice systems also vary significantly as to the applicable legal standard in national criminal adjudication for the determination of responsibility or

---

[17] Compare for example U.S. v. Calley, *infra* note 98 (military); and U.S. v. Barker, 546 F.2d. 940 (D.C. Cir. 1976); and U.S. v. Barker, 514 F.2d. 208 (1975) (criminal).

culpability. One such issue which is particularly relevant to international criminal law is knowledge of the law. Whether knowledge is legally presumed or if the prosecution has to prove actual knowledge are the two divergent legal standards. The application of either one or the other of these standards could have diametrically opposed results with respect to proof of guilt.

The next level of issues is the choice of legal standards and tests. These standards range from the strictly objective to the purely subjective. And the choice of one test over the other can also produce different outcomes as to guilt or innocence.

"Crimes against humanity" are the product of "state action or policy," as discussed in Chapter 6. But only individuals, by commission or omission, are the ones who perform such crimes for or on behalf of, or under color of authority, of their public position, function, or the power they are given by public authority. While that conduct can be ascribable to the state, it extends to each individual person who has been part of the decision-making process or part of the execution of those decisions which resulted in the violation of an existing legal norm. At this point, the question becomes one of apportioning legal responsibility between the individual and the collective decision imputable to the State and to the group of persons. This, at its turn, raises many questions pertaining to the various forms of responsibility, their typology, the means and methods of ascertaining them, the appropriate sanctions and remedies and the enforcement modalities employed. In national systems, certain general doctrines exist which apply to all, or most crimes. In international criminal law, these issues largely depend on the nature of each type of transgression as opposed to their derivation from some abstract principle or doctrine of law, as is the case in most national legal systems. Thus, the elements of criminal responsibility for international crimes which are predicated on "state action or policy," as discussed in Chapter 6, like aggression, "crimes against humanity," genocide, and *apartheid* differ from other international crimes performed by an individual on his own, such as international traffic in drugs or hostage-taking.

All adjudication of individual conduct for purposes of assessing criminal responsibility is necessarily after the fact, and what justifies it is the pre-existence of a law which provides specificity as to the prohibited conduct and whose knowledge is available to those who are expected to heed it or incur the legal consequences of its violation. This three-pronged principle of pre-existing law, specificity of its mandates and knowledge of those to whom it applies is the foundation of every criminal justice system. Yet the boundaries between lawful and unlawful conduct are not always clear in national criminal law,[18] let alone in international criminal law. This is particularly true with respect to the fundamental question of the extent to which a person may be legally held to the knowledge of international criminal law, and more particularly to the requirements of the twenty-two categories of specific international crimes.[19] There are also other questions of law, and mixed questions of law and fact, for which international criminal law does not provide conduct rules. In fact, rules of conduct in international criminal law are mostly inarticulated, because of the absence of a general part. Furthermore, there is no indication as to whether international criminal law is cause-oriented or result-oriented in its inarticulated premises of criminal responsibility.[20]

Some of these unanswered questions make it very difficult to determine other ones such as the secondary basis of criminal responsibility provided by various national criminal law techniques[21] and which are also not articulated in international criminal law. Yet the three general categories of imputability found in the world's major criminal justice systems namely: responsibility for the conduct of another, responsibility for completed crimes arising out of partial conduct, and responsibility for lawful conduct producing an unlawful result, have been relied upon in international prosecutions, but without any explanation.[22] Furthermore, as stated above, international criminal law does not distinguish between risk-creation and risk-taking, which is particularly relevant in the determination of causal responsibility,[23] whose consequences with respect to lesser included offenses are quite significant. This is particularly true with respect to homicides in "crimes against humanity" which are not

---

[18] *See* Robinson, *Rules of Conduct and Principles of Adjudication*, 57 U. OF CHIC. L. REV. 729 (1990).

[19] *See e.g.* BASSIOUNI DRAFT CODE.

[20] *See*, Schulhofer, *Harm and Punishment: A Critique of Emphasis on the Results of Conduct in the Criminal Law,* 122 U. PA. L. REV. 1497 (1974). For a comparison between the United States, English, and German systems *see* G. Fletcher, *supra* note 15 at 759-69 (1978). For a legal-philosophical perspective based on positivism in the common law of England *see* H.L.A. Hart, *supra* note 15 at 13-14 (1968).

[21] For some views of United States problems of criminal imputability and their common law origins *see e.g.* Robinson, *Imputed Criminal Liability*, 93 YALE L.J. 613 (1984); M.C. BASSIOUNI, SUBSTANTIVE CRIMINAL LAW 140-158 and 201-22 (1978); Kirscheimer, *Criminal Omissions*, 55 HARV. L. REV. 615 (1942). For an English Common Law approach *see* J. BENTHAM, COLLECTED WORKS at 164 (1859).

[22] *See e.g.* Chapters 4 and 5.

[23] *See supra* note 20.

"murder" and could be part of "extermination," which does not necessarily include only "murder."[24]

International criminal law does not generally provide for any legal test such as the common law's "ordinary reasonable person"[25] which is so important for the subjective or mental element and for the determination of criminal responsibility and exonerating factors.[26] In most legal systems, these factors are deemed to remove the existence of a culpable state of mind, which is one of the basic requirements for criminal responsibility in the world's major criminal justice systems, even though there are many divergences in and among these systems as to fundamental doctrines and their application.[27] Indeed, the intersection of responsibility and exoneration is the grey area of criminal law in the world's major criminal justice systems, and it is even more so in international criminal law.[28]

Individual criminal responsibility raises, in international criminal law, the same set of legal issues that exist in the national criminal law of all states; starting with concepts of responsibility and culpability. Indeed, the world's major legal systems differ in their conceptual and doctrinal approaches as to the legal bases of criminal responsibility and culpability. This is reflected in the use of such diverse terminology as criminality, culpability, responsibility, and punishability. In some legal systems these terms are predicated on another level of legal abstractions represented by value-laden terms which have different legal significance and impact, they include such terms as: right, wrong, and blameworthiness.

Criminal accountability is also subject to the requirements of certain legal elements, which vary from one legal system to the other. But these elements are also represented by legally significant, though abstract terms such as: *actus reus, mens rea, culpa, dolus, dolus eventualis,* and even causation.

Some legal systems rely on an inarticulated choice of values in ranking the moral-legal significance of these concepts, others do not. Also, the difference in approach and

---

[24]   For a discussion of "murder" and "extermination" *see* Chapter 8 at 290.

[25]   Even though it appears to have become the accepted test with respect to such doctrines as "military necessity," "command responsibility," and defense of "obedience to superior order". *See particularly* Y. DINSTEIN, L.C. GREEN, L. KEIZJER AND E. MÜLLER-RAPPARD *infra* at note 62.

[26]   *See e.g.* Chapter 10; and also *supra* note 16.

[27]   *See* Vassalli, *Colpevolezza, supra* note 15.

[28]   *See* Greenwalt, *The Perplexing Borders of Justification and Excuse*, 89 COLUM. L. REV. 1897 (1989); and Fletcher, *The Right and the Reasonable*, 98 HARV. L. REV. 949 (1985).

in the linkage between: concepts of accountability, the required legal elements for criminal responsibility, and exonerating conditions, vary greatly between the world's major criminal justice systems and they also vary within these systems from country to country. Contemporary penal systems cover this entire range of variables, many without internal consistency, thus providing even a wider range of variables. For example, the German penal system recognizes the concepts of *Schuld* (culpability), *rechtswidrishkiet* (wrongfulness of the act) and *unrecht* (wrongdoing but devoid of culpability or moral connotation). Important distinctions, also exist with respect to the subjective element in the Romanist-Civilist theories which rely on *dolus, dolus eventualis and culpa,* which are the Common Law's counterpart of both specific and general intent. *Dolus* is the fundamental and original form of intent in the Romanist-Civilist and Germanic legal systems. In the latter legal system, *dolus* includes the theories of *Vorsatztheorie* and *Schuldtheorie*. *Dolus* is equivalent to the Common Law's specific intent, and does not include general intent. The latter, represented by recklessness, is found in the Romanist-Civilist-Germanic legal systems' theories of *dolus eventualis* and *culpa,* (Italian), *faute* (French) and *Fahrlässigkeit* (German). All of these legal systems criminalize conduct which ranges from morally blameworthy to socially harmful conduct and each one characterizes responsibility or culpability for such conduct in a different way. All penal law systems have developed a variety of forms of imputed criminal responsibility for certain types of conduct and it is quite unclear as to which one of these different conceptual approaches can be said to apply in international criminal law.

Lastly, it should be noted that national legal systems also differ as to the legal standards and tests they employ to establish legal responsibility and exoneration therefrom. Thus, some systems, mostly common law or common law inspired ones, apply what is referred to as the strictly objective standard to which the applicable test is the mythical ordinary reasonable person in the same circumstances. But, the application of these standards and tests may differ within these systems depending on the type of crime, and that is particularly significant in cases where evidentiary norms create presumptions and shift the burden of proof. Others which derive from the Romanist-Civilist or Germanic tradition, or are inspired therefrom, apply a subjective standard for the more serious offenders, often including motive as part of intent. In some of these legal systems, and with respect to some crimes, one can also find purely utilitaristic approaches which focus on the resulting harm irrespective of particular moral, ethical or legal considerations.

To attempt a synthesis of such a wide range of diversity, which has only been illustrated above, makes the possibility of ascertaining "general principles of law" beyond some fundamental and basic generalities, very difficult, if not impossible. Of course, if the international law requirements for ascertaining "general principles," as discussed in Chapter 7, were changed and allowed extrapolations based on subjective or value-oriented criteria, then it would be possible to formulate such "general principles." But then, it would be akin to a process of progressive codification and it would violate the "principles of legality," as discussed in Chapter 3, particularly if it would be undertaken after the fact.

Most general part issues have yet to be settled in international criminal law. Some of them have been addressed, though inconclusively or insufficiently, in the course of the proceedings before the IMT, IMTFE and Subsequent Proceedings, and some have been decided in the judgments, though mostly without much explanation. But it is shockingly noteworthy that the 1991 version of the Draft Code of Crimes against the Peace and Security of Mankind does not address these issues,[29] thus further reducing its already questionable value as a useful codification of a selective portion of international criminal law, as discussed in Chapter 11.

But, if there is one universally recognized "general principle of law" which can be found in the world's major criminal justice systems, it is that of individual criminal responsibility. The Charter, thus properly recognized it. It is also a basic principle in international criminal law, as evidenced by its explicit or implicit recognition in all 315 international instruments adopted between 1815-1989. Certain corollaries of the principle of individual responsibility also enjoy universal recognition, even though their meanings, contents, and applications differ. They are: the accused's knowledge of the law, and his intent to violate it.

Imputed Criminal Responsibility in the Law of the Charter

As stated above, imputed criminal responsibility varies from one legal system to another. Its different doctrinal bases, and applications also vary within each legal system. It is, therefore, difficult to find sufficient commonality among the world's major legal systems to arrive at a "general principle."

The drafters of the Charter, however, arrived at a formulation in Article 6(a). It states:

---

[29] *See* Draft Code of Crimes Document Section F.5, non-retroactivity article 10, and *non bis im idem* article 9.

Leaders, organizers and accomplices participating in the formulation or execution of a common plan or conspiracy to commit any of the foregoing crimes are responsible for all acts performed by any person in execution of such plan.

On its face, such a formulation derives from the Common Law and it does not have much in common with the Romanist-Civilist-Germanic systems.

The IMT found that this provision did not create a new and separate offence but was merely designed to establish a basis for the responsibility of persons participating in a common plan to prepare, initiate, and wage aggressive war. The IMT did not rely on this provision for "crimes against humanity," though it relied on a concept of vicarious criminal responsibility, better known at Common Law, as flowing from aiding and abetting. The IMT also did not rely on conspiracy in establishing responsibility for belonging to a "criminal organization;" it did so on a different basis which is discussed below. The confusion between different forms of vicarious criminal responsibility and conspiracy later induced the ILC's error in its formulation of the Nuremburg Principles wherein Principle VII held:

Complicity in the commission of a crime against peace, a war crime, or a crime against humanity as set forth in Principle VI is a crime under international law.

This is clearly contrary to the express linkage in the Charter's Article 6(a), as quoted above, between conspiracy and "crimes against peace." The error of the ILC may have been induced by the subtle difference between individual responsibility for participating in the "common plans" of aggression and responsibility for membership in "criminal organizations" which included all three crimes. Even Justice Jackson seems to have fallen into the same confusion when in his *Preface* to the *Report to the President of the United States* he broadly stated:

The charter also enacts the principle that individuals rather than states are responsible for criminal violations of international law and applies to such lawbreakers the principle of conspiracy by which one who joins in a common plan to commit crime becomes responsible for the acts of any other conspirator in executing the plan.[30]

---

[30]   Jackson Report at ix.

But then it should be stated that the cases involving "criminal organizations," as discussed below, are quite confusing as to the basis of criminal responsibility on which they rely. In contrast, the IMTFE, whose Charter was similar to the IMT's, was unrestricted by the narrow concept of individual criminal responsibility and they freely applied their own version of guilt by association. The IMT's record is in this respect far superior to that of the IMTFE, as it only relied in a limited way on "common plan" or "conspiracy" with respect to "crimes against peace" as defined in Article 6(a), but not for other crimes. As to the concept of responsibility for those who "directed, organized, instigated or were accomplices," the target of this basis for criminal responsibility was the decision-making of the ruling Nazi regime. And this is entirely different from the more generalized bases of criminal responsibility under Article II Para. 2 of CCL 10. The latter simply assimilated or joined in one category of criminal responsibility many categories applied differently in the world's major criminal justice systems. Thus, it assimilates those who: conspired to have the crime performed; ordered it; performed it; aided and abetted in its planning, preparation, performance, and concealment; and, those who voluntarily participated in a "criminal organization" implicated in the commission of Article 6 crimes. No distinctions on gradations were made as between principles (and their diverse degrees), accessories (and their diverse degrees) and the different aspects of responsibility for the conduct of another. Such an approach is in essential contradiction with basic principles of individual criminal responsibility and the individualization of punishment existing in the world's major criminal justice systems.

The drafters of CCL 10 clearly wanted to avoid such legal distinctions which would have mired these trials in technical legal arguments for years. They, like the London Charter's drafters, were driven by the facts and the defendants they knew would be accused were to be those who were factually part of or connected to the decision-making and senior level of execution in the chain of command. Above all, they wanted a swift process which would express legally sanctioned retribution of abhorrent collective and also individual conduct.

Articles 9 and 10 of the Charter charged organizations with criminal responsibility, without defining it, and extended such responsibility subject to certain conditions, to its individual components. This notion of group or collective criminal responsibility is different from that of state criminal responsibility,[31] but it is in contradiction with the

---

[31] *See* BASSIOUNI DRAFT CODE at 49-52; Munch, *Criminal Responsibity of States*, 1 BASSIOUNI ICL 123 (1986); F. MALEKIAN, INTERNATIONAL CRIMINAL RESPONSIBILITY OF STATES, (1985). 1991 Draft Code of Crimes, article 5; the ILC Draft Principles of State Responsibility, Article 19 and I. BROWNLIE, SYSTEM

notion of individual criminal responsibility asserted above and discussed in Chapter 5. This issue is particularly significant in light of two other questions, namely: whether there was any basis in international law to apply such a concept of criminal responsibility, and to what extent does it satisfy the requirements of legality, as discussed in Chapter 3. It is this writer's conclusion that both questions should be answered in the negative.

The IMT and Subsequent Proceedings judgments took the approach that "criminal organizations" were in the nature of a "conspiracy in action."[32] But, rather than holding individuals responsible if they were part of a criminal organization, the tribunals held that organizations could be deemed criminal as a result of the individual criminal responsibility of its members.[33] Thereafter, individual members, on certain conditions, could be found guilty of participating in a criminal organization. This completely lopsided approach was intended to serve only one purpose, and that is to brand as criminal such organization as the SS.[34] The problem, however, is what to do with such an anomalous precedent, particularly in light of the trend in the world's major criminal justice systems and in international criminal law to develop a viable approach to the criminal responsibility of states[35] and that of organizations, in addition to individual criminal responsibility. But as the codification of these responsibility bases have yet to occur, it is useful to remember what Professor Donnedieu de Vabres, a judge at the IMT, lamented only one year after the judgment, namely that the absence

---

OF THE LAW AND NATIONS: STATE RESPONSIBILITY 32-33 (vols. 1983). *See also* for earlier works on state responsibility, J. PERSONAZ, LA RÉPARATION DU PRÉJUDICCE EN DROIT INTERNATIONAL PUBLIC (1939); C. EAGLETON, THE RESPONSIBILITY OF STATES IN INTERNATIONAL LAW (1928); C. DE VISSCHER, LA RESPONSIBILITÉ DES ETATS (1924); V.V. PELLA, LA CRIMINALITÉ COLLECTIVE DES ETATS ET LE DROIT PÉNAL DE L'AVENIR (2d. ed. 1925).

[32]   *See* IMT Judgment at 270; and Donnedieu de Vabres, *supra* note 10 at 543.

[33]   Thus the Gestapo was not declared a criminal organization until Kaltenbrunner, who was one of its leaders, was found guilty. *See* Document Section C.4.

[34]   Of the six organizations charged in the Indictment, only three were found criminal, they are: The S.S.; the Gestapo, and the S.D.; and the leadership of organizations of the Nazi Party. The other three which were not found to be criminal organizations are: The S.A.; the Military High Command; and the Reich Cabinet. But individual members of these organizations were found guilty either at the IMT or Subsequent; Proceedings. *See* Document Section C.4.

[35]   *Supra* note 31.

of any codification following Nuremberg can have dire consequences on international justice. He said that it would be "... *funeste au prestige de la justice internationale.*"[36]

The IMT, most mindful of the complexity of such a basis for criminal responsibility, astutely predicated it on three conditions. They are:

1. the public activities of the organization must include one of the Article 6 crimes;
2. the majority of the members of the organization must be volunteers;
3. the majority of the members of the organization must have been knowledgeable or conscious of the criminal nature of the organization's activity.

While the first two of these conditions can be objectively ascertained, the third one is more difficult. But what none of these questions address, singularly or collectively, is how to specifically apply the consequences of a finding of group responsibility? Does it extend to all the members in the same way, and thus become a form of collective strict accountability? The IMT held that there should be an additional finding, namely that each individual have been a volunteer member of the organization. But it did not require that each member have specific knowledge that the organization's purpose was the commission of international crimes.[37] Instead a variety of tests were used to hold persons accountable to knowledge of the organization's moral wrongdoing. To a large extent, one can conclude that a finding of an organization as criminal because a *prima facie* showing against persons individually accused, which they could rebut by showing that they lacked knowledge. Thus, the concept of participatory criminal responsibility articulated in the Law of Charter is that of presumptive individual criminality arising out of the mere voluntary participation in an organization declared to be criminal, on the basis of the above-stated three conditions, but the accused could rebut the presumption. Such a rebuttal would be in the nature of factual denials, and mixed questions of law and facts pertaining to a person's knowledge and intent. These questions of fact and law, at their turn, raise the issue of what legal standard and test to apply. Considering the wide differences between objective and subjective approaches to the adjudicative determination of intent in the world's major criminal justice systems,

---

[36]   *See* Donnedieu de Vabres, *supra* note 10 at 546.

[37]   *Id.* at 548.

the legal issues raised above are far from resolved. It should be noted, however, that a presumptive approach could violate the "general principle of law" of presumption of innocence, which since World War II, has been specifically expressed in international and regional human rights instruments.[38] But it should also be noted that the IMT judgment, and individual judgments in the Subsequent Proceedings repeatedly affirmed the Common Law's principles of presumption of innocence and proof of guilt beyond a reasonable doubt to be established by the prosecution.

It is also notable that the Charter did not provide for any penalties, but that CCL 10 in Article II, para. 2, did, with respect to responsibility for belonging to a "criminal organization." These penalties ranged from the deprivation of certain civil rights to death. Such a range of penalties promulgated after the fact, for a concept of criminal responsibility that already stretches the requirements of legality, may well be said to violate the "principles of legality," as discussed in Chapter 3.

"Crimes against humanity," are by their very nature the product of "state action or policy," as discussed in Chapter 6. What then is the purpose of a concept of group responsibility under the rubric "criminal organizations"? It would have been so much simpler to have relied on German doctrines of imputed criminal responsibility, and participation and to have achieved a better result. One obvious reason why the Allies did not pursue this approach was their rejection of everything German. Another reason may well be that they feared that German criminal law, which they did not know too well, could have defeated the ultimate goal of finding the designated defendants not criminally responsible. But, it could also have been a consequence of the strategic approach to the post-World War II prosecutions in Germany. This approach was that the IMT dealt with the "majors," CCL 10 dealt with the second echelon of those less than majors, and with the "minors." Allied and German Courts would deal with the rest. It could very well be that for expediency's sake and because of the large number of potential defendants, the Allies found the concept of participatory criminal responsibility would give the prosecutors and judges maximum flexibility, and result in swift adjudication. Thus, Article II, para. 2 of CCL 10 became the legislative basis for this new concept of criminal responsibility. But it should be noted, as discussed in Chapter 1, that CCL 10 was not to be deemed part of international law, as it was passed by the legislative authority over Germany, the Allied Control Council, in view of Germany's unconditional surrender. Thus, it must be concluded, on the basis of this

---

[38] *See* Universal Declaration, Article 11; International Covenant on Civil and Political Rights, Article 14; European Human Rights Convention, Article 6; Inter-American Human Rights Convention, Article 8; African Human Rights Convention, Article 7; Draft Arab Human Rights Charter, Article 5.

reasoning, that the CCL 10 and its trials do not constitute a valid international legal precedent, except for its affirmations of certain "general principles." This means that the participatory principles of criminal responsibility that the CCL 10 trials enunciated, prescinding from their validity then, have no subsequent validity in international criminal law. And that is certainly for the best, particularly since the trend in international criminal law on this point is contrary to Article II, para. 1 of CCL 10.[39] The judges at the Subsequent Proceedings were, however, mindful of the troublesome questions posed by Article II, para. 2, as evidenced by the prosecution's opening statement in *The Farben Case* stated:

> This provision, we believe, is not intended to attach criminal guilt automatically to the holders of high positions, but means, rather, that the legitimate and reasonable inferences are to be drawn from the fact that a defendant held such a position, and places upon him the burden of countering the inferences which must otherwise be drawn.

But then the Tribunal went on to state:

> In weighing the evidence and in determining the ultimate facts of guilt or innocence with respect to each defendant, we have sought to apply these fundamental principles of Anglo-American criminal law:
>
> 1. There can be no conviction without proof of personal guilt;
> 2. Guilt must be proved beyond a reasonable doubt;
> 3. Each defendant is presumed to be innocent, and that presumption abides with him throughout the trial;
> 4. The burden of proof is, at all times, upon the prosecution;
> 5. If from credible evidence two reasonable inferences may be drawn, one of guilt and the other of innocence, the latter must prevail. (United States vs. Friedrich Flick, *et al*, Case 5, American Military Tribunal IV, Nurenberg, Germany).

---

[39] These critical views have also been expressed by a number of commentators shortly after the IMT's judgment. *See* Donnedieu de Vabres *supra* note 10 at 546; H. H. JESCHECK, DIE VERANTWORLTICHKEIT DER STÄATSORGAN SEIT NÜREMBERG at 400 *et seq.* (1952); H. MEYROWITZ *supra* note 10 at 365-385; A. VON KNEREIM, THE NUREMBERG TRIALS at 195-230 (1959); Wright, *International Law and Guilt by Association*, 43 AJIL 746 (1947).

In considering the many conflicts in the evidence and the multitude of circumstances from which inferences may be drawn, as disclosed by the voluminous record before us, we have endeavored to avoid the danger of viewing the conduct of the defendants wholly in retrospect. On the contrary, we have sought to determine their knowledge, their state of mind, and their motives from the situation as it appeared, or should have appeared, to them at the time.[40]

Von Knierein comments upon this question by reference to the *Krupp* and *Farben* cases as follows:

In *The Krupp Case* the prosecution went even further and called the provision to establish "at least--at the very least" a presumption of guilt. But none of the Nuremberg Tribunals seems to have gone so far. In *The Farben Case*, Judge Hebert expressly took up the problem in his concurrent opinion, stating quite correctly that:

Paragraph 2(f) does not shift the burden of proof, which remains at all times with the prosecution. Neither does it change the presumption of innocence.[41]

Professor Quincy Wright an advisor to the United States prosecution team who was also consulted on the drafting of the Charter and was a supporter of the post-World War II prosecutions had strong misgivings about "guilt by association," as he called it. He stated:

Advanced systems of criminal law accept the principle that guilt is personal. Guilt is established by evidence that the acts and intentions of the individual were

---

[40]   8 CCL Trials at 1108. Judge Herbert on Count Two of the Charge held:

The indictment charges that the acts were committed unlawfully, wilfully, and knowingly, and that the defendants are criminally responsible "in that they were principals in, accessories to, ordered, abetted, took a consenting part in, were connected with plans and enterprises involving, and were members of organizations or groups, including Farben, which were connected with the commisssion of said crimes."

Id. at 1128.

[41]   *See* A. VON KNEREIM, *supra* note 39 at 206.

criminal. Evidence concerning the acts or intentions of persons with whom he was associated, the programs or policies of organizations of which he was a member, or the behavior of groups or people with whom he was classed have sometimes been admitted as indications of the bad character of the accused, but, in common law, only to rebut the defendant's effort to prove his good character. No matter how bad his character by general reputation or association, the accused must be considered innocent unless his guilt is established by evidence that he himself committed, attempted, or intended the crime charged.[42]

---

[42] Wright, *International Law and Guilt by Association*, 43 AJIL 746, 747 (1946). He further stated:

As I read International Law, the idea of state criminal responsibility has not been favored. The cases where that has been suggested are rare, and on the whole, it has been considered that the state should be only civilly responsible; that is, only bound to make reparations for damages which have resulted from its violation of International Law. I would suggest, on the other hand, that criminal responsibility is based upon psychological considerations and ought therefore to be a responsibility only of individuals. We should, therefore, recognize that the individual is criminally responsible when he commits an act which is an offense against the law of nations, and that the state cannot cover such an act with a blanket of immunity if it is itself under an international obligation not to permit such acts, even though it may be civilly liable to make reparation for the damage.

Id. at 748-49. He quotes A. NUSSBAUM, A CONCISE HISTORY OF THE LAW OF NATIONS (1947) for the proposition that reprisals and other forms of collective, and thus presumably indiscriminate, use of force were a barbaric practice that modern international law does not countenence. *Id.* at 34. *See also supra* note 14 for the positions of Grotius, Vittoria, and Gentili.

Wright goes on to state:

It has also been suggested that the Nuremberg Charter, in authorizing the Tribunal to declare organizations criminal, thus creating a presumption of criminality against all the members of such organizations, accepted the concept of guilt by association. However, in its interpretation of this provision, the Tribunal limited the liability flowing from a finding that an organization was criminal to those who were voluntary members of the organization aware of its criminal purposes at the time the organization was engaging in criminal acts. An individual defendant was assured an opportunity to defend himself on all of these points. With this interpretation the concept of criminal organization was identified with that of conspiracy. No individual could be found guilty unless, in intention or act, he participated in a criminal conspiracy.

Id at 754.

ELEMENTS OF CRIMINAL RESPONSIBILITY

National legal systems vary as to the types, standards and methods of assessing and determining criminal responsibility for participation in its various forms and degrees. In general, one can distinguish between participation in the decision-making and participation in the actual carrying out of the decision. Obviously the more segmented or compartmentalized the carrying out of an unlawful decision, the more difficult it is to establish the knowledge and intent of the person charged with the ultimate consequences of the unlawful act. None of the international criminal law instruments elaborated to date have dealt with these questions. The Geneva Convention of 1949 and the Additional Protocols of 1977, the Genocide Convention and the *Apartheid* Convention have only touched upon these questions with general references and by implication. The 1991 Draft Code of Crimes does not adequate deal with any of these questions.

Knowledge of the Law and Intent

The mental or subjective element is required in major crimes, and in some lesser ones, in almost every legal system of the world. It is considered the essential basis for the determination of criminal responsibility or culpability, depending upon whether national legal systems consider the mental element an element of responsibility or culpability. But in all systems it is predicated on a number of legal assumptions or presumptions, most notably: freedom of will, mental capacity and knowledge of the law.

The London and Tokyo Charters Article 6(c) and 5(c) and CCL 10 Article II, 1(c) declared that the crimes defined are punishable irrespective of whether they constitute a violation of the laws of the State where they were performed. While this provision removes the effect of national legislation designed to "legalize" what would otherwise be criminal,[43] the implications of this provision carry over into the mental element. Thus, if a person engaged in conduct on the basis of a superior's order and relied on the existence of national legislation that permitted such conduct, then for such a person the order cannot be patently unlawful unless that individual has specific knowledge of the wrongdoing. Without such knowledge there is no objective basis to ascertain the existence of intent which would have to include knowledge of the illegality or conscious wrongdoing. The outcome would be exoneration from culpability. Knowledge

---

[43]   *See* Chapter 6 at 253.

of wrongdoing, however, is distinguished by positivists from knowledge of committing a violation of the law. The first conception derives from materialism, while the second from positivism, and the choice between the two is essentially a question of legal philosophy, as discussed in Chapter 2.

In Romanist-Civilist legal systems the problems related to intent and knowledge are more acute than in the Common Law system. In these systems, the mental element is called, *l'élément moral de l'infraction*, which highlights the subjective dimension of intent.[44] In the German system, knowledge does not mean the specific or formal illegal character of the conduct, but its general prohibition or punishability.[45] German legal doctrine and jurisprudence debated that question extensively in the 1920's, particularly with respect to the post-World War I Leipzig trials.[46] But the views of the German dogmatic school, in contradiction to other views, gave rise to many subtleties as to the distinction between the various aspects of knowledge of the lawfulness or unlawfulness of the conduct and the prohibition. The judges and prosecutors at the IMT and Subsequent Proceedings, who were not German scholars, would have been at a significant disadvantage in facing German defense counsels had they been permitted to argue these questions. This is probably another reason that German law was not relied upon in the American, British and French CCL 10 proceedings, though it was relied upon before German courts when they did not apply CCL 10 but German law.[47]

The critical problem with knowledge, or lack thereof can be characterized in the Nazi era, as well as in all totalitarian regimes, in negative terms: it is the will not to know the essential nature of one's wrongdoing or that of others, which one aids and abets.[48] Whether international law had, by 1945, imposed a duty on individuals that went beyond the positive legal norms of national systems is surely questionable. Yet

---

[44]   *See* G. STEFANI, G. LEVASSEUR AND B. BOULAC, *supra* note 15; R. MERLE AND A. VITU, *id.;* and H. DONNEDIEU DE VABRES, *id.*

[45]   *See* H. H. JESCHECK, *supra* 15 at 252-54.

[46]   *See* Hofacker, *Die Leipziger Kriegsverbrecher prozess,* ZSTW 649 *et. seq.* (1922).

[47]   *See* H. MEYROVITZ, *supra* note 10 at 197-98.

[48]   In the case of Funk, the Minister of Economy and President of the Reischbank, he claimed not to have seen nor to have knowledge that the gold deposited by the S.S. with his authorization, in the bank's vaults (actually in the basement of the building where his office was located) had come from dispossessing Jews, including gold that had been removed from the teeth and glasses of those who had been sent to the death camps. Assuming this contention to be true, Mr. Funk must have gone to great length not to see or know what he claimed he didn't see or know existed in his own basement and which was placed there by his authorization. *See* 1 IMT 326.

360

Article 6 specifically enunciated that its provisions applied irrespective of national law. The closest analogy to such a policy is the right, or duty, to disobey an order which is patently unlawful. The German military regulations applicable at the time required it.[49] And later, the Geneva Conventions also contained similar provisions on the nonexecution of a patently unlawful order.[50]

The Roman law maxim, *ignorantia iuris neminem scusat* (ignorance of the law is no defense to anyone) is recognized in the world's major criminal justice systems and as such it constitutes a "general principle" of law applicable to international criminal law. This presumption is, however, predicated on the assumption that the law in question should be known to the person upon whom it imposes criminal responsibility whenever it is breached. The world's major criminal justice systems assume that the proper promulgation and dissemination of information about laws fulfill the legal requirement, which permits the operation of the legal presumption that the criminal law is known to all. Such a presumption of knowledge of the law thus rationalizes the validity of the maxim *ignorantia non scusat*. But the validity of this presumption is not without question or challenge in legal systems, particularly with the contemporary inflation of criminal and quasi-criminal legislation in all countries of the world. Thus, if the question arises in national legal systems as to the reasonableness of this presumption, it surely also arises in international criminal law. What then can be reasonably attributed to the public knowledge of all or some persons throughout the world about international crimes? And what is the degree of specificity of knowledge as to the legal infraction which is required in order to insure the legal validity of such a presumption?

The inarticulated premises of this legal presumption in the national legal systems is that the criminal law is known to everyone because crimes are an emanation of social values which national communities deem so significant that they seek to protect them through penal sanctions, thus, their prohibition is a matter of public and general awareness. Therefore, the absence of these inarticulated premises would deny the legal support for the validity of the irrebuttable presumption of knowledge of the criminal law. Applying these basic considerations to international criminal law in light of the peculiarities of that legal system raises a number of closely related legal issues. They are: 1) whether the presumption of knowledge of international criminal law satisfies

---

[49]   *See* E. SCHMIDT, MILITARSTRAFRECHT (1936). For a German perspective on breaches of the law of war, *see* F. BAUER, DIE KRIEGSVERBRECHERVOR GERICHT (1945).

[50]   As a result of the Geneva Conventions, the military laws of all the parties thereto include a similar provision.

the "principles of legality;" 2) whether it is rebuttable or irrebuttable; 3) whether legal defenses can include ignorance of the law as exoneration by way of justification or excuse; 4) whether ignorance of the law can be viewed as a factor eliminating criminal intent; and 5) whether ignorance of the law, if it is not considered as exonerating, can nevertheless be considered in mitigation of punishment.

The presumption of knowledge of international criminal law is predicated on whether a given international crime satisfies the "principles of legality" of that discipline, as discussed in Chapter 3. But, if legality, at its turn, is predicated on the validity of the presumption of knowledge, the inquiry is a vicious circle, one remanding to the other thus assuming the character of a perpetual *renvoi*. To break the vicious cycle, each of these two concepts must be considered independently of the other.

The peculiarities of international criminal law often result in the formulation of international crimes in a way that is less certain and less specific than what the "principles of legality" in many of the world's major criminal justice systems would require, as discussed in Chapter 3. Thus, the presumption of knowledge of international criminal law cannot be irrebuttable because its inarticulated premises of public knowledge, and certainty and sufficiency of content would be lacking and that would violate minimum standards of legality.

Not all international crimes, however, lack certainty or specificity of content, though their levels differ from crime to crime. The reasons for these differences are: 1) the absence of a singular legislative source; 2) the occasional and even episodic process by which conventional international criminal law develops; 3) as a consequence of the above, the absence of cohesion, harmony and consistency in drafting international instruments; and, 4) the inherent uncertainty and lack of specificity of non-codified customary international criminal law. Thus, the doctrinal dilemma for international criminal law is:

1)   to accept, reject or qualify the presumption of knowledge of international criminal law;

2)   if the presumption is accepted in principle, is it realistic to assume the world public's general knowledge of international criminal law (which is the inarticulated premises upon which the presumed knowledge of national criminal law is founded);

3)   if the presumption is rejected, does it result in a requirement of proving in each case the individual's specific knowledge of the international crime that is charged; and,

4)   if the presumption is accepted as rebuttable or qualified, does ignorance of the law become part of the mental element of the specific crime (which when established, results in removing criminal responsibility) or would it only be a mitigating factor in punishment.

There are two doctrinal approaches as to the presumption of knowledge and ignorance of international criminal law. One approach is to treat the question as part of the mental element of criminal responsibility; and, the other is to treat it as an evidentiary question needed to prove the mental element. The consequence of the first hypothesis is that absence of knowledge or culpability negates responsibility altogether and with respect to the second, it becomes an exonerating factor in the nature of a legal excuse or non-punishability. In both of these instances, however, there are also questions of legal standards and burdens of proof which will depend on a variety of doctrinal approaches as to the questions raised in the various legal systems. Thus, irrebuttable presumptions need no proof by the prosecution and only in cases of rebuttable presumption can the defense raise the question. In this case another question arises and that is the quantum of proof required to rebut the presumption.

Having demonstrated the wide diversity in the world's major criminal justice systems, it is clear that some judgments are needed in international criminal law, and it is this writer's conclusions that they should be as follows:

1)   The presumption of knowledge of international criminal law should exist as a policy-choice for the same reasons recognized in the world's major criminal justice systems, even though in this case with lesser degrees of validity because of the questionable inarticulated premises of public awareness and public knowledge upon which the presumption is founded. But precisely for this reason, the presumption must be rebuttable and not irrebuttable, otherwise it would violate the minimum standards of legality.

2)   Ignorance of the existence of international criminal law is in principle no defense, but ignorance of a specific crime would be a legal excuse if it negates the mental element of the crime.

3)   If the international crime also exists in the national criminal law of the individual's state of nationality or residence, ignorance of the international criminal law should not be deemed as negating the mental element.

4)   Ignorance of a specific violation of international criminal law should, however, be taken into account in mitigation of punishment.

5)   International criminal law should not recognize the principle of strict criminal responsibility, that is responsibility without intent, and intent presupposes actual knowledge of the law.

6)   None of the above should affect other basis of criminal responsibility such as those pertaining to omissions, or responsibility for the conduct of another, except that none of these and other principles of imputed criminal responsibility should be based on strict responsibility.

For the reasons stated above, the legal presumption of knowledge of international criminal law should be deemed a rebuttable presumption. This rebuttable presumption includes knowledge of the illegality of the act performed, based on the standard of reasonableness. Notwithstanding this standard of reasonableness, an individual may present the defense of ignorance of the law. Thus, this legal standard is not ultimately objective, but subjective. This approach reconciles the common law and the Romanistic-Civilist-Germanic legal systems. This standard may be gleaned from various instruments on the regulation of armed conflicts, particularly with respect to norms concerning discretionary judgment, as in the defense of military necessity. With respect to these and other issues, both national and international regulation of armed conflicts indicate that a reasonableness test is applicable, but not as a purely objective one, since it includes the subjective knowledge and intent of the accused.[51] The test for this legal standard can be formulated as follows:

> Whether the ordinary reasonable person, possessed of the intellectual capacity and background of the actor, should have reasonably known or believed the act to be unlawful under international or national law.

---

[51]   *See supra* note 25 and *infra* note 62.

Thus, an actor who knows the act to be unlawful would clearly be found to have satisfied this mental element, as would the actor who intentionally commits the act, with malice at Common Law or with motive in the Romanist-Civilist-Germanic theories of the subjective element. Complete knowledge of all aspects of the international criminality of the act is therefore not necessary. It could also be argued that conscious knowledge of moral wrongdoing should be enough, at least enough to trigger a duty to inquire.[52] Such an inquiry could, however, lead to an interpretation of the law or of a mixed question of law and facts. The outcome of this inquiry could thus lead to the negation of intent and exoneration from criminal responsibility or culpability, as the applicable substantive law would deem such condition to be.

"Crimes against humanity" are *mala in se* acts, which are manifestly contrary to the norms, rules and principles of international criminal law, and to those of the world's major ciminal justice systems, for which most reasonable persons would not have consciousness of wrongdoing. Consequently, a perpetrator cannot take refuge in the Act of State Doctrine or in the defense of "obedience to superior orders" unless exigent circumstances necessitated compliance with such orders, as discussed in Chapter 10. Such a perpetrator must necessarily face individual criminal responsibility for whatever violative acts he committed and for his aiding and abetting others in the commission of such acts. Whether such a perpetrator is found culpable is a question of judicial ascertainment based on the facts and on the applicable substantive criminal law. The latter depends on whether the adjudication jurisdiction will apply its own law, the law of the state wherein the act was committed, or if it is different, the law of the actor's nationality or that of the victim's nationality. International criminal law must, therefore, necessarily rely on "general principles of law," which will either emerge from the national legal systems, or from relevant international legal experiences and practices to determine what substantive law the adjudication jurisdiction will apply.[53]

---

[52] R. CARTIER, LES SECRETS DE LA GUERRE DÉVOILÉS PAR NUREMBERG (1967) wherein the author at 20, reports that Field Marshall Halder stated at his trial that Hitler had told his generals in 1941, that since the U.S.S.R. did not ratify the 1907 Hague Convention, its provisions, particularly those applying to POWs and civilians should not be respected. It is this writer's assumption that, if Hitler, who was not a jurist, made such a statement, it was because some legal adviser had suggested it. Such advice must have been founded on the notion that the 1907 Hague Convention abrogated the 1899 one, and that the Hague rules were not part of the customary international law. But the point here is that knowledge of the law did exist, even though it was erroneously interpreted. And that, at its turn, raises a question as to the consequences of mistake of law which bears on intent and consequently on criminal responsibility. *Id.* at 359.

[53] *See e.g.* H. DONNEDIEU DE VABRES, *supra* note 2. For contemporary works on theories of international criminal jurisdiction, *see* M.C. BASSIOUNI, INTERNATIONAL EXTRADITION IN U.S. LAW AND

International practice, in respect to violations of the regulation of armed conflicts, reveals that the prosecuting state having *in personam* and subject-matter jurisdiction may apply its own precepts of imputability, culpability and punishment.[54] It is not clear, however, what substantive law the adjudicating state can use if it only has *in personam* and not subject-matter jurisdiction. Consequently, one has to turn to that state's rules of private international law applicable to conflicts of laws in the criminal context and which allow the prosecuting state to apply its own conflicts of law rules to determine the applicable general part of substantive criminal law.[55] This in turn, will determine the rules of imputability of criminal responsibility, with all that these rules comport of standards of individual and group responsibility, responsibility for the conduct of another, responsibility based on commission or omission, exonerating conditions (including justifiable and excusable conditions and circumstances), measuring standards of conduct, applying legal tests (i.e., subjective or objective) and the meeting of punishment including, of course, mitigating or aggravating circumstances or conditions. The forum having jurisdiction will thus control both the applicable substantive and procedural law, and with it, of course, all relevant issues bearing on responsibility.[56] But the question remains as to whether international crimes do not impose certain substantive legal requirements which transcend or override the prosecuting state's norms and rules. So far no clear answer is discernible in positive international criminal law because, as stated above, conventional international criminal law has not been formally codified and no general part of international criminal law exists, except for the writings of some scholars.[57]

PRACTICE, Chapter 6, 249-314 (2d. rev. ed. 1987). Blakesley, *Jurisdictional Issues and Conflicts of Jurisdiction,* in LEGAL RESPONSES TO INTERNATIONAL TERRORISM (M.C. Bassiouni ed. 1988); Blakesley, *Extraterritorial Jurisdiction,* in 2 Bassiouni ICL 3-55 (1986); Feller, *Jurisdiction over Offenses with a Foreign Element,* in 2 BASSIOUNI AND NANDA TREATISE, 5-61 (1973).

[54] *See* H.MEYROVITZ, *supra* note 10; A. MAUNOIR, LA REPRESSION DES CRIMES DE GUERRE DEVANT LES TRIBUNAUX FRANÇAIS ET ALLIÉS (1956); Baxter, *The Municipal and International Law Basis of Jurisdiction over War Crimes,* in 2 BASSIOUNI AND NANDA TREATISE 65-96 (1973).

[55] *See supra* notes 2 and 53.

[56] This approach was taken by this writer in the proposal for the establishment of an international criminal court presented to the VIII United Nations Congress on Crime Prevention and the Treatment of Offenders (Havana, August-September 1990) as *Draft Statute for an International Criminal Tribunal,* E/Conf./144/NGO ISISC, 31 July 1990, *reprinted in* 15 NOVA REV. 372 1991.

[57] *See e.g.* Glaser, *supra* notes 8 and 13; Donnevieu de Vabres, *supra* notes 2 and 10.

The Charter and CCL 10 provide that national law cannot be a bar to criminal responsibility for acts constituting international crimes as specified in Article 6. One of the consequences of this principle is that knowledge of national law is displaced by the presumed knowledge of international law. But it does not resolve two basic questions: 1) which specific aspect of international law and under what circumstances does it override national law; and 2) is it proper to place the burden of resolving questions of conflict between international and national law on the individual? This is particularly significant with respect to international criminal law which is not codified and more so with respect to its general part. One way to solve these problems is to revert back to applying the national criminal law of the situs where the crime was committed, or the nationality law of the perpetrator. In this perspective, all Article 6(c) crimes were, except for "persecution," crimes under the 1871 German Penal Code which was in effect in 1945.[58] Thus, there can be no valid claim that the perpetrators did not know of the legal prohibition. But then, they could still argue lack of intent on the basis of mistake of law, if they reasonably believed that their national law obligated them to do what they otherwise perceived to be a crime, or a *malum in se* act. But this presupposes a consciousness of wrongdoing, which also evokes the questions of whether such consciousness is purely moral because of the potential conflict of legal mandates and legal duties. Some of these mandates and legal duties derive from international law, while others derive from national law. How, and on what basis should the individual resolve these conflicts, and how and on what basis is the individual going to be judged, are questions that neither the Law of the Charter nor Post-Charter Legal Developments have addressed, let alone resolved. Furthermore, the interrelationship between knowledge of international and national law, intent, consciousness of wrongdoing, and the factors negating intent such as mistake of law, are also among the questions that neither the Charter, nor the Post-Charter Legal Developments have resolved.

Since the Charter, international criminal law has not significantly evolved these concepts of responsibility but the national laws of several states have. For example, in a civil case involving an assassination plot by Chile against its former Ambassador to the United States, the District Court for the District of Columbia held that:

[T]here is no discretion to commit, or to have one's officers or agents commit, an illegal act. Whatever policy options may exist for a foreign country, it has no

---

[58]   *See* German Penal Code.

discretion to perpetrate conduct designed to result in the assassination of an individual or individuals, action that is clearly contrary to the precepts of humanity as recognized in both national and international law.[59]

Command Responsibility

Policy Considerations

"Command responsibility" includes two different concepts of criminal responsibility. The first is that of direct responsibility for a commander's orders which may be unlawful. The second is that of imputed criminal responsibility for a subordinate's unlawful conduct which is not based on the commander's orders. The latter is essentially based on the commander's failure to act in order to: 1) prevent a specific unlawful conduct; 2) provide for general measures likely to prevent or deter unlawful conduct; 3) investigate allegations of unlawful conduct; and, 4) prosecute, and upon conviction, punish the author of the unlawful conduct. Since these four categories of imputed responsibility for the conduct of another are based on failure to act, the legal standards and tests used to determine whether the omission is culpable or not are outcome determinative of guilt or innocence. Thus, if the legal standard is an objective one, i.e. the ordinary reasonable person having the commander's knowledge of the facts and operating under like circumstances, it will produce a different outcome than a subjective standard which relies on the actual personal knowledge of the commander whether he acted with or without conscious wrongdoing. Similarly, if the test for the objective standard is whether the commander "could have reasonably known," under the circumstances, it would produce a different outcome than if the test is that he "should have known." The former is more speculative than the latter.

The choice of any legal standard and test is ultimately a matter of legal policy. Thus, to place a reasonably higher level duty on commanders on the assumption that this would maximize their vigilance and thus minimize the potential violations of subordinates, is a policy that leads to the adoption of a "should have known" test. To place an unreasonably high standard of responsibility on commanders, particularly in combat situations, is not likely to be accepted nor followed. Commanders cannot be held to be insurers of the proper conduct of their subordinates and no concept of

---

[59] Letelier v. Republic of Chile, 488 F. Supp. 665, 673 (D.D.C. 1980).

imputed criminal responsibility for the conduct of another can deter anyone who is unable to foresee the unlawful conduct which the law requires him to prevent.

A person in command is not necessarily part of a military or para-military organization. If a person in command of a governmental or police unit issues an order for the performance of any of the specific acts within the meaning of "crimes against humanity," and that crime is committed by those under his command, he is criminally responsible. Similarly, such a non-military commander is responsible for his omissions if they lead to the commission of such crimes. The source of law, however, which is applicable to military and para-military personnel is different from that which is applicable to others in the civilian hierarchy of government or in the police, unless they can be linked by an agency relationship to the military. Members of the armed forces are subject to national military law, and the international regulation of armed conflicts. Non-military personnel are subject to national criminal law, unless an agency relationship can be established between such persons and the armed forces, in which case, military law and the international regulation of armed conflicts also applies to them.

The doctrine of command responsibility originated in national military law and gradually become a basis of international criminal responsibility.[60] Command responsibility is the legal and logical concomitant to the defense of "obedience to superior orders," which is discussed in Chapter 10. Indeed, if a subordinate is to be exonerated from criminal responsibility for carrying out a superior's order, that superior should be accountable for the issuance of an order which violates international criminal law. Thus, a nexus exists between the legal policies underlying each of these two conceptions. When a violation of the international regulation of armed conflict takes place, usually such a violation results in harm to protected persons or protected targets. Consequently, the responsibility of the violator must be assessed. The inquiry will usually start with the perpetrator of the violation and then gradually move up the chain of command to the superior who issued the order. Such a chain of command can, depending upon the factual circumstances, reach up to the highest echelon in the military hierarchy. In this respect, the Charter removed any limits up to and including the head of State. Article 7 of the Charter states that "the official position of the

---

[60] *See* Parks, *Command Responsibility for War Crimes*, 62 MIL. L. REV. 1973. *See also* Green, *Superior Orders and Command Responsibility*, 27 CAN. Y.B. INT'L L. 167 (1989).

defendants or responsible officials in Government Departments, should not be considered as freeing themselves for responsibility of mitigation of punishment."[61]

The Charter followed the postulate of Article 227 of the Treaty of Versailles which provided for the prosecution of Kaiser Wilhelm II for the supreme offense against peace. But the Tokyo Charter in Article 6 differed from its counterpart, Article 7 of the London Charter, in that it provided that an official's position could "...be considered in mitigation of punishment if the tribunal determines that justice so requires." Article 6 did not admit mitigation.

Throughout the process of inquiry into the chain of command, different legal standards may apply depending upon whether the person who is the focus of inquiry is the one who committed the violative act, the one who ordered it, or the one who could or should have prevented its occurrence.[62] The reason for such different standards derive from deterrence policy considerations. Criminal responsibility remains, however, personal and is individually judged based on whether such a person issued the order, related the order, or failed to act to prevent illegal conduct by others, or failed to punish a subordinate after the illegal act has been established.

A person who issues an order is obviously responsible for that order. This is clearly a standard of direct personal responsibility; a standard well recognized in the world's major criminal justice systems and in international criminal law. This responsibility is direct, and not secondary as it is in some national legal systems for those who command another to commit a crime. A commander's responsibility for failure to prevent, if no prior knowledge of the possible violation exists, is ancillary, as it is in national criminal law, even though there are separate legal elements and exonerating conditions in military law and international regulation of armed conflicts, such as the doctrine of "military necessity" which have no counterpart in the national criminal law. Furthermore, those in a superior position have the legal duty to supervise, control, and prevent unlawful conduct by subordinates and their failure to do so becomes the basis

---

[61] The IMTFE refused to recognize the diplomatic immunity of Ambassador Oshima, who was sentenced to life imprisonment, *see* Document Section C.10. *See also* BRACKMAN, THE OTHER NUREMBURG, 207 (1987).

[62] For the application of various legal standards to "Command Responsibility and Obedience to Superior Orders" *see* Parks and Green, *supra* note 60. *But see particularly* the four major works on the subject which support the application of the objective standard of reasonableness. N. KEIZJER, MILITARY OBEDIENCE (1978); L.C. GREEN, SUPERIOR ORDERS IN NATIONAL AND INTERNATIONAL LAW 15-242 (1976); Y. DINSTEIN, THE DEFENSE OF "OBEDIENCE TO SUPERIOR ORDERS" IN INTERNATIONAL LAW 5-20 (1965); E. MULLER-RAPPARD, L'ORDRE SUPERIEUR MILITAIRE ET LA RESPONSIBILITÉ DU SUBORDONNÉ 185-251 (1965).

for their criminal responsibility. But these duties differ in military law and national criminal law applicable to civilians. The military standards are higher than their civilian counterparts for essentially two policy reasons: the need to preserve a higher standard of discipline in a military structure, whose concomittant is the superior's responsibility; and, the effectiveness of deterrence within the two contexts.

The difficult problems in military "criminal responsibility" arise in four areas, all of which fall under the general category of omission. They are:

1 - responsibility of a superior who does not initiate an unlawful order but who conveys it to a subordinate;

2 - responsibility for the conduct of a subordinate where that superior ordinarily exercises direct command and control, but in this case fails to do so;

3 - responsibility for the conduct of a subordinate where the superior ordinarily exercises indirect command control, but in this case fails to do so;

4 - responsibility for the conduct of all subordinates under the general command of a senior officer or commanding general officer up to and including the military commander-in-chief, for failure to establish policies and procedures for the prevention of violations and for the punishment of violators, and for failure to implement them.

A subordinate actor's responsibility for a violative act does not necessarily eliminate command responsibility because the latter includes failure to act, failure to prevent, and failure to punish upon discovery of the violation. But failure to act depends on knowledge and opportunity to act: 1) in the prevention of the criminal act; 2) subsequent to the act if the superior failed to supervise, discover, and take remedial action as needed under the circumstances; and 3) prosecute and, if found guilty, punish the violator. Conversely, a subordinate actor's exoneration under the defense of "obedience to superior orders" does not necessarily imply that the immediate superior officer and those in the chain of command above him are criminally responsible if the order was wrongly understood or applied by the subordinate.

Since military law is based on a hierarchical structure of command and control, those in the chain of command have the duty to develop measures designed to prevent the commission of violative acts, to investigate information about violative acts, to punish the perpetrators, and to institute measures to prevent and correct situations leading to potential violations. The essential element in cases of "command responsibility," particularly with respect to those in the higher echelons in the chain of command is that of causation. To establish a chain of cause and effect is more difficult in these cases than in other cases of criminal violation. Thus, the policy of deterrence, as it is perceived by policy-makers, are more determinative than any other legal consideration. Furthermore, the more removed a superior is from the scene of the violative act, the more difficult it is to factually assess his responsibility, particularly in combat situations. The applicable legal standard, which is embodied in the military laws and civilian criminal law of the world's major legal systems is the objective standard of "reasonableness" in light of the existing circumstances; i.e. reasonableness in terms of actual knowledge or knowledge that should have been known. The reasons for this standard are consonant with the policy of criminal law in all legal systems, namely: the personalization of criminal responsibility in light of the potential deterrent of the criminal sanction. Indeed, it is not productive of greater compliance with the requirements of the law if individuals are unable to prevent the conduct which the criminal law seeks to avert. No one can be deterred from conduct beyond the control of the person whose responsibility may be called into question. To hold a superior accountable on the basis of omission for the conduct of a subordinate, therefore, requires intent or knowledge that the omission can actually or reasonably and foreseeably lead to a violative act and that the superior is in a position or has the ability to act in the prevention of the violative act.

The Evolution of Command Responsibility in the Regulation of Armed Conflicts

Issues involving command responsibility are not new. In 500 B.C., Sun Tzu wrote:

When troops flee, are insubordinate, distressed, collapse in disorder, or are routed, it is the fault of the general. None of these disorders can be attributed to natural causes.[63]

---

[63]   See SUN TZU, THE ART OF WAR (S. Griffith trans. 1963) who said several thousand years ago that commanders are responsible for the action of their men. *Id.* at 125. Later, Napoleon emphasized the responsibility of military commanders when he quipped "There are no bad regiments; they are only bad colonels." R. HEINL, DICTIONARY OF MILITARY AND NAVAL QUOTATIONS 56 (1956).

In the Western world, an early comment on command responsibility was made by Grotius, who asserted that rulers "may be held responsible for the crime of a subject if they knew it and do not prevent it when they could and should prevent it."[64] During the same period, in 1621, King Gustavus Adolphus of Sweden promulgated his "Articles of Military Lawwes to be Observed in the Warres," which, in Article 46, provided that: "No Colonel or Captain shall command his soldiers to do any unlawful thing which who so does, shall be punished according to the discretion of the Judges . . . ."[65]

In the United States, the Articles of War, enacted on June 30, 1775, provided that:

Every Officer commanding, in quarters, or on a march, shall keep good order, and to the utmost of his power, redress all such abuses or disorders which may be committed by any Officer or Soldier under his command; if upon complaint made to him of Officers or Soldiers beating or otherwise ill-treating any person, or committing any kind of riots to the disquieting of the inhabitants of this Continent, he, the said commander, who shall refuse or omit to see Justice done to this offender or offenders, and reparation made to the party or parties injured, as soon as the offender's wages shall enable him or them, upon due proof thereof, be punished, as ordered by General Court-Martial, in such manner as if he himself had committed the crimes or disorders complained of.[66]

In 1863, the United States promulgated the Instructions for the Government of the Armies of the United States in the Field, which became known as the Lieber Code. Article 71 provides:

---

[64]   2 H. GROTIUS, DE JURE BELLI AC PACIS 523 (Kelsy transl. 1925). Grotius further stated:

Kings and public officials are liable for neglect if they do not employ the remedies which they can and ought to employ for the prevention of robbery and piracy.

H. GROTIUS, DE JURE BELLI AC PACIS LIBRI TRES, bk II, ch. XVII, pt. xx (1) (Carnegie ed., F. Kelsey trans. 1925) supporting Jean Bodin's similar view in SIX LIVRES DE LA REPUBLIQUE (1577); and A. GENTILI, DE JURE BELLI LIBRI TRES, 99 (Carengie ed., J. Rolfe trans. 1933). See also, Arricle 3 of the fourth Hague Convention; Article 146 of the Fourth Geneva Convention; and Article 86 (I) of Protocol I.

[65]   Quoted in Parks, supra note 60 at 5.

[66]   Lieber Code.

373

Whoever intentionally inflicts additional wounds on an enemy already wholly disabled, or kills such an enemy, or who orders or encourages soldiers to do so, shall suffer death, if duly convicted, whether he belongs to the Army of the United States, or is an enemy captured after having committed his misdeed.[67]

In the late nineteenth century, in the authoritative *Military Law and Precedents*,[68] Winthrop expounds upon the duty of a commander during an armed conflict. He stated:

It is indeed the chief duty of the commander of the army of occupation to maintain order and the public safety, as far as practicable without oppression of the population, and as if the district were a part of the domain of his own nation.

He further adds:

The observance of the rule protecting from violence the unarmed population is especially to be enforced by commanders in occupying or passing through towns or villages of the enemy's country.

All officers or soldiers offending against the rule of immunity of non-combatants or private persons in war forfeit their right to be treated as belligerents, and together with civilians similarly offending, become liable to the severest penalties as violators of the laws of war.[69]

In international conventional law regulating the conduct of armed conflict, Article 1 of the 1907 Hague Convention provides the condition which a combattant must fulfill so as to be accorded the rights of a lawful belligerent. That condition which also exists under the 1949 Geneva Conventions and the 1977 Protocols, requires such a force to be "commanded by a person responsible for his subordinates."[70] This condition affirms the responsibility of commanders. The 1919 Commission on the Responsibility

---

[67] *Id.* art. 71.

[68] W. WINTHROP, MILITARY LAW AND PRECEDENTS (2d. ed. 1895).

[69] *Id.* at 799.

[70] 1907 Hague Convention, Article 1. *See also* Pollock, *The Defense of Superior Orders, Crimes of Responsibility, The Work of the League of Nations*, 35 L.Q. REV. 195 (1919). The same requirements exist in the four Geneva Conventions of 1949, and in the 1977 Additional Protocols.

of the Authors of the War and on Enforcement of Penalties concluded after World War I that:

> The ex-Kaiser and others in high authority were cognizant of and could at least have mitigated the barbarities committed during the course of the war. A word from them would have brought about a different method in the action of their subordinates on land, at sea and in the air....All persons belonging to enemy countries, however high their position may have been, without distinction of rank, including chiefs of State, who have been guilty of offenses against the laws and customs of war or the laws of humanity, are liable to criminal prosecution.[71]

Thus, the Treaty of Versailles called for the trial, by an international military tribunal, of the Kaiser, the Supreme German Commander for the same crime which the Charter in 1945 called "Crimes Against Peace" in Article 6(a). Article 227 of the Versailles Treaty provided that:

> The Allied and Associated Powers publicly arraign William II of Hohenzollen, formerly German Emperor, for a supreme offence against international morality and the sanctity of treaties . . . .

> The Allied and Associated Powers will address a request to the Government of the Netherlands for the surrender to them of the ex-Emperor in order that he may be put on trial.

This provision established the personal responsibility of a Commander-in-Chief. The Versailles Treaty also provided for the prosecution, before an international military tribunal or Allied military tribunals, of those accused of violating the laws of war. Article 228 stated:

> The German Government recognizes the right of the Allied and Associated Powers to bring before military tribunals persons accused of having committed acts in violation of the laws and customs of war. Such persons shall, if found guilty, be

---

[71] *Report of the Majority, and Dissenting Reports of American and Japanese Members of the Commission on the Responsibilities of the Authors of War on Enforcement of Penalties*, VIOLATIONS OF THE LAWS AND CUSTOMS OF WAR, CONFERENCE OF PARIS, 1919, (Carnegie Endowment for International Peace, Division of International Law, Pamphlet No. 32 (1919)), *reprinted in* 14 AM. J. INT'L L. 95, 117 (1920).

sentenced to punishments laid down by law. This provision will apply notwithstanding any proceedings or prosecution before a tribunal in Germany or in the territory of her allies. The German Governor shall hand over to the Allied and Associated Powers, or to such one of them as shall so request, all persons accused of having committed an act in violation of the laws and customs of war, who are specified either by name or by the rank, office, or employment which they held under the German authorities.

As discussed in Chapter 5, the Allies did not form an international military tribunal nor did they prosecute accused German military personnel before their military tribunals.[72] Instead the German Supreme Court, sitting at Leipzig, heard only a handful of cases resulting from criminal acts conducted during the War.[73] Some of these trials, however, dealt with the issues of "obedience to superior orders," and command responsibility.

The issues of command responsibility were plentiful in the post-World War II prosecutions before the IMT, IMTFE, Subsequent Proceedings and other prosecutions discussed in Chapter 5. The most notorious of these trials involved the case of the

---

[72]   The Allies seem to have accepted the objections of the Commission members from the United States, Lansing and Scott, who:

objected to the "unprecedented proposal" to put on trial before an international criminal court the heads of States not only for having directly ordered illegal acts of war but for having abstained from preventing such acts. This would be to subject chiefs of State to a "degree of responsibility hitherto unknown to municipal or international law, for which no precedents are to be found in the modern practice of nations."

GARNER, INTERNATIONAL LAW AND THE WORLD WAR, vol. II, at492, n. 1 (1920).

[73]   *See* Chapter 5; and C. MULLINS, THE LEIPZIG TRIALS (1921).

Japanese General Tomoyuki Yamashita[74] which even today remains a controversial ruling.

General Yamashita served as the commanding general of the Japanese forces in the Philippines as well as the military governor of the islands during the last year of the war. On October 2, 1945, a month after his surrender, Yamashita was served with this Charge:

> Tomoyuki Yamashita, General Imperial Japanese Army, between 9 October 1944 and 2 September 1945, at Manila and at other places in the Philippine Islands, while commander of armed forces of Japan at war with the United States of America and its allies, *unlawfully disregarded and failed to discharge his duty as commander to control the operations of the members of his command, permitting them to commit brutal atrocities and other high crimes* against people of the United States and its allies and dependencies, particularly, the Philippines; and he, General Tomoyuki Yamashita, thereby violated the law of war.[75] (emphasis added)

---

[74] For detailed examinations of the Yamashita trial *see* A.F. REEL (one of Yamashita's defense attorneys), THE CASE OF GENERAL YAMASHITA (1949); and R. LAEL, THE YAMASHITA PRECEDENT: WAR CRIMES AND COMMAND RESPONSIBILITY (1982). *See also* Parks, *supra* note 60, at 22-38. Reel, *supra* provides a first hand account of the trial, he states:

> But let us assume that General Yamashita had been given a fair trial, that the rules of evidence and the constitutional guaranty of due process of law had been adhered to. In my opinion, even then the condemnation was unjust because Yamashita was held accountable for crimes committed by persons other than himself, crimes committed without his knowledge and, in fact, against his orders. He was held so accountable on the basis of a "principle" of command responsibility, a principle that in this perverted form has no basis in either law or logic.

Id. at 242. *See* In Re Yamashita, 327 U.S. 1 (1945) and particularly the dissents of Justices Murphy and Rutledge.

[75] The record of the trial is found in *United States of America v. Tomoyuki*, a Military Commission appointed by General Douglas McArthur by Special Order 110, para. 24 Headquarters United States Army Forces, Western Pacific, dated 1 October 1945, at 23 [hereinafter Commission Record] (emphasis added); *reprinted in* R. LAEL, *supra* note 73, at 80. Colonel Clark, Yamashita's senior defense counsel, commenting on the charge, argued:

> The Accused is not charged with having done something or having failed to do something, but solely with having been something. For the gravamen of the charge is that the Accused was the commander of the Japanese forces, and by virtue of that fact alone, is guilty of every crime committed by every soldier assigned to his command. *Id.* at 82.

Subsequently, the prosecution submitted two separate bills of particulars, which contained an aggregate of 123 specifications.[76] These specific charges included the murder and mistreatment of over 32,000 Filipino civilians and captured Americans, the rape of hundreds of Filipino women and also the arbitrary and unwarranted destruction of private property.[77] These facts notwithstanding, the bills of particulars did not establish a direct link between the perpetration of those unlawful acts and Yamashita.[78]

The trial was before a Military Commission (comprised of American officers, none of whom had legal training) sitting in the Philippines and convened under the authority of General Douglas MacArthur at the United States Army Forces, Western Pacific. It began on October 19, 1945 and, after hearing 286 witnesses and receiving 423 documents into evidence, it ended with a judgment rendered on a particularly significant date, December 7, 1945. During this period, the prosecution "sought to demonstrate the bestiality, enormity, and widespread nature of Japanese war crimes in the Philippines, and sought to convict Yamashita of dereliction of duty."[79] The Military Commission learned how Japanese soldiers executed priests in their churches, murdered patients in their hospitals and burned alive or beheaded American prisoners of war.[80] Two specific instances of Japanese atrocities were more than appalling. One involved a Japanese soldier tossing a baby in the air, driving his bayonet through the child, thereby impaling the baby in the ceiling, and the other involved twenty Japanese soldiers raping a girl and then cutting off her breasts.[81] The prosecution, however, could not prove that General Yamashita had ordered the atrocities, nor that he had direct knowledge of them.[82] Consequently, their case depended on the argument that Yamashita "must have known" of the widespread and enormity of the atrocities. As one author states:

---

[76] *See* Parks, *supra* note 60 at 24.

[77] *See* R. LAEL, *supra* note 74 at 80.

[78] *See id.* at 80-81.

[79] *Id.* at 83.

[80] *Id.*

[81] *Id.* at 83-84.

[82] The prosecution did present two witnesses who linked Yamashita to these crimes, but the two, former Japanese collaborators imprisoned by the Americans, were shown to be not very credible. *See id.* at 84-86, and Parks, *supra* note 60, at 29-30.

378

Of the hundreds of witnesses produced by Kerr and his colleagues [the prosecutors], almost all emphasized the actual commission of atrocities and war crimes rather than any evidence linking them to high-ranking Japanese officers. By proving the commission of the numerous murders and rapes, the prosecution hoped to convince the court that there was no way for Yamashita not to have known, unless he had made a determined effort not to know. In either case, he was guilty of failure to control his men, guilty of failing to exercise his command responsibility.[83]

The Commission accepted this argument. It found General Yamashita guilty and sentenced him to death, stating, *inter alia*:

The Prosecution presented evidence to show that the crimes were so extensive and wide-spread, both as to time and area, that they must have been wilfully permitted by the Accused, or secretly ordered by the Accused . . . .

Clearly, assignment to command military troops is accompanied by broad authority and heavy responsibility. This has been true in all armies throughout recorded history. It is absurd, however, to consider a commander a murderer or rapist because one of his soldiers commits a murder or a rape. Nonetheless, where murder and rape and vicious, revengeful actions are widespread offenses, and there is no effective attempt by a commander to discover and control the criminal acts, such a commander may be held responsible, even criminally liable, for the lawless acts of his troops, depending upon their nature and the circumstances surrounding them. Should a commander issue orders which lead directly to lawless acts, the criminal responsibility is definite and has always been so understood . . . .

The Commission concludes: (1) That a series of atrocities and other high crimes have been committed by members of the Japanese armed forces under your [i.e., Yamashita's] command against people of the United States, their allies and dependencies throughout the Philippine Islands; that they were not sporadic in nature but in many cases were methodically supervised by Japanese officers and

---

[83]   R. LAEL, *supra* note 74 at 86.

noncommissioned officers; (2) that during the period in question you failed to provide effective control of your troops as was required by the circumstances.[84]

Along the same lines, a staff judge advocate, who daily reviewed a summary of the evidence concluded:

The evidence affirmatively shows a complete indifference on the part of the accused as a commanding officer either to restrain those practices or to punish their authors. The evidence is convincing that the overall responsibility lay with the Army Commander, General Yamashita, who was the highest commander in the Philippines; that he was charged with the responsibility of defending the Philippines and that he issued a general order to wipe out the Philippines if possible and to destroy Manila; that subsequently he said he would not revoke the order.

The pattern of rape, murder, mass execution and destruction of property is widespread both in point of time and of area to the extent a reasonable person must logically conclude the program to have been the result of deliberate planning.

From all the fact and circumstances of record, it is impossible to escape the conclusion that the accused knew or had the means to know of the widespread commission of atrocities by members and units of his command; his failure to inform himself through official means available to him of what was common

---

[84]   Commission Record, at 4059-4063. Based on the commission's opinion, Parks concludes that the verdict could have been based on any one of four theories of command responsibility:

(1)   that General Yamashita ordered the offenses committed;

(2)   that, learning about the commission of the offenses, General Yamashita acquiesced in them;

(3)   that, learning about the commission of the offenses, General Yamashita failed to take appropriate measures to prevent their reoccurrence or to halt them;

(4)   the offenses committed by the troops under General Yamashita were so widespread that under the circumstances he exhibited a personal neglect or abrogation of his duties and responsibilities as a commander amounting to wanton, immoral disregard of the action of his subordinates amounting to acquiescence.

Parks, *supra* note 60, at 30-31.

knowledge throughout his command and throughout the civilian population can only be considered as a criminal dereliction of duty on his part.[85]

As a last resort, defense counsel filed a *writ of certiorari* to the United States Supreme Court and *In re Yamashita*[86] was argued before the Court on January 7, 1945. A majority of the Court, in addressing the issue of whether the charge against Yamashita failed to specify an offense against the laws of war, stated:

> [I]t is urged that the charge does not allege that petitioner has either committed or directed the commission of such acts, and consequently that no violation is charged against him. But this overlooks the fact that the gist of the charge is an unlawful breach of duty by petitioner as an army commander to control the operations of the members of his command by "permitting them to commit" the extensive and widespread atrocities specified. The question then is whether the law of war imposes on an army commander a duty to take such appropriate measures as are within his power to control the troops under his command for the prevention of the specified acts which are violations of the law of war and which are likely to attend the occupation of hostile territory by an uncontrolled soldiery, and whether he may be charged with personal responsibility for his failure to take such measures when violations result . . . .
>
> It is evident that the conduct of military operations by troops whose excesses are unrestrained by the orders or efforts of their commander would almost certainly result in violations which it is the purpose of the law of war to prevent. Its purpose to protect the civilian population and prisoners of war from brutality would largely be defeated if the commander of an invading army could with impunity neglect to take reasonable measures for their protection. Hence the law of war presupposes that its violation is to be avoided through the control of the operations of war by commanders who are to some extent responsible for their subordinates.[87]

---

[85] *Cited in* Parks, *supra* note 60, at 32. For other cases which also contributed to the command responsibility doctrine, *see also, id.* at 58-77, which discusses, *inter alia, The Hostage Case* and the trial of Japanese Admiral Toyoda.

[86] 327 U.S. 1 (1945).

[87] *Id.* at 14-15.

The impassioned dissent of Justice Murphy, joined in with a concurring opinion by Justice Rutledge, however, argued that:

He was not charged with personally participating in the acts of atrocity or with ordering or condoning their commission. Not even knowledge of these crimes was attributed to him. It was simply alleged that he unlawfully disregarded and failed to discharge his duty as commander to control the operations of the members of his command, permitting them to commit the acts of atrocity. The recorded annals of warfare and the established principles of international law afford not the slightest precedent for such a charge.[88]

On February 23, 1946, Yamashita was hanged, but the infamous legacy of his trial survived him.

Almost at the same time as the *Yamashita* trial, the Canadian Military Court in Germany was hearing the case of *Brigadefuhrer Kurt Meyer*.[89] The trial was con-

---

[88] *Id.* at 28. Justice Murphy, though, did affirm that "inaction or negligence may give rise to liability, civil or criminal." *Id.* at 39.

General Telford Taylor who succeeded Justice Jackson as Chief U.S. prosecutor at Nuremberg and who supervised the CCL 10 trials in his book NUREMBERG AND VIETNAM: AN AMERICAN TRAGEDY (1970) compares the positions of General Westmoreland and General Yamashita in terms of their ability to supervise their troops. He states:

From General Westmoreland down they were more or less constantly in Vietnam, and splendidly equipped with helicopters and other aircraft, which gave them a degree of mobility unprecedented in earlier wars, and consequently endowed them with every opportunity to keep the course of the fighting and its consequences under close and constant observation. Communications were generally rapid and efficient, so that the flow of information and orders was unimpeded.

These circumstances are in sharp contrast to those that confronted General Yamashita in 1944 and 1945, with his forces reeling back in disarray before the oncoming American military powerhouse. For failure to control his troops so as to prevent the atrocities they committed, Brig. Gens. Egbert F. Mullene and Morris Handwerk and Maj. Gens. James A. Lester, Leo Donovan and Russel B. Reynolds found him guilty of violating the laws of war and sentenced him to death by hanging.

Id. at 181. The conclusion is inescapable: by the Yamashita standards, Westmoreland is guilty.

[89] The extracts quoted here are taken from the unpublished transcript, at 839-45 *as cited in* Green, *Superior Orders and Command Responsibility*, 1989 CAN. Y.B. INT'L L. 167, 196 (1989).

ducted in accordance with the Canadian War Crimes Regulations.[90] Article 10 of these regulations states:

(4) Where there is evidence that more than one war crime has been committed by members of a formation, unit, body, or group while under the command of a single commander, the court may receive that evidence as *prima facie* evidence of the responsibility of the commander for those crimes.

(5) Where there is evidence that a war crime has been committed by members of a formation, unit, body or group and that an officer or non-commissioned officer was present at or immediately before the time when such crime was committed, the court may receive that evidence as *prima facie* evidence of the responsibility of such officer or non-commissioned officer, and of the commander of such formation, unit, body, or group, for that crime.

Meyer was found responsible for inciting and counselling his men to deny quarter to prisoners of war and for the shooting of prisoners at his headquarters.[91] In summation, the Judge Advocate said:

[T]he Regulations do not mean that a military commander is in every case liable to be punished as a war criminal for every war crime committed by his subordinates, but once certain facts have been proved by the Prosecution, there is an onus cast upon the accused to adduce evidence to negative or rebut the inference of responsibility which the Court is entitled to make....The rank of the accused, the duties and responsibilities of the accused by virtue of the command he held, the training of the men under his command, their age and experience, anything relating to the question whether the accused either ordered, encouraged or verbally or tacitly acquiesced in the killing of prisoners, or willfully failed in his duty as a military commander to prevent, or to take action as the circumstances required to endeavour to prevent, the killing of prisoners are matters affecting the question of the accused's responsibility.[92]

---

[90]   War Crimes Regulations (Canada), P.C. 5831, Aug. 30, 1945.

[91]   *See* Green, *supra* note 89 at 197.

[92]   *See* Green, *supra* note 89 at 198.

The controversial standard of command responsibility of "must have known" was not relied upon by the IMT and Subsequent Proceedings. In *United States v. Wilhelm von Leeb*, also known as *The High Command Case*, thirteen German officers who held important staff and/or command positions in Germany's military were on trial. Addressing the issue of command responsibility, the tribunal did not pursue the almost strict liability approach taken by the Yamashita Commission and rejected the theory that a commander could be held criminally responsible solely on the basis of the commander/subordinate relationship in which he is under the duty to know. The tribunal stated:

Military subordination is a comprehensive but not conclusive factor in fixing criminal responsibility. The authority, both administrative and military, of a commander and his criminal responsibility are related but by no means coextensive. Modern war such as the last war entails a large measure of decentralization. A high commander cannot keep completely informed of the details of military operations of subordinates and most assuredly not of every administrative measure. He has the right to assume that details entrusted to responsible subordinates will be legally executed. The President of the United States is Commander in Chief of its military forces. *Criminal acts committed by those forces cannot in themselves be charged to him on the theory of subordination.* The same is true of other high commanders in the chain of command. *Criminality does not attach to every individual in this chain of command from that fact alone. There must be a personal dereliction that can occur only where the act is directly traceable to him or where his failure to properly supervise his subordinates constitutes criminal negligence on his part. In the latter case, it must be a personal neglect amounting to a wanton, immoral disregard of the action of his subordinates amounting to acquiescence.* Any other interpretation of international law would go far beyond the basic principles of criminal law as known to civilized nations.[93] (emphasis added)

With regard to von Leeb, the Tribunal specifically delineates the standard of knowledge by which a commander can be held criminally responsible, stating:

[I]t is not considered under the situation outlined that criminal responsibility attaches to him merely on the theory of subordination and over-all command. He

---

[93]   2 CCL Trials 543-544.

must be shown both to have had knowledge and to have been connected to such criminal acts, either by way of participation or criminal acquiescence.[94]

Thus, clearly a commander must have actual knowledge of criminal conduct or must acquiesce to such conduct. But, it should be noted that the tribunal also recognized that commanders have specific duties, and that their failure to carry them out subjects them to responsibility. *The High Command Case* established the test "should have known,"[95] as was applied by the IMT in another case involving the duty of military commanders in occupied territories wherein it held:

> The commanding general of occupied territories having executive authority as well as military command will not be heard to say that a unit taking unlawful orders from someone other than himself was responsible for the crime and that he is thereby absolved from responsibility. It is here claimed, for example, that certain SS units under the direct command of Heinrich Himmler committed certain of the atrocities herein charged without the knowledge, consent, or approval of these defendants. But this cannot be a defence for the commanding general of occupied territory. The duty and responsibility for maintaining peace and order, and the prevention of crime rests upon the commanding general. He cannot ignore obvious facts and plead ignorance as a defence.[96]

One national prosecution in the United States arising out of the Vietnam war -- is notable because it brings the command responsibility doctrine full circle from Yamashita ("must have known") through *The High Command Case* ("should have known") to simple actual knowledge.[97] The case was that of Captain Medina, the immediate superior to Lieutenant William L. Calley, Jr., who was charged with both ordering his men to kill civilians and with participating in the killings which occurred

---

[94] *Id.* at 555.

[95] *Id.*

[96] *Id.* at 631-32.

[97] U.S. v. Medina, 20 USCMA 403; 43 CMR 243 (1971). *See also* 2 Friedman 1729.

at My Lai (Song My).[98] In his comments to the jury, the military Judge Colonel Kenneth Howard explained a commander's responsibilities:

> After taking action or issuing an order, a commander must remain alert and make timely adjustments as required by a changing situation. Furthermore, a commander is also responsible if he has actual knowledge that troops or other persons subject to his control are in the process of committing or are about to commit a war crime and he wrongfully fails to take the necessary and reasonable steps to insure compliance with the law of war. You will observe that these legal requirements placed upon a commander require actual knowledge plus a wrongful failure to act. Thus mere presence at the scene without knowledge will not suffice. That is, the commander subordinate relationship alone will not allow an inference of knowledge. While it is not necessary that a commander actually see an atrocity being committed, it is essential that he know that his subordinates are in the process of committing atrocities or are about to commit atrocities.[99]

Medina's case, however, seems to be an anomaly in United States jurisprudence on the subject of command responsibility, since the Army Field Manual provides responsibility for actual knowledge of a commander and also knowledge which the commander should have had. Specifically:

---

[98]   U.S. v. Calley (1971,1973) CM 426402, 46 CMR 1131; 48 CMR 19; I MLR 2488; 22 USCMA 534 (1973). *See also* 2 Friedman 1703. In a review of M. BILTON AND K. SIM, FOUR HOURS IN MY LAI: THE SOLDIERS OF CHARLIE COMPANY (1992), Marc Leepson states:

> To Criticize the author's analysis of the war, the Army and the causes of My Lai in no way excuses the reign of terror exacted by most, but by no means all, of the soldiers of Charlie Company (of the American Division's 11th Infantry Brigade). Under Capt. Ernest Medina and Lt. William L. Calley, Jr. the company - which never was fired upon, took no enemy prisoners and recovered no enemy weapons - killed some 400 men, women and children.
> Calley himself murdered dozens of unarmed people, including young children and babies. Medina was aware of what was happening and did nothing to stop the raping, sodomizing and killing. Lt. Col. Frank Barker, Col. Warren K. Henderson and General Samuel H. Koster, the officers directly above Calley and Medina, deliberately suppressed the facts of the massacre. Only Calley was convicted of war crimes, and he was given lenient treatment by the Nixon administration and the army.

Leepson, Book Review, Chicago Tribune, February 23, 1992, Sec. 14, p. 3.

[99]   Cited in R. LAEL, *supra* note 74, at 130-131; *see also* 2 Friedman 1729-1739.

ELEMENTS OF CRIMINAL RESPONSIBILITY

Responsibility for Acts of Subordinates

In some cases, military commanders may be responsible for war crimes committed by subordinate members of the armed forces, or other persons subject to their control. Thus, for instance, when troops commit massacres and atrocities against the civilian population of occupied territory or against prisoners of war, the responsibility may rest not only with the actual perpetrators but also with the commander. Such a responsibility arises directly when the acts in question have been committed in pursuance of an order of the commander concerned. *The commander is also responsible if he has actual knowledge, or other means, that troops or other persons subject to his control are about to commit or have committed a war crime and he fails to take the necessary and reasonable steps to insure compliance with the law of war or to punish violators thereof.*[100] (emphasis added)

This position reflects contemporary international norms on the subject. Article 86 para. 2 of Protocol I provides:

The fact that a breach of the Conventions or of this Protocol was committed by a subordinate does not absolve his superiors from penal disciplinary responsibility, as the case may be, if they knew, or had information which should have enabled him to conclude in the circumstances at the time, that he was committing or was going to commit such a breach and if they did not take all feasible measures within their power to prevent or repress the breach.

Furthermore, Article 87 establishes affirmative duties for the commander to prevent any breaches of the Conventions:

1. The High Contracting Parties and the Parties to the conflict shall require military commanders, with respect to members of the armed forces under their command and other persons under their control, to prevent and, where necessary, to suppress and to report to competent authorities breaches of the Conventions and of this Protocol.

---

[100]   U.S. Dept. of Army, Law of Land Warfare, para. 501 (Field Manual 27-10, 1956).

2.   In order to prevent and suppress breaches, High Contracting Parties and Parties to the conflict shall require that, commensurate with their level of responsibility, commanders ensure that members of the armed forces under their command are aware of their obligations under the Conventions and this Protocol.

3.   The High Contracting Parties and Parties to the conflict shall require any commander who is aware that subordinates or other persons under his control are going to commit or have committed a breach of the Conventions or of this Protocol, to initiate such steps as are necessary to prevent such violations of the Conventions or their Protocol, and where appropriate, to initiate disciplinary or penal actions against violators thereof.[101]

One final post-Charter international instrument is of note since it specifically applies to "crimes against humanity" and imposes command responsibility on a perpetrator of such crimes. Article II of the 1968 Convention on the Non-Applicability of Statutory Limitations to War Crimes and Crimes Against Humanity provides:

If any of the crimes mentioned in article I is committed [i.e., "war crimes" and "crimes against humanity"], the provisions of this Convention shall apply to representatives of the State authority and private individuals who, as principals or accomplices, participate in or who directly incite others to the commission of any of those crimes, or who conspire to commit them, irrespective of the degree of completion, and to representatives of the State authority who tolerate their commission.

The 1991 Draft Code of Crimes, in Article 12, proposes the following:

The fact that a crime against the peace and security of mankind was committed by a subordinate does not relieve his superiors of criminal responsibility, if they knew or had information enabling them to conclude, in the circumstances at the time, that the subordinate was committing or was going to commit such a crime and if they did not take all feasible measures within their power to prevent or repress the crime.

---

[101]   *See also* art. 43, para 1, which provides that armed forces must be placed "under a command responsible ... for the conduct of its subordinates."

388

This formulation differs from the evolution which has taken place since the subsequent proceedings.

The doctrine of "command responsibility" now clearly exists in convential and customary international law. This was recently evidenced by the *Report of the Kahan Commission* set up by Israel to inquire into criminal events that took place at a Palestinian refugee camp after Israel's invasion of Lebanon.[102] On September 16, 1982, the Israeli Defense Forces occupying Beirut after the June invasion of Lebanon permitted a force of Lebanese Christian militia, which was under its control, to enter the Palestinian refugee camps of Sabra and Shatilla.[103] From approximately 6:00 P.M. September 16 until 8:00 A.M. September 18, this force massacred unarmed civilians consisting mostly of older men and women, and children including Palestinians, Lebanese, Iranians, Syrians, Pakistanis and Algerians.[104] The exact number of those killed cannot be determined--bodies having been burned in the ruins, deposited in mass graves and carried from the site in truckloads.[105] Estimates of those massacred have ranged from roughly 300 to as many as 3000 people.[106] The *Kahan Commission* found several Israelis, including Minister of Defense, Ariel Sharon, "indirectly" responsible for the massacres.[107] The *Commission* stated:

> We have found, as has been detailed in this report, that the Minister of Defense bears personal responsibility [for the massacres]. In our opinion, it is fitting that the Minister of Defense draw the appropriate personal conclusions arising out of the defects revealed with regard to the manner in which he discharged the duties of his office...[108]

---

[102] 1973, 22 ILM 473 (1983).

[103] Malone, *The Kahan Report, Ariel Sharon and the Sabra-Shatilla Massacres in Lebanon: Responsibility Under International Law for Massacres of Civilian Populations*, 1985 UTAH L. REV. 373, 374 (1985).

[104] *Id.*

[105] *Id.*

[106] *Id.*

[107] *Id.*

[108] *The Commission of Inquiry Into the Events at the Refugee Camps in Beirut, 1983: Final Report (Authorized Translation), reprinted in* Jerusalem Post, Feb. 9, 1983 (supplement) *as cited in* Malone *supra* note 103.

As one author notes:

> [I]t would appear that the members of the Commission were aware of the relevant
> articles of the Geneva Convention and the Protocols for their comments regarding
> direct and indirect, as well as personal responsibility of the various commanders
> involved, not only reflect these provisions, but may be considered to go beyond
> them.[109]

As the doctrine of "command responsibility" is evident in both conventional and
customary international law, one may wonder as to the responsibility of Captain
Rogers, the commader of the *U.S.S. Vincennes*, who shot down an Iranian civilian
airliner, Flight 665, on a scheduled flight in July 1988.[110] Rogers relied on his crew's
mistaken reading of the instruments due to the stress of the situation and assumed he
was about to be attacked by a military aircraft.[111] As one author states:

> One may apply to the commander, especially in view of his rank and long service,
> responsibility for weakness in organization and morale of his troops and failure to
> show the standards of inspection and training to be expected of a senior officer in
> the American forces.[112]

The history of "command responsibility" doctrine shows that a commander's
responsibility for his troops has long been recognized. It has always been clear that if
a superior orders a subordinate to perform unlawful acts, he is criminally responsible.
Since this precept is so well recognized, much of the literature and opinions of courts,
especially after World War II, have concentrated on the second aspect of the doctrine;
namely that a commander may be held responsible for the unlawful acts of his
subordinates if he failed to act to prevent the unlawful activity when he "knew" or

---

[109] *See* Green, *supra* note 89.

[110] Linnan, *Iran Air Flight 665 and Beyond: Free Passage, Mistaken Self-Defense and State
Responsibility*, 16 YALE J. INT'L L. 245, 248 (1991). *See also* Aerial Incident of 3 July 1988 (Islamic Repulic
of Iran v. United States of America), 13 December 1989, I.C.J. Reports 1989, 132.

[111] *See* Green, *supra* note 89 at 196.

[112] *Id.*

"should have known" of the activity. National courts, however, have set different legal tests ranging from "could have known" to "having actual knowledge."[113]

The Law of the Charter and Post-Charter Legal Developments have not resolved two fundamental legal issues. One is the dilemma of conflicting legal duties which may arise in part by law or by a superior's order which runs contrary to a commander's general or specific legal duty. The other is the range of options and legal standards and tests to determine what a military person must do in the face of superior orders which violate or appear to violate his legal duties.

In *The High Command Case*, the tribunal held:

While, as stated, a commanding officer can be criminally responsible for implementing an illegal order of his superiors, the question arises as to whether or not he becomes responsible for actions committed within his command pursuant to criminal orders passed down independent of him. The choices which he has for opposition in this case are few:

(1) he can issue an order countermanding the order;
(2) he can resign;
(3) he can sabotage the enforcement of the order within a somewhat limited sphere.

As to countermanding the order of his superiors, he has no legal status or power. A countermanding order would not only subject him to the severest punishment, but would undoubtedly have focussed the eyes of Hitler on its rigorous enforcement.

His second choice--resignation--was not much better. Resignation in war time is not a privilege generally accorded to officers in an army. This is true in the Army of the United States. Disagreement with a state policy as expressed by an order affords slight grounds for resignation. In Germany, under Hitler, to assert such a ground for resignation probably would have entailed the most serious consequences for an officer.

---

[113] *See* Parks, *supra* note 60.

Another field of opposition was to sabotage the order. This he could do only verbally by personal contacts. Such verbal repudiation could never be of sufficient scope to annul its enforcement.

A fourth decision he could make is to do nothing.

Control Council No. 10, Article II, paragraph 2, provides in pertinent part as follows:

> "Any person without regard to nationality or the capacity in which he acted, is deemed to have committed a crime as defined in paragraph I of this article, if he...
>
> (b) was an accessory to the commission of any such crime or ordered or abetted the same or
> (c) took a consenting part therein or
> (d) was connected with plans or enterprises involving its commission..."

As heretofore stated, his "connection" is construed as requiring a personal breach of a moral obligation. Viewed from an international standpoint, such has been the interpretation of preceding Tribunals. This connection may however be negative. Under basic principles of command, authority and responsibility, an officer who merely stands by while his subordinates execute a criminal order of his superiors which he knows is criminal, violates a moral obligation under international law. By doing nothing he cannot wash his hands of international responsibility. His only defense lies in the fact that the order was from a superior which Control Council Law No. 10 declares constitutes only a mitigating circumstance...[114]

In this respect, the issue of "Command responsibility" rejoins that of "obedience to superior orders" which is discussed in Chapter 10.

Civilian Command Responsibility

---

[114] 2 CCL Trials.

Civilian superiors in a state hierarchial structure who are not part of the military, or subject to its control, do not fall under the "command responsibility" norms and standards discussed above. They are subject to national criminal laws, which vary significantly from state to state. Whereas national military laws, as a result of the Law of the Charter's influence and the international regulation of armed conflicts, have achieved a high level of conformity, national criminal laws have not. Thus, a major difference exists between "command responsibility" norms and standards in national military law, (applicable to military and in some states also to para-military organization's personnel) and national criminal laws (applicable to civilians in the governmental hierarchy and in most states to law enforcement agencies). Consequently, there are different legal outcomes depending upon the applicable source of law.

In assessing the international norms and standards which have been received in national military laws, in comparison to the norms and standards of civilian "command responsibility" in the world's major criminal justice systems, it appears that the former are more homogenous than the later. This dissimilarity of criminal responsibility levels produces a lack of symmetry in the treatment of those who have engaged in similar conduct resulting in similar harmful outcomes. The essential reason for this situation is the lack of cohesive legislative policy in almost every country in the world which allows the compartmentalization of different aspects of the law. Another explanation, which is, however, related to the essential reason stated above, is the fact that in Post-Charter Legal Developments, particularly the international regulation of armed conflicts under the impetus of the Geneva Conventions, a separate source of law has imposed upon States a duty of conformity with international norms and standards in military law, unparallelled in other aspects of national criminal laws. But since international norms and standards of "command responsibility" penetrate national laws,[115] they should logically extend to all branches of national laws whether they are applicable to military or civilian personnel. That breakthrough, however, has not yet occurred in national criminal justice systems. If any similarities exist between national norms and standards of "command responsibility" in military laws and criminal laws they are usually coincidental.

The differences between these two sources of national laws are a consequence of their respective policies, goals and methods.[116] In the last few decades, however, national criminal laws have introduced a concept of decision-makers' criminal

---

[115]   *See* Chapter 2 at 65.

[116]   *See supra* 368-72.

responsibility, particularly applicable to business structures, similar to that of military "command responsibility." In the United States for example, it first arose in the fields of anti-trust and food and drug control, whereby senior corporate executives up to and including the chief executive officer could be held criminally accountable for their commissions and particularly for their omissions for failure to take appropriate steps to prevent a known or foreseeable harmful result.[117] The increased reliance of national criminal justice systems on concepts of corporate criminal responsibility has also generated new approaches to the individual criminal responsibility of those in the corporate hierarchy.[118] But national criminal justice systems which struggle with these new concepts and policy approaches to the control of harmful behavior produced by organizations (which are of course commanded, controlled or influenced by persons), fail to take into account the international norms and standards of military "command responsibility." This is particularly significant with respect to "crimes against humanity," which are, as discussed in Chapter 6, the product of "state action or policy." And such "state action or policy" is not the exclusive province of the military. In fact, the military may only be a part of it, and in some cases it does not involve the military. Thus, the international and national norms and standards of military "command responsibility" would not be applicable to some or all of those who were part of the processes leading to the decision and/or to its implementation of "state action or policy" leading to the commission of "crimes against humanity." Such non-military perpetrators would be judged in accordance with national norms and standards of civilian criminal laws, and that, of course, does not provide a uniform international legal basis of accountability. To try to develop international civilian norms and standards on the basis of "general principles" would almost be impossible because of the diversity in norms of responsibility and imputability in the world's major criminal justice systems, as discussed above. Civilian government officials, industrialists,

---

117   *See* United States v. Parks, 421 U.S. 658 (1975); and United States v. Dotterwich, 320 U.S. 277 (1943). Both cases are discussed in M.C. BASSIOUNI, SUBSTANTIVE CRIMINAL LAW 148-157 (1978). For the application of the same principle in the areas of Anti-Trust, Securities, and Tax, *see e.g.* INTERNATIONAL CRIMINAL LAW: A GUIDE TO U.S. PRACTICE AND PROCEDURE (V.P. NANDA and M.C. BASSIOUNI EDS. 1987).

118   For an early position, *see* Edgarton, *Corporate Criminal Responsibility*, 36 YALE L.J. 827 (1927). The International Association of Penal Law has devoted several of its Congress subjects and volumes of the RIDP to this topic. *See e.g.* LES SOCIÉTÉS COMMERCIALES ET LE DROIT PÉNAL 58 RIDP 17-165 (1987); *Infractions D'Omission et Responsabilité Pénale pour omission* 55 RIDP 453-1040 (1984); *Conceptions et Principes du Droit Pénal Economique et des Affaires y Compris la Protection du Consommateur* 54 RIDP 17-865 (1983); *Criminalité d'Affaires*, 53 RIDP 21-523 (1982).

business persons and even law enforcement officials who are either part of the decision-making or implementing processes of "crimes against humanity" are, therefore, likely to escape accountability or punishability or to be judged by lesser standards than their counterparts in the military. The Law of the Charter does not address this question, nor do Post-Charter Legal Developments. The 1991 Draft Code of Crimes does not address this question except by general inference which is entirely insufficient. A new international convention on "Crimes Against Humanity," as urged in Chapter 12, is the most appropriate method for dealing with this and other questions pertaining to this international category of crimes, including questions of responsibility raised in this Chapter.

Conclusion

Chapter 9 discusses some of the general part issues of international criminal law by reference to the Law of the Charter, which is the principal source for the elements of criminal responsibility. But the few principles that emerged from the Law of the Charter were not so evident prior to 1945, and the Post-Charter Legal Developments, as discussed in Chapter 11. The 1991 version of the Draft Code of Crimes is far from satisfactory on these questions. One reason for this significant gap may be the assumption of the ILC that the provisions of the Draft Code of Crimes, if and when adopted, would be applied by national courts. Hence, these courts, whether civilian or military would apply the general part of their respective criminal or military laws. But that, of course, ignores the possibility of an international criminal court, unless one can further assume that such a tribunal would apply the law of the State wherein the crime was committed, or alternatively the law of nationality of the victims or the transgressor.[119]

The sparse and eclectic general part norms of international criminal law need systematization and codification, otherwise it would be difficult to understand why a given rule is relied upon, and not another, or from where such a rule derives. As one author states:

---

[119]   *See supra* note 52.

A fact or law is explained only when a sufficient knowledge of the system is reached to enable one to interpret the fact or law in terms of that system, and as one of the actual members [parts] of that coherent and orderly whole."[120]

The similarity between international criminal law and the Common Law of Crimes is greater than acknowledged. Indeed, all systems which evolve without a theory share some common traits. Principal among these is the haphazard emergence of legal proscriptions and their evolution through custom and practice. Such a *cursus* is necessarily conditioned by pragmatic factors which do not usually include consideration for such factors as consistency and cohesion. But in time, particularly after the reaching of a certain level of accumulation of disparate norms and diverse applications, the need for systematization imposes itself. Such systematization, may or may not be based on a theory or on a system, and could simply be an ordering process. The history of the Common Law of Crimes is the most appropriate example of that type of historical evolutionary process as opposed to the Germanic and French-Civilist codifications.

---

[120]   P.H. ROBINSON, THE PRINCIPLES OF REASONING 291 (1947).

CHAPTER 10

DEFENSES AND EXONERATIONS

> "Theirs not to make reply,
> Theirs not to reason why
> Theirs but to do or die."
> A. Tennyson, *The Charge
> of the Light Brigade*
> (1852).

Introduction

The legal defenses discussed in this chapter do not involve questions of fact which negate a criminal accusation, but rather, they involve questions of law which preclude the imposition of responsibility or excuse punishability. These defenses relate to subjective conditions pertaining to the individual actor, or to objective conditions relating to the circumstances of the purported criminal act. But, both subjective and objective factors overlap. In the Common Law system, for example, conditions which negate one of the elements of the offense, namely, the act, intent, concurrence of act and intent, causation and result reflect both objective and subjective factors and affect conditions of responsibility and punishability. The latter are, however, conceptually separate and distinct in the French-Civilist and Germanic legal systems even though their applications are predicated on both subjective and objective factors. Indeed, the world's major criminal justice systems differ significantly as to conditions of responsibility and punishability and their applications to theories of defenses and exonerations as discussed in Chapter 9.[1] Consequently, conditions of exoneration and excuse also differ in the world's major legal systems. Thus their comparative analysis is very difficult. The following categorization is therefore only general.

Legal defenses and exonerating and excusing conditions fall into four categories:

1. Conditions which negate the existence of one or more elements of the crime;

---

[1] *See* Chapter 9 at 339-350.

2. Conditions which relieve the defendant of criminal liability, even though all elements of the crime are present;

3. Conditions that justify the commission of an otherwise criminal act;

4. Legal concessions recognizing that, although a crime has been committed, justice will not be served by imposition of criminal punishment.[2]

The world's major criminal justice systems recognize such defenses as: insanity; self-defense; mistake of law or fact; compulsion (coercion and duress); necessity; and, "obedience to superior orders." Thus, these defenses rise to the level of "general principles," even though national legal systems differ as to the legal nature of these categories of defenses, their doctrinal basis, legal significance, and the scope of their application. Since the purpose of this Chapter is not to develop a comparative criminal law analysis of these defenses, but to evaluate those which are peculiar to "crimes against humanity," the number of potentially applicable defenses are more limited. They are: "obedience to superior orders;" compulsion; reprisals; *Tu quoque*; and immunity of heads of State.[3] Mistake of law is discussed in Chapter 1, and self-defense is not discussed because it is a personal defense which arises under the criminal law of the enforcing state.

A further difficulty exists because the legal source or sources of these defenses differ depending upon the particular defense in question. Thus, some of these defenses and exonerating conditions, like "obedience to superior orders," reprisals and *Tu quoque* arise under international criminal law, national military law and national criminal law. Coercion and necessity arise essentially under national criminal law, but coercion also arises under international criminal law and national military law when it relates to "obedience to superior orders." Lastly, immunity of heads of State arises under public international law and only since the Treaty of Versailles under international criminal law.

---

[2] M.C. BASSIOUNI, SUBSTANTIVE CRIMINAL LAW 441 (1978); J. HALL, GENERAL PRINCIPLES OF CRIMINAL LAW (1947); P.H. ROBINSON, CRIMINAL LAW DEFENCES (4 vols. 1984); JUSTIFICATION AND EXCUSE (A. Eser and G. Fletcher, eds. 1987).

[3] See M.C. BASSIOUNI DRAFT CODE 109-113. See also articles 7 and 8 of the Charter, which respectively negate the act of state doctrine and "obedience to superior orders." See also principles 3 and 4 of the Principles of the Nuremberg Tribunal which negate, respectively, the act of state doctrine and "obedience to superior orders." See also e.g. S. GLASER, INFRACTION INTERNATIONAMLE: SES ÉLÉMENTS CONSTITUTIFS ET SES ASPECTS JURIDIQUES (1957).

It is important to note that international criminal law has historically been shaped by the customary practices of states, and thus in part by national military law and practice. But since World War II, conventional international criminal law has acquired a more preponderant position over that of customary practices. This is particularly true with respect to the 1949 Geneva Conventions which, because of their codified nature, are a more specific and reliable source than custom. But then, many scholars now deem the 1949 Geneva Conventions part of customary law.

The multiplicity of applicable legal sources to the questions raised in this Chapter further evidence the complexity of the multi-disciplinary nature of international criminal law. The problems occasioned by this complex situation also argue for the need to codify the general part of international criminal law. A task that has yet to be formally undertaken by an international body.[4]

"Obedience to Superior Orders"

Rationale

Unlike national criminal law, which is designed to apply to civilians, military law is based on a hierarchical system requiring obedience by subordinates to the orders of superiors. In fact, throughout the history of military law, obedience to superior orders has been one of the highest duties for the subordinate. This obedience exonerates the subordinate from responsibility because of the command responsibility of the superior who issued the order.[5]

This criminal responsibility attaches to the decision-maker and not to the executor of the order who is exonerated. As a counterpart, the subordinate is expected to obey the orders of a superior. This approach to responsibility is predicated on the assumption that the superior can be deterred from wrongful conduct by the imposition of criminal responsibility for unlawful commands. But when this assumption fails, obviously, the overall approach must be reconsidered.

The essential reasons for the defense of "obedience to superior orders" are: (1) the hierarchical nature of the command military structure; (2) the need to maintain

---

[4] *See*, however, Bassiouni Draft Code.

[5] *See* Chapter 9 at 368-394. For a distinction between the military and civilian criminal approaches to the obedience defense, *see id.* Chapter 9, note 98 and accompanying text.

discipline in the military structure; and (3) the fact that a commanding officer is responsible for the acts of his subordinate.

"Crimes against humanity," though committed by individuals, are, because of their nature and scope, the product of "state action or policy."[6] These crimes, like the "crimes against peace" (which, since the United Nations Charter is labelled "aggression"),[7] genocide,[8] and *apartheid*[9] require group participation by individuals whose control over the organs of state can set in motion a chain of events involving a large number of persons whose actions and interaction can produce the criminal outcome irrespective of who or how the original decision was made. But surely in these cases, a certain number of decision-makers have to be involved and a large number of subordinates have to execute their orders. Thus, exonerating the subordinates, particularly those who are in opposition to executing such orders, reduces the prevention of such crimes. All crimes committed as part of "state action or policy" necessarily require the broadening of the criminal responsibility basis in order to maximize prevention. But the question is obviously, how far down the chain of command must the law reach in order to be effective and fair.

In considering the individual responsibility of the different actors carrying out the state-sponsored policy, it is inevitable that some give such orders and others carry them out.[10] In situations where the decision was made exclusively by one person, all those carrying out the policy can claim that they acted pursuant to his "superior order," and thus shield themselves for criminal responsibility. Such an approach was embodied in the *Führerprinzip*, and is necessarily counterproductive to effective deterrence and prevention of these types of crimes. It was therefore rejected by the Law of the Charter.

---

[6]   *See* Chapter 6.

[7]   *See* Bassiouni and Ferencz, *The Crime Against Peace,* in 1 BASSIOUNI ICL 167.

[8]   *See* Bassiouni, *Introduction to the Genocide Convention,* in 1 BASSIOUNI ICL 281.

[9]   *See* Clark, *The Crime of Apartheid,* in 1 BASSIOUNI ICL 299.

[10]   Professor D'Amato finds a paradox when a subordinate and a superior can both be prosecuted and convicted though only one crime was committed. He states that:

> If [the subordinate] is wholly responsible as the perpetrator of the crime, then how could [the superior] be held responsible for issuing an order that legally was required to be ignored by [the subordinate]?

D'Amato, *Agora: Superior Orders vs. Command Responsibility,* 80 AJIL 604 (1986).

DEFENSES AND EXONERATIONS

The military regulations of almost all states prior to the Law of the Charter had essentially provided for an absolute or qualified defense of "obedience to superior orders." For example, the United States Rules of Land Warfare (1940) provided, that:

> Individuals of the armed forces will not be punished for these offenses in case they are committed under the orders or sanction of their government or commanders. The commanders ordering the commission of such acts, or under whose authority they are committed by their troops, may be punished by the belligerent into whose hands they may fall.[11]

Many of the world's military regulations were influenced by Oppenheim's formulation of the defense as stated in the first five editions of his treatise, up to 1940:

> [V]iolations of rules regarding warfare are war crimes only when committed without an order of the belligerent government concerned. If members of the armed forces commit violations by order of their government, they are not war criminals and may not be punished by the enemy; the latter may, however, resort to reprisals.[12]

In the last half of this century, however, most national legal systems, whether in their military laws or their civilian criminal laws, have tended to restrict such defenses

---

[11] U.S. DEP'T OF THE ARMY RULES OF LAND WARFARE § 347 (Field Manual 27-10, 1940). However, on November 15, 1944, a revision added § 345 (1) which stated:

> Individuals and organizations who violate the accepted laws and customs of war may be punished therefor. However, the fact that the acts complained of were done pursuant to the order of a superior or government sanction may be taken into consideration in determining culpability, either by way of defense, or in mitigation of punishment. The person giving such orders may also be punished.

U.S. DEP'T OF ARMY RULES OF LAND WARFARE § 345.1 (1940).

[12] 2 OPPENHEIM, INTERNATIONAL LAW 264-265 (1st ed., 1906) (Subsequent stylistic alterations in later editions replaced the words "cannot" and "can" with "may not" and "may".) The BRITISH MANUAL (1914), No. 443, closely followed Oppenheim:

> Members of armed forces who commit such violations of the recognized rules of warfare as are ordered by their government or by their commander are not war criminals and cannot therefore be punished by the enemy .... "

as "obedience to superior orders"[13] and "coercion" (or compulsion), while also enlarging "command responsibility."[14] Thus, the position of the United States after World War II as embodied in the 1956 Army Field Manual became:

    a)   The fact that the law of war has been violated pursuant to an order of a superior authority, whether military or civil, does not deprive the act in question of its character of a war crime, nor does it constitute a defence in the trial of an accused individual, unless he did not know and could not reasonably have been expected to know that the act ordered was unlawful. In all cases where the order is held not to constitute a defence to an allegation of war crime, the fact that the individual was acting pursuant to orders may be considered in mitigation of punishment.

    b)   In considering the question whether a superior order constitutes a valid defence, the court shall take into consideration the fact that obedience to lawful military orders is the duty of every member of the armed forces; that the latter cannot be expected, in conditions of war discipline, to weigh scrupulously the legal merits of the orders received: that certain rules of warfare may be controversial; or that an act otherwise amounting to a war crime may be done in obedience to orders conceived as a measure of reprisal. At the same time it must be borne in mind that members of the armed forces are bound to obey only lawful orders.[15]

---

[13]   For a survey of such laws and regulations as they appear in various national legal systems, *see* 10 REV. DE DROIT PÉNAL MILITAIRE 87 *et seq.* (1971). This survey contains the position of many states in the world and reveals that there is no absolute defense of "obedience to superior orders" in the military law of national legal systems. *See also* Hancock, *A South African Approach to the Defense of Superior Orders in International Criminal Law*, 2 Responsa Meridiana 188 (1972).

[14]   *See* M.C. BASSIOUNI, *supra* note 1, at 149-157, which, at 156 states: "In furtherance of the policy of the command responsibility model, a person who has a responsible relationship to the violation cannot be shielded from responsibility by claiming a defense of "obedience to superior orders." The rejection of this defense originated in military law and then found its way in a parallel manner into the realm of responsibility of corporate officers and directors." *See also* Chapter 9 at 368.

[15]   U.S. DEP'T OF THE ARMY, LAW OF LAND WARFARE, § 509 (Field Manual 27-10, 1956). Commenting on the provision T. TAYLOR, NUREMBERG AND VIETNAM: AN AMERICAN TRAGEDY (1970), at 51-52, states:

The change in U.S. military regulations corresponded to a change in Oppenheim's treatise in Sir Hersch Lauterpacht's 1952 edition, which stated:

> The fact that a rule of warfare has been violated in pursuance of an order of the belligerent government or of an individual belligerent commander does not deprive the act in question of its character as a war crime: neither does it, in principle, confer upon the perpetrator immunity from punishment by the injured state .... [M]embers of the armed forces are bound to obey lawful orders only and ... cannot therefore escape liability if, in obedience to a command, they commit acts which both violate unchallenged rules of warfare and outrage the general sentiment of humanity.[16]

Policy Considerations

The goal of the humanitarian law of armed conflicts is to prevent certain forms of harm to protected targets. To accomplish this goal -- in light of modern warfare techniques and weapons --requires a broadening of the responsibility base. It became clear, after World War II, that to hold only superiors responsible would not accomplish the goals of deterrence and prevention. Consequently, a new policy approach developed whereby those carrying out unlawful orders would also be held criminally accountable in addition to those who issued such orders.

The differences between the two branches of national law, military and civilian, are essentially characterized by policy considerations predicated on the goals sought to be achieved by each branch. In the military, discipline is a goal which is sought to be accomplished by norms requiring obedience to superior orders. But in the civilian

---

[T]he language [of Par. 509, FM27-10] is well chosen to convey the quality of the factors, imponderable as they are, that must be assessed in a given case. As with so many good rules, the difficulty lies in its application -- in weighing evidence that is likely to be ambiguous or conflicting. Was there a superior order? Especially at the lower levels, many orders are given orally. Was a particular remark or look intended as an order, and if so what was its scope? If the existence and meaning of the order are reasonably clear, there may still be much doubt about the attendant circumstances -- how far the obeying soldier was aware of them, and how well equipped to judge them. If the order was plainly illegal, to what degree of duress was the subordinate subjected? Especially in confused ground fighting of the type prevalent in Vietnam, evidentiary questions such as these may be extremely difficult to resolve.

[16]   2 OPPENHEIM, INTERNATIONAL LAW, 568-569 § 253 (7th ed. H. Lauterpacht ed. 1952).

context, except for law enforcement agencies, discipline is not a value sought to be legally preserved.

With the advent of democracy and the advancement of the rule of law in modern societies, the quest for legality and lawfulness has superceded concerns for discipline irrespective of whether the issue arises under military or non-military law. Consequently, the defense of "obedience to superior orders" has been subordinated to the legality of the order and the lawfulness of its foreseeable outcome. But distinctions still exist between the military and civilian branches of the law. In the military branch, the order is expected to be obeyed unless it is patently illegal or its foreseeable outcome is unlawful. A military order is presumptively lawful and places the burden of assessing its illegality on the subordinate, including the risk of discipline for disobeying it. But military legal systems differ as to the standards of illegality and the judgmental point at which the subordinate must or can disobey the order, and under what circumstances he will be held accountable for carrying out an unlawful order.

The question of legality or lawfulness of a military order does not only derive from the pragmatic goal of insuring discipline, but is also a reflection of legal philosophy. Similarly, in civilian criminal law, whether a person is legally justified or excused from criminal responsibility derives from philosophical conceptions.[17] Thus, authoritarian philosophies presume absolute legality and lawfulness of the hierarchial orders, while democratic conceptions do not. In short, the philosophical issue is whether legality stems from authority or whether authority is subordinated to legality. This dichotomy of perspectives is represented in the works of the English philosophers Hobbes and Locke. Hobbes, who held to an absolute duty of obedience to a superior's order, wrote:

> The King has to determine right and wrong, and therefore the argument is erroneous -- although one can hear it daily expressed -- that only he would be a King who were acting lawfully, and -- which is also defended -- that the King would have to be obeyed only as far as his orders are lawful. Because before the establishment of public authority no lawful or unlawful existed, as their essence derives from a command, and by itself an act is neither right nor wrong. Lawful and unlawful derives from the law of public power. What is ordered by a legitimate King is made lawful by his command and what he forbids is made unlawful by his prohibition. Contrariwise, when single citizens

---

[17] *See* J. HALL, GENERAL PRINCIPLES OF CRIMINAL LAW 377-415 (1947); 2 P.H. ROBINSON, CRIMINAL LAW DEFENCES, at § 171, 259-274, § 177, 347-372 (1984); Dressler, *Exegesis of the Law of Duress: Justifying The Excuse and Searching for Its Proper Limits*, 62 S. CALIF. L. REV. 1331 (1989).

arrogate to themselves to judge right and wrong, they want to make themselves equal to the King, which counters the State's prosperity. The oldest of God's Commandments says: Thou shallst not eat from the tree of knowledge of right and wrong.

When I do, by order, an act which is wrong for the one who commands it, it is not my wrongdoing, as far as the commander is my legitimate master.[18]

Locke, on the other hand, wrote:

Allegiance being nothing but an Obedience according to Law, which when he violates, he has not right to Obedience, nor can claim it otherwise than as the public Person vested with the Power of the Law, and so is to be consider'd as the Image, Phantom or Representative of the Commonwealth, acted by the will of Society, declared in Laws; and thus he has no Will, no Power, but that of the Law.[19]

Locke's position can also be seen in the writings of Hugo Grotius, who subordinates obedience to the legitimacy of the order because that is the only way to resist injustice. The notion of legitimacy of a superior's order is also a consequence of the philosophical conceptions of law and authority which are evidenced in the writings of Montesquieu, Voltaire, Rousseau, Puffendorf, Vattel, Burlemaqui and Bluntschli.

To illustrate this point further, in Germany, in particular during the National-Socialist Regime of the Third Reich, the supremacy of the *Führer's* orders was called the *Führerprinzip*.[20] The legal philosophy of German law at the time was partially

---

[18] T. HOBBES, ELEMENTA PHILOSOPHICA CIVE Ch. 12, §§ 1, 2, *quoted in* N. KEIJZER, MILITARY OBEDIENCE, 146-147 (1978).

[19] *Quoted in* N. KEIJZER, *supra* note 18, at 147.

[20] It should be noted that the German Military Code of that time provided, in Section 47, that:

If the execution of a military order in the course of duty violates the criminal law, then the superior giving the order will bear the sole responsibility therefor. However, the obeying subordinate will share the punishment of the participant: (1) if he has exceeded the order given to him, or (2) if it was within his knowledge that the order of his superior officer concerned an act by which it was intended to commit a civil or military crime or transgression.

based on the views of Hegel, which sublimated the authority of the state. That philosophy became the foundation for the supremacy of the *Führer's* orders and also for their legitimacy.[21] However, unquestioned obedience to superior orders in German legal philosophy was primarily founded on Immanual Kant's philosophy of the *Categorical Imperative,*[22] in which Kant propounds that, apart from inner conscience, every action is legal when it is according to law; this proposition is the basis of external legality as opposed to internal morality. The external law *inbegriff* is what must be obeyed in the social context.[23] According to this legal philosophy, the *Führer's* authority was the legitimate basis for the orders that others followed. Thus, only he, the *Führer*, could be held responsible and everyone else who obeyed his "superior orders" could not. However, this was not the approach taken by German law and doctrine before 1935. The question is, therefore, whether legitimacy flows to the order-giver, as opposed to whether the import or legality of the order controls and that rejoins the discussion of Chapter 2.

Still, positive international law at the time of World War II had no specific norms disallowing the defense and precedents were few and inconclusive.[24] The most important modern precedent was established in the Leipzig trials following World War I, which recognized the defense, but not in absolute terms. Thus, prior to the Charter, neither conventional nor customary international law specifically disallowed the

---

Cited in R.H. JACKSON, THE NÜRNBERG CASE 89 (1947, 2d printing 1971), *quoting* REICHSGESETZBLATT, 1926, No. 37, Art. 47, at 278. Thus, the Code established the responsibility of the superior as a consideration for the exoneration of the subordinate.

[21] *See* G.W.F. HEGEL, INTRODUCTION TO THE PHILOSOPHY OF HISTORY (Loewenberg ed. 1929), at 406, wherein he states: "The State, its laws, its arrangements, constitute the rights of its members; its natural features, its mountains, air, and waters, are their country, their fatherland, their outward material property; the history of this State, their deeds; what their ancestors have produced, belongs to them and lives in their memory. All is their possession, just as they are possessed by it; for it constitutes their existence, their being." *Also cited and discussed in* D'Amato, *The Relation of the Individual to the State in the Era of Human Rights*, 24 TEX. INT'L L.J. 1, 7 (1989).

[22] *See* I. KANT, THE CATEGORICAL IMPERATIVE (1797). *See also* H.J. PATON, THE METAPHYSICS OF MORALS (1947).

[23] While Kant's internal law is based on the natural law maxims of Aristotle, *honeste vivere, nemineim laedere,* and *surim cinque tribuere,* his external law premises are different, and the twain do not meet.

[24] *See* C. MULLINS, THE LEIPZIG TRIALS (1921).

defense. But by resorting to "general principles of law,"[25] it is possible to ascertain that the inarticulated premise of the defense, whether in military or civilian criminal laws, is the legitimacy of the order and the lawfulness of its conduct.

The question thus arises as to whether legality or lawfulness derives from the authority of the order given, its contents, its impact, or from other moral-ethical considerations? Strict positivism argues for the legal authority of the order given irrespective of value-content or impact.[26] However, other legal philosophies may include substantive and procedural legality considerations.[27]

Another view of the defense also deserves careful consideration, namely that the entire question of "obedience to superior orders" should be viewed as part of the mental element and not as a separate defense. This position was asserted by Lauterpacht, who held that "it is necessary to approach the problem of superior orders on the basis of general principles of criminal law, namely as an element in ascertaining the existence of *mens rea* as a condition of accountability."[28]

The multiplicity of legal sources defining the defense makes it difficult to ascertain, with specificity, the scope, contents and legal standards applicable to "obedience to superior orders." The only way to ascertain them is by way of an inductive empirical approach from the world's major criminal justice systems in order to determine whether and to what extent they may be deemed a "general principle of law."[29]

If one is to search for an alternative legal basis to that of national criminal law systems, such a basis is the customary practice of states as evidenced by their international relations and national experiences. In this case, however, the focus is on a much narrower sampling of practices and experiences. Once again, a review of the writings of the most distinguished publicists and the decisions of international tribunals reveals that the same principle exists in national legal systems and in international legal customs and practices. But their application has been widely different. A number of

---

[25] *See* Chapter 7: *Identifying Specific Crimes*, for a methodology of identifying "General Principles."

[26] *See* Chapter 2.

[27] *See Id.*

[28] Lauterpacht, *The Law of Nations and the Punishment of War Criminals*, 21 Brit. Y.B. Int'l L. 58, 87 (1944). *See also* Wise, *War Crimes and Criminal Law*, in Studies in Comparative Criminal Law 35 (E.M. Wise & G.O.W. Mueller eds. 1976).

[29] *See* Bassiouni, *A Functional Approach to 'General Principles of International Law'*, 11 Mich. J. Int'l L. 768 (1990); B. Cheng, General Principles of Law as Applied by International Courts and Tribunals (1953).

legal issues arise with respect to the defense, many of which pertain to doctrinal differences between the different legal systems and some pertain to concepts of culpability and responsibility.[30] Still other issues that pertain to the specifics of the defense include: (1) the type of order; (2) its manifest illegality; (3) what a subordinate can do under the circumstances; (4) how far should the subordinate go in refusing to obey the order; and (5) under what circumstances would the subordinate be subject to a legal condition of coercion. Furthermore, are these issues based on the objective standard of the "ordinary reasonable man" in the Common Law, or on the more subjective one of *dolus* in the Romanist-Civilist-Germanic systems.

There is also a wide array of issues concerning the circumstances which can be deemed "coercion" and involve the question of what are the legal or moral limits of the permissible harm which the subordinate is legally required to face in case of disobedience. Still another important issue is whether one can inflict death or serious bodily harm onto others to avoid similar harm.[31] All of these and other issues are approached with diversity in the military rules and in the civilian criminal laws of the various national legal systems.

Scholarly Views

A number of views on the subject of the defense of "obedience to superior orders" have been expressed by scholars,[32] even though, as one of them stated: "[t]he

---

[30]   *See* Chapter 9.

[31]   *See* J. HALL, *supra* note 17. *See also* the discussion on the defenses of coercion and necessity *infra*.

[32]   *See, e.g.* H. HALLECK, ELEMENTS OF INTERNATIONAL LAW AND THE LAWS OF WAR (1866); J. SPRAIGHT, WAR RIGHTS ON LAND (1911); J. BAKER & H. CROCKER, THE LAW OF LAND WARFARE (1918); W. WINTHROP, MILITARY LAW AND PRECEDENTS (1920); Lauterpacht, *supra* note 28; Sack, *War Criminals and the Defense of Superior Order in International Law*, 5 LAW GUILD REV. 11 (1945); P. GUGGENHEIM, 2 LEHRBUCH DES VÖLKERRECHT (1951); H. KELSEN, PRINCIPLES OF INTERNATIONAL LAW (1952); H.H. JESCHECK, DIE VERANTWÖRTLICHKIET DER STÄTSORGANE NACH VÖLKERSTRAFRECHT (1952); J. PICTET, THE GENEVA CONVENTIONS OF AUGUST 12, 1949: A COMMENTARY (4 Vols. 1956); G. DRAPER, THE RED CROSS CONVENTIONS (1958); G. DAHM, VÖLKERRECHT (1961); II F. BERBER, LEHRLURCH DES VÖLKERRECHT (1962); F. FUHRMANN, DEN HÖHEHE BEFEHL ALS RECHTIFERTUNGUNG IN VÖLKERRECHT (1963); Y. DINSTEIN, THE DEFENCE OF "OBEDIENCE TO SUPERIOR ORDERS" IN INTERNATIONAL LAW (1965); Jescheck, *Befehl und Gehorsam inder Bundeswehr*, in BUNDESWEHR UND RECHT 63 (1965); E. MÜLLER-RAPPARD, L'ORDRE SUPÉRIEUR MILITAIRE ET LA RESPONSIBILITÉ PÉNALE DU SUBORDONNÉ (1965); Wilner, *Superior*

problem raised by the plea of superior orders is, by general admission, one of great complexity both in international and in municipal law."[33]   While each scholar postulates his own particular view on the subject,[34] since World War II, there are essentially two basic approaches to the issue: (1) a subordinate may assert the defense of "obedience to superior orders," but not if the subordinate recognized, or should have recognized, the patent illegality of the order; and, (2) a subordinate may not assert the defense, but may rely on it for mitigation of culpability.[35] In both cases, however,

---

Orders as a Defense to Violations of International Criminal Law, 26 MD. L. REV. 127 (1966); Green, *Superior Orders and the Reasonable Man*, 8 CAN. Y.B. INT'L L. 61 (1970); Hart, *Yamashita, Nuremberg and Vietnam: Command Responsibility Reappraised*, 26 NAVAL WAR COL. REV. 19 (1972); Vogler, *The Defense of 'Superior Orders' in International Criminal Law*, in 1 BASSIOUNI ICL, *supra* note 6, at 619; Daniel, *The Defense of Superior Orders*, 7 U. RICH. L. REV. 477 (1973); L.C. GREEN, SUPERIOR ORDERS IN NATIONAL AND INTERNATIONAL LAW (1976); N. KEIJZER, *supra* note 18, at 140-225; L.C. GREEN, ESSAYS ON THE MODERN LAW OF WAR (1985); Johnson, *The Defence of Superior Orders*, 9 AUST. Y.B. INT'L L. 291 (1985); and Paust, *Superior Orders and Command Responsibility*, in 3 BASSIOUNI ICL 73.

[33]   Lauterpacht, *supra* note 28, at 70.

[34]   For example, Professor Röling contends that the problem of superior orders has two aspects: one of knowledge and the other of fear. As he explains:

1.   The superior order to commit a war crime is a complete defence if it leads to an excusable *error juris*. Certain rules of war are controversial. It may be difficult to come to a correct decision in case of reprisals. It is possible that the alleged criminal did not know and could not reasonably have been expected to know that the act ordered was unlawful. In case he thought, in good faith, that the superior did not order a war crime to be committed, and if he was entitled to come to that conclusion--that is; if there did not exist any negligence on his part--the only conclusion should be that he cannot be punished.

2.   In case he knew that the order was an illegal one, demanding the commission of a crime, then a second defense is feasible. The accused may argue: I knew that what I was going to do was criminal, but I did not dare disobey: I would have been shot on the spot. I was in a clear position of duress, because I realized that serious personal harm would be the consequence of disobedience. This position of duress can have all shades of intensity. Consequently, this line of defence may lead to mitigation of punishment and even to no punishment at all.

Röling, *Criminal Responsibility For Violations of the Laws of War*, 12 REV. BELGE DE DROIT INT'l 8, 18-19 (1976).

[35]   It should be noted of course that there exists a third view on the defense of obedience to superior orders: that the defense is an absolute one (*Befehl ist Befehl*). *See* N. KEIJZER, *supra* note 18, at *xxix*. Although today this approach does not carry much weight, for the greater part of history it was the dominant view. Cicero was of the opinion that, if a subordinate was indeed obliged to obey the superior in the matter

there is a further condition, namely, that the subordinate had a choice in refusing to obey the order; a choice which, similar to "coercion," is that the subordinate would not be subjected to a greater harm than the one he is required to inflict.

The former approach was aptly stated by Francis Wharton who writes:

[W]here a person relies on a command of legal authority as a defence, it is essential that the command be a lawful one, which he was required to obey .... An order which is illegal in itself, and not justified by the rules and usages of war, or which is, in substance, clearly illegal, so that a man of ordinary sense and understanding would know as soon as he heard the order read or given that it was illegal, will afford no protection .... When an act committed by a soldier is a crime, even when done pursuant to military orders, the fact that he was ordered to commit the crime by his military superior is not a defence.[36]

---

to which the order referred, then not he but the superior was the person who had committed the offense. *See id.* at 145 *citing* DE INVENTIONE I, XI, 15. *Also,* as provided in the DIGESTS OF JUSTINIAN, in ancient Rome, "he causes loss who orders it to be caused, but he is without blame who is under the necessity of obeying it." *Quoted in* N. KEIJZER, *supra* note 18, at 144. Even in Shakespeare's day, this view was maintained, for as stated in HENRY V, Act IV, 1, "we [soldiers] know enough if we know we are the Kings subjects: if his cause be wrong, our obedience to the King wipes the crime of it out of us."

For a survey of the approaches taken by various nations to the defense, *see* 10 *Rev. de droit penal militaire* 87 *et seq.* (1971). *See also* MÜLLER-RAPPARD *supra* note 32 for an international and comparative approach.

[36] 1 F. WHARTON, CRIMINAL LAW AND PROCEDURE 257-258, § 118 (1957 ed). For a discussion on the issue of knowledge, *see* Green, *The Man in the Field and the Maxim Ignorantia Juris Non-Excusat,* ARCHIV DES VOLKERRECHTS (Schlochauer ed. 1981) at 169.

The most comprehensive doctrinal statement of the United States' position, and one adopted by the courts, is by Hare:

The question is ... had the accused *reasonable cause for believing in the necessity* of the act which is impugned, and in determining this point a soldier or member of the *posse comitatus* may obviously take the orders of the person in command into view as proceeding from one who is better able to judge and well informed; and, if the circumstances are such that the command may be justifiable, he should not be held guilty for declining to decide that it is wrong with the responsibility incident to disobedience, *unless the case is so plain as not to admit of a reasonable doubt.* A soldier consequently runs little in obeying any order *which a man of common sense so placed would regard as warranted by the circumstances.*

HARE, CONSTITUTIONAL LAW, 920 (1889) (italics added). *See also* Green, *supra* note 32.

Also, Winthrop, a leading American expert on miliary law, who asserted "... a command not lawful may be disobeyed, no matter from what source it proceeds. But to justify an inferior in disobeying an order as illegal, the case must be an extreme one and the illegality not doubtful."[37]

A similar, though less stringent, view was expressed by Sir James Stephen:

[Soldiers] are bound to execute any lawful order which they may receive from their military superior .... Probably ... the order of a military superior would justify his inferiors in executing any orders for giving which they might fairly suppose their superior officer to have good reasons .... [A] soldier should be protected by orders for which he might reasonably believe his officer to have good grounds.[38]

The first approach was also that of Dicey who states:

---

[37] W. WINTHROP, *supra* note 32, at 575.

[38] 1 J. STEPHEN, HISTORY OF THE CRIMINAL LAW 204-206 (1883). Stephen's concern for the subordinate echoes that of St. Augustine, who writes:

... a just man, who happens to serve under an impious king, may justly fight at the latter's command, either if he is certain that the command given him, preserving the order of the public peace, is not contrary to the law of God, or if he is uncertain whether it is so; so that an unjust order may perhaps render the king responsible, while the duty of obedience preserves the innocence of the soldier. AUGUSTINE, CONTRA FAUSTUM MANICHAEM, XXII ch. 76 (Oeuvres Completetes vol. XXVI p. 224), as *quoted in* N. KEIJZER, *supra* note 18, at 146.

THE BRITISH MANUAL (1929), Ch. III, para. 12, defines a lawful command as follows:

"Lawful command" means not only a command which is not contrary to the ordinary civil law, but one which is justified by military law; in other words, a lawful military command to do or not to do, or to desist from doing, a particular act. A superior officer has a right at any time to give a command, for the purpose of the maintenance of good order, or the suppression of a disturbance, or the execution of any military duty or regulation, or for any purpose connected with the amusements and welfare of a regiment or other generally accepted details of military life. But a superior officer has no right to take advantage of his military rank to give a command which does not relate to military duty or usages, or which has for its sole object the attainment of some private end. Such a command, though it may not be unlawful, is not such a lawful command as will make disobedience of it an offence under the Act. In other words, the command must be one relating to military duty, that is to say, the disobedience of it must tend to impede, delay or prevent a military proceeding.

While, however, a soldier runs no substantial risk of punishment for obedience to orders which a man of common sense may honestly believe to involve no breach of law, he ... cannot avoid liability on the ground of obedience to superior orders for any act which a man of ordinary sense must have known to be a crime.[39]

More recently, Justice Keijzer concludes:

The main criterion for the liability of a subordinate acting in compliance with orders is whether the illegality of the order was manifest, meaning that a man of ordinary sense and understanding would in his place have known the order to be illegal. Also, as has become apparent from some cases, if the subordinate himself actually knew of the illegality of the order he could not successfully invoke that order as a defense.[40]

Also, Professor Jescheck writes:

An illegal command cannot justify the deeds ... of the subordinate but is to be considered only as excluding his guilt.... The illegal command does have the effect of an excuse if the subordinate might reasonably rely on its legality. Such reliance is not to be protected if the order was obviously illegal.[41]

---

[39]   A. DICEY, THE LAW OF THE CONSTITUTION 302 (8th ed. 1915). Dicey also explains the dilemma of a soldier forced to decide whether or not he should follow the order. As he states, a soldier's "position is in theory and may be in practice a difficult one. He may ... be liable to be shot by a Court martial if he disobeys an order, and to be hanged by a judge and jury if he obeys it. *Id.* at 299. Dinstein recognized the same dilemma, when he stated that:

... when a soldier is confronted with an [illegal] order to perform an act constituting a criminal offence, the demands of military discipline, as expressed in the duty of obedience to superior orders, come into conflict with the imperative need to preserve the supremacy of the law as manifested in the proscriptions of criminal law: military discipline requires unflinching compliance with orders; the supremacy of law proscribes the commission of criminal acts.

Y. DINSTEIN, *supra* note 32, at 6.

[40]   N. KEIJZER, *supra* note 18, at 169.

[41]   Jescheck, *Befehl und Gehorsam in der Bundeswehr, supra* note 32; *also cited* in Vogler, *supra* note 32.

412

Similarly, Dahm's position is that a soldier does not incriminate himself when acting pursuant to a superior's order unless he either recognizes or should have recognized the illegality of the order.[42]

It is views such as these which allowed Professor Vogler to conclude that the "decisive criterion for the culpability or blamelessness of the subordinate is whether or not he could rely on the legality of the command."[43]

The other basic approach to the superior orders defense is stated in Halsbury:

> The mere fact that a person does a criminal act in obedience to the order of a duly constituted superior does not excuse the person who does the act from criminal liability, but the fact that a person does an act in obedience to a superior whom he is bound to obey, may exclude the inference of malice or wrongful intention which might otherwise follow from the act .... Soldiers and airmen are amenable to the criminal law to the same extent as other subjects .... Obedience to superior orders is not in itself a defence to a criminal charge.[44]

For Professor Guggenheim, the assertion of the defense of having acted pursuant to superior orders does not eliminate the personal criminal culpability of the subordinate, but, in subjective terms, whether or not the subordinate had a choice in the execution of the order needs to be determined for the purpose of mitigation of, or exemption from, the sentence.[45]

---

[42] 3 G. DAHM, *supra* note 32, at 311.

[43] Vogler, *supra* note 32, at 634. But *see* the positivist H.L.A. HART, THE CONCEPT OF LAW (1961), where at 206 he stated: "What surely is most needed in order to make men clear-sighted in confronting the official abuse of power, is that they should preserve the sense that the certification of something as legally valid is not conclusive of the question of obedience, and that, however great the aura of majesty or authority which the official system may have, its demands must in the end be submitted to a moral scrutiny."

[44] 10 HALSBURY, THE LAWS OF ENGLAND §§ 541, 1169 (3rd Simonds ed. 1955). Another author states:

> Superior order is never a justification, unless it itself was lawful. If the order was unlawful, the act done in obedience thereto will also be unlawful, even though, in some cases, the law will excuse the one who did it, or will reduce his punishment.

Sack, *supra* note 32 at 12.

[45] 2 P. GUGGENHEIM, *supra* note 32, at 551.

This position is also supported by Professor Dinstein who is the author of one of the most authoritative works on the subject.[46] Dinstein argues that:

[O]bedience to orders constitutes not a defence *per se* but only a factual element that may be taken into account in conjunction with the other circumstances of the given case within the compass of a defence based on lack of *mens rea*, that is, mistake of law or fact or compulsion.[47]

To Dinstein, "the existence of *mens rea* is the signpost that ought to direct our thoughts and guide us in the attempt to solve the problem of obedience to superior orders."[48] Sir Hersch Lauterpacht had previously expressed the same view, for he states that:

[I]t is necessary to approach the subject of superior orders on the basis of general principles of criminal law, namely, as an element in ascertaining the existence of *mens rea* as a condition of accountability.[49]

As Dinstein further explains:

[O]bedience to orders should be regarded as a factual detail germane to the offence, just like the time when, and the place where, the offence was committed; just like the weapon by which it was carried out; and just like myriads of other circumstantial minutiae. None of these factual details standing alone and out of context is endowed with special traits which radiate special legal significance. When the only thing that we know about a particular offence is that it was performed pursuant to orders, the knowledge does not get us, legally speaking, any farther than if the only thing that we knew were that the offence was committed, for instance, at 6 o'clock p.m. It would have been rash and impetuous on our part, if, on the basis of this knowledge alone, we had jumped to the conclusion that when the offender is brought to trial he must need be relieved of responsibility. No particularly immunizing ingredient is inherent in the mere fact that the offender

---

[46] Y. DINSTEIN, *supra* note 32, also L. GREEN, E. MÜLLER-RAPPARD and N. KEIJZER, *supra* note 32.

[47] *Id.* at 88.

[48] *Id.*

[49] Lauterpacht, *supra* note 28, at 73.

obeyed an order, just as no specially exculpating component is inherent in the fact that the offence was committed at 6 o'clock p.m. Of course, when the scope of our knowledge in respect of the circumstances of the case broadens and all the facts are assembled and evaluated, the fact that the offence was carried out in submission to orders may contribute to the discharge of the defendant from responsibility, just as the fact that the offence was committed at 6 o'clock p.m. may be material in the achievement of the same result.[50]

Thus, in the words of Professor Dinstein: "Superior orders are not a magical talisman which wards off the spirit of justice."[51] Indeed--as another authoritative scholar, Professor Green states--"whether in time of peace or armed conflict, it is clear that while they may constitute ground for mitigating punishment, these orders cannot be accepted as justifying an illegal act."[52]

German military doctrine before 1945 was premised on the maxim *Befehl ist befehl* (an order is an order), and many national military doctrines follwed that view. But the IMT, as discussed below, revoked that view. Instead, in reliance on the Charter, it rejected the defense of "obedience to superior orders" for all unlawful orders irrespective of the actor's state of mind, knowledge, and ability to refuse the order short of imminent threat of death. The Subsequent Proceedings, however, as discussed below, tempered this extreme view with the *caveat* that the actor had no moral choice but to obey. It is this latter perspective that prevailed in the Post-Charter developments in national military law. The prevailing, if not overwhelmingly followed test, is that of reasonableness in light of existing circumstances.

The Judgments of Tribunals

Scholars are not alone in contributing to the development of doctrine regarding the defense of "obedience to superior orders." Military tribunals and other courts have also contributed to the advancement of the superior orders doctrine.

---

[50] Y. DINSTEIN, *supra* note 32, at 88-89.

[51] *Id.* at 89.

[52] Green, *supra* note 32, at 103.

Perhaps the first person to assert the defense of superior orders before a tribunal was Peter von Hagenbach in the year 1474.[53] Charles, the Duke of Burgundy, appointed Hagenbach the Governor (*Landvogt*) of the Upper Rhine, including the fortified town of Breisach. At the behest of Charles, Hagenbach, with the aid of his henchmen, sought to reduce the populace of Breisach to a state of submission by committing such atrocities as murder, rape and illegal confiscation of property.[54] Hagenbach was finally captured and accused of having "trampled under foot the laws of God and man."[55] Hagenbach relied primarily on the defense of "obedience to superior orders." His counsel claimed that Hagenbach "had no right to question the order which he was charged to carry out, and it was his duty to obey. Is it not known that soldiers owe absolute obedience to their superiors?"[56] The Tribunal refused to accept Hagenbach's defense, found him guilty, and sentenced him to death.

Another failed attempt to assert the defense occurred in England, where in 1660, after the restoration of King Charles II, the commander of the guard who presided at the execution of Charles I, Colonel Axtell, was tried for treason and murder. He plead that he was acting upon superior orders, but, the court rejected his plea on the basis that obedience to a treasonable order is itself treasonable.[57]

In the United States, a striking case occurred during the War of 1812. During that war, the populace of the United States was split as to attitudes toward the war, and in New England the United States Navy was not very popular.[58] It happened that while the ship *Independence* was docked in Boston Harbor, a passerby directed abusive language at a marine named Bevans, who was standing guard on the ship. Bevans

---

[53]   *See* 2 G. SCHWARZENBERGER, INTERNATIONAL LAW AS APPLIED BY INTERNATIONAL COURTS 462-466 (1968). *See also* Daniel, *supra* note 32 at 481.

[54]   As Professor Green points out, Hagenbach perpetrated acts which today would be considered "crimes against humanity," Green, *supra* note 32, at 77. *See also* G. SCHWARZENBERGER, *supra* note 53, at 466.

[55]   *See* G. SCHWARZENBERGER, *supra* note 53, at 465. *See also*, A.G. DE BARANTE, 10 HISTOIRE DES DUCS DE BOURGOGNE 1364-1477, 15 (1839).

[56]   *See* G. SCHWARZENBERGER, *supra* 53, at 465; and A.G. DEBARANTE, *supra* note 55, at 16.

[57]   *See* H. MCCOUBREY, INTERNATIONAL HUMANITARIAN LAW 219 (1990). The Court concluded that:

his superior was a traitor, and all that joined him in that act were traitorous and did by that approve the treason; and where the command was traitorous, there the obedience to that command is also traitorous. 84 ENG. REP. 1060 (1660).

[58]   *See* T. TAYLOR, *supra* note 15 at 43-44.

responded by driving his bayonet through the man. Bevans was charged with murder and asserted as a defense that the marines on *Independence* had been ordered to bayonet whomever showed them disrespect. The trial was before Justice Joseph Story who instructed the jury that such an order was illegal and void, and if given and carried out, both the superior and subordinate would be guilty of murder; Bevans was convicted.[59] In another early American case *United States v. Bright*,[60] the court clearly expressed its view on the issue:

> In a state of open and public war, where military law prevails, and the peaceful voice of military law is drowned in the din of arms, great indulgences must necessarily be extended to the acts of subordinate officers done in obedience to the orders of their superiors. But even there the order of a superior officer to take the life of a citizen, or to invade the sanctity of his house and to deprive him of his property, would not shield the inferior against a charge of murder or trespass, in the regular judicial tribunals of this country.[61]

During the Napoleonic Wars, a Scottish court rejected the plea of "superior orders" of a solder who shot and killed a French prisoner. In the case of *Ensign Maxwell*, the court stated:

---

[59] United States v. Bevans, 24 F. Cas. 1138 (C.C.D. Mass. 1816)(No. 14589). Bevans' conviction was later reversed by the Supreme Court on jurisdictional grounds. United States v. Bevans, 3 Wheat. 336 (1818).

[60] 24 F. Cas. 1232 (C.C.D. Pa. 1809)(No. 14647). *See also* Little v. Barrone, 1 U.S. (2 Cranch) 465, 467 (1804) in which Chief Justice Marshall stated:

[i]mplicit obedience which military men usually pay to the orders of their superiors, which indeed is indispensably necessary to every military system, appears to me strongly to imply the principle that those orders, if not to perform a prohibited act, ought to justify the person whose general duty it is to obey them, and who is placed by the laws of his country in a situation which in general requires that he should obey them.

However, as a matter of law, he held:

the instructions cannot change the nature of the transaction, or legalize an act which, without those instructions, would have been a plain trespass. *Id.*

[61] *Id.* at 1237-1238. *See also* Martin v. Mott, 25 U.S. (12 Wheat) 537 (1827). *See*, however, United States v. Jones, 26 f. Cas. 653 (C.C.D. Pa, 1813); and Hyde v. Melvin, 11 Johns (N.Y.) 521 (1814), where the courts did not discuss special rules for the military.

If an officer were to command a soldier to go out to the street and to kill you or me, he would not be bound to obey. It must be a legal order given with reference to the circumstances in which he is placed; and thus every officer has a discretion to disobey orders against the known laws of the land.[62]

Another important prosecution in the development of the "superior orders" doctrine occurred after the American Civil War. At the *Wirz Trial*,[63] the defendant, Major Henry Wirz, was charged with committing atrocities against Union prisoners of war at the Andersonville prison.[64] Wirz was tried before a military commission of six Union generals and two colonels. The Commission heard a prodigious amount of evidence which showed that Union prisoners were given inadequate shelter, inadequate food, and contaminated water. Despite a bountiful harvest in the neighboring country, Wirz turned away farmers offering relief. Further, a stream which constituted the sole source of water was fouled not only by human waste, but also with corpses. As a result some 14,000 prisoners died by the end of the war. Wirz defended himself by providing evidence that his administration of the camp was pursuant to the orders of General John H. Winder, the officer in charge of all Confederate prison camps. The commission found him, *inter alia*, guilty of murder in violation of the laws and customs of war and

---

[62]   2 BUCHANAN, REPORTS OF REMARKABLE TRIALS 3, 58 (1813).

[63]   H.R. Exec. Doc. No. 23, 40th Cong. 2d Sess., 764. *See also* Riggs v. State, 3 Coldwell 85, 91 Am. Dec. 272 (1866). This was one of the most frequently cited cases during this period on the question of obedience. The court found no error in a lower court instruction that:

Any order given by an officer to a private, which does not expressly and clearly show on its face or in the body thereof its own illegality, the soldier would be bound to obey and such an order would be a protection to him .... But an order illegal in itself and not justified by the rules and usages of war, or in its substance being clearly illegal so that a man of ordinary sense and understanding would know as soon as he heard the order read or given that such order was illegal, would afford a private no protection for a crime committed under such order. *Id.* at 273.

[64]   An early American case addressed the issue of "obedience to superior orders" in the context of an action arising from the seizure of property. Chief Justice Taney stated that:

[T]he order given was to do an illegal act; to commit a trespass upon the property of another; and can afford no justification to the person by whom it was executed .... And upon principle, ... it can never be maintained that a military officer can justify himself for doing an unlawful act, by producing the order or his superior. The order may palliate, but it cannot justify.

Mitchell v. Harmony, 13 How. 115, 137 (1851).

sentenced him to hanging.[65] Although no formal judgment was delivered because the case was a military trial, we may assume that the judges shared the view expressed by the Judge Advocate, who stated:

> A superior officer cannot order a subordinate to do an illegal act, and if a subordinate obeys such an order and disastrous consequences result, both the superior and the subordinate must answer for it.[66]

Another notable case is *Regina v. Smith*,[67] which involved a soldier who, under order killed a native for not performing a menial task. Although the court acquitted the soldier, it introduced the "manifest illegality" test, stating:

> It is monstrous to suppose that a soldier would be protected where the order is grossly illegal. [That he] is responsible if he obeys an order that is not strictly legal is an extreme proposition which the Court cannot accept .... Especially in time of war immediate obedience ... is required .... I think it is a safe rule to lay down that if a soldier honestly believes that he is doing his duty in obeying the command of his superior, and if the orders are not so manifestly illegal that he must or ought to have known that they were unlawful, the private soldier would be protected by the orders of his superior.[68]

The issue of "obedience to superior orders" first gained contemporary international significance during the war crimes trials that followed World War I.[69] By virtue of Article 228 of the Treaty of Versailles,[70] Germany submitted to the Allied Powers'

---

[65] *See* T. TAYLOR, *supra* note 15, at 45-46.

[66] H.R. Exec. Doc. No. 23, 40th Cong. 2d Sess., 764, 773.

[67] 17 S.C. 561 (Cape of Good Hope, 1900).

[68] *Id.* at 567-568. A half-century later, an American tribunal also emphasized the manifest illegality of an order. In United States v. Kinder, 14 C.M.R. 742, 774 (1953), the court notes that "of controlling significance in the instant case is the manifest and unmistakable illegality of the order."

[69] *See generally*, Y. DINSTEIN, N. KEIJZER and E. MÜLLER-RAPPARD, *supra* note 32, at 10-20; and Green, *supra* note 32, at 79-81. *See also* C. MULLINS, *supra*, note 24.

[70] Treaty of Versailles, Art. 228. *See also* Chapter III of the 1919 Commission Report which stated:

right to try alleged war criminals. Although the Treaty originally provided that the trials would be administered by the state against whose nationals the alleged crimes were committed,[71] it was subsequently agreed that the German *Reichsgericht* (Supreme Court) sitting at Leipzig would be the court to preside over these cases.[72] The two most notable cases involving the issue of "obedience to superior orders" during the Leipzig Trials[73] were the *Dover Castle*[74] and the *Llandovery Castle*.[75]

In *Dover Castle*, the defendant, Lieutenant Captain Karl Neuman, the commander of a German submarine, was charged with torpedoing the *Dover Castle*, a British hospital ship. The defendant claimed that he was acting pursuant to "superior orders," which were issued by his naval superiors who claimed that they believed that Allied hospital ships were being used for military purposes in violation of the laws of war. The Leipzig Court, acquitted the commander holding:

> It is a military principle that the subordinate is bound to obey the orders of his superiors ... [w]hen the execution of a service order involves an offence against the criminal law, the superior giving the order is alone responsible. This is in accordance with the terms of the German law, § 47, para. 1 of the Military Penal Code ....

> According to § 47 of the Military Penal Code No. 2, a subordinate who acts in conformity with orders is ... liable to punishment as an accomplice, when he knows

---

We desire to say that civil and military authorities cannot be relieved from responsibility by the mere fact that a higher authority might have been convicted of the same offense. It will be for the court to decide whether a plea of superior orders is sufficient to acquit the person charged from responsibility.

14 AJIL 95, 117 (1920).

[71]   *Id.* art. 229.

[72]   As Dinstein explains, because only a relatively few secondary offenders were tried and sentenced at Leipzig, these trials have become synonymous "with a judicial farce." Y. DINSTEIN, *supra* note 32, at 11.

[73]   The superior's orders issue was also addressed in *Robert Neumann's Case, see* 16 AJIL 696 (1922); *see also* C. MULLINS, *supra* note 24, at 87-98. And in the *Stenger and Crusius Case, see* C. MULLINS, *supra* note 24, at 151-167.

[74]   *See Dover Castle*, 16 AJIL 704 (1922). *See also*, C. MULLINS, *supra* note 24, at 99-107, 198, 221-22.

[75]   *See Llandovery Castle*, 16 AJIL 708 (1922). *See also*, C. MULLINS, *supra* note 24, at 107-133, 221.

that his superiors have ordered him to do acts which involve a civil or military crime or misdemeanor. There has been no case of this here. The memoranda of the German Government about the misuse of enemy hospital ships were known to the accused .... He was therefore of the opinion that the measures taken by the German Admiralty against enemy hospital ships were not contrary to international law, but were legitimate reprisals .... The accused ... cannot, therefore, be punished for his conduct.[76]

In the subsequent *Llandovery Castle* case, the same court did not so readily grant the accused a defense of "obedience to superior orders." In that case, also involving a German submarine attack upon a British hospital ship, the submarine commander ordered his subordinates to open fire on the survivors of the torpedoed *Llandovery Castle* who had managed to get into lifeboats. The officers who carried out the order, First Lieutenants Ludwig Dithmar and John Boldt, were charged with the killings and pleaded that they followed the orders of their commander, Helmut Patzik (whom the German authorities failed to apprehend after the war). The court, however, rejected this defense and stated:

The firing on the boats was an offence against the law of nations .... The rule of international law, which is here involved, is simple and is universally known. No possible applicability .... [The commander's] order does not free the accused from guilt. It is true that according to para. 47 of the Military Penal Code, if the execution of an order in the ordinary course of duty involves such a violation the superior giving the order is alone responsible. However, the subordinate obeying such an order is liable to punishment if it was known to him that the order of the superior involved the infringement of civil or military law. This applies in the case of the accused. It is certainly to be urged in favor of the military subordinates, that they are under no obligation to question the order of their superior officer, and they can count upon its legality. But no such confidence can be held to exist, if such an order is universally known to everybody, including also the accused, to be without any doubt whatever against the law.[77]

---

[76] 16 AJIL 707-708 (1922).

[77] 16 AJIL 721-22 (1922). The Court stated further:

In examining the question of the existence of this knowledge, the ambiguity of many rules of international law, as well as the actual circumstances of the case, must be borne in mind, because in

This statement notwithstanding, the court acknowledged that the "superior orders" defense ought to be considered as a factor taken into account for mitigation of punishment, and thereby the court sentenced the accused to only four years of imprisonment.[78]

Professor Dinstein's analysis of the use of the defense of "obedience to superior orders" at the Leipzig trials concluded that:

(1) As a general rule, a subordinate committing a criminal act pursuant to an order should not incur responsibility for it.

(2) This rule is inapplicable if the subordinate knew that the order entailed the commission of a crime, and obeyed it nonetheless.

(3) To determine whether the subordinate was aware of the fact that he had been ordered to perform a criminal act, the Court may use the auxiliary test of manifest illegality.[79]

Undoubtedly, the most important decisions which dealt with the "superior orders" issue was rendered by the IMT at Nuremberg. The importance of those Nuremberg holdings is that for the first time a rule was set down in positive international law which addressed the "superior orders" defense. The Charter[80] of the Nuremberg

---

war time decisions of great importance have frequently to be made on very insufficient material. This consideration, however, cannot be applied to the case at present before the court. *The rule of international law, which is here involved, is simple and is universally known. No possible doubt can exist with regard to the question of its applicability.* The court must in this instance affirm Patzig's guilt of killing contrary to international law.

Id. at 721.

[78] *Id.* at 723.

[79] *See* Y. DINSTEIN, *supra* note 32, at 19.

[80] *See* Document Section C.2.

In 1946, by way of a General Assembly Resolution, the United Nations affirmed the principles of International Law articulated in the Charter; Article 8 included. *See* Affirmation of Nuremberg Principles. Specifically, the Resolution states:

Tribunal, however, specifically articulated a rule applicable to the defense of "obedience to superior orders." Article 8 of the Charter provides:

> The fact that the Defendant acted pursuant to orders of his Government or of a superior shall not free him from responsibility, but may be considered in mitigation of punishment, if the Tribunal determines that Justice so desires.[81]

The General Assembly ... affirms the principles of international law recognized by the Charter of the Nüremberg Tribunal and the Judgment of the Tribunal.

Similarly, in 1950 the ILC affirmed the principles of the Charter. *See* Nuremberg Principles. As to the obedience defence, the Commissions Reports states that:

"The Fact that a person acted pursuant to orders of his government or of a superior does not relieve him from responsibility under international law, provided a moral choice was in fact possible to him." Nuremberg Principles.

[81] Charter, art. 8. The Charter's formulation on this issue resulted as a comprise between the Allies. The United States' original position was:

The fact that a defendant acted pursuant to order of a superior or government sanction shall not constitute an absolute defense but may be considered either in defense or in mitigation of punishment if the Tribunal before which the charges are being tried determines that justice so requires. American Draft of Definitive Proposal, Presented to Foreign Ministers at San Francisco, April 1945, in Jackson's Report at 24.

The Soviet proposal, on the other hand stated that:

The fact that the accused acted under orders of his superior or his government will not be considered as justifying the guilt circumstance. Aide-Mémoire from the Soviet Government, June 14, 1945, in Jackson's Report at 62.

The U.S., however, insisted that superior orders be admissable for purposes of mitigation of punishment and offered another proposal:

The fact that a defendant acted to order of a superior or to government sanction shall not constitute a defense *per se*, but may be considered in mitigation of punishment if the Tribunal determines that justice so requires.

Revised Draft of Agreement and Memorandum Submitted by American Delegation, June 30, 1945, in Jackson's Report at 124.

As Professor Dinstein notes with respect to Nuremberg, "the prosecution and the defence crossed swords many times in the arena of obedience to orders, and the Tribunal seriously pondered the question."[82]

An issue of the obedience defense which was greatly contested at Nuremberg involved the *Führerprinzip* or leadership principle.[83] The Tribunal explained the term in this manner:

The procedure within the [Nazi] party was governed in the most absolute way by the "leadership principle" (*Führerprinzip*).

According to the principle, each *Führer* has the right to govern, administer or decree, subject to no control of any kind and at his complete discretion, subject only to the orders he received from above.

This principle applied in the first instance to Hitler himself as the Leader of the Party, and in a lesser degree to all other party officials. All members of the Party swore an oath of "eternal allegiance" to the Leader."[84]

In light of the *Führerprinzip*, the defense at Nuremberg argued that the Tribunal should relieve the defendants of responsibility since they had not obeyed ordinary orders but orders from the *Führer*. Thus, the accused contended that Article 8 ought not apply because they had obeyed not just a leader, but rather "the Leader," the *Führer* of the Third Reich.[85] As one defense attorney, Dr. Jahrreiss pointed out: "The

---

[82]   Y. DINSTEIN, *supra* note 32 at 125. For individual cases where the defense was raised *see*: 18 IMT 362, Nuremberg Trial, Final Plea for Defendant Doenitz (by Kranzbühler); 18 IMT 362, Nuremberg Trial, Final Plea for Defendant Funk (by Santer); 18 IMT 248, Nuremberg Trial, Final Plea for Defendant Jodl (by Exner); 18 IMT 67, Nuremberg Trial, Final Plea for Defendant Kaltenbrunner (by Kauffmann); 18 IMT 426, Nuremberg Trial, Final Plea for Defendant Raeder (by Siemers); 17 IMT 597-599, Nuremberg Trial, Final Plea for Defendant Ribbentrop (by Horn); 18 IMT 505, Nuremberg Trial, Final Plea for Defendant Sauckel (by Servatius); 19 IMT 72, Nuremberg Trial, Final Plea for Defendant Seyss-Inquart (by Steinbauer); 19 IMT 210, Nuremberg Trial, Final Plea for Defendant Speer (by Flachsner).

[83]   *See e.g.*, 17 IMT 482, 493, Nuremberg Trial, Closing Speech for the Defense (by Jahrreiss).

[84]   *Command Papers* No. 6964, 5, Nuremberg Trial, Judgment, *reprinted in* Y. DINSTEIN, *supra* note 32, at 141.

[85]   *See* Y. DINSTEIN, *supra* note 32, at 140-141.

Führer's orders [had] a special aura of sanctity .... His orders were something quite different from the orders of any official within the hierarchy under him."[86]

The arguments of the defense, however, were dealt with "by one thrust of the sword of logic."[87] The chief Soviet prosecutor, Rudenko, stated in regard to the applicability of Article 8 to orders of the *Führer* that:

> ... it is quite incomprehensible what logical or other methods have led him to assert that the provisions of the Charter, specially drafted for the trial of major war criminals of fascist Germany, did not factually imply the very conditions themselves of the activities of these criminals. What orders then issued by whom and in what country are meant by the Charter of the Tribunal?[88]

Similarly, Justice Jackson, the Chief American Prosecutor, repudiated defense counsel's use of the *Führerprinzip* principle:

> I admit that Hitler was the chief villain. But ... we know that even the head of the state has the same limits to his senses and to the hours of his days as do lesser men. He must rely on others to be his eyes and ears as to most that goes on in a great empire. Other legs must run his errands; other hands must execute his plans. On whom did Hitler rely for such things more than upon these men in the dock? ... These men had access to Hitler and often could control the information that reached him and on which he must base his policy and his orders. They were the Praetorian Guard, and while they were under Caesar's orders, Caesar was always in their hands.[89]

Another Allied prosecutor, Lord Shawcross, commented on the obvious illegality of the orders, regardless of who passes the order:

> By every test of international, of common conscience, of elementary humanity, these orders ... were illegal."[90]

---

[86]   17 IMT 484.

[87]   *See* Y. DINSTEIN, *supra* note 32, at 144.

[88]   19 IMT 577 Nuremberg Trial, Closing Speech for the Prosecution (by Rudenko).

[89]   *Id.* at 430.

[90]   19 IMT 466.

In its Judgment, the Tribunal stood firm in its belief as to the validity of Article 8 of the Charter. The Tribunal stated that:

The provisions of this article are in conformity with the law of all nations. That a soldier was ordered to kill or torture in violation of the international law of war has never been recognized as a defence to such acts of brutality, though, as the Charter here provides, the order may be urged in mitigation of the punishment. The true test, which is found in varying degrees in the criminal law of most nations is not the existence of the order, but whether moral choice was in fact possible.[91]

This oft quoted statement has been the center of much discussion, especially the last sentence, which introduces the "moral choice test." A point of contention is whether the moral choice test undermines the provision in Article 8 which specifically provides that even though an accused "acted pursuant to orders of his Government or of a superior [it] shall not free him from responsibility."[92]

One commentator, Greenspan, contends that the moral choice test does undercut Article 8. He states: "It is clear that the test of moral choice was applied to the question of criminal punishment."[93] This contention, however, contradicts what the Tribunal explicitly asserted previously in the statement; i.e., the Tribunal endorsed the

---

[91] 22 IMT 466, *reprinted in* 41 AJIL, at 221 (1947). Other parts of the Tribunal's Judgments referred to the superior orders issue. The Tribunal stated that:

Participation in ... crimes ... have never been required of any soldier and he cannot now shield himself behind a mythical requirement of soldierly obedience at all costs as his excuse for commission of these crimes. *Id*. at 316.

Ironically, the words used by the Tribunal in its judgment echoed those of Dr. Joseph Goebels, the German Minister of Propaganda, who in May 1944, published an article condemning bombings by the Allies. He exclaimed:

No international law of warfare is in existence which provides that a soldier who has committed a mean crime can escape punishment by pleading as his defence that he followed the commands of his superiors. This holds particularly true if those commands are contrary to all human ethics and opposed to the well-established usage of warfare.

Deutsche Allgemeine Zeitang, 28 May 1944, *quoted in* T. TAYLOR, *supra* note 15, at 48.

[92] Charter, art. 8.

[93] M. GREENSPAN, THE MODERN LAW OF LAND WARFARE 493, n. 343 (1959).

426

provisions of Article 8 when it stated "[t]hat a soldier was ordered to kill or torture in violation of the international law of war has never been recognized as a defence to such acts..."[94]

A more correct view is that of Dinstein who states that "the moral choice test was meant to complement the provision of Article 8 and not to undermine its foundations, and that it does not permit the fact of obedience to orders to be considered for defence purposes."[95]

This author agrees with Professor Dinstein, in that the moral choice test expressed in the Tribunal's Judgment does not allow the consideration of "obedience to superior orders" for defense purposes. In other words, it seems that the Tribunal intended: If, for example, a defendant who was in a position where if he did not comply with the illegal order, he would be killed (i.e., no ability to make a moral choice), then the defendant may be acquitted once all the relevant circumstances were examined pursuant to general principles of law (e.g., the traditional criminal law defense of coercion), without regard to the defense of superior orders. On the other hand, if the defendant was in a position to make a moral choice and nonetheless complied with the illegal order then, applying Article 8, the defendant may not assert the superior orders defense.

One author sums up the obedience defense in relation to Nuremberg in this manner:

Article 8 [of the Nuremberg Charter] provided that "[t]he fact that the defendant acted pursuant to order of his Government or of a superior shall not free him from responsibility, but may be considered in mitigation of punishment, if the Tribunal determines that justice so requires." The Nuremberg Tribunal put a gloss on these words with its statement: "The true test, which is found in varying degrees in the criminal law of most nations, is not the existence of the order, but whether moral choice was in fact possible." Nevertheless, it accepted the basic point -- the defendant's position in the governmental hierarchy and any orders from above were not available as defenses.[96]

---

[94] *Command Papers* No. 6964, p. 42, *cited by* Y. DINSTEIN, *supra* note 32, at 147.

[95] Y. DINSTEIN, *supra* note 32, at 152.

[96] Clark, *Codification of the Principles of the Nuremberg Trial and the Subsequent Development of International Law*, in THE NUREMBERG TRIAL AND INTERNATIONAL LAW 249, 261 (G. Ginsburgs & V.N. Kudriavtsev eds. 1990).

Similar to the Nuremberg Charter, was the Charter of the International Military Tribunal for the Far East,[97] issued at Tokyo on January 19, 1946 by General MacArthur in his capacity as the Supreme Commander for the Allied Powers in the Far East. Article 6 of the Charter provides:

> Neither the official position, at any time, of an accused, nor the fact that an accused acted pursuant to the order of his government or of a superior shall, of itself, be sufficient to free such accused from responsibility for any crime with which he is charged, but such circumstances may be considered in mitigation of punishment if the Tribunal determines that justice so requires.[98]

While the Nuremberg Tribunal and, to a lesser extent, the Tokyo Tribunal serve as important markers in the progression of the superior orders defense, the use of the defense continued.[99] Immediately following Nuremberg, each Allied Power also conducted trials of accused German War criminals, known as the "Subsequent Proceedings." The Subsequent Proceedings were conducted under CCL 10, promulgated on December 20, 1945 by the Control Council of the four Occupying Powers in Germany.[100]

In Article II (4) (b) the CCL 10 states that:

> The fact that any person acted pursuant to the order of his Government or of a superior does not free him from responsibility for a crime, but may be considered in mitigation.[101]

For our purposes, the *Eisatzgruppen* trial serves as the best example of how these tribunals dealt with the superior orders issue, because it did so in a comprehensive manner. The tribunal stated:

---

[97] *See* Tokyo Charter, Document Section C.8.

[98] *Id.* art. 6.

[99] As Dinstein points out, the defense of superior orders has been raised in war crimes trials more frequently than any other. *See* Y. DINSTEIN, *supra* note 32, at 121.

[100] CCL 10. Document Section C.10.

[101] *Id.* Art. II (4)(b).

[T]he obedience of a soldier is not the obedience of an automaton. A soldier is a reasoning agent. He does not respond, and is not expected to respond, like a piece of machinery. It is a fallacy of widespread consumption that a soldier is required to do everything his superior officer orders him to do .... The subordinate is bound to obey only the lawful orders of his superior and if he accepts a criminal order and executes it with a malice of his own, he may not plead Superior Orders in mitigation of his defence. If the nature of the ordered act is manifestly beyond the scope of the superior's authority, the subordinate may not plead ignorance of the criminality of the order. If one claims duress in the execution of an illegal order, it must be shown that the harm caused by obeying the illegal order is not disproportionately greater than the harm which would result from not obeying the illegal order. It would not be an adequate excuse ... if a subordinate, under orders, killed a person known to be innocent, because by not obeying it he himself would risk a few days of confinement. Nor if one acts under duress, may he, without culpability, commit the illegal act once the duress ceases ....[102]

In two other notable cases of the subsequent proceedings, the use of the superior orders defense was also denied.[103] In the case of Field Marshall Milch, the Tribunal stated:

The defendant had his opportunity to join those who refused to do the evil bidding of an evil master, but he cast it aside .... By accepting such attractive and lucrative posts under a head whose power they knew to be unlimited, they ratify in advance his every act, good or bad. They cannot say at the beginning, "The *Führer's* decisions are final; we will have no voice in them; it is not for us to reason why; his will is law," and then, when the *Führer* decrees ... barbarous inhumanities ... to attempt to exculpate themselves by saying, "Oh, we were never in favor of those things ...."[104]

---

[102]   *Eisatzgruppen Case*, 4 CCL Trials 470.

[103]   In fact, as Dinstein notes, in only one case among those published in the *Law Reports of the United Nations War Crimes Commission* was the use of the defense of superior orders successful in gaining an automatic acquittal of the defendant. The one case involved a public prosecutor in a Nazi trial charged with complicity in murder. But as Dinstein states: "This is a unique case, and it seems to be an anomalous phenomenon and an historical anachronism, which does not fall into line with all the other post-Second World War cases." Y. DINSTEIN, *supra* note 32, at 196.

[104]   In Re Milch, 7 LAW REPORTS OF TRIALS OF WAR CRIMINALS 27, 42 (1947).

In another case involving a senior officer, the Tribunal stated:

All of the defendants in this case held official positions in the armed forces of the Third Reich. Hitler, from 1938 on, was Commander-in-Chief of the Armed Forces and was the Supreme Civil and Military Authority in the Third Reich, whose personal decrees had the force and effect of law. Under such circumstances, to recognize as a defence ... that a defendant acted pursuant to the order of his government or of a superior would be in practical effect to say that all the guilt charged ... was the guilt of Hitler alone because he alone possessed the lawmaking power of the State and the supreme authority to issue civil and military directives. To recognize such a contention would be to recognize an absurdity .... The rejection of the defence of superior orders ... would follow of necessity from our holding that the acts ... are criminal ... because they then were crimes under International Common Law. International Common Law must be superior to and, where it conflicts with, take precedence over National Law or directives issued by any governmental authority. A directive to violate International Common Law is therefore void and can afford no protection to one who violates such law in reliance on such a directive .... The defendants ... who received obviously criminal orders were placed in a difficult position but servile compliance with orders clearly criminal for fear of some disadvantage or punishment not immediately threatened cannot be recognized as a defence. To establish the defence of coercion or necessity in the face of danger there must be a showing of circumstances such that a reasonable man would apprehend that he was in such imminent physical peril as to deprive him of freedom to choose the right and refrain from the wrong.[105]

As for more recent cases in the context of war crimes, four are especially deserving of mention. One of these cases was the prosecution in Israel of Adolf Eichmann, who consistently claimed that everything he did was pursuant to superior orders.[106] The District Court of Jerusalem, however, rejected his plea. The Court declared:

We reject absolutely the accused's version that he was nothing more than a 'small cog' in the extermination machine. We find that in the RSHA, which was the

---

[105]   In Re Von Leeb, 12 LAW REPORTS OF TRIALS OF WAR CRIMINALS 1, 71-72 (1948).

[106]   Israel v. Eichmann, 36 I.L.R. 5 (District Court 1961/62). *See* G. HAUSER, JUSTICE IN JERUSALEM 353 *et. seq.* (1966).

430

central authority dealing with the final solution of the Jewish question, the accused was at the head of those engaged in carrying out the final solution. In fulfilling this task, the accused acted in accordance with general directives from his superiors, but there still remained to him wide powers of discretion which extended also to the planning of operations on his own initiative. He was not a puppet in the hands of others; his place was amongst those who pulled the strings.[107]

The second case, which also arose from crimes committed during World War II, is the trial of Klaus Barbie, who after forty years was finally brought to justice by the French Government.[108] Barbie, charged with "crimes against humanity," argued that when an accused is charged with the commission of crimes pursuant to Article 6(c) of the Charter, the presiding judge must follow the mandate of Article 8.[109] Barbie's contention was that the trial court deprived him of the benefit of the Article 8 provisions with respect to mitigating circumstances. Thus, Barbie argued, the trial court committed a prejudicial error. As one author points out, Barbie's counsel misinterpreted Article 8 of the Charter:[110] obedience to a superior's orders is not an excuse under the Charter, nor is it a mandatory mitigating circumstance, but rather, it "may be considered in mitigation of punishment, if the Tribunal determines that justice so requires."[111] On appeal, the *Cour de Cassation* rejected all errors asserted by Barbie, who was sentenced to life imprisonment.

The other two cases involved atrocities committed by United States soldiers during the Vietnam War. In one trial, the accused was found guilty of the premeditated murder of a Vietnamese and sentenced to 35 years of imprisonment. In its judgment, the tribunal stated that:

---

[107]   *Id.* (First Instance) Judgment, § 180.

[108]   *See* Matter of Barbie, Gaz. Pal. Jur. 710 (France, Cass. Crim. Oct. 6, 1983). *See generally* Doman, *Aftermath of Nuremberg: The Trial of Klaus Barbie*, 60 COLO. L. REV. 449 (1989).

[109]   Since the Charter is part of international law, and expressly incorporated into French domestic law by Law No. 64-1326, Barbie argued that it has force in France. He also argued on the basis that Article 55 of the French Constitution of October 1958 decrees that the national law of France must defer to international law. *See* Doman, *supra* note 108, at 467.

[110]   *Id.*

[111]   Charter, art. 8.

[T]he issuance or execution of an order to kill under the circumstances of this case is unjustifiable under the laws of this nation, the principles of international law, or the laws of land warfare. Such an order would have been beyond the scope of authority for a superior to give and would have been palpably unlawful.[112]

In a case arising out of the My Lai (Song My) massacres, that of Lt. Calley, the military judge in his instructions to the court members stated that:

[T]he obedience of a soldier is not the obedience of an automaton, a soldier is a reasoning agent, obliged to respond, not as a machine, but as a person. The law takes these factors into account in assessing criminal responsibility for acts done in compliance with illegal orders.[113]

Post-Charter Developments

Since the Charter's promulgation, a number of international documents have addressed the issue of defence of "obedience to superior orders."[114]

---

[112]   U.S. v. Schultz, 39 M.R. 133, 136 (1966, court martial; 1968 Review Board).

[113]   United States v. First Lieutenant William L. Calley, Jr. (1971), 46 C.M.R. 1131 (1973), *aff'd* 22 U.S.C. M.A. 534, 48 C.M.R. 19 (1973), *reprinted in* 2 Friedman 1703, 1722. At the time of this trial the *United States Manual for Court Martial*, par. 216d (1968) provided that orders requiring the performance of a "military duty may be inferred to be legal," but:

An act performed manifestly beyond the scope of authority, or pursuant to an order that a man of ordinary sense and understanding would know to be illegal, or in a wanton manner in the discharge of a lawful duty, is not excusable.

[114]   One effort between the world wars was put forth, however, it failed. In the 1922 Treaty in Relation to the Use of Submarines and Noxious Gases in Warfare, 6 February 1922, 25 L.N.T.S. 202, 16 AJIL 57 (Supp. official docs, 1922), Article III provided in part that:

The Signatory Powers, desiring to insure the enforcement of the humane rules of existing law declared by them with respect to attacks upon and the seizure and destruction of merchant ships, further declare that any person in the service of any Power who shall violate any of those rules, whether or not such person is under orders of a governmental superior, shall be deemed to have violated the laws of war and shall be liable to trial and punishment as if for an act of piracy and may be brought to trial before the civil or military authorities of any Power within the jurisdiction of which he may be found.

432

The first such example is the 1946 United Nations Resolution on the Affirmation of the Principles of International Law recognized by the Charter of the Nuremberg Tribunal.[115] The Resolution, by affirming the principles enunciated in the Charter, expressly recognizes the validity of the Charter's Article 8, which provides that the fact that an accused acted pursuant to an order of his government or of a superior shall not free him from responsibility, but may be considered in mitigation of punishment.

Shortly after this resolution, the United Nations began to formulate the Genocide Convention.[116] In June of 1947, the Secretariat of the United Nations Organization submitted a Draft Convention, which in Article V provided: "Command of the law or superior orders shall not justify genocide."[117] This article, however, was never incorporated into the final version of the Convention. Those who opposed the article argued that the article would conflict with provisions of national law, which took a different approach to obedience to orders. On the other side, those who advocated the article asserted that rules of international law are superior to those of national law.[118] Nevertheless, a majority of the ad-hoc Committee on Genocide rejected the article and it never appeared in the Convention.

The drafting process of the four Geneva Conventions[119] produced similar results. In late 1948, the International Committee of the Red Cross invited four experts to study

---

Of the five necessary Contracting Parties, Britain, Italy, Japan and the United States ratified, but France refused and thus the treaty never entered into force. This led one author to comment:

It appears to be equally admitted that the defenses of act of state and superior orders ... condition any prosecution for war crimes. The very fact that one writer suggests a reappraisal of these orthodox principles is only further proof of their general acceptance in positive law.

Manner, *The Legal Nature and Punishment of Criminal Acts of Violence Contrary to the Laws of War*, 37 AJIL 406, 433 (1943).

It is interesting to note that France, in order to be consistent with her Allies, enacted an ordinance on August 28, 1944, to the effect that superior orders cannot be pleaded as a justification but can be admitted as "extenuating or exculpating circumstances." *See* 2 OPPENHEIM, INTERNATIONAL LAW 568 N. 1 (7th ed. Lauterpacht 1952).

[115] Affirmation of Nuremberg Principles.

[116] Genocide Convention.

[117] Draft Convention on the Crime of Genocide, E/447.

[118] *See* Y. DINSTEIN, *supra* note 32, at 220-221.

[119] 1949 Geneva Conventions.

the problems surrounding the sanctions imposed for violations of the Conventions. At the behest of the experts, the International Committee recommended to the Diplomatic Conference, convened to formulate and sign the Conventions, to include four articles in each of the four Conventions. The third article provided:

Superior order

The fact that the accused acted in obedience to the orders of a superior or in pursuance of a law or regulation shall not constitute a valid defence, if the prosecution can show that in view of the circumstances the accused had reasonable grounds to assume that he was committing a breach of this Convention. In such a case the punishment may nevertheless be mitigated or remitted, if the circumstances justify.

Full responsibility shall attach to the person giving the order, even if in giving it he was acting in his official capacity as a servant of the State.[120]

The Diplomatic Conference, however, decided not to include this proposed article in the Conventions and like the Genocide Convention the 1949 Geneva Conventions did not make an unequivocal statement as to the obedience defense. The reasons for the rejection included the apprehension that because of lack of general agreement on the subject, the article might hinder the ratification of the Conventions, and the belief that principles of international law relating to the obedience defense were concurrently being examined and formulated by various bodies of the United Nations.[121]

One such body was the ILC, who in 1950 re-formulated the Principles of International Law Recognized in the Charter of the Nürnberg Tribunal and in the Judgment of the Tribunal.[122] Principle IV of the document clearly states that:

---

[120]   1 COMMENTARY: GENEVA CONVENTION FOR THE AMELIORATION OF THE CONDITION OF THE WOUNDED AND SICK IN ARMED FORCES IN THE FIELD 359, n. 1 (J.S. Pictet, ed. 1952).

[121]   *See* Y. DINSTEIN, *supra* note 32, at 224-225. Comparing the efforts of the drafters of the Genocide and Geneva Conventions, he concludes that "[I]n both cases, when the authors of the Conventions encountered the kernel of a problem, they preferred to get rid of it rather than spend time and energy on baring its pith." *Id.* at 225.

[122]   Nuremberg Principles.

The fact that a person acted pursuant to order of his government or of a superior does not relieve him from responsibility under international law, provided a moral choice was in fact possible to him.[123]

In the commentary to the Principle, the Commission explains the connection between its formulation and that of the Nuremberg Tribunal:

105. This text is based on the principle contained in article 8 of the Charter of the Nürnberg Tribunal as interpreted in the judgment. The idea expressed in Principle IV is that superior orders are not a defence provided a moral choice was possible to the accused. In conformity with this conception, the Tribunal rejected the argument of the defence that there could not be any responsibility since most of the defendants acted under the orders of Hitler. The Tribunal declared: "The provisions of this article [article 8] are in conformity with the law of all nations. That a soldier was ordered to kill or torture in violation of the international law of war has never been recognized as a defence to such acts of brutality, though, as the Charter here provides, the order may be urged in mitigation of the punishment. The true test, which is found in varying degrees in the criminal law of most nations, is not the existence of the order, but whether moral choice was in fact possible."

106. The last phrase of article 8 of the Charter "but may be considered in mitigation of punishment, if the Tribunal determines that justice so requires," has not been retained for the reason stated under "Principle III, in paragraph 104 above. [i.e., "The Commission considers that the question of mitigating punishment is a matter for the competent Court to decide."][124]

In addition to the Nuremberg Principles, the ILC also undertook to draft a Code of Offences Against the Peace and Security of Mankind.[125] In 1951, the ILC submitted its first draft of the Code. Article 4 provides:

---

[123]   *Id.* Principle IV.

[124]   *Id.* as *reprinted in* 2 Ferencz 237. For further information on the drafting history of Principle IV, *see* Y. DINSTEIN, *supra* note 32, at 228-241.

[125]   Draft Code of Offenses.

The fact that a person charged with an offence defined in this Code acted pursuant to order of his government or of a superior does not relieve him from responsibility, provided a moral choice was in fact possible to him.[126]

It is clear that this text faithfully follows that of the Nuremberg Principles quoted above. In its report to the General Assembly, the ILC explained the similarities:

The observation on Principle IV, made in the General Assembly during its fifth session, have been carefully studied; no substantial modification, however, has been made in the drafting of this article, which is based on a clear enunciation by the Nürnberg Tribunal. The article lays down the principle that the accused is responsible only if, in the circumstances, it was possible for him to act contrary to superior orders.[127]

Once the ILC submitted the Draft Code to the General Assembly, the Secretary-General requested the various governments to comment upon the draft. With regard to Article 4, a number of governments objected to the "moral choice" test. In taking the comments of the governments into account, the ILC, in 1954, submitted a revised Draft Code with a revised article 4, which no longer contained the language of the moral choice test. The new Article 4, provides:

The fact that a person charged with an offence defined in this Code acted pursuant to an order of his Government or of a superior does not relieve him of responsibility in international law if, in the circumstances at the time, it was possible for him not to comply with that order.[128]

---

[126]   *Report of the ILC*, 2 YEARBOOK OF THE ILC, 1951, 123-124.

[127]   *Id.* at 137.

[128]   *Supra* note 126, art. 4. As the ILC noted in its report to the General Assembly: "Since some Governments had criticized the expression 'moral choice,' the Commission decided to replace it by the wording of the new text." *Report of the ILC*, 2 YEARBOOK OF THE ILC, 1954, 140-173, at 151. The 1991 Draft Code of Crimes states, in Article 11:

The fact that an individual charged with a crime against the peace and security of mankind acted pursuant to an order of a government or a superior does not relieve him of criminal responsibility if, in the circumstances at the time, it was possible for him not to comply with that order.

436

With the exception of the Draft Code of offences and the Draft Code of Crimes, whose formulation leaves something to be desired, it seems that international conventional law has infrequently addressed the issue of "obedience to superior orders." The 1984 Torture Convention[129] is an exception. It provides in Article 2 that "[a]n order from a superior officer or a public authority may not be invoked as a justification of torture."[130] Other international criminal law conventions, however, make no mention of it, or like the *Apartheid* Convention,[131] address it indirectly.[132] A reason for this may be that "obedience to superior orders" as an absolute defense is no longer recognized by customary international law.

Conclusion

A review of scholarly positions, judgments of tribunals and international legislative efforts, lead to the conclusion that "obedience to superior orders" is not a defense, under customary international law, to an international crime when the order is patently illegal and when the subordinate has a moral choice with respect to obeying or refusing to obey the order. But, if the subordinate is coerced or compelled to carry out the order, the norms for the defense of coercion (compulsion) should apply. In such cases, the issue is not justification, but excuse or mitigation of punishment.

In regard to this important issue of "obedience to superior orders," the words of Dr. Lieber are telling. He asserted: "Men who take up arms against one another in public war do not cease on this account to be moral beings, responsible to one another and to God."[133]

The issue of "obedience to superior orders," since 1989, with the fall of the communist regimes in Eastern and Central Europe and the Republics that seceded the

---

[129] Torture Convention; *see* 24 ILM 535 (1985) which contains the substantive changes from the Draft Convention Against Torture and Other Cruel, Inhuman or Degrading Treatment or Punishment, 23 ILM 1027 (1984).

[130] *Id.* art. 2. *See* also the Inter-American Torture Convention which also excludes the defence of superior orders, as well as the act of State defence.

[131] *Apartheid* Convention.

[132] Article III of the Convention, *id.* asserts that international criminal responsibility shall apply, irrespective of the motive involved, to individuals, members of organizations and institutions and representatives of the State. *See* Clark, *supra* note 96, at 261.

[133] *Cited by* T. TAYLOR, *supra* note 15, at 41.

USSR, has arisen once again with the same legal and moral implications raised in connection with the post-World War II prosecutions. These cases as well as some contemplated legislation in some of these countries may have the effect of retroactive application either by declaring certain past laws null and void or by new laws that would not recognize the legal affects of certain prior laws. While this would clearly be a violation of "principles of legality," as discussed in Chapter 3, it nonetheless also relates to superior orders in that the legal basis for the legitimacy of the order that was followed would be removed. Should such a situation prevail, it could apply to many different categories of public officials including but not limited to army, police, and security officials as well as judges and prosecutors. While Command Responsibility, as discussed in Chapter 9, would implicate higher ranking officials, the removal of superior orders would not in this case work as a way of policy prevention but as retributive vengence against those who may have been in a position where they could only assume the legality of the order and may not have been in a position to exercise a different moral choice. The case arose with a February 1992 conviction of two former East German body guards who followed the order "shoot to kill!" against people trying to cross the borders of East Germany. In so doing one of the guards, a soldier age twenty-seven, killed a person fleeing towards West Berlin in February 1989. He was convicted of manslaughter and sentenced to three and a half years in prison. His defense of "obedience to superior orders" was denied, Judge Theodore Sidell holding "Not everything that is legal is right."[134]

Compulsion

This category of defenses includes what different legal systems refer to as duress, coercion, and necessity even though they are different particularly insofar as the origin

---

[134] A recent example demonstrating that "obedience to superior orders" is not a defense under customary international law is the case of two former East German guards who were convicted of slaying an East German citizen who was trying to escape over the Berlin Wall despite the fact that they had orders to do so. The Judge said: "At the end of the 20th Century ..., no one has the right to ignore his conscience when it comes to killing people on behalf of the power structure." Chicago Tribune, January 21, 1992, Sec. 1, p. 3, col. 1. *See also* Time Vol. 139, No. 5, February 3, 1992, 36 which also reports that during the 28 years in which this policy existed there were an estimated 200 people killed and 700 injured and only 38 border guards. *Id.* So far none of the political decision makers or officers who devised the order or carried it out have been accused let alone prosecuted. This case, however, highlights the unfairness of denying the defense of "obedience to superior orders" to the lowest ranking soldier without imposing concommitant responsibility on commanders and decision makers.

of the compulsion they generate upon a person to engage in conduct which is otherwise criminal.

Coercion and duress are closely related to the defense of "obedience to superior orders" but not necessity. Nevertheless, because of differences between German and Continental legal doctrines, on the one hand, and the Common Law on the other, necessity was equated to coercion and duress in the post-World War II prosecutions.

The essential difference between the two defenses is that coercion and duress are the product of compulsion brought about by one person against another, while necessity is the product of natural causes which place a person in a condition of danger. The two sources of compulsion though different may lead a person to harm another in order to avoid a greater or equal personal harm. Both are a concession to the instinct of human survival, but both are limited for policy and moral-ethical reasons, by positive and natural law. The extent to which national legal systems permit such defenses vary significantly, and it is, therefore, very difficult to arrive at a common "general principle" that transcends the recognition of the defense for certain crimes.

From a policy perspective, it is difficult to foresee under what circumstances necessity occasioned by natural factors could justify or excuse "crimes against humanity." From a moral-ethical perspective it is also equally difficult to justify or excuse "crimes against humanity" by reason of coercion. Even at the risk of one's life, how can necessity justify or excuse the taking of multiple lives. But positive international criminal law has given these defenses a limited recognition.

Criminal responsibility in the world's major criminal justice systems embodies basic social values. The proposition is that no matter what thoughts or motives compel an individual to commit a crime, it is possible for that individual to control their conduct. However, the law is not so rigid that it ignores basic human instincts, such as survival. In certain circumstances, an individual is unable to act of free will to conform his conduct to positive or natural law. In these circumstances, where the individual is acting out of necessity or coercion, a defense is recognized.

For Aristotle, "necessity is manifested in eternal phenomena ... We may say that that which is a necessary thing because the conclusion cannot be otherwise ... and the causes of this necessity are the first premises ... The necessary in nature, thèn, is plainly what we call by the name of matter, and the changes in it."[135] To Aristotle, necessity was divided in absolute and hypothetical necessity; absolute necessity being "the starting point," "that which is;" while hypothetical necessity is "that which is to

---

[135] METAPHYSICS 1015a and AQUINAS, SUMMA II-1 § 6 art. 6; T. HOBBES, THE ELEMENTS OF LAW 47-48 (1928); J. HALL, *supra* note 17 at 419.

be." The latter may also be referred to as that which is necessary to attain an end, while the former corresponds to causation, because it is grounded in human experience and common experience. The law, therefore, draws an arbitrary line between the two, somewhere along the lines of common sense of the hypothetically legal standard of the ordinary reasonable person, conditioning it by the fact that "human conduct implies decision, initiative, action and not mere reaction, but at the same time, it is always more or less influenced by external conditions. Hence: 'With regard to the things that are done from fear of greater evils ... it may be debated whether such actions are voluntary or involuntary.'"[136] Thus, the inexorability of the end of self-preservation lies at the base of criminal accountability and will provide legal grounds for those defenses of necessity and coercion. The distinction among these categories is not only a question of degrees but also of qualitative substance. Professor Hall aptly distinguishes necessity and coercion in the following terms:

> There are valid grounds in support of the above noted differences between the doctrines of necessity and coercion. In the former, the pressure which influences the action is physical nature, while in coercion it is the immoral and illegal conduct of a human being that creates the problem. Certain major consequences result. In coercion, the situation may be completely transformed in a split second by the malefactor's change of mind, and he is morally obliged to do that. There can hardly ever be any such very high probability that he will not change his mind, as that no relief will come to alter imminent destructive physical forces. From the viewpoint of the coerced, there are usually far greater chances of removing the evil human coercion -- by positive action or by flight; certainly the cases show that the courts take this view. Even if the execution of the coercer's threat were just as probable as the continuing impact of destructive, physical phenomena, there would frequently be a duty to resist the evildoer -- and that is the meaning of the policy which excludes murder and other serious crimes. In necessity, man bows to the inevitable; but in coercion there is no such inevitability.[137]

The defense of coercion or duress rests essentially on the assumption that a person who commits a crime under the compulsion of a threat by another person may not

---

[136] J. HALL, *supra* note 17, at 420-421, *quoting* ARISTOTLE, METAPHYSICS 1015a and b, and ETHICS b v. III.

[137] J. HALL, *supra* note 17 at 447.

440

choose to protect another over himself.[138] The actor is threatened by a greater harm than the one he is compelled to carry out against another. In this case he can be exonerated from criminal responsibility. In determining whether the defense of coercion should apply to decision makers, such as the defendants at the IMT, or those under their command, the criteria of the defense must necessarily be different for the policy reasons discussed above in the context of "obedience to superior orders."

In most legal systems, the defense is recognized but varies with respect to certain crimes, the nature and type of threats, the immediacy of the harm likely to occur to the actor, the reasonableness of the belief, and the harm inflicted upon others.[139] But, for policy reasons, most national laws do not recognize the defense for the most serious crimes, particularly murder.[140]

At common law, such a defense could be raised with respect to a crime involving death or serious bodily harm when the threat is such as to induce a reasonable fear of immediate death or serious bodily injury to the threatened person.[141] Threats of future injury are not sufficient; the threat must be immediate and present.[142] Thus, threats of violence after defendants had voluntarily participated in a criminal act are not sufficient to allow coercion as a defense.[143] The person seeking to rely on the defense of coercion must have been unable to avoid the circumstances which led to the crime, and the threat must be such as to directly induce the act which the defendant is charged.[144] The defense must always be grounded on a reasonable belief by the actor

---

[138]   M.C. BASSIOUNI, *supra* note 2, at 454.

[139]   *Id.* at 455.

[140]   *Id.*

[141]   *Id.* *See* U.S. v. Bailey et al., 444 U.S. 394, 100 S. Ct. 624 (1980); U.S. v. May 727 F. 2d 764 (8th Cri. 1984); United States v. Nickels, , 502 F.2d 1173 (7th Cir. 1974); Amin v. State, 811 P. 2d 255 (Wyo., 1991); Frasier v. State, 410 S.E. 2d 572 (So. Car., 1991); State v. Migliorino, 150 Wis. 2d 513, 442 N.W. 2d 36 (1989); and State v. Myers, 233 Kan 611; 664 P.2d 834 (1983).

[142]   *Id.*, and United States v. Stevison, 471 F.2d 143 (7th Cir. 1972); R.I. Recreation Center, Inc. v. Aetna Casualty and Surety Co., 177 F.2d 603 (1st Cir. 1949); Shanon v. United States, 76 F.2d 490 (10th Cir. 1935); Nall v. Commonwealth, 208 Ky 700, 271 S.W. 1058 (1925); State v. Ellis, 232 Ore. 70, 374 P.2d 461 (1962).

[143]   *See* M.C. Bassiouni, *supra* note 2 at 455.

[144]   *Id.* at 456.

that a danger to life and personal safety exists.[145] But for policy reasons the Common Law excludes the defense when the resulting harm to another is death.

Many landmark English cases on compulsion deal with treason and the coercion of a wife by her husband.[146] But as Hall states: "The law of the former is uncertain, and the latter has become little more than a vestige of the medieval conception of marriage."[147] As to murder cases, over a century ago, Justice Denman remarked to the jury:

> You probably, gentlemen, never saw two men tried at a criminal bar for an offence which they had jointly committed, where one of them had not been to a certain extent in fear of the other ... yet that circumstance has never been received by the law as an excuse for his crime ... [T]he law is, that no man, from a fear of consequences to himself, has a right to make himself a party to committing mischief on mankind.[148]

In treason cases, it was held that joining or aiding rebels was excusable only on a well-grounded fear of death and if escape were effected as soon as possible.[149]

German and continental laws provide a wider latitude for the defense of necessity[150] than the Common Law. Necessity is defined in this instance as:

> ... characterized by a conflict between a legal duty and an impelling personal interest rather than by one between two incompatible legal duties. In the state of necessity, the personal interest is imperiled in such a way that it cannot be protected except by violation of a legal duty. The problem of state of necessity is thus concerned with the question of determining under what circumstances, if any, a person shall be permitted to disregard a legal duty in order to avert a danger threatening his or another person's interests. The question can be answered easily when the legal duty is insignificant as compared with the magnitude of the harm

---

[145] *Id.* at 457.

[146] J. HALL, *supra* note 17 at 437.

[147] *Id.*

[148] *Id.* at 438.

[149] *Id.*

[150] A. Von Knieriem, *The Nuremberg Trials* (1959) at 259.

442

threatening. Where the interest endangered is one of high value, while that which is sought to be protected by the legal duty in question is of considerably lesser value, it makes good sense to approve of the violation of the legal duty in order to protect the more valuable interests at stake. Hence, a person does not act illegally if he infringes upon an interest of considerably less valuable legal good in order to protect one of higher value. In terms of legal theory, state of necessity, being based upon a comparative evaluation of legal interests, thus constitutes a ground for excluding illegality.[151]

Therefore, necessity in this context includes both coercion and necessity and does distinguish the two, as does the Common Law. In all cases of necessity, however, in German and Continental laws, it is required that the danger not be created by the actor's own fault.[152]

Applying this enlarged concept of necessity to the Nuremberg accused, one author states:

The danger by which the lives and bodily integrity of the Nuremberg accused and their family members had been threatened originated with the National Socialist State rather than the forces of nature. It consisted in the threat of cruel punishment to be expected with certainty for the entire duration of the National Socialist regime. As the regime was clearly in a position always to carry out its threats, all the conditions of the state of necessity were in existence.[153]

Von Knierem goes on to state, however, that:

The conditions that must prevail in order to justify the plea of state of necessity can ... be summarized as follows:

1. The actor must have been in imminent danger to life or limb.
2. It must not be possible to blame the actor for the danger.
3. The actor must not be obliged to live up to the danger.

---

[151] *Id.* at 258.

[152] *Id.* at 259.

[153] *Id.* at 260.

4.   The act committed must be the only possible means by which the actor could have saved himself from the danger.
5.   The actor must have committed the act in a mental state of compulsion rather than of approval.[154]

These conditions closely correspond with the conditions established by the Nuremberg Tribunals. Similarly, in *The Einsatzgruppen Case*, the plea of state of necessity (coercion) was rejected in the following:

> But it is stated that in military law even if the subordinate realizes that the act he is called upon to perform is a crime, he may not refuse its execution without incurring serious consequences, and that this, therefore, constitutes duress. Let it be said at once that there is no law which requires that an innocent man must forfeit his life or suffer serious harm in order to avoid committing a crime which he condemns. The threat, however, must be imminent, real and inevitable. No court will punish a man who, with a loaded pistol at his head, is compelled to pull a lethal lever.

> Nor need the peril be that imminent in order to escape punishment. But were any of the defendants coerced into killing Jews under the threat of being killed themselves if they failed in their homicidal mission? The test to be applied is whether the subordinate acted under coercion or whether he himself approved of the principle involved in the order. If the second proposition be true, the plea of Superior Orders fails.[155]

Another question raised in allowing the defense of coercion for Article 6(c) crimes, is that of the number of victims. Should the defense be allowed when the actor has taken hundreds or thousands of lives? Although the number of victims should not be an issue, can it be a valid defense for a person to pull a lever resulting in many deaths if his life is at stake? Also, what if the actor knows he will have to pull the lever again tomorrow and produce multiple deaths?[156] The fear for one's life should not be allowed to excuse excessive harm to many others.

---

154   *Id.* at 261.

155   *The Einsatzgruppen Case* at 668.

156   A. Von Knierien, *supra* note 150 at 263.

Unlike coercion, necessity is a defense arising whenever a person by reason of natural circumstances beyond his control is compelled to engage in criminal conduct as the most reasonable means available to avoid an impending harm.[157] The threatened or endangered person must weigh the impending material danger against the harm which may result from the criminal violation, and in so doing it must appear that the harm he is going to inflict is lesser than (or at least equal) to the harm that he may incur if the violation were not to take place.[158]

The classical problem of necessity is the survival situation in the context of a shipwreck or planewreck, where the people are on a raft or boat or on an island where the question arises as to who should be sacrificed for the survival of the others.[159]

In two landmark cases, *U.S. v. Homes*,[160] and *Regina v. Dudley and Stevens*,[161] the common law rule was stated respectively by an American and English court that held it unlawful to preserve one life at the expense of another. In the *Holmes* case, an American ship was on a trip from Liverpool to Philadelphia when it struck an iceberg and sank. Forty-two passengers and crew members got into a lifeboat which had a leak and was in danger of swamping due to overcrowding. After twenty-four hours, the crew decided to throw some of the passengers overboard. Women and children were excluded, as were married men and crew members. A total of fourteen men were thrown overboard. On the following day, the lifeboat was rescued. A crewman in the *Holmes* case was convicted of manslaughter on the higher seas. The lenient sentence he received, a $20 fine and 5 months solitary confinement at hard labor, was a result of the great public outcry that had built up surrounding the case, and a tacit recognition of the defense of necessity, to mitigate the punishment, if not excuse the crime.

The facts of *Regina v. Dudley and Stevens* were similar to *Holmes*. In that case, three survivors were in a lifeboat for twenty days, the last eight without food, and without any reasonable prospect of rescue. The two men killed the third, a boy, who was the weakest of the trio and very likely to die anyway. The two men fed off the

---

[157] M.C. BASSIOUNI, *supra* note 2 at 458.

[158] *Id.*

[159] For an interesting discussion of such a situation and the different legal philosophical approaches in determining the guilt of the survivors, *see* Fuller, *The Case of the Speluncean Explorers*, 62 HARV. L. REV. 616 (1949).

[160] 283 at 26 F. Cas. 360 (C.C.E.C.Pa. 1949). These two cases take the same position as have European courts in similar cases among which is the notorious case of *Le Radeau de Le Meduse*.

[161] 14 Q.B.D. 273 (1884).

body of the boy until they were rescued. Though they were convicted of murder, the punishments were light -- the sentences of death were commuted to twenty years hard labor.

In modern statutory formulation, the basic requirements of the defense are as follows:

1. The harm, to be justified, must have been committed under pressure of physical forces;

2. It must have made possible the preservation of at least an equal value; and

3. The commission of the harm must have been the only means of conserving that value.[162]

In addition, however, good faith and a reasonable belief must exist as the motivating factors that acting in derogation of the law is the only possible way to avoid the hardship of the circumstances.[163]

The defense of necessity could not apply to "crimes against humanity" since they are a result of "state action or policy" and not of unforseen natural forces. One case in which it may hypothetically apply to "crimes against humanity" would be an instance of famine in which the State may have to eliminate some of its citizens, or a minority group, for the benefit of other civilians. This issue has not yet been resolved in positive law, though it is under natural law, where a man cannot decide on the fate of another man, only on the basis of the instinct for self-preservation.

---

[162] J. HALL, *supra* note 17 at 426.

[163] M.C. BASSIOUNI, *supra* note 2 at 460; and J. STEPHEN, DIGEST OF THE CRIMINAL LAW, at 32 (1877) wherein he states: "An act which would otherwise be a crime may be excused if the person accused can show that it was done only in order to avoid consequences which could not otherwise be avoided, and which, if they had followed, would have inflicted upon him, or upon others whom he was bound to protect, inevitable and irreparable evil; that no more was done than was reasonalby necessary for that purpose; and that the evil inflicted by it was not disporportionate to the evil avoided." *Id.*

446

Reprisals

Introduction

Reprisals are retributive practices which are recognized in the context of the international regulation of armed conflicts. In time, these practices, which indiscriminately punish persons on a collective basis, became more limited, but they have not reached the level of complete prohibition. Their application to "crimes against humanity" is not, however, permissible. And whatever basis exists for a legal justification or excuse in the context of armed conflicts, should not be applicable to "crimes against humanity."

After the 1907 Hague Convention, reprisals became the method by which to compel a belligerent enemy who violated norms and standards of the regulation of armed conflicts to comply with them. Thus, it continued to be somewhat retributive, though its purposes were narrowed and its justification limited to insure future compliance. Consequently, reprisals had to be proportionate to the violation, as, for example, the use of force in self-defence which contains a proportionality limitation, and there also had to exist a genuine link between the type of original violation and the type of reprisals engaged in as a response to that original violation. Reasonableness, proportionality and counter-part of violations were therefore the three essential elements which the post-World War I developments produced.[164]

---

[164]   Described by one author as:

... both the actor and the addressee of the act are States or other entities enjoying a degree of international personality.

The act must be a retort to a previous act on the part of the addressee which has adversely affected or continues so to affect the interests of the actor and which the latter can reasonably consider a violation of international law. It must, moreover, itself amount to a violation either of the identical or of another norm of international law.

The *prima facie* unlawful act is not authorized by any previous authoritative community decision. Neither is it an act of self-defence, as its aim is not directly to ward off the blow of the addressee's preceding act.

The act, finally, must respect the conditions and limits laid down in international law for justifiable recourse to reprisals; that is, first of all, objectivity, subsidiarity, and proportionality.

Reprisals, no matter whether or how excusable, nonetheless consist of acts which are otherwise violations of international norms and standards of armed conflict regulations. It cannot, therefore, be claimed that reprisals are justified in and of themselves, but they may constitute an excusable condition which exonerates the performing party from responsibility. The legal basis for reprisal is that it is predicated on the assumption that when a belligerent violates its legal obligations, the mutuality of obligations that would otherwise bind the other state to comply with the infringed norms is removed. The exoneration from State responsibility also extends to those individuals who carried out the acts in question, provided they were in conformity with all other legal requirements.

The victims of reprisals, however, are not states, but protected persons and protected targets who unduly suffer from the consequences of a belligerent state's breach of its international obligations. This is the notion of collective punishment which is no longer accepted with respect to protected persons and targets, and with respect to prohibited means of warfare. As Kalshoven states:

> It should be emphasized, however, that "collective responsibility," as understood in this context, is something widely different from real responsibility for an act committed: usually, it will amount to nothing else but a passive attitude and a lack of cooperation in tracing the perpetrators of the act. In any event, it will be a long way off what would constitute a minimum for criminal or civil responsibility; in actual fact, it more closely resembles joint liability of the members of the community, based on the idea of group solidarity, than on anything like responsibility in the proper sense of the term. Exactly the same idea of group solidarity, however, also underlies the retaliatory measures against innocents. This leads to the conclusion that there is no real difference between "punitive" and "deterrent" retaliatory measures against (members of) an occupied population.[165]

Both practices violate the spirit of humanitarian and human rights law applicable to protected persons.

As the notion of humanitarian law progressed, it became clear that the infliction of harm on protected persons and protected targets, while it may induce a state who has breached international obligations to desist from such practice, it nonetheless unduly

---

F. KALSHOVEN, BELLIGERENT REPRISALS, 33 (1971).

[165] *Id.* at 43.

harms those protected persons and protected targets who should be immune from it irrespective of any state's conduct. The notion of humanitarian law, thus, as it gained further recognition, particularly as of the 1949 Geneva Convention, has removed the justification for certain forms of reprisals against protected persons and certain protected targets. But even so the prohibition of reprisals is not absolute. As Kalshoven states:

> ... belligerent reprisals will obviously tend to be in conflict with elementary humanitarian considerations. A number of rules of the law of war have a marginal character, in that their purpose is not so much the realization of some kind of ideally chivalrous combat as the prevention of what is generally felt to be below the standard of what can be tolerated from the viewpoint of humanity, even in the context of warfare. Consequently, a reprisal transgressing such a marginal norm is bound to constitute an inherently inhuman act. In this light, particular importance attaches to the question of whether a rule might have developed to the effect that such sub-marginal acts would be prohibited even by way of reprisals.[166]

Historical Evolution

Reprisals arose under the customary and then the conventional regulation of armed conflicts. The evolution of the concept of reprisals began in the Roman Empire as a private way of compensating an individual for damage caused by a foreigner.[167] Although a private remedy, reprisals were not arbitrary as they were kept in check by regulations.[168] Public reprisals emerged in the 16th century, due to the decentralization of authority in Europe and a lack of means to ensure enforcement short of war, and, although not subject to any limitations, often took the form of seizure in ports or on the high seas of public or private ships of the opposing state.[169]

The breadth of reprisal widened as it was increasingly viewed as an alternative to war and, therefore, removed from the regulations of armed conflict. Reprisals also began to include non-violent actions involving economic, diplomatic, or cultural

---

[166] *Id.* at 39.

[167] *Id.* at 1.

[168] *Id.* at 2.

[169] *Id.*

relations.[170] It was not until the 19th century that reprisals were used to enforce the regulations of armed conflicts and the concept of belligerent reprisals emerged. As Oppenheim stated:

> Whereas reprisals in time of peace are injurious acts committed for the purpose of compelling a State to consent to a satisfactory settlement of a difference created through an international delinquency, reprisals in time of war occur when one belligerent retaliates upon another, by means of otherwise illegitimate acts of warfare, in order to compel him and his subjects and members of his forces to abandon illegitimate acts of warfare and to comply in future with the rules of legitimate warfare. Reprisals between belligerents cannot be dispensed with, for the effect of their use and of the fear of their being used cannot be denied. Every belligerent, and every member of his forces, knows for certain that reprisals are to be expected in case they violate the rules of legitimate warfare.[171]

The concept of belligerent reprisals was specifically alluded to in 1863, in Article 27 of the Lieber Code which states: "[t]he law of war can no more wholly dispense with retaliation than could the law of nations, of which it is a branch." Article 28 of the Lieber Code, however, states:

> Retaliation will, therefore, never be resorted to as a measure of mere revenge, but only as a means of protective retribution, and moreover, cautiously, and unavoidably -- that is to say, retaliation shall only be resorted to after careful inquiry into the real occurrence, and the character of the misdeeds that may demand retribution.
>
> Unjust or inconsiderate retaliation removes the belligerents farther and farther from the mitigating rules of regular war, and by rapid steps leads them nearer to the internecine wars of savages.

Belligerent reprisals were also referred to in Article 84 of the Oxford Manual[172] which states:

---

[170] *Id.* at 4.

[171] 2 OPPENHEIM'S INTERNATIONAL LAW 560 (H. Lauterpacht ed. 7th ed. 1948).

[172] *Reprinted in*, D. SCHINDLER & J. TOMAN, THE LAWS OF ARMED CONFLICTS 35 (1988).

... if the injured party deems the misdeed so serious in character as to make it necessary to recall the enemy to a respect for the law, no other recourse than a resort to reprisals remains.

Reprisals are an exception to the general rule of equity, that an innocent person ought not to suffer for the guilty. They are also at variance with the rule that each belligerent should conform to the rules of war, without reciprocity on the part of the enemy ...[173]

The Oxford Manual, however, places limitations on the right to resort to reprisals in Articles 85-86. Under the Oxford Manual, reprisals may only be used if: 1) the injury complained of has not been redressed; 2) the reprisals are proportionate to the infraction of the law of war; 3) the reprisals are carried out with the authorization of the commander-in-chief; and 4) the reprisals conform to the laws of humanity and morality.[174]

Although the 1899 and 1907 Hague Regulations did not deal with belligerent reprisals for fear that their mention could serve to validate their use,[175] customary practice, prior to the First World War, formed the basis of the law of belligerent reprisals, and states widely agreed that reprisals could be used under the appropriate circumstances.[176]

---

[173] *Id.*

[174] *Id.* at arts. 85-86, *as cited in* Kwakwa, *Belligerent Reprisals in the Law of Armed Conflict*, 27 STANFORD J. INT'L L. 49, 52-53 (1990).

[175] *See* F. KALSHOVEN, *supra* note 164.

[176] Kwakwa, *supra* note 170 at 54. *See also* J. SPAIGHT, WAR RIGHTS ON LAND 463 n.1 (1911) where it is suggested that the Anglo-American War of 1812 provides an example of a "war in which each side deliberately practiced inhumanities on the greatest scale by way of reprisals."

The German MANUAL OF LAND WARFARE (*Kriegsbrauch in Landkriege*) similarly sanctioned the killing of prisoners in unavoidable cases of urgent necessity. The MANUAL distinguished between the *Kriegsraison* (reason, necessity, or convenience of war) and the *Kriegsmanier* (custom of war). The *Kriegsmanier* was deemed to be generally binding on belligerents but could be overruled by the *Kriegsraison* in special circumstances, even for attaining military success. J. STONE, LEGAL CONTROLS OF INTERNATIONAL CONFLICT 352 (1954).

Reprisals were used frequently during the First World War seemingly without any limitations.[177] But the 1919 Commission Report condemned many practices conducted under the guise of reprisals. It was not until the 1929 Geneva Convention, however, that the first express prohibition of reprisals was formulated.[178] Even then the limitations were restricted to the use of reprisals against prisoners of war and they were considered innovative rather than a codification of the customary international law existing at that time.[179] In fact, at that time, the International Law Association thought that there should be a mitigated right of reprisals against prisoners of war, and not a total prohibition.[180] Some argued that even though the use of reprisals against innocent prisoners was detestable, the threat of its use could actually secure better treatment for prisoners.[181]

The uncertainty surrounding the law of belligerent reprisals provided a fertile ground for the large-scale use of reprisals during World War II. Two possible norms in regard to belligerent reprisals existed at the outset of World War II: that belligerent reprisals may not violate humanitarian norms, and the requirement of proportionality.[182] As far as not violating humanitarian norms, none of the belligerents

---

[177]   Oppenheim describes one shocking incident as follows:

> In September 1914, during the First World War, the German armies in Belgium burned the University of Louvain, including its world-famed library, and other buildings in other towns, by way of reprisals, alleging that Belgian civilians had fired upon the German troops. The Belgian Government denied these charges, and maintained that German soldiers in Louvain had shot one another; the civilized world was horrified at these reprisals.

Oppenheim, *supra* note 171 at 564 n.3.

[178]   *See* F. KALSHOVEN, *supra* note 164 at 107; and Kwakwa, *supra* note 174 at 55.

[179]   Kwakwa, *supra* note 174 at 55.

[180]   F. KALSHOVEN, *supra* note 164 at 107.

[181]   *Id.*

[182]   *Id.* at 212-213. The United States' position on reprisals at the time of World War II can be found in U.S. DEP'T OF THE ARMY RULES OF LAND WARFARE § 358 (Field Manual 27-10, 1940) which states:

> 358. Reprisals.--*a. definition.*--Reprisals are acts of retaliation resorted to by one belligerent against the enemy individuals or property for illegal acts of warfare committed by the other belligerent, for the purpose of enforcing future compliance with the recognized rules of civilized warfare.

in World War II showed any great respect for civilian life and property of the enemy, as evidenced by the indiscriminate bombing of enemy towns and the use of economic blockades.[183] In relative contrast, the prohibition of the use of reprisals against prisoners of war fared better;[184] notably, in August 1944, French partisans shot and killed 80 German prisoners after learning that the Germans had executed 80 French prisoners.[185] But proportionality of the reprisals, as well, was more often disregarded

---

b. When and how employed.--Reprisals are never adopted merely for revenge, but only as an unavoidable last resort to induce the enemy to desist from illegitimate practices. They should never be employed by individual soldiers except by direct orders of a commander, and the latter should give such orders only after careful inquiry into the alleged offense. The highest accessible military authority should be consulted unless immediate action is demanded as a matter of military necessity, but in the latter event a subordinate commander may order appropriate reprisals upon his own initiative. Hasty or ill-considered action may subsequently be found to have been wholly unjustified, subject the responsible officer himself to punishment as for a violation of the laws of war, and seriously damage his cause. On the other hand, commanding officers must assume responsibility for retaliative measures when an unscrupulous enemy leaves no other recourse against the repetition of barbarous outrages.

c. Who may commit acts justifying reprisals.--Illegal acts of warfare justifying reprisals may be committed by a government, by its military commanders, or by a community or individuals thereof, whom it is impossible to apprehend, try, and punish.

d. Subjects of reprisals.--The offending forces or populations generally may lawfully be subjected to appropriate reprisals. Hostages taken and held for the declared purpose of insuring against unlawful acts by the enemy forces or people may be punished or put to death if the unlawful acts are nevertheless committed. Reprisals against prisoners of war are expressly forbidden by the Geneva convention of 1929 (See par. 73.)

e. Form of reprisal.--The acts resorted to by way of reprisal need not conform to those complained of by the injured party, but should not be excessive or exceed the degree of violence committed by the enemy. Villages or houses, etc., may be burned for acts of hostility committed from them, where the guilty individuals cannot be identified, tried, and punished. Collective punishments may be inflicted either in the form of fines or otherwise.

f. Procedure.--The rule requiring careful inquiry into the real occurrence will always be followed unless the safety of the troops requires immediate drastic action and the persons who actually committed the offense cannot be ascertained.

[183]   F. Kalshoven, *supra* note 164 at 212-213.

[184]   *Id.*

[185]   Kwakwa, *supra* note 174.

than followed. Proportionality is hard to assess in the case of an economic blockade,[186] but not so in cases of human lives. Hitler's order to kill ten Italian soldiers for every German soldier who was killed in an attack of a truck in Rome was clearly disproportionate.[187] Kalshoven remarking on the use of reprisals in World War II, observes that they were:

> ... in fact virtually useless, for instance, in respect to an enemy who by his whole attitude demonstrates a total disrespect for certain parts of the law of war (as was the case with Germany, particularly where occupation law was concerned). They are equally useless when applied in a situation where the interests at stake are so great as to make it utterly improbable that a belligerent would change his policy merely on account of a certain pressure exerted on him by the enemy: instances of such crucial issues were the strategic air bombardment and the unrestricted submarine warfare, practiced by either side in the course of the Second World War.[188]

The German and Allied practices of indiscriminately bombing civilian populations during World War II were numerous. After the mistaken bombing of London by the German Luftwaffe in September 1940, England bombed Berlin as an act of reprisal. Germany responded by excessive bombing of London and other cities of England and explained it as acts of legitimate reprisals. Then, the Allies fire-bombed the city of Dresden as reprisal for the bombing of Coventry and the entire city of Dresden lay desolate leaving by different estimates 30,000 to 100,000 casualties in its wake. The Allies who bombed German civilian centers extensively during that war were never held accountable for such action. The same tit-for-tat, occurred in the treatment of P.O.W.'s by Germany and Japan, and by the U.S.S.R. An untold number of P.O.W.'s were killed and mistreated in the name of this barbaric practice, yet few of the perpetrators of such crimes were prosecuted; none on the Allies' side.

After World War II, the IMT did not deal with the doctrine of reprisals in its judgment though the question was dealt with in the Subsequent Proceedings. However, a discussion of reprisals did take place during the proceedings due to a remark by

---

186   F. Kalshoven, *supra* note 164 at 213.

187   Kwakwa, *supra* note 174.

188   F. Kalshoven, *supra* note 164 at 214.

Göring that led Justice Jackson to believe that the defense was going to be raised.[189] Jackson, set out the conditions of such a defence as follows:

> First, the defence would have to relate the plea to acts other than against prisoners of war, as reprisals against those persons were specifically prohibited under the P.O.W. Convention of 1929. Then, any act claimed to be justified as a reprisal "must be related to a specific and continuing violation of international law on the other side;" otherwise international law would have no foundation, as any "casual and incidental violation" on one side would "completely absolve the other from any rules of warfare." Next, the act claimed to constitute a reprisal "must follow within a reasonable time" after the offence, and then only after due notice; and the act "must be related reasonably to the offense which it sought to prevent. That is, you cannot by way of reprisal engage in wholesale slaughter in order to vindicate a single murder." A final most important point was that "a deliberate course of violation of international law cannot be shielded as a reprisal ... You cannot vindicate a reign of terror under the doctrine of reprisals."[190]

Thus, Justice Jackson did not view reprisals as a defence to the crimes enunciated in the Charter. Even if the defence did apply to "war crimes" and "crimes against peace," it could not apply to the Article 6(c) "crimes against humanity," as one of the elements of the defence is that the action is against belligerents, not a state's own citizens. The definition of belligerent reprisals quoted above states: "reprisals in time of war occur when one belligerent retaliates against another."[191] Furthermore, Oppenheim states: "... only reprisals against belligerents are admissible."[192]

In *The Hostages Case*, the murder of thousands of civilians from Greece, Yugoslavia, and Albania, by German troops under the command of the defendants was count one of the Indictment.[193] The victims were in two categories: those who were simply rounded up and put in prison camps, and those arbitrarily labelled as

---

[189]   *Id.* at 217.

[190]   9 IMT 323. *Id.* at 217-218.

[191]   *Supra* note 171.

[192]   L. Oppenheim, *supra* note 171 at 562.

[193]   *The Hostages Case* at 765-766.

partisans.[194] Both categories of victims were murdered, without trial, in retaliation for attacks by lawfully constituted enemy military forces and attacks by unknown persons against German troops.[195] The Indictment stated:

... these acts of collective punishment were part of a deliberate scheme of terror and intimidation, wholly unwarranted and unjustified by military necessity and in flagrant violation of the laws and customs of war.[196]

In his opening statement at the Subsequent Proceedings, General Taylor, for the prosecution, stated that:

... the concepts of "hostage" and "reprisal" both derive from relations between nations, or between their opposing armed forces, and not from relations between a nation or its armed forces on the one hand and the civilian population of an occupied territory on the other: retaliatory measures against the latter category could indeed constitute reprisals, but only if these were inflicted for the purpose of persuading the enemy government to discontinue an unlawful course of action, and not for the purpose of punishing the civilian inhabitants themselves .... [T]he execution of hostages, under the circumstances pertinent to this case, [was] quite definitely and clearly a crime under international law.[197]

Defendant's counsel, Dr. Laternser, in his opening statement argued that the hostage killings had been reprisals. He denied that reprisals could not apply in relations of a nation or its armed forces to the population of an occupied territory. He stated:

The action according to plan of inciting the civilian population to acts of sabotage and attacks upon members of the German occupation forces and the fight of the partisans in violation of international law in the occupied territories had the result that during the Second World War reprisals had to be resorted to above all against illegal actions of the civilian population, in order to force the latter to desist from its illegal conduct. It would be absurd to assume that the commanders of the armed

---

194 *Id.*

195 *Id.*

196 *Id.*

197 *Id.* at 841.

forces of a belligerent party had to endure acts of an enemy civilian population in violation of international law, without being able to protect their troops, when necessary, by retaliatory measures.[198]

Thus, he concluded:

... the killing of hostages by way of reprisals was specifically justified by the very operation of the doctrine of reprisals. A contrary opinion might be readily understandable "from the point of view of humanitarian principles, but it is also quite certain that it is incorrect from the point of view of the laws of war."[199]

In its judgment, the Tribunal made a distinction between taking hostages: holding individuals to insure the future good conduct of the other party; and reprisal: holding or punishing individuals for past violations or conduct; and determined that, in this instance, the term hostage was misused to describe reprisals.[200] The Tribunal, after making the distinction, did not treat the subjects differently.[201] The Tribunal determined that the execution of hostages, i.e. reprisal, could only be used as a last resort, that the act could not exceed in severity the unlawful act it was designed to correct, that there had to be publication of proclamations notifying the fact that hostages or reprisal prisoners had been taken, and that there had to be judicial proceedings in order to determine whether the fundamental requirements for shooting hostages or reprisal prisoners had been met.[202] Kalshoven comments on the Tribunal's position as follows:

It is submitted that what the Tribunal considered to be a rule of international law, in reality was its own invention: it is not believed that international law has yet considered the details of the procedure which a military commander ought to follow in order to arrive at a balanced decision in respect to a contemplated execution of hostages or reprisal prisoners. What remains, of course, is the rule at

---

[198] *Id.* at 867.

[199] *See Id.* In particular, the closing statement, pp. 1207-1209, quoted words from 1209.

[200] *Id.* at 1248-49.

[201] F. Kalshoven, *supra* note 164 at 225.

[202] *The Hostages Case* at 1250. *See also* F. Kalshoven, *supra* note 164 at 219-230.

the root of the Tribunal's reasoning, that "the lives of persons may not be arbitrarily taken."[203]

In *The Eisatzgruppen Case* of the Subsequent Proceedings, the justification of belligerent reprisals was raised by the defense for the extermination program of the Jews and other groups.[204] The tribunal, noting that the victims of belligerent reprisals are usually innocent of the acts retaliated against, stated: "... there must at least be such close connection between these persons and these acts as to constitute a joint responsibility."[205] The Tribunal discussed an incident where "... 859 out of 2100 Jews shot in alleged reprisal for the killing of 21 German soldiers near Topola were taken from concentration camps in Yugoslavia, hundreds of miles away."[206] This fact along with the fact that 2100 were killed for 21 deaths led the Tribunal to conclude that it was "... obvious that a flagrant violation of international law had occurred and outright murder has resulted."[207]

In the *High Command Case*, the Tribunal again considered the policy of terror murders in occupied territories. The defendants were charged *inter alia* with having taken part in the policy making and implementation. The Tribunal reduced the views of *The Hostages Case* to the following statement:

> that under certain very restrictive conditions and subject to certain rather extensive safeguards, hostages may be taken, and after a judicial finding of strict compliance with all pre-conditions and as a last desperate remedy hostages may even be sentenced to death. It was held further that similar drastic safeguards, restrictions, and judicial pre-conditions apply to so-called "reprisal prisoners".[208]

Subsequent to World War II, the law of belligerent reprisals emerged as conventional law in the Four Geneva Conventions of 1949. These Conventions prohibit:

---

[203] F. Kalshoven, *supra* note 164 at 228-229.

[204] *The Eisatzgruppen Case* at 411.

[205] *Id.* at 493-494.

[206] *Id.*

[207] *Id.*

[208] F. Kalshoven, *supra* note 164 at 233.

458

1. Reprisals against the wounded, sick, personnel, buildings or equipment protected by the Convention.[209]
2. Reprisals against the wounded, sick and shipwrecked persons, the personnel, the vessels or the equipment protected by the Convention.[210]
3. Measures of reprisals against prisoners of war.[211]
4. Reprisals against civilians and their property.[212]

The use of belligerent reprisals was further restricted in conventional international law by Protocol I to the Geneva Conventions. Because of the strong opposition to a broad article which outlawed the use of all reprisals, many articles were adopted outlawing individual types of reprisals. This virtually had the same effect as a broad prohibition. The relevant articles of Protocol I provide that:

1. Reprisals against the wounded, sick and shipwrecked and against medical transportation are prohibited.[213]
2. Civilian objects shall not be the object of reprisals.[214]
3. Objects indispensable to the survival of the civilian population, such as foodstuffs, agricultural areas for the production of foodstuffs, crops, livestock, drinking water installations and supplies and irrigation works, shall not be made the object of reprisals.[215]
4. Attacks against the civilian population or civilians by way of reprisals are prohibited.[216]
5. Care shall be taken in warfare to protect the natural environment against widespread, long-term and severe damage. This protection includes a prohibition of the use of methods or means of warfare which are intended or

---

[209] Geneva I, art. 46.

[210] Geneva II, art. 47.

[211] Geneva III, art. 13, para. 3.

[212] Geneva IV, art. 33.

[213] Protocol I, art. 20.

[214] Protocol I, art. 52(1).

[215] *Id.* at art. 54(4).

[216] *Id.* at art. 51(6). *See also*, Protocol I, art. 51(5)(6) for prohibition of indiscriminate attack.

may be expected to cause such damage to the natural environment and thereby prejudice the health or survival of the population.[217]

Despite these specific prohibitions seemingly making any act of reprisal illegal, some authors argue that the use of belligerent reprisals is still justified in the absence of any other international enforcement mechanism such as an international criminal court.[218]

Tu Quoque

The argument of *tu quoque* resembles that of reprisal as both presuppose a violation of international law. The former purports to justify the conduct of a state which violates norms and standards of international regulation of armed conflicts on the grounds that the state upon whom or upon whose subjects the harm has been inflicted has engaged in similar conduct. One author states:

> ... the principle of *tu quoque* is invoked not for the purpose of inducing the enemy to desist from its unlawful conduct but as an estoppel against the enemy's subsequent attempt to call into question the lawfulness of the same kind of conduct of the other side. Conduct violating a rule of international law cannot indeed be claimed to have been taken in reprisal by one who at the time was ignorant that the enemy had engaged in the same kind of conduct. But it would still be a mockery of justice if either state could blame the other for the violation of international law or even punish the latter's citizens for it. If it were to try, it would properly be met with the plea of estoppel, unless it were willing to have applied against itself the same sanction which it tries to inflict on the other side.[219]

Tu quoque is essentially a retributive argument based on the Old Testament's "an eye for an eye, and a tooth for a tooth." But the biblical retribution is to be against the offender who inflicted the original harm. In *tu quoque*, the harm is inflicted against

---

217   *Id.* at art. 35 and 55(1).

218   *See* Kwakwa, *supra* note 174.

219   A. VON KNIERIEM, *supra* note 150 at 312.

persons other than those who committed the original violation. Thus, it shares a common denominator with reprisals, that of collective punishment.

Under *tu quoque*, a state would be allowed to reciprocate against another's violation of international law even where such reactions are not justifiable as reprisal.[220] The net result is a situation in which neither state views itself as bound by a rule of international law. This suspension of a rule of international law will last for the duration of the situation, such as a war.[221] Thus, once one state violates a norm, this norm no longer applies to the relations between the violating state and the state against which the violation occurred.[222]

The question of *tu quoque* was raised by the IMT but the Judgment rejected it without discussion. In the trials of Admirals Doenitz and Raeder for violations of the international law concerning submarine warfare, however, the IMT stated:

> In view of all the facts proved, and in particular of an order of the British Admiralty announced on 8 May 1940, according to which all vessels should be sunk at sight in the Skagerrak, and the answer to interrogatories by Admiral Nimitz that unrestricted submarine warfare was carried on in the Pacific Ocean by the United States from the first day that nation entered the war, the sentence of Doenitz is not assessed on the ground of his breaches of the international law of submarine warfare.[223]

The IMT and the Subsequent Proceedings rejected the plea of *tu quoque* in all other respects holding that it did not sit to pass judgment on the violations of international law of other nations.[224] As one author states:

> As far as the *tu quoque* argument is concerned, it need only be mentioned that it is no defence for an individual to claim that a crime for which he is being tried has also been committed by others. Only if there is sufficient evidence to conclude that the act is practiced with impunity by a large number of other persons, would it be

---

[220] *Id.* at 313.

[221] *Id.*

[222] *Id.*

[223] 22 IMT 559. The Tribunal arrived at the same conclusion for Raeder at 563.

[224] A. VON KNIERIEM, *supra* note 150 at 314.

justified to assume that it was not a crime, since international custom and general practice condoned it .... But under no circumstances can the *tu quoque* argument be considered an absolute defence for a crime against international law.[225]

Woetzel further states:

It would be conceivable if such cases where the practice of nations is generally in contravention of certain provisions of international law, that a person responsible for the carrying on of such practices did not act with any *mala intention* or did not intend to violate the law of nations. His action would, therefore, lack sufficient *mens rea* for holding him guilty of committing a crime against international law. This does not, however, represent a recognition of the *tu quoque* argument as justifying a violation of international law.[226]

As discussed above, the argument of *tu quoque* was rejected in the Subsequent Proceedings. In the *Ministries Case*, for example, the defence argued that the Charter and CCL 10 were invalid because Russia, who was a signatory to both, was guilty of the crime against peace in the case of Poland.[227] The Tribunal held that such a defence was inapplicable because these instruments were not new legislations but declarations of existing law, and even if they were new legislation, it had never been recognized that a law was invalid because one of the legislators subscribing to it committed or intended to commit the crime denounced in the law.[228]

Non-Applicability of Reprisals and *Tu Quoque* to "Crimes Against Humanity"

Article 6(c) Crimes are committed by virtue of "state action or policy,"[229] carried out by individuals acting for or on behalf of a state,[230] whose victims are nationals

---

[225] R. WOETZEL, THE NUREMBERG TRIALS IN INTERNATIONAL LAW 120-121 (1962).

[226] *Id.* at 188-189.

[227] *The Ministries Case* at 322-323.

[228] *Id. See also* R. WOETZEL, *supra* note 225 at 226.

[229] *See e.g.* Chapter 6.

[230] *See* Chapter 5 at 192.

of their same state.[231] Reprisals and *tu quoque* are committed against persons who are nationals of another belligerent state. Thus, presumably neither reprisals nor *tu quoque* can be relied upon as an excuse, or even as a mitigating factor in connection with Article 6(c) crimes. The question, however, arises with respect to situations which are predicated on certain legal basis that have no connection with the humanitarian and humanistic basis which protect persons in times of war and peace. These situations can arise as follows: a state, whether belligerent or not, develops a policy or carries out measures which constitute crimes under Article 6(c) against a group of persons within its jurisdiction, whether nationals or residents, who are ethnically, racially or religiously the same as a population group in another state. Can that other state engage in reprisals against the civilian population of the offending state, whether those civilians are within its jurisdiction, or that of the offending state? If the legal basis upon which this question is to be resolved is predicated on nationality and belligerency as opposed to the doctrine of "protected persons," the outcome is certain to be different.

There appears to be an assumption in the writings of post-1960 writers and in the progressive evolution of the ILC's work on "crimes against humanity," that any acts falling within the meaning of Article 6(c) crimes, or however this definition may be construed, are specifically prohibited. But these sources have not specifically addressed the issue of whether such acts can be deemed excusable under the doctrine of reprisals or that of *tu quoque*.

In the context of belligerency, it is clear that no state can inflict certain prohibited harm on "protected persons," provided that such civilians are nationals of another state, irrespective of whether they may be in the original offending state, or in the state claiming to act in reprisal. But since the protective scheme of international humanitarian law does not extend beyond certain defined contexts, there still remains an area of human vulnerability outside this protective scheme. Presumably, international human rights should apply to contexts not regulated by international humanitarian law, and for some the two sources of international legal protection overlap and complement one another. But the uncertainty about what is protected and prohibited, and what is not, needs to be removed by clear and unambiguous international legal norms.

The human vulnerability gap which exists with respect to the situations described above, derives from the distinction between applicable sources of law, i.e. humanitarian regulation of armed conflicts and human rights law, and from the legal distinction based on the contexts of armed conflict and peace and the diversity of nationality

---

[231] *See* Chapter 4 at 176.

between victim and perpetrator. Surely, however, if the goal of international law is the protection of victims, then these distinctions should not apply.[232]

Throughout the world there are a number of population groups inhabiting more than one country, and whose nationality status is different. Kurds, for example, may be Turkish, Iraqis, Iranians, Turkestanis, Syrian, or Lebanese. But, they are minorities in every one of these countries. Can Article 6(c) crimes committed by Iraq against their Kurdish nationals justify reprisals by Turkey against non-Kurdish Iraqi nationals because Turkey has a Kurdish minority? Does the situation differ, if the country claiming reprisals is exclusively of the same ethnic group as the victimized minority of another State? That would be the example of Hungary which has a minority of Hungarians who have been forced after World War II into becoming Romanian nationals? Would Romania's violations against such a Hungarian minority and who are Romanian nationals, be a valid reason for Hungary to engage in reprisals against Romanian nationals who are not of Hungarian ethnic stock?

The same analogy that applied to the emergence of "crimes against humanity" as a jurisdictional extension of war crimes, as discussed in Chapter 4, can be applied with respect to reprisals. Thus, if protected persons cannot be the object of certain reprisals as between belligerents, then the protection of persons under belligerent reprisals is not as extensive as to protect them from all that which Article 6(c) criminalizes. The likely exclusions from the protective scope of Article 6(c) is "deportation" and possibly even some forms of "persecution."

It is, therefore, indispensable that a new codification of "crimes against humanity" include an explicit exclusion of any reprisals and *tu quoque* excusable factors which would be in the nature of Article 6(c) crimes, or as these may further be developed by contemporary codification. The 1991 ILC Draft Code of Crimes regrettably does not address these questions. Thus, a limited defense of reprisals may still be available under international criminal law for such Article 6(c) crimes as "deportation" and "persecution." International human rights norms and standards contain some enunciations protecting persons from such acts, but that does not constitute international crimes.

---

[232] See *International Protection of Victims*, 7 *Nouvelles Etudes Pénales* (M.C. Bassiouni ed.1988); Declaration of Basic Principles of Justice for Victims of Crime and Abuse of Power, U.N.G.A. Res. A/Res. /40/34, 11 December 1985; Bassiouni, *The Protection of "Collective Victims" in International Law*, NEW YORK UNIVERSITY LAW SCHOOL JOURNAL OF HUMAN RIGHTS 239 (1985).

Immunity of Heads of State

Historically, heads of state were not subject to criminal responsibility for their actions, because of the merger of the sovereign and the sovereignty of the state. This is particularly true with respect to monarchies as evidenced by Louis XIV's statement: "*L'état c'est moi.*" It was not until the Treaty of Versailles that immunity of a head of State was removed for the crime of aggression by virtue of that document's Article 227, which provides:

> The Allied and Associated Powers publicly arraign William II of Hohenzollen, formerly German Emperor, for a supreme offence against international morality and the sanctity of treaties ...

> The Allied and Associated Powers will address a request to the Government of the Netherlands for the surrender to them of the ex-Emperor in order that he may be put on trial.[233]

This effort, however, was not carried beyond the stage of its inclusion in a treaty. The Allies did not set up an international tribunal or to seek to secure jurisdiction over Kaiser Wilhelm.[234]

It would surely be difficult to construct a customary rule of international law on this limited basis, but by 1945, the Allies, acting through representatives at the London Conference which produced the London Charter, asserted the principle of heads of States' responsibility for aggression, war crimes, and "crimes against humanity" as if it were both well established and uncontroverted. Article 7 of the Charter states:

> Neither the official position, at any time, of an accused, nor the fact that an accused acted pursuant to order of his government or of a superior shall, of itself, be sufficient to free such accused from responsibility for any crime with which he is charged, but such circumstances may be considered in mitigation of punishment if the Tribunal determines that justice so requires.[235]

---

[233] Treaty of Versailles, art. 227. *See* Document Section A.1.

[234] *See* Chapter 5 at 199.

[235] Charter, art. 7. *See* Document Section C.2.

465

But by 1946, when the IMT convened in Nuremberg, both Hitler and Mussolini had died and thus no prosecutions for heads of State took place in the European theater. In Japan, however, Emperor Hirohito was still alive and the Tokyo Charter equally removed the immunity. In Article 6, the Tokyo Charter states:

> Neither the official position, at any time, of an accused, nor the fact that an accused acted pursuant to order of his government or of a superior shall, of itself, be sufficient to free such accused from responsibility for any crime with which he is charged, but such circumstances may be considered in mitigation of punishment if the Tribunal determines that justice so requires.[236]

But by the good grace of General Douglas McArthur, Hirohito was spared the indignity of being held accountable for his country's acts of aggression against more than one state. Thus, we can find no further practice in support of this proposition.

The ILC's Nuremberg Principles, however, asserted:

> The fact that a person who committed an act which constitutes a crime under international law acted as Head of State or responsible government official does not relieve him from responsibility under international law.[237]

Since then there has not been a single case where a head of State was held responsible for "crimes against humanity." The only example of a head of State being brought to trial, while still head of State, is the trial in the United States of General Noriega.[238] After the Gulf War, the United States vaguely contemplated trying Saddam Hussein,[239] but there were no further developments to these rumblings.

The ILC's 1991 Draft Code of Crimes reaffirms that heads of State should be held accountable for their crimes against the peace and security of mankind. Article 13 provides:

---

[236] Tokyo Charter, art. 6. *See* Document Section C.9.

[237] Nuremberg Principles, Principle III. *See* Document Section C.12.

[238] *See United States v. Noriega*, Case No. 88-0079-CR, United States District Court for the Southern District of Florida.

[239] *See* Hearing before the Subcommittee on International Law, Immigration, and Refugees of the Committee of the Judiciary, House of Representatives, 102nd Congress, 1st Session, March 13, 1991, Serial No. 3.

The official position of an individual who commits a crime against the peace and security of mankind, and particularly the fact that he acts as head of State or Government, does not relieve him of criminal responsibility.[240]

However, despite several international instruments that remove the immunity of a head of State, it is to this writer's dismay that there is no practice to support it, even though there have been many appropriate situations in which to do so.

Conclusion

The problems in identifying a general part for international criminal law, discussed in Chapter 9,[241] also apply to the identification of a general part for "crimes against humanity." Consequently, defenses and exonerating conditions suffer from these very same problems that apply to international criminal law as a whole.

As indicated in Chapter 4, the legal sources of "crimes against humanity" are found in international regulations of armed conflicts and international human rights law.[242] But, neither of these two sources provide for a general part applicable to this criminal category. Also, as discussed in Chapter 1, the emergence of "crimes against humanity" in positive international criminal law was by virtue of the London Agreement of 8 August 1945 which included the London Charter and of course Article 6(c).[243] But the Charter did not contain a general part, though it did specifically exclude the defenses of "obedience to superior orders" and the immunity of heads of State.[244]

The IMT, IMTFE and the Subsequent Proceedings dealt with the defense of "obedience to superior orders" and compulsion, and, in a very limited way, with reprisals and *tu quoque*. These judgments also dealt with the issue of mistake of law as part of command responsibility and "obedience to superior orders." Because the

---

[240] 1991 Draft Code of Crimes, art. 13. *See* Document Section F.5.

[241] *See* Chapter 9 at 339.

[242] *See* Chapter 4 at 165.

[243] *See* Chapter 1 at 5.

[244] *See* Chapter 1 at 5 and Chapter 9 at 339.

467

issues raised were more closely connected with command responsibility, mistake of law was discussed in that section of Chapter 9.[245]

These Judgments did not, however, satisfactorily establish the existence of a pre-Charter legal foundation. And, while there was sufficient pre-existing national legal experience with command responsibility and "obedience to superior orders," there was practically none with the other legal defenses. The London and Tokyo Charters, which were the legislative basis for the IMT and IMTFE, took a significant progressive step by removing the immunity of heads of State and the obedience defenses. The Subsequent Proceedings interpreted this defense in a narrow way, recognizing it whenever the accused actor had no moral alternative, thus transferring it into compulsion, *viz.* duress or coercion. It is interesting to note, in this context, that the IMT and Subsequent Proceedings referred to necessity as the over-arching concept for the compulsion defenses which include necessity and coercion as discussed above.[246] In fact, as pointed out above, the commingling of necessity and coercion could be explained by reason of the different approaches to these defenses and exonerating conditions under the Common Law, the Germanic and the Romanist-Civilist systems.[247]

Post-Charter Legal Developments have not solved the problems raised by the lack of a general part and, with respect to this Chapter, the lack of a reliable legal source with enough specificity to identify defenses and exonerating conditions. The international regulation of armed conflicts and national military laws in the world's major legal systems have, however, contributed to significant clarity with respect to "obedience to superior orders." Also, doctrinal developments in public international law seem to have consolidated the notion that heads of States cannot be immune from prosecution for violations of international criminal law. Even though, as discussed above, there is no international or state practice that can be pointed to as evidence of a customary practice.[248]

---

[245] *See* Chapter 9 at 342.

[246] *See supra* at 442.

[247] *See supra* at 439.

[248] *See supra* at 462, but one exception exists in the U.S. trial of General Manuel Norriga, who was seized by U.S. troops in Panama while he was acting as Head of State. He was brought to trial in Florida on domestic U.S. Criminal charges and was convicted of drug traffic offenses on April 9, 1992. *See supra* note 238. This exception, however, does not prove the point since the charges were not for an international crime, even though drug trafficking is such a crime. Conversely, President Saddam Hussein of Iraq, who was threatened with an international prosecution for aggression and war crimes, was not apprehended as of this

DEFENSES AND EXONERATIONS

The diversity in national criminal justice systems with respect to the conceptual and doctrinal legal basis for criminal responsibility and punishability, including defenses and exonerating conditions, vary significantly. Consequently, it is very difficult to arrive at "general principles" which are sufficiently common to the world's major criminal justice systems and that constitute a legally sufficient basis for all possible applicable defenses. The result is a great deal of legal uncertainty which is compounded by the uncertainties raised with respect to other aspects of the general part.

The obvious solution, as argued in the introduction to this Chapter and throughout this book, is the elaboration of a new convention on "crimes against humanity" which would include a general part more specifically tailored to this criminal category until such time as an international criminal code containing a general part is developed.

---

writing. *See Hearings*, Chapter 12, note 43.

CHAPTER 11

POST-CHARTER LEGAL DEVELOPMENTS

> There is nothing more difficult to take in hand,
> more perilous to conduct, or more uncertain in its
> success, than to take the lead in the introduction
> of a new order of things.
> MACHIAVELLI, THE PRINCE (1537).

Substantive Aspects

Introduction

"Crimes against humanity," as defined in the Charter, as applied by the Nuremberg
and Tokyo Trials, in the Subsequent Proceedings and in national proceedings, and as
built upon by the Post-Charter Legal Developments described below, is a chaotic legal
structure with many unresolved legal issues.[1] There is no codification, systematization,
or even a cohesive policy of harmonizing the different international instruments which
relate to this international category of crimes. Moreover, the Law of the Charter and
substantive Post-Charter Legal Developments are disjoined. Indeed, the ILC, which in
1950 codified the Nuremberg Principles, implicitly repudiated them in its 1954 Draft
Code of Offences against the Peace and Security of Mankind. Thus, no sooner had the
1950 Nuremberg Principles been adopted than they were abandoned in subsequent
efforts to redefine "crimes against humanity" to achieve their intended goals. Since then
the ILC, up to and including the 1991 version of the Draft Code of Crimes, has not,
however, achieved a satisfactory result as is discussed below.

It is this writer's contention that the sum total of the Post-Charter Legal
Developments do not cover all that is included in the Law of Charter, most notably,
mass killings which have occured on a massive scale since World War II. On the
positive side, however, the post-World War II instruments "may all be regarded as
efforts to solidify and concretize the Nuremberg offenses and at the same time an

---

[1]   *See generally*, Bassiouni, *Nuremberg Forty Years After: An Introduction*, 18 CASE W. RES. J. INT'L
L. 261 (1986); and *Forty Years After the Nuremberg Tribunals: The Impact of War Crimes Trials on
International and National Law*, PROCEEDINGS, EIGHTIETH MEETING OF THE AMERICAN SOCIETY OF
INTERNATIONAL LAW (April 9-12, 1986), remarks of J. Paust, T. Taylor, R. Falk, M. C. Bassiouni, and Y.
Onuma, 56-73.

affirmation of those principles by the world community as a whole rather than the smaller number of states that acted at Nuremberg."[2]

"Crimes against humanity" remains a viable international category of crimes, which has not fallen into legal *désuètude*, notwithstanding the absence of consistent state practice. Its continued viability and permeation of other international instruments is evidence that the Charter's Article 6(c) was not only "victor's vengeance," but a foundation block in the building of a new legal structure for the protection of human rights through the criminalization of one of its most serious violations.

The Piece-meal Inclusion of Crimes Against Humanity in Substantive International Instruments

The relevant substantive post-Charter instruments (excluding the general human rights convention) are:

1. United Nations General Assembly Resolution of 11 December 1946, Affirmation of the Principles of International Law Recognized by the Charter of the Nuremberg Tribunal,

2. the 1948 Genocide Convention,

3. Report of the ILC of 29 July 1950,

4. the ILC 1954 Draft Code of Offences and since 1987, the Draft Code of Crimes (up to and including the 1991 version),

5. the 1973 *Apartheid* Convention,

6. the 1984 Torture Convention, and

7. the 1987 European Torture Convention.

---

[2] Clark, *Codification of the Principles of the Nuremberg Trial and the Subsequent Development of International Law*, THE NUREMBERG TRIAL AND INTERNATIONAL LAW 249, 250 (G. Ginsburgs & V.N. Kudriavtsev eds. 1990).

Of these seven instruments, one is a recommendatory general assembly resolution, one is an ILC Report and one is an ILC project none of which have *per se* legally binding effect. Three are international conventions (Genocide, *Aparthied* and Torture) which are binding on their respective parties, and which some sides argue are also binding on non-signatory states because they have become part of *jus cogens*, and one is a regional convention.

There are, however, other substantive instruments but they apply only to the context of armed conflicts, they are:

8.   the 1949 Geneva Conventions, and

9.   the 1977 Protocols.

The 1949 Geneva Conventions are also customary international law; 156 out of 166 member-states of the United Nations have ratified them. Their protections and prohibitions are, therefore, binding upon non-signatory states.

Notwithstanding the breadth of all the above-mentioned instruments, they nevertheless fail to cover all aspects of human depredations which are covered by the Law of Charter, namely mass-killing, as discussed below and in Chapter 12.

The 1949 Geneva Conventions and the two 1977 Additional Protocols incorporate certain components of "crimes against humanity," by including them among the prohibited activities of belligerents in the context of war, whether of an international or non-international character. But they do not fully include the protection of all civilians within the national jurisdiction of a state which is not engaged in an armed conflict. The common articles of all four 1949 Geneva Conventions provide:

> Grave breaches ... shall be those involving any of the following acts, if committed against persons or property protected by the Convention: wilful killing, torture or inhuman treatment, including biological experiments, wilfully causing great suffering or serious injury to body or health, and extensive destruction and appropriation of property, not justified by military necessity and carried out unlawfully and wantonly.[3]

---

[3]   The common articles, with respect to grave breaches, of the four Geneva Conventions of 1949, are: Geneva I, art. L; Geneva II, art. L I; Geneva III, art. CXXX, after "injury to body or health," this article adds, "compelling a prisoner of war to serve in the forces of the hostile power, or wilfully depriving a prisoner of war of the rights of fair and regular trial prescribed by this Convention;" Geneva IV, art. CXLVII, after

472

These and other provisions of the four Conventions and the two Protocols, apply only, as stated above, to certain contexts and to certain protected persons. They do not extend to all civilian populations. The Genocide Convention of 1948 also covers certain manifestations of "crimes against humanity" as defined in the Law of the Charter -- but only with respect to certain specific acts accompanied with a specific intent and against specifically designated groups.[4] Thus, it excludes all other acts and groups not specified in the Convention.

Article II states:

> In the present Convention, genocide means any of the following acts committed with intent to destroy, in whole or in part, a national, ethnic, racial, or religious group, as such:
>
> (a) Killing members of the group;
> (b) Causing serious bodily or mental harm to members of the group;
> (c) Deliberately inflicting on the group, conditions of life calculated to bring about its physical destruction in whole or in part;
> (d) Imposing measures intended to prevent births within the group;
> (e) Forcibly transferring children of the group to another group.

The definition of Genocide clearly excludes situations where the required specific intent does not exist. It also excludes from the protected categories listed in Article II other groups not specifically identified, such as social or political groups. Thus, such instances as "murder, extermination, enslavement, deportation and other inhumane acts," as described in Article 6(c), of groups not included in the Genocide Convention are not protected by the convention, neither are similar acts committed against included groups but without the accompanying specific intent. Thus, one has to ask if it is logical to have a legal scheme whereby the intentional killing of a single person can be genocide and the killing of millions of persons without intent to destroy the

---

"injury to body or health," this article adds, "unlawful deportation or transfer or unlawful confinement of a protected person, compelling a protected person to serve in the forces of a hostile Power, or wilfully depriving a protected person of the rights of fair and regular trial prescribed in the present Convention, taking hostages and extensive destruction and appropriation of property, not justified by military necessity and carried out unlawfully and wantonly."

[4] Lippman, *The Drafting of the 1948 Convention on the Prevention and Punishment of the Crime of Genocide*, 3 B. U. INT'L L.J. 1 (1985); Lemkin, *Le Genocide*, 17 RIDP 25 (1956).

protected group in whole or in part is not an international crime? Yet that is the present situation. Consequently, the Genocide Convention cannot be said to have replaced "crimes against humanity" because it does not provide the same inclusive definition of protected persons and prohibited acts provided under the Laws of the Charter.

The *Apartheid* Convention of 1972, in its Preamble and in Article I, refers to the practices defined in Article II of the Convention as "crimes against humanity:"

> The States parties to the present Convention, ...
> Observing that, in the Convention on the Non-Applicability of Statutory Limitations to War Crimes and Crimes Against Humanity, inhuman acts resulting from the policy of *apartheid* are qualified as crimes against humanity,
> Observing that the General Assembly of the United Nations has adopted a number of resolutions in which the policies and practices of *apartheid* are condemned as a crime against humanity,[5]

and in Article I, the Convention provides:

> The States parties to the present Convention declare that *apartheid* is a crime against humanity and that inhuman acts resulting from the policies and practices of *apartheid* and similar policies and practices of racial segregation and discrimination, as defined in article II of the Convention, are crimes violating the principles of international law, in particular the purposes and principles of the Charter of the United Nations, and constituting a serious threat to international peace and security.

The Advisory Opinion of the ICJ in the case *Legal Consequences for States of the Continued Presence of South Africa in Namibia (South West Africa) Notwithstanding Security Council Resolution 276 (1970)*[6] referred to "crimes against humanity" in the context of *Apartheid* as such:

---

[5] *Apartheid* Convention, Preamble.

[6] Legal Consequences for States of the Continued Presence of South Africa in Namibia (South West Africa) Notwithstanding Security Council Resolution 276 (1970), 1971 I.C.J. Reports 16.

474

[*Apartheid* violates] the fundamental laws of equality and liberty, and nearly all other human rights, to war crimes and *crimes against humanity* when, in the International Convention of 26 November 1968, it declared them liable to prosecution without statutory limitation. Thus, in the eyes of the international community, violations of human rights by the practice of *apartheid*, itself a violation of equality and of the rights which are its corollaries, are no less punishable than the *crimes against humanity* and war crimes upon which the Charter of the Nuremberg Tribunal visited sanctions. General Assembly resolution 2074 (XX) even condemned *apartheid* as constituting "*a crime against humanity*".[7] [emphasis added]

But the specifics of the crime of *apartheid*, as stated in Article II of the Convention are stated as follows:

For the purpose of the present Convention, the term "the crime of *apartheid*," which shall include similar policies and practices of racial segregation and discrimination as practiced in southern Africa, shall apply to the following inhuman acts committed for the purpose of establishing and maintaining domination by one racial group of persons over any other racial group of persons and systematically oppressing them:

(a) Denial to a member or members of a racial group or groups of the right to life and liberty of person:

    (i) By murder of members of a racial group or groups;

    (ii) By the infliction upon the member of a racial group or groups of serious bodily or mental harm, by infringement of their freedom or dignity, or by subjecting them to torture or to cruel inhuman or degrading treatment or punishment.

    (iii) By arbitrary arrest and illegal imprisonment of the members of a racial group or groups;

(b) Deliberate imposition on a racial group or groups of living conditions calculated to cause its or their physical destruction in whole or in part;

---

[7] *Id.*, Separate Opinion of Judge Ammoun, at 79.

(c) Any legislative measures and other measures calculated to prevent a racial group or groups from participating in the political, social, economic and cultural life of the country and the deliberate creation of conditions preventing the full development of such a group or groups, in particular by denying to members of a racial group or groups basic human rights and freedoms, including the right to work, the right to form recognized trade unions, the right to educate, the right to leave and return to their country, the right to a nationality, the right to freedom of movement and residence, the right to freedom of opinion and expression, the right to freedom of peaceful assembly and association;

(d) Any measures, including legislative measures, designed to divide the population along racial lines by the creation of separate reserves and ghettos for the members of a racial group or groups, the prohibition of mixed marriages among members of various racial groups, the expropriation of landed property belonging to a racial group or groups or to members thereof;

(e) Exploitation of the labour of the members of a racial group or groups, in particular by submitting them to forced labour;

(f) Persecution of organization and persons by depriving them of fundamental rights and freedoms, because they oppose *apartheid*.

These specific prohibitions apply to situations where the policies and practices derive from a premise of racial discrimination for the purpose of maintaining the political supremacy of a given racial group. Thus, what Article 6(c) refers to as "murder, extermination, enslavement, deportation and other inhumane acts" which are not committed for the purpose of political supremacy by a given racial group against another one are not covered under the *Apartheid* Convention.[8]

---

[8]   It should be noted with regret that *apartheid* seems to be directed exclusively at the Republic of South Africa, without regard to the universality of application of the prohibited practices. *See* Bassiouni & Derby, *Final Report on the Establishment of an International Criminal Court for the Implementation of the Apartheid Convention and Other Relevant International Instruments*, 9 HOFSTRA L. REV. 523 (1981). *See* Study on Ways and Means of Ensuring the Implementation of International Instruments Such as the International Convention on the Suppression of *Apartheid*, Including the Establishment of the International Jurisdiction Envisioned by Said Convention, E/Cn.4/AC.22/Crp. 19, 25 July 1980. *See also, Report of the Committee on International Jurisdiction*, 7 U.N. GAOR Supp. (No. 11) U.N. Doc. A/2136 (1951); and *Draft*

POST-CHARTER LEGAL DEVELOPMENTS

The major instruments discussed above, the *Apartheid*, Genocide and Geneva Conventions, do not fully cover unlawful human experimentation, which is part of "crimes against humanity" under the Law of the Charter.[9] Such a crime is a "grave breach" under the Geneva Conventions provided it is committed by a belligerant party in the context of an armed conflict. It could also under certain limited circumstances, fall within the meaning of genocide or *apartheid*. But it is otherwise not yet internationally criminalized in time of peace except under "crimes against humanity." This is another serious gap in Post-Charter Legal Development.

Since 1984, the Torture Convention has made torture an international crime, whether in time of peace or in time of war. In the latter context it overlaps with the "grave breaches" provisions of the Geneva Convention and the Additional Protocols. But the 1984 Torture Convention applies only to state parties and non-state parties are not bound by it,[10] unless it can be deemed that torture is also prohibited under customary international law, or under the peremptory norms of *jus cogens*.[11] Thus, several instruments apply to different and sometimes overlapping contexts, and are subject to different requirements, while an anomalous situation exists with respect to unlawful human experimentation, which is prohibited in some contexts and not in others.

Statute for an International Criminal Court (U.N. Report of the 1953 Committee on International Criminal Jurisdiction), U.N. GAOR Supp. (No. 12), U.N. Doc. A/2645 (1953). *See also* footnote 28, Chapter 1.

[9] Bassiouni, Baffes & Evrard, *Le Controle Internationale de L'Experimentation sur L'Homme*, 51 RIDP 267 (1980); Bassiouni, Baffes & Evrad, *An Appraisal of Human Experimentation in International Law and Practice: the Need for International Regulation of Human Experimentation*, 72 J. CRIM. L. & CRIMINOLOGY 1597 (1981).

[10] Torture Convention; *see* 24 ILM 535 (1985) which contains the substantive changes from the Draft Convention Against Torture and Other Cruel, Inhuman or Degrading Treatment or Punishment, 23 ILM 1027 (1984). *See, Draft Convention for the Prevention and Suppression of Torture*, U.N. ECOSOC Doc. E/CN.4/NGO213 (1978) (submitted by the International Association of Penal Law to the 1978 meeting of the U.N. Commission on Human Rights); Bassiouni and Derby, *The Crime of Torture*, in 1 BASSIOUNI ICL 363. *See also* Bassiouni, *The Need for an International Convention for the Prevention and Suppression of Torture*, 48 RIDP 17 (1977); *Draft Convention for the Prevention and Suppression of Torture*, 48 RIDP 265 (1977). J. H. BURGERS AND H. DANELIUS, THE UNITED NATIONS CONVENTION AGAINST TORTURE: A HANDBOOK ON THE CONVENTION AGAINST TORTURE AND OTHER INHUMAN OR DEGRADING TREATMENT OR PUNISHMENT (1988). *See also* J. L. de la Cuesta Arzamendi, EL DELITO DE TORTURA (1990).

[11] For an assertion that torture is proscribed by customary international law under a U.S. legal interpretation, *see* Filartiga v. Pena-Irala, 630 F.2d 876 (2d Cir. 1980).

Article 6(c) of the Charter refers to "other inhumane acts," of a similar character to "murder, extermination, enslavement and deportation." But no post-Charter conventional definition of "inhumane acts" was developed to eliminate the ambiguities and uncertainties in the interpretation of this extension by analogy, particularly in order to avoid the problems of legality discussed in Chapter 3. The non-exhaustive enumeration of the type of inhumane acts listed in Article 6(c) permits resort to the rule *ejusdem generis* -- as a means to interpret the words "other inhumane acts," and, therefore, other serious crimes could be included within the scope of "crimes against humanity," but probably excluding such acts as offenses against property and other human rights violations of a lesser nature.[12] But since the time of the Charter, none of the international criminal law instruments that have been elaborated dealt with this aspect of "crimes against humanity," thus leaving the issue unresolved.

The international protective scheme of human rights, embodied in the Universal Declaration on Human Rights[13] and the International Covenant on Civil and Political Rights,[14] prohibits the commission of all the acts defined in the Law of the Charter, but it does not criminalize any violations of these prescriptions. Furthermore, there is some question as to the binding nature of the Universal Declaration, since it is only a General Assembly Resolution, unless one argues that it is part of "general principles of international law recognized by civilized nations."[15] In that case the argument would be subject to all the difficulties inherent in the application of this source of international law to international criminal law.[16] Also, the International Covenant on Civil and Political Rights applies only to its High Contracting Parties and is subject to whatever limitations these parties may have elected to establish through their Reservations and Declarations.[17] Thus, international human rights law does not provide a criminal scheme as does the Law of the Charter.

---

[12]　　See Schwelb, *Crimes Against Humanity*, 23 Brit. Y.B. Int'l L. 178, 191 (1946); but *see also* Lauterpacht, *The Law of Nations and the Punishments of War Crimes*, 21 Brit. Y.B. Int'l L. 58, 79 (1944).

[13]　　Universal Declaration.

[14]　　U.N. Covenant at 8.

[15]　　See PCIJ Statute art. 38 para. I(3), and ICJ Statute art. 38 para. 1(c). *See generally* B. Cheng, General Principles of Law as Applied by International Tribunals (1987); and Bassiouni, *A Functional Approach to 'General Principles of International Law,'* 11 Mich. J. Int'l L. 768 (1990).

[16]　　*See* Chapter 6.

[17]　　*See* Human Rights: Status of International Instruments (United Nations Publication, 1987), States who ratified the International Covenant on Civil and Political Rights at 25-89.

The piece-meal uncoordinated developments outlined above resulted in:

1. a diversity of legal instruments with differing legal effects, applicable to different and sometimes overlapping contexts and parties,

2. some of the provisions of these instruments are drafted without sufficient specificity, thus offending the "principles of legality,"[18] and

3. they have left gaps in the protective scheme, particularly with respect to mass-killings.

All of this leads to the inescapable conclusion that a comprehensive codification is needed.

Codification of Crimes Against Humanity

Efforts to codify "crimes against humanity" in the post-Charter era have centered on the drafting of a Code of Offences, now Code of Crimes against the Peace and Security of Mankind, which began on November 21, 1947 and has yet to produce a final result.[19]

The General Assembly, in 1947, adopted two resolutions, one which created the ILC -- whose objective was to promote "the progressive development of international

---

[18]   *See* Chapter 3.

[19]   *See* Clark, *supra* note 2, at 249-252. For a detailed analysis *see* Gross, *The Draft Code of Offences Against the Peace and Security of Mankind,* 15 ISRAEL Y.B. H.R. 224 (1985); Williams, *The Draft Code of Offences Against the Peace and Security of Mankind,* 1 BASSIOUNI ICL 109 (1986); Mueller, *The United Nations Draft Code of Offences Against the Peace and Security of Mankind: An American Evolution,* INTERNATIONAL CRIMINAL LAW 597 (G. Mueller & E. Wise eds. 1965). One cannot help muse that if the definition of "crimes against humanity" is taking some fifty years after the promulgation of the Charter, either the drafters of the Charter were more genial men than the distinguished members of the ILC, or that the legal issues are much more complicated than what the Charter enacted. Considering that the 1919 Commission had already attempted to define "crimes against the laws of humanity," it does seem to be taking quite a long time to conclude this effort.

law and its codification"[20] -- while the other directed the ILC to "formulate the principles of international law recognized in the Charter of the Nuremberg Tribunal and in the judgment of the Tribunal."[21]   Additionally, resolution 177 (II) instructed the ILC to prepare a Draft Code of Offenses against the Peace and Security of Mankind. The General Assembly specifically called for the ILC to prepare the Draft Code of Offences "indicating clearly the place to be accorded to the [Nuremberg] principles ...."[22]

At the first session of the ILC in 1949, the Commission considered several drafts of the Nuremberg Principles. It became readily apparent that this formulation was inextricably linked to the preparation of the Draft Code of Offences but for all intents and purposes it elected to consider it a separate undertaking.[23] Professor Jean Spiropoulos, as Special Rapporteur, prepared the draft of the Nuremberg Principles and later prepared a first draft of the Draft Code of Offences.[24]

In 1950, the ILC adopted and submitted to the General Assembly the Principles of International Law Recognized in the Charter of the Nuremberg Tribunal and in the Judgment of the Tribunal, of which Principle VI(c) was the "crimes against humanity" provision. It stated that "crimes against humanity" were:

Murder, extermination, enslavement, deportation and other inhuman acts done against any civilian population, or persecutions on political, racial or religious grounds, when such acts are done or such persecutions are carried on in execution of or in connexion with any crime against peace or any war crime.

---

[20]   U.N.G.A. Res. 174 (II), November 21, 1947.

[21]   U.N.G.A. Res. 177 (II), November 21, 1947.

[22]   *Report of the ILC to the General Assembly, reprinted in* [1949] 1 Y.B. INT'L L. COMM'N 282.

[23]   The Commission considered a set of draft principles authored by Professor Georges Scelle which supported the view that a formulation of the Nuremberg principles should also contain a formulation of the underlying general principles of international law. A majority of the Commission opposed Professor Scelle's position and the ILC found it necessary to appoint a sub-committee. The ILC subsequently considered a first and second draft prepared by the sub-committee on the formulation of the Nuremberg principles. The ILC eventually decided that the Commission's duty was to merely formulate the principles of Nuremberg and not to "express any appreciation" of them.

[24]   *See supra* note 22 at 282-283.

The ILC's formulation of the "crimes against humanity" provision in the Nuremberg Principles omitted the war connection with respect to the first category of enumerated crimes, but retained it for "persecution."[25]

Consistent with the Charter, the ILC's formulation retained the same specific crimes listed in Article 6(c). The ILC made special mention in its report of the second session that it preserved the language, "any civilian population" from Article 6(c) so that the acts mentioned in both Article 6(c) and Principle VI (c), *i.e.*, murder, extermination, enslavement, deportation and other inhumane acts, would be considered "crimes against humanity" regardless of the fact the perpetrator may be acting against his own population.[26] Accordingly, the ILC deemed redundant the language from Article 6(c) "whether or not in violation of the domestic law of the country where perpetrated" and struck it.

Also consistent with the IMT's intent, but not consistent with the language of Article 6(c), the ILC's formulation of the Nuremberg Principles listed those crimes which IMT considered to be within its jurisdiction, though they were not specifically named in the Charter. In so doing, the ILC replaced "any crime within the jurisdiction of the Tribunal" with "any crime against peace or any war crime."[27]

Having completed the formulation of the Nuremberg Principles, Spiropoulos submitted his initial report on the Draft Code of Offenses against the Peace and Security of Mankind in 1950. The Commission considered his comments regarding the place for the Nuremberg Principles in the Draft Code of Offences and decided that they did not have to be incorporated in their entirety into the Draft Code of Offences.[28] In fact, "only a general reference to the corresponding Nüremberg principles was deemed practicable."[29] The ILC also decided that it was free from the specific terms of the Nuremberg Principles in its Draft Code of Offences formulation of "crimes against humanity."[30] Thus, the ILC's formulation of the Nuremberg Principles was not viewed by the very body that produced it as the definitive or binding definition of "crimes against humanity." Indeed, almost half a century later, the ILC has still to

---

[25] *See* discussion of this question in Chapter 1.

[26] *Report of the ILC to the General Assembly, reprinted in* [1950] 2 Y.B. INT'L L. COMM'N 376.

[27] *Id.* at 377.

[28] *Id.* at 380.

[29] *Report of the ILC to the General Assembly, reprinted in* [1951] 2 Y.B. INT'L L. COMM'N 134.

[30] *Id.*

agree on the definition and contents of "crimes against humanity," and has yet to even find the adequate legal formula to include all that which needs to be included within the scope of that category of crimes.

The ILC faced two essential problems: The first was methodological, and the second was substantive. As to the first, it was whether to have a generic or general definition of what constitutes such a crime, or one that defines each and every type of prohibited conduct and specifying its required legal elements. The former approach would have obviously provided more flexibility, but less specificity, and thus risked violating the "principles of legality," as discussed in Chapter 3. The latter risked being too narrow and ran the risk of failing to anticipate specific types of conduct. The second problem concerns the policy of international criminalization and the extent to which human rights violations can or should be internationally criminalized,[31] and if so, how that should be accomplished.

In 1954, Spiropoulos submitted a third and final report to the ILC which was adopted with amendments by the Commission. The "crimes against humanity" provision stated in article 2, para. 11:

> Inhuman acts such as murder, extermination, enslavement, deportation or persecutions, committed against any civilian population on social, political, racial, religious or cultural grounds by the authorities of a State or by private individuals acting at the instigation or with the toleration of such authorities..."

But, the General Assembly delayed consideration of the Draft Code of Offences until a definition of aggression was completed by another special committee and it tabled the Draft Code of Offences.[32]

Article 2(11) of the 1954 Draft Code of Offences incorporated the broad generic definitional approach with some particularities and was the broadest of any prior text,[33] though it clearly contains gaps and insufficiencies.

---

[31] Bassiouni, *The Proscribing Function of International Criminal Law in the International Protection of Human Rights*, 1982, YALE J. WORLD PUB. ORD. 193 (1982), *reprinted in* 1 BASSIOUNI ICL 15; R. LILLICH, INTERNATIONAL HUMAN RIGHTS: PROBLEMS OF LAW, POLICY, AND PRACTICE (2nd ed.1991).

[32] *Report of the ILC*, U.N. G.A.O.R. Supp. (No. 10) (A/38/10) 15-17 *citing*, GAOR 898 (IX) (4 Dec. 1954). *See also, First Report on the Draft Code by Mr. Doudou Thiam, Special Rapporteur*, U.N. Doc. A/CN.4/364, *reprinted in* [1983] Y.B. INT'L L. COMM'N. 137.

[33] *Report of the ILC to the General Assembly*, U.N. Doc. A/2673, *reprinted in* [1954] 2 Y.B. INT'L L. COMM'N 150.

The 1954 Draft Code Article 2(11) differs from the Charter's Article 6(c) in the following ways:

1) Omits the conditional "before or after the war" language in the Charter; "crimes against humanity" under the Draft Code could occur at any time and not necessarily in a time of war;

2) strikes the redundant language of the Charter, "whether or not in violation of domestic law of the country where perpetrated." The ILC was of the view that committing "crimes against humanity" against "any civilian population" adequately included states acting in accordance with their own law against their own populations;

3) adds a new category of discrimination not found in Article 6(c), namely "cultural grounds;"

4) removes the language of the Charter, "in execution of or in connection with any crime ... ;" and

5) requires state involvement, (though not in the same detailed or specific manner as outlined in Chapter 6).

D.H.N. Johnson wrote a critical analysis of the 1954 Draft Code of Offences wherein he made two observations about the changes stated above.[34] He noted that "inhumane acts" were linked to a requirement that they be committed on social, cultural, political, racial, and religious grounds, whereas in the Charter, only "persecutions" were required to be committed on "racial or religious grounds," as discussed in Chapter 1. His concern was that by conditioning "inhumane acts" on the same grounds as "persecutions," there was a heightened burden of proof for the "inhumane acts" which previously only existed for "persecutions" in the Charter.[35]

Johnson also questioned the requirement of state involvement particularly in light of the Genocide Convention. Under the Genocide Convention individuals were

---

[34] Johnson, *Draft Code of Offences Against the Peace and Security of Mankind*, 411 INT'L & COMP. L.Q. 445 (1955).

[35] *Id.* at 465.

responsible under "any circumstance," while under the Draft Code of Offences individuals were only responsible for "crimes against humanity" if a "state action or policy" connection existed, as discussed in Chapter 6.

After 27 years of postponement, in 1981, the General Assembly called for the ILC to resume work on the Draft Code of Offences.[36] In 1982, the ILC appointed Mr. Doudou Thiam as the Special Rapporteur for the Draft Code. Mr. Thiam dutifully and commendably undertook this very difficult task. Among his first decisions was to rethink and redraft the Draft Code *ab initio*. Four years later, in 1986, Mr. Thiam submitted article 12, "Acts constituting crimes against humanity." The proposed article contained four paragraphs. Paragraph one labeled "genocide" became one of the "crimes against humanity;" it relied entirely on the 1948 Convention on the Prevention and Punishment of the Crime of Genocide (art. II).[37] Paragraph two offered two alternative definitions of *apartheid* as another one of the "crimes against humanity." Paragraph three contained a third specific crime "inhumane acts" which reflected the Charter's Article 6(c) and the 1954 Draft Code Article 2(11) but with modifications. And lastly, paragraph four listed an innovation as "crimes against humanity," a breach of an international obligation for safeguarding and preserving the human environment. In 1987, the General Assembly changed the title of the code to the Draft Code of Crimes against the Peace and Security of Mankind.[38] Mr. Thiam, along with a small working group, reworked the "crimes against humanity" provision and in 1989, he resubmitted the Draft Code of Offences in his seventh report to the ILC. But, the "crimes against humanity" article was referred back by the Commission to the working group.[39] Thereafter, new crimes were included such as severe environmental harm and drug trafficking.[40]

---

[36]   U.N. Res. 36/106.

[37]   *Fourth Report of Mr. Doudou Thiam*, Special Rapporteur, U.N. Doc. A/CN.4/398, *reprinted in* [1986] 2 Y.B. INT'L L. COMM'N. 85.

[38]   1991 Draft Code of Crimes at 199, n. 289.

[39]   *Reprinted in* [1989] *Report of the ILC.*, U.N. G.A.O.R. Supp. No. 10 (A/44/10) 132. *See also* 1990 and 1991 Reports.

[40]   *Reprinted in* [1985] *Report of the ILC*, at 171. Adding international drug trafficking to the draft code or slavery is in direct opposition to the intent of the code as expressed by ILC's Report in 1951. The ILC specifically stated the draft code would not cover "piracy, traffic in dangerous drugs, traffic in women and children, slavery, counterfeiting currency, and damage to submarine cables, etc." Johnson, *supra* note 34, at 456. The rationale for omitting these offenses was that the offenses against the peace and security of mankind, as an "indivisible concept," should be "limited to offences which contain a political element and

In 1991, the ILC issued a report on the work of its forty-third session and the ninth report of the Special Rapporteur including the Crimes against the Peace and Security of Mankind.[41] This draft no longer maintains a distinction between crimes against peace, war crimes, and "crimes against humanity." The report states:

> That distinction has provided useful guidelines in determining the approach to be taken in relation to each crime but the Commission felt that, at this stage and pending the receipt of the comments of Governments, it could be dispensed with inasmuch as solutions have emerged as regards both the constituent elements and the attribution of each crime.[42]

There is a sharp contrast between Mr. Thiam's 1991 version of "crimes against humanity" and the 1954 Draft Code of Offences. Unlike the 1954 Draft Code single paragraph provision, the Thiam formulation includes a number of paragraphs with specific categories of crimes. Articles 15-26, thus lists the crimes of: Aggression (Article 15); Threat of aggression (Article 16); Intervention (Article 17); Colonial domination and other forms of alien domination (Article 18); Genocide (Article 19); *Apartheid* (Article 20); Systematic or mass violations of human rights (Article 21); Exceptionally serious war crimes (Article 22); Recruitment, use, financing and training mercenaries (Article 23); International terrorism (Article 24); Illicit traffic in narcotic drugs (Article 25); and Willful and severe damage to the environment (Article 26).[43] It is quite difficult to assess some of the new textual language of the latest ILC formulation, since much of it is not based on prior conventional textual language. But the "crimes against humanity" provision has become a mini-code within the Draft Code of Crimes.

Mr. Thiam's 1991 version is more specific and by far more elaborate than the 1954 Draft Code of Offenses. It does not adhere to the ILC's earlier decisions not to introduce drug trafficking and slavery as crimes against the peace and security of mankind.[44] The Nuremberg Principles were also freely interpreted and enlarged upon, yet it is quite obvious that Mr. Thiam and the Commission were laboring under the

---

which endanger or disturb the maintenance of international peace and security." *Id.*

[41]   [1991] *Report of the ILC*, U.N. G.A.O.R. Supp. No. 10 (A/46/10).

[42]   *Id.* at 259.

[43]   *See* Document Section at C.5.

[44]   *See supra* note 33.

long shadow of Nuremberg. Instead they should unequivically step out of it, without breaking faith with it, in order to elaborate the type of Code which the comtemporary international community expects. It is indeed hard to walk toward the future while looking to the past. Once that healthy psychological break is achieved, it is indispensable that the Commission avail itself of experts in international criminal law and comparative criminal law in order to draft a valid, effective, and enforceable international criminal code. The time for haphazard accumulation of unrelated provisions which, for the most part would not meet the test of legality in most major criminal justice systems, has long passed.

Genocide is incorporated as part of "crimes against humanity" though it was previously viewed by the ILC as a separate and distinct crime.[45] The 1954 Draft Code treated "genocide" and "crimes against humanity" as separate offenses because of their distinct characteristics, which created differing requirements for individual criminal responsibility.[46] Article 2(10) of the Draft Code of Offenses was largely borrowed from Article II of the Genocide Convention, while Article 2(11), "crimes against humanity" was borrowed from Article 6(c) of the Charter. Thus, it can be assumed that the original intent of the 1954 Draft Code of Offenses was that the two crimes should remain separate.[47] The definition of the crime of genocide in the 1991 draft is, however, based entirely on Article II of the Genocide Convention.[48] Thus, this provision sets out a list of acts constituting genocide, rather than the non-exhaustive list of the 1954 Draft Code.[49] Because the genocide provision of the Draft Code of Crimes uses the same wording of the Genocide Convention, the same problems still remain, namely the non-coverage under genocide of mass killings without the requisite intent to eliminate the group in whole or in part, and does not include the mass killing of a group on grounds other than national, ethnic, racial or religious.

---

[45] *Reprinted in* 2 Y.B. INT'L L. COMM'N. 134.

[46] *Id. See also Fourth Report of Mr. Doudou Thiam, reprinted in* [1986], 2 Y.B. INT'L L. COMM'N. 58. The report of the ILC of 1989 suggests that Thiam departs from the 1954 Draft Code by distinguishing genocide from other inhumane acts by devoting a separate provision to it, "because genocide might be regarded as the prototype of a crime against humanity." [1989] *Report of the ILC* Supp. No. 10 (A/44/10) 154. However, this statement is bewildering because from the discussion in the text, the 1954 Draft Code did in fact distinguish genocide from other inhumane acts.

[47] Johnson, *supra* note 34, at 456.

[48] [1991] *Report of the ILC, supra* note 41. *See also* Document Section, F.1. and F.5.

[49] [1991] *Report of the ILC, supra* note 41; and Document Section F.4.

Mr. Thiam's latest version also includes the crime of *apartheid*,[50] whose definition is based on that Convention.[51] The Draft Code of Crimes, however, unlike the *Apartheid* Convention and the 1954 Draft Code, does not contain a reference to southern Africa which limited the scope of application.[52] Though some of the provisions of this crime overlap with genocide, the Draft Code of Crimes does not integrate these violations in a progressive codification fashion.

The 1991 Draft Code of Crimes contains a provision making "systematic or mass violations of human rights" an international crime.[53] It includes "murder," "torture," "slavery," "persecution," and "deportation."[54] But the listing of these "violations of human rights" does not include legal definitions containing sufficient legal elements, thus making such a listing problematic with respect to legality. Such a listing without any more makes it impossible to distinguish between conduct within the national criminal jurisdiction of a given state and conduct subject to international criminal law. Slavery, for example, is mentioned, but the specifics of its application, such as debt bondage and slave-labor, are not defined.[55] Similarly, the crime of deportation does not distinguish between conditions under which deportation is legal and those which are not.[56]

The 1991 Draft Code of Crimes also includes a crime entitled: "Exceptionally serious war crimes."[57] There is no justification for adding this category of crimes which is covered more specifically under the several instruments regulating armed conflicts. Furthermore, the terminology used is vague and ambiguous and violates minimum standards of the "principles of legality." The same critical comments apply to Article 23, "Recruitment, use, financing and training of mercenaries;" Article 24, "International terrorism;" Article 25, "Illicit traffic in narcotic drugs." Furthermore, the

---

[50]   *Id.* at 263.

[51]   *See* Document Section F.2.

[52]   [1991] *Report of the ILC, supra* note 41 at 264. *See also* Document Section F.2. and F.5.

[53]   *Id.* at 265. *See also* Document Section F.5.

[54]   *Id.* at 247.

[55]   *See* Bassiouni, *Enslavement as an International Crime*, 23 N.Y.U. J. INT'L L. & POLITICS 445 (1991).

[56]   The text reads, "deportation of forcible transfer of population..." 1991 Draft Code of Crimes at 247. This is a typographical error, the text should read, "deportation [or] forcible transfer of population..."

[57]   *Id.* at 269. *See also* Document Section.

addition of international drug trafficking to crimes against the peace and security of mankind is unsupported by an international convention, custom, general principle, or writings of the most distinguished publicists, since these crimes are committed by individuals and small groups, which are usually considered part of organized crime, even when they have international ramifications. Such crimes seldom contain the element of "state action or policy" which characterizes "crimes against humanity," and distinguishes such acts from crimes within the national criminal jurisdiction of States. Article 26, "Wilful and severe damage to the environment" is probably the worst example of drafting from a criminal law perspective and violates "principals of legality." It states: "An individual who wilfully causes or orders the causing of widespread, long-term and severe damage to the natural environment shall, on conviction thereof, be sentenced [to...]." If there is ever an example of a normative provision that is overly broad and ambiguous than this is the one. It does not take much legal imagination to see how broad and ambiguous these terms are and how they are fraught with the creation of conflicts between national and international law, and ultimately between states. Nevertheless, it is clear that some of the harmful manifestations of the conduct described must be cognizable under international criminal law. The purposes of this provision are indeed laudable, but its formulation leaves too much to be desired. But then it may well be that the very nature of such violations elude a precise and perspicacious definition.

The confusion between individual and state responsibility is evident in several aspects of the 1991 Draft Code, and the basis for state criminal responsibility is not identified. Furthermore, with respect to those offenses which are the product of "state action or policy," the Draft Code of Crimes fails to identify those pre-requisite legal elements, discussed in Chapter 6, which are indispensable for distinguishing between conduct which is wholly within the national criminal jurisdiction of a given state, and conduct which constitutes an international crime irrespective of national law.

The 1991 Report mentions the establishment of an international criminal court[58] and the recommendations of the Special Rapporteur follow prior models suggested by various scholars.[59]

Aside from the questionable progress discussed above, what the future holds for "crimes against humanity" remains to be seen. But the expectations are bleak that a legally satisfactory codification of "crimes against humanity" will soon emerge. The

---

[58] *Id.* at 201 and 214-235.

[59] BASSIOUNI DRAFT CODE.

danger in producing legally questionable norms is that it gives rise to the opportunity for selective enforcement by a powerful State.

Crimes Against Humanity as Part of Jus Cogens

Under "General Principles of Law Recognized by Civilized Nations," the universal condemnation of the acts contained in Article 6(c) of the Charter rises to the level of *jus cogens*. Post-Charter Legal Developments have added to this baggage of universal condemnation making such a category of crime a clear violation of *jus cogens*. The term *jus cogens* means the compelling law, and as such the hierarchical position of such a rule is presumably above all other principles, norms and rules of both international law and national law.

Some scholars see *jus cogens* and customary international law as similar,[60] while others distinguish between custom and "peremptory norms,"[61] and still others question whether *jus cogens* is simply not another semantical way of describing certain "General Principles" which, for a variety of reasons, rise above other "General Principles".[62] This scholarly debate is, however, essentially one of hierarchy of applicable law no matter how it is described. It is referred to as a "peremptory norm" by the Vienna Convention on the Law of Treaties.[63] It is also referred to in the legal literative as "compelling," "inherent," "inalienable," "essential," "fundamental," and "overriding." It is perhaps as Verdross stated: "no definition is necessary because the idea of *jus cogens* is clear in itself."[64]

---

[60] *See* A. D'AMATO, THE CONCEPT OF CUSTOM IN INTERNATIONAL LAW, 132 (1971).

[61] *See* Christensen, *Jus Cogens: Guarding Interests Fundamental to International Society*, 28 VA. J. INT'L L. 585 (1988). *But see contra*, D'Amato, *It's a Bird, It's a Plane, It's Jus Cogens*, 6 CONN. J. INT'L L. 1 (1990).

[62] Janis, *Jus Cogens: An Artful Not a Scientific Reality*, 3 CONN. INT'L L.J. 370 (1988).

[63] Vienna Convention on the Law of Treaties, with annex, 23 May 1969, U.N. Doc. A/CONF. 39/27, art. 53.

[64] Verdross, *Jus Dispositivium and Jus Cogens in International Law*, 60 AJIL 55, at 57 (1966); and 1 Y.B. INT'L L. COMM'N. 63, 66-67, (1963). The ICJ in Military and Paramilitary Activities in and Against Nicaragua, 1986 ICJ 14, did not define *Jus Cogens* though it relied on it. *See generally, Appraisals of the ICJ's Decision: Nicaragua v. United States*, 81 AJIL 77 *et. seq.* (1987).

This writer's understanding of *jus cogens* is that it is essentially a label placed on a principle whose perceived importance, based on certain values and interests, rises to a level which is acknowledged to be superior to another principle, norm or rule and thus overrides it.

The operative terms used in describing *jus cogens* are value-laden and susceptible of multiple definitions based on different philosophical and jurisprudential conceptions.[65] Nevertheless, the scholarly debate can be characterized as being both methodological and substantive. The range of views among adherents to the positivist school of thought is almost as wide as among adherents to the naturalist one, not to speak of other philosophical and jurisprudential schools.[66] The legal existence and validity of "crimes against humanity" is acknowledged in the naturalist school but not so by positivists, as discussed in Chapter 2.

In addition to the concept of humanitarian law embodied in the 1907 Hague Convention, as discussed in Chapter 4, proponents of *jus cogens* advance that the legal values protecting life and prohibiting the depredations described in Article 6(c) are of a higher "legal" order than any international or national norm or rule which permits their violation. In addition, they would argue that the principles protected by Article 6(c) are well established "General Principles of Law Recognized by Civilized Nations" under both international and national legal sources, as discussed in Chapters 7 and 8. But such arguments may not be sufficiently convincing to rigid positivists, and to those who deem that the requirements of the "principles of legality" particularly *crimen sine lege, nulla poena sine lege* are mandatory in international criminal law.[67]

As demonstrated in Chapters 7 and 8, "General Principles" are a source of international law and they include those specific crimes which are parts of "crimes against humanity." But if "crimes against humanity" rise to the level of *jus cogens*, they would override the "principles of legality" and that would either result in the elimination or substantial diminution of the "principles of legality" with respect to "crimes against humanity." If, however, the "principles of legality" are also deemed to be *jus cogens* than we are confronted with a conflict between two co-equal *jus*

---

[65] *See e.g.*, McDougal, Laswell and Reisman, *The World Constitutive Process of Authoritative Decision Making*, in 1 BLACK AND FALK, THE FUTURE OF THE INTERNATIONAL LEGAL ORDER 73 (1969).

[66] *See generally*, J. HALL, READINGS IN JURISPRUDENCE (1938); C.J. FRIEDRICK, THE PHILOSOPHY OF LAW IN HISTORICAL PERSPECTIVES (1958); and Chapter 2.

[67] *See* Chapter 2.

cogens norms without having a clear basis for making appropriate choices between them.

Genocide[68] is now universally deemed a *jus cogens* violation and its prohibition imposes on states certain duties and obligations *erga omnes*. On the basis of the *erga omnes* rationale for genocide, which some deem to be a species of "crimes against humanity" then this category of crimes as a whole also rises to that level.

The *erga omnes* and *jus cogens* doctrines are often presented as the two sides of the same coin. The term *erga omnes* means "flowing to all," and thus presumably obligations deriving from *jus cogens* are *erga omnes*. Indeed, legal logic supports the proposition that what is "compelling law" must necessarily engender obligation "flowing to all."[69]

The ICJ in the *Barcelona Traction Case* held:

... an essential distinction should be drawn between the obligations of a State towards the international community as a whole, and those arising vis-à-vis another State in the field of diplomatic protection. By their very nature the former are the concern of all States. In view of the importance of the rights involved, all States can be held to have a legal interest in their protection; they are obligations *erga omnes*.[70]

Thus, the first criterion of an obligation rising to the level of *erga omnes* is in the words of the ICJ ... the obligations of a state towards the international Community as a whole ...."[71] The ICJ goes on in Paragraph 34 to give examples[72] but it does not

---

[68]   *See* Advisory Opinion of the International Court of Justice on Reservations to the Genocide Convention, 1951 I.C.J. 15. *See also* Bassiouni, *Introduction to the Genocide Convention*, in 1 BASSIOUNI ICL 281; and *see* Bassiouni, *International Law and the Holocaust*, 9 CALIF. W. INT'L L. J. 201 (1979).

[69]   Randall, *Universal Jurisdiction Under International Law*, 66 TEX L. REV. 785, 829-30 (1988).

[70]   Barcelona Traction (Judgment), 1970 I.C.J. 1.

[71]   *Id.*

[72]   *Id.*, wherein the Court stated:

34. Such obligations derive, for example, in contemporary international law, from the outlawing of acts of aggression, and of genocide, as also from the principles and rules concerning the basic rights of the human person, including protection from slavery and racial discrimination. Some of the corresponding rights of protection have entered into the body of general international law (Reservations to the Convention and punishment of the Crime of Genocide, Advisory Opinion, I.C.J. Reports 1951, 23);

define or list all that could be deemed "obligations of a State towards the International Community as a whole"[73] for the obvious reason that such a listing would be impossible. But clearly a "state action or policy" aimed at committing "crimes against humanity" creates state responsibility for its violation of a *jus cogens* norm. In addition, since there is an international duty to prosecute or extradite such violators, a state that fails to do so would also breach its international legal duty and be in further violation of the principles of state responsibility.[74] Thus, if conduct creates state responsibility because it constitutes the violation of a *jus cogens* norm, then it should follow that those individuals who carry out the "state action or policy" are also in breach of the same *jus cogens* norm.

In an important study bearing on the *erga omnes* and *jus cogens* relationship, particularly as applied to certain international crimes such as genocide, Professor Randall states that "traditionally international law functionally has distinguished the *erga omes* and *jus cogens* doctrines ...."[75] But he recognizes the *sine qua non* relationship of the two with respect to genocide.[76]

---

others are conferred by international instruments of a universal or quasi-universal charter.

[73] *Id.*, at 32.

[74] *See* the work of the ILC in [1976] 2 Y.B. INT'L COMM'N, Part Two, 113; 1 I. BROWNLIE, SYSTEM OF THE LAW OF NATIONS, STATE RESPONSIBILITY (1983). *See also generally* MALEKIAN, INTERNATIONAL CRIMINAL RESPONSIBILITY OF STATES (1985).

[75] Randall, *supra* note 69, at 830.

[76] *Id.* More specifically on the subject, Randall states:

Jus Cogens means compelling law. The *jus cogens* concept refers to "peremptory principles or norms from which no derogatory is permitted, and which may therefore operate to invalidate a treaty or agreement between States to the extent of the inconsistency with any such principles or norms."

While authoritative lists of obligations *erga omnes* and *jus cogens* norms do not exist, any such list likely would include the norms against hijacking, hostage taking, crimes against internationally protected persons, *apartheid*, and torture. Traditionally, international law functionally has distinguished the *erga omnes* and *jus cogens* doctrines, which address violations of individual responsibility. Those doctrines nevertheless, may subsidiarily support the right of all states to exercise universal jurisdiction over the individual offenders. One might argue that "when committed by individuals", violations of *erga omnes* obligations and peremptory norms "may be punishable by any State under the universality principle."

Both the PCIJ and ICJ have recognized the higher law background of *jus cogens* as part of "General Principles" of international law.[77] Furthermore, it is well established that *jus cogens* can derive from principles of *ordre publique* meaning "public policy."[78] The international and national law prohibitions against "crimes against humanity" as evidenced under both international and national legal sources of "General Principles," and whose prohibition is universally condemned, also clearly embody principles of *ordre publique*. This added dimension further reinforces the conclusion that "crimes against humanity" violate a *jus cogens* norm.

The essential characteristic of *jus cogens* as a higher rule is its inderogability.[79] The inderogability of international rules of *ordre publique*, as these may be established in *jus cogens*, also supersedes the principle of national sovereignty. The PCIJ declared in its very first judgment, *The S.S. Wimbledon*,[80] that sovereignty is not inalienable. Indeed sovereignty cannot be claimed as a barrier to the binding nature of *jus cogens* obligations. Professor Schwarzenberger states: "In other words, none of the rules of international customary law governing the principle of sovereignty constitute international *jus cogens*."[81] This means that if *jus cogens* is inderogable and

---

[77] *See* Case Concerning Right of Passage Over Indian Territory (Merits), (Fernandes, J., dissenting) 1960 I.C.J. 123, 135; Judge Fernandes explained, "It is true that, in principle, special rules will prevail over general rules, but to take it as established that in the present case the particular rule is different from the general rule is to beg the question. Moreover, there are exceptions to this principle. Several rules *cogestes* prevail over any special rules. And the general principles to which I shall refer later constitute true rule of *jus cogens* over which no special practice can prevail." *See also* separate opinion of Judge Ammoun in Legal Consequences for States of the Continued Presence of South Africa in Namibia (South West Africa) notwithstanding Security Council Resolution 276 (1970), Advisory Opinion (Ammoun, J. separate opinion), 1971 I.C.J. 66.

[78] Schwelb, *Some Aspects of International Jus Cogens as Formulated by the International Law Commission*, 61 AJIL 946, 949 (1967).

[79] H. KELSEN, PRINCIPLES OF INTERNATIONAL LAW 408-38 (1952). In modern international law the principle of inderogability applies to fundamental human rights and is embodied in relevant conventions, such as the U.N. Covenant and Torture Convention. De Vattel referred to the concept as the "immutable Law of Nations" *See* DE VATTEL, THE LAW OF NATIONS 54-55 (J. Chitty ed, 1855). Also neither general nor special customary international law can derogate to *jus cogens*, see Akehurst, *Customs as a Source of International Law*, 47 BRIT. Y.B. INT'L L. 1 (1974).

[80] The S.S. Wimbledon, 1923 P.C.I.J. (ser. A) No. 1, at 25 (1923). *See also* Case of the European Commission of the Danube, 1927 P.C.I.J. (Ser. B) No. 14, at 6.

[81] Schwarzenberger, *International Jus Cogens*, 43 TEX. L. REV. 455, n. 3 at 655 (1965) the following opinions of the Court of International Justice on the evidentiary source of *jus cogens*:

supersedes national positive law, it cannot be opposed on the grounds of national sovereignty because the latter is neither inalienable nor interrogable. A direct consequence of that hierarchical standing of *jus cogens* makes it controlling over positive law whether international or national.

In 1920, United States Secretary of State Lansing aptly stated:

> This realization compels the conviction that the entire human race ought to be considered, and in fact is, a single community, which awaits the further development of modern civilization to complete its organization and make of all mankind a great, universal political state. There is, therefore, sufficient ground for an examination of sovereignty from this standpoint; and it will be found that,

---

In the Case Concerning the Payment of Various Serbian Loans Issued in France, P.C.I.J., ser A, No. 14, at 46 (1929), in France, P.C.I.J., ser A, No. 15, at 125 (1929), ..., *See also* the Case Concerning the Application of the Convention of 1902 Governing the Guardianship of Infants (Netherlands v. Sweden), (1958) I.C.J. Rep. 55, 122-3 (Spencer, J. Separate opinion).

See Comment, *Jus Dispositivum and Jus Cogens in Light of the Recent Decisions of the German Supreme Constitutional Court*, 60 AJIL 511 (1966). A contrary position to Schwarzenberger which is more supportive of *jus cogens* is that of Professor Verdoss, a member of the International Law Commission: writing in 1966 he said:

> [I]n the field of general international law, there are rules having the character of *jus cogens*. The criterion for these rules consists in the fact that they do not exist to satisfy the needs of the individual states by the higher interest of the whole international community. Hence these rules are absolute. The others are relative, concerning only individual states *inter se*.

Verdross, *supra* note 64, at 58. He points out that the two categories of general international law were also recognized by the International Court of Justice in its Advisory Opinion concerning [*supra* note 68], Reservations to the Genocide Convention, where the Court stated: "The Convention was manifestly adopted for a purely humanitarian and civilizing purpose .... [I]n such a convention the contracting States do not have any interest of their own; they merely have, one and all, a common interest, namely the accomplishment of those high purposes which are the *raison d'etre* of the Convention. Verdross stated that he prepared the article cited for reasons that he "felt obliged to defend article 37 of the International Law Commission's then-existing draft (on the Law of Treaties)" against "criticism directed against it by Professor Schwarzenberger," citing Schwarzenberger, *International Jus Cogens?*, 43 TEX. L. REV. 455, 1965. Verdross, *supra* note 64, at 55. In the French and Latin American literature on private international law, the term *international public policy* is used to denote considerations of *national* public policy which rule out the application of foreign law otherwise relevant under *lex fori*. *See e.g.*, Case Concerning the Application of the Convention of 1902 Governing the Guardianship of Infants (Netherlands v. Sweden), (1958) I.C.J. 55, 1211-22 (Spencer, J., separate opinion).

494

though there has been no formal recognition of the existence of such sovereignty, *the great states of the civilized world have recognized, perhaps unconsciously, its existence in the applied law of nations, just as they have recognized it in the sphere of morals by giving binding effect to the principles of humanity.* (emphasis added)

It has been seen ... that law arising through the decrees of judicial tribunals, when not interpreting enacted laws, is based upon the rational presumption that the sovereign of the state is persistently desirous of directing human conduct in accordance with the principles of natural justice. Thus, although a case may be entirely novel, it is assumed by a municipal court, in the absence of enacted laws applicable to such case, that the sovereign will is in harmony with the principles of natural justice, and the court applying those principles as it understands them renders a decision, and by that act makes known the will of the sovereign and announces the law, since the passive acquiescence of the sovereign is equivalent to a command. The point to be noted is, that the law existed without formal enactment, the court being merely the agent for its announcement in terms. [82]

---

[82] Lansing, *Notes on World Sovereignty*, 15 AJIL 13 (1921). At 22-23, on the subject of "Natural Justice", Lansing states:

It is upon a similar presumption and assumption that the great body of the Law of Nations is founded. The conditions in a state and in the Community of Nations are analogous. The principles of natural justice or absolute justice or strict justice (whichever name most accurately defines the moral intent to be constantly righteous towards others) are by civilized states assumed to be in accord with the dominant sentiment of the human race, that is, with the presumed will of the World Sovereign, except so far as repeated practice between governments has established a custom, in which case, as in that arising in a state, the custom overrules the abstract principle of natural justice. *Consuetudo vincit communem legem.* By these precepts sovereigns and their agents ought to be guided in their intercourse with one another as if the will of the World Sovereign had been declared in the exact terms of enacted law, even as in a state an individual is bound to respect the principles of natural justice in delaying with his fellows as a moral and political duty.

Under the English juridical system the source of the Common Law and of the Law of Nations is recognized as resting on the same assumption of sovereign intent, and the latter is on that account given legal force in the municipal courts of England. Blackstone says: "The Law of Nations (whenever any question arises which is properly the object of its jurisdiction) is here adopted to its full extent by the common law, and is held to be a part of the law of the land." Thus, under the English system the principles of natural justice are applied both internally and externally to the state in the regulation of *all* human relations. A similar recognition of the legal character of the Law of Nations appears in the Constitution of the United States, though it was undoubtedly but the principle expressed by Blackstone

Thus, the doctrine that higher international legal obligations prevail over national legal norms existed before World War II.[83] Subsequently, the ICJ in its Advisory Opinion *Concerning Reservations to the Genocide Convention* held that any reservation to that Convention made by a state by virtue of its sovereignty was illegal, stating that genocide "is contrary to moral law and to the spirit and aims of the United Nations."[84] The Court added conclusively that "principles underlying the Convention are principles which are recognized by civilized nations as binding on States, even without any conventional obligation."[85] Thus as a *jus cogens* norm.

The ICJ also recognized that international law imposes certain obligations upon states, *erga omnes*.[86] Professor Whiteman, in reliance thereon, specifically found the *jus cogens* and *erga omnes* doctrines applicable to genocide, slavery, and racial discrimination, all of which embody "crimes against humanity." She states:

> ... obligations owed to the international community as a whole, stating that such obligations derive, for example, in contemporary international law from the outlawing of acts of aggression, and of *genocide*, as also from the principles and rules concerning *the basic rights of the human person, including protection from slavery and racial discrimination.*[87] (emphasis added)

---

reiterated.

But in 1919 Robert Lansing wrote the dissenting American position to the 1919 Commission Report holding that crimes against the "Laws of Humanity" was not a legally enforceable norm. By 1945 Robert Jackson had to overturn that conclusion in the London Charter's formulation of Article 6(c). The United States had come full circle. But in another flip-flop, the United States has since 1954 opposed the formulation of the Draft Code of crimes and the establishment of an International Criminal Court. Its opposition to an International Criminal Court however, has been softened in 1991-2.

[83]   *See* Wildhaber & Breitenmoser, *The Relationship Between Customary International Law and Municipal Law in Western European Countries*, 48 ZEITSCHRIFT FÜR AUSLÄNDISCHES ÖFFENTLICHES RECHT UND VÖLKERRECHT 163 (1988).

[84]   Reservations to the Genocide Convention, *supra* note 68, at 23-24.

[85]   *Id.*

[86]   *See e.g.*, North Sea Continental Shelf, 1969 I.C.J. 4.

[87]   Whiteman, *Jus cogens in International Law, with a Projected List*, 7 GEO. J. INT'L L. & COMM. L. 609, 610 (1977). *See also* Randall, *supra* note 69, at 829-832.

The position that certain international crimes are *jus cogens* and that they rise not only above treaties but above all sources of law is best expressed by Lord McNair and Sir Gerald Fitzmaurice, whose positions are stated below.[88]

Lord McNair states:

There are, however, many rules of customary international law which stand in a higher category and which cannot be set aside or modified by contracting States; it is easier to illustrate these rules than to define them. They are rules which have been accepted whether expressly by treaty or tacitly by custom, as being necessary to protect the public interests of the society of States or to maintain the standards of public morality recognized by them ... For instance, piracy is stigmatized by customary international law as a crime, in the sense that a pirate is regarded as *hostis humani generis* and can lawfully be punished by any State into whose hands he may fall. Can there be any doubt that a treaty whereby two States agree to permit piracy in a certain area, or against the merchant ships of a certain State, with impunity, would be null and void? Or a treaty whereby two allies agree to wage war by methods which violated the customary rules of warfare, such as the duty to give quarter.[89]

Judge Fitzmaurice states:

There are certain forms of illegal action that can never be justified by or put beyond the range of legitimate complaint by the prior illegal action of another State, even when intended as a reply to such action. These are acts which are not merely illegal, but *malum in se*, such as certain violations of human rights, certain breach of the laws of war, and other rules in the nature of *jus cogens* - that is to say obligations of an absolute character, compliance with which is not dependent on corresponding compliance by others, but is requisite in all circumstances, unless under stress of literal *vis major*. In the conventional field, may be instanced such things as the obligations to maintain certain standards of safety of life at sea. No

---

[88]   Both cited by Whiteman *supra* note 87, at 610-611.

[89]   A. MCNAIR, THE LAW OF TREATIES 213-24 (1951).

amount of noncompliance with the conventions concerned, on the part of other States, could justify a failure to observe their provisions.[90]

In a decisive and rather definitive manner, the Vienna Convention on the Law of Treaties consecrates the notion of peremptory norms of international law as superseding national law and other sources of international law. In Article 53, it establishes:

A treaty is void if at the time of its conclusion, it conflicts with a peremptory norm of general international law. For the purposes of the present Convention, a peremptory norm of international law is a norm accepted and recognized by the community of States as a whole as a norm from which no derogation is permitted and which can be modified only by a subsequent norm of general international law having the same character.[91]

Of great note is the fact that the ILC which drafted the Vienna Convention on the Law of Treaties deemed it to be the embodiment of customary international law.[92]

Since World War II, a number of international and regional instruments on the protection of human rights have been elaborated and entered into effect.[93] These instruments along with numerous United Nations resolutions reaffirm and provide support for the assertion that the protected human interests whose violations are criminalized in "crimes against humanity" have become *jus cogens*.

---

[90] Fitzmaurice, *The General Principles of International Law Considered from the Standpoint of Rules of Law*, 92 RECUEIL DES COURS 120 (1957).

[91] *Supra* note 63.

[92] *See* ELIAS, THE VARIOUS REPORTS OF THE INTERNATIONAL LAW COMMISSIONS BETWEEN 1957-1969. See the various reports of the ILC between 1957-1969. Sir Humphrey Waldock Special Reporter in the Law of Treaties in [1966] 27 Y.B. INT'L L. COMM'N 23 *et seq*. The unanimous acceptance of *jus cogens* is evidenced in *United Nations Conference on the Law of Treaties*, 1st Sess., Vienna, 26 March - 29 May 1968, U.N. Doc. A/Conf. 39/11 and for the second session, 22 May 1969, *see* A/Conf. 39/11 Add. For insight into the *Jus Cogens* question *see* Schwelb, *supra* note 78. Baxter, *Treaties and Custom*, 129 RECEUIL DES COURS DE L'ACADAMIE DE LA HAYE, 104 (1970); and D'Amato, *Manifest Intent and the Customary Rules of International Law*, 64 AJIL 822 (1970). *See also* Paust, *Congress and Genocide: They're Not Going to Get Away With It*, 11 MICH. J. INT'L L. 90 (1989).

[93] *See, United Nations Action in the Field of Human Rights*, ST/HR/2/Rev. 2, U.N. Sales No. E.83 XIV.2 (1983); and HUMAN RIGHTS IN INTERNATIONAL LAW (1985), which provides the texts of many of these instruments. *See also generally* R. LILLICH *supra* note 31.

The connection between international protection of human rights and the international criminalization of its most serious breaches is evident,[94] but, as stated in Chapters 2 and 6, there still must be certain criteria for international criminalization which distinguish between crimes that are within the national criminal jurisdiction of states and those that supercede and override national law in their applicability.

Procedural Aspects

Aut Dedere Aut Iudicare

The essential purpose of criminalizing harmful conduct whether at the national or international level is to prevent such conduct by means of general deterrence. But general deterrence is only as effective as the likelihood of prosecution and punishment. The latter, however, depend upon the existence of a forum for prosecution and an enforcing authority to carry out the eventual sanctions meted out to convicted offenders, and that means: an international criminal jurisdiction and/or universal jurisdiction to be exercised by national criminal justice systems. In addition, prosecution and punishment should not be barred by time limitations. Thus, prosecution and eventual punishment, no matter where or when, are indispensable to the effectiveness of general deterrence which enhances compliance with the mandates of the law and prevents violations.

The maxim *aut dedere aut iudicare*,[95] which this author re-worded from Hugo

---

[94] Bassiouni, *International Criminal Law and Human Rights*, 9 YALE J. PUB. ORD. 193 (1982), *reprinted in* 1 BASSIOUNI ICL 15 (1986); and R. LILLICH *supra* note 31.

[95] *See* Bassiouni, *Characteristics of International Criminal Law Conventions*, 1 BASSIOUNI ICL 3; 1 M.C. BASSIOUNI, INTERNATIONAL EXTRADITION IN UNITED STATES LAW AND PRACTICE Chap. 1 § 2-3 (2nd rev. ed., 1987). For an excellent review of the question, *see* Wise, *Extradition: The Hypothesis of a Civitas Maxima and the Maxim Aut Dedere Aut Judicare*, 62 RIDP 109 (1991). *See also* Costello, *International Terrorism and the Development of the Principle aut dedere aut iudicare*, 10 J. INT'L L. & EC 483 (1925); Wise, *Some Problems of Extradition*, 15 WAYNE L. REV. 709, 720-23 (1968); Bassiouni, *World Public Order and Extradition: A Conceptual Evolution*, in AKTUELLE PROBLEME DES INTERNATIONALEN STRAFRECHTS 10 (D. Oehler and P. Pötz eds., 1970); Bassiouni, *An Appraisal of the Growth and Developing Trends in International Criminal Law*, 45 RIDP 403, 430 (1974); VAN DEN WYNGAERT, THE POLITICAL OFFENSE EXCEPTION TO EXTRADITION: THE DELICATE PROBLEM OF BALANCING THE RIGHTS OF THE INDIVIDUAL AND THE INTERNATIONAL PUBLIC ORDER 8, 132-40 (1980); Bassiouni, *General Report on the Juridical Status of the Requested State Denying Extradition*, 30 AM. J. COMP. L. 610 (1982); Derby, *Duties*

Grotius' *aut dedere aut punire*,[96] because it appropriately mandates prosecution and not punishment in keeping with the presumption of innocence which is a "general principle of law." Punishment, is only a consequence of guilt and its application will depend on a variety of factors such as: the nature of the act, its harmful result, the personality of the actor, and various factors bearing on aggravation and mitigation of sentences. Each of these factors reflects a different philosophical approach to punishment which are beyond the scope of this discussion.[97]

"Crimes against humanity" is a category of international crimes and as such, a general duty exists to prosecute or extradite. This duty, in the opinion of this writer and other scholars, has become a *civitas maxima* and a rule of customary international

---

and Powers Respecting Foreign Crimes, 30 Am. J. Comp. L. 523, 530 n. 40 (Supp. 1982); Wise, *Book Review*, 30 Am. J. Comp. L. 362, 370 n. 64 (1982). Murphy, *The Grotian Vision of World Order*, 76 AJIL 477 (1982). *See also* Wise, *International Crimes and Domestic Criminal Law*, 38 DePaul L. Rev. 923, 932-34 n. 39 and 42 (1989). For expressions of these positions in the 1600's *see* C. Beccaria, Dei Delitti E Delle Poene § 13 (1764) (G.D. Pisapia, trans., ed. 1973); J. Bentham, An Introduction to the Principles of Morals and Legislation (1780) (J.H. Burns, and H.L.A. Hart, eds., 1970).

[96] H. Grotius, De Jure Belli Ac Pacis, Book 2, Chap. XXI, Sections 3, 4, 5(1) and 5(3) (1624). *See also* E. de Vattel, Le Droit des Gens, Book II, Chap. 6, Sections 76-77 (1758); and S. Puffendorf, The Elements of Universal Jurisprudence (1672), Book VII, Ch. 3, Sections 23-24 (Trans. W. Oldfather, 1931).

[97] Helvetius, Beccaria and Bentham were advocates of utilitarianism as a basis for punishment. *See* Helvetius, De L'Esprit (1759) whose influence on Beccaria and Bentham was noticeable; C. Beccaria, on Crimes and Punishment (trans. D. Young, 1986); J. Bentham, An Introduction to the Principles of Morals and Legislation, at Chap. I, Sec. 1-2, and Chap. 2 p. 17-33. Conversely, Kant and Hegel rejected utilitarianism and saw punishment as the natural consequence of the social harm. Thus punishment would vary depending upon the time, place and perception of the significance of the harm. *See* I. Kant, The Metaphysical Elements of Justice - Part I Metaphysics of Morals (ed. and trans. J. Ladd 1965); and G. Hegel's Philosophy of Right (ed. and trans. T.M. Know, 1967). Another approach is expressed by Voltaire, Montesquieu and Rousseau which stresses the legitimacy of the law through the legitimacy of the law-maker. In his Du Contrat Social, Jean-Jacques Rousseau expresses the view that laws are the province of society acting through it's legislator because the making of laws is a fundamental condition of the social contract. *See also* C. Montesquieu, De L'esprit des Lois, Oeuvres Complètes (ed. R. Caillois, Vol. 2, 1951). Locke, however, differs from Rousseau in that he sees the sovereign as the fiduciary of the people to whom the people surrender only that necessary portion of power needed to govern, *see* J. Locke, The Second Treatise of Government (ed. T.P. Peardon, 1952). These and other philosophical perspectives on criminal punishment are discussed in Jenkins, *Varieties of Enlightenment Criminology*, 24 Brit. J. of Criminology 2 (1984).

criminal law.[98] De Vattel argued that international law imposed a definite legal duty on the state to extradite persons accused of serious crimes.[99] In contrast, Puffendorf argued that the duty to extradite was an imperfect obligation, which required an explicit agreement to become binding under international law, thereby securing the reciprocal rights and duties of the contracting states.[100] The modern practice follows the latter view of requiring agreements or treaties, but this view is more valid for common criminality proscribed by individual states than for international crimes which clearly reflects within the scope of *aut dedere aut iudicare*.[101] Support for the validity of the *aut dedere aut iudicare* customary international duty for international crimes and hence, the duty to prosecute or extradite, is found in conventional international criminal law as evidenced by the treaty provisions containing obligations to prosecute or extradite listed in the Document Section.[102]

The duty to prosecute or extradite has not been expressed with sufficient specificity to indicate whether prosecution-extradition are alternative or co-existent duties. Whatever little doctrine exists on the subject, it is unclear as to whether it is disjunctive or co-existent. As stated by this writer:

> This doctrine is unclear as to the meaning of "alternative" or "disjunctive" and "coexistent" obligations to extradite. The following distinction is suggested. If the duty to extradite or prosecute is an alternative or disjunctive one, then there is a primary obligation to extradite if relevant conditions are satisfied, and a secondary obligation to prosecute under national laws if extradition cannot be granted. Thus, the duty to prosecute when it arises under national law leaves the requesting state with no alternative recourse.

> If the duty to extradite or prosecute is co-existent rather than alternative or disjunctive, then the requested state can choose between extradition or prosecution

---

[98] *See* Mueller, *International Criminal Law: Civitas Maxima*, 15 CASE W. RES. J. INT'L L. 1 (1983); and *supra* note 95.

[99] *See* DE VATTEL, *supra* note 96; and GROTIUS *supra* note 96.

[100] *See* S. PUFFENDORF, *supra* note 96.

[101] *See supra* note 95 and text for an explanation of why *aut dedere aut iudicare* is the more correct statement.

[102] *See* Document Section G.4. These provisions also show the non-applicability of statutory limitations to war crimes and "crimes against humanity" as well as other international crimes.

at its discretion. As a result, the state may refuse to extradite the relator to one state, but later agree to extradite him or her to another state or to prosecute. In any event, when a state elects to prosecute then discretion plays a broader role, and can be invoked without a breach of treaty or other international obligations.

The doctrine usually expressed is that the international obligation to extradite or prosecute if it exists would be construed as a co-existent duty provided that national law permits it.[103]

Since "crimes against humanity" are international crimes for which there is universal jurisdiction, as discussed below, any and all states have the alternative duty to prosecute or extradite. Prosecution is premised not only on a state's willingness, but also on it's ability to prosecute fairly and effectively. In the absence of these premises, the duty to extradite to a State willing and capable of prosecuting fairly and effectively arises. A question, however, exists as to whether the duty to extradite supercedes that of prosecution when the national law of the requested State prohibits extradition (e.g. of its nationals), when that State cannot fairly and effectively prosecute. International criminal law has yet to resolve this question.[104]

The goals of *iudicare* include:

1. upholding the principle of fairness through equal application of the law in an impartial legal process;
2. vindication of victim's rights;
3. permitting the accused to atone for his crime and possibly to remove or alleviate the sense of guilt resulting from the secrecy of the crime and the absence of its public vindication;
4. reinforcing public values;
5. increasing public knowledge and awareness of the crime;
6. strengthening general prevention and general deterrence; and,

---

[103] Bassiouni, *The Penal Characteristics of Conventional International Criminal Law*, 15 CASE W. RES. J. INT'L L. 27 (1983).

[104] This situation is exemplified by the case of Libya v. United States where Libya charged that the duty to prosecute under the 1971 Montreal Convention for the Suppression of Unlawful Acts Against the Safety of the Civilian Aircraft, 974 U.N.T.S. 177, 23 September 1971, specifically Articles 6, 7, and 8, supercedes the duty to extradite.

7.   consolidating the *civitas maxima* that all nations must cooperate in the prevention, prosecution, and punishment of international crimes as a means for upholding the international rule of law.

These goals thus combine moral-ethical values with the utilitarian functions of prosecution and punishment and they are indispensable to the effective deterrence, of "crimes against humanity."

The relevant post-Charter procedural instruments, which are discussed below, are:

1.   General Assembly Resolution on War Criminals of 15 December 1970;
2.   U.N. Principles of International Penal Co-operation and Extradition;
3.   U.N. Convention on the Non-Applicability of Statutory Limitations on War Crimes;
4.   European Convention on the Non-Applicability of Statutory Limitations.

Of these four instruments, two are recommendatory general assembly resolutions, one is a regional convention and one is an international convention whose binding nature extends only to its parties. But it could be argued that these instruments, irrespective of their specific binding effect have become part of customary international law and also constitute a "general principle of law." This can be evidenced by their recurrence in a number of other international instruments.[105] The Geneva Convention of August 12, 1949, and Protocol I also contain provisions on the duty to prosecute, extradite and to provide mutual assistance to the High Contracting Parties.[106] These provisions, however, apply to "grave breaches" of the Conventions and the Protocols and do not apply to civilian population under the national jurisdiction of States which are not within the meaning of "protected persons" under the Conventions and the Protocols.

The Post-Charter Duty to Prosecute or Extradite

---

[105]   *See* Document Section G. 4.

[106]   Solf, *Protection of Civilians Against the Effects of Hostilities Under Customary International Law and Under Protocol I*, 1 AM. U. J. INT'L L. & POL'Y 117 (1986); Solf, & Cummings, *A Survey of Penal Sanctions Under Protocol I to the Geneva Conventions of August 12, 1949*, 9 CASE W. RES. J. INT'L L. 205 (1977).

To underscore the duty to prosecute or extradite persons believed to have committed "crimes against humanity," the General Assembly called on States to do so in a 1973 resolution entitled, "Principles of International Co-operation in the Detention, Arrest, Extradition and Punishment of Persons Guilty of War Crimes and Crimes Against Humanity."[107] Its relevant parts state:

1. War crimes and crimes against humanity, wherever they are committed, shall be subject to investigation and the persons against whom there is evidence that they have committed such crimes shall be subject to tracing, arrest, trial and, if found guilty, to punishment ....

3. States shall co-operate with each other on a bi-lateral and multi-lateral basis with a view to halting and preventing war crimes and crimes against humanity, and take the domestic and international measures necessary for that purpose.

4. States shall assist each other in detecting, arresting and bringing to trial persons suspected of having committed such crimes and, if they are found guilty, in punishing them ....

7. States shall not grant asylum to any person with respect to whom there are serious reasons for considering that he has committed a crime against peace, a war crime or a crime against humanity.

The duty to prosecute or extradite is well established in the modern regulation of armed conflicts. The Four Geneva Conventions of 12 August 1949 in their Common Articles on repression of "Grave Breaches" state:

... Each High Contracting Party shall be under the obligation to search for persons alleged to have committed, or to have ordered to be committed, such grave breaches, and shall bring such persons, regardless of their nationality, before its

---

[107] *Principles of International Co-operation in the Detention, Arrest, Extradition and Punishment of Persons Guilty of War Crimes and Crimes Against Humanity*, G.A. Res. 3074 (XXVIII), 28 U.N. GAOR Supp. (No. 30) at 78, U.N. Doc. A/9030, 3 December 1973. *See also* G.A. Res. 2840, (XXVI) 26 U.N. GAOR Supp. (No. 29), at 88, U.N. Doc. A/8429 (1971) affirming that a State's refusal "to cooperate in the arrest, extradition, trial and punishment" of persons accused or convicted of war crimes and crimes against humanity is "contrary to the United Nations Charter and to generally recognized norms of international law."

own courts; it may also, if it prefers, and in accordance with the provisions of its own legislation, hand such persons over for trial to another High Contracting Party concerned ....[108]

Furthermore, Protocol I states:

Article 88 -- Mutual assistance in criminal matters

1. The High Contracting Parties shall afford one another the greatest measure of assistance in connexion with criminal proceedings brought in respect of grave breaches of the Conventions or of this Protocol.
2. Subject to the rights and obligations established in the Conventions and in Article 85, paragraph 1, of this Protocol, and when circumstances permit, the High Contracting Parties shall co-operate in the matter of extradition. They shall give due consideration to the request of the State in whose territory the alleged offence has occurred.
3. The law of the High Contracting Party requested shall apply in all cases. The provisions of the preceding paragraphs shall not, however, affect the obligations arising from the provisions of any other treaty of a bilateral or multilateral nature which governs or will govern the whole or part of the subject of mutual assistance in criminal matters.

Similarly, the Genocide Convention specifies in Article I:[109]

The Contracting Parties confirm that genocide, whether committed in time of peace or in time of war, is a crime under international law which they undertake to prevent and to *punish*. (emphasis added)

The *Apartheid* Convention also specifies in Article IV:[110]

---

[108] *See also*, 1977 Additional Protocols, art. 85 (1) and De Breuker, *La Répression des Infractions Graves aux Dispositions du Premier Protocole Additionnel aux Quatres Conventions de Genève du 12 août 1949*, REV. D. PÉN. MIL. & D. GUERRE, 498 (1977).

[109] Genocide Convention. *See also* Articles V, VI, VII and VIII dealing respectively with jurisdiction, extradition, duty to suppress.

[110] *Apartheid* Convention.

The State Parties to the present Convention undertake:

(a) To adopt any legislative or other measures necessary to *suppress* as well as to prevent any encouragement of the crime of *Apartheid* and similar segregationist policies or their manifestations and to punish persons guilty of that crime;

(b) To adopt legislative, judicial and administrative measures to *prosecute, bring to trial and punish* in accordance with their jurisdiction persons responsible for, or accused of, the acts defined in article II of the present Convention, whether or not such persons reside in the territory of the State in which the acts are committed or are nationals of that State or of some other state or are stateless persons. (emphasis added)

It is to be noted that the *Apartheid* Convention in Article V, and the Genocide Convention in Article VI, provide for jurisdiction of an international criminal tribunal[111] and for universal jurisdiction,[112] thus adding two additional means for the effectiveness of prosecution. Regrettably no international criminal court exists to prosecute violations of the *Apartheid* and Genocide Conventions, though at least with respect to *Apartheid* the United Nations elaborated such a project in 1980, but it remained without progress.[113]

The 1984 Torture Convention also contains a number of provisions on jurisdiction, prosecution, and extradition.[114] These provisions are:

---

[111] This writer was commissioned in 1979 by the United Nations to prepare a draft statute for the establishment of an international criminal tribunal in accordance with Article V of the *Apartheid* Convention. The Report is entitled *Final Report on the Draft Statute for the Creation of an International Criminal Jurisdiction to Implement the International Convention on the Suppression and Punishment of the Crime of Apartheid*, 19 January 1980 U.N. Doc/E/CN/4/1426 (1981). *See also supra* note 8.

[112] *See* section on universal jurisdiction *infra* and Randall *supra* note 69.

[113] *See supra* note 111.

[114] Torture Convention, which contains the substantive changes from the *Draft Convention Against Torture and Other Cruel, Inhuman or Degrading Treatment or Punishment*, 23 ILM 1027 (1984). This writer served as co-chair, along with Niall MacDermot, Secretary General of the International Commission of Jurists, of the *Ad Hoc* Committee of experts meeting at the International Institute of Higher Studies in Criminal Sciences (Siracusa) which prepared the Draft Convention, submitted first by the International Association of Penal Law to the United Nations as U.N. ECOSOC Doc. E/CN/4/NGO-213 (1978); *see* 48 RIDP (1977) devoted to this draft. *See also* Bassiouni and Derby, *The Crime of Torture*, BASSIOUNI ICL *supra* note 10 reprinted with modifications from 48 RIDP 23-103 (1977). The official Swedish text

506

Article 4

1. Each State Party shall ensure that all acts of torture are offences under its criminal law. The same shall apply to an attempt to commit torture and to an act by any person which constitutes complicity or participation in torture.

Article 5

2. Each State Party shall likewise take such measures as may be necessary to establish its jurisdiction over such offenses in cases where the alleged offender is present in any territory under its jurisdiction and it does not extradite him pursuant to Article 8 to any of the States mentioned in paragraph 1 of this Article.

Article 7

1. The State Party in the territory under whose jurisdiction a person is alleged to have committed any offence referred to in Article 4 is found shall in the cases contemplated in Article 5, if it does not extradite him, submit the case to its competent authorities for the purpose of prosecution.

Article 8

1. The offences referred to in Article 4 shall be deemed to be included as extraditable offences in any extradition treaty existing between the States Parties. States Parties undertake to include such offences in every extradition treaty to be concluded between them.

The duty to prosecute or extradite whether alternative or co-existent is clearly established in conventional and customary international criminal law with respect to "crimes against humanity." The national law of a number of states such as Australia,

---

submitted to the United Nations was modelled on the IAPL text, *see* U.N. ECOSOC Doc. E/CN.4/1285 (1978). The IAPL text had a provision concerning the non-applicability of Statutes of Limitations in Article VIII. *See also* J. L. DE LA CUESTA ARZAMENDI, *supra* note 10; J. H. BURGERS AND H. DANELIUS, *supra* note 10.

Belgium, Canada, France, Germany, Israel, the United Kingdom and the United States clearly evidences that the international obligation finds a concomitant application in the internal law and practice of a large number of states.

Non-applicability of Statutes of Limitation

The duties to prosecute or extradite are dependent upon the ability of States to do so and that requires the removal of any impediments that can arise to prevent it. One such impediment is the barring of the criminal action by a statute of limitations. To avoid that, in 1968, the United Nations sponsored an international convention on the "Nonapplicability of Statutes of Limitations to War Crimes and Crimes Against Humanity."[115] Subsequently, the Council of Europe elaborated a similar convention entitled, "European Convention on the Nonapplicability of Statutory Limitations to Crimes Against Humanity and War Crimes."[116]

---

[115] Nonapplicability of Statutory Limitations to War Crimes, 165. The International Association of Penal Law significantly contributed to the adoption of this Convention by publishing a symposium issue of the 37 RIDP 383 *et seq.* (1966) which was widely circulated among U.N. permanent observers, government officials and scholars all over the world. *See also* Van den Wyngaert, *War Crimes, Crimes Against Humanity, and Statutory Limitation*, in 3 BASSIOUNI ICL 89; Glaser, *L'Imprescriptibilité des Crimes de Guerre et des Crimes Contre l'Humanité et l'Extradition de leurs Auteurs à la Lumière du Droit International*, 90 SCHWEIZENRISCHE ZEITSCRIFT FÜR STRAFRECHT 24 (1974); Sottile, *La Prescription des Crimes Contre L'Humanité et le Droit Pénal International*, 43 REVUE DE DROIT INTERNATIONAL, DE SCIENCES DIPLOMATIQUES ET POLITIQUES 5 (1965); Mertens, *L'Imprescriptibilité des Crimes de Guerre et des Crimes Contre l'Humanité*, 51 REVUE DE DROIT PÉNAL ET DE CRIMINOLOGIE 204 (1970); Miller, *The Convention on the Non-Applicability of Statutory Limitations to War Crimes and Crimes Against Humanity*, 65 AJIL 476 (1971); Lerner, *The Convention on the Non-Applicability of Statutory Limitations to War Crimes*, 4 ISRAEL L. REV. 512 (1969). *See also* United Nations Doc. E/CN. 4/906 of 15 February 1966. *See also* Sepalc, *Le rôle Normatif de la Pratique de l'extradition de criminals Nazis*, 13 POLISH Y.B. OF INT'L L. 153 (1984). *See Contra Lithuania Exonerating People Accused As Nazis*, CHICAGO TRIBUNE, Sept. 5, 1991, Sec. 1, at 4, 1.

[116] Nonapplicability of Statutory Limitations to Crimes Against Humanity and War Crimes, E.T.S. No. 82, 25 January 1974, *reprinted in* 13 I.L.M. 540 (1974). *See also* Reports of the Consultative Assembly of the Council of Europe on the applicability of statutes of limitation to war crimes and crimes against humanity (Doc. 1868 of January 27, 1965 and Doc. 2506 of January 15, 1969).

National developments have also occurred which removed any statutory limitations, whether in reliance upon the 1968 Convention or independently of that Convention's obligations.[117]

In the national context, the issue of non-applicability of statutes of limitation arose in *The Barbie Case.*[118] The French Cour de Cassation upheld the post-1968 Conventional international criminal law norm that statutes of limitations do not apply in war crimes and "crimes against humanity."

Supporting the non-applicability of statute of limitations, as early as the 1600's, Cesare Beccaria,[119] writing on impunity, noted that it is tantamount to a betrayal of the nation. In his moral-ethical conception, he could not accept that the public good could benefit from giving a premium to villainy. Adding a utilitarian note, he concluded that such a practice would lead to the reduction of general deterrence and that other villains would be comforted in the belief or expectation that their crimes would also benefit from impunity.[120]

But "crimes against humanity" are not only against a given victim in a single or isolated context whereby forgiveness may be the victim's prerogative. In these crimes, all of humanity is affected by the victimization of a given human group.[121]

The issue in this type of crime is not hatred but retributive and symbolic justice. The first is well established in criminal law doctrine, the second has seldom been

---

[117] For national legislation subsequent to the Charter *see* Herzog, *Etudes des Lois Concernant la Préscription des Crimes Contre l'Humanité*, 20 REVUE DE SCIENCE CRIMINELLE ET DE DROIT COMPARÉ 337 (1965); and authors in 37 RIDP 383 *et seq.* (1966). *See also* Bolle, *La Suisse et L'Imprescriptibilité des Crimes de Guerre et des Crimes Contre l'Humanité*, 93 REVUE PÉNALE SUISSE 308 (1977).

[118] *Matter of Barbie*, GAZ. PAL. JUR 710 (France, Cass. Crim. Oct. 6, 1983). *See generally* Doman, *Aftermath of Nuremberg: The Trial of Klaus Barbie*, 60 COLO. L. REV. 449 (1989).

[119] *See* C. Beccaria, *supra* notes 95 and 97. *See also* Vassalli, *Spunti di Politica Criminale in Cesare Beccaria*, in CESARE BECCARIA AND MODERN CRIMINAL POLICY 23 (1990).

[120] In a recent book FORGIVENESS AND MERCY (1988), authors Jeffrie G. Murphy and Jean Hampton debate the moral-ethical foundations of punishment and the merits of forgiveness and mercy. Reviewed by Dressler, *Hating Criminals: How Can Something That Is So Good Be Wrong*, 88 MICH. L. REV. 1448 (1990). *See also* Pillsbury, *Emotional Justice: Moralizing the passions of Criminal Punishment*, 74 CORNELL L. REV. 655 (1989); Nath, *Wrongdoing and Forgiveness*, 62 PHIL. 499 (1987); J. MURPHY, RETRIBUTION, JUSTICE AND THERAPY (1979), whereby he espouses a Kantian reciprocity of benefits and burdens theory of criminal punishment.

[121] *See* Dressler, *Reflections on Executing Wrongdoers: Moral Theory, New Excuses and the Model Penal Code*, 19 RUT. L. J. 671 (1988); and H.L.A. HART, PUNISHMENT AND RESPONSIBILITY, 3-13 (1968); Weinreb, *Desert, Punishment and Criminal Responsibility*, LAW & CONTEMP. PROBS. 47-49 (1986).

argued because most authors who deal with this question have approached it from the perspective of the traditional victim of domestic crime: the individual. None have dealt with those international crimes that rise to the level of victimizing a large segment of a given society which is part of the world community. The punishability of the actor irrespective of time and place is a necessary ingredient of international criminal responsibility particularly since there is no supra-national enforcement mechanism capable of consistent application of the law.

The virtue of forgiving an individual is a "generosity of judgment"[122] that can be applied in individual cases, but it is no virtue to forgive an entire category of offenders who committed the worst crimes against an entire category of victims. It is thus correct: "to insist that there are occasions when it is not morally appropriate [to forgive] -- in particular, when too much of the person is morally dead."[123] To provide for a statute of limitations is forgiveness by foreswearing justice, retribution, future general deterrence, but it also means accepting the potentiality of future question on moral grounds.

Mercy is a gift, a grant, that a community bestows on a wrongdoer, but only to vindicate the victim's moral value or because it found a moral redeeming value in the perpetrator. It cannot be an abstract decision applicable to an entire category of perpetrators on behalf of a category of victims. To withhold the grant of mercy in these cases is not to uphold hatred or vengence but to express the most basic sense of justice and fairness. To insist on prosecution is in these cases a moral, ethical, legal and pragmatic duty that no amount of passing time should erase.

Statutes of limitation, however, exist in all legal systems, and their removal finds obstacles in many of these systems for a variety of reasons, some of which raise such a bar to the level of a principle of fundamental justice. Thus, a conflict exists between the development at the international level of non-applicability of statutes of limitation to "crimes against humanity" and the principled existence of the bar in national criminal justice systems. This conflict has yet to be resolved as both concepts continue in parallel coexistence.

Universal Jurisdiction

---

122   FORGIVENESS AND MERCY, *supra* note 120, at 84.

123   *Id.*, at 83.

Jurisdiction may be defined as "the authority of states to prescribe their law, to subject persons and things to adjudication in their courts and other tribunals, and to enforce their law, both judicially and nonjudicially."[124] There are five basic theories of jurisdiction recognized by international law as giving rise to a state's rule-making and rule-enforcing power. These theories are: (1) Territorial, which is based on the place where the offense was committed; (2) Active Personality or Nationality, which is based on the nationality of the accused; (3) Passive Personality, which is based on the nationality of the victim; (4) Protective, which is based on the national interest affected; and (5) Universality, which is based on the international character of the offense. While the first four jurisdictional theories require some connection or nexus between the state desiring to assert jurisdiction and the offense, the universality theory rests upon different ground. As stated by Carnegie:

A State claiming to act under this [universality] principle claims to exercise jurisdiction over any offender irrespective of any question of nationality or place of commission of the offence, or of any link between the prosecuting State and the offender.[125]

Recently, three states, Australia, Canada and the United Kingdom enacted enabling statutes to prosecute war criminals based on a modified version of universal jurisdiction couched in terms of extended and retrospective national criminal jurisdiction.[126] The Australian War Crimes Amendment Act of 1988 allows for the prosecution, in national courts, of war criminals whose crimes were committed between September 1, 1939 and

---

[124] RESTATEMENT (THIRD) OF THE FOREIGN RELATIONS LAW OF THE UNITED STATES, § 402 (1)(a) and comment c (1987).

[125] Carnegie, *Jurisdiction Over Violations of the Laws and Customs of War*, 39 BRIT. Y.B. INT'L L. 402, 405 (1963).

[126] *See generally*, Note, *U.S. Prosecution of Past and Future War Criminals and Criminals Against Humanity: Proposals for Reform Based on the Canadian and Australian Experience*, 29 VIR. J. INT'L L. 887 (1989), which calls for the United States to enact legislation asserting universal jurisdiction over war criminals. Most recently an enactment of law giving a court jurisdiction over war criminals occurred in May 1991, in the United Kingdom, which would allow British courts to try Nazi war criminals. The law came into being despite the rejection by the House of Lords. Ironically, Lord Shawcross, Britain's chief prosecutor at Nuremberg, argued against the law on the ground that it was not possible to conduct fair trials in Britain nearly fifty years after the alleged crimes were committed in central Europe. CHICAGO TRIBUNE, May 2, 1991, Sec. 1, at 18.

May 8, 1945.[127] Although limited in time, the statute is based upon an application of universal jurisdiction, since it applies to crimes committed outside of Australia and by and against individuals with whom Australia had only a tenuous connection at the time of the crime. The Canadian legislation on the other hand is not so temporally limited. The 1987 Act to amend the Criminal Code provides that any person who commits a war crime or crime against humanity "shall be deemed to [have] committ[ed] that [crime] in Canada at the time of the act or omission, if the crime, if committed in Canada would constitute an offence against the laws of Canada in force at [that] time."[128]

The rationale for universal jurisdiction, in general or with regard to specific statutes, such as those referred to above, is that there exist certain offenses, which due to their very nature, affect the interests of all states, even when committed in another state or against another state, victim or interest.[129] As previously stated by this author,

---

[127] War Crimes Amendment Act 1988, § 9, 1989 Aust. Acts 926; 119 Parl. Deb., S. 497 (1987); 157 Parl. Deb., H.R. 1613 (1987).

[128] Act to amend the Criminal Code, ch. 37, 1987 Can. Stat. 1107. Section 1.96 of the Act defines the crimes thusly:

Crime against humanity means murder, extermination, enslavement, deportation, persecution or any other inhumane act or omission that is committed against any civilian population or any identifiable group of persons ... and that, at that time and in that place constitutes a contravention of customary international law or is criminal according to general principles recognized by the community of nations;

War crimes means an act or omission that is committed during an international armed conflict ... and that, at that time and in that place, constitutes a contravention of the customary international law or conventional international law applicable in international armed conflicts.

[129] *See* MARTIN'S ANNUAL CRIMINAL CODE 1990 (E.L. Greenspan ed. 1989) § 7 (3.71). *See also* Green, *Canadian Law, War Crimes and Crimes Against Humanity,* 59 BRIT. Y.B. INT'L L. 217 (1988); Green, *Canadian Law and the Punishment of War Crimes,* 28 CHITTY'S L.J. 249 (1980); Jacquart, *La notion de crime contre l'humanité en droit international contemporain et en droit Canadien,* 21 REVUE GÉNÉRALE DE DROIT 607 (1990); Regina v. Finta, 50 C.C.C. (3d) 247, 61 D.L.R. 85 (4th, 1989); Williams, *The Criminal Law Amendment Act of 1985: Implications for International Criminal Law,* 23 CAN. Y.B. INT'L. L. 226 (1985). *See also, Report of the War Crimes Inquiry of the Parliament of the United Kingdom,* CM 744 (1989), which was the basis of the War Crime Bill adopted by the House of Commons, May 2, 1991. *See also,* Australian Crimes Amendment Act of 1988 which was approved by the Senate and the House of Representatives of the Commonwealth of Australia, 25 January 1989. *See also e.g.* 1 M.C. BASSIOUNI, INTERNATIONAL EXTRADITION: UNITED STATES LAW AND PRACTICE, (2nd Rev. 1987) at 298.

512

the "gravamen of such an offense is that it constitutes a violation against mankind."[130] Thus, the principle of universal jurisdiction assumes that each state has an interest in exercising jurisdiction to combat offenses which all nations have condemned.[131]

Although during the Middle Ages, towns in northern Italy prosecuted certain types of criminals called *banditi, vagabundi, and assassini,* who were within their jurisdiction, regardless of where they committed their criminals acts,[132] the history of universal jurisdiction stems from the customary international practices regarding pirates and brigands in the 1600's; even "[b]efore International Law in the modern sense of the term was in existence, a pirate was already considered an outlaw, a *hostis humani generis.*"[133]   Since then, however, the concept of a universal right to

---

[130]   M.C. BASSIOUNI, *supra* note 129.

[131]   *See* Randall, *Universal Jurisdiction Under International Law*, 66 TEX. L. REV. 785, 788 (1988); *see also* L. HENKIN, R. PUGH, O. SCHACHTER & H. SMIT, INTERNATIONAL LAW 823 (2d ed. 1987). At § 404, *Universal Jurisdiction to Define and Punish Certain Offenses*, THE FOREIGN RELATIONS LAW OF THE UNITED STATES, *supra* note 124, states that

> A state has jurisdiction to define and prescribe punishment for certain offenses recognized by the community of nations as of universal concern, such as piracy, slave trade, attacks on or hijacking of aircraft, genocide, war crimes, and perhaps certain acts of terrorism, ...

See also infra notes 132 and 133.

[132]   H. DONNEDIEU DE VABRES, LES PRINCIPES MODERNES DU DROIT PÉNAL INTERNATIONAL 136 (1928).

[133]   1 OPPENHEIM, INTERNATIONAL LAW: A TREATISE 609 (8th ed. H. Lauterpacht ed. 1955). Many authors from Hugo Grotius to contemporary ones have amply documented these practices of states exercising jurisdiction over pirates, even when the pirate and his victim were not nationals of the prosecuting state. *See also,* H. GROTIUS, *supra* note 96; A. GENTILE, DE JURE BELLI LIBRE TRES, Bk. I, Chap. XXV (Classics of International Law, J. Scott ed. 1933); C. MALLORY, DE JURE MARITINO ET NAVOLI (1676) Bk. I Chap. IV § iv (1682 ed.), which, at 54, refers to Pirates as *hostis humani generis,* cited by Green, *Terrorism and the Law of the Sea,* INTERNATIONAL LAW AT A TIME OF PERPLEXITY, 249, 252-53 (Y. Dinstein ed., 1989); Cowles, *Universality of Jurisdiction Over War Crimes,* 33 CALIF. L.R. 177, at 188-189 (1945); Wortley, *Pirata Non Mutat Dominium,* 24 BRIT. Y.B. INT'L L. 258 (1947); A. NUSSBAUM, A CONCISE HISTORY OF THE LAW OF NATIONS 30-31 (1954); Rubin, *The Law of Piracy,* 15 DENVER J. INT'L L. & POL. 173 (1987). *See also e.g.* A. RUBIN, THE LAW OF PIRACY (1988). It should be noted that while the Seventeenth century is generally considered as the time when pirates were universally considered *hostis humani generis,* C. PHILLIPSON, 2 THE INTERNATIONAL LAW AND CUSTOM OF ANCIENT GREECE, 375, (1911), claims that the writings of Justinian and Demosthenes assert that in both ancient Rome and Greece:

prosecute and a universal right to punish has been recognized grudgingly. This has been the case notwithstanding Grotius' approval of the right of states to try crimes committed outside of their territorial jurisdiction, if these crimes violated the law of nature or the law of nations. As he states:

> ... Kings, and those who are invested with a Power equal to that of Kings, have a Right to exact Punishments, not only for Injuries committed against themselves or their Subjects, but likewise, for those which do not peculiarly concern them, but which are, in any Persons whatsoever, grievous Violations of the Law of Nature or Nations. For the Liberty of consulting the Benefit of human Society, by Punishments, does now, since Civil Societies, and Courts of Justice, have been instituted, reside in those who are possessed of the supreme Power, and that properly, not as they have an Authority over others, but as they are in Subjection to none. For ... it is so much more honourable, to revenge other Peoples Injuries rather than their own .... Kings, besides the Charge of their particular Dominions, have upon them the care of human Society in general.[134]

To some scholars of international criminal law it is clear that a crime *delicti juris gentium*, committed by a *hostes humani generis*, can indeed be prosecuted by any state and the perpetrator punished by any state.

Professor Feller writes:

> Sometimes the criminal law is applied by virtue of a principle which reflects the special quality of the class of offenses known as *delicta juris gentium*, crimes under international law. These crimes threaten to undermine the very foundations of the enlightened international community as a whole; and it is this quality that gives each one of the members of that community the right to extend the incidence of its criminal law to them, even though they are committed outside the state's

---

"pirates, no matter how large their bans, and how organised they were, were not regarded as 'regular enemies,' *iusti hostes*, but as enemies of mankind generally; so that the usual formalities relating to the commencement of war, and the mitigations conceded in the case of other belligerents, were held not to be applicable to them."

[134] GROTIUS, *supra* note 96, Book II, Chap XX.

boundaries and the offender has no special connection with the state ... Hence, too, the name "universality principle."[135]

And, as Professor Jordan Paust states:

[U]niversal enforcement has been recognized over "crimes against mankind," "crimes against the whole world" and the "enemies of the whole human family," or those persons who become *hostis humani generis* by the commission of international crimes.[136]

It should be noted that in the "Draft Convention on Jurisdiction with Respect to Crime" (prepared by the Harvard Research in International Law),[137] universal jurisdiction over certain crimes is contemplated. With carefully chosen language, Article 10 provides:

A State has jurisdiction with respect to any crime committed outside its territory by an alien, other than the crimes mentioned in Articles 6 ["Persons Assimilated to Nationals"], 7 ["Protection-Security of the State"], 8 ["Protection-Counterfeiting"] and 9 ["Piracy"], as follows:

(a) When committed in a place not subject to its authority but subject to the authority of another State, if the act or omission which constitutes the crime is also an offence by the law of the place where it was committed, if surrender of the alien for prosecution has been offered to such other State or States and the offer remains unaccepted, and if prosecution is not barred by lapse of time under the law of the place where the crime was committed. The

---

[135] Feller, *Jurisdiction over Offenses with a Foreign Element*, in 2 BASSIOUNI & NANDA TREATISE 5, 32-33.

[136] Paust, *Universality and the Responsibility to Enforce International Criminal Law: No U.S. Sanctuary for Alleged Nazi War Criminals*, 11 HOU. J. INT'L L. 337, 340 (1989). *See* Murphy, *Protected Persons and Diplomatic Facilities*, LEGAL ASPECTS OF INTERNATIONAL TERRORISM 227, 285 (A. Evans & J. Murphy eds. 1978), states that universal jurisdiction applies "to crimes that affect the international community and are against international law." *See also* M.C. BASSIOUNI, INTERNATIONAL EXTRADITION: UNITED STATES LAW AND PRACTICE, *supra* note 95, at 298. "Such crimes are appropriately called *delicti jus gentium*." *Id.* at 298.

[137] As *reprinted in* 29 AJIL 439 (Supp. 1935).

penalty imposed shall in no case be more severe than the penalty prescribed for the same act or omission by the law of the place where the crime was committed.

(b) When committed in a place not subject to the authority of any State, if the act or omission which constitutes the crime is also an offence by the law of a State of which the alien is a national, if surrender of the alien for prosecution has been offered to the State or States of which he is a national and the offer remains unaccepted, and if prosecution is not barred by lapse of time under the law of a State of which the alien is a national. The penalty imposed shall in no case be more severe than the penalty prescribed for the same act or omission by the law of a State of which the alien is a national.

(c) When committed in a place not subject to the authority of any State, if the crime was committed to the injury of the State assuming jurisdiction, or of one of its nationals, or of a corporation or juristic person having its national character.

(d) When committed in a place not subject to the authority of any State and the alien is not a national of any State.[138]

Conventional international law on the subject, however, is not so clear and at best it is inconsistent. Since 1815, there have been sixty-four international criminal law conventions that contain reference to one or more of the recognized theories of jurisdiction.[139] Among those, only a few contain a provision that could be interpreted as providing universal jurisdiction. Among those conventions which provide a universal jurisdiction provision are the Four Geneva Conventions of 1949, which maintain, in common articles, that:

The High Contracting Parties undertake to enact any legislation necessary to provide effective penal sanctions for persons committing, or ordering to be

---

[138]   *Id.* at 440-441. As the language indicates, this Article is "distinctly subsidiary and one which will be rarely invoked .. .. [still, because of] its utility in occasional cases as a subsidiary principle, it seems clear that it should have a place in the present Convention." *Id.* at 573-574. For further commentary on this article *see id.* at 573-592.

[139]   *See* Document Section at G.4.

committed, any of the grave breaches of the present Convention defined in the following Article.

Each High Contracting Party shall be under the obligation to search for persons alleged to have committed, or to have ordered to be committed, such grave breaches, and shall bring such persons, regardless of their nationality, before its own courts. It may also, if it prefers, and in accordance with the provisions of its own legislation, hand such persons over for trial to another High Contracting Party concerned, provided such High Contracting Party has made out a *prima facie* case.

Each High Contracting Party shall take measures necessary for the suppression of all acts contrary to the provisions of the present Convention other than the grave breaches defined in the following Article.

Grave breaches to which the preceding Article relates shall be those involving any of the following acts, if committed against persons or property protected by the Convention: wilful killing, torture or inhuman treatment, including biological experiments, wilfully causing great suffering or serious injury to body or health, and extensive destruction and appropriation of property, not justified by military necessity and carried out unlawfully and wantonly.[140]

Thus, the language of the Conventions supports universal jurisdiction.[141]

Another convention which is clear on the principle of universality is the *Apartheid* Convention which in Article IV provides:

---

[140]   *Supra* note 107; COMMENTARY ON THE ADDITIONAL PROTOCOLS 583-1124 (Y. Sandoz, C. Swinarski, B. Zimmerman, eds. 1987); and NEW RULES FOR VICTIMS OF ARMED CONFLICTS 273-489 (M. Bothe, K. J. Patsch, W. A. Solf, eds. 1982. *See also* Solf, *Protections of Civilians Against the Effects of Hostilities Unver Customary International Law and Under Protocol I*, 1 AM. U. J. INT'L L. & POL'Y 117 (1986); Solf & Cummings, *A Survey of Penal Sanctions Under Protocol I to the Geneva Conventions of August 12, 1949*, 9 CASE W. RES. J. INT'L L. 205 (1977).

[141]   Not all commentators are in agreement with this statement. Röling, *The Law of War and the National Jurisdiction Since 1945*, 100 RECUIEL DES COURS 329, 362 (1960), argues that the Conventions do not contain the universality principle but only the principle of extended protection, which "means that neutrals do not have the obligation to search for alleged war criminals, and that they do not have the obligation to try war criminals, in cases where extradition does not take place."

(b) To adopt legislative, judicial and administrative measures to prosecute, bring to trial and punish in accordance with their jurisdiction persons responsible for, or accused of, the acts defined in article II of the present Convention, whether or not such persons reside in the territory of the State in which the acts are committed or are nationals of that State or some other State or are stateless persons.

Also, Article V provides that:

Persons charged with the acts enumerated in article II of the present Convention may be tried by a competent tribunal of any State Party to the Convention which may acquire jurisdiction over the person of the accused or by an international penal tribunal having jurisdiction with respect to those State Parties which shall have accepted its jurisdiction.

These two articles taken together show that under this Convention a state may assert either territorial or universal jurisdiction.

Universal jurisdiction over piracy, which, as noted above, has been recognized under customary law for centuries, is also recognized under conventional law. The 1982 United Nations Convention on the Law of the Sea at Article 105,[142] which is identical to article 19 of the 1958 Convention on the High Seas, [143] provides that:

On the high seas, or in any other place outside the jurisdiction of any State, every State may seize a pirate ship or aircraft, or ship or aircraft taken by piracy and under the control of pirates, and arrest the persons and seize the property on board. The Courts, of the State which carried out the seizure may decide upon penalties to be imposed, and may also determine the action to be taken with regard to the ship, aircraft or property, subject to the rights of third parties acting in good faith.[144]

---

[142] United Nations Convention on the Law of the Sea, done in Montego Bay, 10 December 1982, *reprinted in* THE LAW OF THE SEA, U.N. Doc. A/CONF. 62/122.

[143] Convention on the High Seas, done 29 April 1958, 13 U.S.T. 2312, T.I.A.S. No. 5200, 450 U.N.T.S. 82.

[144] Convention on the Law of the Sea, *supra* note 142, at art. 105.

Also, the Law of the Sea Convention implicitly recognizes universal jurisdiction for slave trading, as provided in Article 110, which states that "a warship which encounters on the high seas a foreign ship ... is not justified in boarding it unless there is reasonable ground for suspecting that ... the ship is engaged in the slave trade .... "[145]

Several other treaties can be interpreted as conferring universal jurisdiction for certain international crimes. These offenses include torture, hostage taking, hijacking and sabotage of aircraft and crimes against internationally protected persons. All of these conventions contain a similar provision, with minor variation, as the following one from the 1979 Hostages Convention:

> The State Party in the territory of which the alleged offender is found shall, if it does not extradite him, be obliged, without exception whatsoever and whether or not the offense was committed in its territory, to submit the case to its competent authorities for the purpose of prosecution, through proceedings in accordance with the laws of the State.[146]

But, the greater number of international criminal law conventions do not provide for universal jurisdiction.[147] The Genocide Convention in Article 6 provides that:

---

[145]   *Id.* at art. 110. This author has taken the position that the widespread attempts to abolish slavery and slave trading permits the use of universal jurisdiction over slave trading, either under customary law or under "General Principles of International Law." Bassiouni, *Theories of Jurisdiction and Their Application in Extradition Law and Practice,* 5 CALIF. W. INT'L L.J. 1, 54 (1974). For an examination of the international movement against slavery, *see* Bassiouni & Nanda, *Slavery and Slave Trade: Steps Toward Its Eradication,* 12 SANTA CLARA REV. 424 (1972). *See also* Bassiouni, *Enslavement As An International Crime,* 23 N.Y.U. J. INT'L L. & POLITICS 445 (1991).

[146]   International Convention Against the Taking of Hostages, 4 December 1979, U.N. G.A. Res. 34/146, 34 U.N. GAOR Supp. (No. 39), U.N. Doc. A/C.6/34 L.23, *reprinted in* 18 I.L.M. 1456 (1979), art. 8 (1). Very similar provisions are found in: Convention for the Suppression of Unlawful Seizure of Aircraft, The Hague, 16 December 1970, 22 U.S.T. 1641, T.I.A.S. No. 7192, 860 U.N.T.S. 105, *reprinted in* 10 I.L.M. 133 (1971), art. 7; Convention for the Suppression of Unlawful Acts Against the Safety of Civil Aviation, Montreal, 23 September 1971, 24 U.S.T. 565, T.I.A.S. No. 7570, 974 U.N.T.S. 177, *reprinted in* 10 I.L.M. 1151 (1971), art. 7; Convention on the Prevention and Punishment of Crimes Against Internationally Protected Persons, Including Diplomatic Agents, 14 December 1973, 28 U.S.T. 1975, T.I.A.S. No. 8532, 1035 U.N.T.S. 167, G.A. Res. 3166, 27 U.N. GAOR Supp. (No. 10), U.N. Doc. A/Res/3166 (1974), art. 7; Convention Against Torture and Other Cruel, Inhuman or Degrading Treatment or Punishment, *supra* note 10, at art. 7 (1).

[147]   *See* Document Section G.4. *See also* Clark, *Offenses of International Concern: Multilateral State Treaty Practice in the Forty Years Since Nuremberg,* 57 NORDIC J. INT'L L. 49, 51-63 (1988), which

"[p]ersons charged with genocide ... shall be tried by a competent tribunal of the State in the territory of which the act was committed, or by such international penal tribunal as may have jurisdiction." Thus, the Convention requires the parties to exercise jurisdiction based on the territoriality principle, which is concurrent to the jurisdiction of an international criminal court, should one be created. While genocide is not subject to the universality principle under conventional law, universal jurisdiction may be applied to the crime under customary international law.[148] This application under customary law is proper as stated by the district court in *The Eichman Case*: "[T]he reference in Article 6 to territorial jurisdiction is not exhaustive. Every sovereign State may exercise its existing powers within the limits of customary international law ... "[149] Specific support for applying the universality principle to genocide under customary international law is found in the Restatement (Third) of the Foreign Relations Law of the United States which considers genocide an offense for which a state has universal jurisdiction to prescribe punishment because genocide is an offense "recognized by the community of nations as of universal concern."[150]

War crimes are also among the limited number of offenses subject to universal jurisdiction under customary international law. The BRITISH MANUAL OF MILITARY LAW declares the existence of this jurisdictional basis:

> War crimes are crimes *ex jure gentium* and are thus triable by the Courts of all States .... British Military Courts have jurisdiction outside the United Kingdom over war crimes committed not only by members of the enemy armed forces, but also by enemy civilians and other persons of any nationality, including those of British nationality or the nationals of allied and neutral powers.[151]

---

delineates and examines post-Nuremberg "Treaties on the basis of whether they contemplate universal jurisdiction, or negative on universal jurisdiction, are obscure on universal jurisdiction, or treaties which contemplate 'fallback' jurisdiction."

[148]   For those who espouse this view, *see* Randall, *supra* note 131, at 834 *et seq.*

[149]   Attorney Gen. of Israel v. Eichmann, 36 I.L.R. 18, 39 (Isr. Dist. Ct.--Jerusalem 1961), *aff'd*, 36 I.L.R. 277 (Isr. Sup. Ct. 1962); Baade, *The Eichman Trial: Some Legal Aspects*, 1961 DUKE L.J. 400, 418; Lasok, *The Eichmann Trial*, 11 INT'L L. & COMP. L. Q. 355, 364 (1962). *But see* Fawcett, *The Eichmann Case*, 38 BRIT. Y.B. INT'L L. 181, 205-07 (1962).

[150]   FOREIGN RELATIONS LAW OF THE UNITED STATES, *supra* note 131 at § 404.

[151]   3 BRITISH MANUAL OF MILITARY LAW, para. 637, (1958 ed.).

520

The foundation for the application of the universality principal to war crimes, as well as "crimes against humanity," stems from the proceedings before the IMT and the subsequent prosecutions.[152] The IMT makes one indistinct reference to the universality principal in its judgment wherein it states:

> The Signatory Powers created this Tribunal, defined the law it was to administer, and made regulations for the proper conduct of the Trial. In doing so, they have done together what any one of them might have done singly; for it is not to be doubted that any nation has the right thus to set up special courts to administer law.[153]

It may be inferred from this statement that "any nation" would have jurisdiction to prosecute the war criminals, whether or not the nation had a nexus with the offenses at issue. This conclusion is supported by a memorandum prepared by the United Nations Secretary General, which states:

> [I]t is ... possible and perhaps ... probable, that the [Nuremberg Tribunal] considered the crimes under the Charter to be, as international crimes, subject to the jurisdiction of every State. The case of piracy would then be the appropriate parallel. This interpretation seems to be supported by the fact that the Court affirmed that the Tribunal had made use of a right belonging to any nation.[154]

---

[152] It should be noted however, that in 1919 the Report of the Commission on the Responsibility of the Authors of the War and on Enforcement of Penalties declared that:

> Every belligerent has, according to international law the power and authority to try the individuals alleged to be guilty of .. . violations of the Laws and Customs of War, if such persons have been taken prisoner or have otherwise fallen into its power. Each belligerent has, or has power to set up .. . an appropriate tribunal, military or civil, for the trial of such cases.

Report Presented to the Preliminary Peace Conference by the Commission on the Responsibility of the Authors of the War and on Enforcement of Penalties (1919), *reprinted in* 14 AJIL 95, 121 (1920). The United States, which dissented from the majority report concurred on this point. *See* Carnegie, *supra* note 125.

[153] 22 Trial of the Major War Criminals, Judgment 461 (1948), *reprinted in* 41 AJIL 172, 216 (1947).

[154] *The Charter and Judgment of the Nürnberg Tribunal,* U.N. Doc. A/CN.4/5 (1949) (memorandum submitted by the Secretary General).

521

The subsequent proceedings, conducted by the Allied Powers in the territories under their administration also relied on the universality principle. One such trial, held pursuant to CCL 10, was *In re List,*[155] known as *The Hostages Case* because the defendant German officers were charged with the execution of hundreds of thousands of civilian hostages. The tribunal explained that:

> An international crime is ... an act universally recognized as criminal, which is considered a grave matter of international concern and for some valid reason cannot be left within the exclusive jurisdiction of the state that would have control over it under ordinary circumstances.[156]

In the *Alemelo Trial,*[157] a British military court sitting in the Netherlands declared that "every independent state has in International Law jurisdiction to punish pirates and war criminals in its custody regardless of the nationality of the victim or the place where the offense was committed."[158] In yet another case, *In re Eisentrager,*[159] the United States Military Commission sitting in Shanghai also declared its reliance upon the universality principle:

> A war crime ... is not a crime against the law or criminal code of any individual nation, but a crime against the *jus gentium*. The laws and usages of war are of universal application, and do not depend for their existence upon national laws and frontiers. Arguments to the effect that only a sovereign of the *locus criminis* has jurisdiction and that only the *lex loci* can be applied, are therefore without any foundation.[160]

Two other important judicial proceedings, which occurred many years after the post-war trials but still involve crimes committed during World War II, also bear upon

---

155 *The Hostage Case.*

156 *Id.* at 1241. The court further asserts that a state that captures a war criminal may either "surrender the alleged criminal to the state where the offense was committed, or .. . retain the alleged criminal for trial under its own legal processes." *Id.* at 1242.

157 1 LAW REPORTS OF TRIALS OF WAR CRIMINALS 35 (1949).

158 *Id.* at 42.

159 14 LAW REPORTS OF TRIALS OF WAR CRIMINALS 8 (1949).

160 *Id.* at 15 (footnote omitted).

the use of the universality principle as to war crimes and "crimes against humanity." In *The Eichmann*[161] *Case*, the Israeli courts relied in part upon universal jurisdiction to prosecute the defendant, who was accused, amongst other things, of war crimes and "crimes against humanity." The district court of Jerusalem explained how:

> The State of Israel's "right to punish" the accused derives ... from two cumulative sources: a universal source (pertaining to the whole of mankind) which vests the right to prosecute and punish crimes of this order in every state within the family of nations; and a specific national source, which gives the victim nation the right to try any who assault their existence."[162]

Along the same lines, Israel's supreme court concluded:

> [T]here is full justification for applying here the principal of universal jurisdiction since the international character of "crimes against humanity" ... dealt with in this instant case is no longer in doubt .... [T]he basic reason for which international law recognizes the right of each State to exercise such jurisdiction in piracy offenses -- notwithstanding the fact that its own sovereignty does not extend to the scene of the commission of the offence ... and the offender is a national of another State

---

[161]   Attorney General of Israel v. Eichmann, *supra* note 149; *see also* 56 AJIL 805 (1962) for an unofficial translation of the district court opinion.   For criticism of the courts reliance on universal jurisdiction, *see* R. WOETZEL, THE NUREMBERG TRIALS IN INTERNATIONAL LAW WITH A POSTLUDE ON THE EICHMAN CASE 245-272 (1962), arguing that an extension of the universality principle to crimes against humanity could not be considered as generally accepted in international law at the time of the Eichmann trial. As he states in more detail, at 271:

> The basis for jurisdiction of the court in the Eichmann case may be criticised mainly from the point of view of the territoriality and nationality principles: the crimes did not take place in the territory of Israel nor were nationals of Israel in the accepted legal sense involved, since the state of Israel did not exist at the time the actions charged were committed. The trial has been justified on the grounds of an extension of the universal principle of jurisdiction to crimes against humanity involving genocide. The enlargement of the scope of this principle, however, could not at the time of the holding of the trial be considered as generally accepted in international law. It was not reflected in the Genocide Convention or international practice and agreement since the Nuremberg trials. In these respects the legal basis of the Eichmann trial can be considered controversial.

[162]   Eichmann, *supra* note 149, 36 I.L.R. 18, at 50.

523

or is stateless -- applies with even greater force to the above-mentioned crimes."[163]

To the fact that Eichmann's alleged crimes occurred during World War II, before Israel came into existence, the supreme court explained:

> Not only do all the crimes attributed to the appellant bear an international character, but their harmful and murderous effects were so embracing and widespread as to shake the international community to its very foundations. The State of Israel therefore was entitled, pursuant to the principle of universal jurisdiction and in the capacity of a guardian of international law and an agent for its enforcement, to try the appellant. That being the case, no importance attaches to the fact that the State of Israel did not exist when the offenses were committed.[164]

More recently, in 1985, a United States Circuit Court of Appeals ruled in *Demjanjuk v. Petrovsky*[165] that the United States could extradite an alleged Nazi concentration camp guard to Israel based on Israel's right to exercise universal jurisdiction over the accused.[166] The court recognized that the acts committed by

---

[163]   Eichmann, *supra* note 149, 36 I.L.R. 277, at 299.

[164]   *Id.*, at 304.

[165]   Demjanjuk v. Petrovsky, 776 F.2d 571 (6th Cir. 1985), *cert. denied*, 475 U.S. 1016 (1986). For the opinion at the district court level, which the sixth circuit affirmed, *see* Matter of Extradition of Demjanjuk, 612 F.Supp. 544 (N.D. Ohio 1985). The court determined that Israel's jurisdiction to prosecute the alleged concentration camp guard "conforms with the international law principle of 'universal jurisdiction.'" *Id.* at 555.

[166]   For other cases in the United States which have recently relied upon the universality principle, *see* United States v. Layton, 509 F.Supp. 212, 223 (N.D. Cal.) (which recognized universal jurisdiction to define and prosecute terrorist acts against internationally protected persons), *appeal dismissed*, 645 F.2d 681 (9th Cir.), *cert. denied*, 452 U.S. 972 (1981); Von Dardel v. Union of Soviet Socialist Republics, 623 F.Supp. 246, 254 (D.D.C. 1955) (which refers to the "concept of extraordinary judicial jurisdiction over acts in violation of significant international standards ... embodied in the principle of 'universal' violations of international law"). *See also* Filartiga v. Pena-Irala, 630 F.2d 876, 890 (2d Cir. 1980) (exclaiming that "the torturer has become--like the pirate and slave trader before him--*hostis humani generis*, an enemy of all mankind."). *See also*, U.S. v. Yunis, 681 F. Supp. 896 (D.D.C. 1988), where a federal district court held that it had jurisdiction over a defendant prosecuted for his alleged involvement in the hijacking and destruction of a civilian aircraft under, *inter alia*, the universal principle of international law that conferred jurisdiction

Nazis and Nazi collaborators are "crimes universally recognized and condemned by the community of nations,"[167] and that these "crimes are offenses against the law of nations or against humanity and that the prosecuting nation is acting for all nations."[168] Thus the court concluded:

> This being so, Israel or any other nation, regardless of its status in 1942 or 1943, may undertake to vindicate the interest of all nations by seeking to punish the perpetrators of such crimes.[169]

In sum, it is appropriate to say that universal jurisdiction for all international crimes is a position supported by some of the "most distinguished publicists," even if the universality principal has been evidenced in only some conventions on international criminal law. Conversely, however, the customary practice of States has been limited in recognizing universal jurisdiction. Sir Hersch Lauterpacht stated over thirty years ago:

> There is an implied recognition of the protection, by International Law, of the fundamental rights of the individual in so far as it prohibits and penalizes crimes against humanity, conceived as offences of the gravest character against the life and liberty of the individual, irrespective of whether acts of that nature have been perpetrated in obedience to the law of the State ....

> While no general rule of positive International Law can as yet be asserted which gives to States the right to punish foreign nationals for crimes against humanity in the same way as they are, for instance, entitled to punish acts of piracy, there are clear indications pointing to the gradual evolution of a significant principle of International Law to that effect. That principle consists both in the adoption of the rule of universality of jurisdiction and in the recognition of the supremacy of the law of humanity over the law of the sovereign State when

---

on any forum that obtained the physical custody of a perpetrator of certain offenses considered particularly heinous and harmful to humanity.

[167] Demjanjuk, *supra* note 165, at 582.

[168] *Id.*, at 583.

[169] *Id.*

enacted or applied in violation of elementary human rights in a manner which may justly be held to shock the conscience of mankind.[170]

Lauterpacht's statement is given further credence by the 1973 United Nations Resolution on Principles of International Cooperation in the Detection, Arrest, Extradition, and Punishment of Persons Guilty of War Crimes and Crimes Against Humanity, which declares:

1. War crimes and crimes against humanity, wherever they are committed, shall be subject to investigation and the persons against whom there is evidence that they have committed such crimes shall be subject to tracing, arrest, trial and, if found guilty, to punishment ...

3. States shall co-operate with each other on a bilateral and multi-lateral basis with a view to halting and preventing war crimes and crimes against humanity, and take the domestic and international measures necessary for that purpose.

4. States shall assist each other in detecting, arresting and bringing to trial persons suspected of having committed such crimes and, if they are found guilty, in punishing them ...

7. States shall not grant asylum to any person with respect to whom there are serious reasons for considering that he has committed a crime against peace, a war crime or a crime against humanity.[171]

The Law of the Charter, the Post-Charter Legal Developments, the 1949 Geneva Conventions, the *Apartheid* Convention and the Torture Convention, as other international instruments, recent national legislation and judicial decisions, and the writings of the most distinguished publicists all add up to the conclusion that "crimes against humanity" is subject to universal jurisdiction.

---

[170] 1 OPPENHEIM, INTERNATIONAL LAW 752-753 (H. Lauterpacht ed. 8th ed. 1955). *See also* UNWCC 191-220.

[171] G.A. Res. 3074, 28 U.N. GAOR Supp. (No. 30) at 78, U.N. Doc. A/9030 (1973).

The value and importance of universal jurisdiction is more significant insofar as the world community does not yet have an international criminal court to prosecute international crimes.[172]

Conclusion

The significance of these Post-Charter Developments, lies in their cumulative effect which reinforces the conventional and customary international criminal law aspects of "crimes against humanity." Even though the post-Charter procedural developments do not add to the substantive contents of the criminal category, they contribute to that mosaic which still has to be assembled in a cohesive whole.

These Post-Charter Developments demonstrate the continued concern and interest of the world community in sustaining the Law of the Charter and give continued expression to the fact that the Charter, the Nuremberg and Tokyo prosecutions, their sequels and other national sequels were not a singular manifestation of international action about such a crime, but a continuing one.

The progressive development of international instruments subsequent to the Charter, also supports the proposition that even if no post-Charter codification of "crimes against humanity" has yet occurred, the legal viability of this category of international crimes has been consistently reinforced.

But while these Post-Charter Developments have addressed some of the issues concerning "principles of legality,"[173] "obedience to superior orders,"[174] the duties to prosecute or extradite, and the nonapplicability of statutory limitation, there are still many unresolved issues due to the absence of a comprehensive codification of the substantive and procedural aspects of "crimes against humanity."[175]

Change, when it comes, invariably affects or inconveniences those who bring it about as well as those who have to bear its consequences; even when it is for the best. Thus, change never comes easy.

---

[172] *See* footnote 28, Chapter 1.

[173] *See* Chapter 3.

[174] *See* Chapter 10 at 398.

[175] *See* Chapter 12.

527

CHAPTER 12

CONCLUDING ASSESSMENT

Those Who Forget the Lessons of the Past are
Condemned to Repeat Their Mistakes.
George Santayana

Until the advent of World War II, history had never witnessed on such a scale the conduct defined in Article 6(c). Even though the facts superceeded the expectations of the law, which were embodied in a general prohibition under the rubric "laws of humanity,"[1] its legal sufficiency raised questions of legality.[2]

Whether the Charter was declarative or innovative depends firstly on the existence of preceding international law and secondly on the sufficiency of its normative proscriptions. The determination of these questions, however, hinges upon the sources of international law relied upon, and among these, whether "general principles of law" constitutes a legally sufficient source of international criminal law.[3]

The mere pre-existence of prescriptive international law does not necessarily mean that it can be deemed to criminally proscribe certain conduct no matter how abhorrent it may be. And this leads once again to the question of whether the Charter's Article 6(c) formulation satisfies the minimum requirements of legality.[4]

The answers to these questions ultimately depend upon the choice of an underlying theory of legal philosophy.[5]

The Charter was the first international instrument which dealt specifically with "crimes against humanity" as a distinct category of international crimes,[6] even though the contents of the Charter's Article 6(c) definition substantially incorporate similar conduct previously prohibited under the conventional and customary regulation of armed conflicts. Indeed, the conduct prohibited by Article 6(c) constitutes war crimes,

---

[1]   See Chapter 4.

[2]   See Chapter 3.

[3]   See Chapter 7.

[4]   See Chapter 3.

[5]   See Chapter 2.

[6]   See Chapters 1 and 4.

528

if committed by a member of the belligerent forces of one state against a member of the civilian population of another state.[7] The Charter, however, extended these violations to encompass the protection of the civilian population of the same state as that of the perpetrators. Thus, the two categories of crimes are predicated on the same values and seek to achieve the same protections for civilians during the course of armed conflicts. But their respective international elements differ in part.

A war crime contains four international elements: (1) the conduct[8] is committed by a member of the armed forces of one state against a member of the armed forces or a civilian of another state in the context of an armed conflict; (2) it involves a transnational activity; (3) it affects more than one state; and (4) it is contrary to the international regulation of armed conflicts (which embodies the "laws of humanity"). [9]

"Crimes against humanity" as formulated in the Charter's Article 6(c) extends criminal responsibility, to encompass persons who do not have a different nationality than the victims, and sometimes, to conduct which is not transnational. Thus, it does not have the first two international elements of war crimes. However, the two other international elements of war crimes are present in "crimes against humanity" insofar as the conduct may affect more than one state and is contrary to the basic "laws of humanity." But another international element exists in "crimes against humanity" which is not needed for war crimes, that the conduct must be the product of "state action or policy."[10] Indeed, war crimes, unlike "crimes against humanity," can be committed by individuals without "state action or policy" supporting it and that is the essential difference in the nature of these two categories of international crimes. The requirement of "state action or policy" is a peculiarity of "crimes against humanity," which essentially distinguishes the specific crimes contained within this international category of crimes from other international and national crimes.

The Charter's formulation of "crimes against humanity" can be viewed as a jurisdictional extension of the international protection afforded to civilian population from violations committed against it by those of the same nationality in connection with war. Taken in the context of the overarching concept of the "laws of humanity" embodied in the 1907 Hague Convention, as reinforced by the Versailles Treaty, 1919 Commission Report and Post World War I Prosecutions and other international

---

[7] *See* Chapter 4.

[8] *See* 1 BASSIOUNI ICL 1-13.

[9] *See* Chapter 4.

[10] *See* Chapter 6.

instruments. Thus, it can be argued that this jurisdictional extension was declarative of international law and not innovative. The declarative theory can rely on the cumulative weight of pre-1945 conventional and customary law which made "crimes against humanity," at the time, an emerging customary international law crime.[11] Justice Jackson, aptly argued that the "institution [of the new] customs . . . [would] themselves become sources of a newer and strengthened international law."[12] But to reach this conclusion requires the rejection of positivism in international law,[13] and the acceptance of "general principles" as a limited source of international criminal law subject to the requirements of the "principles of legality."[14] In addition, it can be argued that the very nature of international law necessarily requires freedom from the limitations of positivism because it is a discipline which, "is not static, but a continual adaptation which follows the needs of a changing world."[15] Thus, Jackson stated in his opening statement before the IMT:

> It is true, of course, that we have no judicial precedent for the Charter. But International Law is more than a scholarly collection of abstract and immutable principles. It is an outgrowth of treaties and agreements between nations and of accepted customs. Yet every custom has its origin in some single act, and every agreement has to be initiated by the action of some state. Unless we are prepared to abandon every principle of growth for International Law, we cannot deny that our own day has the right to institute customs and to conclude agreements that will themselves become sources of a newer and strengthened International Law. International Law is not capable of development by the normal process of legislation for there is no continuing international legislative authority. Innovations and revisions in International Law are brought about by the action of governments designed to meet a change in circumstances. It grows, as did the Common Law, through decisions reached from time to time in adapting settled principles to new situations. The fact is that when the law evolves by the case method, as did the Common Law and as international law must do if it is to advance at all, it advances at the expense of those who wrongly guessed the law and learned too late

---

[11] See Bassiouni, *International Law and the Holocaust*, 9 CALIF. INT'L L.J. 202 (1978).

[12] Jackson's Report.

[13] See Chapter 2.

[14] See Chapter 3.

[15] 1 IMT 221.

their error. The Law, so far as international law can be decreed, has been clearly pronounced when these acts took place. Hence, I am not disturbed by the lack of judicial precedent for the inquiry we propose to conduct.[16]

These views led the IMT to conclude that the Charter did not represent "an arbitrary exercise of power on the part of the victorious nations but was the expression of international law existing at the time of its creation."[17] The IMTFE accepted this basic proposition as did the Subsequent Proceedings and all judgments of national tribunals since then. Critics of this position, however, argue that subsequent reiteration, no matter how frequent does not necessarily add to the validity of an otherwise flawed premise. The flaw, in the opinion of these critics, is based essentially on three considerations: the violation of the "principles of legality"; the setting aside of positive national law by *ad hoc* promulgation made by the victors after the fact; and the double-standard of applying the newly enacted norms exclusively to the vanquished.

Critics of the Charter deem "crimes against humanity" to be *lex desiderata* because its formulation represents the embodiment of morality as a substitute for positive law.[18] But the words of Lord Coolidge in *The Queen v. Dudley and Stephens* (1884), though totally unrelated to the Charter, nonetheless eloquently answer that critique:

Though Law and morality are not the same, and many things may be immoral which are not necessarily illegal, yet the absolute divorce of law from morality would be of fatal consequence.[19]

It can be said that international law, like the Common Law and other legal systems developed gradually on the basis of states' practices, conventional international law,

---

[16] 2 IMT 147.

[17] 1 IMT 218.

[18] *See* D'Amato, *The Moral Dilemma of Positivism*, 20 VAL. U. L. REV. 43 (1985) wherein at 43, he states: "Not only do positivists insist upon separating law from morality, but they also appear to be unable to deal with moral questions raised by law once the two are separated. This inability stems, I believe, from their simultaneous attempt to assert and to prove that law and morality are separate; the argument reduces to a vicious circle." *See also* A. D'AMATO, JURISPRUDENCE: A DESCRIPTIVE AND NORMATIVE ANALYSIS OF LAW 294-302 (1984); *Contra*, Hart, *Positivism and the Separation of Law and Morals*, 71 Harv. L. Rev. 593, 624-29 (1958); and Professor Fuller's response, *Positivism and Fidelity to Law; A Reply to Professor Hart*, 71 HARV. L. REV. 630 (1958).

[19] 19 Q.B.D. 273, at 287 (1884).

and case-law.[20] In 1877, Sir James Stephen described the evolution of case-law as follows:

> [it is] like an art or a science, the principles of which are first enunciated vaguely, and are gradually reduced to precision by their application to particular circumstances.[21]

Consequently, the requirements of legality in a case-law system are necessarily different from those of a codified one.[22] It was no accident, therefore, that Stephen's definition of the Common Law's case-law evolution was also expressed, in 1945, by Mr. Justice Robert Jackson in his opening address at the IMT at Nuremberg as quoted above.[23] In the same vein, Professor Quincy Wright, a supporter of the declarative nature of the Charter, described it, as follows:

> Considering international law as a progressive system, the rules and principles of which are to be determined at any moment by examining all its sources "general principles of law", "international customs" and the "teachings of the most highly qualified publicity" no less than "international conventions" and "judicial decisions", there can be little doubt that international law had designated as crimes

---

[20]   Donnedieu de Vabres, a Judge at the IMT, recognized this trait of international law when he stated in his incisive analysis of the Nuremberg Trial: *"Il est de l'essence du droit international d'être, en fait, un droit coutumier."* *See* H. Donnedieu de Vabres, *Le Procès de Nuremberg devant les principes Modernes du Droit Pènal International*, 70 RECEUIL DES COURS 481 at 575 (1947).

[21]   *See* J. STEPHEN, DIGEST OF CRIMINAL LAW § 160 (1877), *quoted by* F. WHARTON, A TREATISE ON CRIMINAL LAW at 19 (8th ed. 1880). For the history of the Common Law of Crimes and juridically created crimes *see also* J. STEPHEN, A HISTORY OF THE CRIMINAL LAW OF ENGLAND at 359-60 (1883). For the nature of Common Law misdemeanors *see* Rex v. Manley (1933) K.B. 529 (1932) commented upon in Stylbass, *Public Mischief*, 49 L.Q. 183 (1933); and Jackson, *Common Law Misdemeanors*, 6 COM. L. REV. 193 (1937); Shaw v. Director of Public Prosecutions, A.C. 220 (1960) *discussed in* Brownlie & Williams, *Judicial Legislation in Criminal Law*, 42 CAN. B. REV. 561 (1964). For the proposition that the International Law is part of the Common Law, *see* C.M. PICCIOTTO, THE RELATION OF INTERNATIONAL LAW TO THE LAW OF ENGLAND AND OF THE UNITED STATES at 75 *et. seq.* (1915).

[22]   *See* Chapter 3.

[23]   *See supra* note 16 and accompanying text.

["crimes against humanity"] the acts so specified in the Charter long before the acts charged against the defendants were committed.[24]

Yet there can be no doubt that the formulation of Article 6(c) was the product of the London Charter's drafters.

The position that Article 6(c) did not innovate a new type of violation in international criminal law is based on the assumption that the new normative proscription only extended pre-existing violations to the same category of victims, (i.e., innocent civilians), but in a different context. Thus, the substance of the legal prohibition remained the same, as did the basic principles of law upon which it was predicated. One can therefore conclude that the Charter's "crimes against humanity" was a progressive codification of a declaratory nature, as discussed in Chapter 1. But the nagging question remains as to whether the undisputed wrongs committed against innocent civilians, hitherto outside the limited contextual application of war crimes, did constitute a new crime under international law in accordance with certain requirements of legality in international criminal law.[25] Since the basic values embodied in the protection of these victims in international criminal law have never been at issue, only whether they can be embodied in normative proscriptions formulated after the fact, is the assumption that notice of the violation can be found in other legal sources sufficient to satisfy the requirements of legality in international criminal law? One answer can be found in the Common Law of crimes as expressed by Wharton:

---

[24]   Wright, *The Law of the Nuremberg Trial*, in INTERNATIONAL LAW IN THE TWENTIETH CENTURY at 623 and 641 (L. Gross ed. 1969) (emphasis added); *See also* Bassiouni, *Crimes Against Humanity*, in 3 BASSIOUNI ICL 51 (1987); E. ARONEAUNU, LE CRIME CONTRE L'HUMANITE (1961); P. DROST, THE CRIME OF STATE (2 vols. 1959); A. QUINTANO-RIPOLES, TRATADO DE DERECHO PÉNAL INTERNACIONÁL Y PENAL INTERNACIONÁL at 607 *et seq.* (1955); *See also* Graven, *Les Crimes Contre l'Humanité*, in 1 RECEUIL DES COUR DE L'ACADEMIE DE DROIT INTERNATIONAL DE LA HAYE, p. 443 (1950); Boissarie, *Rapport sur les Definitions du Crime Contre l'Humanité*, 18 RIDP 201 (1947); Dautricourt, *La Definition du Crime Contre l'Humanité*, in REVUE DE DROIT PÉNAL ET DE CRIMINOLOGIE 47 (1947); H. Donnedieu de Vabres, *Le Procés de Nuremberg devant les principles modernes du Droit Penal International*, in 70 RECEUIL DES COURS 485 (1947). The author was one of the four chief judges at Nuremberg. His earlier work LES PRINCIPLES MODERNES DU DROIT PÉNAL INTERNATIONAL (1928), also supports this view.

[25]   *See* Chapter 3.

The presumption of knowledge of the unlawfulness of crimes *mala in se* is not limited by state boundaries. The unlawfulness of such crimes is assumed wherever civilization exists.[26]

The same rationale of the *mala in se* Common Law crimes holds true for "crimes against humanity." as defined in the Charter, because the same acts are unlawful under "general principles of law."[27] Indeed, murder, manslaughter, battery, rape, torture and the like are crimes in every legal system.[28] Sir James Stephen held that:

> In all cases in which force is used against the person of another, both the person who orders such force to be used and the person using that force is responsible for its use, and neither of them is justified by the circumstances that he acts in obedience to orders given him by a civil or military superior . . .[29]

The framers of the Charter and the members of the IMT recognized the valid legal existence of "crimes against humanity" under international law on the basis of the cumulative effect of all three sources of international law, namely conventional, customary and "general principles." But arguments challenging the legality of the Charter's enunciation of "crimes against humanity" were consistently raised at the Nuremberg[30] and Tokyo trials,[31] the post-Nuremberg prosecutions under CCL 10,[32] before the proceedings conducted by the Allies in their occupation zones,[33] and in the

---

[26] F. WHARTON, *supra* note 21, § 285, p. 311.

[27] *See* Chapters 7 and 8.

[28] *See* Chapters 7 and 8.

[29] J. STEPHEN, A DIGEST OF CRIMINAL LAW, *supra* note 21, art. 202, *quoted in* F. WHARTON, *supra* note 21, at 130.

[30] *See* Chapter 2, note 55.

[31] *See generally*, R.H. MINEAR, VICTOR'S JUSTICE: THE TOKYO WAR CRIMES TRIAL (1971); THE TOKYO WAR CRIMES TRIAL (C., Hosoya, N. Ando, Y. Onuma, R. Minear eds. 1986).

[32] *See* H. MEYROWITZ, LA REPRESSION PAR LES TRIBUNAUX ALLEMANDS DES CRIMES CONTRE L'HUMANITÉ ET DE L'APPARTENANCE A LEUR ORGANIZATION CRIMINELLE (1960).

[33] *See generally*, A. MAUNOIR, LA REPRESSION DES CRIMES DE GUERRE DEVANT LES TRIBUNAUX FRANCAIS ET ALLIÉS (1956).

special military tribunals set up by the United States in the Far East.[34] Similar claims were also raised in national tribunals, such as in the Eichmann[35] and Barbie[36] trials held, respectively, in Israel and France. They have always been rejected. Justice Jackson dealt with these arguments in his closing address before the IMT:

> The defendants complain that our pace is too fast. In drawing the Charter of this Tribunal, we thought we were recording an accomplished advance in International Law. But they say that we have outrun our times, that we have anticipated an advance that should be, but has not yet been made. The Agreement of London, whether it originates or merely records, at all events marks a transition in International Law which roughly corresponds to that in the evolution of local law when men ceased to punish local crime by "hue and cry" and began to let reason and inquiry govern punishment. The society of nations has emerged from the primitive "hue and cry," the law of "catch and kill." It seeks to apply sanctions to enforce International Law, but to guide their application by evidence, law, and reason instead of outcry. The defendants denounce the law under which their accounting is asked. Their dislike for the law which condemns them is not original. It has been remarked before [quoting Shakespeare] that no man e'er felt the halter draw, With good opinion of the law.[37]

Concern for legality is never to be taken lightly no matter how atrocious the violation or how abhorrent the violator.[38] The observance of the "Rule of Law" is far more important than the prosecution or punishment of any offender or group of offenders. We should never forget that if it were not for such offenders' transgression of the "Rule of Law," violations embodied in "crimes against humanity" could not have

---

[34]   *See* In re Yamashita, 327 U.S. 1 (1946); Homma v. Untied States, 327 U.S. 759 (1946). Both cases have been criticized because they established an unprecedented criteria for command responsibility: the two generals in question should have known or should have prevented the war crimes committed by soldiers under their command and the great dissents of Justices Murphy and Rutledge, *id.* at 26 *et seq. See generally* F. REEL, THE CASE OF GENERAL YAMASHITA (1949).

[35]   *See* Attorney General of Israel v. Eichmann, (Israel Dist. Court 1962) 36 I.L.R. 5 (1962) (Supreme Court of Israel) 36 I.L.R. 277 (1962). *See generally* G. HAUSER, JUSTICE IN JERUSALEM (1966).

[36]   *See* Matter of Barbie, Gaz. Pal. Jur. 710 (France, Cass. Crim. Oct. 6, 1983). *See generally*, Doman, *Aftermath of Nuremberg: The Trial of Klaus Barbie*, 60 COLO. L. REV. 449 (1989).

[37]   19 IMT 398.

[38]   *See* Chapter 3.

occurred. To disregard legality and the due process of the law in both its substantive and procedural meanings and applications reduces us to arguing that better reasons or higher motives justify or excuse that which others have also done, but for different reasons or motives. Competing values should not be the only distinction as between those who sit in judgment and those who stand accused. History has all too well and all too frequently recorded that ends do not justify the means, Machiavelli's advice to the Prince notwithstanding.

In the celebrated dissents of Justice Murphy and Rutledge in *The Yamashita Case*,[39] we find admonitions that should always be remembered. Justice Rutledge said:

> At a time like this when emotions are understandably high it is difficult to adopt a dispassionate attitude toward a case of this nature. Yet now is precisely the time when that attitude is most essential. While peoples in other lands may not share our beliefs as to due process and the dignity of the individual, we are not free to give effect to our emotions in reckless disregard of the rights of others. We live under the Constitution, which is the embodiment of all the high hopes and aspirations of the new world. And it is applicable in both war and peace. We must act accordingly. Indeed, an uncurbed spirit of revenge and retribution, masked in formal legal procedure for purposes of dealing with a fallen enemy commander, can do more lasting harm than all of the atrocities giving rise to that spirit. The people's faith in the fairness and objectiveness of the law can be seriously undercut by that spirit. The fires of nationalism can be further kindled. And the hearts of all mankind can be embittered and filled with hatred, leaving forlorn and impoverished the noble ideal of malice toward none and charity to all. These are the reasons that lead me to dissent in these terms.[40]

And Justice Murphy said:

> If we are ever to develop an orderly international community based upon a recognition of human dignity it is of the utmost importance that the necessary punishment of those guilty of atrocities be as free as possible from the ugly stigma of revenge and vindictiveness.[41]

---

[39] *Supra* note 34.

[40] *Id.* at 41.

[41] *Id.* at 29.

CONCLUDING ASSESSMENT

Presumably, the contentious questions concerning the validity of "crimes against humanity" under the Law of the Charter should have been settled with respect to violations committed after 1946 when the IMT rendered its judgment. Regrettably, this was not the case.[42] Since World War II, the world community has once again settled into complacency, leaving the post-World War II experiences in international criminal adjudication to become part of the baggage of an unpleasant phase of history that the world community seems to deem as best forgotten. It shouldn't.

If someday there is to be a prosecution for "crimes against humanity" based on the Law of the Charter, the argument is likely to be raised by the defense that these *ad hoc* tribunals were special tribunals set up by the victors to carry out retribution upon the defeated, in a way that purported to legitimize the intended outcome of punishing only the losers. They would add, as evidence of their contention, that the General Assembly has passed only one Resolution -- requiring the ILC to codify the Nuremberg principles, which they completed in 1950,[43] and that no international convention has been elaborated to make "crimes against humanity" a conventional international crime. Also, they would add, that no international criminal court has been established since Nuremberg and Tokyo even though several proposals were developed by the United Nations, non-governmental organizations and individual scholars,[44] and that indeed the major powers behind Nuremberg and Tokyo, the United States, the United Kingdom, and France, today oppose the establishment of an international criminal court.[45]

---

[42] *See* Chapter 11.

[43] *See, Affirmation of the Nuremberg Principles. Principles of International Law Recognized in the Charter of the Nuremberg Tribunal and in the Judgment of the Tribunal* (ILC), 29 July 1950, 5 U.N. GAOR Supp. (No. 12), 11 U.N. Doc. A/1316 (1950).

[44] *See* Chapter 5, note 85.

[45] *See Hearing before the Subcommittee on International Law, Immigration, and Refugees of the Committee of the Judiciary, House of Representatives,* 102ND CONG., 1ST SESS. (March 13, 1991); *Report of the Judicial Conference of the United States on the Feasibility of and the Relationship to the Federal Judiciary of an International Criminal Court,* Approved By the Judicial Conference of the United States on September, 1991, submitted to the Senate Judiciary Committee on October 28, 1991. *See also* Bassiouni and Blakesley, *The Need for an International Criminal Court in the New International World Order,* 25 VAND. J. TRANS. L. 137 (1992); and Bassiouni, *The Time Has Come for an International Criminal Court,* 1 IND. INT'L & COMP. L. REV. 1 (1991).

The Charter and its related post-Charter instruments[46] were essentially directed at those who were to enforce these normative provisions. These instruments were formulated in a way that was much less directed toward guiding the conduct of those for whom such directives were intended to apply than to those who were to enforce them. That is why specific content,[47] general part requirements;[48] and all that is necessary to guide public and individual conduct is substantially wanting. It almost appears as if the Charter and Post-Charter Developments were not intended to inform the public at large, as is required by the "principles of legality" in the world's major criminal justice systems, but to provide a certain type of general prevention engendered by the fear of selective enforcement. Thus, the Charter, and its related post-Charter instruments legitimizes the selective transmission of decision-rules that are easily adaptable by the occasional enforcer.[49] And that does not make for sound international criminal justice policy.

The Genocide Convention of 1948[50] -- which was to serve as the legal instrument *par excellence* to resolve the legal issues and deficiencies of the Charter's formulation of "crimes against humanity" -- is of limited use to counteract the arguments presented above, because it fails to cover all the depredations that are included in Article 6(c) of the Charter. Indeed genocide applies only to instances where the killing is done with the "intent to eliminate," a narrowly defined group, "in whole or in part."[51] Thus, "murder, extermination, enslavement, deportation, and other inhuman acts," as stated in Article 6(c) of the Charter, when committed without the intent to eliminate a group in whole or in part on the basis of race or religion remains outside the scope of the Genocide Convention. Consequently, the Genocide Convention is less encompassing than "crimes against humanity."[52] The 1991 Draft Code of Crimes regrettably does

---

[46]   *See* Chapter 11.

[47]   *See* Chapters 7 and 8.

[48]   *See* Chapters 9 and 10.

[49]   *See* Dan-Cohen, *Decision for Rules and Conduct Rules: On Acoustic Separation in Criminal Law*, 97 HARV. L. REV. 625 (1984).

[50]   *See* Genocide Convention and Chapter 11 for its discussion in connection with "Post Charter Legal Developments."

[51]   *Id.* Article II; and *see* Bassiouni, *Introduction to the Genocide Convention*, in 1 BASSIOUNI ICL 271.

[52]   *See* Chapter 11.

not fill these gaps as it incorporates, without change, the text of the Genocide Convention, and its other provisions are both deficient and insufficient.

The scattered and inconclusive Post-Charter Legal Developments,[53] leave so many unresolved questions which are made more evident by the numerous tragic events which have occurred since World War II. Sadly, these events seem to have also become footnotes in history, their tragic lessons either forgotten, or relegated to memories of unpleasant events. They include: the Stalin purges of the 1950's, which resulted in an estimable number in the millions of persons killed;[54] the 1960's civil war of Nigeria where an estimated one million Nigerian Biafrans were killed;[55] the 1970's war of secession between East and West Pakistan which resulted in one million Bangladeshi deaths before the creation of the independent state of Bangladesh;[56] the estimated two million Cambodians (40 percent of the population) killed by the Khmer Rouge during the 1980's;[57] the intentionally induced famine of the Ukraine;[58] and the practices of *Apartheid* in South Africa.[59] There have also been countless other tragedies of lesser magnitude, though nonetheless noteworthy. Among them were: Paraguay's genocide-like practices visited upon native Indian tribes in the 1970's; the brutal repressive tribal killings of Burundi and Uganda during the 1960's and 1970's; the plight of the Kurds in Iraq and Turkey; and Israel's repression of Palestinians since the late 1960's.[60] The list could go on and on.[61] These, and so many other similar

---

[53]   *Id.*

[54]   *See* R. CONQUEST, THE GREAT TERROR: STALIN'S RAGE OF THE THIRTIES (1973).

[55]   *See* J. STRENLAW, THE INTERNATIONAL POLITICS OF THE NIGERIAN CIVIL WAR 1967-1970 (1977).

[56]   *See* L. KUPER, GENOCIDE (1981), who cites three million Bangladeshi deaths. *See also* MacDermot, *Crimes Against Humanity in Bangladesh*, 7 INT'L L.J. 476 (1973).

[57]   *See* H. Hannum, *International Law and Cambodian Genocide: The Sounds of Silence*, 11 HUMAN RIGHTS QUARTERLY 71 (1989); Report of the Cambodian Genocide Project (1984); Blodgett, *Cambodian Case*, 71 ABA JOURNAL 31 (1985); *I.C.J. Report on Democratic Kampuchea*, 20 I.C.J. REV. 19 (1978); KAMPUCHEA: DECADE OF THE GENOCIDE (R. Kiljunen ed. 1984); Paust, *Political Oppression in the Name of National Security*, 9 YALE J. WORLD PUB. ORD. 178 (1982); Bazyler, *Re-examining the Doctrine of Humanitarian Intervention in Light of the Atrocities in Kampuchea and Ethiopia*, 23 STANFORD J. INT'L. L. 547 (1987); Stomton, *Kampuchean Genocide and The World Court*, 2 CONN. J. INT'L. L. 341 (1987).

[58]   *See* M. DOLOT, EXECUTION BY HUNGER: THE HIDDEN HOLOCAUST (1985).

[59]   *See* Ö. ÖZGÜR, *APARTHEID*: THE UNITED NATIONS AND PEACEFUL CHANGE IN SOUTH AFRICA (1982); J. LELYRELD, MOVE YOUR SHADOW: SOUTH AFRICA, BLACK AND WHITE (1985).

[60]   *See* R. Falk and B. Weston, *The Relevance of International Law to Palestinian Rights in the West*

deeds affecting large and small groups of people in all regions of the world, have regrettably elicited, but only the most superficial reactions from the international community. They have not revived nor revitalized the Law of the Charter, and they have not given rise to new institutions or measures to prevent, control and suppress such occurrences. Instead, the Khmer Rouge who are responsible for what is probably the worst national holocaust since what happened to the Jews in World War II were dignified in October 1991 with signing an agreement for the end of the civil war that gives them the legitimacy of being part of the new government.

To underscore the indifference and at times, politically motivated disregard, in opposing significant human rights depredations, we must recall the words Hitler is reported to have said in a speech in Munich in 1936 in reference to his policies against the Jews: "Who after all is today speaking about the destruction of the Armenians?"[62] Perhaps, if the world community had remembered or had showed more concern for these victims, the Gypsies, the Slavs, the mentally ill, and so many others, the horrors

---

Bank and Gaza: In Legal Defence of the Intifada, 32 HARV. INT'L L.J. 129 (1991); THE PALESTINIAN INTIFADA - DECEMBER 9, 1987-DECEMBER 8, 1988: A RECORD OF ISRAEL: REPRESSION (M.C. Bassiouni and L. Caincar eds. 1989); *Living Conditions of the Palestinian People in the Occupied Territories*, U.N. Report (1985); S. COHEN AND D. GOLAN, THE INTERROGATION OF PALESTINIANS DURING THE INTIFADA: ILL-TREATMENT, MODERATE PHYSICAL PRESSURE OR TORTURE? (1991); *Prison Conditions in Israel and the Occupied Territories*, HUMAN RIGHTS WATCH REPORT (April 1991); THE ANNUAL REPORT OF THE PALESTINE HUMAN RIGHTS INFORMATION CENTER: PALESTINIAN HUMAN RIGHTS UNDER ISRAELI OCCUPATION (1990).

[61] *See* L. KUPER, *supra* note 56 at 138-185. *See also* R. GAUCHER, THE TERRORISTS: FROM TSARIST RUSSIA TO THE O.A.S. (1978); S.T. HOMER, VIET CONG REPRESSION AND ITS IMPLICATIONS FOR THE FUTURE (1970); A. PARRY, TERRORISM FROM ROBESPIERRE TO ARAFAT (1976); REPORT OF AMNESTY INTERNATIONAL: IRAQ/OCCUPIED KUWAIT: HUMAN RIGHTS VIOLATIONS SINCE 2 AUGUST, AI Index: MDE 14/16/90, Distr: SC/CO/GR (December, 1990); *The Bombing of Iraqi Cities: Middle East Watch Condemns Bombing without Warning of air Raid Shelter in Baghdad's Al Ameriyya District on February 13*, NEWS FROM MIDDLE EAST WATCH (March 6, 1991); *Kuwait: Deteriorating Human Rights Conditions since the Early Occupation*, NEWS FROM MIDDLE EAST WATCH (November 16, 1990). For the synthesis of these reports and relevant legal analysis *see Needless Deaths in the Gulf War* (A MIDDLE EAST WATCH REPORT, 1991); M. BILTON AND K. SIM, FOUR HOURS IN MY LAI: THE SOLDIERS OF CHARLIE COMPANY (1992); Leepson, *Book Review*, CHICAGO TRIBUNE, February 23, 1992, Sec. 14, p. 3.

[62] *See* J.F. WILLIS, PROLOGUE TO NUREMBERG 173 (1982) citing to Sir G. Ogilvie-Forbes report of 25 August 1939, with enclosures of Hitler's speech to Chief Commanders and Commanding Generals, 22 August 1939, Great Britain, Foreign Office, DOCUMENTS ON BRITISH FOREIGN POLICY, 1919-1939 (E.L. Woodward et al., 3rd series, 9 vols., 1949-55), 7:258. For an analysis of the various versions of Hitler's speech, *see* Winfried Baumgart, *Zür Ansprache Hitlers vor den Führen der Wehrmacht am 22 August 1939: Eine Quellenkritische Untersuchung*, VIERTELJAHRSHEFTE FÜR ZEITGESCHICHTE 16 (April 1968):120-49.

540

that befell the Jews would not have occurred. And perhaps, if the world community had learned the lesson of World War II, the many atrocities that have since occurred may have also been avoided; if not in whole, at least in part.

The legal viability of "crimes against humanity" as an international crime separate and apart from genocide and from war crimes is still very much needed. But, its legal vulnerability is clearly owed to the shameful inattention given to this subject by those in a position to shape the development and evolution of international criminal law. We only need to recall that after World War I, the opportunity to establish, in positive international law, the international crime of "Crimes Against the Laws of Humanity" was foregone for political reasons.[63] At that time, it was probably seen by pragmatic United States' policy-makers and others as merely foregoing the prosecution of Turkish nationals for the estimated killing of several hundred thousand Armenians (some estimate the number killed at more than 1 million) in exchange for a new political ally.[64] But when World War II began to empty its horrors, the lack of a solid precedent was significantly felt and the Allies had to rely upon the 1919 Commission Report for support, despite explicit rejection of the Report's use of the terms "laws of humanity" by the United States.[65]

Perhaps someday in the future, prosecutors will rely on the Nuremberg and Tokyo Judgments in the same way that the prosecutors at these two tribunals relied on the 1919 precedents, and they too, like their predecessors, will lament the absence of conventional international criminal law that could have definitely closed the door on arguments challenging the legal viability of "crimes against humanity" as applicable to post-World War II events.

As a consolation, however, it should be noted, that the veneer of international law has thickened since 1945 through the advancement of human rights. In the post-Charter era, the continuum in the legal reinforcement of "crimes against humanity" as an international crime has been consistently evidenced by international legal norms and principles. Also, some states -- notably, Canada -- have enacted specific national

---

[63]   *See* Chapter 4 at 169.

[64]   *See generally* A.J. TOYNBEE, ARMENIAN ATROCITIES: THE MURDER OF A NATION (1915); and Dadrian, *Genocide as a Problem of National and International Law: The World War I Armenian Case and its Contemporary Ramifications*, 14 YALE J. INT'L L. 221 (1989).

[65]   The Dissenting Report of the United States and Japan are found in Annex II and III respectively of the 1919 Commission Report.

legislation.[66] Thus, the legal fabric of "crimes against humanity" grows stronger.[67] Surely the awareness and concern of peoples all over the world have become more acute as evidenced by the increasing reference and usage of the "crimes against humanity," even though in a legally inaccurate way, to a variety of human rights depredations. Nevertheless, the practice of prosecuting and punishing post-World War II offenders, other than Germans for World War II, crimes is blatantly absent. Once again, the practice of states has not been equal to the mandate of the law and to the

---

[66] MARTIN'S CRIMINAL CODE 1989 (E.L. Greenspan ed.). § 7 (3.71) provides that:

Notwithstanding anything in this Act or any other Act, every person who, either before or after the coming into force of this subsection, commits an act or omission outside Canada that constitutes a war crime or a crime against humanity and that, if committed in Canada, would constitute an offence against the laws of Canada in force at the time of the act or omission shall be deemed to commit that act or omission in Canada at that time if,

(a)   at the time of the act or omission.

    (i)   that person is a Canadian citizen or is employed by Canada in a civilian or military capacity,

    (ii)   that person is a citizen of, or is employed in a civilian or military capacity by, a state that is engaged in an armed conflict against Canada, or

    (iii)   the victim of the act or omission is a Canadian citizen of a state that is allied with Canada in an armed conflict; or

(b)   at the time of the act or omission, Canada could, in conformity with international law, exercise jurisdiction over the person with respect to the act or omission on the basis of the person's presence in Canada and, subsequent to the time of the act or omission, the person is present in Canada.

See Green, Canadian Law, War Crimes and Crimes Against Humanity, 59 BRIT. Y.B. INT'L L. 217 (1988); Green, Canadian Law and the Punishment of War Crimes, 28 CHITTY'S LAW J. 249 (1980); Jacquart, La Notion de crime contre l'humanité en droit international contemporain et en droit canadian, 21 REVUE GENERALE DE DROIT 607 (1990). REPORT OF COMMISSION OF INQUIRY ON WAR CRIMINALS: PUBLIC (J. Deschênes ed. 1986); Williams, The Criminal Law Amendment Act 1985: Implications for International Criminal Law, 23 CAN. Y.B. INT'L L. 226 (1985). See also Regina v. Finta, 50 C.C.C. (3d.) 247, 61 D.L.R. 85 (4th, 1989). For the opposite approach, see Lithuania Exonerating People Accused as Nazis, CHICAGO TRIBUNE, Sec. 1, p. 4, col. 1, September 5, 1991.

[67] See Proceedings, Eightieth Annual Meeting The American Society of International Law, FORTY YEARS AFTER THE NUREMBERG TRIBUNALS: THE IMPACT OF THE WAR CRIMES TRIALS ON INTERNATIONAL AND NATIONAL LAW (April 9-12, 1986), remarks of M.C. Bassiouni, at 59-65.

expectations of humankind. There are indeed a number of instances which occurred since World War II, as stated above, that fall within the definition of "crimes against humanity" as established by the Charter -- and applied, for good or for bad, by the Nuremberg and Tokyo trials and their sequels -- which to the disgrace of the human race, have gone unpunished.

Law is part of history, and history, like a river, occasionally runs sluggish and stagnates in the pools of time, or it may run deep and forceful, rushing toward unpredictable destinations. The Law of the Charter was a deep and forceful thrust cutting across legal hurdles and creating a new course for history. It opened a new channel for international criminal law and provided a means to strengthen the international legal process and the "Rule of Law." Regrettably, the current has, since 1945, become sluggish once again, stagnating in the pools of time, even in the face of the great need for its constant thrusts in the direction that had been outlined since the 1919 Peace Treaty of Versailles, and for which the Law of the Charter opened a new course. But the stagnation in time rather than invigorating the Law of the Charter with new impetus, has clogged it with the debris of history, and threatens it with *desuétude*.[68] To a large extent the Law of the Charter is unsatisfactory, and for this writer, so are the Post-Charter Legal Developments, as discussed in Chapter 11. But while the former may be explained by the exigencies of that time, the subsequent neglect cannot be excused. Professor Donnedieu de Vabres, a judge at the IMT, commented in 1947:

> *Il serait étrange qu'après l'expérience récente et les critiques en partie justifiées qu'elle a fait naître, cette lacune ne fût pas comblée. Il serait étrange qu'á chaque manifestation de la criminalité internationale dût succéder la fondation d'un tribunal d'occasion. L'affirmation des principes de Nuremberg est illusoire, s'il n'existe pas d'organe préconstitué et permanent, digne de les sanctionner. Or il se manifeste, á cet égard, au sein de l'Organisation des Nations Unies elle-même, d'inquiétantes hésitations.*

> *Les années qui viennent marqueront sans doute un moment critique de l'histoire, qui a vu s'entremêler jusqu'ici les agressions de la violence et les triomphes du droit. Si la violence prévaut, le jugement de Nuremberg restera comme un fait historique caractéristique d'une tendance, á un moment donné de l'évolution; mais*

---

[68]   *Id.*

543

il ne sera rien de plus. Sinon, il sera un précédent, d'une portée incomparable. Seules, une saine compréhension de l'intérêt humain, un sursaut de la conscience universelle peuvent conjurer le péril . . . . [69]

A historical parallel thus exists between the complacency of governments after World War I in formulating norms of positive international criminal law, and the post-World War II complacency which left us with a similarly weak normative framework.[70]

Can the new era of human rights of the nineties prevent the recurrence of horrible and senseless violence by man against man, as we have witnessed during World War II and thereafter? Perhaps it can. But if it cannot, then we must at the very least express our reprobation and affirm our values in opposition to these practices. Our historical legacy must include our unequivocal condemnation of such grave human depredations. Yet even that is substantially lacking.

To neglect the codification of "crimes against humanity" in a legally sufficient and enforceable way and to forego the prosecution of its perpetrators is to negate the bond of faith we must maintain with our humanity. As the Prophet Muhammad said in a *hadith*: "If you see a wrong you must redress it, with your hand [action] if you can, otherwise with your tongue [vocal condemnation], otherwise with your eyes [reprobation], otherwise in your heart and that is the weakest manifestation of your faith [conviction]."

To pursue the goal of effective prevention, control and suppression of "crimes against humanity," requires a new comprehensive international convention on "crimes against humanity" that foresees future needs on the basis of past experiences. The forty-four year effort of the ILC in preparing, what since 1987 is called the Draft Code of Crimes against the Peace and Security of Mankind, has gone far too long and its present stage indicates many weaknesses that need to be corrected. If these weaknesses remain, the Draft Code of Crimes will only be a standard-setting instrument and not an enforceable normative code. But maybe that is precisely the politically-motivated intention of some, namely: to give the appearance of progress without providing much substance to it. Maybe that effort is also intended to produce an instrument whose loose and legally questionable formulations are intended to legitimize eventual future selective action by those with the power to enforce it. As the late Sir Hersch Lauterpacht warned:

---

[69]   *Supra* note 20 at 577.

[70]   *Id.*, and *also* Chapter 11.

CONCLUDING ASSESSMENT

There is an element of apprehension that attempts at codification may leave things in a condition worse than they were before by casting doubt upon principles hitherto generally accepted and by enabling some governments to cloak political claims for a change of the law in the garb of existing legal rules as they purport to see them.[71]

Maybe that is also why we do not yet have an international criminal court capable of fair and impartial application of international criminal law. Even though we clearly need an international criminal court that can effectively express the higher values of our legal civilization in the fair and impartial adjudication of international crimes. An institution which, to paraphrase Aristotle, would offer the same law whether in Athens or Rome, and apply equally to all peoples of the world, not only because it is law, but because as Aristotle also said, it is "the right reason."[72] As eloquently stated by Thomas Paine:

"He that would make his own liberty secure must guard even his enemy from oppression; for if he violates this duty he establishes a precedent that will reach to himself."[73]

Justice Robert Jackson in the last sentence of his Report to the President on the Nuremberg trials stated: "I am consoled by the fact that in proceedings of this novelty, errors and missteps may also be instructive to the future."[74] But have we learned? Or are we, paraphrasing George Santayana: condemned to repeat our mistakes because we have not learned the lessons of the past.

---

[71]   Lauterpacht, *Codification and Development of International Law*, 49 AJIL 16, 33 (1955). *See also* Baxter, *The Effects of Ill-conceived Codification and Development of International Law*, in RECUEIL D'ETUDES DE DROIT INTERNATIONAL EN HOMMAGE A PAUL GUGGENHEIM (1952).

[72]   For a contemporary perspective on Universal Application, *see* J. DONNELLY, UNIVERSAL HUMAN RIGHTS IN THEORY AND PRACTICE (1989); *see also* THE FUTURE OF HUMAN RIGHTS PROTECTION IN A CHANGING WORLD: FIFTY YEARS SINCE THE FOUR FREEDOMS ADDRESS (A. Aide and J. Helgesen eds. 1991).

[73]   THOMAS PAINE, 2 THE COMPLETE WRITINGS OF THOMAS PAINE 588 (Foner ed. 1945).

[74]   Jackson's Report 440. Also as one author stated:

This task must, if it is to have permanent value, be performed without any preconceived ideas, in the spirit of law and of justice, which cannot be the task of a single people, or of individual power groups, but it must be the concern of the whole human race.

Ehard, *The Nuremberg Trial Against the Major War Criminals and International Law*, 43 AJIL 224 (1949). *See also* Kelsen, *Will the Judgment in the Nuremberg Trial Constitute a Precedent*, 1 INT. L.Q. 167 (1947).

DOCUMENTS SECTION

A. **Documents Relating to International Prosecutions Arising Out of World War I**

B. **Documents Relating to International Prosecutions Preceding the Charter**

C. **Documents Relating to the Charter**

DOCUMENTS SECTION

DOCUMENTS SECTION

A. DOCUMENTS RELATING TO INTERNATIONAL PROSECUTIONS ARISING OF WORLD WAR I

1. **TREATY OF PEACE BETWEEN THE ALLIED AND ASSOCIATED POWERS AND GERMANY, Versailles, 28 June 1919**
(Excerpts)

11 Martens (3rd) 323. *Reprinted in* 2 Bevans 43; 1 Friedman 417.

Part VII - Penalties

Article 227

The Allied and Associated Powers publicly arraign William II of Hohenzollen, formerly German Emperor, for a supreme offence against international morality and the sanctity of treaties.

A special tribunal will be constituted to try the accused, thereby assuring him the guarantees essential to the right of defence. It will be composed of five judges, one appointed by each of the following Powers: namely the United States of America, Great Britain, France, Italy, and Japan.

In its decision the tribunal will be guided by the highest motives of international policy, with a view to vindicating the solemn obligations of international undertaking and the validity of international morality. It will be its duty to fix the punishment which it considers should be imposed.

The Allied and Associated Powers will address a request to the Government of the Netherlands for the surrender to them of the ex-Emperor in order that he may be put on trial.

CRIMES AGAINST HUMANITY

Article 228

The German Government recognizes the right of the Allied and Associated Powers to bring before military tribunals persons accused of having committed acts in violation of the laws and customs of war. Such persons shall, if found guilty, be sentenced to punishments laid down by law. This provision will apply notwithstanding any proceedings or prosecution before a tribunal in Germany or in the territory of her allies.

The German Governor shall hand over to the Allied and Associated Powers, or to such one of them as shall so request, all persons accused of having committed an act in violation of the laws and customs of war, who are specified either by name or by the rank, office, or employment which they held under the German authorities.

Article 229

Persons guilty of criminal acts against the nationals of one of the Allied and Associated Powers will be brought before the military tribunals of that Power.

Persons guilty of criminal acts against the nationals of more than one of the Allied and Associated Powers will be brought before military tribunals composed of members of the military tribunals of the Powers concerned.

In every case the accused will be entitled to name his own counsel.

Article 230

The German Government undertakes to furnish all documents and information of every kind, the production of which may be considered necessary to ensure the full knowledge of the incriminating acts, the discovery of offenders, and the just appreciation of responsibility.

2. **REPORT PRESENTED TO THE PRELIMINARY PEACE CONFERENCE BY THE COMMISSION ON THE RESPONSIBILITY OF THE AUTHORS OF THE WAR AND ON ENFORCEMENT OF PENALTIES Versailles, March, 1919**

(Excerpts)

(Conference of Paris 1919 Carnegie Endowment for International Peace, Division of International Law), Pamphlet No. 32 (1919). *Reprinted in* 14 AJIL 95 (1920) (Supp.); 1 Friedman 842.

CHAPTER II
VIOLATIONS OF THE LAWS AND CUSTOMS OF WAR

On the second point submitted by the Conference, the facts as to breaches of the laws and customs of war committed by the forces of the German Empire and their allies on land, on sea, and in the air, during the present war, the Commission has considered a large number of documents. The Report of the British Commission drawn up by Lord Bryce, the labours of the French Commission presided over by M. Payelle, the numerous publications of the Belgian Government, the memorandum submitted by the Belgian Delegation, the Memorandum of the Greek Delegation, the documents lodged by the Italian Government, the formal denunciation by the Greeks at the Conference of the crimes committed against Greek populations by the Bulgars, Turks and Greeks, the Memorandum of the Serbian Delegation, the Report of the Inter-Allied Commission on the violations of the Hague Conventions and of international law in general, committed between 1915 and 1918 by the Bulgars in occupied Serbia, the summary of the Polish Delegation, together with the Roumanian and Armenian Memoranda, supply abundant evidence of outrages of every description committed on land, at sea, and in the air, against the laws and customs of war and of the laws of humanity.

In spite of the explicit regulations, of established customs, and of the clear dictates of humanity, Germany and her allies have piled outrage upon outrage. Additions are daily and continually being made. By way of illustration, a certain number of examples have been collected in Annex I. It is impossible to imagine a list of cases so diverse and so painful. Violations of the rights of combatants, of the rights of civilians, and of the rights of both, are multiplied in this list of the most cruel practices which primitive barbarism, aided by all the resources of modern science, could devise for the execution of a system of terrorism carefully planned and carried out to the end. Not even prisoners, or wounded, or women, or children have been respected by belligerents who deliberately sought to strike terror into every heart for the purpose of repressing all resistance. Murders and massacres, tortures, shields formed of living human beings, collective penalties, the arrest and execution of hostages, the requisitioning of services for military purposes, the arbitrary destruction of public and private property, the aerial bombardment of open towns without there being any regular siege, the destruction of merchant ships without previous visit and without any precautions for the safety of passengers and crew, the massacre of prisoners, attacks on hospital ships, the poisoning of springs and of wells, outrages and profanations without regard for religion or the honour of individuals, the issue of counterfeit money reported by the Polish Government, the methodical and deliberate destruction of industries with no other object than to promote German economic supremacy after the war, constitute the most striking list of crimes that has ever been drawn up to the eternal shame of those who committed them. The facts are established. They are numerous and so vouched for that they admit of no doubt and cry for justice. The Commission, impressed by their number and gravity, thinks there are good grounds for the constitution of a special Commission, to collect and classify all outstanding information for the purpose of preparing a complete list of the charges under the following heads:

The following is the list arrived at:

(1.) Murders and massacres; systematic terrorism.
(2.) Putting hostages to death.
(3.) Torture of civilians.
(4.) Deliberate starvation of civilians.
(5.) Rape.
(6.) Abduction of girls and women for the purpose of enforced prostitution.
(7.) Deportation of civilians.
(8.) Internment of civilians under inhuman conditions.
(9.) Forced labour of civilians in connection with the military operations of the enemy.
...
(14.) Confiscation of property.
...

CHAPTER III
PERSONAL RESPONSIBILITY

... In view of the grave charges which may be preferred against -- to take one case -- the ex-Kaiser -- the vindication of the principles of the laws and customs of war and the laws of humanity which have been violated would be incomplete if he were not brought to trial and if other offenders less highly placed were punished....

CONCLUSION

All persons belonging to enemy countries, however high their position may have been, without distinction of rank, including Chiefs of States, who have been guilty of offences against the laws and customs of war or the laws of humanity, are liable to criminal prosecution.

CHAPTER IV
CONSTITUTION AND PROCEDURE OF AN APPROPRIATE TRIBUNAL

...

(b)   Violations of the Laws and Customs of War and the Laws of Humanity

...

VIOLATIONS OF THE LAWS AND CUSTOMS
OF WAR AND OF THE LAWS OF HUMANITY

...

(3) The law to be applied by the tribunal shall be 'the principles of the law of nations as they result from the usages established among civilized peoples, from the laws of humanity and from the dictates of public conscience.'

...

CONCLUSIONS

The Commission has consequently the honour to recommend:
   1. That a High Tribunal be constituted as above set out.

   2. That it shall be provided by the Treaty of Peace
   (a)   That the enemy Governments shall, notwithstanding that Peace may have been declared, recognize the jurisdiction of the National Tribunals and the

555

High Tribunal, that all enemy persons alleged to have been guilty of offences against the laws and customs of war and the laws of humanity shall be excluded from any amnesty to which the belligerents may agree, and that the Governments of such persons shall undertake to surrender them to be tried.

(b) That the enemy Governments shall undertake to deliver up and give in such manner as may be determined thereby:

(i) The names of all persons in command or charge of or in any way exercising authority in or over all civilian internment camps, prisoner-of-war camps, branch camps, working camps and 'commandos' and other places where prisoners were confined in any of their dominions or in territory at any time occupied by them, with respect to which such information is required, and all orders and instructions or copies of orders or instructions and reports in their possession or under their control relating to the administration and discipline of all such places in respect of which the supply of such documents as aforesaid shall be demanded;

(ii) All orders, instructions, copies of orders and instructions, General Staff plans of campaign, proceedings in Naval or Military Courts and Courts of Enquiry, reports and other documents in their possession or under their control which relate to acts or operations, whether in their dominions or in territory at any time occupied by them, which shall be alleged to have been done or carried out in breach of the laws and customs of war and the laws of humanity;

...

4. That the five States represented on the Prosecuting Commission shall jointly approach Neutral Governments with a view to obtaining the surrender for trial of persons within their territories who are charged by such States with violations of the laws and customs of war and the laws of humanity.

COMMISSION ON THE RESPONSIBILITY OF THE
AUTHORS OF THE WAR AND ON ENFORCEMENT OF PENALTIES

ANNEX I TO THE REPORT OF THE COMMISSION

DOCUMENTS SECTION

Summary of Examples of Offences committed by the Authorities of Forces of the Central Empires and their Allies against the Laws and Customs of War and the Laws of Humanity.

{Note. -- As has already been stated in the Report, this tabular analysis does not by any means purport to be exhaustive or complete. The object is simply to give a number of typical examples. The crimes imputable to the Central Empires and their allies run into thousands. The list under each of the heads given below could be very greatly extended.}

CONTENTS

ANNEX II

Memorandum of Reservations presented by the Representatives of the United States to the Report of the Commission on Responsibilities, April 4, 1919.

...

To the unprecedented proposal of creating an international criminal tribunal and to the doctrine of negative criminality the American members refused to give their assent.

...

The duty of the Commission was, therefore, to determine whether the facts found were violations of the laws and customs of war. It was not asked whether these facts were violations of the laws or of the principles of humanity. Nevertheless, the report of the Commission does not, as in the opinion of the American Representatives it should, confine itself to the ascertainment of the facts and to their violation of the laws and customs of war, but, going beyond the terms of the mandate, declares that the facts found and acts committed were in violation of the laws and of the elementary principles of humanity. The laws and customs of war are a standard certain, to be found in books of authority and in the practice of nations. The laws and principles of humanity vary with the individual, which, if for no other reason, should exclude them from consideration in a court of justice, especially one charged with the administration of criminal law. The American Representatives, therefore, objected to the references to the laws and principles of humanity, to be found in the report, in what they believed was meant to be a judicial proceeding, as, in their opinion, the facts found were to be violations or breaches of the laws and customs of war, and the persons singled out for trial and punishment for acts committed during the war were only to be those persons guilty of acts which should have been committed in violation of the laws and customs of war. With this reservation as to the invocation of the principles of humanity, the American Representatives are in substantial accord with the conclusions reached by the Commission on this head that:

...

III

The third question submitted to the Commission on Responsibilities requires an expression of opinion concerning 'the degree of responsibility for these offences attaching to particular members of the enemy forces, including members of the General Staffs, and other individuals, however highly placed.' The conclusion which the Commission reached, and which is stated in the report, is to the effect that 'all persons belonging to enemy countries, however high their position may have been, without distinction of rank, including Chiefs of States, who have been guilty of offences against the laws and customs of war or the laws of humanity, are liable to criminal prosecution.' The American Representatives are unable to agree with this conclusion, in so far as it subjects to criminal, and, therefore, to legal prosecution, persons accused of offences against 'the laws of humanity,' and in so far as it subjects Chiefs of States to a degree of responsibility hitherto unknown to municipal or international law, for which no precedents are to be found in the modern practice of nations.

...

558

IV

A judicial tribunal only deals with existing law and only administers existing law, leaving to another forum infractions of the moral law and actions contrary to the laws and principles of humanity. A further objection lies in the fact that the laws and principles of humanity are not certain, varying with time, place, and circumstance, and according, it may be, to the conscience of the individual judge. There is no fixed and universal standard of humanity. The law of humanity, or the principle of humanity, is much like equity, whereof John Selden, as wise and cautious as he was learned, aptly said:

'Equity is a roguish thing. For Law we have a measure, know what to trust to; Equity is according to the conscience of him that is Chancellor, and as that is larger or narrower, so is Equity. 'Tis all one as if they should make the standard for the measure we call a 'foot' a Chancellor's foot; what an uncertain measure would this be! One Chancellor has a long foot, another a short foot, a third an indifferent foot. 'Tis the same thing in the Chancellor's conscience.'

...

Under these conditions and with these limitations the American Representatives considered that the United States might be a party to a High Tribunal, which they would have preferred to call, because of its composition, the Mixed or United Tribunal or Commission. They were averse to the creation of a new tribunal, of a new law, of a new penalty, which would be *ex post facto* in nature, and thus contrary to an express clause of the Constitution of the United States and in conflict with the law and practice of civilized communities. They believed, however, that the United States could co-operate to this extent by the utilization of existing tribunals, existing laws, and existing penalties. However, the possibility of co-operating was frustrated by the insistence on the part of the majority that criminal liability should, in excess of the mandate of the Conference, attach to the laws and principles of humanity, in addition to the laws and customs of war, and that the jurisdiction of the High Court should be specifically extended to 'the heads of States.'

CRIMES AGAINST HUMANITY

Memorandum on the Principles which should Determine Inhuman and Improper Acts of War

To determine the principles which should be the standard of justice in measuring the charge of inhuman or atrocious conduct during the prosecution of a war, the following propositions should be considered:

1. Slaying and maiming men in accordance with generally accepted rules of war are from their nature cruel and contrary to the modern conception of humanity.

2. The methods of destruction of life and property in conformity with the accepted rules of war are admitted by civilized nations to be justifiable and no charge of cruelty, inhumanity, or impropriety lies against a party employing such methods.
...

7. While an act may be essentially reprehensible and the perpetrator entirely unwarranted in assuming it to be necessary from a military point of view, he must not be condemned as wilfully violating the laws and customs of war or the principles of humanity unless it can be shown that the act was wanton and without reasonable excuse.
...

ANNEX IV

Provisions for Insertion in Treaties with Enemy Governments

ARTICLE I

The Enemy Government admits that even after the conclusion of peace, every Allied and Associated State may exercise, in respect of any enemy or former enemy, the right which it would have had during the war to try and punish any enemy who fell within its power and who had been guilty of a violation of the principles of the law of nations as these result from the usages established among civilized peoples, from the laws of humanity and from the dictates of public conscience.

ARTICLE II

The Enemy Government recognizes the right of the Allied and Associated States, after the conclusion of peace, to constitute a High Tribunal composed of members named by the Allied and Associated States in such numbers and in such proportions as they may think proper, and admits the jurisdiction of such tribunal to try and punish enemies or former enemies guilty during the war of violations of the principles of the law of nations as these result from the usages established among civilized peoples, from the laws of humanity and from the dictates of public conscience. It agrees that no trial or sentence by any of its own courts shall bar trial and sentence by the High Tribunal or by a national court belonging to one of the Allied or Associated States....

B. DOCUMENTS RELATING TO INTERNATIONAL PROSECUTIONS PROCEEDING THE CHARTER

1. THE PUNISHMENT OF WAR CRIMINALS: RECOMMENDATIONS OF THE LONDON INTERNATIONAL ASSEMBLY (WHAT CRIMES SHOULD BE TREATED AS "WAR CRIMES") (Report of Commission I) 1944

(Excerpts)

It is essential that the categories of crimes in respect of which post-war punishment is required, be stated as precisely as possible. After much discussion, the majority of the Commission recommended that a comprehensive view should be taken, including not only the customary violations of the laws of war, but any other serious crime against the local law committed in time of war, the perpetrator of which has not been visited by appropriate punishment. Moreover, in accordance with Stalin's views as expressed on November 6th, 1943, the Commission recommended that those responsible for the "crime of war", i.e. unprovoked aggression, should be branded as criminals and adequately punished. In respect of the extermination of Jews, it was recommended that punishment should be imposed not only when the victims were Allied Jews, but even when the crimes had been committed against stateless Jews or any other Jews, in Germany or elsewhere. Finally, for a speedy punishment of crimes such as those that were perpetrated after the last war against peace-minded Germans who were assisting the Allies in re-establishing law and order, it was recommended that crimes committed after the cessation of hostilities with a view to preventing the restoration of peace, should also be treated as war crimes (i.e. tried by Allied, and not by German or other ex-enemy courts).

SUPERIOR ORDER

...

The Assembly has furthermore proposed that even compulsion shall not exonerate the doer when the act ordered was so obviously and glaringly a crime that it could not be accomplished without revolting the conscience of the average human being. Nor should it be a justification when the perpetrator belonged to an organization the membership of which implied blind obedience to any orders, criminal though they may be.

...

RECOMMENDATIONS

...

1. CONCERNING THE DEFINITION OF WAR CRIMES.

...

From this point of view the Commission regard as war crimes especially:

...

(c) all crimes committed either within an Axis country or outside such country for the extermination of a race, nation or political party (referred to in the United Nations' Declaration of December 17th, 1942);

3. CONCERNING AN INTERNATIONAL-OR UNITED NATIONS-CRIMINAL COURT.

Law to be applied by an International Criminal Court.

(i) Until a convention laying down the main principles of international criminal law, defining the crimes and affixing penalties to them has been agreed upon, the Court shall apply:

(a) international custom, as evidence of a general practice accepted as law;

  (b) international treaties, conventions and declarations, whether general or particular, recognized by the High Contracting Parties;

  (c) the general principles of criminal law recognized by the United Nations;

  (d) judicial decisions and doctrines of highly qualified publicists as subsidiary means for the determination of rules of law.

(ii) No act may be tried as an offence unless it is specified as a criminal offence either by the law of the country of the accused, or by the law of his residence at the time of the commission of the act, or by the law of the place where the act was carried out, provided in each case that such law is in accordance with the general principles of criminal law recognized by the United Nations.

...

5. CONCERNING THE APPREHENSION OF THE CRIMINALS

...

APPENDIX I.--VIOLATIONS OF THE LAWS OF WAR.

B.   Acts whether or not directly connected with warfare, which have caused death, illness or bodily harm or loss of liberty to those to whom they were applied, such as:

  (1) Crimes committed without order or authority: Serious crimes against persons, punishable by ordinary criminal law, committed without any pretence of legal authority or order (including e.g.: murder, manslaughter, infliction of grievous bodily harm, torture, false imprisonment, rape, etc.).

  (2) Crimes ordered by or committed under order of or with approval of authorities:

    (a)   Common murder--or mass murder of civilians or prisoners of war.

    (b)   Putting hostages to death.

    (c)   Execution, bodily disablement or prolonged deprivation of liberty ordered by a court which was either (a) composed of persons some of whom have no authority to sit on it, or (b) without jurisdiction as to the person or the act, or (c) imposing a sentence in violation of the law or without due respect for the rights of the defence.

    (d)   Wilful starvation of populations, excessive removal of foodstuffs, or depriving persons of shelter, clothing and/or other means of sustenance.

    (e)   Compulsory enlistment of civilians or prisoners of war in enemy forces, or in dangerous war work.

    (f)   Internment or segregation in inhuman conditions.

    (g)   Mass deportation.

    (h)   Abduction of women with the object of prostitution.

    (i)   Abduction of children.

    (j)   Serious ill-treatment or torture of civilians or prisoners of war.

    (k)   Compelling sick or wounded, women, children or old people to a work which is out of proportion with their condition, age or sex.

    (l)   Imposing collective punishments.

    (m)   Other violations of the Hague Convention IV or of the Conventions of Geneva.

C.   Serious crimes against property, such as:

  (1) Crimes committed without authority of doer: Crimes against property under ordinary criminal law (theft-looting-robbery-arson, etc.).

  (2) Crimes committed under order or with approval of authorities:

(a)   Wanton destruction of property unrelated to military events, carried out by the occupying authorities, in occupied countries.

(b)   Plundering or removal of property belonging to the State, Associations, Churches, Schools, etc., or private individuals.

2.   HISTORY OF THE UNITED NATIONS WAR CRIMES COMMISSION AND THE DEVELOPMENT OF THE LAWS OF WAR COMPILED BY THE UNITED NATIONS WAR CRIMES COMMISSION, 1948
(Excerpts)

Crimes Against Humanity

...

The notion of crimes against humanity, as it evolved in the Commission, was based upon the opinion that many offences committed by the enemy could not technically be regarded as war crimes *stricto sensu* on account of one or several elements, which were of a different nature. In this respect the victims' nationality played a prominent role, as was exemplified in the case of German and Austrian Jews, as well as of Jews of other Axis satellite countries, such as Hungary and Roumania. The victims were subjected to the same treatment as Allied nationals in occupied territories; they were deported and interned under inhuman conditions in concentration camps, systematically ill-treated or exterminated. It was felt that, but for the fact that the victims were technically enemy nationals, such persecutions were otherwise in every respect similar to war crimes.

As a consequence, the rule stressed during the first days of the Commission's activities, that narrow legalisms were to be disregarded and the field of the violations of the laws of war extended so as to meet the requirements of justice, was applied in respect of this class of crimes.

The development of the subject in the Commission took, technically speaking, the course of extending the concept of war crimes to a wider notion than that hitherto restricting it to the laws and customs of war. Accordingly, along with the notion of war crimes *stricto sensu*, there evolved the concept of war crimes in a wider, non-technical sense, as a common denominator devised so as to include crimes against humanity, and, as will be seen later, also that of crimes against peace.

...

It was therefore suggested that the Commission should include within its competence crimes other than those technically designated as war crimes *stricto sensu*. These were described as crimes committed "in violation of the criminal laws of the countries invaded or otherwise affected, of the laws and customs of war, of the general principles of criminal law as recognized by civilized nations, or of the laws of humanity and the dictates of the public conscience as provided in the Hague Preamble". This formula was then applied to crimes against humanity, which, as distinct from war crimes proper, were defined as "crimes committed against any person without regard to nationality, stateless persons included, because of race, nationality, religious or political belief, irrespective of where they have been committed". It should be noted that this definition was to be adopted in substance in Article 6 of the Nuremberg Charter.

DEVELOPMENTS IN THE CONCEPTS OF CRIMES AGAINST HUMANITY, WAR CRIMES AND CRIMES AGAINST PEACE
CRIMES AGAINST HUMANITY

Developments Preceding the Charter of 1945

Introductory

Articles 6 and 5 respectively of the Charters of the International Military Tribunals at Nuremberg and Tokyo, and Article II of the Control Council (for Germany) Law No. 10 which laid down the jurisdiction of the International Military Tribunals and of the other courts in Germany which were to try war criminals, specify three types of crimes: (a) crimes against peace, (b) war crimes and (c) crimes against humanity.

As will be shown later, the terms "crimes against humanity" and "war crimes", as defined in these documents, and the concepts they represent, are juxtaposed and inter-related to the extent that while all acts enumerated under the heading "war crimes" are also "crimes against humanity", the reverse is not necessarily true. For instance, acts committed on enemy occupied territory or against allied nations may be war crimes as well as crimes against humanity, whereas acts committed either when a state of war does not exist, or against citizens of neutral states, or against enemy nations or on enemy territory, are crimes against humanity, but are not violations of the laws and customs of war, and hence not war crimes. It might be added that crimes against peace, namely the planning, preparation, initiation and waging of a war of aggression, which were declared by the Nuremberg Tribunal to be the supreme international crime, constitute also, in a general non-technical sense, a crime against humanity, since in certain circumstances they involve violations of human rights.

The terms "crimes against peace", "war crimes" and "crimes against humanity", although used in the documents as technical terms, do not represent conceptions entirely novel or without precedent. As was pointed out earlier, in connection with the development of the laws of war prior to the First World War, all reference to "humanity", such as "interests of humanity", "principles of humanity" "and laws of humanity" as appear in the Fourth Hague Convention of 1907 and in the other documents and enactments of that period, have been used in a non-technical sense, and certainly not with the intention of indicating a set of norms different from the "laws and customs of war", which are covered by the term "war crimes" in the documents of 1945 and 1946.

It was also pointed out that the term "crimes against humanity" in a non-technical sense, was used for the first time in the Declaration of 28th May, 1915, which dealt precisely with the category of crimes that the modern conception of the term is intended to cover, namely inhumane acts committed by a Government against its own subjects. Finally, stress was laid on the fact that the two categories of offences with which the Commission of Fifteen was concerned--violations of the laws and customs of war on the one hand, and violations of the laws of humanity on the other correspond generally speaking to "war crimes" and "crimes against humanity" as they are used in the documents of 1945-1946. It is not, however, known whether the Commission, in using the term "crimes against the laws of humanity", had in mind offences which were not covered by the other expression. It has also been shown what was the outcome of the recommendations put forward by the Commission of Fifteen as concerns the provisions of the Peace Treaties of 1919-1923.

The Italo-Abyssinian War of 1935-36

During the Italo-Abyssinian conflict a number of protests, appeals and declarations were issued by Haile Selassie, the Emperor of Ethiopia, denouncing the many and various crimes committed by Italian forces and authorities against the Ethiopian population, both during the campaign and after the annexation of Ethiopia by Italy on 9th May, 1936. One category of these crimes was the use of poison gas by the Italian Army and Air Force. This was considered by an *ad hoc* Committee of Thirteen of the League of Nations, which pointed out that both parties had signed the Geneva Convention prohibiting the use of gases in any form or circumstance, and reference was made to the numerous confirmations of gas-poisoning received from impartial sources.

In his personal address to the Sixteenth Assembly of the League of Nations of 4th July, 1936, the Emperor of Ethiopia described how the Italian Government had made war not only on the armed forces, but had also attacked populations far removed from hostilities. He stated that towards the end of 1935 the Italians had used tear gas and then mustard gas, and later had extended the same technique to vast areas of Ethiopian territory, drenching not only soldiers but also women, children, cattle, rivers, lakes and pastures with this "deadly rain", systematically killing all living creatures.

On 17th March, 1937, the Emperor requested the Secretary General of the League to appoint a Commission of Inquiry to investigate the horrors committed in Ethiopia by the Italian Government. In addition to other crimes committed, the Emperor denounced the execution of Ras Desta, a prisoner of war, and the massacre of over 6,000 persons in Addis Ababa which occurred in February, 1937. These allegations indicated that crimes coming within different notions had been committed in Ethiopia.

The Peace Treaty with Italy signed in Paris on 10th February, 1947, contains in Article 45 provisions relating to Italy's obligations regarding the apprehension and surrender of war criminals in general. The persons in respect of whom Italy must take all necessary steps to ensure apprehension and surrender, are those accused of having committed, ordered or abetted war crimes and crimes against peace or humanity. With regard to Ethiopia's right to prosecute Italian nationals for crimes committed in that country, the relevant Article 38 reads as follows:

"The date from which the provisions of the present Treaty shall become applicable as regards all measures and acts of any kind whatsoever entailing the responsibility of Italy or of Italian nationals towards Ethiopia, shall be held to be October 3rd, 1935."

The reference to "all measures and acts of any kind whatsoever" clearly indicates that the provisions of Article 45 relating to war criminals in general apply also to the Italo-Ethiopian war. It may thus be seen that the crimes, committed in Ethiopia during the war 1935-36 have been qualified by these provisions as both war crimes and crimes against humanity.

568

DOCUMENTS SECTION

The Spanish Conflict

A further example of the use between the two World Wars of the expression dictates of humanity, in a non-technical sense, may be found in the "International Agreement for Collective Measures against Piratical Attacks in the Mediterranean by Submarines" signed at Nyon on 14th September, 1937, and supplemented three days later by an agreement signed at Geneva in respect of similar acts by surface vessels and aircraft. The agreement declares attacks committed during the Spanish conflict against merchant ships not belonging to either of the conflicting Spanish parties to be violations of the rules of international law and to "constitute acts contrary to the most elementary dictates of humanity, which should be treated as acts of piracy".

Other Developments

During the Second World War innumerable official and semi-official declarations and pronouncements dealing with the problem of crimes against humanity were issued. In 1943, the London International Assembly passed a resolution to the effect that this was one of the crimes for which the major war criminals should be indicted.

The United Nations War Crimes Commission, as has been shown in the preceding chapter, recommended early in its existence that crimes against stateless or other persons on account of their race or religion should be considered as war crimes in the wider sense, and were, therefore, within the Commission's terms of reference.

All these documents and recommendations show that the insertion of the provisions concerning "crimes against humanity" in the Charters of the International Military Tribunals at Nuremberg and Tokyo was due to the desire that the retributive action of those United Nations should not be limited to bringing to justice those who had committed war crimes in the traditional and narrow sense that is, violations of the laws and customs of war, perpetrated on Allied territory or against Allied citizens--but that atrocities committed on Axis territory and against persons of other than Allied nationality should also be punished.

Article 6(c) and the general attitude of the Tribunal

While the Nuremberg Charter is the first legal enactment to formulate the definition of crimes against humanity, though the concept was not without precedent, sub-paragraph

569

(c) of Article 6 of the Charter appears *prima facie* to lay down a set of novel principles, or at least to pave the way to considerable progress in the relationship between the community of nations, its members states and individuals citizens of these states, and between international law and municipal law. The following three elements of the definition of crimes against humanity, as laid down in Article 6(c) appear to contain these novel principles:

(1) "before and during the war",

(2) "against any civilian population",

(3) "Whether or not in violation of the domestic law of the country where perpetrated".

The first principle indicated by the words "before or during the war" apparently implies that international law contains penal sanctions against individuals, applicable not only in time of war, but also in time of peace. This presupposes the existence of a system of international law under which individuals are responsible to the community of nations for violations of rules of international criminal law, and according to which attacks on the fundamental liberties and constitutional rights of peoples and individual persons, that is inhuman acts, constitute international crimes not only in time of war, but also, in certain circumstances, in time of peace. The embodiment of this principle in the Charter, taken in conjunction with the principle that it is irrelevant whether or not such crimes are committed in violation of the domestic law of the country where perpetrated, meant that the Tribunal had the competence to override the national sovereignty and municipal law of the States of which the perpetrators are subject, and where the crimes had been committed. This principle was, however, restricted by the special qualification laid down in the provision, as amended in the Berlin Protocol, that in order to constitute crimes against humanity which call for international penal sanction, the inhumane acts specifically enumerated in Article 6(c) must be committed in "execution of or in connection with any crime within the jurisdiction of the Tribunal", that is, they must be connected with a crime against peace or a war crime proper. This qualification, therefore, limited the scope of the concept of crimes against humanity, with a further consequence that their greatest practical importance in peace time is seriously affected.

The second principle expressed by the words "against any civilian population" is that any civilian population is under the protection of international criminal law and that the nationality of the victims is irrelevant. It seems to imply that such protection is also extended to cases where the alleged violations of human rights have been perpetrated by

570

a State against its own subjects. The term, therefore, includes crimes against both allied and enemy nationals.

In particular, it follows that a civilian population remains under the protection of the provisions regarding crimes against humanity irrespective of its status or otherwise of belligerent occupation; whether it is (a) the population of a territory under belligerent occupation, effected with or without resort to war (e.g. Austria and parts of Czechoslovakia in 1938 and 1939); or (b) the population of other States not under occupation, in which armed forces of one belligerent are stationed (e.g. German forces in Italy); or of countries adjacent to a belligerent (e.g. cases of kidnapping and other violence); or (c) the population of a belligerent itself (e.g. German or Italian nationals of the same or different race as the respective State authorities).

The words *"civilian population"* appear to indicate that "crimes against humanity" are restricted to inhumane acts committed against civilians as opposed to members of the armed forces, while the use of the word population appears to indicate that a larger body of victims is visualized, and that single or isolated acts against individuals may be considered to fall outside the scope of the concept.

As already mentioned, the violation of a certain human right, coming within the scope of Article 6(c), may also constitute a violation of the laws and customs of war, as enumerated under Article 6(b). The provision dealing with war crimes (Article 6(b)) expressly states that its enumeration of specific criminal acts is not exhaustive. No such statement which is to be found in Article 6(c) is also not exhaustive, at least so far as substance is concerned.

There are two types of crimes against humanity; crimes of the "murder-type" such as murder, extermination, enslavement, deportation, etc., and "persecutions". With regard to the latter the provision requires that they must have been committed on political, racial or religious grounds.

The acts of the "murder-type" enumerated in Article 6(c) as crimes against humanity are similar to, but not identical with, those mentioned as war crimes in Article 6(b). Murder appears under both headings. Extermination, mentioned only in Article 6(c), is apparently to be interpreted as murder on a large scale--mass murder. The inclusion of both "extermination" and "murder" may be taken to mean that implication in the policy of extermination, without any direct connection with actual criminal acts of murder, may be punished as complicity in the crime of extermination.

It is difficult to tell whether there is any difference between "deportation to slave labour and for other purposes" as mentioned under (b), and the two separate items of "enslavement" and "deportation" mentioned under (c). "Ill-treatment" is mentioned under (b), but is omitted in (c). However, this particular crime might fall under the category of "other inhumane acts".

Finally, the third principle that it is irrelevant whether an offence alleged to be a crime against humanity was or was not committed in violation of the domestic law of the country where it was perpetrated, means that it is no defence that the act alleged to be a crime against humanity was legal under the domestic law of that country. The exclusion of this plea is closely connected with the provisions of Article 8 of the Charter regarding the defence of superior orders.

As concerns the attitude of the Tribunal to the law relating to crimes against humanity, its general considerations were given as follows:

"With regard to crimes against humanity, there is no doubt whatever that political opponents were murdered in Germany before the war, and that many of them were kept in concentration camps in circumstances of great horror and cruelty. The policy of terror was certainly carried out on a vast scale, and in many cases was organized and systematic. The policy of persecution, repression and murder of civilians in Germany before the war of 1939 who were likely to be hostile to the Government, was most ruthlessly carried out. The persecution of the Jews during the same period is established beyond all doubt. To constitute crimes against humanity, the acts relied on before the outbreak of war must have been in execution of, or in connection with, any crime within the jurisdiction of the Tribunal. The Tribunal is of the opinion that revolting and horrible as many of these crimes were, it has not been satisfactorily proved that they were done in execution of, or in connection with, any such crime. The Tribunal therefore cannot make a general declaration that the acts before 1939 were crimes against humanity within the meaning of the Charter, but from the beginning of the war in 1939 war crimes were committed on a vast scale, which were also crimes against humanity; and insofar as the inhuman acts charged in the Indictment, and committed after the beginning of the war, did not constitute war crimes, they were all committed in the execution of or in connection with, the aggressive war, and therefore constituted crimes against humanity".

It may thus be seen that the Tribunal applied the principle of the Berlin Protocol and restricted both crimes, of the murder type and persecutions, by the provision that they must have been committed in connection with crimes coming within the competence of the Tribunal.

This does not imply that no crime committed prior to 1st September, 1939, can be considered as a crime against humanity. Acts committed in connection with crimes against peace, perpetrated before 1st September, 1939, were recognized by the Tribunal as constituting crimes against humanity. On the other hand, in cases where inhumane acts were committed after the beginning of the war and did not constitute war crimes, their connection with the war was presumed by the Tribunal , and they were therefore considered as crimes against humanity. Although in theory it remains irrelevant whether a crime against humanity was committed before or during the war, in practice it is difficult to establish a connection between what is alleged to be a crime against humanity and a crime within the jurisdiction of the Tribunal if the act was committed before the war.

3. THE MOSCOW CONFERENCE, October 19-30, 1943 (DECLARATION OF GERMAN ATROCITIES), 1 November 1943

1943 FOR. REL. (I) 749 at 768. *Reprinted in* 38 AJIL 3, at 7 (1944) (Supp.); 3 Bevans 816, at 834.

The United Kingdom, the United States and the Soviet Union have received from many quarters evidence of atrocities, massacres and cold-blooded mass executions which are being perpetrated by the Hitlerite forces in the many countries they have overrun and from which they are now being steadily expelled. The brutalities of Hitlerite domination are no new thing and all the peoples or territories in their grip have suffered from the worst form of government by terror. What is new is that many of these territories are now being redeemed by the advancing armies of the liberating Powers and that in their desperation, the recoiling Hitlerite Huns are redoubling their ruthless cruelties. This is now evidenced with particular clearness by monstrous crimes of the Hitlerites on the

573

territory of the Soviet Union which is being liberated from the Hitlerites, and on French and Italian territory.

Accordingly, the aforesaid three allied Powers, speaking in the interests of the thirty-two [thirty-three] United Nations, hereby solemnly declare and give full warning of their declaration as follows:

At the time of the granting of any armistice to any government which may be set up in Germany, those German officers and men and members of the Nazi party who have been responsible for, or have taken a consenting part in the above atrocities, massacres and executions, will be sent back to the countries in which their abominable deeds were done in order that they may be judged and punished according to the laws of these liberated countries and of the free governments which will be created therein. Lists will be compiled in all possible detail from all these countries having regard especially to the invaded parts of the Soviet Union, to Poland and Czechoslovakia, to Yugoslavia and Greece, including Crete and other islands, to Norway, Denmark, the Netherlands, Belgium, Luxembourg, France and Italy.

Thus, the Germans who take part in wholesale shootings of Italian officers or in the execution of French, Dutch, Belgian or Norwegian hostages or of Cretan peasants, or who have shared in the slaughters inflicted on the people of Poland or in territories of the Soviet Union which are now being swept clear of the enemy, will know that they will be brought back to the scene of their crimes and judged on the spot by the peoples whom they have outraged. Let those who have hitherto not imbrued their hands with innocent blood beware lest they join the ranks of the guilty, for most assuredly the three allied Powers will pursue them to the uttermost ends of the earth and will deliver them to their accusers in order that justice may be done.

The above declaration is without prejudice to the case of the major criminals, whose offences have no particular geographical localization and who will be punished by the joint decision of the governments of the Allies.

ROOSEVELT, CHURCHILL AND STALIN
Signed at Moscow, November 1, 1943

4. THE TEHRAN CONFERENCE (DECLARATION OF THE THREE POWERS), 1 December 1943

DEP'T. OF STATE BULL. 409-410 (Dec. 11, 1943). *Reprinted in* 1943 FOR. REL. 640; 3 Bevans 859; A. DECADE OF AMERICAN FOREIGN POLICY: BASIC DOCUMENTS 1941-1949 21-22 (1985).

We--the President of the United States, the Prime Minister of Great Britain, and the Premier of the Soviet Union, have met these four days past, in this, the Capital of our Ally, Iran, and have shaped and confirmed our common policy.

We express our determination that our nations shall work together in war and in the peace that will follow.

As to war--our military staffs have joined in our round table discussions, and we have concerted our plans for the destruction of the German forces. We have reached complete agreement as to the scope and timing of the operations to be undertaken from the east, west and south.

The common understanding which we have here reached guarantees that victory will be ours.

And as to peace--we are sure that our concord will win an enduring Peace. We recognize fully the supreme responsibility resting upon us and all the United Nations to make a peace which will command the goodwill of the overwhelming mass of the peoples of the world and banish the scourge and terror of war for many generations.

With our Diplomatic advisors we have surveyed the problems of the future. We shall seek the cooperation and active participation of all nations, large and small, whose peoples in heart and mind are dedicated, as are our own peoples, to the elimination of tyranny and slavery, oppression and intolerance. We will welcome them, as they may choose to come, into a world family of Democratic Nations.

No power on earth can prevent our destroying the German armies by land, their U Boats by sea, and their war plants from the air.

Our attack will be relentless and increasing.

575

Emerging from these cordial conferences we look with confidence to the day when all peoples of the world may live free lives, untouched by tyranny, and according to their varying desires and their own consciences.

We came here with hope and determination. We leave here, friends in fact, in spirit and in purpose.

ROOSEVELT, CHURCHILL AND STALIN
Signed at Tehran, December 1, 1943

5.   THE BERLIN (POTSDAM) CONFERENCE, (PROTOCOL OF PROCEEDINGS), 2 August 1945
(Excerpts)

1945 FOR. REL. Conference of Berlin (Potsdam II) 1499. *Reprinted in* 3 Bevans 1207; 39 AJIL 245 (1945) (Supp.).

The Berlin Conference of the Three Heads of Government of the U.S.S.R., U.S.A., and U.K., which took place from July 17 to August 2, 1945, came to the following conclusions:

....

II. THE PRINCIPLES TO GOVERN THE TREATMENT OF GERMANY
IN THE INITIAL CONTROL PERIOD.

A. POLITICAL PRINCIPLES.

1.   In accordance with the Agreement on Control Machinery in Germany, supreme authority in Germany is exercised, on instructions from their respective Governments, by the Commanders-in-Chief of the armed forces of the United States of America, the

United Kingdom, the Union of Soviet Socialist Republics, and the French Republic, each in his own zone of occupation, and also jointly, in matters affecting Germany as a whole, in their capacity as members of the Control Council.

2. So far as is practicable, there shall be uniformity of treatment of the German population throughout Germany.

3. The purposes of the occupation of Germany by which the Control Council shall be guided are:

(i) The complete disarmament and demilitarization of Germany and the elimination or control of all German industry that could be used for military production. To these ends:--

   (a) All German land, naval and air forces, the S.S., S.A., S.D., and Gestapo, with all their organizations, staffs and institutions, including the General Staff, the Officers' Corps, Reserve Corps, military schools, war veterans' organizations and all other military and semi-military organizations, together with all clubs and associations which serve to keep alive the military tradition in Germany, shall be completely and finally abolished in such manner as permanently to prevent the revival or reorganization of German militarism and Nazism;

   (b) All arms, ammunition and implements of war and all specialized facilities for their production shall be held at the disposal of the Allies or destroyed. The maintenance and production of all aircraft and all arms, ammunition and implements of war shall be prevented.

(ii) To convince the German people that they have suffered a total military defeat and that they cannot escape responsibility for what they have brought upon themselves, since their own ruthless warfare and the fanatical Nazi resistance have destroyed the German economy and made chaos and suffering inevitable.

(iii) To destroy the National Socialist Party and its affiliated and supervised organizations, to dissolve all Nazi institutions, to ensure that they are not revived in any form, and to prevent all Nazi and militarist activity or propaganda.

(iv) To prepare for the eventual reconstruction of German political life on a democratic basis and for eventual peaceful cooperation in international life by Germany.

4. All Nazi laws which provided the basis of the Hitler regime or established discrimination on grounds of race, creed, or political opinion shall be abolished. No such discrimination, whether legal, administrative or otherwise, shall be tolerated.

5. War criminals and those who have participated in planning or carrying out Nazi enterprises involving or resulting in atrocities or war crimes shall be arrested and brought to judgment. Nazi leaders, influential Nazi supporters and high officials of Nazi organizations and institutions and any other persons dangerous to the occupation or its objectives shall be arrested and interned.

6. All members of the Nazi Party who have been more than nominal participants in its activities and all other persons hostile to Allied purposes shall be removed from public and semi-public office, and from positions of responsibility in important private undertakings. Such persons shall be replaced by persons who, by their political and moral qualities, are deemed capable of assisting in developing genuine democratic institutions in Germany.

7. German education shall be so controlled as completely to eliminate Nazi and militarist doctrines and to make possible the successful development of democratic ideas.

8. The judicial system will be reorganized in accordance with the principles of democracy, of justice under law., and of equal rights for all citizens without distinction of race, nationality or religion.

9. The administration in Germany should be directed towards the decentralization of the political structure and the development of local responsibility. To this end:--

(i)   local self-government shall be restored throughout Germany on democratic principles and in particular through elective councils as rapidly as is consistent with military security and the purposes of military occupation;

(ii)   all democratic political parties with rights of assembly and of public discussion shall be allowed and encouraged throughout Germany;

(iii)   representative and elective principles shall be introduced into regional, provincial and state (Land) administration as rapidly as may be justified by the successful application of these principles in local self-government;

578

(iv)   for the time being, no central German Government shall be established. Notwithstanding this, however, certain essential central German administrative departments, headed by State Secretaries, shall be established, particularly in the fields of finance, transport, communications, foreign trade and industry. Such departments will act under the direction of the Control Council.

10. Subject to the necessity for maintaining military security, freedom of speech, press and religion shall be permitted, and religious institutions shall be respected. Subject likewise to the maintenance of military security, the formation of free trade unions shall be permitted.
....

VI. War Criminals

The Three Governments have taken note of the discussions which have been proceeding in recent weeks in London between British, United States, Soviet and French representatives with a view to reaching agreement on the methods of trial of those major war criminals whose crimes under the Moscow Declaration of October, 1943 have no particular geographical localization. The three Governments reaffirm their intention to bring these criminals to swift and sure justice. They hope that the negotiations in London will result in speedy agreement being reached for this purpose, and they regard it as a matter of great importance that the trial of these major criminals should begin at the earliest possible date. The first list of defendants will be published before 1st September.

C. DOCUMENTS RELATING TO THE CHARTER

1. **AGREEMENT FOR THE PROSECUTION AND PUNISHMENT OF MAJOR WAR CRIMINALS OF THE EUROPEAN AXIS, London, 8 August 1945**

8 U.N.T.S. 279; 59 Stat. 1544, 8AS No. 472. *Reprinted in* 39 AJIL 257 (1945) (Supp.); 1 Ferencz 454; 1 Friedman 863; Schindler/Toman 823.

AGREEMENT by the Government of the UNITED STATES OF AMERICA, the Provisional Government of the FRENCH REPUBLIC, the Government of the UNITED

KINGDOM OF GREAT BRITAIN AND NORTHERN IRELAND and the Government of the UNION OF SOVIET SOCIALIST REPUBLICS for the Prosecution and Punishment of the MAJOR WAR CRIMINALS of the EUROPEAN AXIS

WHEREAS the United Nations have from time to time made declarations of their intention that War Criminals shall be brought to justice;

AND WHEREAS the Moscow Declaration of the 30th October 1943 on German atrocities in Occupied Europe stated that those German Officers and men and members of the Nazi Party who have been responsible for or have taken a consenting part in atrocities and crimes will be sent back to the countries in which their abominable deeds were done in order that they may be judged and punished according to the laws of these liberated countries and of the free Governments that will be created therein;

AND WHEREAS this Declaration was stated to be without prejudice to the case of major criminals whose offenses have no particular geographical location and who will be punished by the joint decision of the Governments of the Allies;

NOW THEREFORE the Government of the United States of America, the Provisional Government of the French Republic, the Government of the United Kingdom of Great Britain and Northern Ireland and the Government of the Union of Soviet Socialist Republics (hereinafter called "the Signatories") acting in the interests of all the United Nations and by their representatives duly authorized thereto have concluded this Agreement.

Article 1 There shall be established after consultation with the Control Council for Germany an International Military Tribunal for the trial of war criminals whose offenses have no particular geographical location whether they be accused individually or in their capacity as members of organizations or groups or in both capacities.

Article 2 The constitution, jurisdiction and functions of the International Military Tribunal shall be those set out in the Charter annexed to this Agreement, which Charter shall form an integral part of this Agreement.

Article 3 Each of the Signatories shall take the necessary steps to make available for the investigation of the charges and trial of the major war criminals detained by them who are to be tried by the International Military Tribunal. The Signatories shall also use their best endeavors to make available for investigation of the charges against and the trial before the International Military Tribunal of such of the major war criminals as are not in the territories of any of the Signatories.

Article 4 Nothing in this Agreement shall prejudice the provisions established by the Moscow Declaration concerning the return of war criminals to the countries where they committed their crimes.

Article 5 Any Government of the United Nations may adhere to this Agreement by notice given through the diplomatic channel to the Government of the United Kingdom, who shall inform the other signatories and adhering Governments of each such adherence.

Article 6 Nothing in this Agreement shall prejudice the jurisdiction or the powers of any national or occupation court established or to be established in any allied territory or in Germany for the trial of war criminals.

Article 7 This Agreement shall come into force on the day of signature and shall remain in force for the period of one year and shall continue thereafter, subject to the right of any Signatory to give, through the diplomatic channel, one month's notice of intention to terminate it. Such termination shall not prejudice any proceedings already taken or any findings already made in pursuance of this Agreement.

IN WITNESS WHEREOF the Undersigned have signed the present Agreement.

DONE in quadruplicate in London this 8th day of August 1945 each in English, French and Russian, and each text to have equal authenticity.

For the Government of the United States of America
ROBERT H. JACKSON

For the Provisional government of the French Republic
ROBERT FALCO

For the Government of the United Kingdom of
Great Britain and Northern Ireland
C. JOWITT

For the Government of the Union of Soviet Socialist Republics
I. NIKITCHENKO
A. TRAININ

2. **CHARTER OF THE INTERNATIONAL MILITARY TRIBUNAL, ANNEXED TO THE LONDON AGREEMENT, 8 August 1945**

I. Constitution of the International Military Tribunal

Article 1 In pursuance of the Agreement signed on the 8th day of August 1945 by the Government of the United States of America, the Provisional Government of the French Republic, the Government of the United Kingdom of Great Britain and Northern Ireland and the Government of the Union of Soviet Socialist Republics, there shall be established an International Military Tribunal (hereinafter called "the Tribunal") for the just and prompt trial and punishment of the major war criminals of the European Axis.

Article 2 The Tribunal shall consist of four members, each with an alternate. One member and one alternate shall be appointed by each of the Signatories. The alternates shall, so far as they are able, be present at all sessions of the Tribunal. In case of illness of any member of the Tribunal or his incapacity for some other reason to fulfill his functions, his alternate shall take his place.

Article 3 Neither the Tribunal, its members nor their alternates can be challenged by the prosecution, or by the Defendants or their Counsel. Each Signatory may replace its member of the Tribunal or his alternate for reasons of health or for other good reasons, except that no replacement may take place during a Trial, other than by an alternate.

Article 4
(a) The presence of all four members of the Tribunal or the alternate for any absent member shall be necessary to constitute the quorum.
(b) The members of the Tribunal shall, before any trial begins, agree among themselves upon the selection from their number of a President, and the President shall hold office during that trial, or as may otherwise be agreed by a vote of not less than three members. The principle of rotation of presidency for successive trials is agreed. If, however, a session of the Tribunal takes place on the territory

of one of the four Signatories, the representative of that Signatory on the Tribunal shall preside.

(c) Save as aforesaid the Tribunal shall take decisions by a majority vote and in case the votes are evenly divided, the vote of the President shall be decisive: provided always that convictions and sentences shall only be imposed by affirmative votes of at least three members of the Tribunal.

Article 5 In case of need and depending on the number of the matters to be tried, other Tribunals may be set up; and the establishment, functions, and procedure of each Tribunal shall be identical, and shall be governed by this Charter.

II. Jurisdiction and General Principles

Article 6 The Tribunal established by the Agreement referred to in Article 1 hereof for the trial and punishment of the major war criminals of the European Axis countries shall have the power to try and punish persons who, acting in the interests of the European Axis countries, whether as individuals or as members of organizations, committed any of the following crimes.

The following acts, or any of them, are crimes coming within the jurisdiction of the Tribunal for which there shall be individual responsibility:

(a) **CRIMES AGAINST PEACE:** namely, planning, preparation, initiation or waging of a war of aggression, or a war in violation of international treaties, agreements or assurances, or participation in a common plan or conspiracy for the accomplishment of any of the foregoing;

(b) **WAR CRIMES:** namely, violations of the laws or customs of war. Such violations shall include, but not be limited to, murder, ill-treatment or deportation to slave labor or for any other purpose of civilian population of or in occupied territory, murder or ill-treatment of prisoners of war or persons on the seas, killing of hostages, plunder of public or private property, wanton destruction of cities, towns or villages, or devastation not justified by military necessity;

(c) **CRIMES AGAINST HUMANITY:** namely, murder, extermination, enslavement, deportation, and other inhuman acts committed against any civilian population, before or during the war; or persecutions on political, racial or religious grounds in execution of or in connection with any crime within the

583

jurisdiction of the Tribunal whether or not in violation of the domestic law of the country where perpetrated.

Leaders, organizers, instigators and accomplices participating in the formulation or execution of a common plan or conspiracy to commit any of the foregoing crimes are responsible for all acts performed by any persons in execution of such plan.

Article 7 The official position of defendants, whether as Heads of State or responsible officials in Government Departments, shall not be considered as freeing them from responsibility or mitigating punishment.

Article 8 The fact that the Defendant acted pursuant to order of his Government or of a superior shall not free him from responsibility, but may be considered in mitigation of punishment, if the Tribunal determines that justice so requires.

Article 9 At the trial of any individual member of any group or organization the Tribunal may declare (in connection with any act of which the individual may be convicted) that the group or organization of which the individual was a member was a criminal organization.

After receipt of the Indictment the Tribunal shall give such notice as it thinks fit that the prosecution intends to ask the Tribunal to make such declaration and any member of the organization will be entitled to apply to the Tribunal for leave to be heard by the Tribunal upon the question of the criminal character of the organization. The Tribunal shall have power to allow or reject the application. If the application is allowed, the Tribunal may direct in what manner the applicants shall be represented and heard.

Article 10   In cases where a group or organization is declared criminal by the Tribunal, the competent national authority of any Signatory shall have the right to bring individuals to trial for membership therein before national, military or occupation courts. In any such case the criminal nature of the group or organization is considered proved and shall not be questioned.

Article 11   Any person convicted by the Tribunal may be charged before a national, military or occupation court, referred to in Article 10 of this Charter, with a crime other than of membership in a criminal group or organization and such court may, after convicting him, impose upon him punishment independent of and additional to the punishment imposed by the Tribunal for participation in the criminal activities of such group or organization.

Article 12   The Tribunal shall have the right to take proceedings against a person charged with crimes set out in Article 6 of this Charter in his absence, if he has not been found or if the Tribunal, for any reason, finds it necessary, in the interests of justice, to conduct the hearing in his absence.

Article 13   The Tribunal shall draw up rules for its procedure. These rules shall not be inconsistent with the provisions of this Charter.

3.   PROTOCOL TO AGREEMENT AND CHARTER, London, 6 October 1945

Whereas an Agreement and Charter regarding the Prosecution of War Criminals was signed in London on the 8th August 1945, in the English, French, and Russian languages,

And whereas a discrepancy has been found to exist between the originals of Article 6, paragraph (c), of the Charter in the Russian language, on the one hand, and the originals in the English and French languages, on the other, to wit, the semi-colon in Article 6, paragraph (c), of the Charter between the words "war" and "or", as carried in the English and French texts, is a comma in the Russian text, And whereas it is desired to rectify this discrepancy:

Now, THEREFORE, the undersigned, signatories of the said Agreement on behalf of their respective Governments, duly authorized thereto, have agreed that Article 6, paragraph (c), of the Charter in the Russian text is correct, and that the meaning and intention of the text should be changed to a comma, and that the French text should be amended to read as follows:

c)   **LES CRIMES CONTRE L'HUMANITE:**   c'est à dire l'assassinat, l'extermination, la réduction en esclavage, la déportation, et tout autre acte inhumain commis contre toutes populations civiles, avant ou pendant la guerre, ou bien les persécutions pour des motifs politiques, raciaux, ou réligieux, lorsque ces actes ou persécutions, qu'ils aient constitué ou non une violation du droit interne du pays où ils ont été perpétrés, ont été commis à la suite de tout crime rentrant dans la compétence du Tribunal, ou en liaison avec ce crime.

IN WITNESS WHEREOF the Undersigned have signed the present Protocol.

DONE in quadruplicate in Berlin this 6th day of October, 1945, each in English, French, and Russian, and each text to have equal authenticity.

For the Government of the United States of America
Robert H. Jackson

For the Provisional Government of the French Republic
F. DeMenthon

For the Government of the United Kingdom of Great
Britain and Northern Ireland
Hartley Shawcross

For the Government of the Union of Soviet Socialist Republics
R. Rudenko

4. DISPOSITION AND OUTCOME OF THE NUREMBERG TRIAL

Bormann, Martin (Head of Nazi Party Chancellery) - Convicted, in absentia, of Counts 3 and 4 and sentenced to hang. He played an important role in subjugating the occupied territories, maltreating slave laborers and persecuting Jews.

Doenitz, Karl (Commander in Chief of Navy) - Convicted of Counts 2 and 3 and sentenced to 10 years of imprisonment.

Frank, Hans (Chief administrator of occupied Poland) - Convicted of Counts 3 and 4 and sentenced to hang. As head of occupied Poland, he ruthlessly applied Nazi principles of economic exploitation and racism.

Frick, Wilhelm (Minister of Interior) - Convicted of Counts 2, 3 and 4 and sentenced to hang. He prepared laws to persecute Jews, restrict Christian churches and suppress domestic opposition.

Fritzsche, Hans (Propaganda official) - Acquitted.

Funk, Walter (Minister of Economics) - Convicted of Counts 2, 3 and 4 and sentenced to life imprisonment. He organized and executed the economic exploitation of the conquered territories and had a place on the board which supervised the slave-labor system.

Goering, Hermann (Reich Marshal) - Convicted of all four Counts and sentenced to hang. He helped establish and carry out Nazi programs, *inter alia*, for looting art and destroying the economies of occupied territories. He also signed the only extant written order calling for the "final solution of the Jewish question."

Hess, Rudolf (Close confidant to Hitler) - Convicted of Counts 1 and 2 and sentenced to life imprisonment.

Jodl, Alfred (Chief of the Operations Staff of the High Command of the Armed Forces) - Convicted of all four Counts and sentenced to hang. He ordered a scorched-earth retreat from Norway.

Kaltenbrunner, Ernst (Secret police chief) - Convicted of Counts 3 and 4 and sentenced to hang. He presided over the Gestapo and subsections of these secret police organizations which carried out the "final solution of the Jewish question." Also, he personally gave execution orders and directives.

Keitel, Wilhelm (Commander of armed forces) - Convicted of all four Counts and sentenced to hang. He signed orders affecting military acts which would constitute "Crimes Against Humanity."

von Neurath, Constantin F. (Protector of Bohemia and Moravia) - Convicted of all four Counts and sentenced to 15 years of imprisonment. He signed orders calling for repressive measures including persecution of Jews and killing of students.

von Papen, Franz (Diplomat) - Acquitted.

Raeder, Erich (Commanding admiral of the German fleet) - Convicted of Counts 1, 2 and 3 and sentenced to life imprisonment.

von Ribbentrop, Joachim (Foreign Minister) - Convicted of all four Counts and sentenced to hang. He and the Foreign Ministry were closely involved with carrying out the deportation of Jews to extermination camps.

Rosenberg, Alfred (Minister of occupied Eastern territories and headed effort to collect cultural (e.g. art) resources) - Convicted of all four Counts and sentenced to hang. He presided over ruthless occupational system in the Eastern territories and was responsible for looting art treasures of Europe.

Sauckel, Hjalmar (Plenipotentiary for Labor) - Convicted of Counts 3 and 4 and sentenced to hang. He was responsible for forcing workers from the occupied territories to work in Germany.

Schacht, Hjalmar (Minister of Economics) - Acquitted.

Schirach, Baldur (Gauleiter of Vienna; formerly "Leader of Youth") - Convicted of Count 4 and sentenced to 20 years of imprisonment. He implemented a forced labor system and deported Jews.

Seyss-Inquart, Arthur (Austrian agent of the Nazis) - Convicted of all four Counts and sentenced to hang. Held responsible for police terror, forced labor and deportation of Jews.

Speer, Albert (Armaments Minister) - Convicted of Counts 3 and 4 and sentenced to 20 years of imprisonment. He called for labor quotas, which he knew would be filled with forced foreign labor.

Streicher, Julius (Propagandist) - Convicted of Count 4 and sentenced to hang. He was held responsible for advocating and encouraging the extermination of the Jews even though he knew about the activities in the death camps.

4. DISPOSITION AND OUTCOME OF THE NUREMBERG TRIAL

Defendant	Count 1 Common Plan	Count 2 Crimes vs. Peace	Count 3 War Crimes	Count 4 Crimes vs. Humanity	Sentence
Goering	Guilty	Guilty	Guilty	Guilty	Death[1]
Hess	Guilty	Guilty	Acquitted	Acquitted	Life Imprisonment[2]
Von Ribbentrop	Guilty	Guilty	Guilty	Guilty	Death
Gen. Keitel	Guilty	Guilty	Guilty	Guilty	Death
Kaltenbrunner	Acquitted	—	Guilty	Guilty	Death
Rosenberg	Guilty	Guilty	Guilty	Guilty	Death
Frank	Acquitted	—	Guilty	Guilty	Death
Frick	Acquitted	Guilty	Guilty	Guilty	Death
Streicher	Acquitted	—	—	Guilty	Death
Funk	Acquitted	Guilty	Guilty	Guilty	Life Imprisonment
Schacht	Acquitted	Acquitted	—	—	None[3]
Adm. Doenitz	Acquitted	Guilty	Guilty	—	Ten years
Adm. Raeder	Guilty	Guilty	Guilty	—	Life Imprisonment
Von Schirach	Acquitted	—	—	Guilty	Twenty years
Sauckel	Acquitted	Acquitted	Guilty	Guilty	Death
Gen. Jodl	Guilty	Guilty	Guilty	Guilty	Death
Von Papen	Acquitted	Acquitted	—	—	None[4]
Seyss-Inquart	Acquitted	Guilty	Guilty	Guilty	Death
Speer	Acquitted	Acquitted	Guilty	Guilty	Twenty years
Von Neurath	Guilty	Guilty	Guilty	Guilty	Fifteen years
Fritzsche	Acquitted	—	Acquitted	Acquitted	None[5]
Bormann	Acquitted	—	Guilty	Guilty	Death[6]
Gestapo				Criminal, with limitations	
SD				Criminal, with limitations	
Leadership Corps, Nazi Party				Criminal, with limitations	
SA				Not declared criminal	
Reich Cabinet				Not declared criminal	
General Staff and High Command				Not declared criminal	

1 Committed suicide after sentencing and before execution.
2 Soviet dissent from refusal to impose death sentence.
3 Soviet dissent.
4 Soviet dissent.
5 Soviet dissent.
6 Tried in absentia; if he is found, the penalty is subject to reduction by the Control Council.

589

5.   ALLIED CONTROL COUNCIL LAW No. 10 PUNISHMENT OF PERSONS GUILTY OF WAR CRIMES, CRIMES AGAINST PEACE AND AGAINST HUMANITY, 20 December 1945

OFFICIAL GAZETTE OF THE CONTROL COUNCIL FOR GERMANY, No. 3, Berlin, 31 January 1946. *Reprinted in* 1 Ferencz 488; 1 Friedman 908.

In order to give effect to the terms of the Moscow Declaration of 30 October 1943 and the London Agreement of 8 August 1945, and the Charter issued pursuant thereto and in order to establish a uniform legal basis in Germany for the prosecution of war criminals and other similar offenders, other than those dealt with by the International Military Tribunal, the Control Council enacts as follows:

Article I

The Moscow Declaration of 30 October 1943 "Concerning Responsibility of Hitlerites for Committed Atrocities" and the London Agreement of 8 August 1945 "Concerning Prosecution and Punishment of Major War Criminals of the European Axis" are made integral parts of this Law. Adherence to the provisions of the London Agreement by any of the United Nations, as provided for in Article V of that Agreement, shall not entitle such Nation to participate or interfere in the operation of the Law within the Control Council area of authority in Germany.

Article II

1.   Each of the following acts is recognized as a crime:

(a)   **Crimes against Peace**. Initiation of invasions of other countries and wars of aggression in violation of international laws and treaties, including but not limited to planning, preparation, initiation or waging a war of aggression, a war in violation of international treaties, agreements or assurances, or participation in a common plan or conspiracy for the accomplishment of any of the foregoing.

(b)   **War Crimes**. Atrocities or offences against persons or property, constituting violations of the laws or customs of war, including but not limited to, murder, ill treatment or deportation to slave labour or for any other purpose, of civilian population from occupied territory, murder or ill treatment of prisoners of war or persons on the seas, killing of hostages, plunder of public or private property, wanton destruction of cities, towns or villages, or devastation not justified by military necessity.

(c) **Crimes against Humanity**. Atrocities and offences, including but not limited to murder, extermination, enslavement, deportation, imprisonment, torture, rape, or other inhumane acts committed against any civilian population, or persecutions on political, racial or religious grounds whether or not in violation of the domestic laws of the country where perpetrated.

(d) Membership in categories of a criminal group or organization declared criminal by the International Military Tribunal.

2. Any person without regard to nationality or the capacity in which he acted, is deemed to have committed a crime as defined in paragraph 1 of this Article, if he was:

(a) a principal or;

(b) was an accessory to the commission of any such crime or ordered or abetted the same or;

(c) took a consenting part therein or;

(d) was connected with plans or enterprises involving its commission or;

(e) was a member of any organization or group connected with the commission of any such crime or

(f) with reference to paragraph 1(a), if he held a high political, civil or military (including General Staff) position in Germany or in one of its Allies, co-belligerents or satellites or held high position in the financial, industrial or economic life of any such country.

3. Any person found guilty of any of the Crimes above mentioned may upon conviction be punished as shall be determined by the tribunal to be just. Such punishment may consist of one or more of the following:

(a) Death.

(b) Imprisonment for life or a term of years, with or without hard labour.

(c) Fine, and imprisonment with or without hard labour, in lieu thereof.

(d) Forfeiture of property.

(e) Restitution of property wrongfully acquired.

(f) Deprivation of some or all civil rights.

4. Any property declared to be forfeited or the restitution of which is ordered by the Tribunal shall be delivered to the Control Council for Germany, which shall decide on its disposal.

(a) The official position of any person, whether as Head of State or as a responsible official in a Government Department, does not free him from responsibility for a crime or entitle him to mitigation of punishment.

(b) The Fact that any person acted pursuant to the order of his Government or of a superior does not free him from responsibility for a crime, but may be considered in mitigation.

5. In any trial or prosecution for a crime herein referred to, the accused shall not be entitled to the benefits of any statute of limitation in respect of the period from 30 January 1933 to 1 July 1945, nor shall any immunity, pardon or amnesty granted under the Nazi regime be admitted as a bar to trial or punishment.

Article III

1. Each occupying authority, within its Zone of occupation.

(a) shall have the right to cause persons within such Zones suspected of having committed a crime, including those charged with crime by one of the United Nations, to be arrested and shall take under control the property, real and personal, owned or controlled by the said persons, pending decisions as to its eventual disposition.

(b) shall report to the Legal Directorate the names of all suspected criminals, the reasons for and the places of their detention, if they are detained, and the names and location of witnesses.

(c) shall take appropriate measures to see that witnesses and evidence will be available when required.

(d) shall have the right to cause all persons so arrested and charged, and not delivered to another authority as herein provided, or released, to be brought to trial before an appropriate tribunal. Such tribunal may, in the case of crimes committed by persons of German citizenship or nationality against other persons of German citizenship or nationality, or stateless persons, be a German Court, if authorized by the occupying authorities.

2. The tribunal by which persons charged with offenses hereunder shall be tried and the rules and procedure thereof shall be determined or designated by each Zone Commander for his respective Zone. Nothing herein is intended to, or shall impair or limit the jurisdiction or power of any court or tribunal now or hereafter established in any Zone by the Commander thereof, or of the International Military Tribunal established by the London Agreement of 8 August 1945.

3. Persons wanted for trial by an International Military Tribunal will not be tried without the consent of the Committee of Chief Prosecutors. Each Zone Commander will deliver such persons who are within his Zone to that committee upon request and will make witnesses and evidence available to it.

4. Persons known to be wanted for trial in another Zone or outside Germany will not be tried prior to decision under Article IV unless the fact of their apprehension has been reported in accordance with Section 1(b) of this Article, three months have elapsed thereafter, and no request for delivery of the type contemplated by Article IV has been received by the Zone Commander concerned.

5. The execution of death sentences may be deferred by not to exceed one month after the sentence has become final when the Zone Commander concerned has reason to believe that the testimony of those under sentence would be of value in the investigation and trial of crimes within or without his Zone.

6. Each Zone Commander will cause such effect to be given to the judgments of courts of competent jurisdiction, with respect to the property taken under his control pursuant hereto, as he may deem proper in the interest of justice.

Article IV

1. When any person in a Zone in Germany is alleged to have committed a crime, as defined in Article II, in a country other than Germany or in another Zone, the government of that nation or the Commander of the latter Zone, as the case may be, may request the Commander of the Zone in which the person is located for his arrest and delivery for trial to the country or Zone in which the crime was committed. Such request for delivery shall be granted by the Commander receiving it unless he believes such person is wanted for trial or as a witness by an International Military Tribunal, or in Germany, or in a nation other than the one making the request, or the Commander is not

satisfied that delivery should be made, in any of which cases he shall have the right to forward the said request to the Legal Directorate of the Allied Control Authority. A similar procedure shall apply to witnesses, material exhibits and other forms of evidence.

2. The Legal Directorate shall consider all requests referred to it, and shall determine the same in accordance with the following principles, its determination to be communicated to the Zone Commander.

(a) A person wanted for trial or as a witness by an International Military Tribunal shall not be delivered for trial or required to give evidence outside Germany, as the case may be, except upon approval of the Committee of Chief Prosecutors acting under the London Agreement of 8 August 1945.

(b) A person wanted for trial by several authorities (other than an International Military Tribunal) shall be disposed of in accordance with the following priorities:

(1) If wanted for trial in the Zone in which he is, he should not be delivered unless arrangements are made for his return after trial elsewhere;

(2) If wanted for trial in a Zone other than that in which he is, he should be delivered to that Zone in preference to delivery outside Germany unless arrangements are made for his return to that Zone after trial elsewhere;

(3) If wanted for trial outside Germany by two or more of the United Nations, of one of which he is a citizen, that one should have priority;

(4) If wanted for trial outside Germany by several countries, not all of which are United Nations, United Nations should have priority;

(5) If wanted for trial outside Germany by two or more of the United Nations, then, subject to Article IV 2(b)(3) above, that which has the most serious charges against him, which are moreover supported by evidence, should have priority.

Article V

The delivery, under Article IV of this Law, of persons for trial shall be made on demands of the Governments or Zone Commanders in such a manner that the delivery of criminals to one jurisdiction will not become the means of defeating or unnecessarily delaying the carrying out of justice in another place. If within six months the delivered person has not been convicted by the Court of the Zone or country to which he has been delivered, then such person shall be returned upon demand of the Commander of the Zone where the person was located prior to delivery. Done at Berlin, 20 December 1945.

JOSEPH T. MCNARNY
General

B.L. MONTGOMERY
Field Marshal

L. KOELTZ
Général de Corps d'Armée

G. ZHUKOV
Marshal of the Soviet Union

6. MILITARY GOVERNMENT--GERMANY UNITED STATES ZONE ORDINANCE NO. 7, ORGANIZATION AND POWERS OF CERTAIN MILITARY TRIBUNALS, 18 October 1946

ARTICLE I

The purpose of this Ordinance is to provide for the establishment of military tribunals which shall have power to try and punish persons charged with offenses recognized as crimes in Article II of Control Council Law No. 10, including conspiracies to commit any such crimes. Nothing herein shall prejudice the jurisdiction or the powers of other courts established or which may be established for the trial of any such offenses.

ARTICLE II

(a) Pursuant to the powers of the Military Governor for the United States Zone of Occupation within Germany and further pursuant to the powers conferred upon the Zone Commander by Control Council Law No. 10 and Articles 10 and 11 of the Charter of the International Military Tribunal annexed to the London Agreement of 8 August 1945 certain tribunals to be known as "Military Tribunals" shall be established hereunder.

(b) Each such tribunal shall consist of three or more members to be designated by the Military Governor. One alternate member may be designated to any tribunal if deemed advisable by the Military Governor. Except as provided in subsection (c) of this Article, all members and alternates shall be lawyers who have been admitted to practice, for at least five years, in the highest courts of one of the United States or its territories or of the District of Columbia, or who have been admitted to practice in the United States Supreme Court.

(c) The Military Governor may in his discretion enter into an agreement with one or more other zone commanders of the member nations of the Allied Control Authority providing for the joint trial of any case or cases. In such cases the tribunals shall consist of three or more members as may be provided in the agreement. In such cases the tribunals may include properly qualified lawyers designated by the other member nations.

(d) The Military Governor shall designate one of the members of the tribunal to serve as the presiding judge.

(e) Neither the tribunals nor the members of the tribunals or the alternates may be challenged by the prosecution or by the defendants or their counsel.

(f) In case of illness of any member of a tribunal or his incapacity for some other reason, the alternate, if one has been designated, shall take his place as a member in the pending trial. Members may be replaced by reasons of health or for other good reasons, except that no replacement of a member may take place, during a trial, other than by the alternate. If no alternate has been designated, the trial shall be continued to conclusion by the remaining members.

(g) The presence of three members of the tribunal or of two members when authorized pursuant to subsection (f) *supra* shall be necessary to constitute a quorum. In the case of tribunals designated under (c) above the agreement shall determine the requirements for a quorum.

(h) Decisions and judgments, including convictions and sentences, shall be by majority vote of the members. If the votes of the members are equally divided, the presiding member shall declare a mistrial.

ARTICLE III

(a) Charges against persons to be tried in the tribunals established hereunder shall originate in the Office of the Chief of Counsel for War Crimes, appointed by the Military Governor pursuant to paragraph 3 of the Executive Order Numbered 9679 of the President of the United States dated 16 January 1946. The Chief of Counsel for War Crimes shall determine the persons to be tried by the tribunals and he or his designated representative shall file the indictments with the Secretary General of the tribunals (see Article XIV, *infra*) and shall conduct the prosecution.

(b) The Chief of Counsel for War Crimes, when in his judgment it is advisable, may invite one or more United Nations to designate representatives to participate in the prosecution of any case.

ARTICLE IV

In order to ensure fair trial for the defendants, the following procedure shall be followed:

(a) A defendant shall be furnished, at a reasonable time before his trial, a copy of the indictment and of all documents lodged with the indictment, translated into a language which he understands. The indictment shall state the charges plainly, concisely and with sufficient particulars to inform defendant of the offenses charged.

(b) The trial shall be conducted in, or translated into, a language which the defendant understands.

(c) A defendant shall have the right to be represented by counsel of his own selection, provided such counsel shall be a person qualified under existing regulations to conduct cases before the courts of defendant's country, or any other person who may be specially authorized by the tribunal. The tribunal shall appoint qualified counsel to represent a defendant who is not represented by counsel of his own selection.

(d) Every defendant shall be entitled to be present at his trial except that a defendant may be proceeded against during temporary absences if in the opinion of the tribunal defendant's interests will not thereby be impaired, and except further as provided in Article VI (c). The tribunal may also proceed in the absence of any defendant who has applied for and has been granted permission to be absent.

(e) A defendant shall have the right through his counsel to present evidence at the trial in support of his defense, and to cross-examine any witness called by the prosecution.

(f) A defendant may apply in writing to the tribunal for the production of witnesses or of documents. The application shall state where the witness or document is thought to be located and shall also state the facts to be proved by the witness or the document and the relevancy of such facts to the defense. If the tribunal grants the application, the defendant shall be given such aid in obtaining production of evidence as the tribunal may order.

ARTICLE V

The tribunals shall have the power:

(a) to summon witnesses to the trial, to require their attendance and testimony and to put questions to them;

(b) to interrogate any defendant who takes the stand to testify in his own behalf, or who is called to testify regarding any other defendant;

(c) to require the production of documents and other evidentiary material;

(d) to administer oaths;

(e) to appoint officers for the carrying out of any task designated by the tribunals including the taking of evidence on commission;

(f) to adopt rules of procedure not inconsistent with this Ordinance. Such rules shall be adopted, and from time to time as necessary, revised by the members of the tribunal or by the committee of presiding judges as provided in Article XIII.

ARTICLE VI

The tribunals shall:

(a) confine the trial strictly to an expeditious hearing of the issues raised by the charges;

(b) take strict measures to prevent any action which will cause unreasonable delay, and rule out irrelevant issues and statements of any kind whatsoever;

(c) deal summarily with any contumacy, imposing appropriate punishment, including the exclusion of any defendant or his counsel from some or all further proceedings, but without prejudice to the determination of the charges.

ARTICLE VII

The tribunals shall not be bound by technical rules of evidence. They shall adopt and apply to the greatest possible extent expeditious and non-technical procedure, and shall admit any evidence which they deem to have probative value. Without limiting the foregoing general rules, the following shall be deemed admissible if they appear to the tribunal to contain information of probative value relating to the charges: affidavits, depositions, interrogations, and other statements, diaries, letters, the records, findings, statements and judgments of the military tribunals and the reviewing and confirming authorities of any of the United Nations, and copies of any document or other secondary evidence of the contents of any document, if the original is not readily available or cannot be produced without delay. The tribunal shall afford the opposing party such opportunity to question the authenticity or probative value of such evidence as in the opinion of the tribunal the ends of justice require.

ARTICLE VIII

The tribunals may require that they be informed of the nature of any evidence before it is offered so that they may rules upon the relevance thereof.

ARTICLE IX

The tribunals shall not require proof of facts of common knowledge but shall take judicial notice thereof. They shall also take judicial notice of official governmental documents and reports of any of the United Nations, including the acts and documents of the committees set up in the various Allied countries for the investigation of war crimes,and the records and findings of military or other tribunals of any of the United Nations.

ARTICLE X

The determinations of the International Military Tribunal in the judgment in Case No. 1 that invasions, aggressive acts, aggressive wars, crimes, atrocities or inhumane acts were planned or occurred, shall be binding on the tribunals established hereunder and shall not be questioned except insofar as the participation therein or knowledge thereof by any particular person may be concerned. Statements of the International Military Tribunal in the judgment in Case No. 1 constitute proof of the facts stated, in the absence of substantial new evidence to the contrary.

ARTICLE XI

The proceedings at the trial shall take the following course:

(a) The tribunal shall inquire of each defendant whether he has received and had an opportunity to read the indictment against him and whether he pleads "guilty" or "not guilty."

(b) The prosecution may make an opening statement.

(c) The prosecution shall produce its evidence subject to the cross examination of its witnesses.

(d) The defense may make an opening statement.

(e) The defense shall produce its evidence subject to the cross examination of its witnesses.

(f) Such rebutting evidence as may be held by the tribunal to be material may be produced by either the prosecution or the defense.

(g) The defense shall address the court.

(h) The prosecution shall address the court.

(i) Each defendant may make a statement to the tribunal.

(j) The tribunal shall deliver judgement and pronounce sentence.

ARTICLE XII

A Central Secretariat to assist the tribunals to be appointed hereunder shall be established as soon as practicable. The main office of the Secretariat shall be located in Nurnberg. The Secretariat shall consist of a Secretary General and such assistant secretaries, military officers, clerks, interpreters and other personnel as may be necessary.

ARTICLE XIII

The Secretary General shall be appointed by the Military Governor and shall organize and direct the work of the Secretariat. He shall be subject to the supervision of the members of the tribunals, except that when at least three tribunals shall be functioning, the presiding judges of the several tribunals may form the supervisory committee.

ARTICLE XIV

The Secretariat shall:

(a) Be responsible for the administrative and supply needs of the Secretariat and of the several tribunals.

(b) Receive all documents addressed to tribunals.

(c) Prepare and recommend uniform rules of procedure, not inconsistent with the provisions of this Ordinance.

(d) Secure such information for the tribunals as may be needed for the approval or appointment of defense counsel.

(e) Serve as liaison between the prosecution and defense counsel.

(f) Arrange for aid to be given defendants and the prosecution in obtaining production of witnesses or evidence as authorized by the tribunals.

(g) Be responsible for the preparation of the records of the proceedings before the tribunals.

(h) Provide the necessary clerical, reporting and interpretative services to the tribunals and its members, and perform such other duties as may be required for the efficient conduct of the proceedings before the tribunals, or as may be requested by any of the tribunals.

ARTICLE XV

The judgments of the tribunals as to the guilt or the innocence of any defendant shall give the reasons on which they are based and shall be final and not subject to review. The sentences imposed may be subject to review as provided in Article XVII, *infra*.

ARTICLE XVI

The tribunal shall have the right to impose upon the defendant, upon conviction, such punishment as shall be determined by the tribunal to be just, which may consist of one or more of the penalties provided in Article II, Section 3, of Control Council Law No. 10.

ARTICLE XVII

(a) Except as provided in (b) *infra*, the record of each case shall be forwarded to the Military Governor who shall have the power to mitigate, reduce or otherwise alter the sentence imposed by the tribunal, but may not increase the severity thereof.

(b) In cases tried before tribunals authorized by Article II (c), the sentence shall be reviewed jointly by the zone commanders of the nations involved, who may mitigate, reduce or otherwise alter the sentence by majority vote, but may not increase the severity thereof. If only two nations are represented, the sentence may be altered only by the consent of both zone commanders.

ARTICLE XVIII

No sentence of death shall be carried into execution unless and until confirmed in writing by the Military Governor. In accordance with Article III, Section 5, of Law No.

10, execution of the death sentence may be deferred by not to exceed one month after such confirmation if there is reason to believe that the testimony of the convicted person may be of value in the investigation and trial of other crimes.

ARTICLE XIX

Upon the pronouncement of a death sentence by a tribunal established thereunder and pending confirmation thereof, the condemned will be remanded to the prison or place where he was confined and there be segregated from the other inmates, or be transferred to a more appropriate place of confinement.

ARTICLE XX

Upon the confirmation of a sentence of death the Military Governor will issue the necessary orders for carrying out the execution.

ARTICLE XXI

Where sentence of confinement for a term of years has been imposed the condemned shall be confined in the manner directed by the tribunal imposing sentence. The place of confinement may be changed from time to time by the Military Governor.

ARTICLE XXII

Any property declared to be forfeited or the restitution of which is ordered by a tribunal shall be delivered to the Military Governor, for disposal in accordance with Control Council Law No. 10, Article II (3).

ARTICLE XXIII

Any of the duties and functions of the Military Governor provided for herein may be delegated to the Deputy Military Governor. Any of the duties and functions of the Zone Commander provided for herein may be exercised by and in the name of the Military Governor and may be delegated to the Deputy Military Governor.

602

AMENDMENT TO MILITARY GOVERNMENT ORDINANCE NO. 7 OF 18 OCTOBER 1946, ORGANIZATION AND POWERS OF CERTAIN MILITARY TRIBUNALS By ORDINANCE NO. 11

ARTICLE I

Article V of Ordinance No. 7 is amended by adding thereto a new subdivision to be designated "(g)," reading as follows:

"(g) The presiding judges, and, when established, the supervisory committee of presiding judges provided in Article XIII shall assign the cases brought by the Chief of Counsel for War Crimes to the various Military Tribunals for trial."

ARTICLE II

Ordinance No. 7 is amended by adding thereto a new article following Article V to be designated Article V-B, reading as follows:

"(a) A joint session of the Military Tribunals may be called by any of the presiding judges thereof or upon motion, addressed to each of the Tribunals, of the Chief of Counsel for War Crimes or of counsel for any defendant whose interests are affected, to hear argument upon and to review any interlocutory ruling by any of the Military Tribunals on a fundamental or important legal question either substantive or procedural, which ruling is in conflict with or is inconsistent with a prior ruling of another of the Military Tribunals.

"(b) A joint session of the Military Tribunals may be called in the same manner as provided in subsection (a) of this Article to hear argument upon and to review conflicting or inconsistent final rulings contained in the decisions or judgments of any of the Military Tribunals on a fundamental or important legal question, either substantive or procedural. Any motion with respect to such final ruling shall be filed within ten (10) days following the issuance of decision or judgment.

"(c) Decisions by joint sessions of the Military Tribunals, unless thereafter altered in another joint session, shall be binding upon all the Military Tribunals. In the case of the review of final rulings by joint sessions, the judgments reviewed may be confirmed or remanded for action consistent with the joint decision.

"(d) The presence of a majority of the members of each Military Tribunal then constituted is required to constitute a quorum.

"(e) The members of the Military Tribunals shall, before any joint session begins, agree among themselves upon the selection from their number of a member to preside over the joint session.

"(f) Decisions shall be by majority vote of the members. If the votes of the members are equally divided, the vote of the member presiding over the session shall be decisive."

ARTICLE III

Subdivisions (g) and (h) of Article XI of Ordinance No. 7 are deleted; subdivision (i) is relettered "(h)"; subdivision (j) is relettered "(i)"; and a new subdivision, to be designated "(g)," is added, reading as follows:

"(g) The prosecution and defense shall address the court in such order as the Tribunal may determine."

This Ordinance becomes effective 17 February 1947.

7. PROCLAMATION BY THE SUPREME COMMANDER FOR THE ALLIED POWERS, Tokyo, 19 January 1946

T.I.A.S. 1589. *Reprinted in* 4 Bevans 20; 1 B. FERENCZ, DEFINING INTERNATIONAL AGGRESSION 522 (1975); Friedman 894.

WHEREAS, the United States and the Nations allied therewith in opposing the illegal wars of aggression of the Axis Nations, have from time to time made declarations of their intentions that war criminals should be brought to justice;

Whereas, the Governments of the Allied Powers at war with Japan on the 26th July 1945 at Potsdam, declared as one of the terms of surrender that stern justice shall be meted out to all war criminals including those who have visited cruelties upon our prisoners;

Whereas, by the Instrument of Surrender of Japan executed at Tokyo Bay, Japan, on the 2nd September 1945, the signatories for Japan, by command of and in behalf of the Emperor and the Japanese government, accepted the terms set forth in such Declaration at Potsdam;

DOCUMENTS SECTION

Whereas, by such Instrument of Surrender, the authority of the Emperor and the Japanese Government to rule the state of Japan is made subject to the Supreme Commander for the Allied Powers, who is authorized to take such steps as he deems proper to effectuate the terms of surrender;

Whereas, the undersigned has been designated by the Allied Powers as Supreme Commander for the Allied Powers to carry into effect the general surrender of the Japanese armed forces;

Whereas, the Governments of the United States, Great Britain and Russia at the Moscow Conference, 26th December 1945, having considered the effectuation by Japan of the Terms of Surrender, with the concurrence of China have agreed that the Supreme Commander shall issue all Orders for the implementation of the Terms of Surrender.

Now, therefore, I, Douglas MacArthur, as Supreme Commander for the Allied Powers, by virtue of the authority so conferred upon me, in order to implement the Term of Surrender which requires the meting out of stern justice to war criminals, do order and provide as follows:

Article 1: There shall be established an International Military Tribunal for the Far East for the trial of those persons charged individually, or as members of organizations, or in both capacities, with offenses which include crimes against peace.

Article 2: The Constitution, jurisdiction and functions of this Tribunal are those set forth in the Charter of the International Military Tribunal for the Far East, approved by me this day.

Article 3:   Nothing in this Order shall prejudice the jurisdiction of any other international, national or occupation court, commission or other tribunal established or to be established in Japan or in any territory of a United Nation with which Japan has been at war, for the trial of war criminals.

Given under my hand at Tokyo, this 19th of January, 1946.
Douglas MacArthur
General of the Army,
United States Army Supreme Commander
for the Allied Powers

8. CHARTER OF THE INTERNATIONAL MILITARY TRIBUNAL FOR THE FAR EAST, Tokyo, 19 January 1946

T.I.A.S. 1589 *Reprinted in* 1 B. FERENCZ, DEFINING INTERNATIONAL AGGRESSION 523; 1 Friedman 895.

Section I

CONSTITUTION OF TRIBUNAL

Article 1: Tribunal Established. The International Military Tribunal for the Far East is hereby established for the just and prompt trial and punishment of the major war criminals in the Far East. The permanent seat of the Tribunal is in Tokyo.

Article 2: Members. The tribunal shall consist of not less than six members nor more than eleven members, appointed by the Supreme Commander for the Allied Powers from the names submitted by the Signatories to the Instrument of Surrender, India, and the Commonwealth of the Philippines.

Article 3: Officers and Secretariat.
a. *President.* The Supreme Commander for the Allied Powers shall appoint a Member to be President of the Tribunal.
b. *Secretariat.*
  (1) The Secretariat of the Tribunal shall be composed of a General Secretary to be appointed by the Supreme Commander for the Allied Powers and such assistant secretaries, clerks, interpreters, and other personnel as may be necessary.
  (2) The General Secretary shall organize and direct the work of the Secretariat.
  (3) The Secretariat shall receive all documents addressed to the Tribunal, maintain the records of the Tribunal, provide necessary clerical services to the Tribunal and its members, and perform such other duties as may be designated by the Tribunal.

Article 4: Convening and Quorum, Voting, and Absence.
a. *Convening and Quorum.* When as many as six members of the Tribunal are present, they may convene the Tribunal in formal session. The presence of a majority of all members shall be necessary to constitute a quorum.

606

b.   *Voting*. All decisions and judgments of this Tribunal, including convictions and sentences, shall be by a majority vote of those members of the Tribunal present. In case the votes are evenly divided, the vote of the President shall be decisive.

c.   *Absence*. If a member at any time is absent and afterwards is able to be present, he shall take part in all subsequent proceedings; unless he declares in open court that he is disqualified by reason of insufficient familiarity with the proceedings which took place in his absence.

Section II

JURISDICTION AND GENERAL PROVISIONS

Article 5: Jurisdiction Over Persons and Offenses. The Tribunal shall have the power to try and punish Far Eastern war criminals who as individuals or as members of organizations are charged with offenses which include Crimes against Peace. The following acts, or any of them, are crimes coming within the jurisdiction of the Tribunal for which there shall be individual responsibility:

a.   *Crimes against Peace*: Namely, the planning, preparation, initiation or waging of a declared or undeclared war of aggression, or a war in violation of international law, treaties, agreements or assurances, or participation in a common plan or conspiracy for the accomplishment of any of the foregoing;

b.   *Conventional War Crimes*: Namely, violations of the laws or customs of war;

c.   *Crimes against Humanity*:   Namely, murder, extermination, enslavement, deportation, and other inhumane acts committed before or during the war, or persecutions on political or racial grounds in execution of or in connection with any crime within the jurisdiction of the Tribunal, whether or not in violation of the domestic law of the country where perpetrated.   Leaders, organizers, instigators and accomplices participating in the formulation or execution of a common plan or conspiracy to commit any of the foregoing crimes are responsible for all acts performed by any person in execution of such plan.

Article 6: Responsibility of Accused. Neither the official position, at any time, of an accused, nor the fact that an accused acted pursuant to order of his government or of a superior shall, of itself, be sufficient to free such accused from responsibility for any crime with which he is charged, but such circumstances may be considered in mitigation of punishment if the Tribunal determines that justice so requires.

Article 7: Rules of Procedure. The Tribunal may draft and amend rules of procedure consistent with the fundamental provisions of this Charter.

Article 8: Counsel.

a. *Chief of Counsel.* The Chief of Counsel designated by the Supreme Commander for the Allied Powers is responsible for the investigation and prosecution of charges against war criminals within the jurisdiction of this Tribunal and will render such legal assistance to the Supreme Commander as is appropriate.

b. *Associate Counsel.* Any United Nation with which Japan has been at war may appoint an Associate Counsel to assist the Chief of Counsel.

Section III

FAIR TRIAL FOR ACCUSED

Article 9: Procedure for Fair Trial. In order to insure a fair trial for the accused the following procedure shall be followed:

a. *Indictment.* The indictment shall consist of a plain, concise, and adequate statement of each offense charged. Each accused shall be furnished, in adequate time for defense, a copy of the indictment, including any amendment, and of this Charter, in a language understood by the accused.

b. *Language.* The trial and related proceedings shall be conducted in English and in the language of the accused. Translations of documents and other papers shall be provided as needed and requested.

c. *Counsel for Accused.* Each accused shall have the right to be represented by counsel of his own selection, subject to the disapproval of such counsel at any time by the Tribunal. The accused shall file with the General Secretary of the Tribunal the name of his counsel. If an accused is not represented by counsel and in open court requests the appointment of counsel, the Tribunal shall designate counsel for him. In the absence of such request the Tribunal may appoint counsel for an accused if in its judgment such appointment is necessary to provide for a fair trial.

d. *Evidence for Defense.* An accused shall have the right, through himself or through his counsel (but not through both), to conduct his defense, including the right to examine any witness, subject to such reasonable restrictions as the Tribunal may determine.

e. *Production of Evidence for the Defense.* An accused may apply in writing to the Tribunal for the production of witnesses or of documents. The application shall state where the witness or document is thought to be located. It shall also state the facts proposed to be proved by the witness or the document and the relevancy of such facts to the defense. If the Tribunal grants the application the Tribunal shall be given such aid in obtaining production of the evidence as the circumstances require.

Article 10: Applications and Motions before Trial. All motions, applications, or other requests addressed to the Tribunal prior to the commencement of trial shall be made in writing and filed with the General Secretary of the Tribunal for action by the Tribunal.

Section IV

POWERS OF TRIBUNAL AND CONDUCT OF TRIAL

Article 11: Powers. The Tribunal shall have the power:

a. To summon witnesses to the trial, to require them to attend and testify, and to question them.
b. To interrogate each accused and to permit comment on his refusal to answer any question.
c. To require the production of documents and other evidentiary material.
d. To require of each witness an oath, affirmation, or such declaration as is customary in the country of the witness, and to administer oaths.
e. To appoint officers for the carrying out of any task designated by the Tribunal, including the power to have evidence taken on commission.

Article 12: Conduct of Trial. The Tribunal shall:

a. Confine the trial strictly to an expeditious hearing of the issues raised by the charges.
b. Take strict measures to prevent any action which would cause any unreasonable delay and rule out irrelevant issues and statements of any kind whatsoever.
c. Provide for the maintenance of order at the trial and deal summarily with any contumacy, imposing appropriate punishment, including exclusion of any accused or his counsel from some or all further proceedings, but without prejudice to the determination of the charges.

d.   Determine the mental and physical capacity of any accused to proceed to trial.

Article 13: Evidence.

a.   *Admissibility.* The Tribunal shall not be bound by technical rules of evidence. It shall adopt and apply to the greatest possible extent expeditious and non-technical procedure, and shall admit any evidence which it deems to have probative value. All purported admissions or statements of the accused are admissible.

b.   *Relevance.* The Tribunal may require to be informed of the nature of any evidence before it is offered in order to rule upon the relevance.

c.   *Specific evidence admissible.* In particular, and without limiting in any way the scope of the foregoing general rules, the following evidence may be admitted:

(1) A document, regardless of its security classification and without proof of its issuance or signature, which appears to the Tribunal to have been signed or issued by any officer, department, agency or member of the armed forces of any government.

(2) A report which appears to the Tribunal to have been signed or issued by the International Red Cross or a member thereof, or by a doctor of medicine or any medical service personnel, or by an investigator or intelligence officer, or by any other person who appears to the Tribunal to have personal knowledge of the matters contained in the report.

(3) An affidavit, deposition or other signed statement.

(4) A diary, letter or other document, including sworn or unsworn statements, which appear to the Tribunal to contain information relating to the charge.

(5) A copy of a document or other secondary evidence of its contents, if the original is not immediately available.

d.   *Judicial Notice.* The Tribunal shall neither require proof of facts of common knowledge, nor of the authenticity of official government documents and reports of any nation or of the proceedings, records, and findings of military or other agencies of any of the United Nations.

e.   *Records, Exhibits, and Documents.* The transcript of the proceedings, and exhibits and documents submitted to the Tribunal, will be filed with the General Secretary of the Tribunal and will constitute part of the Record.

Article 14: Place of Trial. The first trial will be held in Tokyo, and any subsequent trials will be held at such places as the Tribunal decides.

Article 15: Course of Trial Proceedings. The proceedings of the Trial will take the following course:

a.   The indictment will be read in court unless the reading is waived by all accused.

b.   The Tribunal will ask each accused whether he pleads "guilty" or "not guilty."

c.   The prosecution and each accused (by counsel only, if represented) may make a concise opening statement.

d.   The prosecution and defense may offer evidence, and the admissibility of the same shall be determined by the Tribunal.

e.   The prosecution and each accused (by counsel only, if represented) may examine each witness and each accused who gives testimony.

f.   Accused (by counsel only, if represented) may address the Tribunal.

g.   The prosecution may address the Tribunal.

h.   The Tribunal will deliver judgment and pronounce sentence.

Section V

JUDGMENT AND SENTENCE

Article 16: Penalty. The Tribunal shall have the power to impose upon an accused, on conviction, death, or such other punishment as shall be determined by it to be just.

Article 17: Judgment and Review. The judgment will be announced in open court and will give the reasons on which it is based. The record of the trial will be transmitted directly to the Supreme Commander for the Allied Powers for his action. Sentence will be carried out in accordance with the Order of the Supreme Commander for the Allied Powers, who may at any time reduce or otherwise alter the sentence, except to increase its severity.

By command of General MacArthur:

Richard J. Marshall
Major General, General Staff Corps,
Chief of Staff

9.   INTERNATIONAL MILITARY TRIBUNAL FOR THE FAR EAST, EXCERPTS FROM THE JUDGMENT IN THE TOKYO WAR CRIMES TRIAL, 12 November 1948

1 B. FERENCZ, DEFINING INTERNATIONAL AGGRESSION 539 (2 vols. 1975).

THE UNITED STATES OF AMERICA, THE REPUBLIC OF CHINA, THE UNITED KINGDOM OF GREAT BRITAIN AND NORTHERN IRELAND, THE UNION OF SOVIET SOCIALIST REPUBLICS, THE COMMONWEALTH OF AUSTRALIA, CANADA, THE REPUBLIC OF FRANCE, THE KINGDOM OF THE NETHERLANDS, NEW ZEALAND, INDIA, AND THE COMMONWEALTH OF THE PHILIPPINES

AGAINST

ARAKI, Sadao	KIDO, Koichi	OSHIMA, Hiroshi
DOHIHARA, Kenji	KIMURA, Heitaro	SATO, Kenryo
HASHIMOTO, Kingoro	KOISO, Kuniaki	SHIGEMITSU, Mamoru
HATA, Shunroku	MATSUI, Iwane	SHIMADA, Shigetaro
HIRANUMA, Kiichiro	MATSUOKA, Yosuke	SHIRATORI, Toshio
HIROTA, Koki	MINAMI, Jiro	SUZUKI, Teiichi
HOSHINO, Naoki	MUTO, Akira	TOGO, Shigenori
ITAGAKI, Seishiro	NAGANO, Osami	TOJO, Hideki
KAYA, Okinori	OKA, Takasumi	UMEZU, Yoshijiro
OKAWA, Shumei		

CHAPTER I. ESTABLISHMENT AND PROCEEDINGS OF THE TRIBUNAL

The Tribunal was established in virtue of and to implement the Cairo Declaration of the lst of December, 1943, the Declaration of Potsdam of the 26th of July, 1945, the Instrument of Surrender of the 2nd of September, 1945, and the Moscow Conference of the 26 of December, 1945....

The Declaration of Potsdam ... was made by the President of the United States of America, the President of the National Government of the Republic of China, and the Prime Minister of Great Britain and later adhered to by the Union of Soviet Socialist Republics. Its principal relevant provisions are:

"Japan shall be given an opportunity to end this war...

"There must be eliminated for all time the authority and influence of those who have deceived and misled the people of Japan into embarking on world conquest, for we insist that a new order of peace, security and justice will be impossible until irresponsible militarism is driven from the world ....

"We do not intend that the Japanese people shall be enslaved as a race or destroyed as a nation, but stern justice shall be meted out to all war criminals including those who have visited cruelties upon our prisoners."

[Twenty-eight Japanese were indicted, all but one pleaded guilty--seven were sentenced to death, 16 imprisoned for life, 2 prison sentences--Emperor Hirohito was not indicted, nor was any industrialist. Paraphrases of judgment.]

(a) *Jurisdiction of the Tribunal*

In our opinion the law of the Charter is decisive and binding on the Tribunal. This is a special tribunal set up by the Supreme Commander under authority conferred on him by the Allied Powers. It derives its jurisdiction from the Charter. In this trial its members have no jurisdiction except such as is to be found in the Charter. The Order of the Supreme Commander, which appointed the members of the Tribunal, states: "The responsibilities, powers, and duties of the members of the Tribunal are set forth in the Charter thereof .... " In the result, the members of the Tribunal, being otherwise wholly without power in respect to the trial of the accused, have been empowered by the documents, which constituted the Tribunal and appointed them as members, to try the accused but subject always to the duty and responsibility of applying to the trial the law set forth in the Charter.

The foregoing expression of opinion is not to be taken as supporting the view, if such view be held, that the Allied Powers or any victor nations have the right under international law in providing for the trial and punishment of war criminals to enact or promulgate laws or vest in their tribunals powers in conflicts with recognized international law or rules of principles thereof. In the exercise of their right to create tribunals for such a purpose and in conferring powers upon such tribunals belligerent powers may act only within the limits of international law.

The substantial grounds of the defence challenge to the jurisdiction of the Tribunal to hear and adjudicate upon the charges contained in the Indictment are the following:

613

(1) The Allied Powers acting through the Supreme Commander have no authority to include in the Charter of the Tribunal and to designate as justiciable "Crimes against Peace" (Article 5(a));
(2) Aggressive war is not per se illegal and the Pact of Paris of 1928 renouncing war as an instrument of national policy does not enlarge the meaning of war crimes nor constitute war a crime;
(3) War is the act of a nation for which there is no individual responsibility under international law;
(4) The provisions of the Charter are "ex post facto" legislation and therefore illegal;
(5) The Instrument of Surrender which provides that the Declaration of Potsdam will be given effect imposes the condition that Conventional War Crimes that are recognized by international law at the date of the Declaration (26 July 1945) would be the only crimes prosecuted;
(6) Killings in the course of belligerent operations except in so far as they constitute violations of the rules of warfare or the laws and customs of war are the normal incidents of war and are not murder;
(7) Several of the accused being prisoners of war are triable by court martial as provided by the Geneva Convention of 1929 and not by this Tribunal.

Since the law of the Charter is decisive and binding upon it, this Tribunal is formally bound to reject the first four of the above seven contentions advanced for the Defence but in view of the great importance of the questions of law involved the Tribunal will record its opinion on these questions.

After this Tribunal had in May 1946 dismissed the defence motions and upheld the validity of its Charter and its jurisdiction thereunder, stating that the reasons for this decision would be given later, the International Military Tribunal sitting at Nuremberg delivered its verdicts on the first of October 1946 ...

(b) *Responsibility for War Crimes Against Prisoners*

Prisoners taken in war and civilian internees are in the power of the Government which captures them. This was not always the case. For the last two centuries, however, this position has been recognized and the customary law to this effect was formally embodied in the Hague Convention No. IV in 1907 and repeated in the Geneva Prisoners of War Convention of 1929. Responsibility for the care of prisoners of war and of civilian internees (all of whom we will refer to as "prisoners") rests therefore with the

Government having them in possession. This responsibility is not limited to the duty of mere maintenance but extends to the prevention of mistreatment. In particular, acts of inhumanity to prisoners which are forbidden by the customary law of nations as well as by conventions are to be prevented by the Government having responsibility for the prisoners.

In the discharge of these duties to prisoners Governments must have resort to persons. Indeed the Governments responsible, in this sense, are those persons who direct and control the functions of Government. In this case and in the above regard we are concerned with the members of the Japanese Cabinet. The duty to prisoners is not a meaningless obligation cast upon a political abstraction. It is a specific duty to be performed in the first case by those persons who constitute the Government. In the multitude of duties and tasks involved in modern government, there is of necessity an elaborate system of subdivision and delegation of duties. In the case of the duty of Governments to prisoners held by them in time of war those persons who constitute the Government have the principal and continuing responsibility for their prisoners, even though they delegate the duties of maintenance and protection to others.

In general the responsibility for prisoners held by Japan may be stated to have rested upon:
(1) Members of the Government;
(2) Military or Naval Officers in command of formations having prisoners in their possession;
(3) Officials in those departments which were concerned with the well-being of prisoners;
(4) Officials, whether civilian, military, or naval, having direct and immediate control of prisoners.

It is the duty of all those on whom responsibility rests to secure proper treatment of prisoners and to prevent their ill-treatment by establishing and securing the continuous and efficient working of a system appropriate for these purposes. Such persons fail in this duty and become responsible for ill-treatment of prisoners if:
(1) They fail to establish such a system.
(2) If having established such a system, they fail to secure its continued and efficient working.

Each of such persons has a duty to ascertain that the system is working and if he neglects to do so he is responsible. He does not discharge his duty by merely instituting an appropriate system and thereafter neglecting to learn of its application. An Army Commander or a Minister of War, for example, must be at the same pains to ensure obedience to his orders in this respect as he would in respect of other orders he has issued on matters of the first importance.

Nevertheless, such persons are not responsible if a proper system and its continuous efficient functioning be provided for and conventional war crimes be committed unless:
(1) They had knowledge that such crimes were being committed, and having such knowledge they failed to take such steps as were within their power to prevent the commission of such crimes in the future, or
(2) They are at fault in having failed to acquire such knowledge.

If such a person had, or should, but for negligence or supineness, have had such knowledge he is not excused for inaction if his Office required or permitted him to take any action to prevent such crimes. On the other hand, it is not enough for the exculpation of a person, otherwise responsible, for him to show that he accepted assurances from others more directly associated with the control of the prisoners if having regard to the position of those others, to the frequency of reports of such crimes, or to any other circumstances he should have been put upon further enquiry as to whether those assurances were true or untrue. That crimes are notorious, numerous and widespread as to time and place are matters to be considered in imputing knowledge.

A member of a Cabinet which collectively, as one of the principal organs of the Government, is responsible for the care of prisoners is not absolved from responsibility if, having knowledge of the commission of the crimes in the sense already discussed, and omitting or failing to secure the taking of measures to prevent the commission of such crimes in the future, he elects to continue as a member of the Cabinet. This is the position even though the Department of which he has the charge is not directly concerned with the care of prisoners. A Cabinet member may resign. If he has knowledge of ill-treatment of prisoners, is powerless to prevent future ill-treatment, but elects to remain in the Cabinet thereby continuing to participate in its collective responsibility for protection of prisoners he willingly assumes responsibility for any ill-treatment in the future.

Army or Navy Commanders can, by order, secure proper treatment and prevent ill-treatment of prisoners. So can Ministers of War and of the Navy. If crimes are committed against prisoners under their control, of the likely occurrence of which they had, or should have had, knowledge in advance, they are responsible for those crimes. If, for example, it be shown that within the units under his command conventional war crimes have been committed of which he knew or should have known, a commander who takes no adequate steps to prevent the occurrence of such crimes in the future will be responsible for such future crimes.

Departmental Officials having knowledge of ill-treatment of prisoners are not responsible by reason of their failure to resign; but if their functions included the administration of the system of protection of prisoners and if they had or should have had knowledge of crimes and did nothing effective, to the extent of their powers, to prevent their occurrence in the future then they are responsible for such future crimes ....

(c) *The Indictment*

Under the heading of "Crimes Against Peace" the Charter names five separate crimes. These are planning, preparation, initiation and waging aggressive war or a war in violation of international law, treaties, agreements or assurances; to these four is added the further crime of participation in a common plan or conspiracy for the accomplishment of any of the foregoing. The Indictment was based upon the Charter and all the above crimes were charged in addition to further charges founded upon other provisions of the Charter.

A conspiracy to wage aggressive or unlawful war arises when two or more persons enter into an agreement to commit that crime. Thereafter, in furtherance of the conspiracy, follows planning and preparing for such war. (p. 32) Those who participate at this stage may be either original conspirators or later adherents. If the latter adopt the purpose of the conspiracy and plan and prepare for its fulfillment they become conspirators. For this reason, as all the accused are charged with the conspiracies, we do not consider it necessary in respect of those we may find guilty of conspiracy to enter convictions also for planning and preparing. In other words, although we do not question the validity of the charges we do not think it necessary in respect of any defendants who may be found guilty of conspiracy to take into consideration or to enter convictions upon Counts 6 to 17 inclusive.

A similar position arises in connection with the counts of initiating and waging aggressive war. Although initiating aggressive war in some circumstances may have another meaning, in the Indictment before us it is given the meaning of commencing the hostilities. In this sense it involves the actual waging of the aggressive war. After such a war has been initiated or has been commenced by some offenders others may participate in such circumstances, as to become guilty of waging the war. This consideration, however, affords no reason for registering convictions on the counts of initiating as well as of waging aggressive war. We propose therefore to abstain from consideration of Counts 18 to 26 inclusive.

Counts 37 and 38 charge conspiracy to murder. Article 5, sub-paragraphs (b) and (c) of the Charter, deal with Conventional War Crimes and Crimes against Humanity. In sub-paragraph (c) of Article 5 occurs this passage: "Leaders, organizers, instigators and accomplices participating in the formulation or execution of a common plan or conspiracy to commit any of the foregoing crimes are responsible for all acts performed by any person in execution of such plan." (p. 33). A similar provision appeared in the Nuremberg Charter although there it was an independent paragraph and was not, as in our Charter, incorporated in sub-paragraph (c). The context of this provision clearly relates it exclusively to sub-paragraph (a), Crimes against Peace, as that is the only category in which a "common plan or conspiracy" is stated to be a crime. It has no application to Conventional War Crimes and Crimes against Humanity as conspiracies to commit such crimes are not made criminal by the Charter of the Tribunal. The Prosecution did not challenge this view but submitted that the counts were sustainable under Article 5(a) of the Charter. It was argued that the waging of aggressive war was unlawful and involved unlawful killing which is murder. From this it was submitted further that a conspiracy to wage war unlawfully was a conspiracy also to commit murder. The crimes triable by this Tribunal are those set out in the Charter. Article 5(a) states that a conspiracy to commit the crimes therein specified is itself a crime. The crimes, other than conspiracy, specified in Article 5(a) are "planning, preparation, initiating or waging" of a war of aggression. There is no specification of the crime of conspiracy to commit murder by the waging of aggressive war or otherwise. We hold therefore that we have no jurisdiction to deal with charges of conspiracy to commit murder as contained in Counts 37 and 38 and decline to entertain these charges.

10. DISPOSITION AND OUTCOME OF INTERNATIONAL MILITARY TRIBUNAL FOR THE FAR EAST

Araki, Sadao; General (Former Minister of War; senior adviser to cabinet) - Convicted of Counts 1 and 27. Sentenced to life imprisonment.

Doihara, Kenji; General (Supreme War Council; army commander) - Convicted of Counts 1, 27, 29, 31, 32, 35, 36 and 54. Sentenced to death.

Hashimoto, Kingoro; Colonel (Held various commands) - Convicted of Counts 1 and 27. Sentenced to life imprisonment.

Hata, Shunroku; Field Marshall (Former Minister of War; Commander of China Expeditionary Force) - Convicted on Counts 1, 27, 29, 31, 32 and 55. Sentenced to life imprisonment.

Hiranuma, Kiichiro; Baron (Former Premier; President of Privy Council) - Convicted of Counts 1, 27, 29, 31, 32 and 36. Sentenced to life imprisonment.

Hirota, Koki; Baron (Former Premier and Foreign Minister) -Convicted of Counts 1, 27 and 55. Sentenced to death.

Hoshino, Naoki (Chief cabinet secretary) - Convicted of Counts 1, 27, 31 and 32. Sentenced to life imprisonment.

Itagaki, Seishiro; General (Former Minister of War; Supreme War Council) - Convicted of Counts 1, 27, 29, 31, 32, 35, 36 and 54. Sentenced to death.

Kaya, Okinori (Minister of Finance) - Convicted of Counts 1, 27, 29, 31 and 32. Sentenced to life imprisonment.

Kido, Koichi; Marquis (Lord Keeper of the Privy Seal) - Convicted of Counts 1, 27, 31 and 32. Sentenced to life imprisonment.

Kimura, Heitaro; General (Vice Minister of War; Supreme War Council; Army Commander) - Convicted of Counts 1, 27, 29, 31, 32, 54 and 55. Sentenced to death.

Koiso, Kuniaki; General (Governor-General of Korea; Premier) - Convicted of Counts 1, 27, 29, 31, 32 and 55. Sentenced to death.

Matsui, Iwane; General (Commander, China Expeditionary Force) - Convicted of Count 55. Sentenced to death.

Matsuoka, Yosuke (Foreign Minister) - Died during the course of the trial.

Minami, Jiro; General (Governor-General, Korea; Privy Council) - Convicted of Counts 1 and 27. Sentenced to life imprisonment.

Muto, Akira; General (Director of Military Affairs Bureau; army commander) - Convicted of Counts 1, 27, 29, 31, 32, 54 and 55. Sentenced to death.

Nagano, Osami; Admiral (Navy Chief of Staff; Naval advisor to Emperor) - Died during trial.

Oka, Takasumi; Admiral (Chief of Naval Affairs Bureau; vice-Minister of the Navy) - Convicted of Counts 1, 27, 29, 31 and 32. Sentenced to life imprisonment.

Okawa, Shumei (Held no formal government position, but a major intellectual advocate of Japanese militarists) - Assigned to psychiatric ward.

Oshima, Hiroshi; General (Ambassador to Germany) - Convicted of Count 1. Sentenced to life imprisonment.

Sato, Kenryo; General (Chief of Military Affairs Bureau; army commander) - Convicted of Counts 1, 27, 29, 31, 32. Sentenced to life imprisonment.

Shigemitsu, Mamoru (Diplomat; Foreign Minister) - Convicted of Counts 27, 29, 31, 32, 33 and 55. Sentenced to seven years in prison.

Shimad, Shigetaro; Admiral (Navy Minister; Supreme War Council) - Convicted of Counts 1, 27, 29, 31 and 32. Sentenced to life imprisonment.

Shiratori, Toshio (Career diplomat) - Convicted of Count 1. Sentenced to life imprisonment.

Suzuki, Teiichi; General (President, Cabinet Planning Board; advisor to cabinet) - Convicted of Count 1. Sentenced to life imprisonment.

Togo, Shigenori (Diplomat; Foreign Minister) - Convicted of Counts 1, 27, 29, 31 and 32. Sentenced to twenty years in prison.

Tojo, Hideki; General (Premier; Minister of War) - Convicted of Counts 1, 27, 29, 31, 32, 33 and 54. Sentenced to death.

Umezu, Yoshijiro; General (army commander; Army Chief of Staff) - Convicted of Counts 1, 27, 29, 31 and 32. Sentenced to life imprisonment.

10. DISPOSITION AND OUTCOME OF THE INTERNATIONAL MILITARY TRIBUNAL FOR THE FAR EAST

Verdicts

Count	1	27	29	31	32	33	35	36	54	55
ARAKI	G	G	A	A	A	A	A	A	A	A
DOIHARA	G	G	G	G	G	A	G	G	G	0
HASHIMOTO	G	G	A	A	A		A		A	A
HATA	G	G	G	G	G	A	A	A	A	G
HIRANUMA	G	G	G	G	G	A	A	G	A	A
HIROTA	G	G	A	A	A	A	G		A	G
HOSHINO	G	G	G	G	G				A	A
ITAGAKI	G	G	G	G	G	A		G	A	A
KAYA	G	G	G	G	G				A	A
KIDO	G	G	G	G	G				A	A
KIMURA	G	G	G	G	G	A	A	A	A	G
KOISO	G	G	G	G	A				A	G
MATSUI	A	A	A	A	A	A		A	A	G
MINAMI	G	G	A	A	G				A	A
MUTO	G	G	G	G	G	A		A	G	G
OKA	G	G	A	A	A				A	A
OSHIMA	G	A	G	G	G				A	A
SATO	G	G	G	G	G	A			A	A
SHIGEMITSU	G	G	A	A	A	A		A	A	G
SHIMADA	G	G	G	G	G				A	A
SHIRATORI	G	A	G	G	G		A		A	A
SUZUKI	G	G	A	A	A		A	A	A	A
TOGO	G	G	G	G	G	G	A	A	A	A
TOJO	G	G	G	G	G		A	A	A	0
UMEZU	G	G	G	G	G		A	A	A	A

KEY: Blank --Not indicted on the count.   G --Guilty.

      A --Acquitted.   0 --Charged but no finding made by the Tribunal.

Count 1 --The Over-all Conspiracy.

Count 27 --Waging war against China.   Count 33 --Waging war against France.

Count 29 --Waging war against the United States.   Count 35 --Waging war against USSR at Lake Khassan.

Count 31 --Waging war against the British Commonwealth.   Count 36 --Waging war against the Mongolian People's Republic and the USSR

Count 32 --Waging war against the Netherlands.   Count 54 --Ordering, authorizing or permitting atrocities.

     Count 55 --Disregard of duty to secure observance of and prevent breaches of Laws of War

622

11. UNITED NATIONS GENERAL ASSEMBLY RESOLUTION ON AFFIRMATION OF THE PRINCIPLES OF INTERNATIONAL LAW RECOGNIZED BY THE CHARTER OF THE NUREMBERG TRIBUNAL, 11 December 1946

UNITED NATIONS GENERAL ASSEMBLY RESOLUTION 95

1 U.N. GAOR (Part II) at 188, U.N. Doc. A/64/Add. 1 (1946). *Reprinted in* 2 Friedman 1027; Schnidler/Toman 833.

THE GENERAL ASSEMBLY,

Recognizes the obligation laid upon it by Article 13, paragraph 1, subparagraph a of the Charter, to initiate studies and make recommendations for the purpose of encouraging the progressive development of international law and its codification; and

Takes note of an Agreement for the establishment of an International Military Tribunal for the prosecution and punishment of the major war criminals of the European Axis signed in London on 8 August 1945, and of the Charter annexed thereto, and of the fact that similar principles have been adopted in the Charter of the International Military Tribunal for the trial of the major war criminals in the Far East, proclaimed at Tokyo on 19 January 1946;

Therefore,

Affirms the principles of international law recognized by the Charter of the Nürnberg Tribunal and the judgment of the Tribunal;

Directs the Committee on codification of international law established by the resolution of the General Assembly of 11 December 1946, to treat as a matter of primary importance plans for the formulation, in the context of a general codification of offences against the peace and security of mankind, or of an International Criminal Code, of the principles recognized in the Charter of the Nürnberg Tribunal and in the judgment of the Tribunal.

LAW OF WAR

[Shortly after the Nuremberg judgment was rendered, President Harry S. Truman addressing the United Nations General Assembly, gave high praise to the principles of law applied at Nuremberg. He said it pointed the "path along which agreement might be sought, with hope of success," among the people of all countries "upon principles of law and justice." The Secretary General of the UN, Trygve Lie, endorsed the idea that the Nuremberg principles be made a permanent part of international law: "In the interests of peace and in order to protect mankind against future wars, it will be of decisive significance to have the principles which were implied in the Nuremberg trials ... made a permanent part of the body of international law as quickly as possible." On November 15, 1946 the United States delegation introduced a resolution to that effect before the General Assembly, and after some modifications, it was adopted unanimously in the above language on December 11, 1946.]

12. **INTERNATIONAL LAW COMMISSION REPORT ON PRINCIPLES OF THE NUREMBERG TRIBUNAL, 29 July 1950**
(Excerpts)

5 U.N. GAOR Supp. (No. 12) 11, U.N. Doc. A/1316 (1950). *Reprinted in* 4 AJIL 126 (1950) (Supp.) 2 Ferencz 235.

Part III. Formulation of the Nuremberg Principles

*Principles of International Law Recognized in the Charter of the
Nuremberg Tribunal and in the Judgment of the Tribunal*

Principle I. Any person who commits an act which constitutes a crime under international law is responsible therefore and liable to punishment.

Principle II. The fact that internal law does not impose a penalty for an act which constitutes a crime under international law does not relieve the person who committed the act from responsibility under international law.

Principle III. The fact that a person who committed an act which constitutes a crime under international law acted as Head of State or responsible government official does not relieve him from responsibility under international law.

Principle IV. The fact that a person acted pursuant to an order of his government or of a superior does not relieve him from responsibility under international law, provided a moral choice was in fact possible to him.

Principle V. Any person charged with a crime under international law has the right to a fair trial on the facts and law.

Principle VI. The crimes hereinafter set out are punishable as crimes under international law:
a. Crimes Against Peace:
    (i)   Planning, preparation, initiation or waging of a war of aggression, of a war in violation of international treaties, agreements or assurances;
    (ii) Participation in a common plan or conspiracy for the accomplishment of any of the acts mentioned under (i).
b. War Crimes:
    Violations of the laws or customs of war which include, but are not limited to, murder, ill-treatment or deportation to slave-labour or for any other purpose of civilian population of or in occupied territory, murder, or ill-treatment of prisoners of war, of persons on the seas, killing of hostages, plunder of public or private property, wanton destruction of cities, towns, or villages, or devastation not justified by military necessity.
c. Crimes Against Humanity:
    Murder, extermination, enslavement, deportation and other inhuman acts done against any civilian population, or persecutions on political, racial or religious grounds, when such acts are done or such persecutions are carried on in execution of or in connexion with any crime against peace or any war crime.

Principle VII. Complicity in the commission of a crime against peace, a war crime, or a crime against humanity as set forth in Principle VI is a crime under international law.
b. Crimes against humanity whether committed in time of war or in time of peace as they are defined in the Charter of the International Military Tribunal, Nuremberg, of August 8, 1945, and confirmed by resolutions 3 (I) of February

13, 1946, and 95 (I) of December 11, 1946, of the General Assembly of the United Nations, evicted by armed attack or occupation and inhuman acts resulting from the policy of *apartheid*, and the crime of genocide as defined in the 1948 Convention on the Prevention and Punishment of the Crime of Genocide, even if such acts do not constitute a violation of the domestic law of the country in which they were committed.

D. DOCUMENTS RELATING TO THE INTERNATIONAL REGULATION OF ARMED CONFLICT

1.   INSTRUCTIONS FOR THE GOVERNMENT OF ARMIES OF THE UNITED STATES IN THE FIELD, (Lieber Code), Washington D.C., 24 April 1863

(Excerpts)

War Dept. Classification No. 1.12:   October 8, 1863 (Washington, D.C., 1863). *Reprinted in* 1 Friedman 158.

Section I-Martial Law-Military Jurisdiction-
Military Necessity-Retaliation.

Article IV

Martial Law is simply military authority exercised in accordance with the laws and usages of war. Military oppression is not Martial Law; it is the abuse of the power which that law confers. As Martial Law is executed by military force, it is incumbent upon those who administer it to be strictly guided by the principles of justice, honor, and humanity--virtues adorning a soldier even more than other men, for the very reason that he possesses the power of his arms against the unarmed.

Article XIV

Military necessity, as understood by modern civilized nations, consists in the necessity of those measures which are indispensable for securing the ends of the war, and which are lawful according to the modern law and usages of war.

Article XV

Military necessity admits of all direct destruction of life or limb of armed enemies, and of other persons whose destruction is incidentally unavoidable in the armed contests of the war; it allows of the capturing of every armed enemy, and every enemy of importance to the hostile government, or of peculiar danger to the captor; it allows

627

of all destruction of property, and obstruction of the ways and channels of traffic, travel, or communication, and of all withholding of sustenance or means of life from the enemy; of the appropriation of whatever an enemy's country affords necessary for the subsistence and safety of the army, and of such deception as does not involve the breaking of good faith either positively pledged, regarding agreements entered into during the war, or supposed by the modern law of war to exist. Men who take up arms against one another in public war do not cease on this account to be moral beings, responsible to one another and to God.

Article XVI

Military necessity does not admit of cruelty--that is, the infliction of suffering for the sake of suffering or for revenge, nor of maiming or wounding except in fight, nor of torture to extort confessions. It does not admit of the use of poison in any way, nor of the wanton devastation of a district. It admits of deception, but disclaims acts of perfidy; and, in general, military necessity does not include any act of hostility which makes the return to peace unnecessarily difficult.

Article XXII

Nevertheless, as civilization has advanced during the last centuries, so has likewise steadily advanced, especially in war on land, the distinction between the private individual belonging in a hostile country and the hostile country itself, with its men in arms. The principle has been more and more acknowledged that the unarmed citizen is to be spared in person, property, and honor as much as the exigencies of war will admit.

Article XXIII

Private citizens are no longer murdered, enslaved, or carried off to distant parts, and the inoffensive individual is as little disturbed in his private relations as the commander of the hostile troops can afford to grant in the overruling demands of a vigorous war.

Article XXIV

The almost universal rule in remote times was, and continues to be with barbarous armies, that the private individual of the hostile country is destined to suffer every

628

privation of liberty and protection, and every disruption of family ties. Protection was, and still is with uncivilized people, the exception.

Article XXV

In modern regular wars of the Europeans, and their descendants in other portions of the globe, protection of the inoffensive citizen of the hostile country is the rule; privation and disturbance of private relations are the exceptions.

Article XXX

Ever since the formation and coexistence of modern nations, and ever since wars have become great national wars, war has come to be acknowledged not to be its own end, but the means to obtain great ends of state, or to consist in defense against wrong; and no conventional restriction of the modes adopted to injure the enemy is any longer admitted; but the law of war imposes many limitations and restrictions on principles of justice, faith, and honor.

SECTION II--Public and Private Property of the Enemy-Protection of Persons, and Especially of Women, of Religion, the Arts and Sciences-Punishment of Crimes against the Inhabitants of Hostile Countries.

Article XXXIII

It is no longer considered lawful--on the contrary, it is held to be a serious breach of the law of war--to force the subjects of the enemy into the service of the victorious government, except the latter should proclaim, after a fair and complete conquest of the hostile country or district, that it is resolved to keep the country, district, or place permanently as its own and make it a portion of its own country.

Article XXXVII

The United States acknowledge and protect, in hostile countries occupied by them, religion and morality; strictly private property; the persons of the inhabitants, especially those of women; and the sacredness of domestic relations. Offenses to the contrary shall be rigorously punished.

629

CRIMES AGAINST HUMANITY

Article XLII

Slavery, complicating and confounding the ideas of property (that is, of a thing), and of personality (that is, of humanity), exists according to municipal or local law only. The law of nature and nations has never acknowledged it. The digest of the Roman law enacts the early dictum of the pagan jurist, that "so far as the law of nature is concerned, all men are equal." Fugitives escaping from a country in which they were slaves, villains, or serfs, into another country, have, for centuries past, been held free and acknowledged free by judicial decisions of European countries, even though the municipal law of the country in which the slave had taken refuge acknowledged slavery within its own dominions.

Article XLIII

Therefore, in a war between the United States and a belligerent which admits of slavery, if a person held in bondage by that belligerent be captured by or come as a fugitive under the protection of the military forces of the United States, such person is immediately entitled to the rights and privileges of a freeman. To return such person into slavery would amount to enslaving a free person, and neither the United States nor any officer under their authority can enslave any human being. Moreover, a person so made free by the law of war is under the shield of the law of nations, and the former owner or State can have, by the law of postliminy, no belligerent lien or claim of service.

Article XLIV

All wanton violence committed against persons in the invaded country, all destruction of property not commanded by the authorized officer, all robbery, all pillage or sacking, even after taking a place by main force, all rape, wounding, maiming, or killing of such inhabitants, are prohibited under the penalty of death, or such other severe punishment as may seem adequate for the gravity of the offense.

A soldier, officer or private, in the act of committing such violence, and disobeying a superior ordering him to abstain from it, may be lawfully killed on the spot by such superior.

Article XLVII

Crimes punishable by all penal codes, such as arson, murder, maiming, assaults, highway robbery, theft, burglary, fraud, forgery, and rape, if committed by an American soldier in a hostile country against its inhabitants, are not only punishable as at home, but in all cases in which death is not inflicted, the severer punishment shall be preferred.

SECTION III--Deserters-Prisoners of War-Hostages-Booty on the Battlefield.

Article LVI

A prisoner of war is subject to no punishment for being a public enemy, nor is any revenge wreaked upon him by the intentional infliction of any suffering, or disgrace, by cruel imprisonment, want of food, by mutilation, death, or any other barbarity.

Article LVII

So soon as a man is armed by a sovereign government and takes the soldier's oath of fidelity, he is a belligerent; his killing, wounding, or other warlike acts are not individual crimes or offenses. No belligerent has a right to declare that enemies of a certain class, color, or condition, when properly organized as soldiers, will not be treated by him as public enemies.

Article LVIII

The law of nations knows of no distinction of color, and if an enemy of the United States should enslave and sell any captured persons of their army, it would be a case for the severest retaliation, if not redressed upon complaint.

The United States cannot retaliate by enslavement; therefore death must be the retaliation for this crime against the law of nations.

631

CRIMES AGAINST HUMANITY

Article LIX

A prisoner of war remains answerable for his crimes committed against the captor's army or people, committed before he was captured, and for which he has not been punished by his own authorities.

All prisoners of war are liable to the infliction of retaliatory measures.

Article LX

It is against the usage of modern war to resolve, in hatred and revenge, to give no quarter. No body of troops has the right to declare that it will not give, and therefore will not expect, quarter; but a commander is permitted to direct his troops to give no quarter, in great straits, when his own salvation makes it *impossible* to cumber himself with prisoners.

Article LXI

Troops that give no quarter have no right to kill enemies already disabled on the ground, or prisoners captured by other troops.

Article LXVIII

Modern wars are not internecine wars, in which the killing of the enemy is the object. The destruction of the enemy in modern war, and indeed, modern war itself, are means to obtain that object of the belligerent which lies beyond the war.

Unnecessary or revengeful destruction of life is not lawful.

Article LXX

The use of poison in any manner, be it to poison wells, or food, or arms, is wholly excluded from modern warfare. He that uses it puts himself out of the pale of the law and usages of war.

Article LXXI

Whoever intentionally inflicts additional wounds on an enemy already wholly disabled, or kills such an enemy, or who orders or encourages soldiers to do so, shall suffer death, if duly convicted, whether he belongs to the Army of the United States, or is an enemy captured after having committed his misdeed.

Article LXXII

Money and other valuables on the person of a prisoner, such as watches or jewelry, as well as extra clothing, are regarded by the American Army as the private property of the prisoner, and the appropriation of such valuables or money is considered dishonorable, and is prohibited.

Nevertheless, if large sums are found upon the persons of prisoners, or in their possession, they shall be taken from them, and the surplus, after providing for their own support, appropriated for the use of the army, under the direction of the commander, unless otherwise ordered by the government. Nor can prisoners claim, as private property, large sums found and captured in their train, although they have been placed in the private luggage of the prisoners.

Article LXXV

Prisoners of war are subject to confinement or imprisonment such as may be deemed necessary on account of safety, but they are to be subjected to no other intentional suffering or indignity. The confinement and mode of treating a prisoner may be varied during his captivity according to the demands of safety.

Article LXXVI

Prisoners of war shall be fed upon plain and wholesome food, whenever practicable, and treated with humanity.

They may be required to work for the benefit of the captor's government, according to their rank and condition.

Article LXXIX

Every captured wounded enemy shall be medically treated, according to the ability of the medical staff.

Article LXXX

Honorable men, when captured, will abstain from giving to the enemy information concerning their own army, and the modern law of war permits no longer the use of any violence against prisoners in order to extort the desired information or to punish them for having given false information.

2. **CONVENTION FOR THE AMELIORATION OF THE CONDITION OF THE WOUNDED IN ARMIES IN THE FIELD, Geneva, 22 August 1864**
(Excerpts)

18 Martens 607, 22 Stat. 940, T.S. No. 377.

Article V

Inhabitants of the country who bring help to the wounded shall be respected and shall remain free. Generals of the belligerent Powers shall make it their duty to notify the inhabitants of the appeal made to their humanity, and of the neutrality which humane conduct will confer.

The presence of any wounded combatant receiving shelter and care in a house shall ensure its protection. An inhabitant who has given shelter to the wounded shall be exempted from billeting and from a portion of such war contributions as may be levied.

3. **CONVENTION WITH RESPECT TO THE LAWS AND CUSTOMS OF WAR ON LAND, The Hague, 29 July 1899**
(Excerpts)

26 Martens (2d) 949, 32 Stat. 1803, T.S. No. 403. *Reprinted in* 1 AJIL 129 (1907) (Supp.); 1 Friedman 221; Schindler/Toman 57.

Preambular Language

...

"Until a more complete code of the laws of war is issued, the High Contracting Parties think it right to declare that in cases not included in the Regulations adopted by them, populations and belligerent remain under the protection and empire of the principles of international law, as they result from the usages established between civilized nations, from the laws of humanity, and the requirements of the public conscience; ..."

4. LAWS AND CUSTOMS OF WAR ON LAND, ANNEX TO THE CONVENTION REGULATIONS RESPECTING THE LAWS AND CUSTOMS OF WAR ON LAND (HAGUE II)--The Hague, 29 July 1899 (Excerpts)

26 Martens (2d) 949, 32 Stat. 1803, T.S. No. 403. *Reprinted in* 1 AJIL 129 (1907) (Supp.); 1 Friedman 221; Schindler/Toman 57.

SECTION 1

ON BELLIGERENTS

CHAPTER 1

On The Qualifications of Belligerents

Article 1:   The laws, rights, and duties of war apply not only to armies, but also to militia and volunteer corps fulfilling the following conditions:
   1. To be commanded by a person responsible for his subordinates;
   2. To have a fixed distinctive emblem recognizable at a distance;
   3. To carry arms openly; and
   4. To conduct their operations in accordance with the laws and customs of war.

In countries where militia or volunteer corps constitute the army, or form part of it, they are included under the denomination "army."

Article 2:   The population of a territory which has not been occupied who, on the enemy's approach, spontaneously take up arms to resist the invading troops without having time to organize themselves in accordance with Article 1, shall be regarded as belligerents, if they carry arms openly and if they respect the laws and customs of war.

Article 28: The pillage of a town or place, even when taken by assault, is prohibited.

Section III

ON MILITARY AUTHORITY OVER HOSTILE TERRITORY

Article 42: Territory is considered occupied when it is actually placed under the authority of the hostile army.

The occupation applies only to the territory where such authority is established, and in a position to assert itself.

Article 43: The authority of the legitimate power having actually passed into the hands of the occupant, the latter shall take all steps in his power to re-establish and insure, as far as possible, public order and safety, while respecting, unless absolutely prevented, the laws in force in the country.

Article 44: Any compulsion of the population of occupied territory to take part in military operations against its own country is prohibited.

Article 45: It is forbidden to compel the inhabitants of occupied territory to swear allegiance to the hostile Power.

Article 46: Family honour and rights, the lives of persons, and private property, as well as religious convictions and practice, must be respected.

Private property cannot be confiscated.

Article 47: Pillage is formally prohibited.

Article 48: If, in the territory occupied, the occupant collects the taxes, dues, and tolls imposed for the benefit of the State, he shall do so, as far as is possible, in accordance with the rules of assessment and incidence in force, and shall in consequence be bound to defray the expenses of the administration of the occupied territory to the same extent as the legitimate Government was so bound.

Article 49:   If, in addition to the taxes mentioned in the above article, the occupant levies other money contributions in the occupied territory, this shall only be for the needs of the army or of the administration of the territory in question.

Article 50:   No general penalty, pecuniary or otherwise, shall be inflicted upon the population on account of the acts of individuals for which they cannot be regarded as jointly and severally responsible.

Article 51:   No contribution shall be collected except under a written order, and on the responsibility of a commander-in-chief.

The collection of the said contribution shall only be effected as far as possible in accordance with the rules of assessment and incidence of the taxes in force.

For every contribution a receipt shall be given to the contributors.

Article 52:   Neither requisitions in kind nor services can be demanded from communes or inhabitants except for the necessities of the army of occupation. They must be in proportion to the resources of the country, and of such a nature as not to involve the population in the obligation of taking part in military operations against their country.

These requisitions and services shall only be demanded on the authority of the commander in the locality occupied.

The contributions in kind shall, as far as possible, be paid for in ready money; if not, their receipt shall be acknowledged.

Article 56:   The property of the communes, that of religious, charitable, and educational institutions, and those of arts and science, even when State property, shall be treated as private property.

All seizure of, and destruction, or intentional damage done to such institutions, to historical monuments, works of art or science, is prohibited, and should be made the subject of legal proceedings.

637

5. **CONVENTION RESPECTING THE LAWS AND CUSTOMS OF WAR ON LAND, ANNEX TO THE CONVENTION REGULATIONS RESPECTING THE LAWS AND CUSTOMS OF WAR ON LAND (HAGUE IV), The Hague, 18 October 1907**

(Excerpts)

3 Martens (3d) 461, 36 Stat. 2277, T.S. No. 539. *Reprinted in* 2 AJIL 90 (1908) (Supp.); 1 Bevans 631; 1 Friedman 308.

Preambular Language

...

"Until a more complete code of the laws of war has been issued, the High Contracting Parties deem it expedient to declare that, in cases not included in the Regulations adopted by them, the inhabitants and the belligerent remain under the protection and the rule of the principles of the law of nations, as they result from the usages established among civilized peoples, from the laws of humanity, and the dictates of the public conscience."

6. **LAWS AND CUSTOMS OF WAR ON LAND, ANNEX TO THE CONVENTION REGULATIONS RESPECTING THE LAWS AND CUSTOMS OF WAR ON LAND (HAGUE IV), The Hague, 18 October 1907**

(Excerpts)

SECTION I

ON BELLIGERENTS

CHAPTER 1

The Qualifications of Belligerents

Article 1: The laws, rights, and duties of war apply not only to armies, but also to militia and volunteer corps fulfilling the following conditions;

1. To be commanded by a person responsible for his subordinates;
2. To have a fixed distinctive emblem recognizable at a distance;
3. To carry arms openly; and
4. To conduct their operations in accordance with the laws and customs of war.

In countries where militia or volunteer corps consitute the army, or form part of it, they are included under the denomination "army."

Article 2:   The inhabitants of a territory which has not been occupied, who, on the approach of the enemy, spontaneously take up arms to resist the invading troops without having had time to organize themselves in accordance with Article 1, shall be regarded as belligerents if they carry arms openly and if they respect the laws and customs of war.

Article 28:   The pillage of a town or place, even taken by assault, is prohibited.

Section III

MILITARY AUTHORITY OVER THE TERRITORY OF THE HOSTILE STATE

Article 42:   Territory is considered occupied when it is actually placed under the authority of the hostile army.

The occupation extends only to the territory where such authority has been established and can be exercised.

Article 43:   The authority of the legitimate power having in fact passed into the hands of the occupant, the latter shall take all the measures in his power to restore, and ensure, as far as possible, public order and safety, while respecting, unless absolutely prevented, the laws in force in the country.

Article 44:   A belligerent is forbidden to force the inhabitants of territory occupied by it to furnish information about the army of the other belligerent, or about its means of defence.

Article 45: It is forbidden to compel the inhabitants of occupied territory to swear allegiance to the hostile Power.

Article 46: Family honour and rights, the lives of persons, and private property, as well as religious convictions and practice, must be respected.

Article 47: Pillage is formally forbidden.

Article 48: If, in the territory occupied, the occupant collects the taxes, dues, and tolls imposed for the benefit of the State, he shall do so, as far as is possible, in accordance with the rules of assessment and incidence in force, and shall in consequence be bound to defray the expenses of the administration of the occupied territory to the same extent as the legitimate Government was so bound.

Article 49: If, in addition to the taxes mentioned in the above Article, the occupant levies other money contributions in the occupied territory, this shall only be for the needs of the army or of the administration of the territory in question.

Article 50: No general penalty, pecuniary or otherwise, shall be inflicted upon the population on account of the acts of individuals for which they cannot be regarded as jointly and severally responsible.

Article 51: No contribution shall be collected except under a written order, and on the responsibility of a Commander-in-Chief.

The collection of the said contribution shall only be effective as far as possible in accordance with the rules of assessment and incidence of the taxes in force.

For every contribution a receipt shall be given to the contributors.

Article 52: Requisitions in kind and services shall not be demanded from municipalities or inhabitants except for the needs of the army of occupation. They shall be in proportion to the resources of the country, and of such a nature as not to involve the inhabitants in the obligation of taking part in military operations against their own country.

Such requisitions and services shall only be demanded on the authority of the commander in the locality occupied.

Contributions in kind shall as far as possible be paid for in case; if not, a receipt shall be given and the payment of the amount due shall be made as soon as possible.

Article 53: An army of occupation can only take possession of cash, funds, and realizable securities which are strictly the property of the State, depots of arms, means of transport, stores and supplies, and, generally, all movable property belonging to the State which may be used for military operations.

All appliances, whether on land, at sea, or in the air, adapted for the transmission of news, or for the transport of persons or things, exclusive of cases governed by naval law, depots of arms, and, generally, all kinds of ammunition of war, may be seized, even if they belong to private individuals, but must be restored and compensation fixed when peace is made.

Article 54: Submarine cables connecting an occupied territory with a neutral territory shall not be seized or destroyed except in the case of absolute necessity. They must likewise be restored and compensation fixed when peace is made.

Article 55: The occupying state shall be regarded only as administrator and usufructuary of public buildings, real estate, forests, and agricultural estates belonging to the hostile State, and situated in the occupied country. It must safeguard the capital of these properties, and administer them in accordance with the rules of usufruct.

Article 56: The property of municipalities, that of institutions dedicated to religion, charity and education, the arts and sciences, even when State property, shall be treated as private property.

All seizure of, destruction or wilful damage done to institutions of this character, historic monuments, works of art and science, is forbidden, and should be made the subject of legal proceedings.

7. **CONVENTION FOR THE AMELIORATION OF THE CONDITION OF THE WOUNDED AND SICK IN ARMIES IN THE FIELD, Geneva, 6 July 1906**

(Excerpts)

2 Martens (3d) 620, 35 Stat. 1885, T.S. No. 464.

CHAPTER I--The Sick and Wounded.

CRIMES AGAINST HUMANITY

Article I

Officers, soldiers, and other persons officially attached to armies, who are sick or wounded, shall be respected and cared for, without distinction of nationality, by the belligerent in whose power they are.

A belligerent, however, when compelled to leave his wounded in the hands of his adversary, shall leave with them, so far as military conditions permit, a portion of the personnel and material of his sanitary service to assist in caring for them.

Article III

After every engagement the belligerent who remains in possession of the field of battle shall take measures to search for the wounded and to protect the wounded and dead from robbery and ill treatment.

He will see that a careful examination is made of the bodies of the dead prior to their internment or incineration.

Article V

Military authority may make an appeal to the charitable zeal of the inhabitants to receive and, under its supervision, to care for the sick and wounded of the armies, granting to persons responding to such appeals special protection and certain immunities.

CHAPTER II--Sanitary Formations and Establishments.

Article VI

Mobile sanitary formations (i.e., those which are intended to accompany armies in the field) and the fixed establishments belonging to the sanitary service shall be protected and respected by belligerents.

CHAPTER III--Personnel.

Article IX

The personnel charged exclusively with the removal, transportation, and treatment of the sick and wounded, as well as with the administration of sanitary formations and establishments, and the chaplains attached to armies, shall be respected and protected under all circumstances. If they fall into the hands of the enemy they shall not be considered as prisoners of war.

8. CONVENTION FOR THE AMELIORATION OF THE CONDITION OF THE WOUNDED AND SICK OF ARMIES IN THE FIELD, Geneva, 27 July 1929

(Excerpts)

118 L.N.T.S. 303, 47 Stat. 2074, T.S. No. 847.

CHAPTER I - The Wounded and Sick

ARTICLE I

Officers, soldiers, and other persons officially attached to the armies who are wounded or sick shall be respected and protected in all circumstances; they shall be humanely treated and cared for without distinction of nationality by the belligerent in whose power they are.

A belligerent, however, when compelled to leave his wounded or sick in the hands of his adversary, shall leave with them, so far as military exigencies permit, a portion of the personnel and material of his sanitary service to assist in caring for them.

CHAPTER III - Personnel.

ARTICLE IX

The personnel charged exclusively with the removal, transportation, and treatment of the wounded and sick, as well as with the administration of sanitary formations and establishments, and the chaplains attached to armies, shall be respected and protected under all circumstances. If they fall into the hands of the enemy they shall not be treated as prisoners of war....

9. CONVENTION FOR THE AMELIORATION OF THE CONDITION OF THE WOUNDED AND SICK IN ARMED FORCES IN THE FIELD, Geneva, 12 August 1949

(Excerpts)

75 U.N.T.S. 31, 6 U.S.T. 3114, T.I.A.S. 3362. *Reprinted in* 1 Friedman 525; Schnidler/Toman 305.

ARTICLE III

In the case of armed conflict not of an international character occurring in the territory of one of the High Contracting Parties, each Party to the conflict shall be bound to apply, as a minimum, the following provisions:

1. Persons taking no active part in the hostilities, including members of armed forces who have laid down their arms and those placed hors de combat by sickness, wounds, detention, or any other cause, shall in all circumstances be treated humanely, without any adverse distinction founded on race, colour, religion or faith, sex birth or wealth, or any other similar criteria.

To this end, the following acts are and shall remain prohibited at any time and in any place whatsoever with respect to the above-mentioned persons:
   (a) violence to life and person, in particular murder of all kinds, mutilation, cruel treatment and torture;
   (b) taking of hostages;

(c) outrages upon personal dignity, in particular humiliating and degrading treatment;

(d) the passing of sentences and the carrying out of executions without previous judgment pronounced by a regularly constituted court, affording all the judicial guarantees which are recognized as indispensable by civilized peoples.

2. The wounded and sick shall be collected and cared for.

An impartial humanitarian body, such as the International Committee of the Red Cross, may offer its services to the Parties to the conflict.

The Parties to the conflict should further endeavour to bring into force, by means of special agreements, all or part of the other provisions of the present Convention.

The application of the preceding provisions shall not affect the legal status of the Parties to the conflict.

CHAPTER II - Wounded and Sick

ARTICLE XII

Members of the armed forces and other persons mentioned in the following Article, who are wounded or sick, shall be respected and protected in all circumstances.

They shall be treated humanely and cared for by the Party to the conflict in whose power they may be, without any adverse distinction founded on sex, race, nationality, religion, political opinions, or any other similar criteria. Any attempts upon their lives, or violence to their persons, shall be strictly prohibited; in particular, they shall not be murdered or exterminated, subjected to torture or to biological experiments; they shall not wilfully be left without medical assistance and care, nor shall conditions exposing them to contagion or infection be created.

Only urgent medical reasons will authorize priority in the order of treatment to be administered.

Women shall be treated with all consideration due to their sex.

The Party to the conflict which is compelled to abandon wounded or sick to the enemy shall, as far as military considerations permit, leave with them a part of its medical personnel and material to assist in their care.

ARTICLE XVIII

The military authorities may appeal to the charity of the inhabitants voluntarily to collect and care for, under their direction, the wounded and sick, granting persons who have responded to this appeal the necessary protection and facilities. Should the adverse Party take or retake control of the area, he shall likewise grant these persons the same protection and the same facilities.

The military authorities shall permit the inhabitants and relief societies, even in invaded or occupied areas, spontaneously to collect and care for wounded or sick of whatever nationality. The civilian population shall respect these wounded and sick, and in particular abstain from offering them violence.

No one may ever be molested or convicted for having nursed the wounded or sick.

The provisions of the present Article do not relieve the occupying Power of its obligation to give both physical and moral care to the wounded and sick.

CHAPTER III - Medical Units and Establishments

ARTICLE XIX

Fixed establishments and mobile medical units of the Medical Service may in no circumstances be attacked, but shall at all times be respected and protected by the Parties to the conflict. Should they fall into the hands of the adverse Party, their personnel shall be free to pursue their duties, as long as the capturing Power has not itself ensured the necessary care of the wounded and sick found in such establishments and units.

The responsible authorities shall ensure that the said medical establishments and units are, as far as possible, situated in such a manner that attacks against military objectives cannot imperil their safety.

CHAPTER IV - Personnel

ARTICLE XXIV

Medical personnel exclusively engaged in the search for, or the collection, transport or treatment of the wounded or sick, or in the prevention of disease, staff exclusively engaged in the administration of medical units and establishments, as well as chaplains attached to the armed forces, shall be respected and protected in all circumstances.

CHAPTER IV - Medical Transports

ARTICLE XXXV

Transports of wounded and sick or of medical equipment shall be respected and protected in the same way as mobile medical units.

Should such transports or vehicles fall into the hands of the adverse Party, they shall be subject to the laws of war, on condition that the Party to the conflict who captures them shall in all cases ensure the care of the wounded and sick they contain.

The civilian personnel and all means of transport obtained by requisition shall be subject to the general rules of international law.

CHAPTER IX - Repression of Abuses and Infractions

ARTICLE XLIX

The High Contracting Parties undertake to enact any legislation necessary to provide effective penal sanctions for persons committing, or ordering to be committed, any of the grave breaches of the present Convention defined in the following Article.

Each High Contracting Party shall be under the obligation to search persons alleged to have committed, or to have ordered to be committed, such grave breaches, and shall bring such persons, regardless of their nationality, before its own courts. It may also, if it prefers, and in accordance with the provisions of its own legislation, hand such persons over for trial to another High Contracting Party concerned, provided such High Contracting Party has made out a prima facie case.

Each High Contracting Party shall take measures necessary for the suppression of all acts contrary to the provisions of the present Convention other than the grave breaches defined in the following Article.

In all circumstances, the accused persons shall benefit by safeguards of proper trial and defence, which shall not be less favourable than those provided by Article CV and those following of the Geneva Convention relative to the Treatment of Prisoners of War of August 12, 1949.

10. CONVENTION FOR THE AMELIORATION OF THE CONDITION OF WOUNDED, SICK AND SHIPWRECKED MEMBERS OF ARMED FORCES AT SEA, Geneva, 12 August 1949
(Excerpts)

75 U.N.T.S. 85, 6 U.S.T. 3217, T.I.A.S. No. 3363. *Reprinted in* 1 Friedman 570; Schindler/Toman 333.

ARTICLE III

In the case of armed conflict not of an international character occurring in the territory of one of the High Contracting Parties, each Party to the conflict shall be bound to apply, as a minimum, the following provisions:

1. Persons taking no active part in the hostilities, including members of armed forces who have laid down their arms and those placed hors de combat by sickness, wounds, detention, or any other cause, shall in all circumstances be treated humanely, without any adverse distinction founded on race, colour, religion or faith, sex or wealth, or any other similar criteria.

To this end, the following acts are and shall remain prohibited at any time and in any place whatsoever with respect to the above-mentioned persons:

    (a) violence to life and person, in particular murder of all kinds, mutilation, cruel treatment and torture;

    (b) taking of hostages;

    (c) outrages upon personal dignity, in particular, humiliating and degrading treatment;

    (d) the passing of sentences and the carrying out of executions without previous judgment pronounced by a regularly constituted court, affording all the judicial guarantees which are recognized as indispensable by civilized peoples.

2. The wounded, sick and shipwrecked shall be collected and cared for.

An impartial humanitarian body,, such as the International Committee of the Red Cross, may offer its services to the Parties to the conflict.

The Parties to the conflict should further endeavor to bring into force, by means of special agreements, all or part of the other provisions of the present Convention.

The application of the preceding provisions shall not affect the legal status of the Parties to the conflict.

CHAPTER II - Wounded, Sick and Shipwrecked

ARTICLE XII

Members of the armed forces and other persons mentioned in the following Article, who are at sea and who are wounded, sick or shipwrecked, shall be respected and protected in all circumstances, it being understood that the term "shipwreck" means shipwreck from any cause and includes forced landings at sea by or from aircraft.

Such persons shall be treated humanely and cared for by the Parties to the conflict in whose power they may be, without any adverse distinction founded on sex, race, nationality, religion, political opinions, or any other similar criteria. Any attempts upon their lives, or violence to their persons, shall be strictly prohibited; in particular, they shall not be murdered or exterminated, subjected to torture or to biological experiments; they shall not wilfully be left without medical assistance and care, nor shall conditions exposing them to contagion or infection be created.

Only urgent medical reasons will authorize priority in the order of treatment to be administered.

Women shall be treated with all consideration due to their sex.

ARTICLE XVIII

After each engagement, Parties to the conflict shall, without delay, take all possible measures to search for and collect the shipwrecked, wounded and sick, to protect them against pillage and ill-treatment, to ensure their adequate care, and to search for the dead and prevent their being despoiled.

Whenever circumstances permit, the Parties to the conflict shall conclude local arrangements for the removal of the wounded and sick by sea from a besieged or encircled area and for the passage of medical and religious personnel and equipment on their way to that area.

CHAPTER IV - Personnel

ARTICLE XXXVI

The religious, medical and hospital personnel of hospital ships and their crews shall be respected and protected; they may not be captured during the time they are in the service of the hospital ship, whether or not there are wounded and sick on board.

CHAPTER VIII - Repression of Abuses and Infractions

ARTICLE L

The High Contracting Parties undertake to enact any legislation necessary to provide effective penal sanctions for persons committing, or ordering to be committed, any of the grave breaches of the present Convention defined in the following Article.

650

Each High Contracting Party shall be under the obligation to search for persons alleged to have committed, or to have ordered to be committed, such grave breaches, and shall bring such persons, regardless of their nationality, before its own courts. It may also, if it prefers, and in accordance with the provisions of its own legislation, hand such persons over for trial to another High Contracting Party concerned, provided such High Contracting Party has made out a prima facie case.

Each High Contracting Party shall take measures necessary for the suppression of all acts contrary to the provisions of the present Convention other than the grave breaches defined in the following Article.

In all circumstances, the accused persons shall benefit by safeguards of proper trial and defence, which shall not be less favorable than those provided by Article CV and those following of the Geneva Convention relative to the Treatment of Prisoners of War of August 12, 1949.

ARTICLE LI

Grave breaches to which the preceding Article relates shall be those involving any of the following acts, if committed against persons or property protected by the Convention: wilful killing, torture or inhuman treatment, including biological experiments, wilfully causing great suffering or serious injury to body or health, and extensive destruction and appropriation of property, not justified by military necessity and carried out unlawfully and wantonly.

ARTICLE LII

No High Contracting Party shall be allowed to absolve itself or any other High Contracting Party of any liability incurred by itself or by another High Contracting Party in respect of breaches referred to in the preceding Article.

651

11. CONVENTION RELATIVE TO THE TREATMENT OF PRISONERS OF WAR, Geneva, 12 August 1949

(Excerpts)

75 U.N.T.S. 135, 6 U.S.T. 3316, T.I.A.S. No. 3364. *Reprinted in* 1 Friedman 641; Schindler/Toman 427.

ARTICLE XIII

Prisoners of war must at all times be humanely treated. Any unlawful act or omission by the Detaining Power causing death or seriously endangering the health of a prisoner of war in its custody is prohibited, and will be regarded as a serious breach of the present Convention. In particular, no prisoner of war may be subjected to physical mutilation or to medical or scientific experiments of any kind which are not justified by the medical, dental or hospital treatment of the prisoner concerned and carried out in his interest.

Likewise, prisoners of war must at all times be protected, particularly against acts of violence or intimidation and against insults and public curiosity.

Measures of reprisal against prisoners of war are prohibited.

ARTICLE XIV

Prisoners of war are entitled in all circumstances to respect for their persons and their honour.

Women shall be treated with all the regard due to their sex and shall in all cases benefit by treatment as favourable as that granted to men.

Prisoners of war shall retain the full civil capacity which they enjoyed at the time of their capture. The Detaining Power may not restrict the exercise, either within or without its own territory, of the rights such capacity confers except in so far as the captivity requires.

PART III. CAPTIVITY

SECTION I. BEGINNING OF CAPTIVITY

ARTICLE XVII

Every prisoner of war, when questioned on the subject, is bound to give only his surname, first names and rank, date of birth, and army, regimental, personal or serial number, or failing this, equivalent information.

If he wilfully infringes these rule, he may render himself liable to a restriction of the privileges accorded to his rank or status.

Each Party to a conflict is required to furnish the persons under its jurisdiction who are liable to become prisoners of war with an identity card showing the owner's surname, first names, rank, army, regimental, personal or serial number or equivalent information, and date of birth. The identity card may, furthermore, bear the signature or the fingerprints, or both, of the owner, and may bear, as well, any other information the Party to the conflict may wish to add concerning persons belonging to its armed forces. As far as possible the card shall measure 6.5 X 10 CM. and shall be issued in duplicate. The identity card shall be shown by the prisoner of war upon demand, but may in no case be taken away from him.

No physical or mental torture, nor any other form of coercion, may be inflicted on prisoners of war to secure from them information of any kind whatever. Prisoners of war who refuse to answer may not be threatened, insulted, or exposed to unpleasant or disadvantageous treatment of any kind.

Prisoners of war who, owing to their physical or mental condition, are unable to state their identity, shall be handed over to the medical service. The identity of such prisoners shall be established by all possible means, subject to the provisions of the preceding paragraph.

The questioning of prisoners of war shall be carried out in a language which they understand.

CRIMES AGAINST HUMANITY

ARTICLE XX

The evacuation of prisoners of war shall always be effected humanely and in conditions similar to those for the forces of the Detaining Power in their changes of station.

The Detaining Power shall supply prisoners of war who are being evacuated with sufficient food and potable water, and with the necessary clothing and medical attention. The Detaining Power shall take all suitable precautions to ensure their safety during evacuation, and shall establish as soon as possible a list of the prisoners of war who are evacuated.

If prisoners of war must, during evacuation, pass through transit camps, their stay in such camps shall be as brief as possible.

SECTION II. INTERNMENT OF PRISONERS OF WAR

CHAPTER I - General Observations

ARTICLE XXII

Prisoners of war may be interned only in premises located on land and affording every guarantee of hygiene and healthfulness. Except in particular cases which are justified by the interest of the prisoners themselves, they shall not be interned in penitentiaries.

Prisoners of war interned in unhealthy areas, or where the climate is injurious for them, shall be removed as soon as possible to a more favourable climate.

The Detaining Power shall assemble prisoners of war in camps or camp compounds according to their nationality, language and customs, provided that such prisoners shall not be separated from prisoners of war belonging to the armed forces with which they were serving at the time of their capture, except with their consent.

ARTICLE XXIII

No prisoner of war may at any time be sent to, or detained in areas where he may be exposed to the fire of the combat zone, nor may his presence be used to render certain points or areas immune from military operations.

Prisoners of war shall have shelters against air bombardment and other hazards of war, to the same extent as the local civilian population. With the exception of those engaged in the protection of their quarters against the aforesaid hazards, they may enter such shelters as soon as possible after the giving of the alarm. Any other protective measure taken in favour of the population shall also apply to them.

Detaining Powers shall give the Powers concerned, through the intermediary of the Protecting Powers, all useful information regarding the geographical locations of prisoner of war camps.

Whenever military considerations permit, prisoner of war camps shall be indicated in the day-time by the letters PW or PG, placed so as to be clearly visible from the air. The Powers concerned may, however, agree upon any other system of marking. Only prisoner of war camps shall be marked as such.

CHAPTER II - Quarters, Food and Clothing of Prisoners of War

ARTICLE XXV

Prisoners of war shall be quartered under conditions as favourable as those for the forces of the Detaining Power who are billeted in the same area. The said conditions shall make allowance for the habits and customs of the prisoners and shall in no case be prejudicial to their health.

The foregoing provisions shall apply in particular to the dormitories of prisoners of war as regards both total surface and minimum cubic space, and the general installations, bedding and blankets.

The premises provided for the use of prisoners of war, as well as men, are accommodated, separate dormitories shall be provided for them.

655

ARTICLE XXVI

The basic daily food rations shall be sufficient in quantity, quality and variety to keep prisoners of war in good heath and to prevent loss of weight or the development of nutritional deficiencies. Account shall also be taken of the habitual diet of the prisoners.

The Detaining Power shall supply prisoners of war who work with such additional rations as are necessary for the labour on which they are employed.

Sufficient drinking water shall be supplied to prisoners of war. The use of tobacco shall be permitted.

Prisoners of war shall, as far as possible, be associated with the preparation of their meals; they may be employed for that purpose in the kitchens. Furthermore, they shall be given the means of preparing, themselves, the additional food in their possession.

Adequate premises shall be provided for messing.

Collective disciplinary measures affecting food are prohibited.

CHAPTER III - Hygiene and Medical Attention

ARTICLE XXIX

The Detaining Power shall be bound to take all sanitary measures necessary to ensure the cleanliness and healthfulness of camps and to prevent epidemics.

Prisoners of war shall have for their use, day and night, conveniences which conform to the rules of hygiene and maintained in a constant state of cleanliness. In any camps in which women prisoners of war are accommodated, separate conveniences shall be provided for them.

Also, apart from the baths and showers with which the camps shall be furnished, prisoners of war shall be provided with sufficient water and soap for their personal toilet and for washing their personal laundry; the necessary installations, facilities and time shall be granted them for that purpose.

ARTICLE XXX

Every camp shall have an adequate infirmary where prisoners of war may have the attention they require, as well as an appropriate diet. Isolation wards shall, if necessary, be set aside for cases of contagious or mental disease.

Prisoners of war suffering from serious disease, or whose condition necessitates special treatment, a surgical operation or hospital care, must be admitted to any military or civilian medical unit where such treatment can be given, even if their repatriation is contemplated in the near future. Special facilities shall be afforded for the care to be given to the disabled, in particular to the blind, and for their rehabilitation, pending repatriation.

Prisoners of war shall have the attention, preferably, of medical personnel of the Power on which they depend and, if possible, of their nationality.

Prisoners of war may not be prevented from presenting themselves to the medical authorities for examination. The detaining authorities shall, upon request, issue to every prisoner who has undergone treatment, an official certificate indicating the nature of his illness or injury, and the duration and kind of treatment received. A duplicate of this certificate shall be forwarded to the Central Prisoners of War Agency.

The costs of treatment, including those of any apparatus necessary for the maintenance of prisoners of war in good health, particularly dentures and other artificial appliances, and spectacles, shall be borne by the Detaining Power.

CHAPTER IV - Medical Personnel and Chaplains Retained to Assist Prisoners of War

ARTICLE XXXIII

Members of the medical personnel and chaplains while retained by the Detaining Power with a view to assisting prisoners of war, shall not be considered as prisoners of war. They shall, however, receive as a minimum the benefits and protection of the present Convention, and shall also be granted all facilities necessary to provide for the medical care of, and religious ministration to prisoners of war.

They shall continue to exercise their medical and spiritual functions for the benefit of prisoners of war, preferably those belonging to the armed forces upon which they depend, within the scope of the military laws and regulations of the Detaining Power and under the control of its competent services, in accordance with their professional etiquette. They shall also benefit by the following facilities in the exercise of their medical or spiritual functions:

(a) They shall be authorized to visit periodically prisoners of war situated in working detachments or in hospitals outside the camp. For this purpose, the Detaining Power shall place at their disposal the necessary means of transport.

(b) The senior medical officer in each camp shall be responsible to the camp military authorities for everything connected with the activities of retained medical personnel. For this purpose, Parties to the conflict shall agree at the outbreak of hostilities on the subject of the corresponding ranks of the medical personnel, including that of societies mentioned in Article XXVI of the Geneva Convention for the Amelioration of the Condition of the Wounded and Sick in Armed Forces in the Field of August 12, 1949. This senior medical officer, as well as chaplains, shall have the right to deal with the competent authorities of the camp on all questions relating to their duties. Such authorities shall afford them all necessary facilities for correspondence relating to these questions.

(c) Although they shall be subject to the internal discipline of the camp in which they are retained, such personnel may not be compelled to carry out any work other than that concerned with their medical or religious duties.

During hostilities, the Parties to the conflict shall agree concerning the possible relief of retained personnel and shall settle the procedure to be followed.

None of the preceding provisions shall relieve the Detaining Power of its obligations with regard to prisoners of war from the medical or spiritual point of view.

CHAPTER V - Religious, Intellectual and Physical Activities

ARTICLE XXXIV

Prisoners of war shall enjoy complete latitude in the exercise of their religious duties, including attendance at the service of their faith, on condition that they comply with the disciplinary routine prescribed by the military authorities.

Adequate premises shall be provided where religious services may be held.

ARTICLE XXXVIII

While respecting the individual preferences of every prisoner, the Detaining Power shall encourage the practice of intellectual, educational, and recreational pursuits sports and games amongst prisoners, and shall take the measures necessary to ensure the exercise thereof by providing them with adequate premises and necessary equipment.

CHAPTER VIII - Transfer of Prisoners of War
After Their Arrival in Camp

ARTICLE XLVI

The Detaining Power, when deciding upon the transfer of prisoners of war, shall take into account the interest of the prisoners themselves, more especially so as not to increase the difficulty of their repatriation.

The transfer of prisoners of war shall always be effected humanely and in conditions not less favourable than those under which the forces of the Detaining Power are transferred. Account shall always be taken of the climatic conditions to which the prisoners of war are accustomed and the conditions of transfer shall in no case be prejudicial to their health.

The Detaining Power shall supply prisoners of war during transfer with sufficient food and drinking water to keep them in good health, likewise with the necessary clothing, shelter and medical attention. The Detaining Power shall take adequate precautions, especially in case of transport by sea or by air, to ensure their safety during transfer, and shall draw up a complete list of all transferred prisoners before their departure.

ARTICLE XLVII

Sick or wounded prisoners of war shall not be transferred as long as their recovery may be endangered by the journey, unless their safety imperatively demands it.

If the combat zone draws closer to a camp, the prisoner of war in the said camp shall not be transferred unless their transfer can be carried out in adequate conditions of safety, or unless they are exposed to greater risks by remaining on the spot than by being transferred.

Part VI - Execution of Convention

Section 1 - General Provisions

ARTICLE CXXIX

The High Contracting Parties undertake to enact any legislation necessary to provide effective penal sanctions for persons committing, or ordering to be committed, any of the grave breaches of the present Convention defined in the following Article.

Each High Contracting Party shall be under the obligation to search for persons alleged to have committed, or to have ordered to be committed, such grave breaches, and shall bring such persons, regardless of their nationality, before its own courts. It may also, if it prefers, and in accordance with the provisions of its own legislation, hand such persons over for trial to another High Contracting Party concerned, provided such High Contracting Party has made out a prima facie case.

Each High Contracting Party shall take measures necessary for the suppression of all acts contrary to the provisions of the present Convention other than the grave breaches defined in the following Article.

In all circumstances, the accused persons shall benefit by safeguards of proper trial and defence, which shall not be less favourable than those provided by Article CV and those following of the present Convention.

ARTICLE CXXX

Grave breaches to which the preceding Article relates shall be those involving any of the following acts, if committed against persons or property protected by the Convention: wilful killing, torture or inhuman treatment, including biological experiments, wilfully causing great suffering or serious injury to body or health, compelling a prisoner of war to serve in the forces of the hostile Power, or wilfully depriving a prisoner of war of the rights of a fair and regular trial prescribed in this Convention.

ARTICLE CXXXI

No High Contracting Party shall be allowed to absolve itself or any other High Contracting Party of any liability incurred by itself or by another High Contracting Party in respect of breaches referred to in the preceding Article.

12. CONVENTION RELATIVE TO THE PROTECTION OF CIVILIAN PERSONS IN TIME OF WAR, Geneva, 12 August 1949
(Excerpts)

75 U.N.T.S. 287, 6 U.S.T. 3516, T.I.A.S. 3365. *Reprinted in* 1 Friedman 641; Schindler/Toman 427.

ARTICLE III

In the case of armed conflict not of an international character occurring in the territory of one of the High Contracting Parties, each Party to the conflict shall be bound to apply, as a minimum, the following provisions:

1. Persons taking no active part in the hostilities, including members of armed forces who have laid down their arms and those placed *hors de combat* by sickness, wounds, detention, or any other cause, shall in all circumstances be treated humanely,

without any adverse distinction founded on race, colour, religion or faith, sex, birth or wealth, or any other similar criteria.

To this end, the following acts are and shall remain prohibited at any time and in any place whatsoever with respect to the above-mentioned persons:

(a) violence to life and person, in particular murder of all kinds, mutilation, cruel treatment and torture;
(b) taking of hostages;
(c) outrages upon personal dignity, in particular humiliating and degrading treatment;
(d) the passing of sentences and the carrying out of executions without previous judgment pronounced by a regularly constituted court, affording all the judicial guarantees which are recognized as indispensable by civilized peoples.

2. The wounded and sick shall be collected and cared for.

An impartial humanitarian body, such as the International Committee of the Red Cross, may offer its services to the Parties to the conflict.

The Parties to the conflict should further endeavour to bring into force, by means of special agreements, all or part of the other provisions of the present Convention.

The application of the preceding provisions shall not affect the legal status of the Parties to the conflict.

ARTICLE IV

Persons protected by the Convention are those who, at a given moment and in any manner whatsoever, find themselves, in case of a conflict or occupation, in the hands of a Party to the conflict or Occupying Power of which they are not nationals.

Nationals of a State which is not bound by the Convention are not protected by it. Nationals of a neutral State who find themselves in the territory of a belligerent State, and nationals of a co-belligerent State, shall not be regarded as protected persons while the State of which they are nationals has normal diplomatic representation in the State in whose hands they are.

The provisions of Part II are, however, wider in application, as defined in Article XIII.

Persons protected by the Geneva Convention for the Amelioration of the Condition of the Wounded and Sick in Armed Forces in the Field of August 12, 1949, or by the Geneva Convention for the Amelioration of the Condition of Wounded, Sick and Shipwrecked Members of Armed Forces at Sea of August 12, 1949, or by the Geneva Convention relative to the Treatment of Prisoners of War of August 12, 1949, shall not be considered as protected persons within the meaning of the present Convention.

ARTICLE V

Where in the territory of a Party to the conflict, the latter is satisfied that an individual protected person is definitely suspected of or engaged in activities hostile to the security of the State, such individual person shall not be entitled to claim such rights and privileges under the present Convention as would, if exercised in the favour of such individual person, be prejudicial to the security of such State.

Where in occupied territory an individual protected person is detained as a spy or saboteur, or as a person under definite suspicion of activity hostile to the security of the Occupying Power, such person shall, in those cases where absolute military security so requires, be regarded as having forfeited rights of communication under the present Convention.

In each case, such persons shall nevertheless be treated with humanity, and in case of trial, shall not be deprived of the rights of fair and regular trial prescribed by the present Convention. They shall also be granted the full rights and privileges of a protected person under the present Convention at the earliest date consistent with the security of the State or Occupying Power, as the case may be.

PART II. GENERAL PROTECTION OF POPULATIONS AGAINST CERTAIN CONSEQUENCES OF WAR

ARTICLE XIII

The provisions of Part II cover the whole of the populations of the countries in conflict, without any adverse distinction based, in particular, on race, nationality, religion or political opinion, and are intended to alleviate the sufferings caused by war.

ARTICLE XVI

The wounded and sick, as well as the infirm, and expectant mothers, shall be the object of particular protection and respect.

As far as military considerations allow, each Party to the conflict shall facilitate the steps taken to search for the killed and wounded, to assist the shipwrecked and other persons exposed to grave danger, and to protect them against pillage and ill-treatment.

ARTICLE XVII

The Parties to the conflict shall endeavour to conclude local agreements for the removal from besieged or encircled areas, of wounded, sick, infirm, and aged persons, children and maternity cases, and for the passage of ministers of all religions, medical personnel and medical equipment on their way to such areas.

ARTICLE XVIII

Civilian hospitals organized to give care to the wounded and sick, the infirm and maternity cases, may in no circumstances be the object of attack, but shall at all times be respected and protected by the Parties to the conflict.

States which are Parties to a conflict shall provide all civilian hospitals with certificates showing that they are civilian hospitals and that the buildings which they occupy are not used for any purpose which would deprive these hospitals of protection in accordance with Article XIX.

Civilian hospitals shall be marked by means of the emblem provided for in Article XXVIII of the Geneva Convention for the Amelioration of the Condition of the Wounded and Sick in Armed Forces in the Field of August 12, 1949, but only if so authorized by the State.

The Parties to the conflict shall, in so far as military considerations permit, take the necessary steps to make the distinctive emblems indicating civilian hospitals clearly visible to the enemy land, air and naval forces in order to obviate the possibility of any hostile action.

In view of the dangers to which hospitals may be exposed by being close to military objectives, it is recommended that such hospitals be situated as far as possible from such objectives.

ARTICLE XXIV

The Parties to the conflict shall take the necessary measures to ensure that children under fifteen, who are orphaned or are separated from their families as a result of the war, are not left to their own resources, and that their maintenance, the exercise of their religion and their education are facilitated in all circumstances. The education shall, as far as possible, be entrusted to persons of a similar cultural tradition.

The Parties to the conflict shall facilitate the reception of such children in a neutral country for the duration of the conflict with the consent of the Protecting Power, if any, and under due safeguards for the observance of the principles stated in the first paragraph.

PART III. STATUS AND TREATMENT OF PROTECTED PERSONS

SECTION I. PROVISIONS COMMON TO THE TERRITORIES OF THE PARTIES TO THE CONFLICT AND TO OCCUPIED TERRITORIES

ARTICLE XXVII

Protected persons are entitled, in all circumstances, to respect for their persons, their honour, their family rights, their religious convictions and practices, and their manners and customs. They shall at all times be humanely treated, and shall be protected especially against all acts of violence or threats thereof and against insults and public curiosity.

Women shall be especially protected against any attack on their honour, in particular against rape, enforced prostitution, or any form of indecent assault.

Without prejudice to the provisions relating to their state of health, age and sex, all protected persons shall be treated with the same consideration by the Party to the conflict in whose power they are, without any adverse distinction based, in particular, on race, religion or political opinion.

However, the Parties to the conflict may take such measures of control and security in regard to protected persons as may be necessary as a result of the war.

ARTICLE XXXI

No physical or moral coercion shall be exercised against protected persons, in particular to obtain information from them or from third parties.

ARTICLE XXXII

The High Contracting Parties specifically agree that each of them is prohibited from taking any measure of such a character as to cause the physical suffering or extermination of protected persons in their hands. This prohibition applies not only to murder, torture, corporal punishment, mutilation and medical or scientific experiments not necessitated by the medical treatment of a protected person, but also to any other measures of brutality whether applied by civilian or military agents.

ARTICLE XXXIII

No protected person may be punished for an offence he or she has not personally committed. Collective penalties and likewise all measures of intimidation or of terrorism are prohibited.

Pillage is prohibited.

Reprisals against protected persons and their property are prohibited.

ARTICLE XXXIV

The taking of hostages is prohibited.

SECTION II. ALIENS IN THE TERRITORY OF A PARTY TO THE CONFLICT

ARTICLE XXXVIII

With the exception of special measures authorized by the present Convention, in particular by Articles XXVII and XLI thereof, the situation of protected persons shall continue to be regulated, in principle, by the provisions concerning aliens in time of peace. In any case, the following rights shall be granted to them:

1. They shall be enabled to receive the individual or collective relief that may be sent to them.

2. They shall, if their state of health so requires, receive medical attention and hospital treatment to the same extent as the nationals of the State concerned.

3. They shall be allowed to practice their religion and to receive spiritual assistance from ministers of their faith.

4. If they reside in an area particularly exposed to the dangers of war, they shall be authorized to move from that area to the same extent as the nationals of the State concerned.

5. Children under fifteen years, pregnant women and mothers of children under seven years shall benefit by any preferential treatment to the same extent as the nationals of the State concerned.

ARTICLE XLIX

Individual or mass forcible transfers, as well as deportations of protected persons from occupied territory to the territory of the Occupying Power or to that of any other country, occupied or not, are prohibited, regardless of their motive.

Nevertheless, the Occupying Power may undertake total or partial evacuation of a given area if the security of the population or imperative military reasons so demand. Such evacuations may not involve the displacement of protected persons outside the bounds of the occupied territory except when for material reasons it is impossible to avoid such displacement. Persons thus evacuated shall be transferred back to their homes as soon as hostilities in the area in question have ceased.

The Occupying Power undertaking such transfers or evacuations shall ensure, to the greatest practicable extent, that proper accommodation is provided to receive the protected persons, that the removals are effected in satisfactory conditions of hygiene, health, safety and nutrition, and that members of the same family are not separated.

The Protecting Power shall be informed of any transfers and evacuations as soon as they have taken place.

The Occupying Power shall not detain protected persons in an area particularly exposed to the dangers of war unless the security of the population or imperative military reasons so demand.

The Occupying Power shall not deport or transfer parts of its own civilian population into the territory it occupies.

ARTICLE LV

To the fullest extent of the means available to it, the Occupying Power has the duty of ensuring the food and medical supplies of the population; it should, in particular, bring in the necessary foodstuffs, medical stores and other articles if the resources of the occupied territory are inadequate.

The Occupying Power may not requisition foodstuffs, articles or medical supplies available in the occupied territory, except for use by the occupation forces and administration personnel, and then only if the requirements of the civilian population have been taken into account. Subject to the provisions of other international Conventions, the Occupying Power shall make arrangements to ensure that fair value is paid for any requisitioned goods.

The Protecting Power shall, at any time, be at liberty to verify the state of the food and medical supplies in occupied territories, except where temporary restrictions are made necessary by imperative military requirements.

ARTICLE LVI

To the fullest extent of the means available to it, the Occupying Power has the duty of ensuring and maintaining, with the cooperation of national and local authorities, the medical and hospital establishments and services, public health and hygiene in the occupied territory, with particular reference to the adoption and application of the prophylactic and preventive measures necessary to combat the spread of contagious diseases and epidemics. Medical personnel of all categories shall be allowed to carry out their duties.

If new hospitals are set up in occupied territory and if the competent organs of the occupied State are not operating there, the occupying authorities shall, if necessary, grant them the recognition provided for in Article XVIII. In similar circumstances, the occupying authorities shall also grant recognition to hospital personnel and transport vehicles under the provisions of Articles XX and XXI.

In adopting measures of health and hygiene and in their implementation, the Occupying Power shall take into consideration the moral and ethical susceptibilities of the population of the occupied territory.

ARTICLE LVII

The Occupying Power may requisition civilian hospitals only temporarily and only in cases of urgent necessity for the care of military wounded and sick, and then on condition that suitable arrangements are made in due time for the care and treatment of the patients and for the needs of the civilian population for hospital accommodation.

The material and stores of civilian hospitals cannot be requisitioned so long as they are necessary for the needs of the civilian population.

ARTICLE LVIII

The Occupying Power shall permit ministers of religion to give spiritual assistance to the members of their religious communities.

The Occupying Power shall also accept consignments of books and articles required for religious needs and shall facilitate their distribution in occupied territory.

Section IV. Regulations for the Treatment of Internees

CHAPTER I - General Provisions

ARTICLE LXXIX

The Parties to the conflict shall not intern protected persons, except in accordance with the provisions of Articles XLI, XLII, XLIII, LXVIII and LXXVIII.

ARTICLE LXXX

Internees shall retain their full civil capacity and shall exercise such attendant rights as may be compatible with their status.

ARTICLE LXXXI

Parties to the conflict who intern protected persons shall be bound to provide free of charge for their maintenance, and to grant them also the medical attention required by their state of health.

No deduction from the allowances, salaries or credits due to the internees shall be made for the repayment of these costs.

The Detaining Power shall provide for the support of those dependent on the internees, if such dependents are without adequate means of support or are unable to earn a living.

ARTICLE LXXXII

The Detaining Power shall, as far as possible, accommodate the internees according to their nationality, language and customs. Internees who are nationals of the same country shall not be separated merely because they have different languages.

Throughout the duration of their internment, members of the same family, and in particular parents and children, shall be lodged together in the same place of internment, except when separation of a temporary nature is necessitated for reasons of employment of health or for the purposes of enforcement of the provisions of Chapter IX of the present Section. Internees may request that their children who are left at liberty without parental care shall be interned with them.

Wherever possible, interned members of the same family shall be housed in the same premises and given separate accommodation from other internees, together with facilities for leading a proper family life.

CHAPTER II - Places of Internment

ARTICLE LXXXV

The Detaining Power is bound to take all necessary and possible measures to ensure that protected persons shall, from the outset of their internment, be accommodated in buildings or quarters which afford every possible safeguard as regards hygiene and health, and provide efficient protection against the rigors of the climate and the effects of the war. In no case shall permanent places of internment be situated in an unhealthy area or have a climate which is harmful to his health, he shall be removed to a more suitable place of internment as rapidly as circumstances permit.

The premises shall be fully protected from dampness, adequately heated and lighted, in particular between dusk and lights out. The sleeping quarters shall be sufficiently spacious and well ventilated, and the internees shall have suitable bedding and sufficient blankets, account being taken of the climate, and the age, sex, and state of health of the internees.

Internees shall have for their use, day and night, sanitary conveniences which conform to the rules of hygiene and are constantly maintained in a state of cleanliness. They shall be provided with sufficient water and soap for their daily personal toilet and for washing their personal laundry; installations and facilities necessary for this purpose shall be granted to them. Showers or bathe shall also be available. The necessary time shall be set aside for washing and for cleaning.

Whenever it is necessary, as an exceptional and temporary measure, to accommodate women internees who are not members of a family unit in the same place of internment as men, the provision of separate sleeping quarters and sanitary conveniences for the use of such women internees shall be obligatory.

ARTICLE LXXXVI

The Detaining Power shall place at the disposal of interned persons, of whatever denomination, premises suitable for the holding of their religious services.

CHAPTER III - Food and Clothing

ARTICLE LXXXIX

Daily food rations for internees shall be sufficient in quantity, quality and variety to keep internees in a good state of health and prevent the development of nutritional deficiencies. Account shall also be taken of the customary diet of the internees.

Internees shall also be given the means by which they can prepare for themselves any additional food in their possession.

Sufficient drinking water shall be supplied to internees. The use of tobacco shall be permitted.

Internees who work shall receive additional rations in proportion to the kind of labour which they perform.

Expectant and nursing mothers, and children under fifteen years of age, shall be given additional food, in proportion to their physiological needs.

672

ARTICLE XC

When taken into custody, internees shall be given all facilities to provide themselves with the necessary clothing, footwear and change of underwear, and later on, to procure further supplies if required. Should any internees not have sufficient clothing account being taken of the climate, and be unable to procure any, it shall be provided free of charge to them by the Detaining Power.

The clothing supplied by the Detaining Power to internees and the outward markings placed on their own clothes shall not be ignominious nor expose them to ridicule.

Workers shall receive suitable working outfits, including protective clothing, whenever the nature of their work so requires.

CHAPTER IV - Hygiene and Medical Attention

ARTICLE XCI

Every place of internment shall have an adequate infirmary, under the direction of a qualified doctor, where internees may have the attention they require, as well as an appropriate diet. Isolation wards shall be set aside for cases of contagious or mental diseases.

Maternity cases and internees suffering from serious diseases, or whose condition requires special treatment, a surgical operation or hospital care, must be admitted to any institution where adequate treatment can be given and shall receive care not inferior to that provided for the general population.

Internees shall, for preference, have the attention of medical personnel of their own nationality.

Internees may not be prevented from presenting themselves to the medical authorities for examination. The medical authorities of the Detaining Power shall, upon request, issue to every internee who has undergone treatment an official certificate showing the nature of his illness or injury, and the duration and nature of the treatment given. A duplicate of this certificate shall be forwarded to the Central Agency provided for in Article CXL.

Treatment, including the provision of any apparatus necessary for the maintenance of internees in good health, particularly dentures and other artificial appliances and spectacles, shall be free of charge to the internee.

CHAPTER V - Religious, Intellectual and Physical Activities

ARTICLE XCIII

Internees shall enjoy complete latitude in the exercise of their religious duties, including attendance at the services of their faith, on condition that they comply with the disciplinary routine prescribed by the detaining authorities.

Ministers of religion who are interned shall be allowed to minister freely to the members of their community. For this purpose, the Detaining Power shall ensure their equitable allocation amongst the various places of internment in which there are internees speaking the same language and belonging to the same religion. Should such ministers be too few in number, the Detaining Power shall provide them with the necessary facilities, including means of transport, for moving from one place to another, and they shall be authorized to visit any internees who are in hospital. Ministers of religion shall be at liberty to correspond on matters concerning their ministry with the religious authorities in the country of detention and, as far as possible, with the international religious organizations of their faith. Such correspondence shall not be considered as forming a part of the quota mentioned in Article CVII. It shall, however, be subject to the provisions of Article CXII.

When internees do not have at their disposal the assistance of ministers of their faith, or should these latter be too few in number, the local religious authorities of the same faith may appoint, in agreement with the Detaining Power, a minister of the internees' faith, or if such a course is feasible from a denominational point view, a minister of similar religion or a qualified layman. The latter shall enjoy the facilities granted to the ministry he has assumed. Persons so appointed shall comply with all regulations laid down by the Detaining Power in the interests of discipline and security.

ARTICLE XCIV

The Detaining Power shall encourage intellectual, educational and recreational pursuits, sports and games amongst internees, whilst leaving them free to take part in them or not. It shall take all practicable measures to ensure the exercise thereof, in particular by providing suitable premises.

All possible facilities shall be granted to internees to continue their studies or to take up new subjects. The education of children and young people shall be ensured; they shall be allowed to attend schools either within the place of internment or outside.

Internees shall be given opportunities for physical exercise, sports and outdoor games. For this purpose, sufficient open spaces shall be set aside in all places of internment. Special playgrounds shall be reserved for children and young people.

ARTICLE XCV

The Detaining Power shall not employ internees as workers, unless they so desire. Employment which, if undertaken under compulsion by a protected person not in internment, would involve a breach of Articles XLI or LI of the present Convention, and employment on work which is of a degrading or humiliating character are in any case prohibited.

After a working period of six weeks, internees shall be free to give up work at any moment, subject to eight days' notice.

These provisions constitute no obstacle to the right of the Detaining Power to employ interned doctors, dentists and other medical personnel in their professional capacity on behalf of their fellow internees, or to employ internees for administrative and maintenance work in places of internment and to detail such persons for work in the kitchens or for other domestic tasks, or to require such persons to undertake duties connected with the protection of internees against aerial bombardment or other war risks. No internee may, however, be required to perform tasks for which he is, in the opinion of a medical officer, physically unsuited.

The Detaining Power shall take entire responsibility for all working conditions, for medical attention, for the payment of wages, and for ensuring that all employed

675

internees receive compensation for occupational accidents and diseases. The standards prescribed for the said working conditions and for compensation shall be in accordance with the national laws and regulations, and with the existing practice; they shall in no case be inferior to those obtaining for work of the same nature in the same district. Wages for work done shall be determined on an equitable basis by special agreements between the internees, the Detaining Power, and, if the case arises, employers other than the Detaining Power, due regard being paid to the obligation of the Detaining Power to provide for free maintenance of internees and for the medical attention which their state of health may require. Internees permanently detailed for categories of work mentioned in the third paragraph of this Article, shall be paid fair wages by the Detaining Power. The working conditions and the scale of compensation for occupational accidents and diseases to internees thus detailed shall not be inferior to those applicable to work of the same nature in the same district.

CHAPTER VI - Personal Property and Financial Resources

Article XCVII

Internees shall be permitted to retain articles of personal use. Monies, cheques, bonds, etc., and valuables in their possession may not be taken from them except in accordance with established procedure. Detailed receipts shall be given therefor.

The amounts shall be paid into the account of every internee as provided for in Article XCVIII. Such amounts may not be converted into any other currency unless legislation in force in the territory in which the owner is interned so requires or the internee gives his consent.

Articles which have above all a personal or sentimental value may not be taken away.

A woman internee shall not be searched except by a woman.

On release or repatriation, internees shall be given all articles, monies or other valuables taken from them during internment and shall receive in currency the balance of any credit to their accounts kept in accordance with Article XCVIII, with the exception of any articles or amounts withheld by the Detaining Power by virtue of its legislation in force. If the property of an internee is so withheld, the owner shall receive a detailed receipt....

ARTICLE C

The disciplinary regime in places of internment shall be consistent with humanitarian principles, and shall in no circumstances include regulations imposing on internees any physical exertion dangerous to their health or involving physical or moral victimization. Identification by tattooing or imprinting signs or markings on the body is prohibited.

In particular, prolonged standing and roll-calls, punishment drill, military drill and manoeuvres, or the reduction of food rations are prohibited.

Chapter VIII - Relations with the Exterior

ARTICLE CVIII

Internees shall be allowed to receive, by post or by any other means, individual parcels or collective shipments containing in particular foodstuffs, clothing, medical supplies, as well as books and objects of a devotional, educational or recreational character which may meet their needs. Such shipments shall in no way free the Detaining Power from the obligations imposed upon it by virtue of the present Convention.

Should military necessity require the quantity of such shipments to be limited, due notice thereof shall be given to the Protecting Power and to the International Committee of the Red Cross, or to any other organization giving assistance to the internees and responsible for the forwarding of such shipments.

The conditions for the sending of individual parcels and collective shipments shall, if necessary, be the subject of special agreements between the Powers concerned, which may in no case delay the receipt by the internees of relief supplies. Parcels of clothing and foodstuffs may not include books. Medical relief supplies shall, as a rule, be sent in collective parcels.

677

CHAPTER XII - Release, Repatriation and Accommodation in Neutral Countries

ARTICLE CXXXII

Each interned person shall be released by the Detaining Power as soon as the reasons which necessitated his internment no longer exist.

The Parties to the conflict shall, moreover, endeavour during the course of hostilities, to conclude agreements for the release, the repatriation, the return to places of residence or the accommodation in a neutral country of certain classes of internees, in particular children, pregnant women and mothers with infants and young children, wounded and sick, and internees who have been detained for a long time.

Part IV
Execution of the Convention

Section 1 - General Provisions

ARTICLE CXLVI

The High Contracting Parties undertake to enact any legislation necessary to provide effective penal sanctions for persons committing, or ordering to be committed, any of the grave breaches of the present Convention defined in the following Article.

Each High Contracting Party shall be under the obligation to search for persons alleged to have committed, or to have ordered to be committed, such grave breaches, and shall bring such persons, regardless of their nationality, before its own courts. It may also, if it prefers, and in accordance with the provisions of its own legislation, hand such persons over for trial to another High Contracting Party concerned, provided such High Contracting Party has made out a prima facie case.

Each High Contracting Party shall take measures necessary for the suppression of all acts contrary to the provisions of the present Convention other than the grave breaches defined in the following Article.

In all circumstances, the accused persons shall benefit by safeguards of proper trial and defence, which shall not be less favourable than those provided by Article CV and

678

those following of the Geneva Convention relative to the Treatment of Prisoners of War of August 12, 1949.

ARTICLE CXLVII

Grave breaches to which the preceding Article relates shall be those involving any of the following acts, if committed against persons or property protected by the present Convention: wilful killing, torture or inhuman treatment, including biological experiments, wilfully causing great suffering or serious injury to body or health, unlawful deportation or transfer or unlawful confinement of protected persons, compelling a protected person to serve in the forces of a hostile Power, or wilfully depriving a protected person of the rights of a fair and regular trial prescribed in the present Convention, taking of hostages and extensive destruction and appropriation of property, not justified by military necessity and carried out unlawfully and wantonly.

ARTICLE CXLVIII

No High Contracting Party shall be allowed to absolve itself or any other High Contracting Party of any liability incurred by itself or by another High Contracting Party in respect of breaches referred to in the preceding Article.

13. **PROTOCOL ADDITIONAL TO THE GENEVA CONVENTIONS OF 12 AUGUST 1949, AND RELATING TO THE PROTECTION OF VICTIMS OF INTERNATIONAL ARMED CONFLICTS (PROTOCOL I), Geneva, 12 December 1977**

(Excerpts)

U.N. Doc. A/32/144 Annex I. *Reprinted in* 16 ILM 1391 (1977); Schindler/Toman 551.

INTRODUCTORY NOTE: The present Protocol brings mainly the following innovations:

Article 1(4) provides that armed conflicts in which peoples are fighting against colonial domination, alien occupation or racist regimes are to be considered international conflicts.

Part II (Articles 8-34) develops the rules of the First and the Second Geneva Conventions on wounded, sick and shipwrecked. It extends the protection of the Conventions to civilian medical personnel, equipment and supplies and to civilian units and transports and contains detailed provisions on medical transportation.

Part III and several chapters of Part IV (Articles 35-60) deal with the conduct of hostilities, i.e. questions which hitherto were regulated by the Hague Conventions of 1899 and 1907 and by customary international law. Their reaffirmation and development is important in view of the age of the Hague Conventions and of the new States which had no part in their elaboration Articles 43 and 44 give a new definition of armed forces and combat. Among the most important Articles are those on the protection of the civilian population against the effects of hostilities. They contain a definition of military objectives and prohibitions of attack on civilian persons and objects. Further Articles (61-79) deal with the protection of civil defence organizations, relief actions and the treatment of persons in the power of a party to the conflict.

Part V (Articles 80-91) brings some new elements to the problem on execution of the Conventions and the Protocol.

ENTRY INTO FORCE: 7 December 1978

PROTOCOL I ADDITIONAL TO THE GENEVA CONVENTIONS, 1977

PREAMBLE

Proclaiming their earnest wish to see peace prevail among peoples,

Recalling that every State has the duty, in conformity with the Charter of the United Nations, to refrain in its international relations from the threat or use of force against the sovereignty, territorial integrity or political independence of any State, or in any other manner inconsistent with the purposes of the United Nations,

Believing it necessary nevertheless to reaffirm and develop the provisions protecting the victims of armed conflicts and to supplement measures intended to reinforce their application,

Expressing their conviction that nothing in this Protocol or in the Geneva Conventions of 12 August 1949 can be construed as legitimizing or authorizing any act of aggression or any other use of force inconsistent with the Charter of the United Nations,

Reaffirming further that the provisions of the Geneva Conventions of 12 August 1949 and of this Protocol must be fully applied in all circumstances to all persons who are protected by those instruments, without any adverse distinction based on the nature or origin of the armed conflict or on the causes espoused by or attributed to the Parties to the conflict,

Have agreed on the following:

PART I

GENERAL PROVISIONS

Article 1 - General principles and scope of application

1. The High Contracting Parties undertake to respect and to ensure respect for this Protocol in all circumstances.

2. In cases not covered by this Protocol or by other international agreements, civilians and combatants remain under the protection and authority of the principles of international law derived from established custom, from the principles of humanity and from the dictates of public conscience.

3. This Protocol, which supplements the Geneva Conventions of 12 August 1949 for the protection of war victims, shall apply in the situations referred to in Article 2 common to those Conventions.

4. The situations referred to in the preceding paragraph include armed conflicts in which peoples are fighting against colonial domination and alien occupation and against racist regimes in the exercise of their right of self-determination, as enshrined in the Charter of the United Nations and the Declaration on Principles of International Law

681

concerning Friendly Relations and Co-operation among States in accordance with the Charter of the United Nations.

Part III Methods and Means of Warfare Combatant and Prisoner-of-War Status

Section II Combatant and Prisoner-of-War Status

...

Article 45--Protection of persons who have taken part in hostilities

1. A person who takes part in hostilities and falls into the power of an adverse Party shall be presumed to be a prisoner of war, and therefore shall be protected by the Third Convention, if he claims the status of prisoner of war, or if he appears to be entitled to such status, or if the Party on which he depends claims such status on his behalf by notification to the Detaining Power or to the Protecting Power. Should any doubt arise as to whether any such person is entitled to the status of prisoner of war, he shall continue to have such status and, therefore, to be protected by the Third Convention and this Protocol until such time as his status has been determined by a competent tribunal.

2. If a person who has fallen into the power of an adverse Party is not held as a prisoner of war and is to be tried by that Party for an offence arising out of the hostilities, he shall have the right to assert his entitlement to prisoner-of-war status before a judicial tribunal and to have that question adjudicated. Whenever possible under the applicable procedure, this adjudication shall occur before the trial for the offence. The representatives of the Protecting Power shall be entitled to attend the proceedings in which that question is adjudicated, unless, exceptionally, the proceedings are held in camera in the interest of State security. In such a case the Detaining Power shall advise the Protecting Power accordingly.

3. Any person who has taken part in hostilities, who is not entitled to prisoner-of-war status and who does not benefit from more favourable treatment in accordance with the Fourth Convention shall have the right at all times to the protection of Article 75 of this Protocol. In occupied territory, any such person, unless he is held as a spy,

shall also be entitled, notwithstanding Article 5 of the Fourth Convention, to his rights of communication under that Convention.

PART IV
CIVILIAN POPULATION

SECTION I

GENERAL PROTECTION AGAINST EFFECTS OF HOSTILITIES

Chapter I

BASIC RULE AND FIELD OF APPLICATION

Article 48 - Basic rule

In order to ensure respect for and protection of the civilian population and civilian objects, the Parties to the conflict shall at all times distinguish between the civilian population and combatants and between civilian objects and military objectives and accordingly shall direct their operations only against military objectives.

Article 49 - Definition of attacks and scope of application

1. "Attacks" means acts of violence against the adversary, whether in offence or in defence.

2. The provisions of this Protocol with respect to attacks apply to all attacks in whatever territory conducted, including the national territory belonging to a Party to the conflict but under the control of an adverse Party.

3. The provisions of this Section apply to any land, air or sea warfare which may affect the civilian population, individual civilians or civilian objects on land. They further apply to all attacks from the sea or from the air against objectives on land but do not otherwise affect the rules of international law applicable in armed conflict at sea or in the air.

4.   The provisions of this Section are additional to the rules concerning humanitarian protection contained in the Fourth Convention, particularly in Part II thereof, and in other international agreements binding from the High Contracting Parties, as well as to other rules of international law relating to the protection of civilians and civilian objects on land, at sea or in the air against the effects of hostilities.

Chapter II

CIVILIANS AND CIVILIAN POPULATION

Article 50 - Definition of civilians and civilian population

1.   A civilian is any person who does not belong to one of the categories of persons referred to in Article 4 A (1), (2), (3) and (6) of the Third Convention and in Article 43 of this Protocol. In case of doubt whether a person is a civilian, that person shall be considered to be a civilian.

2.   The civilian population comprises all persons who are civilians.

3.   The presence within the civilian population of individuals who do not come within the definition of civilians does not deprive the population of its civilian character.

Article 51 - Protection of the civilian population

1.   The civilian population and individual civilians shall enjoy general protection against dangers arising from military operations. To give effect to this protection, the following rules, which are additional to other applicable rules of international law, shall be observed in all circumstances.

2.   The civilian population as such, as well as individual civilians, shall not be the object of attack. Acts or threats of violence the primary purpose of which is to spread terror among the civilian population are prohibited.

3.   Civilians shall enjoy the protection afforded by this Section, unless and for such time as they take a direct part in hostilities.

4. Indiscriminate attacks are prohibited. Indiscriminate attacks are:

(a) those which are not directed at a specific military objective;
(b) those which employ a method or means of combat which cannot be directed at a specific military objective; or
(c) those which employ a method or means of combat the effects of which cannot be limited as required by this Protocol;

and consequently, in each such case, are of a nature to strike military objectives and civilians or civilian objects without distinction.

5. Among others, the following types of attacks are to be considered as indiscriminate:

(a) an attack by bombardment by any methods or means which treats as a single military objective a number of clearly separated and distinct military objectives located in a city, town, village or other area containing a similar concentration of civilians or civilian objects; and
(b) an attack which may be expected to cause incidental loss of civilian life, injury to civilians, damage to civilian objects, or a combination thereof, which would be excessive in relation to the concrete and direct military advantage anticipated.

6. Attacks against the civilian population or civilians by way of reprisals are prohibited.

7. The presence or movements of the civilian population or individual civilians shall not be used to render certain points or areas immune from military operations, in particular in attempts to shield military objectives from attacks or to shield, favour or impede military operations. The Parties to the conflict shall not direct the movement of the civilian population or individual civilians in order to attempt to shield military objectives from attacks or to shield military operations.

8. Any violation of these prohibitions shall not release the Parties to the conflict from their legal obligations with respect to the civilian population and civilians, including the obligation to take the precautionary measures provided for in Article 57.

Chapter III

CIVILIAN OBJECTS

Article 52 - General Protection of Civilian Objects

1. Civilian objects shall not be the object of attack or of reprisals. Civilian objects are all objects which are not military objectives as defined in paragraph 2.

2. Attacks shall be limited strictly to military objectives. In so far as objects are concerned, military objectives are limited to those objects which by their nature, location, purpose or use make an effective contribution to military action and whose total or partial destruction, capture or neutralization, in the circumstances ruling at the time, offers a definite military advantage.

3. In case of doubt whether an object which is normally dedicated to civilian purposes, such as a place of worship, a house or other dwelling or a school, is being used to make an effective contribution to military action, it shall be presumed not to be so used.

Article 53 - Protection of cultural objects and of places of worship

Without prejudice to the provisions of the Hague Convention for the Protection of Cultural Property in the Event of Armed Conflict of 14 May 1954, and of other relevant international instruments, it is prohibited:

(a) to commit any acts of hostility directed against the historic monuments, works of art or places of worship which constitute the cultural or spiritual heritage of peoples;
(b) to use such objects in support of the military effort;
(c) to make such objects the object of reprisals.

Article 54 - Protection of objects indispensable to the survival of the civilian population

1. Starvation of civilians as a method of warfare is prohibited.

2. It is prohibited to attack, destroy, remove or render useless objects indispensable to the survival of the civilian population, such as foodstuffs, agricultural areas for the production of foodstuffs, crops, livestock, drinking water installations and supplies and irrigation works, for the specific purpose of denying them for their sustenance value to the civilian population or to the adverse Party, whatever the motive, whether in order to starve out civilians, to cause them to move away, or for any other motive.

3. The prohibitions in paragraph 2 shall not apply to such of the objects covered by it as are used by an adverse Party:

(a) as sustenance solely for the members of its armed forces; or
(b) if not as sustenance, then in direct support of military action, provided, however, that in no event shall actions against these objects be taken which may be expected to leave the civilian population with such inadequate food or water as to cause its starvation or force its movement.

4. These objects shall not be made the object of reprisals.

5. In recognition of the vital requirements of any Party to the conflict in the defence of its national territory against invasion, derogation from the prohibitions contained in paragraph 2 may be made by a Party to the conflict within such territory under its own control where required by imperative military necessity.

Article 55 - Protection of the natural environment

1. Care shall be taken in warfare to protect the natural environment against widespread, long-term and severe damage. This protection includes a prohibition of the use of methods or means of warfare which are intended or may be expected to cause such damage to the natural environment and thereby to prejudice the health or survival of the population.

2. Attacks against the natural environment by way of reprisals are prohibited.

14. PROTOCOL ADDITIONAL TO THE GENEVA CONVENTIONS OF 12
    AUGUST 1949, AND RELATING TO THE PROTECTION OF VICTIMS
    OF NON-INTERNATIONAL ARMED CONFLICTS, (PROTOCOL II),
    Geneva, 12 December 1977
                              (Excerpts)

U.N. Doc. A/32/144 Annex II. *Reprinted in* 13 ILM 1391 at 1442 (1977);
Schindler/Toman 619.

INTRODUCTORY NOTE. The only provision applicable to non-international armed
conflicts before the adoption of the present Protocol was Article 3 common to all four
Geneva Conventions of 1949. This Article proved to be inadequate in view of the fact
that about 80% of the victims of armed conflicts since 1945 have been victims of non-
international conflicts and that non-international conflicts are often fought with more
cruelty than international conflicts. The aim of the present Protocol is to extend the
essential rules of the law of armed conflicts to internal wars. The fear that the Protocol
might affect State sovereignty, prevent governments from effectively maintaining law
and order within their borders and that it might be invoked to justify outside
intervention led to the decision of the Diplomatic Conference at its fourth session to
shorten and simplify the Protocol. Instead of the 47 Articles proposed by the ICRC the
Conference adopted only 28. The essential substance of the draft was, however,
maintained. The part on methods and means of combat was deleted, but its basic
principles are to be found in Article 4 (fundamental guarantees). The provisions of the
activity of impartial humanitarian organizations were adopted in a less binding form
than originally foreseen. The restrictive definition of the material field of application
in Article I will have the effect that Protocol II will be applicable to a smaller range
of internal conflicts than Article 3 common to the Conventions of 1949.

ENTRY INTO FORCE: 7 December 1978

                              PREAMBLE

The High Contracting Parties.

Recalling that the humanitarian principles enshrined in Article 3 common to the Geneva Conventions of 12 August 1949, constitutes the foundation of respect for the human person in cases of armed conflict not of an international character,

Recalling furthermore that international instruments relating to human rights offer a basic protection to the human person,

Emphasizing the need to ensure a better protection for the victims of those armed conflicts,

Recalling that, in cases not covered by the law in force, the human person remains under the protection of the principles of humanity and the dictates of the public conscience,

Have agreed on the following:

PART I

SCOPE OF THIS PROTOCOL

Article I - Material field of application

1. This Protocol, which develops and supplements Article 3 common to the Geneva Conventions of 12 August 1949 without modifying its existing conditions of application, shall apply to all armed conflicts which are not covered by Article I of the Protocol Additional to the Geneva Conventions of 12 August 1949, and relating to the Protection of Victims of International Armed Conflicts (Protocol I) and which take place in the territory of a High Contracting Party between its armed forces and dissident armed forces or other organized armed groups which, under responsible command, exercise such control over a part of its territory as to enable them to carry out sustained and concerted military operations and to implement this Protocol.

2. This Protocol shall not apply to situations of internal disturbances and tensions, such as riots, isolated and sporadic acts of violence and other acts of a similar nature, as not being armed conflicts.

PART II

HUMANE TREATMENT

Article 4 - Fundamental guarantees

1. All persons who do not take a direct part or who have ceased to take part in hostilities, whether or not their liberty has been restricted, are entitled to respect for their person, honour and convictions and religious practices. They shall in all circumstances be treated humanely, without any adverse distinction. It is prohibited to order that there shall be no survivors.

2. Without prejudice to the generality of the foregoing, the following acts against the persons referred to in paragraph 1 are and shall remain prohibited at any time and in any place whatsoever:

(a) violence to the life, health, and physical or mental well-being of persons, in particular murder as well as cruel treatment such as torture, mutilation or any form of corporal punishment;

(b) collective punishments;

(c) taking of hostages;

(d) acts of terrorism;

(e) outrages upon personal dignity, in particular humiliating and degrading treatment, rape, enforced prostitution and any form of indecent assault;

(f) slavery and the slave trade in all their forms;

(g) pillage;

(h) threats to commit any of the foregoing acts.

3. Children shall be provided with the care and aid they require, and in particular:

(a) they shall receive an education, including religious and moral education, in keeping with the wishes of their parents or, in the absence of parents, of those responsible for their care;

(b) all appropriate steps shall be taken to facilitate the reunion of families temporarily separated;

(c) children who have not attained the age of fifteen years shall neither be recruited in the armed forces or groups nor allowed to take part in hostilities;

(d) the special protection provided by this Article to children who have not attained the age of fifteen years shall remain applicable to them if they take a direct part in hostilities despite the provisions of sub-paragraph (c) and are captured;

(e) measures shall be taken, if necessary, and whenever possible with the consent of their parents or persons who by law or custom are primarily responsible for their care, to remove children temporarily from the area in which hostilities are taking place to a safer area within the country and ensure that they are accompanied by persons responsible for their safety and well-being.

Article 5 - Persons whose liberty has been restricted

1. In addition to the provisions of Article 4, the following provisions shall be respected as a minimum with regard to persons deprived of their liberty for reasons related to the armed conflict, whether they are interned or detained:

(a) the wounded and the sick shall be treated in accordance with Article 7;

(b) the persons referred to in this paragraph shall, to the same extent as the local civilian population, be provided with food and drinking water and be afforded safeguards as regards health and hygiene and protection against the rigors of the climate and the dangers of the armed conflict;

(c) they shall be allowed to receive individual or collective relief;

(d) they shall be allowed to practice their religion and, if requested and appropriate, to receive spiritual assistance from persons, such as chaplains, performing religious functions;

(e) they shall, if made to work, have the benefit of working conditions and safeguards similar to those enjoyed by the local civilian population.

2. Those who are responsible for the internment or detention of the persons referred to in paragraph 1 shall also, within the limits of their capabilities, respect the following provisions relating to such persons:

(a) except when men and women of a family are accommodated together, women shall be held in quarters separated from those of men and shall be under the immediate supervision of women;

(b) they shall be allowed to send and receive letters and cards, the number of which may be limited by competent authority if it deems necessary;

(c) places of internment and detention shall not be located close to the combat zone. The persons referred to in paragraph 1 shall be evacuated when the places where they are interned or detained become particularly exposed to danger arising out of the armed conflict, if their evacuation can be carried out under adequate conditions of safety;

(d) they shall have the benefit of medical examinations;

(e) their physical or mental health and integrity shall not be endangered by any unjustified act or omission. Accordingly, it is prohibited to subject the persons described in this Article to any medical procedure which is not indicated by the state of health of the person concerned, and which is not consistent with the generally accepted medical standards applied to free persons under similar medical circumstances.

3. Persons who are not covered by paragraph 1 but whose liberty has been restricted in any way whatsoever for reasons related to the armed conflict shall be treated humanely in accordance with Article 4 and with paragraphs 1 (a), (c) and (d), and 2(b) of this Article.

4. If it is decided to release persons deprived of their liberty, necessary measures to ensure their safety shall be taken by those so deciding.

Article 6 - Penal prosecutions

1. This Article applies to the prosecution and punishment of criminal offences related to the armed conflict.

2. No sentence shall be passed and no penalty shall be executed on a person found guilty of an offence except pursuant to a conviction pronounced by a court offering the essential guarantees of independence and impartiality. In particular:

(a) the procedure shall provide for an accused to be informed without delay of the particulars of the offence alleged against him and shall afford the accused before and during his trial all necessary rights and means of defence;

(b) no one shall be convicted of an offence except on the basis of individual penal responsibility;

(c) no one shall be held guilty of any criminal offence on account of any act or omission which did not constitute a criminal offence, under the law, at the time when it was committed; nor shall a heavier penalty be imposed than that which was applicable at the time when the criminal offence was committed; if, after the commission of the offence, provision is made by law for the imposition of a lighter penalty, the offender shall benefit thereby;

(d) anyone charged with an offence is presumed innocent until proven guilty according to law;

(e) anyone charged with an offence shall have the right to be tried in his presence;

(f) no one shall be compelled to testify against himself or to confess guilt.

3. A convicted person shall be advised on conviction of his judicial and other remedies and of the time-limits within which they may be exercised.

4. The death penalty shall not be pronounced on persons who were under the age of eighteen years at the time of the offence and shall not be carried out on pregnant women or mothers of young children.

5. At the end of hostilities, the authorities in power shall endeavour to grant the broadest possible amnesty to persons who have participated in the armed conflict, or those deprived of their liberty for reasons related to the armed conflict, whether they are interned or detained.

PART III

WOUNDED, SICK AND SHIPWRECKED

Article 7 - Protection and care

1. All the wounded, sick and shipwrecked, whether or not they have taken part in the armed conflict, shall be respected and protected.

2. In all circumstances they shall be treated humanely and shall receive, to the fullest extent practicable and with the least possible delay, the medical care and attention required by their condition. There shall be no distinction among them founded on any grounds other than medical ones.

Article 8 - Search

Whenever circumstances permit, and particularly after an engagement, all possible measures shall be taken, without delay, to search for and collect the wounded, sick and shipwrecked, to protect them against pillage and ill-treatment, to ensure their adequate care, and to search for the dead, prevent their being despoiled, decently dispose of them.

Article 9 - Protection of medical and religious personnel

1. Medical and religious personnel shall be respected and protected and shall be granted all available help for the performance of their duties. They shall not be compelled to carry out tasks which are not compatible with their humanitarian mission.

2. In the performance of their duties medical personnel may not be required to give priority to any person except on medical grounds.

Article 10 - General protection of medical duties

1. Under no circumstances shall any person be punished for having carried out medical activities compatible with medical ethics, regardless of the person benefiting therefrom.

2. Persons engaged in medical activities shall neither be compelled to perform acts nor to carry out work contrary to, nor be compelled to refrain from acts required by, the rules of medical ethics or other rules designed for the benefit of the wounded and sick, or this Protocol.

3. The professional obligations of persons engaged in medical activities regarding information which they may acquire concerning the wounded and sick under their care shall, subject to national law, be respected.

4. Subject to national law, no person engaged in medical activities may be penalized in any way for refusing or failing to give information concerning the wounded and sick who are, or who have been, under his care.

Article 11 - Protection of medical units and transports

1.   Medical units and transports shall be respected and protected at all times and shall not be the object of attack.

2.   The protection to which medical units and transports are entitled shall not cease unless they are used to commit hostile acts, outside their humanitarian function. Protection may, however, cease only after a warning has been given setting, whenever appropriate, a reasonable time-limit, and after such warning has remained unheeded.

Article 12 - The distinctive emblem

Under the direction of the competent authority concerned, the distinctive emblem of the red cross, red crescent or red lion and sun on a white ground shall be displayed by medical and religious personnel and medical units, and on medical transports. It shall be respected in all circumstances. It shall not be used improperly.

PART IV

CIVILIAN POPULATION

Article 13 - Protection of the civilian population

1.   The civilian population and individual civilians shall enjoy general protection against the dangers arising from military operations. To give effect to this protection, the following rules shall be observed in all circumstances.

2.   The civilian population as such, as well as individual civilians, shall not be the object of attack. Acts or threats of violence the primary purpose of which is to spread terror among the civilian population are prohibited.

3.   Civilians shall enjoy the protection afforded by this Part, unless and for such time as they take a direct part in hostilities.

Article 14 - Protection of objects indispensable to the survival of the civilian population

Starvation of civilians as a method of combat is prohibited. It is therefore prohibited to attack, destroy, remove or render useless, for that purpose, objects indispensable to the survival of the civilian population, such as foodstuffs, agricultural areas for the population of foodstuffs, crops, livestock, drinking water installations and supplies and irrigation works.

Article 15 - Protection of works and installations containing dangerous forces

Works or installations containing dangerous forces, namely dams, dykes and nuclear electrical generating stations, shall not be made the object of attack, even where these objects are military objectives, if such attack may cause the release of dangerous forces and consequent severe losses among the civilian population.

Article 16 - Protection of cultural objects and of places of worship

Without prejudice to the provisions of the Hague Convention for the Protection of Cultural Property in the Event of Armed Conflict of 14 May 1954, it is prohibited to commit any acts of hostility directed against historic monuments, works of art or places of worship which constitute the cultural or spiritual heritage of peoples, and to use them in support of the military effort.

Article 17 - Prohibition of forced movement of civilians

1. The displacement of the civilian population shall not be ordered for reasons related to the conflict unless the security of the civilians involved or imperative military reasons so demand. Should such displacements have to be carried out, all possible measures shall be taken in order that the civilian population may be received under satisfactory conditions of shelter, hygiene, health, safety and nutrition.

2. Civilians shall not be compelled to leave their own territory for reasons connected with the conflict.

Article 18 - Relief societies and relief actions

1. Relief societies located in the territory of the High Contracting Party, such as for the performance of their traditional functions in relation to the victims of the armed conflict. The civilian population may, even on its own initiative, offer to collect and care for the wounded, sick and shipwrecked.

2. If the civilian population is suffering undue hardship owing to a lack of the supplies essential for its survival, such as foodstuffs and medical supplies, relief actions for the civilian population which are of an exclusively humanitarian and impartial nature and which are conducted without any adverse distinction shall be undertaken subject to the consent of the High Contracting Party concerned.

E. DOCUMENTS RELATING TO PROSECUTION EXTRADITION AND NON-APPLICABILITY OF STATUTES OF LIMITATIONS

1. UNITED NATIONS RESOLUTION ON WAR CRIMINALS, 15 December 1970

GENERAL ASSEMBLY RESOLUTION 2712 U.N.G.A. Res. 2538 (XXIV). *Reprinted in* 1 Friedman 754.

THE GENERAL ASSEMBLY,

Recalling its resolution 2583 (XXIV) of 15 December 1969 on the punishment of war criminals and of persons who have committed crimes against humanity,

Welcoming with satisfaction the fact that the Convention on the Non-Applicability of Statutory Limitations to War Crimes and Crimes against Humanity entered into force on 11 November 1970,

Noting with regret that the numerous decisions adopted by the United Nations on the question of the punishment of war criminals and of persons who have committed crimes against humanity are still not being fully complied with,

Expressing deep concern at the fact that in present-day conditions, as a result of aggressive wars and the policies and practices of racism, *apartheid* and colonialism and other similar ideologies and practices, war crimes and crimes against humanity are being committed in various parts of the world,

Convinced that a thorough investigation of war crimes and crimes against humanity, as well as the arrest, extradition and punishment of persons guilty of such crimes-- wherever they may have been committed--and the establishment of criteria for determining compensation to the victims of such crimes, are important elements in the prevention of similar crimes now and in the future, and also in the protection of human rights and fundamental freedoms, the strengthening of confidence and the development of co-operation between peoples and the safeguarding of international peace and security,

1. *Draws attention* to the fact that many war criminals and persons who have committed crimes against humanity are continuing to take refuge in the territories of certain States and are enjoying protection;

2. *Calls upon* all States to take measures, in accordance with recognized principles of international law, to arrest such persons and extradite them to the countries where

they have committed war crimes and crimes against humanity, so that they can be brought to trial and punished in accordance with the laws of those countries;

3. *Condemns* the war crimes and crimes against humanity at present being committed as a result of aggressive wars and the policies of racism, *apartheid* and colonialism and calls upon the States concerned to bring to trial persons guilty of such crimes;

4. *Also calls upon* all the States concerned to intensify their co-operation in the collection and exchange of information which will contribute to the detection, arrest, extradition, trial and punishment of persons guilty of war crimes and crimes against humanity;

5. *Once again requests* the States concerned, if they have not already done so, to take the necessary measures for the thorough investigation of war crimes and crimes against humanity, as defined in article I of the Convention on the Non-Applicability of Statutory Limitations to War Crimes and Crimes against Humanity, and for the detection, arrest, extradition and punishment of all war criminals and persons guilty of crimes against humanity who have not yet been brought to trial or punished;

6. *Requests* States which have not yet become parties to the Convention on the Non-Applicability of Statutory Limitations to War Crimes and Crimes against Humanity to do so as soon as possible;

7. *Appeals* to Governments to provide the Secretary-General with information on the measures which they have taken or are taking to become parties to the Convention on the Non-Applicability of Statutory Limitations to War Crimes and Crimes against Humanity;

8. *Also appeals* to States which have not yet become parties to the Convention on the Non-Applicability of Statutory Limitations to War Crimes and Crimes against Humanity strictly to observe the provisions of General Assembly resolution 2583 (XXIV) to the effect that they should refrain from action running counter to the main purposes of that Convention;

9. *Requests* the Secretary-General to continue, in the light of the comments and observations submitted by Governments, the study of the question of the punishment of war crimes and crimes against humanity and the criteria for determining compensation to the victims of such crimes, in order to submit a report on this question to the General Assembly at its twenty-sixth session.

Article II

If any of the crimes mentioned in article I are committed, the provisions of this Convention shall apply to representatives of the state authority and private individuals who, as principals or accomplices, participate in or who directly incite others to the commission of any of those crimes, or who conspire to commit them, irrespective of the degree of completion, and to representatives of the state authority who tolerate their commission.

Article III

The states parties to the present Convention undertake to adopt all necessary domestic measures, legislative or otherwise, with a view to making possible the extradition, in accordance with international law, of the persons referred to in article II of this Convention.

Article IV

The states parties to the present Convention undertake to adopt, in accordance with their respective constitutional processes, any legislative or other measures necessary to insure that statutory or other limitations shall not apply to the prosecution and punishment of the crimes referred to in articles I and II of this Convention and that, where they exist, such limitations shall be abolished.

Article V

This Convention shall, until December 31, 1969, be open for signature by any state member of the United Nations or member of any of its specialized agencies or of the International Atomic Energy Agency, by any state party to the Statute of the International Court of Justice, and by any other state which has been invited by the General Assembly of the United Nations to become a party to this Convention.

Article VI

This Convention is subject to ratification. Instruments of ratification shall be deposited with the Secretary-General of the United Nations.

Article VII

This Convention shall be open to accession by any state referred to in article V. Instruments of accession shall be deposited with the Secretary-General of the United Nations.

Article VIII

1. This Convention shall enter into force on the nineteenth day after the date of the deposit with the Secretary-General of the United Nations of the tenth instrument of ratification or accession.

2. For each state ratifying this Convention or acceding to it after the deposit of the tenth instrument of ratification or accession, the Convention shall enter into force on the ninetieth day after the date of the deposit of its own instrument of ratification or accession.

Article IX

1. After the expiry of a period of ten years from the date on which this Convention enters into force, a request for the revision of the Convention may be made at any time by any contracting party by means of a notification in writing addressed to the Secretary-General of the United Nations.

2. The General Assembly of the United Nations shall decide upon the steps, if any, to be taken in respect of such a request.

Done at Strasbourg, this 25th day of January 1974, in the English and French languages, both texts being equally authoritative, in a single copy which shall remain deposited in the archives of the Council of Europe. The Secretary General of the Council of Europe shall transmit certified copies to each of the signatory and acceding States.

2. **UNITED NATIONS RESOLUTION ON PRINCIPLES OF INTERNATIONAL CO-OPERATION IN THE DETECTION, ARREST, EXTRADITION AND PUNISHMENT OF PERSONS GUILTY OF WAR CRIMES AND CRIMES AGAINST HUMANITY, 3 December 1973**

General Assembly resolution 3074 (XXVIII) of 3 December 1973, 1973 Y.B. OF THE U.N. 572. *Reprinted in* 13 ILM 230 (1974).

The General Assembly,

Recalling its resolutions 2583 (XXIV) of 15 December 1969, 2712 (XXV) of 15 December 1970, 2840 (XXVI) of 18 December 1971 and 3020 (XXVII) of 18 December 1972.

CRIMES AGAINST HUMANITY

Taking into account the special need for international action in order to ensure the prosecution and punishment of persons guilty of war crimes and crimes against humanity,

Having considered the draft principles of international co-operation in the detection, arrest, extradition and punishment of persons guilty of war crimes and crimes against humanity,

Declares that the United Nations, in pursuance of the principles and purposes set forth in the Charter concerning the promotion of co-operation between peoples and the maintenance of international peace and security, proclaims the following principles of international co-operation in the detection, arrest, extradition and punishment of persons guilty of war crimes and crimes against humanity:

1. War crimes and crimes against humanity, wherever they are committed, shall be subject to investigation and the persons against whom there is evidence that they have committed such crimes shall be subject to tracing, arrest, trial and, if found guilty, to punishment.

2. Every State has the right to try its own nationals for war crimes or crimes against humanity.

3. States shall co-operate with each other on a bilateral and multilateral basis with a view to halting and preventing war crimes and crimes against humanity, and shall take the domestic and international measures necessary for that purpose.

4. States shall assist each other in detecting, arresting and bringing to trial persons suspected of having committed such crimes and, if they are found guilty, in punishing them.

5. Persons against whom there is evidence that they have committed war crimes and crimes against humanity shall be subject to trial and, if found guilty, to punishment, as a general rule in the countries in which they committed those crimes. In that connexion, States shall co-operate on questions of extraditing such persons.

6. States shall co-operate with each other in the collection of information and evidence which would help to bring to trial the persons indicated in paragraph 5 above and shall exchange such information.

7. In accordance with article 1 of the Declaration on Territorial Asylum of 14 December 1967, States shall not grant asylum to any person with respect to whom there are serious reasons for considering that he has committed a crime against peace, a war crime or a crime against humanity.

8. States shall not take any legislative or other measures which may be prejudicial to the international obligations they have assumed in regard to the detection, arrest,

extradition and punishment of persons guilty of war crimes and crimes against humanity.

9. In co-operating with a view to the detection, arrest and extradition of persons against whom there is evidence that they have committed war crimes and crimes against humanity and, if found guilty, their punishment. States shall act in conformity with the provisions of the Charter of the United Nations and of the Declaration on Principles of International Law concerning Friendly Relations and Co-operation among States in accordance with the Charter of the United Nations.

3. CONVENTION ON THE NON-APPLICABILITY OF STATUTORY LIMITATIONS TO WAR CRIMES AND CRIMES AGAINST HUMANITY, New York, 26 November 1968
(Excerpts)

754 U.N.T.S. 73. *Reprinted in* 8 ILM 68 (1969); Schindler/Toman 837.

Article I

No statutory limitation shall apply to the following crimes, irrespective of the date of their commission:

a. War crimes as they are defined in the Charter of the International Military Tribunal, Nuremberg, of August 8, 1945 and confirmed by Resolutions 3(I) of February 13, 1946, and 95(I) of December 11, 1946, of the General Assembly of the United Nations, particularly the "grave breaches" enumerated in the Geneva Conventions of August 12, 1949, for the protection of war victims;

b. Crimes against humanity whether committed in time of war or in time of peace as they are defined in the Charter of the International Military Tribunal, Nuremberg, of August 8, 1945, and confirmed by resolutions 3(I) of February 13, 1946 and 95(I) of December 11, 1946, of the General Assembly of the United Nations, of *apartheid*, and the crime of genocide as defined in the 1948 Convention on the Prevention and Punishment of the Crime of Genocide, even if such acts do not constitute a violation of the domestic law of the country in which they were committed.

Article II

If any of the crimes mentioned in article I are committed, the provisions of this Convention shall apply to representatives of the state authority and private individuals

703

who, as principals or accomplices, participate in or who directly incite others to the commission of any of those crimes, or who conspire to commit them, irrespective of the degree of completion, and to representatives of the state authority who tolerate their commission.

Article III

The states parties to the present Convention undertake to adopt all necessary domestic measures, legislative or otherwise, with a view to making possible the extradition, in accordance with international law, of the persons referred to in article II of this Convention.

Article IV

The states parties to the present Convention undertake to adopt, in accordance with their respective constitutional processes, any legislative or other measures necessary to insure that statutory or other limitations shall not apply to the prosecution and punishment of the crimes referred to in articles I and II of this Convention and that, where they exist, such limitations shall be abolished.

Article V

This Convention shall, until December 31, 1969, be open for signature by any state member of the United Nations or member of any of its specialized agencies or of the International Atomic Energy Agency, by any state party to the Statute of the International Court of Justice, and by any other state which has been invited by the General Assembly of the United Nations to become a party to this Convention.

Article VI

This Convention is subject to ratification. Instruments of ratification shall be deposited with the Secretary-General of the United Nations.

Article VII

This Convention shall be open to accession by any state referred to in article V. Instruments of accession shall be deposited with the Secretary-General of the United Nations.

Article VIII

1. This Convention shall enter into force on the nineteenth day after the date of the deposit with the Secretary-General of the United Nations of the tenth instrument of ratification or accession.

2. For each state ratifying this Convention or acceding to it after the deposit of the tenth instrument of ratification or accession, the Convention shall enter into force on the nineteenth day after the date of the deposit of its own instrument of ratification or accession.

Article IX

1. After the expiry of a period of ten years from the date on which this Convention enters into force, a request for the revision of the Convention may be made at any time by any contracting party by means of a notification in writing addressed to the Secretary-General of the United Nations.

2. The General Assembly of the United Nations shall decide upon the steps, if any, to be taken in respect of such a request.

4. **EUROPEAN CONVENTION ON THE NON-APPLICABILITY OF STATUTORY LIMITATION TO CRIMES AGAINST HUMANITY AND WAR CRIMES, Strasbourg, 25 January 1974**

E.T.S. No. 82. *Reprinted in* 13 ILM 540 (1974).

The member States of the Council of Europe, signatory hereto, Considering the necessity to safeguard human dignity in time of war and in time of peace;

Considering that crimes against humanity and the most serious violations of the laws and customs of war constitute a serious infraction of human dignity;

Concerned in consequence to ensure that the punishment of those crimes is not prevented by statutory limitations whether in relation to prosecution or to the enforcement of the punishment;

Considering the essential interest in promoting a common criminal policy in this field, the aim of the Council of Europe being to achieve a greater unity between its members,

Have agreed as follows:

CRIMES AGAINST HUMANITY

Article 1

Each Contracting State undertakes to adopt any necessary measures to secure that statutory limitation shall not apply to the prosecution of the following offences, or to the enforcement of the sentences imposed for such offences, in so far as they are punishable under its domestic law:

1. the crimes against humanity specified in the Convention on the Prevention and Punishment of the Crime of Genocide adopted on 9 December 1948 by the General Assembly of the United Nations;

2. (a) the violations specified in Article 50 of the 1949 Geneva Convention for the Amelioration of the Condition of the Wounded and Sick in Armed Forces in the Field, Article 51 of the 1949 Geneva Convention for the Amelioration of the Condition of Wounded, Sick and Shipwrecked Members of Armed Forces at Sea, Article 130 of the 1949 Geneva Convention Relative to the Treatment of Prisoners of War and Article 147 of the 1949 Geneva Convention Relative to the Protection of Civilian Persons in Time of War, (b) any comparable violations of the laws of war having effect at the time when this Convention enters into force and of customs of war existing at that time, which are not already provided for in the above-mentioned provisions of the Geneva Conventions, when the specific violation under consideration is of a particularly grave character by reason either of its factual and intentional elements or of the extent of its foreseeable consequences;

3. any other violation of a rule or custom of international law which may hereafter be established and which the Contracting State concerned considers according to a declaration under Article 6 as being of a comparable nature to those referred to in paragraph 1 or 2 of this Article.

Article 2

1. The present Convention applies to offences committed after its entry into force in respect of the Contracting State concerned.

2. It applies also to offences committed before such entry into force in those cases where the statutory limitation period had not expired at that time.

Article 3

1. This Convention shall be open to signature by the member States of the Council of Europe. It shall be subject to ratification or acceptance. Instruments of ratification or acceptance shall be deposited with the Secretary General of the Council of Europe.

2. The Convention shall enter into force three months after the date of deposit of the third instrument of ratification or acceptance.

3. In respect of a signatory State ratifying or accepting subsequently, the Convention shall come into force three months after the date of the deposit of its instrument of ratification or acceptance.

Article 4

1. After the entry into force of this Convention, the Committee of Ministers of the Council of Europe may invite any non-member State to accede thereto, provided that the resolution containing such invitation receives the unanimous agreement of the Members of the Council who have ratified the Convention.

2. Such accession shall be effected by depositing with the Secretary General of the Council of Europe an instrument of accession which shall take effect three months after the date of its deposit.

Article 5

1. Any State may, at the time of signature or when depositing its instrument of ratification, acceptance or accession, specify the territory or territories to which this Convention shall apply.

2. Any State may, when depositing its instrument of ratification, acceptance or accession or at any later date, by declaration addressed to the Secretary General of the Council of Europe, extend this Convention to any other territory or territories specified in the declaration and for whose international relations it is responsible or on whose behalf it is authorized to give undertakings.

3. Any declaration made in pursuance of the preceding paragraph may, in respect of any territory mentioned in such declaration, be withdrawn according to the procedure laid down in Article 7 of this Convention.

Article 6

1. Any Contracting State may, at any time, by declaration addressed to the Secretary General of the Council of Europe, extend this Convention to any violations provided for in Article 1, paragraph 3 of this Convention.

2. Any declaration made in pursuance of the preceding paragraph may be withdrawn according to the procedure laid down in Article 7 of this Convention.

Article 7

1. This Convention shall remain in force indefinitely.

2. Any Contracting State may, insofar as it is concerned, denounce this Convention by means of a notification addressed to the Secretary General of the Council of Europe.

3. Such denunciation shall take effect six months after the date of receipt by the Secretary General of such notification.

Article 8

The Secretary General of the Council of Europe shall notify the member States of the Council and any State which has acceded to this Convention of:
   (a) any signature;
   (b) any deposit of an instrument of ratification, acceptance or accession;
   (c) any date of entry into force of this Convention in accordance with Article 3 thereof;
   (d) any declaration received in pursuance of the provisions of Article 5 or Article 6;
   (e) any notification received in pursuance of the provisions of Article 7 and the date on which the denunciation takes effect.

In witness whereof the undersigned, being duly authorized thereto, have signed this Convention.

Done at Strasbourg, this 25th day of January 1974, in the English and French languages, both texts being equally authoritative, in a single copy which shall remain deposited in the archives of the Council of Europe. The Secretary General of the Council of Europe shall transmit certified copies to each of the signatory and acceding States.

F. CODIFICATION

1. **CONVENTION ON THE PREVENTION AND SUPPRESSION OF THE CRIME OF GENOCIDE, 9 December 1948**
(Excerpts)

78 U.N.T.S. 277. *Reprinted in* 45 AJIL 7 (1951) (Supp.); 2 Ferencz 174; 1 Friedman 692.

The Contracting Parties,

Having considered the declaration made by the General Assembly of the United Nations in its resolution 96(I) dated 11 December 1946 that genocide is a crime under international law, contrary to the spirit and aims of the United Nations and condemned by the civilized world;

Recognizing that at all periods of history genocide has inflicted great losses on humanity; and

Being convinced that, in order to liberate mankind from such an odious scourge, international cooperation is required,

Hereby agree as hereinafter provided:

Article I

The Contracting Parties confirm that genocide, whether committed in time of peace or in time of war, is a crime under international law which they undertake to prevent and to punish.

Article II

In the present Convention, genocide means any of the following acts committed with intent to destroy, in whole or in part, a national, ethnic, racial, or religious group, as such:

(a) Killing members of the group;
(b) Causing serious bodily or mental harm to members of the group;
(c) Deliberately inflicting on the group, conditions of life calculated to bring about its physical destruction in whole or in part;
(d) Imposing measures intended to prevent births within the group;
(e) Forcibly transferring children of the group to another group.

Article III

The following acts shall be punishable:

(a) Genocide;
(b) Conspiracy to commit genocide;
(c) Direct and public incitement to commit genocide;
(d) Attempt to commit genocide;
(e) Complicity in genocide.

Article IV

Persons committing genocide or any of the other acts enumerated in article III shall be punished, whether they are constitutionally responsible rulers, public officials, or private individuals.

Article V

The Contracting Parties undertake to enact, in accordance with their respective Constitutions, the necessary legislation to give effect to the provisions of the present Convention and, in particular, to provide effective penalties for persons guilty of genocide or of any of the other acts enumerated in article III.

Article VI

Persons charged with genocide or any of the other acts enumerated in article III shall be tried by a competent tribunal of the State in the territory of which the act was committed, or by such international penal tribunal as may have jurisdiction with respect to those Contracting Parties which shall have accepted its jurisdiction.

Article VII

Genocide and the other acts enumerated in article III shall not be considered as political crimes for the purpose of extradition.

The Contracting Parties pledge themselves in such cases to grant extradition in accordance with their laws and treaties in force.

Article VIII

Any Contracting Party may call upon the competent organs of the United Nations to take such action under the Charter of the United Nations as they consider appropriate for the prevention and suppression of acts of genocide or any of the other acts enumerated in article III.

Article IX

Disputes between the Contracting Parties relating to the interpretation, application, or fulfillment of the present Convention, including those relating to the responsibility of a State for genocide or for any of the other acts enumerated in article III, shall be submitted to the International Court of Justice at the request of any of the parties to the dispute.

2.   CONVENTION ON THE SUPPRESSION AND PUNISHMENT OF THE CRIME OF *APARTHEID*, 30 November 1973
(Excerpts)

Adopted and opened for signature and ratification by General Assembly resolution 3068 (XXVIII) of 30 November 1973

U.N. GAOR Supp. (No. 30), at 75, U.N. Doc. A/9030 (1973). *Reprinted in* 13 ILM 50 (1974).

ENTRY INTO FORCE: 18 July 1976, in accordance with article XV.

The States Parties to the present Convention, Recalling the provisions of the Charter of the United Nations, in which all Members pledged themselves to take joint and separate action in co-operation with the Organization for the achievement of universal respect for, and observance of, human rights and fundamental freedoms for all without distinction as to race, sex, language or religion,

Considering the Universal Declaration of Human Rights, which states that all human beings are born free and equal in dignity and rights and that everyone is entitled to all the rights and freedoms set forth in the Declaration, without distinction of any kind, such as race, colour or national origin,

Considering the Declaration on the Granting of Independence to Colonial Countries and Peoples, in which the General Assembly stated that the process of liberation is irresistible and irreversible and that, in the interests of human dignity, progress and justice, an end must be put to colonialism and all practices of segregation and discrimination associated therewith.

Observing that, in accordance with the International Convention on the Elimination of All Forms of Racial Discrimination, States particularly condemn racial segregation and *apartheid* and undertake to prevent, prohibit and eradicate all practices of this nature in territories under their jurisdiction.

Observing that, in the Convention on the Prevention and Punishment of the Crime of Genocide, certain acts which may also be qualified as acts of *apartheid* constitute a crime under international law.

Observing that, in the Convention on the Non-Applicability of Statutory Limitations to War Crimes and Crimes Against Humanity, "inhuman acts resulting from the policy of *apartheid*" are qualified as crimes against humanity,

Observing that the General Assembly of the United Nations has adopted a number of resolutions in which the policies and practices of apartheid are condemned as a crime against humanity,

Observing that the Security Council has emphasized that *apartheid* and its continued intensification and expansion seriously disturbs and threatens international peace and security,

Convinced that an International Convention on the Suppression and Punishment of the Crime of *Apartheid* would make it possible to take more effective measures at the international and national levels with a view to the suppression and punishment of the crime of *apartheid*.

Have agreed as follows:

Article I

1. The States Parties to the present Convention declare that *apartheid* is a crime against humanity and that inhuman acts resulting from the policies and practices of *apartheid* and similar policies and practices of racial segregation and discrimination, as defined in article II of the Convention, are crimes violating the principles of international law, in particular the purposes and principles of the Charter of the United Nations, and constituting a serious threat to international peace and security.

2. The States Parties to the present Convention declare criminal those organizations, institutions and individuals committing the crime of *apartheid*.

Article II

For the purpose of the present Convention, the term "the crime of *apartheid*", which shall include similar policies and practices of racial segregation and discrimination as practiced in southern Africa, shall apply to the following inhuman acts committed for the purpose of establishing and maintaining domination by one racial group of persons over any other racial group of persons and systematically oppressing them:

(a) Denial to a member or members of a racial group or groups of the right to life and liberty of person:
   (i) By murder of members of a racial group or groups;
   (ii) By the infliction upon the members of a racial group or groups of serious bodily or mental harm, by the infringement of their freedom or dignity, or by subjecting them to torture or to cruel, inhuman or degrading treatment or punishment;
   (iii) By arbitrary arrest and illegal imprisonment of the members of a racial group or groups;

(b) Deliberate imposition on a racial group or groups of living conditions calculated to cause its or their physical destruction in whole or in part;

(c) Any legislative measures and other measures calculated to prevent a racial group or groups from participation in the political, social, economic and cultural life of the country and the deliberate creation of conditions preventing the full development of such a group or groups, in particular by denying to members of a racial group or groups basic human rights and freedoms, including the right to work, the right to form recognized trade unions, the right to education, the right to leave and to return to their country, the right to a nationality, the right to freedom of movement and residence, the right to freedom of opinion and expression, and the right to freedom of peaceful assembly and association;

(d) Any measures, including legislative measures, designed to divide the population along racial lines by the creation of separate reserves and ghettos for the members of a racial group or groups, the prohibition of mixed marriages among members of various racial groups, the expropriation of landed property belonging to a racial group or groups or to members thereof;

(e) Exploitation of the labour of the members of a racial group or groups, in particular by submitting them to forced labour;

714

(f) Persecution of organizations and persons, by depriving them of fundamental rights and freedoms, because they oppose *apartheid*.

3.   CONVENTION AGAINST TORTURE AND OTHER CRUEL, INHUMAN OR DEGRADING TREATMENT OR PUNISHMENT, New York, 10 December 1984

(Excerpts)

U.N.G.A. Res. 39/46. *Reprinted in* 24 ILM 535 (1985); 23 ILM 1027 (1984).

The States Parties to this Convention,

Considering that, in accordance with the principles proclaimed in the Charter of the United Nations, recognition of the equal and inalienable rights of all members of the human family is the foundation of freedom, justice and peace in the world,

Recognizing that those rights derive from the inherent dignity of the human person,

Considering the obligation of States under the Charter, in particular Article 55, to promote universal respect for, and observant of, human rights and fundamental freedoms,

Having regard to article 5 of the Universal Declaration of Human Rights and Article 7 of the International Covenant on Civil and Political Rights, both of which provide that no one may be subjected to torture or to cruel, inhuman or degrading treatment or punishment,

Having regard also to the Declaration on the Protection of All Persons from Being Subjected to Torture and Other Cruel, Inhuman or Degrading Treatment or Punishment, adopted by the General Assembly on 9 December 1975 (resolution 3452 (XXX)),

Desiring to make more effective the struggle against torture and other cruel, inhuman or degrading treatment or punishment throughout the world,

Have agreed as follows:

Part I

Article 1

1. For the purposes of this Convention, torture means any act by which severe pain or suffering, whether physical or mental, is intentionally inflicted on a person for such purposes as obtaining from him or a third person information or a confession, punishing him for an act he or a third person has committed or is suspected of having committed, or intimidating or coercing him or a third person, or for any reason based on discrimination of any kind, when such pain or suffering is inflicted by or at the instigation of or with the consent or acquiescence of a public official or other person acting in an official capacity. It does not include pain or suffering arising only from, inherent in or incidental to lawful sanctions.

2. This article is without prejudice to any international instrument or national legislation which does or may contain provisions of wider application.

Article 2

1. Each State Party shall take effective legislative, administrative, judicial or other measures to prevent acts of torture in any territory under its jurisdiction.

2. No exceptional circumstances whatsoever, whether a state of war or a threat or war, internal political instability or any other public emergency, may be invoked as a justification of torture.

3. An order from a superior officer or a public authority may not be invoked as a justification of torture.

Article 3

1. No State Party shall expel, return ("*refouler*") or extradite a person to another State where there are substantial grounds for believing that he would be in danger of being subjected to torture.

2. For the purpose of determining whether there are such grounds, the competent authorities shall take into account all relevant considerations including, where applicable, the existence in the State concerned of a consistent pattern of gross, flagrant or mass violations of human rights.

Article 4

1. Each State Party shall ensure that all acts of torture are offences under its criminal law. The same shall apply to an attempt to commit torture and to an act by any person which constitutes complicity or participation in torture.

2. Each State Party shall make these offences punishable by appropriate penalties which take into account their grave nature.

Article 5

1. Each State Party shall take such measures as may be necessary to establish its jurisdiction over the offences referred to in article 4 in the following cases:

(a) When the offences are committed in any territory under its jurisdiction or on board a ship or aircraft registered in that State;

(b) When the alleged offender is a national of that State;

(c) When the victim is a national of that State if that State considers it appropriate.

2. Each State Party shall likewise take such measures as may be necessary to establish its jurisdiction over such offences in cases where the alleged offender is present in any territory under its jurisdiction and it does not extradite him pursuant to article 8 to any of the States mentioned in paragraph 1 of this article.

3. This Convention does not exclude any criminal jurisdiction exercised in accordance with internal law.

Article 6

1. Upon being satisfied, after an examination of information available to it, that the circumstances so warrant, any State Party in whose territory a person alleged to have committed any offence referred to in article 4 is present, shall take him into custody

717

or take other legal measures to ensure his presence. The custody and other legal measures shall be as provided in the law of that State but may be continued only for such time as is necessary to enable any criminal or extradition proceedings to be instituted.

2. Such State shall immediately make a preliminary inquiry into the facts.

3. Any person in custody pursuant to paragraph 1 of this article shall be assisted in communicating immediately with the nearest appropriate representative of the State of which he is a national, or, if he is a stateless person, to the representative of the State where he usually resides.

4. When a State, pursuant to this article, has taken a person into custody, it shall immediately notify the States referred to in article 5, paragraph 1, of the fact that such person is in custody and of the circumstances which warrant his detention. The State which makes the preliminary inquiry contemplated in paragraph 2 of this article shall promptly report its findings to the said States and shall indicate whether it intends to exercise jurisdiction.

Article 7

1. The State Party in territory under whose jurisdiction a person alleged to have committed any offence referred to in article 4 is found, shall in the cases contemplated in article 5, if it does not extradite him, submit the case to its competent authorities for the purpose of prosecution.

2. These authorities shall take their decision in the same manner as in the case of any ordinary offence of a serious nature under the law of that State. In the cases referred to in article 5, paragraph 2, the standards of evidence required for prosecution and conviction shall in no way be less stringent than those which apply in the cases referred to in article 5, paragraph 1.

3. Any person regarding whom proceedings are brought in connection with any of the offences referred to in article 4 shall be guaranteed fair treatment at all stages of the proceedings.

Article 8

1. The offences referred to in article 4 shall be deemed to be included as extraditable offences in any extradition treaty existing between States Parties. States Parties undertake to include such offences as extraditable offences in every extradition treaty to be concluded between them.

2. If a State Party which makes extradition conditional on the existence of a treaty receives a request for extradition from another State Party with which it has no extradition treaty, it may consider this Convention as the legal basis for extradition in respect of such offences. Extradition shall be subject to the other conditions provided by the law of the requested State.

3. States Parties which do not make extradition conditional on the existence of a treaty shall recognize such offences as extraditable offences between themselves subject to the conditions provided by the law of the requested State.

4. Such offences shall be treated, for the purpose of extradition between States Parties, as if they had been committed not only in the place in which they occurred but also in the territories of the States required to establish their jurisdiction in accordance with article 5, paragraph 1.

Article 9

1. States Parties shall afford one another the greatest measure of assistance in connection with criminal proceedings brought in respect of any of the offences referred to in article 4, including the supply of all evidence at their disposal necessary for the proceedings.

2. States Parties shall carry out their obligations under paragraph 1 of this article in conformity with any treaties of mutual judicial assistance that may exist between them.

Article 10

1. Each State Party shall ensure that education and information regarding the prohibition against torture are fully included in the training of law enforcement personnel civil or military, medical personnel, public officials and other persons who

may be involved in the custody, interrogation or treatment of any individual subjected to any form of arrest, detention or imprisonment.

2. Each State Party shall include this prohibition in the rules or instructions issued in regard to the duties and functions of any such persons.

Article 11

Each State Party shall keep under systematic review interrogation rules, instructions, methods and practices as well as arrangements for the custody and treatment of persons subjected to any form of arrest, detention or imprisonment in any territory under its jurisdiction, with a view to preventing any cases of torture.

Article 12

Each State Party shall ensure that its competent authorities proceed to a prompt and impartial investigation, wherever there is reasonable ground to believe that an act of torture has been committed in any territory under its jurisdiction.

Article 13

Each State Party shall ensure that any individual who alleges he has been subjected to torture in any territory under its jurisdiction has the right to complain to and to have his case promptly and impartially examined by its competent authorities. Steps shall be taken to ensure that the complainant and witnesses are protected against all ill-treatment or intimidation as a consequence of his complaint or any evidence given.

Article 14

1. Each State Party shall ensure in its legal system that the victim of an act of torture obtains redress and has an enforceable right to fair and adequate compensation including the means for as full rehabilitation as possible. In the event of the death of the victim as a result of an act of torture, his dependants shall be entitled to compensation.

2. Nothing in this article shall affect any right of the victim or other persons to compensation which may exist under national law.

DOCUMENTS SECTION

Article 15

Each State Party shall ensure that any statement which is established to have been made as a result of torture shall not be invoked as evidence in any proceedings, except against a person accused of torture as evidence that the statement was made.

Article 16

1. Each State Party shall undertake to prevent in any territory under its jurisdiction other acts of cruel, inhuman or degrading treatment or punishment which do not amount to torture as defined in article 1, when such acts are committed by or at the instigation of or with the consent or acquiescence of a public official or other person acting in an official capacity. In particular, the obligations contained in articles 10, 11, 12 and 13 shall apply with the substitution for references to torture or references to other forms of cruel, inhuman or degrading treatment or punishment.

2. The provisions of this Convention are without prejudice to the provisions of any other international instrument or national law which prohibits cruel, inhuman or degrading treatment or punishment or which relates to extradition or expulsion.

Part II

Article 17

1. There shall be established a Committee against Torture (hereinafter referred to as the Committee) which shall carry out the functions hereinafter provided. The Committee shall consist of 10 experts of high moral standing and recognized competence in the field of human rights, who shall serve in their personal capacity. The experts shall be elected by the States Parties, consideration being given to equitable geographical distribution and to the usefulness of the participation of some persons having legal experience.

2. The members of the Committee shall be elected by secret ballot from a list of persons nominated by States Parties. Each State Party may nominate one person from among its own nationals. States Parties shall bear in mind the usefulness of nominating persons who are also members of the Human Rights Committee established under the

International Covenant on Civil and Political Rights and are willing to serve on the Committee against Torture.

3. Elections of the members of the Committee shall be held at biennial meetings of States Parties convened by the Secretary-General of the United Nations. At those meetings, for which two thirds of the States Parties shall constitute a quorum, the persons elected to the Committee shall be those who obtain the largest number of votes and an absolute majority of the votes of the representatives of States Parties present and voting.

4. The initial election shall be held no later than six months after the date of the entry into force of this Convention. At least four months before the date of each election, the Secretary-General of the United Nations shall address a letter to the States Parties inviting them to submit their nominations within three months. The Secretary-General shall prepare a list in alphabetical order of all persons thus nominated, indicating the States Parties which have nominated them, and shall submit it to the States Parties.

5. The members of the Committee shall be elected for a term of four years. They shall be eligible for re-election if renominated. However, the term of five of the members elected at the first election shall expire at the end of two years; immediately after the first election the names of these five members shall be chosen by lot by the chairman of the meeting referred to in paragraph 3.

6. If a member of the Committee dies or resigns or for any other cause can no longer perform his Committee duties, the State Party which nominated him shall appoint another expert from among its nationals to serve for the remainder of his term, subject to the approval of the majority of the States Parties. The approval shall be considered given unless half or more of the States Parties respond negatively within all six weeks after having been informed by the Secretary-General of the United Nations of the proposed appointment.

7. States Parties shall be responsible for the expenses of the members of the Committee while they are in performance of Committee duties.

Article 18

1. The Committee shall elect its officers for a term of two years. They may be re-elected.

2. The Committee shall establish its own rules of procedure, but these rules shall provide, *inter alia*, that:

(a) Six members shall constitute a quorum;
(b) Decisions of the Committee shall be made by a majority vote of the members present.

3. The Secretary-General of the United Nations shall provide the necessary staff and facilities for the effective performance of the functions of the Committee under this Convention.

4. The Secretary-General of the United Nations shall convene the initial meeting of the Committee. After its initial meeting, the Committee shall meet at such time as shall be provided in its rules of procedure.

5. The State Parties shall be responsible for expenses incurred in connection with the holding of meetings of the States Parties and of the Committee, including reimbursement to the United Nations for any expenses, such as the cost of staff and facilities, incurred by the United Nations pursuant to paragraph 3 above.

Article 19

1. The States Parties shall submit to the Committee, through the Secretary-General of the United Nations, reports on the measures they have taken to give effect to their undertakings under this Convention, within one year after the entry into force of this Convention for the State Party concerned. Thereafter the States Parties shall submit supplementary reports every four years on any new measures taken, and such other reports as the Committee may request.

2. The Secretary-General shall transmit the reports to all States Parties.

3. Each report shall be considered by the Committee which may make such comments or suggestions on the report as it may consider appropriate, and shall forward these to the State Party concerned. That State Party may respond with any observations it chooses to the Committee.

4. The Committee may, at its discretion, decide to include any comments or suggestions made by it in accordance with paragraph 3, together with the observations it hereon received from the State Party concerned, in its annual report made in accordance with article 24. If so requested by the State Party concerned, the Committee may also include a copy of the report submitted under paragraph 1.

Article 20

1. If the Committee receives information which appears to it to contain reliable indications that torture is being systematically practised in the territory of a State Party, the Committee shall invite that State Party to submit observations with regard to the information concerned.

2. Taking into account any observations which may have been submitted by the State Party concerned as well as any other relevant information available to it, the Committee may, if it decides that this is warranted, designate one or more of its members to make a confidential inquiry and to report to the Committee urgently.

3. If an inquiry is made in accordance, with paragraph 2, the Committee shall seek the co-operation of the State Party concerned. In agreement with that State Party, such an inquiry may include a visit to its territory.

4. After examining the findings of its member or members submitted in accordance with paragraph 2, the Committee shall transmit these findings to the State Party concerned together with any comments or suggestions which seem appropriate in view of the situation.

5. All the proceedings of the Committee referred to in paragraphs 1-4 of this article shall be confidential, and at all stages of the proceedings the cooperation of the State Party shall be sought. After such proceedings have been completed with regard to an inquiry made in accordance with paragraph 2, the Committee may, after consultations

with the State Party concerned, decide to include a summary account of the results of the proceedings in its annual report made in accordance with article 24.

Article 21

1. A State Party to this Convention may at any time declare under this article that it recognizes the competence of the Committee to receive and consider communications to the effect that a State Party claims that another State Party is not fulfilling its obligations under this Convention. Such communications may be received and considered according to the procedures laid down in this article only if submitted by a State Party which has made a declaration recognizing in regard to itself the competence of the Committee. No communication shall be dealt with by the Committee under this article if it concerns a State Party which has not made such a declaration. Communications received under this article shall be dealt with in accordance with the following procedure:

(a) If a State Party considers that another State Party is not giving effect to the provisions of this Convention, it may, by written communication, bring the matter to the attention of that State Party. Within three months after the receipt of the communication the receiving State shall afford the State which sent the communication an explanation or any other statement in writing clarifying the matter which should include, to the extent possible and pertinent, reference to domestic procedures and remedies taken, pending, or available in the matter.

(b) If the matter is not adjusted to the satisfaction of both States Parties concerned within six months after the receipt by the receiving State of the initial communication, either State shall have the right to refer the matter to the Committee by notice given to the Committee and to the other State.

(c) The Committee shall deal with a matter referred to it under this article only after it has ascertained that all domestic remedies have been invoked and exhausted in the matter, in conformity with the generally recognized principles of international law. This shall not be the rule where the application of the remedies is unreasonably prolonged or is unlikely to bring effective relief to the person who is the victim of the violation of this Convention.

(d) The Committee shall hold closed meetings when examining communications under this article.

(e) Subject to the provisions of subparagraph (c), the Committee shall make available its good offices to the States Parties concerned with a view to a friendly solution of the matter on the basis of respect for the obligations provided for in the present Convention. For this purpose, the Committee may, when appropriate, set up an *ad hoc* conciliation commission.

(f) In any matter referred to it under this article, the Committee may call upon the States Parties concerned, referred to in subparagraph (5), to supply any relevant information.

(g) The States Parties concerned, referred to in subparagraph (b), shall have the right to be represented when the matter is being considered by the Committee and to make submissions orally and/or in writing.

(h) The Committee shall, within 12 months after the date of receipt of notice under subparagraph (b), submit a report.

(i) If a solution within the terms of subparagraph (e) is reached, the Committee shall confine its report to a brief statement of the facts and of the solution reached.

(j) If a solution within the terms of subparagraph (e) is not reached, the Committee shall confine its report to a brief statement of the facts; the written submissions and record of the oral submissions made by the States Parties concerned shall be attached to the report.

In every matter, the report shall be communicated to the States Parties concerned.

2. The provisions of this article shall come into force when five States Parties to this Convention have made declarations under paragraph 1 of this article. Such declarations shall be deposited by the States Parties with the Secretary-General of the United Nations, who shall transmit copies thereof to the other States Parties. A declaration may be withdrawn at any time by notification to the Secretary-General. Such a withdrawal shall not prejudice the consideration of any matter which is the

subject of a communication already transmitted under this article; no further communication by any State Party shall be received under this article after the notification of withdrawal of the declaration has been received by the Secretary-General, unless the State Party concerned has made a new declaration.

Article 22

1.   A State Party to this Convention may at any time declare under this article that it recognizes the competence of the Committee to receive and consider communications from or on behalf of individuals subject to its jurisdiction who claim to be victims of a violation by a State Party of the provisions of the Convention. No communication shall be received by the Committee if it concerns a State Party to the Convention which has not made such a declaration.

2.   The Committee shall consider inadmissible any communication under this article which is anonymous, or which it considers to be an abuse of the right of submission of such communications or to be incompatible with the provisions of this Convention.

3.   Subject to the provisions of paragraph 2, the Committee shall bring any communications submitted to it under this article to the attention of the State Party to this Convention which has made a declaration under paragraph 1 and is alleged to be violating any provisions of the Convention. Within six months, the receiving State shall submit to the Committee written explanations or statements clarifying the matter and the remedy, if any, that may have been taken by that State.

4.   The Committee shall consider communications received under this article in the light of all information made available to it by or on behalf of the individual and by the State Party concerned.

5.   The Committee shall not consider any communications from an individual under this article unless it has ascertained that:

(a) The same matter has not been, and is not being, examined under another procedure of international investigation or settlement;
(b) The individual has exhausted all available domestic remedies: this shall not be the rule where the application of the remedies is unreasonably prolonged or is

727

unlikely to bring effective relief to the person who is the victim of the violation of this Convention.

6.   The Committee shall hold closed meetings when examining communications under this article.

7.   The Committee shall forward its views to the State Party concerned and to the individual.

8.   The provisions of this article shall come into force when five States Parties to this Convention have made declarations under paragraph 1 of this article.   Such declarations shall be deposited by the States Parties with the Secretary-General of the United Nations, who shall transmit copies thereof to the other States Parties.   A declaration may be withdrawn at any time by notification to the Secretary-General. Such a withdrawal shall not prejudice the consideration of any matter which is the subject of a communication already transmitted under this article; no further communication by or on behalf of an individual shall be received under this article after the notification of withdrawal of the declaration has been received by the Secretary-General, unless the State Party concerned has made a new declaration.

Article 23

The members of the Committee, and of the *ad hoc* conciliation commissions which may be appointed under article 21, paragraph 1 (e), shall be entitled to the facilities, privileges and immunities of experts on mission for the United Nations as laid down in the relevant sections of the Convention on the Privileges and Immunities of the United Nations.

4. INTERNATIONAL LAW COMMISSION DRAFT CODE OF OFFENCES AGAINST THE PEACE AND SECURITY OF MANKIND, 28 July 1954

(Excerpts)

9 U.N. GAOR Supp. (No. 9) at 11, U.N. Doc. A/2693 (1954). *Reprinted in* 45 AJIL 123 (1954) (Supp.); 2 Ferencz 460.

INTRODUCTION

54. By resolution 177 (II) of 21 November 1947, the General Assembly decided:

"To entrust the formulation of the principles of international law recongnized in the Charter of the Nürnberg Tribunal and in the judgment of the Tribunal to the International Law Commission, the members of which will, in accordance with resolution 174 (II), be elected at the next session of the General Assembly,"

and directed the Commission to

"(a) Formulate Charter of the Nürnberg Tribunal and in the judgment of the Tribunal, and
"(b) Prepare a draft code of offences against the peace and security of mankind, indicating clearly the place to be accorded to the principles mentioned in sub-paragraph (a) above."

In 1950, the International Law Commission reported to the General Assembly its formulation under sub-paragraph (a) of resolution 177 (II). By resolution 488 (V) of 12 December 1950, the General Assembly invited the Governments of Member States to express their observations on the formulation, and requested the Commission:

"In preparing the draft code of offences against the peace and security of mankind, to take account of the observations made on this formulation by delegations during the fifth session of the General Assembly and of any observations which may be made by Governments."

55. The preparation of a draft code of offences against the peace and security of mankind was given preliminary consideration by the Commission at its first session, in 1949, when the Commission appointed Mr. J. Spiropoulos special rapporteur on the

729

subject, and invited him to prepare a working paper for submission to the Commission at its second session. The Commission also decided that a questionnaire should be circulated to Governments inquiring what offences, apart from those recognized in the Charter and judgment of the Nürnberg Tribunal, should be included in the draft code.

56.   At its second session, in 1950, Mr. Spiropoulos presented his report (A/CN.4/25) to the Commission, which took it as a basis of discussion. The subject was considered by the Commission at its 54th to 62nd and 72nd meetings. The Commission also took into consideration the replies received from Governments (A/CN.4/19, Part II, A/CN.4/19/Add.1 and Add.2) to its questionnaire. In the light of the deliberations of the Commission, a drafting committee, composed of Messrs. Alfaro, Hudson and Spiropoulos, prepared a provisional text (A/CN.4/R.6) which was referred by the Commission without discussion to Mr. Spiropoulos, who was requested to continue the work on the subject and to submit a new report to the Commission at its third session.

57.   At the third session, in 1951, Mr. Spiropoulos submitted a second report (A/CN.4/44) containing a new draft of a code and also a digest of the observations on the Commission's formulation of the Nürnberg principles made by delegations during the fifth session of the General Assembly. The Commission also had before it the observations received from Governments (A/CN.4/45 and Corr. 1, A/CN.4/45/Add.1 and Add.2) on this formulation. Taking into account the observations referred to above, the Commission considered the subject at its 89th to 92nd, 106th to 111th, 129th and 133rd meetings, and adopted a draft Code of Offences against the Peace and Security of Mankind as set forth herein below.

58.   In submitting this draft code to the General Assembly, the Commission wishes to present the following observations as to some general questions which arose in the course of the preparation of the text:

(a) The Commission first considered the meaning of the term "offences against the peace and security of mankind," contained in resolution 177 (II). The view of the Commission was that the meaning of this term should be limited to offences which contain a political element and which endanger or disturb the maintenance of international peace and security. For these reasons, the draft code does not deal with questions concerning conflicts of legislation and jurisdiction in international criminal matters; nor does it include such matters as piracy, traffic in dangerous drugs, traffic in women and children, slavery, counterfeiting currency, damage to submarine cables, etc.

(b) The Commission thereafter discussed the meaning of the phrase "indicating clearly the place to be accorded to" the Nürnberg principles. The sense of the Commission was that this phrase should not be interpreted as meaning that the Nürnberg principles would have to be inserted in their entirety in the draft code. The Commission felt that the phrase did not preclude it from suggesting modification or development of these principles for the purpose of their incorporation in the draft code. It was not thought necessary to indicate the exact extent to which the various Nürnberg principles had been incorporated in the draft code. Only a general reference to the corresponding Nürnberg principles was deemed practicable.

(c) The Commission decided to deal with the criminal responsibility of individuals only. It may be recalled in this connexion that the Nürnberg Tribunal stated in its judgment: "Crimes against international law are committed by men, not by abstract entities, and only by punishing individuals who commit such crimes can the provisions of international law be enforced."

(d) The Commission has not considered itself called upon to propose methods by which a code may be given binding force. It has therefore refrained from drafting an instrument for implementing the code. The offences set forth are characterized in Article 1 as international crimes. Hence, the Commission has envisaged the possibility of an international tribunal for the trial and punishment of persons committing such offences. The Commission has taken note of the action of the General Assembly in setting up a special committee to prepare draft conventions and proposals relating to the establishment of an international criminal court. Pending the establishment of a competent international criminal court, a transitional measure might be adopted providing for the application of the code by national courts. Such a measure would doubtless be considered in drafting the instrument by which the code would be put into force.

TEXT OF THE DRAFT CODE

59. The Draft Code of Offences against the Peace and Security of Mankind, as adopted by the Commission, reads as follows:

Article 1

Offences against the peace and security of mankind, as defined in this Code, are crimes under international law, for which the responsible individuals shall be punishable.

This article is based upon the principle of individual responsibility for crimes under international law. This principle is recognized by the Charter and judgment of the Nürnberg Tribunal, and in the Commission's formulation of the Nürnberg principles it is stated as follows: "Any person who commits an act which constitutes a crime under international law is responsible therefor and liable to punishment."

Article 2

The following acts are offences against the peace and security of mankind:

(1) Any act of aggression, including the employment by the authorities of a State of armed force against another State for any purpose other than national or collective self-defence or in pursuance of a decision or recommendation by a competent organ of the United Nations.

In laying down that any act of aggression is an offence against the peace and security of mankind, this paragraph is in consonance with resolution 380 (V), adopted by the General Assembly on 17 November 1950, in which the General Assembly solemnly reaffirms that any aggression "is the gravest of all crimes against peace and security throughout the world."

The paragraph also incorporates, in substance, that part of Article 6, paragraph (a), of the Charter of the Nürnberg Tribunal, which defines as "crimes against peace," *inter alia*, the "initiation or waging of a war of aggression...."

While every act of aggression constitutes a crime under paragraph (1), no attempt is made to enumerate such acts exhaustively. It is expressly provided that the employment of armed force in the circumstances specified in the paragraph is an act of aggression. It is, however, possible that aggression can be committed also by other acts, including some of those referred to in other paragraphs of Article 2.

Provisions against the use of force have been included in many international instruments, such as the Covenant of the League of Nations, the Treaty for the Renunciation of War of 27 August 1928, the Anti-War Treaty of Non-Aggression and Conciliation, signed at Rio de Janeiro, 10 October 1933, the Act of Chapultepec of 8 March 1945, the Pact of the Arab League of 22 March 1945, the Iner-American Treaty of Reciprocal Assistance of 2 September 1947, and the Charter of the Organization of American States, signed at Bogotà, 30 April 1948.

The use of force is prohibited by Article 2, paragraph 4, of the Charter of the United Nations, which binds all Members to "refrain in their international relations from the ... use of force against the territorial integrity or political independence of any State, or in any other manner inconsistent witht he purposes of the United Nations." The same prohibition is contained in the draft Declaration on Rights which, in Article 9, provides that "Every State has the duty to refrain from resorting to war as an instrument of national policy, and to refrain from the ... use of force against the territorial integrity or political independence of another State, or in any other manner inconsistent with international law and order."

The offence defined in this paragraph can be committed only by the authorities of a State. A criminal responsibility of private individuals under international law may, however, arise under the provisions of paragraph (12) of the present article.

(2) Any threat by the authorities of a State to resort to an act of aggression against another State.

This paragraph is based upon the consideration that not only acts of aggression but also the threat of aggresion present a grave danger to the peace and security of mankind and should be regarded as an international crime.

Article 2, paragraph 4, of the Charter of the United Nations prescribes that all Members shall "refrain in their international relations from the threat ... of force against the territorial integrity or political independence of any State, or in any

733

other manner inconsistent with the Purposes of the United Nations." The same prohibition is contained in the draft Declaration on Rights and Duties of States, prepared by the International Law Commission, which, in Article 9, provides that "Every State has the duty ... to refrain from the threat of another State, or in any other manner inconsistent with international law and order."

The offence defined in this paragraph can be committed only by the authorities of a State. A criminal responsibility of private individuals under international law may, however, arise under the provisions of paragraph (12) of the present article.

(3) The preparation by the authorities of a State for the employment of armed force against another State for any purpose other than national or collective self-defence or in pursuance of a decision or recommendation by a competent organ of the United Nations.

In prohibiting the preparation for the employment of armed force (except under certain specified conditions) this paragraph incorporates in substance that part of Article 6, paragraph (a), of the Charter of the Nürnberg Tribunal which defines as "crimes against peace," *inter alia*, "planning" and "preparation" of "a war of aggression ..." As used in this paragraph the term "preparation" includes "planning." It is considered that "planning" is punishable only if it results in preparatory acts and thus becomes an element in the preparation for the employment of armed force.

the offence defined in this paragraph can be committed only by the authorities of a State. A criminal responsibility of private individuals under international law may, however, arise under the provisions of paragraph (12) of the present article.

(4) The incursion into the territory of a State from the territory of another State by armed bands acting for a political purpose.

The offence defined in this paragraph can be committed only by the members of the armed bands, and they are individually responsible. A criminal responsibility of the authorities of a State under international law may, however, arise under the provisions of paragraph (12) of the present article.

(5) The undertaking or encouragement by the authorities of a State of activities calculated to foment civil strife in another State, or the toleration by the authorities of a State or organized activities calculated to foment civil strife in another State.

In its resolution 380 (V) of 17 November 1950, the General Assembly declared that "fomenting civil strife in the interest of foreign Power" was aggression.

The draft Declaration on Rights and Duties of States prepared by the International Law Commission provides, in Article 4: "Every State has the duty to refrain from fomenting civil strife in the territory of another State, and to prevent the organization within its territory of activities calculated to foment such civil strife."

The offence defined in this paragraph can be committed only by the authorities of a State. A criminal responsibility of private individuals under international law may, however, arise under the provisions of paragraph (12) of the present article.

(6) The undertaking or encouragement by the authorities of a State of terrorist activities in another State, or the toleration by the authorities of a State of organized activities calculated to carry out terrorist acts in another State.

Article 1 of the Convention for the Prevention and Punishment of Terrorism of 16 November 1937 contained a prohibition of the encouragement by a State of terrorist activities directed against another State.

The offence defined in this paragraph can be committed only by the authorities of a State. A Criminal responsibility of private individuals under international law may, however, arise under the provisions of paragraph (12) of the present article.

(7) Acts by the authorities of a State in violation of its obligations under a treaty which is designed to ensure international peace and security by means of restrictions or limitations on armaments, or on military training, or on fortifications, or of other restrictions of the same character.

It may be recalled that the League of Nations' Committee on Arbitration and Security considered the failure to observe conventional restrictions such as those mentioned in this paragraph as raising, under many circumstances, a presumption of aggression. (Memorandum on Articles 10, 11 and 16 of the Covenant, submitted by Mr. Rutgers, League of Nations document C.A.S. 10., 6 February, 1928.)

The offence defined in this paragraph can be committed only by the authorities of a State. A criminal responsibility of private individuals under international law may, however, arise under the provisions of paragraph (12) of the present article.

(8) Acts by authorities of a State resulting in the annexation, contrary to international law, of territory belonging to another State or of territory under an international régime.

Annexation of territory in violation of international law constitutes a distinct offence, because it presents a particularly lasting danger to the peace and security of mankind. The Covenant of the League of Nations, in Article 10, provided that "The Members of the League undertake to respect and preserve as against external aggression the territorial integrity and existing political independence of all Members of the League." The Charter of the United Nations, in Article 2, paragraph 4, stipulates that "All Members shall refrain in their international relations from the threat or use of force against the territorial integrity or political independence of any State ...." Illegal annexation may also be achieved without overt threat or use of force, or by one or more of the acts defined in the other paragraphs of the present article. For this reason the paragraph is not limited to annexation of territory achieved by the threat or use of force.

The term "territory under an international régime" envisages territories under the international trusteeship system of the United Nations as well as those under any other form of international régime.

The offence defined in this paragraph can be committed only by the authorities of a State. A criminal responsibility of private individuals under international law may, however, arise under the provisions of paragraph (12) of the present article.

(9) **Acts by the authorities of a State or by private individuals, committed with intent to destroy, in whole or in part, a national, ethnical, racial or religious group as such, including:**

(i)   **Killing members of the group;**

(ii)   **Causing serious bodily or mental harm to members of the group;**

(iii)   **Deliberately inflicting on the group conditions of life calculated to bring about its physical destruction in whole or in part;**

(iv)   **Imposing measures intended to prevent births within the group;**

(v)   **Forcibly transferring children of the group to another group.**

The text of this paragraph follows the definition of the crime of genocide contained in Article II of the Convention on the Prevention and Punishment of the Crime of Genocide.

the offence defined in this paragraph can be committed both by authorities of a State and by private individuals.

(10) **Inhuman acts by the authorities of a State or by private individuals against any civilian population, such as murder, orextermination, or enslavement or deportation, or persecutions on political, racial, religious or cultural grounds, when such acts are committed in execution of or in connexion with other offences defined in this article.**

This paragraph corresponds substantially to Article 6, paragraph (c) of the Charter of the Nürnberg Tribunal, which defines "crimes against humanity." It has, however, been deemed necessary to prohibit also inhuman acts on cultural grounds, since such acts are no less detrimental to the peace and security of mankind than those provided for in the said Charter. There is another variation from the Nürnberg provision. While, according to the Charter of the Nürnberg Tribunal, any of the inhuman acts constitutes a crime under international law only if its is committed in execution of or in connexion with any crime against peace or war crime as defined in that Charter, this paragraph characterizes as crimes under international law inhuman acts when these acts are committed in execution of or in connexion with other offences defined in the present article.

The offence defined in this paragraph can be committed both by authorities of a State and by private individuals.

(11) Acts in violation of the laws or customs of war.

This paragraph corresponds to Article 6, paragraph (b), of the Charter of the Nürnberg Tribunal. Unlike the latter, it does not include an enumeration of acts which are in violation of the laws or customs of war, since no exhaustive enumeration has been deemed practicable.

The question was considered whether every violation of the laws or customs of war should be regarded as a crime under the code or whether only acts of a certain gravity should be characterized as such crimes. The first alternative was adopted.

This paragraph applies to all cases of declared war or of any other armed conflict which may rise between two or more States, even if the existence of a state of war is recognized by none of them.

The United Nations Educational, Scientific and Cultural Organiztion has urged that wanton destruction, during an armed conflict, of historical monuments, historical documents, works of art or any other cultural objects should be punishable under international law. (Letter of 17 March 1950 from the Director-General of UNESCO to the International Law Commission transmitting a "Report on the International Protection of Cultural Property, by Penal Measures, in the Event of Armed Conflict," document 5C/PRG/6 Annex I/UNESCO/MUS/Conf.1/20 (rev.), 8 March 1950.) It is understood that such destruction comes within the purview of the present paragraph. Indeed, to some extent, it is forbidden by Article 56 of the Regulations annexed to the 4th Hague Convention of 1907 respecting the Laws and Customs of War on Land, and by Article 5 of the 9th Hague Convention of 1907 respecting Bombardment by Naval Forces in Time of War.

The offence defined in this paragraph can be committed both by authorities of a State and by private individuals.

(12) Acts which constitute:

(i)   **Conspiracy to commit any of the offences defined in the preceding paragraphs of this article; or**

(ii)   **Direct incitement to commit any of the offences defined in the preceding paragraphs of this article; or**

(iii)   **Attempts to commit any of the offences defined in the preceding paragraphs of this article; or**

(iv)   **Complicity in the commission of any of the offences defined in the preceding paragraphs of this article.**

The notion of conspiracy is found in Article 6, paragraph (a), of the Charter of the Nürnberg Tribunal and the notion of complicity in the last paragraph of the same article. The notion of conspiracy in the said Charter is limited to the "planning, preparation, initiation or waging of a war of aggression, or a war in violation of international treaties, agreements or assurances," while the present paragraph provides for the application of the notion to all offences against the peace and security of mankind.

The notions of incitement and of attempt are found in the Genocide Convention as well as in certain national enactments on war crimes.

In including "complicity in the commission of any of the offences defined in the preceding paragraphs" among the acts which are offences against th epeace and security of mankind, it is not intended to stipulate that all those contributing, in the normal exercise of their duties, to the perpetration of offences against the peace and security of mankind could, on that ground alone, be considered as accomplices in such crimes. There can be no question of punishing as accomplices in such an offence all the members of the armed forces of a State or the workers in war industries.

Article 3

The fact that a person acted as Head of State or as responsible government official does not relieve him from responsibility for committing any of the offences defined in this Code.

This article incorporates, with modifications, Article 7 of the Charter of the Nürnberg Tribunal, which article provides: "The official position of defendants, whether as Heads of State or responsible officials in government departments, shall not be considered as freeing them from responsibility or mitigating punishment."

Principle III of the Commission's formulation of the Nürnberg Principles reads: "The fact that a person who committed an act which constitutes a crime under international law acted as Head of State or responsible Government official does not relieve him from responsibility under international law."

The last phrase of Article 7 of the Nürnberg Charter "or mitigating punishment" was not retained in the above-quoted principle as the question of mitigating punishment was deemed to be a matter for the competent court to decide.

Article 4

The fact that a person charged with an offence defined in this Code acted pursuant to order of his Government or of a superior does not relieve him from responsibility, provided a moral choice was in fact possible to him.

Principle IV of the Commission's formulation of the Nürnberg Principles, on the basis of the interpretation given by the Nürnberg Tribunal to Article 8 of its Charter, states: "The fact that a person acted pursuant to order of his Government or of a superior does not relieve him from responsibility under international law, provided a moral choice was in fact possible to him."

The observations on Principle IV, made in the General Assembly during its fifth session, have been carefully studied; no substantial modification, however, has been made int he drafting of this article which is based on a clear enunciation by the Nürnberg Tribunal. The article lays down the principle that the accused is responsible only if, in the circumstances, it was possible for him to act contrary to superior orders.

Article 5

The penalty for any offence defined in this Code shall be determined by the tribunal excercising jurisdiction over the individual accused, taking into account the gravity of the offence.

The article provides for the punishmetn of the offences defined in the Code. Such a provision is considered desirable in view of the generally accepted principle *nulla poena sine lege*. However, as it is not deemed practicable to prescribe a definite penalty for each offence, it is left to the competent tribunal to determine the penalty, taking into consideration the gravity of the offence committed.

5. INTERNATIONAL LAW COMMISION REPORT ON THE DRAFT CODE OF CRIMES AGAINST THE PEACE AND SECURITY OF MANKIND, 19 July 1991

(Excerpts)

U.N. G.A.O.R. Supp. No. 10 (A/46/10) 238.

PART I

CHAPTER 1. DEFINITION AND CHARACTERIZATION

Article 1

Definition

The crimes (under international law) defined in this Code constitute crimes against the peace and security of mankind.

CRIMES AGAINST HUMANITY

Article 2

Characterization

The characterization of an act or omission as a crime against the peace and security of mankind is independent of internal law. The fact that an act or omission is or is snot punishable under internal law does not affect this characterization.

CHAPTER 2. GENERAL PRINCIPLES

Article 3

Responsibility and punishment

1. An individual who commits a crime against the peace and security of mankind is responsible therefor and is liable to punishment.

2. An individual who aids, abets or provides the means for the commission of a crime against the peace and security of mankind or conspires in or directly incites the commission of such a crime is responsible therefor and is liable to punishment.

3. An individual who commits an act constituting an attempt to commit a crime against the peace and security of mankind (as set out in arts ...) is responsible therefor and is liable to punishment. Attempt means any commencement of execution of a crime that failed or was halted only because of circumstances independent of the perpetrator's intention.

Article 4

Motives

Responsibility for a crime against the peace and security of mankind is not affected by any motives invoked by the accused which are not covered by the definition of the crime.

Article 5

Responsibility of States

Prosecution of an individual for a crime against the peace and security of mankind does not relieve a State of any responsibility under international law for an act or omission attributable to it.

Article 6

Obligation to try to extradite

1. A State in whose territory an individual alleged to have committed a crime against the peace and security of mankind is present shall either try or extradite him.

2. If extradition is requested by several States, special consideration shall be given to the request of the State in whose territory the crime was committed.

3. The provisions of paragraphs 1 and 2 do not prejudge the establishment and the jurisdiction of an international criminal court.

Article 7

Non-applicability of statutory limitations

No statutory limitation shall apply to crimes against the peace and security of mankind.

Article 8

Judicial guarantees

An individual charged with a crime against the peace and security of mankind shall be entitled without discrimination to the minimum guarantees due to all human beings with regard to the law and the facts. In particular, he shall have the right to be presumed innocent until proved guilty and have the rights:

(a)   in the determination of any charge against him, to have a fair and public hearing by a competent, independent and impartial tribunal duly established by law or by treaty;

(b)   to be informed promptly and in detail in a language which he understands of the nature and cause of the charge against him;

(c)   to have adequate time and facilities for the preparation of his defence and to communicate with counsel of his own choosing;

(d)   to be tried without undue delay;

(e)   to be tried in his presence, and to defend himself in person or through legal assistance of his own choosing; to be informed, if he does not have legal assistance, of this right; and to have legal assistance assigned to him and without payment by him in any case if he does not have sufficient means to pay for it;

(f)   to examine, or have examined, the witnesses against him and to obtain the attendance and examination of witnesses on his behalf under the same conditions as witnesses against him;

(g)   to have the free assistance of an interpreter if he cannot understand or speak the language used in court;

(h)   not to be compelled to testify against himself or to confess guilt.

Article 9

Non bis in idem

1. No one shall be tried or punished for a crime under this Code for which he has already been finally convicted or acquitted by an international criminal court.

2. Subject to paragraphs 3, 4 and 5, no one shall be tried or punished for a crime under this Code in respect of an act for which he has already been finally convicted or acquitted by a national court, provided that, if a punishment was imposed, it has been enforced or is in the process of being enforced.

3. Notwithstanding the provisions of paragraph 2, an individual may be tried and punished by an international criminal court or by a national court for a crime under this Code if the act which was the subject of a trial and judgment as an ordinary crime corresponds to one of the crimes characterized in this Code.

4. Notwithstanding the provisions of paragraph 2, an individual may be tried and punished by a national court of another State for a crime under this Code:

    (a)   if the act which was the subject of the previous judgment took place in the territory of that State; or

    (b)   if that State has been the main victim of the crime.

5. In the case of a subsequent conviction under this Code, the court, in passing sentence, shall deduct any penalty imposed and implemented as a resuslt of a previous conviction for the same act.

Article 10

Non-retroactivity

1. No one shall be convicted under this Code for acts committed before its entry into force.

2. Nothing in this article shall preclude the trial and punishment of anyone for any act which, at the time when it was committed, was criminal in accordance with international law or domestic law applicable in conformity with international law.

Article 11

Order of a Government or a superior

The fact that an individual charged with a crime against the peace and security of mankind acted pursuant to an order of a Government or a superior does not relieve him of criminal responsibility if, in the circumstances at the time, it was possible for him not to comply with that order.

CRIMES AGAINST HUMANITY

Article 12

Responsibility of the superior

The fact that a crime against the peace and security of mankind was committed by a subordinate does not relieve his superiors of criminal responsibility, if they knew or had information enabling them to conclude, in the circumstances at the time, that the subordinate was committing or was going to commit such a crime and if they did not take all feasible measures within their power to prevent or repress the crime.

Article 13

Official position and responsibility

The official position of an individual who commits a crime against the peace and security of mankind, and particularly the fact that he acts as head of State or Government, does not relieve him of criminal responsibility.

Article 14

Defences and extenuating circumstances

1. The competent court shall determine the admissibility of defences under the general principles oflaw, in the light of the character of each crime.

2. In passing sentence, the court shall, where appropriate, take into account extenuating circumstances.

PART II

CRIMES AGAINST THE PEACE AND SECURITY OF MANKIND

Article 15

Aggression

1. An individual who as leader or organizer plans, commits or orders the commission of an act of aggression shall, on conviction thereof, be sentenced (to ...).

2. Aggression is the use of armed force by a State against the sovereignty, territorial integrity or political independence of another State, or in any other manner inconsistent with the Charter of the United Nations.

3. The first use of armed force by a State in contravention of the Charter shall constitute *prima facie* evidence of an act of aggression, although the Security Council may, in conformity with the Charter, conclude that a determination that an act of aggression has been committed would not be justified in the light of other relevant circumstances, including the fact that the acts concerned or their consequences are not of sufficient gravity.

4. Any of the following acts, regardless of a declaration of war, constitutes an act of aggression, due regard being paid to paragraphs 2 and 3:

   (a)   the invasion or attack by the armed forces of a State of the territory of another State, or any military occupation, however temporary, resulting from such invasion or attack, or any annexation by the use of force of the territory of another State or part thereof;

   (b)   bombardment by the armed forces of a State against the territory of another State or the use of any weapons by a State against the territory of another State;

   (c)   the blockade of the ports or coasts of a State by the armed forces of another State;

747

(d)   an attack by the armed forces of a State on the land, sea or air forces, or marine and air fleets of another State;

(e)   the use of armed forces of one State which are within the territory of another State with the agreement of the receiving State, in contravention of the conditions provided for in the agreement, or any extension of their presence in such territory beyond the termination of the agreement;

(f)   the action of a State in allowing its territory, which it has placed at the disposal of another State, to be used by that other State for perpetrating an act of aggression against a third State;

(g)   the sending by or on behalf of a State of armed bands, groups, irregulars or mercenaries, which carry out acts of armed force against another State of such gravity as to amount to the acts listed above, or its substantial involvement therein;

(h)   any other acts determined by the Security Council as constituting acts of aggression under the provisions of the Charter;

(i)   any determination by the Security Council as to the existence of an act of aggression is binding on national courts.)

5. Nothing in this article shall be interpreted as in any way englarging or diminishing the scope of the Charter of the United Nations including its provisions concerning cases in which the use of force is lawful.

6. Nothing in this article could in any way prejudice the right to self-determination, freedom and independence, as derived from the Charter, of peoples forcibly deprived of that right and referred to in the Declaration on Principles of International Law concerning Friendly Relations and Cooperation among States in accordance with the Charter of the United Nations, particularly peoples under colonial and racist regimes or other forms of alien domination; nor the right of these peoples to struggle to that end and to seek and receive support, in accordance with the principles of the Charter and in conformity with the above-mentioned Declaration.

Article 16

Threat of aggression

1. An individual who as leader or organizer commits or orders the commission of a threat of aggression shall, on conviction thereof, be sentence (to ...).

2. Threat of aggression consists of declarations, communications, demonstrations of force or any other measures which would give good reason to the Government of a State to believe that aggression is being seriously contemplated against that State.

Article 17

Intervention

1. An individual who as leader or organizer commits or orders the commission of an act of intervention in the internal or external affairs of a State shall, on conviction thereof, be sentenced (to ...).

2. Intervention in the internal or external affairs of a State consists of fomenting (armed) subversive or terrorist activities or by organizing, assisting or financing such activities, or supplying arms for the purpose of such activities, thereby (seriously) undermining the free exercise by that State of its sovereign rights.

3. Nothing in this article shall in any way prejudice the right of peoples to self-determination as enshrined in the Charter of the United Nations.

Article 18

Colonial domination and other forms of alien domination

An individual who as leader or organizer establishes or maintains by force or orders the establishment or maintenance by force of colonial domination or any other form of alien domination contrary to the right of peoples to self-determination as enshrined in the Charter of the United Nations shall, on conviction thereof, be sentenced (to ...).

CRIMES AGAINST HUMANITY

Article 19

Genocide

1. An individual who commits or orders the commission of an act of genocide shall, on conviction thereof, be sentenced (to ...).

2. Genocide means any of the following acts committed with intent to destroy, in whole or in part, a national, ethnic, racial or religious group as such:

    (a)   killing members of the group;

    (b)   causing serious bodily or mental harm to members of the group;

    (c)   deliberately inflicting on the group conditions of life calculated to bring about its physical destruction in whole or in part;

    (d)   imposing measures intended to prevent births within the group;

    (e)   forcibly transferring children of the group to another group.

Article 20

Apartheid

1. An individual who as leader or organizer commits or orders the commission of the crime of *apartheid* shall, on conviction thereof, be sentenced (to ...).

2. *Apartheid* consists of any of the following acts based on policies and practices of racial segregation and discrimination committed for the purpose of establishing or maintaining domination by one racial group over any other racial group and systematically oppressing it:

    (a)   denial to a member of members of a racial group of the right to life and liberty of person;

(b)   deliberate imposition on a racial group of living conditions calculated to cause its physical destruction in whole or in part;

(c)   any legislative measures and other measures calculated to prevent a racial group from participating in the political, social, economic and cultural life of the country and the deliberate creation of conditions preventing the full development of such a group;

(d)   any measures, including legislative measures, designed to divide the population along racial lines, in particular by the creation of separate reserves and ghettos for the members of a racial group, the prohibition of marriages among members of various racial groups or the expropriation of landed property belonging to a racial group or to members thereof;

(e)   exploitation of the labour of the members of a racial group, in particular by submitting them to forced labour;

(f)   persecution of organizations and persons, by depriving them of fundamental rights and freedoms, because they oppose *apartheid.*

Article 21

Systematic or mass violations of human rights

An individual who commits or orders the commission of any of the following violations of human rights:

-    murder

-    torture

-    establishing or maintaining over persons a status of slavery, servitude or forced labour

-    persecution on social, political, racial, religious or cultural grounds in a systematic manner or on a mass scale; or

-    deportation of forcible transfer of population shall, on conviction thereof, be sentenced (to ...).

Article 22

Exceptionally serious war crimes

1. An individual who commits or orders the commission of an exceptionally serious war crime shall, on conviction thereof, be sentenced (to ...).

2. For the purposes of this Code, an exceptionally serious war crime is an exceptionally serious violation of principles and rules of international law applicable in armed conflict consisting of any of the following acts:

(a)   acts of inhumanity, cruelty or barbarity directed against the life, dignity or physical or mental integrity of persons (in particular wilful killing, torture, mutilation, biological experiments, taking of hostages, compelling a protected person to serve in the forces of a hostile Power, unjustifiable delay in the repatriation of prisoners of war after the cessation of active hostilities, deportation or transfer of the civilian population and collective punishment);

(b)   establishment of settlers in an occupied territory and changes to the demographic composition of an occupied territory;

(c)   use of unlawful weapons;

(d)   employing methods or means of warfare which are intended or may be expected to cause widespread, long-term and severe damage to the natural environment;

(e)   large-scale destruction of civilian property;

(f)   wilful attacks on property of exceptional religious, historical or cultural value.

Article 23

Recruitment, use, financing and training of mercenaries

1. An individual who as an agent or representative of a State commits or orders the commission of any of the following acts:

- recruitment, use, financing or training of mercenaries for activities directed against another State or for the purpose of opposing the legitimate exercise of the inalienable right of peoples to self-determination as recognized under international law shall, on conviction thereof, be sentenced (to ...).

2. A mercenary is any individual who:

(a)   is specially recruited locally or abroad in order to fight in an armed conflict;

(b)   is motivated to take part in the hostilities essentially by the desire for private gain and, in fact, is promised, by or on behalf of a party to the conflict, material compensation substantially in excess of that promised or paid to combatants of similar rank and functions in the armed forces of that party;

(c)   is neither a national of a party to the conflict nor a resident of territory controlled by a party to the conflict;

(d)   is not a member of the armed forces of a party to the conflict; and

(e)   has not been sent by a State which is not a party to the conflict on official duty as a member of its armed forces.

3. A mercenary is also any individual who, in any other situation:

(a)   is specially recruited locally or abroad for the purpose of participating in a concerted act of violence aimed at:

    (i)   overthrowing a Government or otherwise undermining the constitutional order of a State; or

753

(ii)   undermining the territorial integrity of a State;

(b)   is motivated to take part therein essentially by the desire for significant private gain and is prompted by the promise or payment of material compensation;

(c)   is neither a national nor a resident of the State against which such an act is directed;

(d)   has not been sent by a State on official duty; and

(e)   is not a member of the armed forces of the State in whose territory the act is undertaken.

Article 24

International terrorism

An individual who as an agent or representative of a State commits or orders the commission of any of the following acts:

-       undertaking, organizing, assisting, financing, encouraging or tolerating acts against another State directed at persons or property and of such a nature as to create a state of terror in the minds of public figures, groups of persons or the general public shall, on conviction thereof, be sentenced (to ...).

Article 25

Illicit traffic in narcotic drugs

1. An individual who commits or orders the commission of any of the following acts:

-       undertaking, organizing, facilitating, financing or encouraging illicit traffic in narcotic drugs on a large scale, whether within the confines of a State or in a transboundary context shall, on conviction thereof, be sentenced (to ...).

2. For the purposes of paragraph 1, facilitating or encouraging illicit traffic in narcotic drugs includes the acquisition, holding, conversion or transfer of property by an

individual who knows that such property is derived from the crime described in this article in order to conceal or disguise the illicit origin of the property.

3. Illicit traffic in narcotic drugs means any production, manufacture, extraction, preparation, offering, offering for sale, distribution, sale, delivery on any terms whatsoever, brokerage, dispatch, dispatch in transit, transport, importation or exportation of any narcotic drug or any psychotropic substance contrary to internal or international law.

Article 26

Wilful and severe damage to the environment

An individual who wilfully causes or orders the causing of widespread, long-term and severe damage to the natural environment shall, on conviction thereof, be sentenced (to ...).

G. OTHER RELEVANT DOCUMENTS

1. CHRONOLOGICAL EXCERPTS OF THE TEXTUAL FORMULATIONS LEADING TO THE ADOPTION OF ARTICLE 6(c)

1. American Draft of Definitive Proposal,
Presented to Foreign Ministers at
San Francisco, April 1945

DECLARATION REGARDING THE CRIMINAL ACTS
TO BE CHARGED

6. The parties to this Agreement agree to bring to trial, in the names of their respective peoples, the persons referred to in Article 5 for their responsibility for the following criminal acts:

a. Violation of the customs and rules of warfare.
b. Invasion by force or threat of force of other countries in violation of international law or treaties.
c. Initiation of war in violation of international law or treaties.
d. Launching a war of aggression.
e. Recourse to war as an instrument of national policy or for the solution of international controversies.

7. This declaration shall also include the right to charge and try defendants under this Agreement for violations of law other than those recited above, including but not limited to atrocities and crimes committed in violation of the domestic law of any Axis Power or satellite or of any of the United Nations.

---

2. British Memorandum of May 28, 1945

DRAFTING AMENDMENTS

Substitute for Paragraph 6:

6. The parties to this Agreement agree to bring to trial, in the names of their respective peoples, the persons referred to in Article 5 for their responsibility for the following criminal acts:

a. Violation of the customs and rules of warfare.
b. Pursuing a systematic policy for the purpose of dominating Europe by a war of aggression and in the carrying out of that policy.
   (1) Initiating and making attacks on other countries in violation of International Law, treaties or assurances.
   (2) Resorting to war as an instrument of national policy.

---

3. Revision of American Draft of Proposed Agreement, June 14, 1945

EXECUTIVE AGREEMENT RELATING TO THE PROSECUTION OF EUROPEAN AXIS WAR CRIMINALS

DECLARATION OF LEGAL PRINCIPLES

b. Atrocities and offenses, including atrocities and persecutions on racial or religious grounds, committed since 1 January 1933 in violation of any applicable provision of the domestic law of the country in which committed.

---

4. Amendments Proposed by the United Kingdom, June 28, 1945

PROPOSED AMENDMENTS BY THE UNITED KINGDOM DELEGATION TO THE UNITED STATES DRAFT PROTOCOL

(e) Atrocities and persecutions and deportations on political, racial or religious grounds, in pursuance of the common plan or enterprise referred to in sub-paragraph (d) hereof whether or not in violation of the domestic law of the country where perpetrated.

5. Minutes of Conference Session of
June 29, 1945

{EXPLANATION OF UNITED KINGDOM MEMORANDUM}

Then (e) deals with atrocities and persecutions in pursuance of the plan and whether they are in violation of the domestic law of the country where perpetrated; that is, it would include atrocities and persecutions in Germany if they were legal by German law.

6. Revised Draft of Agreement and
Memorandum Submitted by American
Delegation, June 30, 1945

EXECUTIVE AGREEMENT RELATING TO THE PROSECUTION OF
EUROPEAN AXIS WAR CRIMINALS

(e)   Atrocities and persecutions and deportations on political, racial, or religious grounds, in pursuance of the common plan or enterprise referred to in subparagraph (d) hereof, whether or not in violation of the domestic law of the country where perpetrated.

7. Draft Showing Soviet and American
Proposals in Parallel Columns

EXECUTIVE AGREEMENT

LAST DRAFT OF SOVIET STATUTE

I. GENERAL PROVISIONS

Article 2
Range of Crimes

Among the crimes coming under the jurisdiction of the Tribunal are:

c)   atrocities and violence in regard to civilian populations, deportations of civilians to slave labour, murder and ill-treatment of prisoners of war, destruction of towns and villages, plunder and other violations of the laws and customs of war;

LAST DRAFT OF AMERICAN ANNEX

5.   The Tribunal shall be bound by this declaration of the Signatories that the following acts are criminal violations of International Law:

(a) Violations of the laws, rules, and customs of war. Such violations shall include, but shall not be limited to, mass murder and ill-treatment of prisoners of war and civilian populations and the plunder of such populations.

---

8. Draft of Agreement and Charter,
Reported by Drafting Subcommittee,
July 11, 1945

A G R E E M E N T by the Governments of the UNITED KINGDOM OF GREAT BRITAIN AND NORTHERN IRELAND, of the UNITED STATES OF AMERICA, of the Provisional Government of the FRENCH REPUBLIC and of the UNION OF SOVIET SOCIALIST REPUBLICS for the Prosecution and Punishment of the MAJOR WAR CRIMINALS of the EUROPEAN AXIS POWERS

JURISDICTION AND GENERAL PRINCIPLES

6.   The following acts shall be considered criminal violations of International Law and shall come within the jurisdiction of the Tribunal:

(e)   Atrocities and persecutions and deportations on political, racial or religious grounds in [pursuance of a common plan or enterprise referred to in subparagraph (d) hereof, whether or not in violation of the domestic law of the country where perpetrated].

759

---

9. Draft Article on Definition of
"Crimes", Submitted by French Delegation,
July 19, 1945

DRAFT ARTICLE ON THE DEFINITION
OF CRIMES

The Tribunal will have jurisdiction to try any person who has, in any capacity whatsoever, directed the preparation and conduct of:

ii) the policy of atrocities and persecutions against civilian populations;

and who is responsible for the violations of international law, the laws of humanity and the dictates of the public conscience, committed by the armed forces and civilian authorities in the service of those enemy Powers.

---

10. Proposed Revision of Definition of
"Crimes" (Article 6), Submitted by British
Delegation, July 20, 1945

The Tribunal shall have power to try, convict and sentence any person who has, in any capacity whatever directed or participated in the planning, furtherance, or conduct of any or all of the following acts, designs, or attempts namely:

2. Systematic atrocities against or systematic terrorism or ill-treatment or murder of civilians;

and who is hereby declared therefore to be personally answerable for the violations of international law, of the laws of humanity, and of the dictates of the public conscience, committed in the course of carrying out the said acts, designs or attempts by the forces and authorities whether armed, civilian or otherwise, in the service of any of the European Axis Powers.

---

11. Redraft of Definition of "Crimes",
Submitted by Soviet Delegation, July 23, 1945

DRAFT ARTICLE 6 OF THE CHARTER

The Tribunal shall have power to try any person who has in any capacity whatever directed or participated in the preparation or conduct of any or all of the following acts, designs or attempts namely:

b)   Atrocities against the civilian population including murder and ill-treatment of civilians, the deportation of civilians to slave labour and other violations of the laws and customs of warfare;

and who is therefore personally answerable for the violation of international law, of the laws of humanity and of the dictates of the public conscience, committed in the course of carrying out the said acts, designs or attempts by the forces and authorities whether armed, civilian or otherwise, in the service of any of the European Axis Powers.

---

12. Redraft of Charter, Submitted by
British Delegation, July 23, 1945

A G R E E M E N T by the Government of the UNITED KINGDOM OF GREAT BRITAIN AND NORTHERN IRELAND, the UNITED STATES OF AMERICA, the Provisional Government of the FRENCH REPUBLIC and the Government of the UNION OF SOVIET SOCIALIST REPUBLICS for the Prosecution and Punishment of the MAJOR WAR CRIMINALS of the EUROPEAN AXIS

CHARTER

CONSTITUTION OF THE INTERNATIONAL MILITARY
TRIBUNAL
JURISDICTION AND GENERAL PRINCIPLES

Article 6

The following acts shall be considered criminal violations of International Law and shall come within the jurisdiction of the Tribunal:

(e)   Atrocities and persecutions and deportations on political, racial or religious grounds [in pursuance of a common plan or enterprise referred to in sub-paragraph (d) hereof, whether or not in violation of the domestic law of the country where perpetrated.]

---

13. Redraft of Soviet Definition of "Crimes"
(Article 6), Submitted by British
Delegation, July 23, 1945

The following acts or designs or attempts at any of them shall be deemed crimes on conviction of which punishment may be imposed by the Tribunal upon any person who is proved to have in any capacity whatever directed or participated in the preparation or planning for or carrying out of any or all of such acts designs or attempts:

(b)   Atrocities against civilian populations including, *inter alia*, murder and ill-treatment of civilians and deportation of civilians to slave labour, and persecutions on racial or religious grounds where such persecutions were inflicted in pursuance of the aggression or domination referred to in paragraph (a) above;

14. Redraft of Definition of "Crimes",
Submitted by Soviet Delegation, July 25, 1945

The following acts, designs or attempts at any of them shall be deemed crimes and shall come within the jurisdiction of the Tribunal:

b) Atrocities against civilian populations including murder and ill-treatment of civilians and deportation of civilians to slave labour, and persecutions on racial or religious grounds inflicted in pursuance of the aggression or domination referred to in paragraph (a) above;

15. Redraft of Definition of "Crimes",
Submitted by American Delegation,
July 25, 1945

DEFINITION OF CRIMES PROPOSED BY
UNITED STATES REPRESENTATIVE

6.   The following acts shall be deemed criminal violations of International Law, and the Tribunal shall have power and jurisdiction to convict any person who committed any of them on the part of the European Axis powers:

(b)   Persecutions, exterminations, or deportations on political, racial or religious grounds, whether or not in violation of domestic law of the country where perpetrated, when in pursuance of a common plan, enterprise or policy to prepare for or wage a war of aggression;

---

16. Revised Definition of "Crimes", Prepared
by British Delegation and Accepted by
French Delegation, July 28, 1945

For the purpose of the trials before the Tribunal established by the Agreement referred to in Article 1 hereof, the following acts or designs or attempts at any of them shall be deemed to be crimes coming within the jurisdiction of the Tribunal:

(b)   Atrocities against civilian populations other than those referred to in paragraph (a). These include but are not limited to murder and ill-treatment of civilians and deportations of civilians to slave labour and persecution on political, racial or religious grounds committed in pursuance of the common plan or conspiracy referred to in paragraph (d) below.

---

17. Revised Definition of "Crimes",
Prepared by British Delegation To Meet Views
of Soviet Delegation, July 28, 1945

763

For the purpose of the trials of the major war criminals of the European Axis Powers before the Tribunal established by the Agreement referred to in Article 1 hereof, the following acts or designs or attempts at any of them shall be deemed to be crimes coming within the jurisdiction of the Tribunal:

(c)   Atrocities against civilian populations other than those referred to in paragraph (b). These include murder and ill-treatment of civilians and deportations of civilians to slave labour and persecution on political, racial or religious grounds committed in pursuance of the common plan or conspiracy referred to in paragraph (a) above.

---

18. Revised Definition of "Crimes", Submitted by American Delegation, July 30, 1945

The Tribunal established by the Agreement referred to in Article 1 hereof shall have power and jurisdiction to hear, try and determine charges of crime against only those who acted in aid of the European Axis Powers.

The following acts, designs, or attempts at any of them, shall be deemed to be crimes coming within its jurisdiction:

(c)   Atrocities against civilian populations other than those referred to in paragraph (b). These include but are not limited to murder and ill-treatment of civilians and deportations of civilians to slave labour or persecution on political, racial or religious grounds committed in any country, at any time, in pursuance of the common plan or conspiracy referred to in paragraph (a) above.

---

19. Notes on Proposed Definition of "Crimes", Submitted by American Delegation, July 31, 1945

4.   In (c) we should insert words to make clear that we are reaching persecution, etc. of Jews and others in Germany as well as outside of it, and before as well as after commencement of the war.

20. Revision of Definition of "Crimes",
Submitted by American Delegation,
July 31, 1945

ARTICLE 6. DEFINITION OF CRIMES

The Tribunal established by the Agreement referred to in Article 1 hereof shall have power and jurisdiction to try and determine charges of crime against individuals who and organizations which acted in aid of the European Axis Powers and to impose punishments on those found guilty.

The following acts, or any of them, are crimes coming within its jurisdiction for which there shall be individual responsibility:

(c)   CRIMES AGAINST HUMANITY, namely, murder extermination, enslavement, deportation, and other inhumane acts committed against any civilian population, before or during the war, or persecutions on political, racial, religious grounds, in furtherance of or in connection with any crime within the jurisdiction of the International Tribunal, whether or not in violation of the domestic law of the country where perpetrated.

---

21. Agreement and Charter, August 8, 1945

Charter of the International Military Tribunal

II. JURISDICTION AND GENERAL PRINCIPLES

Article 6. The Tribunal established by the Agreement referred to in Article 1 hereof for the trial and punishment of the major war criminals of the European Axis countries shall have the power to try and punish persons who, acting in the interests of the European Axis countries, whether as individuals or as members of organizations, committed any of the following crimes.

The following acts, or any of them, are crimes coming within the jurisdiction of the Tribunal for which there shall be individual responsibility:

765

(c)   CRIMES AGAINST HUMANITY: namely, murder, extermination, enslavement, deportation, and other inhumane acts committed against any civilian population, before or during the war; or persecutions on political, racial or religious grounds in execution of or in connection with any crime within the jurisdiction of the Tribunal, whether or not in violation of the domestic law of the country where perpetrated.

---

22.   Protocol to Agreement and Charter,
October 6, 1945

PROTOCOL

Whereas an Agreement and Charter regarding the Prosecution of War Criminals was signed in London on the 8th August 1945, in the English, French, and Russian languages,

And whereas a discrepancy has been found to exist between the originals of Article 6, paragraph (c), of the Charter in the Russian language, on the one hand, and the originals in the English and French languages, on the other, to wit, the semi-colon in Article 6, paragraph (c), of the Charter between the words "war" and "or", as carried in the English and French texts, is a comma in the Russian text,

And whereas it is desired to rectify this discrepancy:

NOW, THEREFORE, the undersigned, signatories of the said Agreement on behalf of their respective Governments, duly authorized thereto, have agreed that Article 6, paragraph (c), of the Charter in the Russian text is correct, and that the meaning and intention of the Agreement and Charter require that the said semi-colon in the English text should be changed to a comma, and that the French text should be amended to read as follows:

c) LES CRIMES CONTRE L'HUMANITE: c'est à dire l'assassinat, l'extermination, la réduction en esclavage, la déportation, et tout autre acte inhumain commis contre toutes populations civiles, avant ou pendant la guerre, ou bien les persécutions pour des motifs politiques, raciaux, ou réligieux, lorsque ces actes ou persécutions, qu'ils aient constitué ou non une violation du droit interne du pays où ils ont été perpétrés, ont été commis à la suite de tout crime rentrant dans la compétence du Tribunal, ou en liaison avec ce crime.

2. INTERNATIONAL SLAVERY INSTRUMENTS

1. The 1815 Declaration Relative to the Universal Abolition of the Slave Trade [Congress of Vienna Act. XV] declared slave trade as repugnant. It noted governments resolved to put an end to the slave trade and that all powers with colonies had recognized by legislative acts, treaties and other formal undertakings the obligation and necessity of abolishing it. This instrument implicitly recognized the penal nature of slave trade by establishing a duty to prohibit, prevent, prosecute, punish, or the like, in paragraphs 3 and 4. It did not, however, contain enforcement provisions for the abolition of slave trade, nor did it make it an international crime. [2 Martens 432, *reprinted in* 63 Parry's 473].

2. The 1822 Declaration Respecting the Abolition of the Slave Trade (Congress of Verona) embodied the signatories' declaration of intentions to abolish slave trade and reaffirmed their opposition to slave trade, but contained no criminalization of the conduct. [6 Martens 139, *reprinted in* 73 Parry's 32].

3. The 1841 Treaty for the Suppression of the African Slave Trade (Treaty of London) equated slave trade to piracy and thus, made it an international crime. With respect to the act of slave trade, this instrument established duties to prohibit, punish or the like, (Articles I and III), prosecute (Article X), and cooperate in prosecution and punishment (Article XV). Articles VI, VII, X and Annex B establish a criminal jurisdictional basis. Specifically, States were empowered to search the ships of other signatory states on the high seas and detain the vessel and crew if they found that the vessel was carrying slaves. A trial would be held in the country which seized the vessel in question and if it was found to have been engaged in the slave trade, the vessel would be confiscated. The confiscation was in the nature of a penal sanction. [10 Martens 392, *reprinted in* 92 Parry's 437].

4. The 1863 Instruction for Armies in the Field (Lieber Code) provided instructions for the Union troops during the United States' Civil War and noted that deportation and reduction to servitude of the civilian population of conquered States by the conqueror were no longer practiced in the conduct of war and thus the practice was impermissible. The Code was widely

followed by other countries, and was even officially adopted by the German Government in the Franco-German War of 1870. [Promulgated as INSTRUCTIONS FOR OFFICERS AND NON-COMMISSIONED OFFICERS ON OUTPOST AND PATROL DUTY AND TROOPS IN CAMPAIGN BY ORDER OF THE SECRETARY OF WAR, in Washington, D.C. (War Dep't Classification No. w1.12: Oct. 8, 1863). *Reprinted in* 1 Friedman 158].

5. The 1874 Project of an International Declaration Concerning the Laws and Customs of War (Declaration of Brussels, Brussels Conference on the Laws and Customs of War, No. 18) and the Final Protocol (Brussels Conference on the Laws and Customs of War, No. 19) contain articles dealing specifically with slavery and forced labor. Art. XXV prohibited slavery and forced labor. Art. XXXVI prohibited compulsory enlistment of the civilian population. The instrument was not legally binding but is evidence of customary International Law and "General Principles" of International Law. [*See* 4 Martens (2d) 219, *reprinted in* 1 AJIL 96 (1907)].

6. The 1885 General Act of the Conference Respecting the Congo (General Act of Berlin) provided in Article 6 that Powers exercising sovereignty or influence in the Congo Basin undertook to suppress slavery and the slave trade. The Act in Chapter II, Article 9, established duties to prohibit, prevent, prosecute, and punish. Slave trade was prohibited in accordance with the principles of "le droit des gens." Each Power undertook to use all means in its power to put an end to the trade and punish those engaging in it. [10 Martens (2d) 414, *reprinted in* 3 AJIL 7 (1909). This Act was revised by the Convention Revising the General Act of Berlin, 26 February 1885, and the General Act and Declaration of Brussels, 2 July 1890, 10 September 1919; *see also* 1 BASSIOUNI DIGEST 425 (1986)].

7. The 1890 Convention Relative to the Slave Trade and Importation into Africa of Firearms, Ammunition, Spirituous Liquors (general Act of the Brussels Conference) established broader and stricter penalties for the continuing practice of slave trade within the signatory states by regulating firearms and spirituous liquors in Africa on the assumption that their elimination would aid in the achievement of their principal goal of eradicating slavery. Articles criminalizing slave trade and duties to repress slavery are:

DOCUMENTS SECTION

Articles I, II, III, V, VIII, IX, XV, XVII, XIX, XX, XXV, XL, LXII, LXVII and LXX contained duties to prohibit, prevent, prosecute, punish or the like.

Articles V, XII, XIX, LXVII and LXX criminalized the proscribed conduct.

Articles V, XII, XIX, XL, LIX, LXVII and LXXXVII contained the duty or right to punish the proscribed conduct.

Article LXVII contained the duty or right to extradite for the crime of slavery.

Articles XXVI, XLV, LXXI, LXXII, LXXVIII, LXXIX and Section II contained the duty or right to cooperate in prosecution and punishment (including judicial assistance).

Articles LIV, LVI, LX, LXX, XXIX and LII contained the establishment of a criminal jurisdictional basis.

Under Article 5, contracting Powers obligated themselves to enact or introduce penal legislation to punish serious offenses against individuals - those responsible for mutilating male adults and children anyone participating in the capture of slaves by force as well as provisions concerning violations of the liberty of individuals and those engaged in transporting or trafficking in slaves.

Those guilty of any of the crimes were to be brought to justice in the place where they were found, thus establishing universal jurisdiction for those violating the terms of the treaty. [17 Martens (2d) 345, 27 Stat. 886, T.S. No. 383, *reprinted in* 173 Parry's 293. The Act was revised by the Convention Respecting the Liquor Traffic in Africa, signed at Brussels, 8 June 1899, *see* 25 Martens (3d) 722, T.S. 467. It was not, however, adopted wholesale by every country. As Oppenheim notes, "France, in ratifying the General Act of the Brussels Anti-Slavery Conference of July 2, 1890, excepted from ratification Articles 21 to 23 and 42 to 61, and the Powers acquiesced in this partial ratification, so that France was not bound by these twenty-three articles," *see* 1 OPPENHEIM, INTERNATIONAL LAW: A TREATISE 641, 912 (H. Lauterpacht ed. 8th ed. 1955) (citing Martens, 22 N.R.G. (2d) 260)].

8. In the 1890 Treaty Between Great Britain and Spain for the Suppression of the African Slave Trade, the signatories agreed to prohibit all trade in slaves carried on by them and to punish all persons engaged in such traffic. [18 Martens (2d) 168, *reprinted in* PARLIAMENTARY PAPERS, 1892, vol. XCV, p. 735, T.S. No. 3 (1892)].

9. In the 1899 Convention with Respect to the Laws and Customs of War on Land (First Hague, II) and (a) Regulations Respecting the Laws and Customs of War on Land, Articles 27, 28 and 44 recognized the criminal nature of slavery by establishing duties to prohibit, prevent, prosecute, punish, or the like. [26 Martens (2d) 949, 32 Stat. 1803, T.S. No. 403, *reprinted in* 1 AJIL 129 (Supp. official doc. 1907). Sections II and III of this Convention and its Regulations were supplemented by Sections II and III of the Regulations supplemented by the Geneva Convention Relative to the Protection of Civilians in Time of War, 12 August 1949, 75 U.N.T.S. 287, as between contracting parties to both conventions; Chapter II of the Regulations complemented by the Geneva Convention Relative to the Treatment of Prisoners of War, 27 July 1929, *infra* note 18, and the Geneva Convention Relative to the Treatment of Prisoners of War, 12 August 1949, 75 U.N.T.S. 135, as between contracting parties. The Convention was replaced by the Convention Respecting the Laws and Customs of War on Land (Second Hague, IV), 18 October 1907, *infra* note 11, as between contracting parties to the later convention].

10. The 1905 International Agreement for the Suppression of the "White Slave Traffic" in Articles 1, 2 and 3 established the duty or right to cooperate in prosecution and punishment (including judicial assistance). [1 L.N.T.S. 83 *reprinted in* 195 Parry's 326. This Agreement was subsequently amended by the Protocol Amending the International Agreement for the Suppression of the White Slave Traffic, 18 May 1904, and the International Convention for the Suppression of White Slave Traffic, signed at Paris, on 4 May 1910, signed at Lake Success, New York, 4 May 1949, 30 U.N.T.S. 23. It was

subsequently replaced by the International Agreement for the Suppression of the White Slave Traffic, signed at Paris on 18 May 1904 as amended by the Protocol signed at Lake Success, New York, 4 May 1949, 92 U.N.T.S. 19].

11.   The 1907 Convention Respecting the Laws and Customs of War on Land (Second Hague, IV and (a) Regulations Respecting the Laws and Customs of War of on Land, 18 October 1907 (Hague Regulations) prohibited certain types of forced labor from prisoners of war in Article 1 and referred to Slavery and related crimes in Arts. 6, 44 and 52, while Article 6 contemplated the use by the belligerent State of the labor of prisoners of war and stated that the tasks should not be excessive and should have no connection to the war effort. [3 Martens (3d) 461, 36 Stat. 2277, T.S. No. 539. *Reprinted in* 2 AJIL 90 (1908) (Supp.); 1 Bevans 631; 1 Friedman 308. This convention was supplemented by the Convention for the Protection of Cultural Property in the Event of Armed Conflict, signed at the Hague, 14 May 1954, 249 U.N.T.S. 240. Sections II and III of the Regulations were supplemented by the Geneva Convention Relative to the Protection of Civilian Persons in Time of War, 12 August 1949, *see infra* note 54, as between contracting parties to both conventions, Chapter II of the Regulations complemented by the Geneva Convention Relative to the Treatment of Prisoners of War, 27 July 1929, *infra* note 18, and the Geneva Convention Relative to the Treatment of Prisoners of War, 12 August 1949, *see infra* note 53, as between contracting parties to both conventions.

Austria, Germany, Hungary, Japan, Montenegro, Turkey and the Union of Soviet Socialist Republics all made reservations upon signature, ratification or accession. *See* 1 BASSIOUNI DIGEST 172].

12.   The 1910 International Convention for the Suppression of the White Slave Traffic implicitly recognized the penal nature of the act by establishing a duty to prohibit, prevent, prosecute, punish, or the like in Articles I, II, III, V and the Closing Protocol. Articles I, II and the Closing Protocol establish a criminal jurisdictional basis, and Articles VI and VII call for a duty or right to cooperate in prosecution and punishment (including judicial assistance), and further, Article V contains a duty or right to extradite. [7 Martens (3d) 252, *reprinted in* 211 Parry's 45. This Convention was amended by the Protocol Amending the International Agreement for the Suppression of the White Slave

Traffic, signed at Paris, on 4 May 1910, signed at Lake Success, New York, 4 May 1949, *see infra* note 48. The Convention was subsequently replaced by the International Convention for the Suppression of the White Slave Traffic, signed at Paris on 4 May 1910, and as Amended by the Protocol Signed at Lake Success, New York, 4 May 1949, 98 U.N.T.S. 101].

13. The 1919 Convention Revising the General Act of Berlin, 26 February 1885, and the General Act and Declaration of Brussels, 2 July 1890 (Treaty of Saint-Germain-en-Laye) implicitly recognized the penal nature of the act by establishing a duty to prohibit, prevent, prosecute, punish, or the like found in Article 11. [8 L.N.T.S. 25, 49 Stat. 3027, T.S. 877, *reprinted in* 14 Martens (3d) 12. The General Act of Berlin was abrogated by this treaty, as was the General Act of Brussels].

14. The 1921 International Convention for the Suppression of the Traffic in Women and Children implicitly recognized the penal nature of the act by establishing a duty to prohibit, prevent, prosecute, punish, or the like is found in Articles 2 and 3. Article 4 contains a duty or right to prosecute. [9 L.N.T.S. 415, *reprinted in* 18 AJIL 130 (1924). This instrument was subsequently amended by the Protocol to Amend the International Convention for the Suppression of the Traffic in Women and Children, concluded at Geneva on 30 September 1921, and the Convention for the Suppression of Trafficin Women of Full Age, concluded at Geneva on 11 October 1933, signed at Lake Success, New York, 12 November 1947, *infra* note 44. It was subsequently replaced by the International Convention for the Suppression of the Traffic in Women and Children of 30 September 1921 as Amended by the Protocol Signed at Lake Success, New York, 12 November 1947, *infra* note 45].

15. The 1922 Treaty Relating to the Use of Submarines and Noxious Gases in Warfare [London Naval Treaty] never entered into force for failure to receive necessary notifications but is evidence of customary International Law and "General Principles" of International Law. Article 3 dealt with piracy and the prohibition of transporting slaves in submarines. [25 L.N.T.S. 202, *reprinted in* 13 Martens (3d) 643, and 16 AJIL 57 (1922)].

16.   The 1926 Slavery Convention recognized the penal nature of the act by establishing a duty to prohibit, prevent, prosecute, punish or the like in Articles 2, 3 and 6. Furthermore, Article 4 contains a duty to cooperate in prosecution, and punishment (including judicial assistance). [60 .N.T.S. 253, 46 Stat. 2183, T.S. No. 778, *reprinted in* 21 AJIL 171 (1927). This Convention was amended by the Protocol Amending the Slavery Convention signed at Geneva on 25 September 1926, signed at New York, 7 December 1953, *infra* note 57, as between the contracting parties to the Protocol. It was subsequently replaced by the Slavery Convention Signed at Geneva on 25 September 1926 and Amended by the Protocol Opened for Signature or Acceptance at the Headquarters of the United Nations, New York, on 7 December 1953, *infra* note 58].

17.   In the 1928 Bellot Rules, Article 25 provided that an occupier may not force inhabitants of occupied territory to take part in the war effort. Article 28 provided that an occupier must pay normal wages for services rendered by inhabitants. [*See* International Law Association *Report of the Thirty-Fifth Conference held at Warsaw, August 9th to 16th 1928*, pp. 238-290 (1929)].

18.   The 1929 Geneva Convention Relative to the Treatment of Prisoners of War addressed Slavery and related crimes in Articles 27 and 29, and regulation of prisoners of war labor in Articles 30, 31, 32 and 33. [118 L.N.T.S. 343, 47 Stat. 2021, T.S. No. 846, *reprinted in* 30 Martens (3d) 846, and 27 AJIL 59 (1933). This Convention was supplemented by the Regulations Respecting the Laws and Customs of War on Land, 18 October 1907, *supra* note 11. It was replaced by the Geneva Convention Relative to the Treatment of Prisoners of War, 12 August 1949, *see infra* note 53, as between contracting parties to the later convention, later supplemented by Protocol I Additional to the Geneva Conventions of 12 August 1949, 12 December 1977, *infra* note 66, and Protocol II Additional to the Geneva Conventions of 12 August 1949, 12 December 1977, *infra* note 67, as between contracting parties to each later convention].

19.   The 1930 Convention Concerning Forced or Compulsory Labor in Article 21, "penal offense," recognized such conduct as constituting an international crime, or a crime under international law. The duty to prohibit, prevent, prosecute, punish, or the like is found in Articles 1, 4, 5, 10, 18 and 20.

Article 25 covers the state parties' rights to prosecute and punish the proscribed conduct. [*See* 5 HUDSON 609. This treaty was modified by the Final Articles Revision Convention, signed at Montreal, 9 October 1946, *see* 38 U.N.T.S. 3].

20.   The 1933 International Convention for the Suppression of the Traffic in Women of Full Age in Article 1, recognized the penal nature of the act by establishing a duty to prohibit, prevent, prosecute or the like. Articles 1 and 2 criminalized the proscribed conduct and contained a duty or right to punish. Article 3 contained a duty or right to cooperate in prosecution and punishment (including judicial assistance). Article 4 refers to the establishment of an international criminal court or tribunal. [150 L.N.T.S. 431, *reprinted in* 6 Hudson 469. The Convention was subsequently amended by the Protocol to Amend the Convention for the Suppression of the Traffic in Women and Children, Concluded at Geneva on 30 September 1921, and the Convention for the Suppression of Traffic in Women of Full Age, Concluded at Geneva, on 11 October 1933, signed at Lake Success, New York, 12 November 1947, *see infra* note 44. It was subsequently replaced by the International Convention for the Suppression of the Traffic in Women of Full Age, Concluded at Geneva on 11 October 1933, as Amended by the Protocol signed at Lake Success, New York, on 12 November 1947, *see infra* note 45].

21.   The 1943 Instrument of Surrender of Italy provided for the surrender and punishment of persons who engaged in enslavement during the course of the war. [61 Stat. 2742, T.I.A.S. No. 1604, *reprinted in* 3 Bevans 775. This instrument was amended by the Protocol Amending the Instrument of Surrender of Italy of 29 September 1943, 9 November 1943, *infra* note 24; and was terminated 15 September 1947, upon the entry into force of the Treaty of Peace with Italy, 10 February 1947, T.I.A.S. No. 1648].

22.   The 1943 Declaration Regarding Italy [Moscow Conference of Foreign Secretaries, Secret Protocol, Annex 4] embodied the provisions enunciated in the Instrument of Surrender of Italy with regards to slavery. [1943 FOR. REL. (I) 749, at 759, *reprinted in* 38 AJIL 3, 6 (1944)].

23.   The 1943 Declaration of German Atrocities [Moscow Conference of Foreign Secretaries, Secret Protocol, Annex 4] stated in detail the intentions of the

Allies with respect to the post-war prosecution of German war criminals with respect to, *inter alia*, the enslavement and deportation of civilians. [1943 FOR. REL. (I) 749, at 768, *reprinted in* 38 AJIL 3, 7 (1944)].

24.   The 1943 Protocol Amending the Instrument of Surrender of Italy of 29 September 1943 amends the prior instrument by adding a jurisdictional provision to the same category of crimes. [61 Stat. 2761, T.I.A.S. No. 1604, *reprinted in* 3 Bevans 854. This protocol was terminated 15 September 1947, upon the entry into force of the Treaty of Peace with Italy, 10 February 1947, *see supra* note 21].

25.   The 1944 Agreement Concerning an Armistice with Romania allowed for the surrender and prosecution of persons found to have engaged in slavery. [59 Stat. 1712, E.A.S. No. 490, *reprinted in* 39 AJIL 88 (1945). This treaty was replaced by Treaty of Peace with Romania, 10 February 1947, 42 U.N.T.S. 3].

26.   The 1944 Agreement Concerning an Armistice with Bulgaria allowed for the surrender and prosecution of persons found to have engaged in slavery. [58 Stat. 1498, E.A.S. 437, *reprinted in* 3 Bevans 909. This treaty was replaced by the Treaty of Peace with Bulgaria, 10 February 1947, 41 U.N.T.S. 21].

27.   The 1945 Report of the Crimea (Yalta) Conference. Slavery and related crimes are addressed in Article II. [1945 FOR. REL. (Conferences at Malta and Yalta) 968, *reprinted in* 3 Bevans 1005].

28.   The 1945 Declaration Regarding the Defeat of Germany and the Assumption of Supreme Authority with Respect to Germany. In Article 11, the Declaration specified the surrender for prosecution of persons having engaged in War Crimes, including enslavement and the deportation of civilians for use in slave or forced labor. [68 U.N.T.S. 189, 60 Stat. 1649, T.I.A.S. No. 1520, *reprinted in* 39 AJIL 171 (1945). This Declaration was supplemented by the Agreement on Certain Additional Requirements to be Imposed on Germany, 20 September 1945].

29. The 1945 Proclamation by the Heads of Governments, United States, China and the United Kingdom (Terms for Japanese Surrender) [Berlin (Potsdam) Conference].

The Proclamation allowed for the surrender and prosecution of persons found to have engaged in, *inter alia*, slavery and other War Crimes in Article 6. [1945 FOR. REL. (Conference of Berlin [Potsdam] II) 1474, *reprinted in* 3 Bevans 1204].

30. The 1945 Protocol of Proceedings [Berlin (Potsdam) Conference]. Slavery and related crimes are addressed in Articles II, A, 5, and VI. [1945 FOR. REL. (Conference of Berlin [Potsdam] II) 1478, *reprinted in* 3 Bevans 1207].

31. The 1945 Report on the Tripartite Conference of Berlin [Berlin (Potsdam) Conference]. Slavery and related crimes are addressed in Articles III, A, 5, and VII. [1945 FOR. REL. (Conference of Berlin [Potsdam] II) 1499, also *reprinted in* 39 AJIL 245 (1945)].

32. The 1945 Agreement for the Prosecution and Punishment of Major War Criminals of the European Axis (London Agreement). The Charter affixed to the Agreement considers slavery, deportation to slave labor and forced labor as a "War Crime" or "Crimes Against Humanity." [2 U.N.T.S. 279, 59 Stat. 1544, E.A.S. No. 472, also *reprinted in* 39 AJIL 257 (1945). This treaty was supplemented by Protocol on the Prosecution and Punishment of Major War Criminals of the European Axis, 6 October 1945, 59 Stat. 1586, E.A.S. 472, 3 Bevans 1286, rectifying a discrepancy in Article 6 of the Charter of the International Military Tribunal; supplemented with respect to Crimes Against Humanity (same state parties), Tehran Conference, Declaration of the Three Powers, 1 December 1943, 1943 FOR. REL. (Conferences of Cairo and Tehran) 640, 3 Bevans 859. *Also* Control Council Law No. 10 (Punishment of Persons Guilty of War Crimes, Crimes Against Peace and Against Humanity), 20 December 1945, *infra* note 34].

33. The 1945 Charter of the International Military Tribunal annexed to the London Agreement. In Article 6, the Charter classified enslavement, deportation to slave labor, and forced labor as crimes subject to punishment as either "War Crimes" or "Crimes Against Humanity." [*See supra* note 32.

See also Affirmation of the Principles of International Law Recognized by the Charter of Nuremberg Tribunal, *infra* note 38; Principles of International Law Recognized in Charter of the Nuremberg Tribunal and in the Judgment of the Tribunal (International Law Commission), *infra* note 56].

34. The 1945 Control Council Law No. 10 (Punishment of Persons Guilty of War Crimes, Crimes Against Peace and Against Humanity). This Law, following the lead of the Charter, allowed for the Surrender to prosecution before a military tribunal, persons accused of, *inter alia*, enslavement and deportation to slave labor. [OFFICIAL GAZETTE OF THE CONTROL COUNCIL FOR GERMANY, No. 3, Berlin, 31 January 1946, *reprinted in* 1 Ferencz 488].

35. The 1946 Special Proclamation: Establishment of an International Military Tribunal for the Far East. The accompanying Charter classified enslavement, deportation to slave labor and forced labor as either "War Crimes" or "Crimes Against Humanity." [T.I.A.S. No. 1589, 4 Bevans 20. This treaty was amended 26 April 1946].

36. The 1946 Charter of the International Military Tribunal for the Far East. In Article 5, the Charter classified enslavement, deportation to slave labor and forced labor as crimes subject to punishment as either "War Crimes" or "Crimes Against Humanity." [*Id*].

37. The 1946 Agreement on the Machinery of Control of Austria. Slavery and related crimes are addressed in Article 5. [138 U.N.T.S. 85, 62 Stat. 4036, T.I.A.S. No., 2097, *reprinted in* 4 Bevans 79. This Treaty was terminated on 27 July 1955, upon the entry into force of the State Treaty for the Re-Establishment of An Independent and Democratic Austria, signed at Vienna, 15 May 1955, 6 U.S.T.S. 2369, T.I.A.S. No. 3298].

38. The 1946 Affirmation of the Principles of International Law Recognized by the Charter of the Nuremberg Tribunal (United Nations General Assembly Resolution). Since the resolution expressly affirmed the Nuremberg Charter, it accepts the principles of enslavement, deportation to forced labor as constituting either "War Crimes" or "Crimes Against Humanity." [U.N. G.A. Res. 95 (I), U.N. Doc. A/64/Add. 1 (1946), *reprinted in* 1 Friedman 1027].

39.   The 1947 Treaty of Peace with Bulgaria. Slavery and related crimes are
       addressed in Article 5. [41 U.N.T.S. 21, 61 Stat. 1915, T.I.A.S. No. 1650,
       reprinted in 42 AJIL 179 (1948)].

40.   The 1947 Treaty of Peace with Hungary. Slavery and related crimes are
       addressed in Article 6. [41 U.N.T.S. 135, 61 Stat. 2065, T.I.A.S. No. 1651,
       reprinted in 42 AJIL 225 (1948)].

41.   The 1947 Treaty of Peace with Romania. Slavery and related crimes are
       addressed in Article 6. 1649, *reprinted in* 42 AJIL 252 (1948)].

42.   The 1947 Treaty of Peace with Italy. Slavery and related crimes are
       addressed in Article 45. [49 & 50 U.N.T.S., 61 Stat. 1245, T.I.A.S. No.
       1648, *reprinted in* 42 AJIL 47 (1948). This Treaty was supplemented by the
       Declaration on the Italian Peace Treaty, signed at Washington, 26 September
       1951, and Exchange of Notes at Washington, effecting the release of Italy
       from certain of its obligations to the United States].

43.   The 1947 Treaty of Peace Between the Allied Powers and Finland. Slavery
       and related crimes are addressed in Article 9. [48 U.N.T.S. 203, *reprinted in*
       42 AJIL 203 (1948)].

44.   The 1947 Protocol to Amend the Convention for the Suppression of the
       Traffic in Women and Children, Concluded at Geneva on 30 September 1921,
       and the Convention for the Suppression of Traffic in Women of Full Age,
       Concluded at Geneva on 11 October 1933, with (a) Annex to the Protocol to
       Amend the Convention for the Suppression of the Traffic in Women and
       Children, Concluded at Geneva on 30 September 1921, and the Convention
       for the Suppression of Traffic in Women of Full Age, Concluded at Geneva
       on 11 October 1933. The Protocol and Annex indicated the modifications
       made in the original League of Nations Conventions and denoted the
       acceptance of the United Nations to perform all duties in place of the League
       of Nations. [53 U.N.T.S. 13].

45.   The 1947 International Convention for the Suppression of the Traffic in
       Women and Children, Concluded at Geneva on 30 September 1921, as
       Amended by the Protocol signed at Lake Success, New York, on 12

November 1947. This Convention's penal characteristics are the same as those of the original League of Nations Convention. [53 U.N.T.S. 39].

46. The 1947 International Convention for the Suppression of the Traffic in Women of Full Age, Concluded at Geneva on 11 October 1933, as Amended by the Protocol signed at Lake Success, New York, on 12 November 1947. This document incorporates the text of the original Convention as modified by the applicable Protocol and as such this Convention's penal characteristics are the same as those of the original Convention. [53 U.N.T.S. 49].

47. The 1948 Convention on the Prevention and Punishment of the Crime of Genocide. The Convention addresses slavery and related crimes in Article II, which defines Genocide, as, *inter alia*, "[f]orcibly transferring children of the group to another group." [78 U.N.T.S. 277, *reprinted in* 45 AJIL 7 (1951)].

48. The 1949 Protocol Amending the International Agreement for the Suppression of the White Slave Traffic, Signed at Paris, on 18 May 1904, and the International Convention for the Suppression of the White Slave Traffic, Signed at Paris, on 4 May 1910, and (a) Annex to the Protocol Amending the International Agreement for the Suppression of the White Slave Traffic, Signed at Paris, on 4 May 1910. The Protocol and Annex indicated the modifications made in the original League of Nations Conventions and denoted the acceptance of the United Nations to perform all duties in place of the League of Nations. [30 U.N.T.S. 23, 2 U.S.T. 1997, and T.I.A.S. No. 2332].

49. The 1949 International Agreement for the Suppression of the White Slave Traffic, Signed at Paris on 18 May 1904, as Amended by the Protocol signed at Lake Success, New York, 4 May 1949. This document incorporates the text of the original agreement as modified by the Protocol and as such the penal characteristics are the same as those of the original agreement. [92 U.N.T.S. 19].

50. The 1949 International Convention for the Suppression of White Slave Traffic, Signed at Paris on 4 May 1910, and as Amended by the Protocol Signed at Lake Success, New York, 4 May 1949. This document incorporates the text of the original Convention as modified by the Protocol

and as such the Protocol's penal characteristics are the same as those of the original Convention. [98 U.N.T.S. 101].

51.   The 1949 Geneva Convention for the Amelioration of the Condition of the Wounded and Sick in Armed Forces in the Field. Slavery and related crimes are addressed in Articles 3 and 50. [75 U.N.T.S. 31, U.S.T. 3114, T.I.A.S. No. 3362, *reprinted in* 1 Friedman 525. This Convention was supplemented by Protocols I and II Additional to the Geneva Conventions of 12 August 1949, 12 December 1977, *infra* notes 66 and 67].

52.   The 1949 Geneva Convention for the Amelioration of the Condition of Wounded, Sick and Shipwrecked Members of Armed Forces at Sea. Slavery and related crimes are addressed in Articles 3 and 51. [75 U.N.T.S. 85, 6 U.S.T. 3217, T.I.A.S. No. 3363, *reprinted in* 1 Friedman 570. This Convention was supplemented by Protocols I and II Additional to the Geneva Conventions of 12 August 1949, 12 December 1977, *infra* notes 66 and 67].

53.   The 1949 Geneva Convention Relative to the Treatment of Prisoners of War. Slavery and related crimes are addressed in Articles 3, 49, 50, 51, 52, 53, 54, 55, 56, 57 and 130. All but Articles 3 and 130 specifically regulate the labor of prisoners of war. [75 U.N.T.S. 135, 6 U.S.T. 3316, T.I.A.S. No. 3364, *reprinted in* 47 AJIL 119 (1953). This Convention was supplemented by Protocols I and II Additional to the Geneva Conventions of 12 August 1949, 12 December 1977, *infra* notes 66 and 67].

54.   The 1949 Geneva Convention Relative to the Protection of Civilian Persons in Time of War. Slavery and related crimes are addressed in Articles 3, 49, 51, 52 and 147. [75 U.N.T.S. 287, 6 U.S.T. 3516, T.I.A.S. No. 3365, *reprinted in* 50 AJIL 724 (1956). This Convention was supplemented by Protocols I and II Additional to the Geneva Conventions of 12 August 1949, 12 December 1977, *infra* notes 66 and 67].

55.   The 1950 Convention for the Suppression of the Traffic in Persons and of the Exploitation of the Prostitution of Others. The penal characteristics of this Convention establish an implicit recognition of the penal nature of the act by establishing in Articles 1, 2, 3 and 4, a duty to prohibit, prevent, prosecute, and punish the act. Also, the duty or right to prosecute may be found in

Articles 1, 2, 3, 4 and 9. The duty or right to extradite is found in Article 8, while the duty or right to cooperate in prosecution and punishment is found in Article 13. The establishment of a criminal jurisdictional basis is found in Articles 11 and 15. [96 U.N.T.S. 271].

56. The 1950 Principles of International Law Recognized in the Charter of the Nuremberg Tribunal and in the Judgment of the Tribunal (International Law Commission). This document reaffirms the principles of the Nuremberg Charter and therefore recognizes enslavement and deportation to slave labor as acts punishable as either "War Crimes" or "Crimes Against Humanity." [5 U.N. GAOR (No. 12), at 11, U.N. Doc. A/1316 (1950), *reprinted in* 2 Ferencz 236, and 44 AJIL 126 (1950)].

57. The 1953 Protocol Amending the Slavery Convention Signed at Geneva on 25 September 1926 and (a) Annex to the Protocol Amending the Slavery Convention signed at Geneva on 25 September 1926. The Protocol and Annex indicate all modifications to be made in the original Convention and the acceptance of the United Nations of the Convention. [182 U.N.T.S. 51, U.S.T. 479, T.I.A.S. No. 3532].

58. The 1953 Slavery Convention Signed at Geneva on 25 September 1926 and Amended by the Protocol Opened for Signature or Acceptance at the Headquarters of the United Nations, New York, on 7 December 1953. This document incorporates the text of the original Convention as modified by the applicable Protocol and as such this Convention's penal characteristics are the same as those of the original Convention. [212 U.N.T.S. 17].

59. The 1954 Draft Code of Offenses Against the Peace and Security of Mankind (International Law Commission). Although the Code has yet to enter into force, the current tentative definition of Crimes Against Humanity includes slavery and other forms of bondage. [9 U.N. GAOR Supp. (No. 9) at 11, U.N. Doc. A/2693 (1954), *reprinted in* 45 AJIL 123 (1951)].

60. The 1956 Supplementary Convention on the Abolition of Slavery, the Slave Trade, and Institutions and Practices Similar to Slavery. The penal characteristics of the Convention explicitly or implicitly recognize, in Articles 2 and 5, the proscribed conduct as constituting not only a crime but an

international crime. The implicit recognition of the penal nature of the act by establishing a duty to prohibit, prevent, prosecute, punish, or the like is found in Articles 1 and 3. Criminalization of the proscribed conduct is found in Articles 1, 2 and 5. The duty or right to prosecute is implicitly found in Articles 2 and 5, as is the duty or right to punish the proscribed conduct. The duty or right to cooperate in prosecution and punishment is found in Article 8. [266 U.N.T.S. 3, 18 U.S.T. 3201, T.I.A.S. No. 6418].

61. The 1957 Convention (No. 105) Concerning the Abolition of Forced Labor. Implicit recognition of the penal nature of the act, by establishing a duty to prohibit, prevent, prosecute, punish or the like is found in Articles 1 and 2 (the latter of which contains the duty to abolish forced labor). [320 U.N.T.S. 291].

62. The 1958 Convention on the High Seas (Geneva Convention on the Law of the Sea.) Implicit recognition of the penal nature of the act, by establishing a duty to prohibit, prevent, prosecute, punish or the like is found in Article 13, as is the criminalization of the proscribed conduct. [450 U.N.T.S. 82, 13 U.S.T. 2312, T.I.A.S. No. 5200].

63. The 1966 International Convention of the Elimination of All Forms of Racial Discrimination. Slavery and related crimes are addressed in Articles 2, 3, and 4 (implicitly insofar as they may be the basis of conduct defined in that category of crime). [See 660 U.N.T.S. 195, reprinted in 5 ILM 352 (1966)].

64. The 1968 Convention on the Non-Applicability of Statutory Limitations to War Crimes and Crimes Against Humanity. Slavery and related crimes are addressed in Article I. [754 U.N.T.S. 73, reprinted in 8 ILM 68 (1969)].

65. The 1974 European Convention on the Non-Applicability of Statutory Limitations to Crimes Against Humanity and War Crimes (Inter-European). Slavery and related crimes are addressed in Article I. [E.T.S. No. 82, reprinted in 13 ILM 540 (1974)].

66. The 1977 Protocol I Additional to the Geneva Conventions of 12 August 1949. Slavery and related crimes are considered a "grave breach" in Article

85 which prohibits, *inter alia*, the deportation of civilians. [U.N. Doc. A/32/144 Annex I, *reprinted in* 16 ILM 1391 (1977)].

67. The 1977 Protocol II Additional to the Geneva Conventions of 12 August 1949. Article 4 specifically prohibits slavery and the slave-trade in all its forms. [U.N. Doc. A/32/144 Annex II, *reprinted in* 16 ILM 1442 (1977)].

68. The 1980 Draft Convention Defining Torture as an International Crime (Inter-American). Slavery and related crimes are addressed in Article 2. [OAS Doc. OEA/Ser. G, CP/Doc. 1061/80 (1980), *reprinted in* 19 ILM 619 (1980)].

69. The 1982 Convention on the Law of the Sea (Montego Bay Convention). The implicit recognition of the penal nature of the act by establishing a duty to prohibit, prevent, prosecute, punish or the like, is found in Article 99. [U.N. Doc. A/CONF.62/122].

70. The 1983 Draft European Convention on the Protection of Detainees From Torture and From Cruel, Inhuman or Degrading Treatment or Punishment (Inter-European). [*See Report on the Protection of Detainees from Torture and from Cruel, Inhuman or Degrading Treatment or Punishment to the Parliamentary Assembly of the Council of Europe*, Doc. No. 5099 Appendix (1983)].

71. The 1984 Convention Against Torture and Other Cruel, Inhuman or Degrading Treatment or Punishment. Slavery and related crimes are implicitly addressed in Article 1. [U.N. G.A. Res. 39/46. *See* 24 I.L.M. 535 which contains the substantive changes from the Draft Convention Against Torture and Other Cruel, Inhuman or Degrading Treatment or Punishment, 23 ILM 1027 (1984)].

3. DEFINITIONS OF THE TERMS "PERSECUTE" AND "PERSECUTION"*

Language: Arabic
Source: "AL-BUSTANI" DICTIONARY by SHEIKH ABDULLAH AL-BUSTANI AL-LUBNANI, Amir Kaniya Press, Beirut, 1930.
Definition: *âdyâhu bisababi 'l-madyhabi* -- he harmed/wronged/ molested him because of his beliefs/creed/views/ opinions.

Language: Danish
Source: DICTIONARY OF THE DANISH LANGUAGE, by VERNER DAHLERUP, Volume 5 (Flyve-Frette), Copenhagen 1923, Gyldendalske Bokhandel-Nordisk Forlag, Printed by H.H. Thiele (Issued by the Danish Language and Literature Society).
Definition: *Forfolge* -- to pursue with a hostile purpose; to seek, to affect with continuous attacks; to torment; to victimize.

Language: Dutch
Source: VAN DALE'S BIG DICTIONARY OF THE NETHERLANDS LANGUAGE by JOHAN HENDRIK VAN DALE, Sixth Edition, The Hague, Martinus Nijhoff, 1924, Leiden, A.W. Sijthoff's Publ. Co.
Definition: *Vervolgen* -- to follow with hostile intentions: to go after (someone) with rocks, with pejorative words; to persecute for reason of one's faith; to pester, hound, plague.

Language: English
Source: OXFORD UNIVERSAL ENGLISH DICTIONARY, by WILLIAM LITTLE, H.W. Fowler, J. Coulson, revised and edited by C.T. Onions, Volume VII (Pel-Rel), Oxford University Press, Doubleday, Doran & Co. 1937.
Definition: *Persecute* -- to pursue with malignancy or injurious action, especially to oppress for holding a heretical opinion or belief; to harass, worry.
Persecution -- the infliction of death, torture, or penalties for adherence to a particular religious belief or opinion; a particular course or period of systematic infliction of punishment directed against those holding a particular (religious) belief.

* Translated from official dictionaries

784

Language: French
Source: DICTIONNAIRE DE L'ACADÉMIE FRANÇAISE, Eighth edition, Volume II (H-Z), Librairie Hoehette, 1935.
Definition: *Persecute* -- to harass, torment relentlessly by unjust means, with violent pursuit.
Persécution -- unjust and violent pursuit, vexation.

Language: German
Source: CONCISE DICTIONARY OF THE GERMAN LANGUAGE, by DANIEL SANDERS, Eighth edition, by J. Ernst Wülfing, Bibliographical Institute, Leipzig, 1924.
Definition: *Verfolgen* -- to seek to obtain or attain an object by pursuing; in hostile intent, follow, pursue, harass someone with stones, defamations, wanted posters, etc.; to follow someone in a hostile manner showing him active hatred, not to allow him (like harassed game) a minute's rest for fear.

Language: Greek
Source: GREAT DICTIONARY OF THE GREEK LANGUAGE, by Demetrios Demetrakos, Athens, 1939.
Definition: [*Katadiökö*] -- to run after someone in order to capture or kill him; to pursue in order to do harm.

Language: Hungarian
Source: DICTIONARY OF THE HUNGARIAN LANGUAGE, by JÓZSEF BALASSA, Volume I (A-K), Károly Grill Publishers, Budapest, 1940.
Definition: *Kínoz* -- pester, cause torment/suffering; cause anguish (mental torment).

Language: Italian
Source: DICTIONARY OF THE ITALIAN LANGUAGE, by GUILIO CAPPUCCINI, 13th edition, G.B. Paravia & Co., Torino, 1938.
Definition: *Perseguitare* -- to go or keep after for the purpose of harming; harass, bother in order to achieve an end.

Language: Japanese
Source: LARGE DICTIONARY, by YATARO SHIMONAKA, Volume 20, Heibonsha Co., Tokyo, 1936.
Definition: [*Persecution*, p. 435] -- to cause harm in a pressing fashion; to cause suffering; to oppress.

Language: Norwegian
Source: THE STANDARD NORWEGIAN DICTIONARY, by TRYGVE KNUDSEN and ALF SOMMERFELT ET AL., Volume I (For-Laavevegg), H. Aschehoug & Co. (issued by the Standard Norwegian Language Committee), Olso 1937.
Definition: *Forfolge* -- to pursue, chase, hunt (with intent to spy on, harm, capture, etc.); to go with intent to harm, torment.

Language: Polish
Source: ILLUSTRATED DICTIONARY OF THE POLISH LANGUAGE, by M. ARCT, Warsaw, 1916.
Definition: *Przesladowac* -- to bother, annoy; to oppress, pester, worry, grind down, harass; to torment, torture, bother, distress, afflict.

Language: Portuguese
Source: COMPLETE DICTIONARY OF THE PORTUGUESE LANGUAGE, by AUGUSTO MORENO, Third edition, Oporto, 1941.
Definition: *Perseguir* -- to follow closely, accuse, harass, cause to be punished, pursue, provoke so as to injure.

Language: Romanian
Source: ILLUSTRATED ENCYCLOPEDIC DICTIONARY, "CARTEA ROMANEASCA," BULEVARDUL REGLE CAROL I, No. 3-5, Bucharest, 1931.
Definition: *Persecuta* -- to pursue; to trouble through wrongful, violent pressure, to oppress.

Language: Spanish
Source: DICTIONARY OF THE SPANISH LANGUAGE, by the Real Academia Espanola, Madrid, 1939.
Definition: *Perseguir* -- to bother, harass, inflict suffering, cause maximum injury; to pester or annoy with persistent entreaties.

786

Language: Swedish
Source: DICTIONARY OF MODERN SWEDISH, by OLAF OSTERGREN, Volume II (F-G), Wahlstrom & Widstrand, Stockholm, 1926.
Definition: *Forfolja* -- to haunt, not leave in peace, continuously harass, pester, attack, continue to torment or harm or trouble, annoy, or oppress.

Language: Turkish
Source: TURKISH DICTIONARY: THE ETYMOLOGICAL AND LITERARY DICTIONARIES OF THE TURKISH LANGUAGE, by HUSEYIN KAZIM KADRI, Volume 3, The Maarif Printing House, Istanbul, 1943.
Definition: *Magduriyet* -- the state of being unjustly treated, wronged, or victimized; oppression, victimization.

As these definitions show, the terms "persecute" and "persecution" generally entail that someone, with hostile purposes or intentions, pursues another to harass, torment, oppress or harm that person, usually on account of that person's religious beliefs, views or opinions.

The criminal laws of most countries of the world do not have a crime called "persecution" because the acts comprised within the general meaning of persecution, which produce harmful results, are criminalized. Thus, to determine the legal meaning of persecution one has to examine the specific acts committed in order to determine whether they constituted a crime.

Therefore, no specific international crime of "persecution" exists under any source of international law. It is possible to construct a reasoning that "persecution" as defined above, when resulting in a specific violation can be deemed an aggravating factor. Another approach is to hold that a state policy of persecution of a class of persons by virtue of which common crimes are made lawful, or unenforced become international crimes; that is probably the basis for the *Apartheid* Convention.

4. COMPILATION OF INTERNATIONAL CRIMINAL LAW CONVENTIONS CONTAINING PROVISIONS ESTABLISHING THE DUTY TO PROSECUTE OR EXTRADITE

A.   *Prohibition Against War*

1.   Treaty of Peace with Germany (Treaty of Versailles), signed at Versailles, 28 June 1919, 11 Martens (3d) 323, 1919 For. Rel. (Paris Peace Conference XIII) 55, 743, (entered into force 10 January 1920).
      Article 227 (duty to prosecute and hand over Kaiser)
      Article 228 (duty to prosecute and hand over alleged war criminals)
      Article 229 (duty to prosecute if alleged offender not extradited)

2.   General Treaty for the Renunciation of War as an Instrument of National Policy (Kellogg-Briand Pact or Pact of Paris), 27 August 1928, 94 L.N.T.S. 57, 46 Stat. 2343, T.S. No. 796 (entered into force 24 July 1929; entered into force with respect to the United States 24 July 1929).

3.   Agreement for the Prosecution and Punishment of the Major War Criminals of the European Axis (London Charter), 8 August 1945, 82 U.N.T.S. 279, 59 Stat. 1544, E.A.S. No. 472 (entered into force with respect to the United States 8 August 1945).
      Article 6(a)/(Charter) (recognition of aggression as crime against peace)
      Article 3/(agreement) (duty to cooperate in investigation and prosecution of alleged war criminals)

4.   Charter of the International Military Tribunal: Far East, 19 January and amended 26 April 1946, T.I.A.S. No. 1589.
      Article 5(a) (recognition of aggression as a crime against peace)

5.   Definition of Aggression, 14 December 1974, U.N. G.A. Res. 3314 (XXIX), 29 U.N. GAOR Supp. (No. 31), at 142, U.N. Doc. A/9631 (1974).
      Article 5 (recognition of aggression as crime against peace)

B. *Prohibition of Certain Means and Methods in the Conduct of War (Humanitarian Law of Armed Conflict)*

1. Geneva Convention for the Amelioration of the Condition of the Wounded and Sick in Armies in the Field (Second Red Cross Convention), 6 July 1906, 35 Stat. 1885, T.S. No. 464, 2 Martens (3d) 620.
   Articles 27 and 28 (duty to criminalize)

2. Convention for the Adaptation to Maritime Warfare of the Principles of the Geneva Convention (Second Hague, X), 18 October 1907, 36 Stat. 2371, T.S. No. 543, 3 Martens (3d) 630.
   Article 21 (duty to criminalize)

3. Geneva Convention for the Amelioration of the Condition of the Wounded and Sick in Armies in the Field (Third Red Cross Convention), 27 July 1929, 47 Stat. 2074, T.S. No. 847, 118 L.N.T.S. 303.
   Article 29 (duty to criminalize)

4. Geneva Convention for the Amelioration of the Condition of the Wounded and Sick in the Armed Forces in the Field, 12 August 1949, 6 U.S.T. 3114, T.I.A.S. No. 3362, 75 U.N.T.S. 31.
   Article 49 (duty to search for and prosecute)
   Article 50 (recognition as a crime)

5. Geneva Convention for the Amelioration of the Condition of the Wounded, Sick and Shipwrecked Members of Armed Forces at Sea, 12 August 1949, 6 U.S.T. 3217, T.I.A.S. No. 3363, 75 U.N.T.S. 85.
   Article 50 (duty to search for and prosecute)
   Article 51 (recognition as a crime)

6. Geneva Convention Relative to the Treatment of Prisoners of War, 12 August 1949, 6 U.S.T. 3316, T.I.A.S. No. 3364, 75 U.N.T.S. 135.
   Article 129 (duty to search for and prosecute)
   Article 130 (recognition as a crime)

7. Geneva Convention Relative to the Protection of Civilian Persons in Time of War, 12 August 1949, 6 U.S.T. 3516, T.I.A.S. No. 3365, 75 U.N.T.S. 287.

789

Article 146 (duty to search for and prosecute)
Article 147 (recognition as a crime)

8. Protocol I Additional to the 1949 Geneva Conventions, 12 Dec. 1977, U.N. Doc. A/32/144 Annex I (1977); INTERNATIONAL REVIEW OF THE RED CROSS (special issue August-September 1977).
Article 88 (duty to cooperate with other states in prosecution and extradition)

9. Convention for the Prohibition of the Development, Production, and Stockpiling of Bacteriological (Biological) and Toxic Weapons and on Their Destruction, 10 April 1972, 26 U.S.T. 583, T.I.A.S. No. 8062, 1015 U.N.T.S. 163.
Articles IV and IX (duty to prohibit and prevent)

C.   *Prohibition of Emplacement of Weapons in Certain Areas*

1. Treaty on Antarctica, 1 December 1959, 12 U.S.T. 794, T.I.A.S. No. 4780, 402 U.N.T.S. 71.
Articles I, V and X (duty to prohibit)

2. Treaty Banning Nuclear Weapon Tests in the Atmosphere, in Outer Space, and Under Water, 5 August 1963, 14 U.S.T. 1313, T.I.A.S. No. 5433, 480 U.N.T.S. 43.
Article I (duty to prevent and prohibit)

D.   *Prohibition Against Genocide*

1. Convention on the Prevention and Punishment of the Crime of Genocide, 9 December 1948, 78 U.N.T.S. 277.
Article I (recognition as international crime; duty to prevent and punish)
Article IV (duty to criminalize)
Article IV (duty to prosecute)
Article IV (duty to extradite; duty not to apply political offense exception)

790

E. *Prohibition Against Apartheid*

1. International Convention on the Suppression and Punishment of the Crime of *Apartheid*, 30 November 1973, U.N. G.A. Res. 3068 (XXVIII), 28 U.N. GAOR Supp. (No. 30), at 75, U.N. Doc. A/9030 (1973).
   Articles I and III (recognition as international crime)
   Article IV (duty to suppress and criminalize)
   Article IV (duty to prosecute)
   Article XI (duty to extradite; duty not to apply political offense exception)

F. *Prohibition Against Torture*

1. Convention Against Torture and Other Cruel, Inhuman or Degrading Treatment or Punishment, 7 December 1984, U.N. Doc. A/RES/39/46.
   Article I (recognition as international crime)
   Article IV (duty to criminalize)
   Article IX (duty to establish jurisdiction)
   Article X (duty to extradite)
   Article XI (duty to provide cooperation and juridical assistance)
   Article XII (duty not to apply political offense exception)

G. *Prohibition Against Slavery and Slave-Related Practices*

1. Treaty for the Suppression of the African Slave Trade (Treaty of London), 20 December 1841, 2 Martens (1st) 392.
   Article I (recognized as a crime)
   Article X (duty to prosecute and punish)

2. Treaty for the Suppression of the African Slave Trade (Washington Treaty), Great Britain-United States, 7 April 1862, 12 Stat. 1225, T.S. No. 126, 17 Martens (2d) 259.
   Article II (duty to prosecute)
   Article IX (duty to "transfer")

3. Brussels Convention, 2 July 1890, 27 Stat. 886, T.S. No. 383, 17 Martens (2d) 345.

Article V (duty to punish, prosecute, and return)

4. International Convention for the Suppression of White Slave Traffic, 4 May 1910, 7 Martens (3d) 252.
    Articles 1 and 2 (duty to punish)
    Article 3 (duty to criminalize)
    Article 5 (duty to extradite)
    Articles 4 and 6 (duty to cooperate in prosecution)

5. St. Germain-en-Laye Convention, 10 September 1919, 49 Stat. 3027, T.S. No. 877, 8 L.N.T.S. 25.
    Article II (duty to suppress)

6. International Convention for the Suppression of Traffic in Women and Children, 30 September 1921, 9 L.N.T.S. 416.
    Article 2 (duty to prosecute)
    Article 3 (duty to punish)
    Article 4 (duty to extradite)

7. Slavery Convention, 25 September 1926, 24 Stat. 2183, T.S. No. 778, 60 *L.N.T.S.* 253.
    Article 2 (duty to prevent and suppress)
    Article 4 (duty to cooperate in abolition)
    Article 6 (duty to criminalize)

8. Convention (No. 29) Concerning Forced or Compulsory Labour, 28 June 1930, 39 U.N.T.S. 55.
    Article 1 (duty to suppress)
    Article 25 (duty to prosecute and punish)

9. International Convention for the Suppression of Traffic in Women of Full Age, 11 October 1933, 150 L.N.T.S. 431.
    Article 1 (duty to punish)
    Article 2 (duty to criminalize)
    Article 3 (duty to cooperate in suppression)

10. Convention for the Suppression of the Traffic in Persons and of the Exploitation of the Prostitution of Others, 21 March 1950, 96 U.N.T.S. 271.
    Articles 1, 2, 3 and 4 (duty to punish)
    Article 6 (duty to criminalize)
    Article 8 (duty to extradite)
    Article 9 (duty to prosecute if not extradited)
    Articles 13, 14 and 15 (duty to criminalize in prosecution)

11. Supplementary Convention on the Abolition of Slavery, the Slave Trade, and Institutions and Practices Similar to Slavery, 7 September 1956, 18 U.S.T. 3201, T.I.A.S. No. 6418, 266 U.N.T.S. 3.
    Article I (duty to abolish)
    Articles 3, 5 and 6 (duty to criminalize and punish)
    Article 8 (duty to cooperate in prosecution)

12. Convention (No. 105) Concerning the Abolition of Forced Labour, 25 June 1957, 320 U.N.T.S. 291.
    Article 1 (duty to suppress)
    Article 2 (duty to enact legislation to abolish)

13. Convention on the High Seas, 29 April 1958, 13 U.S.T. 2312, T.I.A.S. No. 5200, 450 U.N.T.S. 82.
    Article 13 (duty to prevent and punish)

H. *Prohibition Against Piracy*

1. Convention on the High Seas, 29 April 1958, 13 U.S.T. 2312, T.I.A.S. No. 5200, 450 U.N.T.S. 82.
    Article 13 (duty to punish)

2. Convention of the Law of the Sea (Montego Bay Convention), 10 December 1982 U.N. Doc. A/CONF. 62/122.

3. Convention and Protocol From the International Conference on the Suppression of Unlawful Acts Against the Safety of Maritime Navigation,

adopted by the International Maritime Organization, at Rome, 10 March 1988, I.M.O. Doc. SVA/CON/15.

Article 3 (definition of offence)
Article 5 (duty to punish)
Article 6 (duty to establish jurisdiction)
Article 10 (duty to prosecute)
Article 11 (duty to extradite)
Article 12 (duty to mutual assistance in prosecution)

I.   *Prohibition Against Aircraft Hijacking and Related Offenses*

1.   Convention on Offences and Certain Other Acts Committed on Board Aircraft (Tokyo Hijacking Convention), 14 September 1963, 20 U.S.T. 2941, T.I.A.S. No. 6768, 704 U.N.T.S. 219.

Article 1(a) (recognition as crime)
Article 3 (duty to establish jurisdiction)
Article 13 (duty to take into custody)

2.   Convention for the Suppression of Unlawful Seizure of Aircraft (Hague Hijacking Convention), 16 December 1970, 22 U.S.T. 1641, T.I.A.S. No. 7192, 860 U.N.T.S. 105.

Article I (recognition as crime)
Article II (duty to punish)
Article IV (duty to establish jurisdiction)
Article V (duty to take into custody)
Article VII (duty to prosecute if not extradited)
Article X (duty to cooperate in prosecution)

3.   Convention for the Suppression of Unlawful Acts Against the Safety of Civil Aviation (Montreal Hijacking Convention), 23 September 1971, 24 U.S.T. 564, T.I.A.S. No. 7570, 974 U.N.T.S. 177.

Article 1 (recognition as crime)
Article 3 (duty to punish)
Article 5 (duty to establish jurisdiction)
Article 6 (duty to take into custody)
Article 7 (duty to prosecute if not extradited)
Article 8 (duty to extradite)

794

Article 11 (duty to cooperate in prosecution)

4. Protocol for the Suppression of Unlawful Acts of Violence at Airports Servicing Civil Aviation, adopted by the International Civil Aviation Organization, at Montreal, 24 February 1988, 27 I.L.M. 627 (1988).
    Article II (definition of offence)
    Article III (Duty to prosecute or extradite)

J. *Prohibition Against Seizure of Diplomats, Internationally Protected Persons and Civilian Hostages*

1. Organization of American States Convention to Prevent and Punish the Acts of Terrorism Taking the Form of Crimes Against Persons and Related Extortion that are of International Significance, 2 February 1971, 27 U.S.T. 3949, T.I.A.S. No. 8413.
    Article 1 (duty to prevent and punish)
    Article 2 (recognition as crime)
    Articles 3 and 7 (duty to extradite)
    Article 5 (duty to prosecute if not extradite)
    Article 8 (duty to criminalize)

2. Convention on the Prevention and Punishment of Crimes Against Internationally Protected Persons, Including Diplomatic Agents, 14 December 1973, 28 U.S.T. 1975, T.I.A.S. 8532.
    Article 2 (recognition as crime)
    Article 3 (duty to establish jurisdiction)
    Article 4 (duty to prevent)
    Article 6 (duty to prosecute or extradite)
    Article 7 (duty to prosecute if not extradited)
    Article 8 (duty to extradite)
    Article 10 (duty to provide juridical assistance)

3. International Convention Against the Taking of Hostages, 18 December 1979, U.N. G.A. Res. 34/145 (XXXIV), 34 U.N. GAOR Supp. (No. 46), at 245, U.N. Doc. A/34/146.
    Article 1 (recognition as crime)
    Article 2 (duty to punish)

Article 4 (duty to prevent)
Article 5 (duty to establish jurisdiction)
Article 6 (duty to take into custody)
Article 7 (duty to prosecute)
Article 8 (duty to prosecute if not extradited)
Articles 9 and 10 (duty to extradite)
Article 11 (duty to provide juridical assistance)

K.   *Prohibition Against the Use of the Mails for Violence*

1.   Treaty on the Creation of a Universal Postal Union, 9 October 1874, 1 Martens (2d) 651.
     Article 11 (duty to prohibit)

2.   Universal Postal Union, 26 May 1906, 1 Martens (3d) 355, 35 Stat. 1639.
     Article XVI (duty to prohibit)
     Article XVIII (duty to criminalize)

3.   Universal Postal Convention (Berne Convention), 11 July 1952, 4 U.S.T. 1118, T.I.A.S. No. 2800, 169 U.N.T.S. 3.
     Article 59 (duty to prohibit)

4.   Agreement Concerning Insured Letters and Boxes, 11 July 1952, 170 U.N.T.S. 3.
     Article 5 (duty to prohibit)

L.   *General Conventions Against Terrorism*

1.   Convention for the Prevention and Punishment of Terrorism, 16 November 1937, 19 League of Nations Official Journal 23 (1938), L.N. Doc. C.546 (I), M383 (I), 1937. V (1938).
     Articles 2 and 3 (duty to criminalize)
     Article 8 (duty to extradite)
     Articles 9, 10 and 11 (duty to prosecute if not extradited)
     Article 17 (duty to provide judicial assistance)

DOCUMENTS SECTION

2.   European Convention on the Suppression of Terrorism, 22 January 1977, E.T.S. No. 90.
   Articles 1 and 2 (duty to apply political offense exception)
   Articles 3 and 4 (duty to extradite)
   Article 6 (duty to establish jurisdiction)
   Article 7 (duty to prosecute if not extradited)
   Article 8 (duty to provide judicial assistance)

M.   *Prohibition Against International Traffic in Drugs*

1.   International Opium Convention, 23 January 1912, 38 Stat. 1912, T.S. No. 612, 8 L.N.T.S. 187.
   Articles III, VI, VII, XI and XV (duty to prevent, suppress, or prohibit)
   Article XX (duty to criminalize)

2.   Agreement Concerning the Suppression of the Manufacture of, Internal Trade in and Use of, Prepared Opium, 11 February 1925, 51 L.N.T.S. 337.
   Articles II, V and VI (duty to prohibit)
   Article VIII (duty to cooperate in suppression)
   Article IX (duty to criminalize)

3.   Convention Relating to Dangerous Drugs, 19 February 1925, 81 L.N.T.S. 317.
   Articles 2, 5, 7 and 11 (duty to prohibit)
   Articles 28 and 29 (duty to criminalize)
   Article 30 (duty to cooperate in suppression)

4.   Convention for Limiting the Manufacture and Regulating the Distribution of Narcotic Drugs, 13 July 1931, 48 Stat. 1543, T.S. No. 863, 139 L.N.T.S. 301.
   Articles 10, 11 and 12 (duty to prohibit)
   Article 15 (duty to criminalize)
   Articles 21 and 23 (duty to cooperate in suppression)

5.   Agreement Concerning the Suppression of Opium Smoking, 27 November 1931, 177 L.N.T.S. 373.
   Article II(1) (duty to prohibit)
   Article II(2) (duty to punish)

797

6. Convention for the Suppression of Illicit Traffic in Dangerous Drugs, and Protocol of Signature, 26 June 1936, 198 L.N.T.S. 204.
   Articles 2 and 5 (duty to criminalize and punish)
   Article 3 (duty to criminalize) ·
   Articles 7, 8 and 9 (duty to extradite)
   Articles 6 and 13 (duty to provide judicial assistance)

7. Single Convention on Narcotic Drugs, 30 March 1961, 18 U.S.T. 1407, T.I.A.S. No. 6298, 520 U.N.T.S. 204.
   Article 36(1), (2)(a) (duty to criminalize)
   Article 36(2)(b) (desirable to extradite)

8. Convention on Psychotropic Substances, 21 February 1971, 32 U.S.T. 543, T.I.A.S. No. 9725, 1019 U.N.T.S. 399.
   Article 22 (duty to criminalize and extradite)

9. Protocol Amending the 1961 Single Convention on Narcotic Drugs, 8 August 1975, 26 U.S.T. 1439, T.I.A.S. No. 8118, 976 U.N.T.S. 3.
   Article 36(1), (2)(a) (duty to criminalize)
   Article 36(a)(b) (duty to extradite)

10. United Nations Convention Against Illicit Traffic in Narcotic Drugs and Psychotropic Substances, 19 December 1988, U.N. Doc. E/CONF. 82/15.
   Article 3 (duty to criminalize and to prosecute)
   Article 4 (criminal jurisdiction)
   Article 6 (duty to extradite)
   Articles 7, 9 and 10 (duty to provide mutual assistance)

N. *Prohibition Against Counterfeiting*

1. International Convention for the Suppression of Counterfeiting Currency, 20 April 1929, 112 L.N.T.S. 371.
   Article 3 (duty to punish)
   Articles 8 and 9 (duty to prosecute if not extradited)
   Article 16 (duty to provide judicial assistance)

O.   *Protection of National and Archaeological Treasures*

1.   Convention on the Protection of Cultural Property in the Event of an Armed Conflict, 14 May 1954, 249 U.N.T.S. 240.
Article 28 (duty to prosecute)

2.   UNESCO Convention on the Means of Prohibiting and Preventing the Illicit Import, Export and Transfer of Ownership of Art Treasures, 14 November 1970, 823 U.N.T.S. 231, *reprinted in* 10 I.L.M. 289 (1971).
Article 8 (duty to penalize)

P.   *Protection of International Means of Communication*

1.   Convention for the Protection of Submarine Cables, 14 March 1884, 24 Stat. 989, T.S. No. 380, 11 Martens (2d) 281.
Article II (duty to punish)
Article XII (duty to criminalize)

Q.   *Prohibition of International Traffic in Obscene Publications*

1.   International Convention for the Suppression of the Circulation of and Traffic in Obscene Publications, 12 September 1923, 27 L.N.T.S. 213, 7 Martens (3d) 266.
Article 1 (duty to prosecute and punish)
Article 4 (duty to criminalize)
Article 6 (duty to cooperate in suppression)

R.   *Prohibition Against Bribery*

1.   Draft International Agreement to Eliminate and Prevent Illicit Payments, U.N. ECOSOC Report of the *Ad Hoc* Intergovernmental Working Group on the Problem of Corrupt Practices in International Commercial Transactions, 5 July 1977, U.N. Doc. E/6006.
Article III.1(i) (duty to criminalize)
Articles III.1(ii) and III.5 (duty to prohibit)
Article III.1(iii) (duty to prosecute)
Article III.1(iv) (duty to punish)

Article IV.2 (duty to provide judicial assistance)
Article IV.3 (duty to extradite)

5. CANADIAN CRIMINAL CODE § 7 (3.71-3.77)

MARTIN'S ANNUAL CRIMINAL CODE 1990

(E.L. Greenspan ed. 1989).

(3.71)   Notwithstanding anything in this Act or any other Act, every person who, either before or after the coming into force of this subsection, commits an act or omission outside Canada that constitutes a war crime or a crime against humanity and that, if committed in Canada, would constitute an offence against the laws of Canada in force at the time of the act or omission shall be deemed to commit that act or omission in Canada at that time if,

(a)   at the time of the act or omission,

   (i)   that person is a Canadian citizen or is employed by Canada in a civilian or military capacity,

   (ii)   that person is a citizen of, or is employed in a civilian or military capacity by, a state that is engaged in an armed conflict against Canada, or

   (iii)   the victim of the act or omission is a Canadian citizen or a citizen of a state that is allied with Canada in an armed conflict; or

(b)   at the time of the act or omission, Canada could, in conformity with international law, exercise jurisdiction over the person with respect to the act or omission on the basis of the person's presence in Canada and, subsequent to the time of the act or omission, the person is present in Canada.

(3.72)   Any proceedings with respect to an act or omission referred to in subsection (3.71) shall be conducted in accordance with the laws of evidence and procedure in force at the time of the proceedings.

(3.73)   In any proceedings under this Act with respect to an act or omission referred to in subsection (3.71), notwithstanding that the act or omission is an offence under the laws of Canada in force at the time of the act or omission, the accused may, subject to subsection 607(6), rely on any justification, excuse or defence available under the laws of Canada or under international law at that time or at the time of the proceedings.

(3.74)   Notwithstanding subsection (3.73) and section 15, a person may be convicted of an offence in respect of an act or omission referred to in subsection (3.71) even if the act or omission is committed in obedience to or in conformity with the law in force at the time and in the place of its commission.

(3.75)   Notwithstanding any other provision of this Act, no proceedings may be commenced with respect to an act or omission referred to in subsection (3.71) without the personal consent in writing of the Attorney General or Deputy Attorney General of Canada, and such proceedings may only be conducted by the Attorney General of Canada or counsel acting on his behalf.

(3.76)   For the purposes of this section, "conventional international law" means

(a)   any convention, treaty or other international agreement that is in force and to which Canada is a party, or

(b)   any convention, treaty or other international agreemtn that is in force and the provisions of which Canada has agreed to accept and apply in an armed conflict in which it is involved;

"crime against humanity" means murder, extermination, enslavement, deportation, persecution or any other inhumane act or omission that is committed against any civilian population or any identifiable group of persons, whether or not it constitutes a contravention of the law in force at the time and in the place of its commission, and that, at that time and in that place, constitutes a contravention of customary international law or conventional international law or is criminal according to the general principles of law recognized by the community of nations;

"war crime" means an act or omission that is committed during an international armed conflict, whether or not it constitutes a contravention of the law in force at the time and in the place of its commission, and that, at that time and in that place, constitutes a contravention of the customary international law or conventional international law applicable in international armed conflicts.

(3.77) In the definitions "crime against humanity" and "war crime" in subsection (3.76), "act or omission" includes, for greater certainty, attempting or conspiring to commit, counselling any person to commit, aiding or abetting any person in the commission of, or being an accessory after the fact in relation to, an act or omission.

INDEX

INDEX

INDEX

INDEX

INDEX